New Zea   Division

1916 - 1919

A Popular History
Based on Official Records

BY

COL. H. STEWART, C.M.G., D.S.O., M.C.

(Late Comdg. 2nd Bn., Canterbury Regt.)

Printed and bound by Antony Rowe Ltd, Eastbourne

Dedicated to

The Lasting Memory of
The New Zealand Division

Preface

In accordance with instructions received from the New Zealand Government, this history is designed for the intelligent general reader. Technicalities have been simplified as far as possible, and the meanings of non-obvious terms have been explained. The narrative deals almost exclusively with movements and engagements. No detailed review of administration has been attempted, and I have eschewed statistics. On the other hand, individual acts of gallantry receive an amount of notice which in a work addressed to the serious student would be disproportionate.

With a small self-contained unit like the New Zealand Division it is possible to see how a complete accurate and vivid record might have been compiled by a "Historian," as distinct from a Press Correspondent, writing contemporaneously with the Division's actions. Endowed with the necessary qualifications of tact, energy, patience, sanity, technical knowledge, and a passion for accuracy, and living at Divisional headquarters, he would have been able to interview participants, down to section commanders if necessary, and thereby check statements, amplify official narratives, elucidate obscurities, catch the atmosphere of the time and describe the country at leisure from actual observation. He might have produced a picture unique for truthfulness and interest.

As it was , the opportunity was overlooked. The actors are now dispersed, and the historian must fall back on written records. Such records can be supplemented by the recollections of officers and men, but owing to the unreliability of the human memory and for various other reasons this latter source of information must be used with the greatest caution. Battalion and Company Commanders writing first-hand descriptions on the morrow of an engagement know the difficulties in the way of setting out detailed truth. A year or more afterwards the task of recapturing facts is a desperate undertaking.

The authorities used for this book are:—

(i) The monthly War Diaries of Units, with their appendices. These are of varying value. Those of Division (G.S.) and of Brigades are generally good. Those of Battalions, in 1916 highly inadequate, improved considerably in the latter

part of the war. None fortunately are so laconic as that of a
certain English unit, whose sole reference to a highly successful advance on the Messines Ridge on 7th June 1917 is
limited to the words "Took part in the Battle of Messines."
Many, however, written under the pressure of other work, are
scrappy and inaccurate, and all are necessarily somewhat dry
and colourless. I have read all the diaries of every unit in
the Division, and studied extensively those of the different
Armies and Corps, of which the Division from time to time
formed part, together with those of flank Divisions Brigades
and Battalions, without knowledge of which one's view is
inevitably circumscribed and frequently wrong.

(ii) Operation Orders, including those of Armies and
Corps.

(iii) Corps Division Brigade and Battalion Intelligence
Summaries, memoranda on tactical situations, &c.

(iv.) Narratives of operations, as and when compiled by
Armies Corps[1] and smaller formations.

(v) Orders issued and messages and reports submitted
during operations, and records of telephone conversations.

(vi) N.Z.E.F. Orders and Gradation Lists, and Divisional
Routine Orders.

(vii) Recommendations for Honours and Awards.

(viii) Reports rendered by the G.O.C., N.Z. Division, and
the G.O. i/c Administration to the G.O.C., N.Z.E.F., for trans-
mission to the New Zealand Government.

(ix) Various, such as personal diaries, copies of private
letters to New Zealand, statements on oath by repatriated
prisoners of war, the Official Correspondent's despatches, &c.
Of the histories which I have consulted, I have found Col.
Buchan's volumes ("Nelson's History of the War") much
the most valuable. Though frequently incorrect in details,
they present a well-informed and vividly expressed narrative
of political tendencies and of the changing military situation
and general military operations. Lt.-Col. Weston's "Three
Years with the New Zealanders" gives a graphic account of
a battalion's experiences in war. Lt.-Col. S. S. Allen's
admirable "2nd Auckland, 1918," was published after the
bulk of my own book had gone to press, but I have been able
to derive useful information from it for my later chapters.

(x) Haig's Despatches.

---

1 A particularly valuable resumé of its part in the Battles of Bapaume and
Havrincourt-Epehy was issued by the IV. Corps.

In September 1919 I paid a visit to all the Division's battlefields to determine certain topographical obscurities.

Exactitude was not perhaps the most conspicuous virtue of pre-war Regimental Histories. Every possible care has been taken in this narrative to ensure accuracy, but I cannot hope to have avoided altogether errors of detail. With the fallibility of the more important original sources, not overmuch reliance can be put in the most rigorously scientific methods to recover facts from them. The insecurity of the historian of previous wars and ages, dependent often as he is on second-hand authorities, has been impressed on me during these investigations with great force. For any corrections sent me at the undermentioned address I shall be grateful. I trust, however, that substantial accuracy will be found to have been attained. Certain cruces of no special importance, arising from conflicting or inadequate information, are perhaps now insoluble. In cases where marked discrepancies exist, as to captures of prisoners objectives &c., I have found it a good principle to select the less favourable account. Certain diaries, it may be added, afford entertaining or exasperating illustrations of the preference shown by amour propre to camouflage rather than to confession. Apart from the actual facts I have endeavoured to convey a faithful and sober idea of the atmosphere of war in which the Division existed, of its complex machinery, its demand for strenuous and incessant labour, its hardship squalor waste, and its challenge to fortitude self-denial and gallantry.

A few points of treatment may be noted. The material necessary for the complete presentation of the main outlines of the war is not yet available. As a background to the story of the Division, I have thought it essential to give concise summaries of the general operations of the time, but do not pretend to look on these as conclusive. To avoid prolixity and obscurity, the smallest infantry unit mentioned by name is the Battalion, and except on special occasions Companies are not distinguished by title or letter. These will receive due recognition in the various Regimental histories. In the nomenclature of the Territorial Battalions I have preferred to maintain generally the curious idiosyncrasy and all but invariable usage of the Division and have called the 1st Battalion Auckland Regiment "1st Auckland" rather than "the 1st Aucklands," or "Auckland" rather than "the Aucklanders." On the other hand, the Rifle Brigade Battalions are for conciseness distinguished as "the 1st Rifles,"

&c., terms which were rarely if ever used in the Division.[1]
The New Zealand Field Artillery Brigades are numbered
without further definition, and the word "English" or
"British" is added in the case of Imperial artillery units.
Unless when the coherence of the narrative demands otherwise, units are mentioned from right to left. Initials, except
when their omission makes for ambiguity, are not repeated.
Names of officers commanding battalions in battle are given
only when the Battalion Commander himself is for any reason
absent. In several maps contours have for the sake of clearness been omitted. The illustrations except those of persons
or where stated otherwise have been selected from the
official N.Z.E.F. photographs. One example of the Army
aeroplane photographs is shown.

Throughout my work the Historical Section of the War
Cabinet allowed me free access to all the records I wanted, and
I have to thank their officials, Brig.-Gen. J. E. Edmonds, C.B.,
C.M.G., D.S.O., R.E., Major H. C. Ferguson, C.M.G., Welsh
Guards, and particularly Major C. T. Atkinson, for their
courtesy and assistance. Major J. T. Treloar, O.B.E., Aus-
tralian War Records, with similar readiness put all his
serviceable material at my disposal.

In a still greater degree I received the utmost help from
Major H. S. Westmacott, Auckland Regiment, who was in
charge latterly of the New Zealand War Records. The most
troublesome and inconvenient demands were met by him and
his staff always cheerfully and ungrudgingly.

I have also to acknowledge assistance from many officers
and men, and more particularly from the understated: Lt.-Gen.
Sir A. J. Godley, Major-Gen. Sir A. H. Russell, Brig.-Gen.
G. N. Johnston, Brig.-Gen. C. W. Melvill, Brig.-Gen. R.
Young, Lt.-Col. F. Symon, Lt.-Col. J. Studholme, Lt.-Col. H. E.
Barrowclough, all of whom have read the work in type and
made valuable suggestions. The well-known French anti-
quarian, M. Léon Contil, procured for me information, un-
obtainable in England, about the Butte de Polygon. I
owe a special debt to Capt. S. Cory Wright, Divisional
Intelligence Officer, who most unselfishly scrutinised the
whole narrative with minute care, and supplemented it from
his unrivalled store of precise information. On points of
detail I have received help from Brig.-Gen. G. S. Richardson,

---

1 Usually "1st Bn., etc., N.Z.R.B." Colloquially the Rifle Brigade Battalions
were known as "Dinks," a term applied to them on their arrival in Egypt, 1916, and
alluding to the special patronage which they enjoyed of the Governor-General of the
Dominion, and to their peculiarities of drill and dress.

Lt -Col. E. H. Northcroft, Lt.-Col. C. H. D. Evans, Major J. L. C. Merton, Capt. V. G. Jervis, Capt. W. J. Organ, Lt. L. C. L. Averill.

All these officers have given me valuable information on obscure points and helped me to avoid or eliminate inaccuracies. For such as may remain I am solely responsible. I have also to acknowledge the unwearied energy and painstaking, scholarly care of my secretary, Sergt. R. S. Gilmour; and the excellent work done, under my general supervision, in the preparation of the maps by Messrs. E. D. Broadhead, J. L. Martin and E. Pfankuch, of the Lands and Survey Department. The task of proof-correcting has been materially lightened by the assistance of my wife and Mr. T. W. Cane. Finally, I desire to thank Mr. Louis Whitcombe and his staff for their unfailing vigilance courtesy and consideration.

H.S.

Canterbury College,
Christchurch, 1st July 1920.

Contents

List of Illustrations

List of Maps

Foreword by Field-Marshal Earl Haig, of Bemersyde, K.T., G.C.B., O.M., Etc.

G.H.Q. The Forces in Great Britain,

Horse Guards,

London, S.W.1.

14th August, 1919

The story of New Zealand's share in the Great War needs no introduction from anyone, but I am grateful for the opportunity to express to the people of New Zealand my high opinion of the troops they sent to fight under my command. I can assure them that my opinion is shared by everyone with whom New Zealand troops came in contact.

The pages of this book will tell you of the exploits of your Division. I can only add that no Division in France built up for itself a finer reputation, whether for the gallantry of its conduct in battle or for the excellence of its behaviour out of the line. Its record does honour to the land from which it came and to the Empire for which it fought.

D. Haig.

Field-Marshal

Foreword by Lt.-General Sir G. M. Harper, K.C.B., D.S.O., Commanding IV. Corps

After the evacuation of Gallipoli the New Zealand Division was ordered to France and arrived in April, 1916.

At the time both sides were involved in trench warfare. The British, in conjunction with the French, attacked during the autumn on the Somme. The enemy was not sufficiently reduced in numbers, armament or moral, for a decision to be obtained. It was not then considered justifiable to attack at various periods on several portions of the front. Communication had not been sufficiently perfected, nor was the artillery considered adequate. In an offensive on a comparatively narrow front the enemy was naturally able to concentrate his artillery and reserves against the particular portion attacked, with comparative safety to the remainder of his front.

In 1917 the British plan was more ambitious. The Arras offensive in April was succeeded by the attack on Messines Ridge, afterwards by the Ypres offensive in July, and later, in November, by the Cambrai attack supported by tanks. In each case, however, the attack definitely ceased before being undertaken elsewhere. As in the preceding year, the enemy, after suffering initial losses, was able to concentrate in such force as to make further attacks very costly.

In these offensives the success of a Division depended mainly upon artillery support. If the plan had been well devised, if the artillery support was adequate, and further, if the infantry had been well trained and practised in the tasks they had to carry out, they generally took their objective with comparatively slight loss. It was, however, in the consolidation after the attack that losses were chiefly incurred. Divisions therefore suffered heavy losses from machine guns if unsuccessful in the first instance, and if successful, from artillery fire in the later stages. In either case, after a few days' fighting they had to be withdrawn to recuperate and refit. It was thus impracticable for a Division to make a prolonged sustained effort against the enemy.

During this period the New Zealand Division made several gallant attacks, but for the reasons given above, they were not able to make their individuality properly felt, nor impress their full fighting powers upon the enemy. Their opportunity came, however, when, in 1918, the Division joined the I V. Corps at the critical time in March, when it completely checked the enemy's advance at Beaumont-Hamel and Colincamps, and closed the gap between the IV. and V. Corps. By a brilliant stroke it drove the enemy from the commanding ground at La Signy Farm, south of Hébuterne. This enabled observation to be obtained over the enemy's lines. A period of trench warfare then ensued. During this time the New Zealanders established a complete ascendency over the enemy. By carefully considered and well executed raids they gave him no respite, and identifications of the hostile units were obtained whenever required. It was this ascendency which compelled the enemy to evacuate the ground about Rossignol Wood.

In the great attack which commenced in August 1918 the New Zealand Division played a most brilliant part in the operations on the IV. Corps front. Its efforts were crowned with almost continual success. Of these the most notable were the capture of Bapaume, after having driven the enemy from Grévillers and Biefvillers; the brilliant night advance from Welsh Ridge, which, on the 1st October, led to the capture of Crèvecoeur; and subsequently the great attack on the 8th October, when the Division broke through the northern portion of the strongly organised Masnières Line and penetrated far into the enemy's line at Esnes and Haucourt. These successes were finally crowned by the skilful attack which led to the surrender of the fortress of Le Quesnoy and the driving of the enemy through the Forest of Mormal.

During the period the New Zealanders were in the IV. Corps they captured from the enemy 287 officers, 8745 other ranks, 145 guns, 1419 machine guns, and 2 tanks, besides much other material. These continued successes constituted a record which it is safe to say was unsurpassed in the final series of attacks which led to the armistice.

What were the causes which conduced to these successes? Firstly, the New Zealander was endowed to a marked degree with bravery, individuality and initiative. Every man fought intelligently. If a portion of the attacking line was checked, the remainder worked their way forward, dealt with the enemy opposing the advance, or relieved the situation so that an advance was possible on the whole front. Secondly, the Division was kept up to strength throughout the operations. It was thus possible to retain brigades of four battalions, whereas in the British Divisions a reduction to three had become necessary.

The Division was kept up in physique as well as numbers; but numbers, endowed with intelligence and bravery, are not in themselves sufficient to ensure victory.

The Division was particularly fortunate in its commander. Major-General Sir A. H. Russell was a soldier by training and by nature. Imbued with sound tactical ideas, he was able to launch the Division in attack with a sound plan and a reasonable chance of success. He thought out problems beforehand, in fact, he was always thinking ahead. He inspired those whom he served and those who served him with the utmost confidence. His staff was thoroughly efficient, as was not surprising with a commander of this calibre. The Division was also fortunate in its brigadiers and subordinate commanders, who were selected in accordance with their fighting capacity. The consequence was that throughout the Division there was mutual confidence and whole-hearted co-operation. It was this that contributed to success as much as, and even more than, the qualities of the individual fighting soldier.

New Zealand may well be proud of the Division that contributed so largely to the ultimate defeat of the enemy. Its achievements were splendid, and as such, they should be recorded in history.

G. M. Harper

Lt.-General,
Commanding IV. Corps.

MAJOR-GENERAL SIR A. H. RUSSELL, K.C.B. K.C.M.G.

The New Zealand Division

CHAPTER I

The Formation of the Division

It does not fall within the province of this book to describe the raising and despatch of the original New Zealand Expeditionary Force, the formation of the New Zealand and Australian Division, which consisting predominantly of New Zealanders included an Australian infantry brigade and other Australian units, or the achievements of the composite Division in Egypt and Gallipoli.[1] The present narrative has for its subject the history of the New Zealand Division, whose inception dates from the early spring of 1916 with the transference of the Australian units of the old composite Division to Australian formations and the raising of fresh units to take their place and to complete the establishment of a purely New Zealand Division.

This reorganisation followed after a short interval the inevitable abandonment of the Peninsula in December 1915 and January 1916. The policy of evacuation had made for a necessarily piecemeal arrival in Egypt, but by the end of the first week in January the 1st and 2nd Australian Divisions (less mounted troops) were concentrated at Tel-el-Kebir, and the New Zealand and Australian Division (less mounted troops) at Moascar, near Ismailia, on the Suez Canal.[2] The latter neighbourhood was already familiar to the New Zealand infantry as the scene of their first experience of battle, for it was here that a year previously they had participated in the repulse of the Turkish attack on the Canal. Anzac Corps Headquarters moved from Cairo to Ismailia on 4th January. Subsequently to Lieut.-General Sir

---

1 For the early history of the New Zealand Expeditionary Force, the New Zealand and Australian Division, and the Australian and New Zealand Army Corps, see Waite, *The New Zealanders at Gallipoli*.

2 The 3 Australian Light Horse Brigades and the New Zealand Mounted Rifles Brigade had been despatched to Zeitoun in the vicinity of Cairo.

W. R. Birdwood's assuming temporary command of the
Dardanelles Army, Major-General (now Lieut.-General) Sir
A. J. Godley had been in November 1915 promoted from
command of the New Zealand and Australian Division to
temporary command of the Anzac Corps. He had been
succeeded as Divisional commander by Brigadier-General (now
Major-General) Sir A. H. Russell. While giving up command
of the Division, General Godley retained control of the New
Zealand Expeditionary Force as a whole.

Pending the development of the renewed Turkish threat
at the Canal, the role of the Mediterranean Expeditionary
Force was defined by the Chief of the Imperial Staff as being
that of the strategical reserve of the Empire. With this
function in view, the depleted ranks were immediately filled
up from accumulated reinforcements, and the troops, who
despite the rigours of the Gallipoli campaign and its tragic
dénouement were in excellent health and fine morale, embarked without delay on a vigorous course of training. The
main principles governing military policy in Egypt were
two. On the one hand there was the possibility of an attack
on the Canal, and on the other the probability that the
various Corps quartered for the moment in the country would
be required for operations in some other theatre of war in
the spring. To meet the Turkish attack, extensive fortifications and engineering works were in process of construction
east of the Canal. It was, however, the latter principle that
was to affect the New Zealand and Australian Division for
the first 2 months of the year. General Headquarters and
Corps emphasised the urgency of intensive training. Thus,
on 17th January, the Australasian Divisions received from
Corps a memorandum whose nature is indicated by the following extract:—

> "There is little enough time in which to fit ourselves to
> take the field against the Germans, which may be our
> next move, and every moment is precious. Each officer
> and man must make the fullest use of his opportunity for
> training. Except on one, or possibly two, days in the
> week, at the discretion of Divisional commanders, lunch
> should now be taken in the field, and troops should be
> clear of camp by 7.30 a.m., and should not return before
> 4 p.m., at the earliest."

A few days later G.H.Q. issued secret instructions impressing
the necessity of taking every measure to ensure complete
preparation for the field.

The New Zealand and Australian Division had all round its quarters a practically unlimited area, admirably suited alike for barrack-square drill, musketry, field firing and tactical operations. The broken surface of the desert, the tortuous wadis, the deep unexpected hollows, the glacis or sheer declivities of the yellow sand hills, the mud villages and the palm plantations lent themselves readily for all manner of schemes. In view, too, of the possibility of having to deliver a counter-attack through the front line defences, the Division was frequently exercised in moving over the desert on a broad front and in passing through "gaps" of a size similar to those left for the purpose of counter-attack in the defence system. Night operations were practised twice a week, with the object of training the troops to carry out close formation marches and to execute attacks over the featureless desert in the dark with confidence and facility. Many courses of instruction were held. In addition to Divisional and brigade manoeuvres, a feature was made of "staff rides," including a series for junior officers. A first acquaintance was made in the machine gun school at Ismailia with the recently invented Lewis gun, the far-reaching potentialities of which were to win speedy recognition.

Owing to shortage of equipment and to other reasons, the new artillery units, whose formation will be referred to presently, were confined to general or theoretical work; the other batteries fired practices with live shell, and occasionally in co-operation with aeroplane observers. Apart from their technical training and reorganisation, the Engineers were employed in pontoon-building on the Sweet Water Canal, near Ismailia, and on the Suez Canal at Ballah Scrapeum and El Ferdan; in general camp improvements, such as pipe-laying and the provision of water supply; the building of huts; the supervision of native labour in the construction of tramways and of light piers; and in the development of the field works at Abu Arak and other points in the Canal defences. On 16th January the Division was inspected by Sir Archibald Murray, the new Commander-in-Chief of the Mediterranean Force, who had relieved Sir C. C. Munro a week previously.

On arrival in Egypt from Gallipoli, administration had been hampered by more than the usual difficulties attendant on the redistribution of large forces. The baggage sent from Anzac had not arrived, and owing to insufficiency of camp equipment the troops were at first obliged to bivouac in the open. There was also a shortage of supplies due to the enormous congestion on the railways, so that for the first few days less than half the bread ration and no jam or bacon were procurable. The provision of an adequate water system presented grave difficulties. The Supply Units had only temporary structures formed of biscuit-boxes covered with tarpaulins to protect their most perishable commodities from the sun's rays. They surmounted all obstacles, however, just as rapidly as they circumvented the craftiness of the native dealers, who increased the weight of their bales of green feed by a judicious use of the roadside watering pipes and inserted stones in every crutch or cavity of their consignments of wood. Brick sheds with wooden roofs and Venetian ventilators were erected, and the services of native carpenters were engaged to expedite the construction of tables and benches for offices canteens and mess-rooms. Tents and marquees rose gradually in orderly formations, followed by baths canteens and cinema halls. With such amenities, with plenty of food, with undisturbed sleep and freedom from anxiety, with the unrivalled winter air of the desert, even the very strenuous training was an extraordinary relaxation after the hardships of Gallipoli. Ismailia, in addition, though less cosmopolitan than Cairo, provided diverse opportunities for amusement. The deep clear waters of Lake Timsah, reflecting the blue sky and the bare yellow hills, afforded scope for bathing and swimming. Football and athletic competitions gave relief from training and re-organisation, and mounted steeplechases were held over the sand-dunes and the network of little canals. All around were the habiliments of war—guns horses aeroplanes warships—but the trials and horrors of battle and of the trenches seemed remote and unreal.

Shortly after Sir Archibald Murray had assumed command, the Mediterranean Expeditionary Force in Egypt, augmented by the large forces returned from the Peninsula, was reconstituted and located, from the southern extremity of the defences northwards, as follows. The IX. Corps (Lieut.-General Hon. Sir J. Byng) with headquarters at Suez and comprising the 29th 46th and 10th (Indian) Divisions, was responsible for the area from Suez to Kabrit inclusive. The intermediate section from Kabrit to El Ferdan, both exclusive, was in charge of the Anzac Corps. Northwards from El Ferdan to Port Said extended the XV. Corps (Lieut.-General H. S. Horne), with the 11th 13th and 31st Divisions.

In general reserve at Tel-el-Kebir was the VIII. Corps, consisting of the 42nd and 52nd Divisions under Lieut.-General Sir F. J. Davies.

To the defensive front allotted to the Anzac Corps the 2 Australian Divisions began to move from Tel-el-Kebir on 24th January. The New Zealand and Australian Division remained in Corps reserve at Moascar. At the same time the New Zealand Mounted Rifles Brigade under Brigadier-General E. W. C. Chaytor, who had succeeded General Russell, began a wearisome trek from Zeitoun to the Corps area. They bivouacked alongside the infantry at Moascar on the night of 28th/29th January, whence they reached their destination at Serapeum on the following day. The Light Horse Brigades followed by rail.

The fact that the New Zealand and Australian Division was thus left in reserve facilitated the complex task of re-organisation. By the beginning of 1916 there had been a remarkable expansion of the Australasian forces in Egypt owing to the piling up of sick and wounded, and particularly to the steady flow of reinforcements from the Dominions. These had been temporarily drafted into makeshift formations, training brigades, and the like, but their numbers demanded some radical reorganisation. The problem now pressed for solution. It was earnestly considered at Corps Headquarters during the latter part of January and was reviewed from all aspects. On 21st January Sir Archibald Murray wired in code to the Chief of the Imperial Staff:—

"I find there is now a very large accumulation of Australian and New Zealand reinforcements here which cannot be absorbed in existing organisations. It is essential that these should be formed into definite units with the least possible delay, both for reasons of training and discipline. I have consulted General Birdwood, and we are of the opinion that it is possible to form immediately four new Australian brigades, four Australian Pioneer battalions, and another New Zealand brigade. The New Zealand Division[1] at present contains the 4th Australian Brigade and two dismounted Light Horse and Mounted Rifles brigades. The dismounted brigades are being replaced by the New Zealand Rifles Brigade; and the formations, if additional to New Zealand brigade, from reinforcements in Egypt will enable a complete New Zealand Division to be formed and will release the 4th Aus-

_____
[1] _i.e._ the New Zealand and Australian Division.

tralian Brigade." (The proposed Australian formations of 2 fresh Divisions to be raised in Egypt in addition to the Division to be raised in Australia are then discussed.) "I understand that General Birdwood has the confidence of the Australian and New Zealand Governments, and if these proposals are agreed to, I propose to organise at once, and it will simplify and hasten matters if General Birdwood is permitted to arrange all details in direct communication with the relative Defence Ministers."

On reference to the Dominions the War Office was notified by Australia that she agreed to the proposals. The New Zealand Government, however, having already sent the Rifle Brigade in excess of the numbers originally contemplated, desired further information in view of the necessity that would arise of maintaining 3 infantry brigades with reinforcements arranged for only 2, and with no increase on the scale in force possible before the autumn. General Murray was therefore instructed by the War Office on 5th February to notify General Birdwood that he must await instructions with regard to the proposed New Zealand Division. On the 8th the Commander-in-Chief replied to the War Office that while quite understanding the situation as regards New Zealand, he trusted that he might be permitted to form a third infantry brigade at once, as there were sufficient men available for it in excess of the establishment of the 2 existing brigades.

"The formation of such a brigade is necessary in any case for the purpose of training and discipline. In addition to the surplus of infantry reinforcements who are available for the formation of a third infantry brigade, there is a large number of surplus Mounted Rifles who are available and willing to come forward either for artillery or infantry brigade. Reinforcements are coming in every month at the rate of 20% in excess of establishment, and there seems little chance in the near future of absorbing this surplus in existing units. It therefore seems practically certain that we could keep up the proposed New Zealand Division to approximate strength until New Zealand can increase the present scale of reinforcements."

The position was thus clearly stated, and on 10th February, pending formal sanction from the Governments, the arrangements made for forming a second Anzac Corps were put into operation. At the same time it was decided that the

LIEUT.-GENERAL SIR A. J. GODLEY, K.C.B., K.C.M.G.

BRIG.-GEN. G. NAPIER JOHNSTON, C.M.G., D.S.O.

BRIG.-GEN. F. EARL JOHNSTON, C.B.

I. Anzac Corps (General Godley) should consist, as at present constituted, of the 1st and 2nd Australian Divisions and the New Zealand and Australian Division, while the II. Anzac Corps should be composed of the 3rd Division (still in Australia) and of the new 4th and 5th Australian Divisions. General Godley's Corps would continue to hold its sector of the defences, while II. Anzac would be left undisturbed at Tel-el-Kebir to complete its reorganisation. The old Corps Staff was divided between the two Corps. The Staff of Headquarters, Australian and New Zealand Forces (General Birdwood), with that of the II. Anzac Corps, now split off from the I. Anzac Corps and set up offices in separate buildings. Brigadier-General C. B. B. White's appointment of B.G.G.S. on the staff of II. Anzac was temporarily filled by Colonel C. M. Wagstaff, while the former acted as D.A. and Q.M.G. of the Australian and New Zealand Forces. General Godley's Chief Staff Officer was Colonel (now Brigadier-General) C. W. Gywnn, C.M.G., D.S.O., R.E.

Meanwhile Generals Birdwood and Godley had been in communication with the New Zealand Government, and the latter formally notified its approval of the proposals contemplated to the War Office, which cabled to Headquarters Mediterranean Expeditionary Force to that effect in the middle of February.

The organisation of the new Division was based in the main on War Establishments, Part VII., as laid down in 1915 for the New Armies. There were some minor modifications. Thus a Cyclist Company[1] and a Motor Machine Gun Battery were not raised, nor an Ammunition Sub Park, nor a Divisional Supply Column. A squadron of the former Divisional cavalry, the Otago Mounted Rifles Regiment, now with the Mounted Brigade at Serapeum, was on 23rd February designated Divisional Mounted Troops, and the remainder of the Regiment was drafted into the newly-formed Pioneer Battalion. Their horses were sent to the new artillery infantry and pioneer units. Even then a remount demand for over 1800 horses had to be rendered to complete the Division's establishment. The formation of an Australian and New Zealand Mounted Division, mooted by the War Office as early as 29th December, and now on the point of accomplishment, absorbed the Light Horse Brigades and the New Zealand Mounted Rifles Brigade.

---

[1] A Cyclist Company was formed, however, in New Zealand in April 1916, by voluntary transfers from the Mounted Rifles units in training at that time, and arrived in France in July of the same year: see p. 59.

The problems faced in artillery expansion were complicated by the lack of trained personnel. It was even proposed at one time to adhere to the inadequate establishments laid down for British Territorial Divisions operating in Egypt. Eventually, however, it was decided not to be satisfied with half-measures, but to adopt boldly Part VII. Establishments, with the one exception that the Howitzer Brigade should consist of 3 instead of 4 batteries. Eight new 18-pounder batteries were therefore formed,[1] the 7th and 8th being added to the old 1st Brigade; the 9th and 10th being added to the old 2nd Brigade, and the 11th 12th 13th and 14th constituting the new 3rd Brigade. An additional Howitzer Battery (the 15th) completed the 4th (Howitzer) Brigade. The artillery therefore now consisted of three 18-pounder brigades of four batteries each and one howitzer brigade of three batteries. In the training of the raw artillery material the experience of the C.R.A. (Brigadier-General Napier Johnston) on the Instructional Staff of the British Army was invaluable.

To bring the Engineers up to establishment, the Field Troop New Zealand Engineers was transferred from the Mounted Rifles Brigade and expanded with the addition of skilled tradesmen drawn from the infantry into a third Field Company.

By the middle of January the 2nd Battalion of the New Zealand Rifles Brigade had arrived at Moascar from Alexandria, where it had acted as Lines of Communication troops in the Western Frontier campaign against the Senussi. It was followed towards the end of the month by the 1st Battalion, which had received instructive experience, seen some fighting, and suffered its first casualties at Jebel Medwa in December. The 3rd and 4th Battalions did not arrive from New Zealand till the middle of March.

In the formation of the 2nd New Zealand Infantry Brigade the same principle which governed the raising of the additional artillery batteries was followed, namely, the expansion of each of the 4 original "regiments" into 2 battalions, the 2nd Battalions of the regiments forming the 2nd Brigade.[2] A complete cadre of officers was provided from

1 The 1st Artillery Brigade had consisted of the 1st 3rd and 6th (How.) Batteries; the 2nd of the 2nd 5th and 4th (How.) Batteries.

2 The original N.Z. Infantry Brigade was formed of 4 "Regiments" drawn from the 4 military districts. Auckland Canterbury Otago Wellington. In the "Regiment," each company was drawn from and designated by the number and title of the regiment in the N.Z. Military Forces from whose area it was raised. Thus the Canterbury companies were the 1st (Canterbury); the 2nd (South Canterbury); the 12th (Nelson and Marlborough); the 13th (North Canterbury and Westland).

the original infantry brigade, with the addition of a limited number of officers from the Mounted Rifles Brigade. A certain number of non-commissioned officers was transferred from the original brigade, but the rank and file were provided almost entirely from the reinforcements of all branches of the service and by the transfer of a certain number of men surplus in existing units. Brigadier-General W. G. Braithwaite relinquished his command of the as yet incomplete Rifle Brigade to take command of the 2nd Brigade. He was succeeded in command of the Rifle Brigade by Lt.-Col. H. T. Fulton (2nd King's Own Gurkha Rifles), commanding the 1st Battalion, who was then granted the temporary rank of Brigadier-General.

A happy solution lay to hand for the formation of a Pioneer Battalion. After the August operations on the Peninsula the remainder of the original Maori contingent, together with reinforcements which had joined them, had been divided up by tribes among the 4 infantry regiments. The same course was adopted with the reinforcements which arrived at this time and were welcomed with ancient Maori ceremonial on the Egyptian desert. These now constituted the nucleus of the Pioneer Battalion, the remainder being drawn, as mentioned above, from the headquarters and the 2 surplus squadrons of the Otago Mounted Rifles. The appointment of battalion commander was given to Major (now Lt.-Col.) G. A. King, N.Z.S.C., who had been Staff Captain of the Mounted Brigade. Further reinforcements arrived on 15th March, consisting of 112 Maoris, 125 Niue Islanders,[1] and 45 Rarotongans. In the formation of each company the 2 leading platoons were composed of Maoris or Islanders in tribes, and the other 2 of pakehas.[2]

A machine gun corps was created by the formation of 3 machine gun companies drawn from the machine gun sections in the battalions; 2 companies from those of the original (now the 1st) Infantry Brigade, and the third from those of the Rifle Brigade. Two new field ambulances were raised by the expansion of the existing organisation and by building upon a No. 2 Field Ambulance section which had arrived from New Zealand in December. A Divi-

1 Climatic conditions proved too severe for the Niue Islanders of the tropical Pacific. Some of them were sent home from Egypt, the remainder from France in May. Of the Address despatched by the Chief of Niue to England in 1914 the opening words merit quotation here: "To King George V., all those in authority and the brave men who fight: I am the island of Niue, a small child that stands up to help the Kingdom of King George . . . ."

2 Pakeha, Maori for "European."

sional Sanitary Section was formed on 7th February. The
Army Service Corps branch was expanded, and in addition
5 Depot Units of Supply, with Field Bakery and Field
Butchery, were formed as Lines of Communication Units, not
incorporated in the Division. The 2 Veterinary Sections
despatched from New Zealand in December 1914 were disbanded, the personnel being absorbed in 2 Mobile Veterinary
Sections, one of which was attached to the Division and
the other to the Mounted Rifles Brigade.

The expansion of old and the formation of new units not
merely absorbed the excess personnel of the disbanded Otago
Mounted Rifles Regiment and all accumulated 7th 8th and
9th Reinforcements, but also drained the Mounted Rifles'
surplus reinforcements in New Zealand as well as in Egypt.
The natural reluctance of the horseman to leave his particular arm was overcome firstly by the precedent set on
Gallipoli, where Mounted Rifles and Light Horse had served
in the open as in trenches on foot, and secondly by the
reflection, not unreasonable at this stage of the evolution of
tactics, that there was a brighter prospect of seeing fighting
in other branches of the service. The spirit with which all
ranks transferred is given generous recognition by General
Godley in an order issued on 3rd June:—

"The G.O.C. wishes to place on record his appreciation
and that of the New Zealand Government of the patriotic
and public-spirited action of the many officers, n.c.o.s,
and men of the Mounted Rifles who have voluntarily
transferred, both in Egypt and in New Zealand, to the
infantry and other arms when it became known that men
were urgently required for these services.

"That so large a number of all ranks should have
readily and cheerfully responded to the call to place the
interests of the Force before everything else is a most
gratifying and convincing proof that the N.Z.E.F. has in
it that first essential for efficiency and success—the true
soldierly spirit."

Towards the end of February, while all these augmentations
were in progress, the 4th Australian Infantry Brigade left
the Division at Moascar to join their comrades at Tel-el-
Kebir. Their movement had been delayed by a shortage of
tents and camp equipment in their new quarters, but now a
battalion marched out daily, and by the evening of 28th February the 16th Battalion and the 4th Field Ambulance, the
last of the Australians of the old composite Division, had

gone. They were given a spontaneous and moving send-off by the New Zealanders who had shared with them dangers and privations on the Anzac ridges and had partaken of their open-handed hospitality at Moascar. The separation from these old comrades, though inevitable and indeed desirable from the administrative point of view in both forces, was keenly and genuinely regretted on personal grounds. On 1st March authority was given for the assumption of the title "The New Zealand Division" instead of "The New Zealand and Australian Division," and the new formations and units were taken on strength. The labour travails were over and the new Division born.

Meanwhile the Turkish debacle in the Caucasus[1] had compelled the Porte not merely to reduce to garrison strength its forces in Thrace Gallipoli and Western Anatolia, but even to divert the Syrian Army northwards. Thus the danger to the Canal and nodal centre of the Empire was daily receding. The Egyptian garrison was therefore reduced by the despatch of the 29th and other British Divisions to the Western Front. The first results of the German blow at Verdun, its repercussions in the political atmosphere, and the desirability of relieving a French Army on a sector of the defensive front[2] made it, however, increasingly obvious that there would be a further call on the troops in Egypt.

The call came to the I. Anzac Corps at the beginning of March. It was arranged thereupon that General Birdwood should reassume command of I. Anzac, and that General Godley should take that of II. Anzac. General Godley would naturally have preferred to retain his New Zealanders under his own command, but as neither of the newly-formed 4th and 5th Australian Divisions was as yet sufficiently trained to complete General Birdwood's Corps for service in France, he magnanimously insisted that the New Zealand Division should be retained by and accompany I. Anzac pending his own arrival in France with II. Anzac.

Arrangements had already been made for the relief of the 2nd Australian Division in the defensive zone, and the New Zealand Division had begun to take over their area east of the Canal. In the front line 2 Australian infantry brigades were relieved by the New Zealand Mounted Rifles Brigade, which was now for this purpose temporarily attached to the Division. They disposed 1 squadron at each previous

---

1 The Russians entered Erzerum on 16th February.
2 Haig's Despatch of 29th May, 1916, paras. 1 and 10.

battalion headquarters, 6 squadrons in all being in the front line and 1 regiment at railhead. Similarly the 3rd Light Horse Brigade took over the 1st Australian Division's frontage to the south. The guns remained in situ, and were served till the arrival of the relieving New Zealand batteries by personnel detailed for transfer to the 4th and 5th Australian Divisions. On the same date the 1st New Zealand Infantry Brigade relieved the reserve Australian brigade at the bridgehead at Ferry Post. By 8th March the movement of the Division was completed. Headquarters were at Albury Hill, the 1st Infantry Brigade at Ferry Post, the Rifle Brigade a mile east of it, the newly-formed 2nd Brigade half a mile west of Albury Hill. The 2nd Australian Division was now assembled at Moascar, making the final arrangements for entraining and embarkation.

The contrast between the Canal defences now and at the time of the Turkish fiasco a year previously was most striking. Then there had been a few bridgeheads on the eastern bank, but the general situation had been described by an inspecting General, not less justly than caustically, as one in which the Canal protected the troops instead of the troops defending the Canal. Now railways and metalled roads ran eastwards into the desert, and elaborate provision had been made for the supply of water. The first line of defence was now not on the Canal, but 7 miles distant. It had been selected by Major-General Horne, afterwards in turn XV. Corps and First Army Commander in France, who had been specially sent to Egypt for the purpose. The engineering operations and the administration were carried out by the Director of Railways and the Director of Works under the control of Major-General Sir H. V. Cox, who acted as Staff Officer (ad hoc) to Sir John Maxwell.

Gradually if slowly the Turks were pushing their Palestine railway system south of Beersheba, but even assuming an improbably high rate of progress it was certain that in face of transport difficulties over the sand they could bring up only a limited amount of guns and ammunition. The concealment of trenches, while not so important as on the Western front, was far more difficult in the open desert. Moreover, the scarcity of water would compel the enemy either to win a victory in two or three days or to retire. He could not sit down to a systematic bombardment and trench warfare. For these reasons, therefore, our defence positions were selected more with a view to good all-round and to effective

BRIG.-GEN. W. G. BRAITHWAITE, C.B., C.M.G., D.S.O.

BRIG.-GEN. G. S. RICHARDSON, C.B., C.M.G., C.B.E.

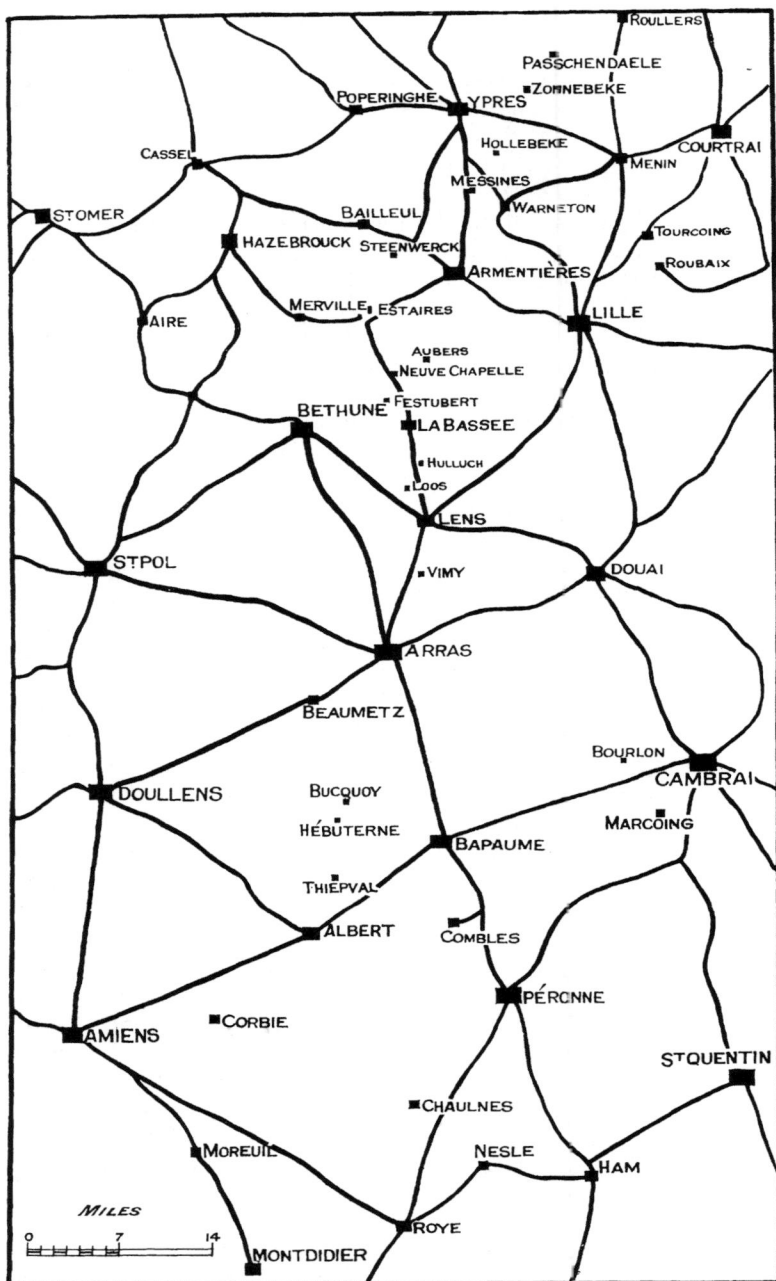

N.W. FRANCE

cross fire than to concealment from prolonged and intense artillery concentration. The first line included all the important points from which observed fire could be directed on the Canal and shipping. The second line ran about 4,500 yards in rear of the first, and although it surrendered many points whence an enemy could observe the Canal, it was sufficiently advanced to prevent any serious interference with traffic. The third line consisted of the strengthened original defences. The ships allotted to the Anzac Sector under command of Capt. A. P. Davidson, R.N., were the *Cornwallis*, the Monitor *Sir Thomas Picton*, Monitor No. 15, and the French coast defence battleship *Requin*.

The front line system which the Mounted Brigade now took over was still in process of organisation. Wide and formidable entanglements were laid out in the light of most recent experience, concealed in hollows and with deceptive pockets to allure the assault on to enfilade and co-ordinated machine gun fire. The trenches themselves were not continuous, but constituted a series of fortified "localities," the garrisons of which would vary from a battalion or less up to a brigade. The primary role of these garrisons was defined to be passive defence. With a touch of imagery rare in military "Defence Schemes" they were compared to rocks round which a torrent might surge without sweeping them away. Between them were left gaps free from obstacles for the development of counter-strokes by other troops.

The Mounted patrols rode out daily well in front of the position and supplemented the mostly negative information brought in by aeroplanes, Arab agents of varying reliability, and the Bikanir Camel Corps. Though the enemy strength remained meagre, nothing was left to chance as far as the defence system was concerned. Nelson Camp, Hagley Park, Sphinx Post and all the other positions were solidly entrenched and wired. The Engineers supervising the working parties had their troubles through the drifting sand with which an occasional khamseen choked the trenches. Apart from reconnoitring the positions in the line which they would occupy in the event of a strong attack, the infantry remained in support in rear, training and perfecting their organisation. They were visited on 21st March by the youthful Prince of Wales who rode round informally and watched them at drill. He was just in time to receive a haka[1] in the Maori

---

1 Maori for "dance," here of welcome.

lines, before the Pioneers set out on the dusty march back across the Canal to Moascar.

For it was now the turn of the New Zealanders to follow the 2nd and 1st Australian Divisions to France.   On 23rd March, when the Chief of the Imperial Staff directed that the Division should follow immediately the 1st Australian Division, it was already concentrated at Moascar, with the exception of Divisional Headquarters which remained with the Mounted Brigade till the sector was transferred on the 30th to the 5th Australian Division from Tel-el-Kebir.   The War Office pressed for expedition of despatch and chafed against the necessity of exchanging the long rifles for the short rifles firing the new ammunition used in France.   It was too late, however, to modify the arrangements made with the 11th Division for the exchange.

A farewell inspection of the Division was held by General Murray on 3rd April.   His satisfaction was indicated in the following congratulatory message from General Godley to the Divisional Commander:—

"The Commander-in-Chief has directed me to convey to you and all ranks under your command his high appreciation of the fine turn-out and soldierly bearing of your Division at his inspection of it this afternoon.   The steadiness and good marching of the troops were all that could be desired, and the staff arrangements were excellent. I need hardly tell you how proud I am to be the medium of communication of such a message to my old Division, or how pleased I was to see it acquit itself so creditably."

A day or two later the Division entrained for Alexandria and Port Said, where embarkation of advanced parties commenced on 5th April.   Divisional Headquarters sailed on the *Minnewaska*, and in all 16 transports were employed. Guns and wheeled vehicles with the exception of the artillery telephone carts were left in Egypt.   Many regrets were expressed by the artillery at losing their pre-war New Zealand guns which had been used on Gallipoli, nor were they ever to get such good pieces again.

The following was the composition of the Division at this date.

HEADQUARTERS

General Officer Commanding—Major-Gen. Sir A. H. Russell, K.C.M.G.

Aides-de-Camp—Lt. (Hon. Capt.) O. B. Ryrie, (A.I.F.), Lt. R. F. R. Beetham

General Staff Officer, 1st Grade—Major (Temp. Lt.-Col.) W. R. Pinwill, King's Liverpool Regiment (Imperial General Staff)

General Staff Officer, 2nd Grade—Major A. C. Temperley (Norfolk
  Regiment)
General Staff Officer, 3rd Grade—Capt. W. H. Hastings (92nd Punjabis)
A.A. and Q.M.G.—Major (Temp. Lt.-Col.) H. G. Reid, R.A.S.C.
D.A.A. and Q.M.G.—Major W. C. Morrison, N.Z.S.C.
D.A.Q.M.G.—Capt. M. H. Jackson (29th Lancers)
A.D.M.S.—Col. C. M. Begg, C.M.G.
D.A.D.M.S.—Major A. R. D. Carbery
A.D.V.S.—Lt.-Col. A. R. Young
D.A.D.O.S.—Lt.-Col. H. Herbert
A.P.M.—Capt. D. Kettle

DIVISIONAL MOUNTED TROOPS
1 Squadron Otago Mounted Rifles—Lt.-Col. R. R. Grigor

DIVISIONAL ARTILLERY
Commander—Lt.-Col. (Temp. Brig.-Gen.) G. N. Johnston, R.A.
A.D.C.—Lt. F. S. Wilding
Brigade Major—Capt. J. M. Richmond, R.N.Z.A.
Staff Captain—Capt. H. J. Daltry
1st Brigade N.Z.F.A.—Lt.-Col. F. Symon, C.M.G., R.N.Z.A.
2nd Brigade N.Z.F.A.—Lt.-Col. F. B. Sykes, D.S.O., R.A.
3rd Brigade N.Z.F.A.—Lt.-Col. I. T. Standish, D.S.O., R.N.ZA.
4th (Howitzer) Brigade—Major (Temp. Lt.-Col.) N. S. Falla, D.S.O.
D.A.C.—Lt.-Col. M. M. Gard'ner, R.N.Z.A.

DIVISIONAL ENGINEERS
Officer Commanding—Lt.-Col. G. R. Pridham, R.E.
Three Field Companies
One Signal Company

1st NEW ZEALAND INFANTRY BRIGADE
Commander—Major (Temp. Brig.-Gen.) F. E. Johnston, C.B. (North
  Staffordshire Regiment)
Brigade Major—Major R. O. Chesney, N.Z.S.C.
Staff Captain—Capt. H. M. W. Richardson, N.Z.S.C.
1st Bn., Auckland Regiment—Lt.-Col. A. Plugge, C.M.G.
1st Bn., Canterbury Regiment—Lt.-Col. R. Young, C.M.G., D.S.O.
1st Bn., Otago Regiment—Lt.-Col. A. B. Charters
1st Bn., Wellington Regiment—Lt.-Col. H. Hart, D.S.O.

NEW ZEALAND RIFLE BRIGADE
Commander—Major (Temp. Brig.-Gen.) H. T. Fulton, D.S.O. (2nd
  King's Own Gurkha Rifles)
Brigade Major—Capt. (Temp. Major) T. R. Eastwood (Rifle Brigade)
Staff Captain—Capt. R. G. Purdy, N.Z.S.C.
1st Bn., Rifle Brigade—Lt.-Col. W. S. Austin
2nd Bn., Rifle Brigade—Lt.-Col. A. E. Stewart
3rd Bn., Rifle Brigade—Lt.-Col. J. A. Cowles
4th Bn., Rifle Brigade—Lt.-Col. C. W. Melvill, N.Z.S.C.

2nd NEW ZEALAND INFANTRY BRIGADE
Commander—Lt.-Col. (Temp. Brig.-Gen.) W. G. Braithwaite, D.S.O.
  (Royal Welsh Fusiliers)
Brigade Major—Major F. H. Lampen, N.Z.S.C.
Staff Captain—Major E. Puttick
2nd Bn., Auckland Regiment—Lt.-Col. W. W. Alderman, A.I.F. Staff
2nd Bn., Canterbury Regiment—Lt.-Col. H. Stewart, M.C.

2nd Bn., Otago Regiment—Lt.-Col. A. Moore, D.S.O. (Royal Dublin
　　Fusiliers)
2nd Bn., Wellington Regiment—Lt.-Col. W. H. Cunningham
New Zealand Pioneer Bn.,—Lt. Col. G. A. King, N.Z.S.C.
　　　　　　3 Machine Gun Companies
New Zealand Divisional Train—Lt.-Col. N. C. Hamilton, R.A.S.C.
1st New Zealand Field Ambulance—Lt.-Col. E. J. C'Neill, D.S.O.
2nd New Zealand Field Ambulance—Lt.-Col. D. N. W. Murray
3rd New Zealand Field Ambulance—Lt.-Col. J. Hardie Neil
　　　　　New Zealand Sanitary Section.
　　　　　New Zealand Mobile Veterinary Section
In addition the following units accompanied the Division:—
　　　　　　5 Depot Units of Supply
　　　　　　1 Field Butchery
　　　　　　1 Field Bakery
　　　　　　1 Infantry Base Depot
　　　　　　Divisional Record Section
　　　　　　Postal Corps Details

The voyage to Marseilles over a calm sea was uneventful.
Transports took different courses, and some touched at Malta.
In addition to the ordinary routine, emphasis was laid on gas
lectures, and gas helmets were issued.　Every precaution
was taken against submarines.　No lights were allowed on
deck between sunset and reveille, and all lights below were
carefully shaded and deadlights closed.　The minimum of
noise was enjoined after dark.　All ranks worked ate and
slept in lifebelts.　''Boat stations'' were regularly practised,
and besides machine and Lewis gun sentries a submarine
guard was on duty throughout on each vessel.　This
consisted of 2 platoons, 1 in the forward-well deck, 25 men
armed with loaded rifles on each side of the ship, and 1
platoon in the aft-well deck, similarly divided.　Wireless
messages announced the presence of submarines off Marseilles, and observers on one transport sighted or thought
they sighted a periscope 800 yards astern.　But all the
vessels reached Marseilles, from 11th April onwards, without
incident.　A few units received a demonstration of welcome
from the populace, but for the most part unobtrusively and
expeditiously the New Zealand Division entrained for the
British sector away in the North.

Although the Corps was thus despatched to France and
a Base Depot formed at Etaples, near Boulogne, it was not
proposed at first to shift the Australian or New Zealand bases
from Egypt, which was for the Australasian forces more
favourably situated than England.　The War Office definitely
approved this policy on 24th March.　The N.Z.E.F. Headquarters therefore remained in the Kasr-el-nil barracks in
Cairo, under the control of Col. J. J. Esson, where they

had been established in January.   On Col. Esson's returning on duty to New Zealand in March he was succeeded
by Col. V. S. Smyth, N.Z.S.C.   The Chief Staff Officer
was Lt.-Col. G. T. Hall, who had during 1915 commanded
the New Zealand Base Details Camp at Zeitoun.   In the
beginning of the year Col. W. H. Parkes was appointed
D.D.M.S. to the Force, and Major J. Studholme became
General Godley's Assistant Military Secretary.

There were at this time in England about 2000 convalescent
New Zealand soldiers who had come in hospital ships from the
Dardanelles.   Originally after being discharged fit these had
been quartered in an Australian depot at Weymouth, but by
March they had been concentrated partly in an English
camp at Epsom and principally at an exclusively New Zealand
depot at Hornchurch.   This was at first commanded by
Major T. H. Dawson, who was succeeded in April by
Major C. H. J. Brown, N.Z.S.C.   Throughout this early
period a committee of New Zealanders under Lord Plunket,
a former Governor of the Dominion, had set up various
organisations for the well-being of the troops, in particular a
small hospital at Walton-on-Thames, which was conducted by
Major B. Myers.   Administration in England was carried
on by the High Commissioner's staff.   The work thus
imposed on Sir Thomas Mackenzie's office not only in the way
of records pay and other details of administration, but also
in correspondence with the War Office and the New Zealand
Government was excessive; and with the best will in the world
the system was not conducive to military discipline or general
efficiency.   It was therefore decided to attach to the High
Commissioner's staff a Military Representative who should
undertake liaison duties with the War Office and at the same
time act as Commandant of the Hornchurch depot.   At the
instance of the New Zealand Government a cable was
accordingly sent in February to the Salonika Army asking for
the release of Brigadier-General G. S. Richardson, who had
at the outbreak of war been acting as New Zealand Representative at the War Office and at this time held the appointment
of D.A. and Q.M.G. in the XII. Corps.   He arrived in
England in March, and following on recommendations
submitted by General Godley to the New Zealand Government,
assumed the larger duties of Commandant New Zealand
Troops in England, in addition to those of Military
Representative for the Dominion.   The appointment was
subsequently defined as that of General Officer in charge

of Administration. His headquarters was at first a room in the High Commissioner's office with administrative personnel detached in 2 buildings in Victoria Street.

This arrangement, however inconvenient, might have sufficed to deal with the handful of troops that might be expected to be in England on the assumption that the base remained in Egypt. A conference, however, on various questions connected with the Australasian forces was held at the War Office on 28th April between General Birdwood and the Heads of Departments concerned, at which also the Australian and New Zealand Military Representatives were present. To facilitate administration and effect economy in man-power by providing opportunities for speedier recovery under more favourable climatic conditions from wounds or sickness, it was then agreed that the bases for the Australasian troops in France should be transferred from Egypt to England. At the same time the position of the New Zealand High Commissioner was defined. It was decided that he should be kept informed by the Representative on all military matters affecting New Zealand, but that his office should no longer be the channel for correspondence with the War Office. Following on this interview, the New Zealand Base arrived in London early in May, and suitable accommodation was secured for all offices in Southampton Row. In the beginning of June a "Command Depot" (Major J. A. Mackenzie) was established on the edge of Salisbury Plain at Codford. This term had been introduced to distinguish the depots specially devoted to the reception of unfit men from the ordinary Infantry or General Base depots where reinforcements and fit men were in training and readiness to proceed to the front. As a training depot the War Office shortly afterwards assigned Sling Camp, also on Salisbury Plain. There the training units brought from Egypt under Colonel Smyth were concentrated. The infantry were organised in 3 reserve battalions for the respective brigades in the field. At this time, and for some little time afterwards, various Imperial officers were loaned for instructional duties.

In July the Walton-on-Thames hospital was taken under military control and expanded. Major (now Lt.-Col.) B. Myers, who had supervised it for the committee, was promoted A.D.M.S. and transferred to Medical Headquarters. His place was taken by Lt.-Col. T. Mill.[1] Walton thus became

1   Succeeded in December 1917 by Col. E. J. O'Neill, D.S.O.

No. 2 New Zealand General Hospital. The former 2nd Stationary Hospital (Lt.-Col. D. S. Wylie) on being transferred in May to England had been designated No. 1 New Zealand General Hospital.[1] It was established at Brockenhurst in the luxuriant woodland scenery of the New Forest. By July a No. 3 General Hospital (Lt.-Col. M. Holmes)[2] had been organised near the Command Depot at Codford. In June Major C. H. Tewsley took over the administration of the Hornchurch Depot from Major (now Lt.-Col.) Brown to enable the latter to proceed to the command of the 2nd Auckland Battalion in France. In the course of the following month the engineers were centralised at Christchurch, the signallers at Hitchin, and the machine gunners at Grantham, where the foundations of the great British Army machine gun school were already laid. In the last week of September 1916 the Australians and New Zealanders training on and about Salisbury Plain were inspected by H.M. the King. Such were the early stages in the development of the organisation and establishments in England which were afterwards to expand to a scale not then visualised.

1 Lt.-Col. Wylie was succeeded in January 1918 by Col. P. S. Fenwick, C.M.G.

2 Succeeded in turn by Col. Fenwick, (Aug. 1916); Lt.-Col. H. J. McLean, (Jan. 1918); Lt.-Col. G. Home, O.B.E. (Nov. 1918); Major (Temp. Lt.-Col.) H. M. Buchanan, (Jan. 1919).

CHAPTER II

SUMMER AT ARMENTIÈRES

The tedium of the 58-hour journey northwards in the trucks of the French military train was relieved at the outset by the exquisite scenery of the Rhone Valley. The fresh green of the trees and rich grasses, the early flowers in the meadows, and the sunny woodlands, tricked out with the blossoms and pageantry of Spring, were in striking contrast with the monotony of the parched desert. The troops were in the highest spirits. With lively curiosity they eyed the riverside mansions and trim villages, and exchanged pleasantries with the fishermen on the banks and the cheering girls at the stations. A detour was made round Paris. Thereafter the grey rain-sodden skies, bleak country and bitter winds of the north formed a more appropriate setting for the grim business that lay in front.

Divisional Headquarters had proceeded by mail train to the concentration area, of which Hazebrouck was the centre, and the advanced party reached the railhead, Steenbecque, on 13th April. The troops began to arrive there on the 15th. Divisional Headquarters and the artillery were at Blaringhem. The 1st Infantry Brigade was concentrated round Morbecque, the Rifle Brigade round Steenbecque, and the 2nd Brigade round Roquetoire. The transport personnel, with the horses, had been detrained at Abbeville to be issued with wagons. They trekked the remaining 60 miles in 3 days. For animals just landed from a 6 days' voyage and a 2 days' train journey this proved a severe trial, even with empty wagons. The transition from the warmth of Egypt also affected them, especially the mules, and one or two animals died. The artillery were in a similar way diverted to Havre, where, with remarkable expedition, they were equipped with vehicles and guns, and despatched to the concentration area by train.

Thus assembled in the last week of April, the Division passed again under the command of the I. Anzac Corps, which in its turn formed part of the Second Army under General Plumer. The 2 Australian Divisions had in the middle of April taken over a sector of the front line system from Fleurbaix to Armentières. Corps Headquarters was at

BRIG.-GEN. H. T. FULTON, C.M.G., D.S.O.

GENERAL RUSSELL ADDRESSING TROOPS

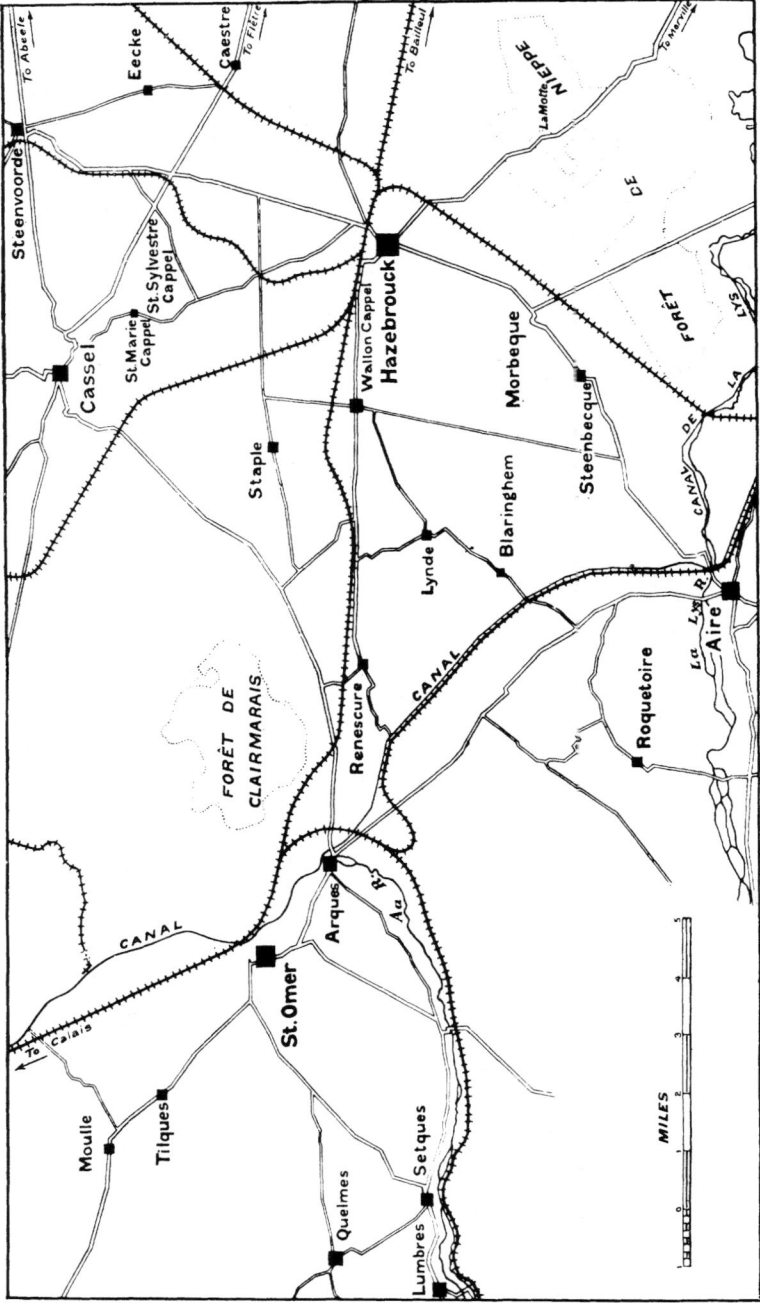

St. Omer and Hazebrouck

the picturesque village of La Motte, amid the oaks elms and beeches of the extensive Forêt de Nieppe. This concentration area was somewhat more diversified by wooded declivities than is usual in the Département du Nord. Amid the unfenced fields, intensively and untiringly cultivated by women and old men, lay the agricultural villages, each marked by its tall church spire, its red brick houses, its substantial tree-shaded chateau on the outskirts, and its slatternly farms with clay-walled byres and insanitary manure-heaps in the courtyards. In the near neighbourhood was the ancient fortress-town of Aire. From the uplands one commanded a wide view of the low-lying country as far south as Lens, where the slag-heaps and high pit-heads looked for all the world like transplanted pyramids. In these flats the British Command had staged their first costly but useful experiments in the offensive. From that direction occasionally a dull far-off rumble was audible, and in the evening, beyond the glow of the blast furnaces near Aire, the rockets and flares of the trenches described slow parabolas on the screen of the dark heavens.

The continuously cold wet weather which followed the arrival of the Division necessitated the issue of a second blanket, turned all gun parks and horse lines into quagmires, and interfered gravely with training. Nor had the artillery ground available for field firing. Batteries were sent, however, to Calais for a day in turn for shoots with indirect laying at visible targets. Otherwise artillery training was limited to gun-drill and route-marching. This last formed a standing dish for the infantry, whom it was vital to accustom to the hard-metalled or pavé roads of France after the yielding sand of the desert. Parties of all ranks were sent to the different Army and Corps schools which stimulated so effectively the military education of junior officers, non-commissioned officers and specialists in every ramification of scientific warfare. On their pattern the Division was to found its own schools[1] at Armentières, and the principle was later to be extended to brigades and even battalions. Every unit was now put through a gas demonstration, and the issue of the new P.H. gas masks was completed.

At the same time a study had to be made of the formidable mass of pamphlets and circulars dealing with every

[1] Grenade School, Gas School, Trench Warfare School, Physical and Bayonet Training School, Machine Gun School.

phase of military life in France, with which each mail flooded orderly rooms. If it was a matter for regret to find the possession of a camera so sternly forbidden, it was an occasion for rejoicing to receive, appropriately enough on 25th April, notification of the allotment of leave to England. Carefully worked out by G.H.Q. to give the whole of the British forces a proportionate allowance in accordance with the ferry capacity, the allotment was similarly adjusted in the Division. The privilege exercised an incalculable influence on morale. In the early days of the war, individuals with a taste for attracting attention, or with the object of evoking sympathy, had crossed to London unshaven and bespattered with mud to represent the life of the trenches; now insistence was laid on smartness of appearance, as on cleanliness of person, and new uniforms were if necessary issued.

During the interval which elapsed before the Division moved forward, informal visits were paid to various units by General Haig and General Plumer. Now that the New Zealanders were to play a role on the principal stage of operations, under the eye and exposed to the criticism of British and Allied forces and of Generals and war correspondents, it became more than ever desirable that the saluting and general soldierly bearing of the troops should be of the highest standard, and reflect as brightly as possible their proved fighting qualities. A Divisional Order issued at the time dealt with this continually recurring question in terms of candour and common sense:—

"The G.O.C. expects every officer and man to help in making the New Zealand Division a credit to the Dominion.

"Saluting and general bearing are not really matters of discipline to be dealt with as such, but are matters of self-respect, and in so far as they are good or bad reflect credit or discredit on the Division.

"Men who fail to salute when they should, are untidy in dress, lounge about the streets, and fail to keep their eyes sufficiently open and their wits sufficiently wide awake to see when an officer is passing, may or may not be good fighters, but they certainly make a bad impression. To be smart and alert isn't servility. It is exactly the opposite. Every officer and man of the Division should walk about as if he had £10,000 a year, and must be as jealous of our reputation as a woman of her honour."

Various alterations were made at this time in the organisation of the Division.   Experience in France had shown
that much of the independence of action and movement
formerly belonging to a Division had now passed to the
Corps. The mounted troops, originally allotted with a view
to providing the Divisional Commander with a small mobile
force under his immediate control for reconnaissance and protective and escort duty, had become under the prevailing
conditions of stationary warfare something of a luxury.   So
far from a Division moving independently, and with one
or more roads allotted for its exclusive use, it seemed at this
stage that movement would be by Corps marching and fighting in depth on a comparatively narrow frontage; nor was
it till the closing months of the war that the evolution of
tactics favoured a reversion to the original conception.
General Headquarters therefore decided that the mounted
troops of Divisions in a Corps should be assembled under the
direct control of the Corps Commander and be organised as
a Corps unit.   Accordingly, the squadron of the Otago
Mounted Rifles and the 2 squadrons of Light Horse of the
Australian Divisions were grouped in a composite regiment
which was called the 1st Anzac Light Horse Regiment.   The
command was given to Lt.-Col. R. R. Grigor.[1]   On the
same principle, pending the arrival of the New Zealand
cyclist company,[2] a Corps Cyclist Battalion was formed by
the expansion of the 2 Australian companies.

The organisation of the artillery also now underwent
changes designed to promote greater efficiency in the field.
The Howitzer Brigade was split up, and one howitzer battery
was transferred to each of the 18-pounder brigades. In place
of it, they each lost their respectively highest numbered
battery, and these three batteries, namely, the 8th 10th and
14th, were formed into a reconstituted 4th Brigade of three
batteries. This new organisation of three brigades, each of three
18-pounder batteries and one howitzer battery, and one
brigade of three 18-pounder batteries was to hold good till
the beginning of 1917.[3]   At the same time the Brigade Ammunition Columns were absorbed into the Divisional Ammunition Column.   A new development was the formation of
trench mortar batteries.   One heavy and three[4] medium
batteries were raised as an integral portion of the Divisional

1   p. 15.
2   pp. 7, 59.
3   p. 140.
4   Lettered respectively XNZ, YNZ, ZNZ.

Artillery. The six light trench mortar batteries, which were now made part of infantry brigades and were formed of personnel drawn from infantry units, were shortly afterwards organised into three batteries of eight guns each.

It was now also that the title of the New Zealand Rifle Brigade was altered to 3rd New Zealand (Rifle) Brigade, the Brigade itself taking precedence next after instead of before the 2nd Brigade as hitherto. Motor transport was allotted to the Field Ambulance, and in accordance with the orders obtaining in France all transport vehicles of the Division were marked by the fern-leaf as the Divisional identification. Reference should be made also to the appointment of the Divisional Gas Officer and his staff, and to the formation of the Divisional Salvage Company, whose function it was to check waste by collecting abandoned Government property in billets and areas.

While the Division was thus being trained and organised, the first party of Maori bushmen was attached to the Forest Control in the Nieppe Forest. Here their sterling performances speedily won them a widespread reputation. In a contest held at the end of April, they actually beat the French bucherons in their own style, which consisted in felling the tree level with the ground, and trimming the small stump so as to leave a rounded top that would not hold water. In the following month they won 2 first and 2 second places in the 4 events of a competition with Australians and Canadians for which General Birdwood presented the prizes.

On 1st May the Division marched forward into the reserve area of the Corps. Headquarters moved to Estaires, the 2nd Infantry Brigade to the Doulieu area, and the 3rd Brigade to Estaires and its neighbourhood. The 1st Brigade remained for the time at Morbecque. This first move with regimental transport involved for some units a march of over 20 miles, and it was manifest that while benefiting by their recent training, the infantry were not yet adequately hardened. Substantial improvement in this respect was to be effected by the formation in June of a School of Chiropody, at which non-commissioned officers were trained for work in the units. On arrival in the new area, parties of Sappers and Pioneers were at once detached for work on the Lys bridgeheads and rear lines of trenches in the neighbourhood of Sailly, where they remained till the Division went to Armentières.

Detailed information was received on 5th May as to the relief of the 17th Division of the II. Corps which held the front line to the north of the 2 Australian Divisions of I. Anzac. On 9th May the 1st and 3rd Infantry Brigades exchanged areas, so as to enable the former to take over the line with the 2nd Brigade. Representatives of all arms visited their "opposite numbers" in the line and received unbounded kindness and help. The artillery parties profited by a stay of several days with the British gunners. Commanding officers, company commanders, and specialists, such as intelligence personnel and signallers, remained in the trenches for a period of 24 hours in order to familiarise themselves with the methods of relief and of holding the line, the principles of artillery co-operation, the question of water supply, the location of cemeteries, and all the hundred and one points of their new business.

The infantry relief was commenced on 13th May by the 1st Brigade. Moving with the usual intervals between platoons to minimise the risk of hostile shelling, they took over the l'Epinette subsector on the right. On the following day the 2nd Brigade went into the Houplines subsector, with their left flank on the river Lys. The 3rd Brigade marched up to Armentières to be in reserve. By noon on the 16th the relief was complete with the exception of certain artillery units, and the command of the sector passed to the New Zealand Division. Thereupon I. Anzac, having now all its 3 Divisions in the trenches, assumed responsibility for the extended line. The trenches in the reduced II. Corps sector on the north bank of the river were held at the moment by the 9th Division. The New Zealand artillery exchanged their new guns for those of the 17th Division, and had completed their relief by the 19th. Some of the gun positions were in factories on the outskirts of the town behind sliding doors, but most emplacements were hidden away under the cover of hedges walls or artificial camouflage.[1] The batteries were divided into 3 groups, one of the three 4th Brigade batteries being attached to each group. The 4th Brigade Commander, Lt.-Col. Falla, thus left temporarily unemployed, was appointed Divisional Artillery Intelligence Officer.

The German trenches lay for the most part 200 or 300 yards, but in places only some 60 yards, across No

1 The outgoing gunners had taken advantage of the quiet period in the spring of 1916 to brighten the vicinity of many of the guns and dugouts with carefully tended flower borders and vegetable gardens. These made the battery positions very conspicuous, and in the active period which began in July were speedily destroyed.

Man's Land. They were held by troops of the German XIX. Corps, known also as the 2nd Royal Saxon Corps, under General von Laffert. At the end of October 1914 they had been included in the force engaged in the outflanking race northwards, when they were attacked by the British cavalry and by the advanced guard of the III. Corps, and driven back on their present line between the Lille-Armentières railway and the river Douve by Messines. Von Laffert's sector was bisected by the Lys, which here forms the frontier between France and Belgium. It remained a German Corps sector till the line was broken in our Messines offensive, and is an example of the German practice of including an obstacle like the Lys within a sector of command rather than, as was the British wont, making a boundary of it. This frontier district had often in previous history been the scene of conflicts, and Armentières itself had more than once experienced the ravages of invading armies.

The first trench system occupied by the New Zealanders in France extended for some 4 miles to the east and south-east of Armentières from Pear Tree Farm, just south of the Armentières-Lille railway, to the river Lys, in front of its suburb Houplines. The whole of this front area was composed of low-lying flats, criss-crossed by canals and railways, in the basin of the muddy, sluggish, canalised Lys. It lay intermediate between the black country to the south and the agricultural district to the north, and reflected characteristics of both regions. In Armentières itself and the villages on the river, Sailly, Bac St. Maur, and Erquinghem, about a third of the civil population remained, and the isolated tree-surrounded brick farms two to three miles behind the trenches were still inhabited. But for the most part the fields on the enemy bank of the Lys, with their pollarded willows, lay unkempt and melancholy, crossed by bands of wire and seamed with trenches. Farm implements rusted where the retreating owner had abandoned them in the German advance. Long scrim barricades hid the exposed parts of the poplar-bordered roads from enemy observation. The German country in front, sparsely wooded and marked by occasional farms, was similarly flat till the ground rose, a mile back, in the Pérenchies ridge behind which lay Lille. The ridge dominated all the low country of the trenches. Very prominent on it was a water tower, used as an observation post. And all along it were set the western forts of Lille, on which was lavished all the strength that German science and industry could contrive.

Experience had early demonstrated the power of modern artillery to break a shallow defence position, and the efficacy, as a counter-measure, of a series of trenches in depth. Behind the front system, for the defence and maintenance of which the Division was responsible, stretched several others in a more or less complete state of organisation. The second line, known as the A.B.C. line, ran in a chain of fortified localities from the southern boundary at Charred Post to Bois Grenier, and thence north to the Ferme de la Hallerie. In the rear of its northern sector again were 2 alternative positions, also formed by a series of posts, to meet the pressure on our salient at Armentières; and with the same object an alternative defence position had been constructed from Armentières to Fleurbaix, which pivoting on the latter village joined up with the posts southwards. Behind this system lay the bridgeheads along the river Lys at Nouveau Monde and Sailly and Bac St. Maur, and extending from the Sailly defences a line ran north to Steenwerck. The whole formed the third or X.Y.Z. line.

As compared with the trench warfare at Anzac, though the essentials remained the same—the immemorial ceremony of "stand-to," the sentry system, the co-ordination of machine gun positions, the fight against vermin, the sleeping in boots and accoutrements, the incessant labour with spade and sandbag—there were, however, many marked differences. After the deep-dug saps on the Gallipoli ridges, the open trenches in these water-sodden flats, protected by breastworks built up above the ground level, seemed perilously insecure. It had yet to be realised that more elaborate trenches were impossible owing to climatic conditions, the low-lying nature of the country, and the infinitely heavier weight of artillery. Nor were they, as on Gallipoli, manned continuously throughout. Even had the supply of troops been adequate, such a policy, in view of the development of artillery, would have been not merely wasteful of man-power from everyday bombardments and exposure to physical and moral strain, but would also have involved sacrifice of life not less futile than costly against modern methods of attack. The odds in favour of an assault delivered with powerful artillery preparation were conceded, and the likelihood of the enemy's winning a temporary footing in our front line was recognised. But it was the general policy in such an eventuality to restore the

3

situation by counter-attack rather than seek to prevent it by an accumulation of troops in the front line. The quicker such a counter-attack could be delivered, before the enemy had time to reorganise and consolidate his gains, the better; and therefore definite plans were drawn up for this action by reserve troops in each and every part of the line. Should this immediate counter-attack fail, and the enemy succeed in establishing a firm hold on our front line or in penetrating deeper, it was not the principle to fritter away reserves in a series of weak efforts, but to deliver under Corps arrangements a grand counter-attack after an interval sufficient to allow the employment of adequate artillery and the maximum force of troops available.

In accordance with this policy, it had already become the general practice to divide a sector into garrisoned "localities" separated by so-called "gaps" of about 200 yards or less. These gaps were carefully enfiladed from wing trenches of the localities on either flank and were also capable of being raked by fire from the support trench in rear. To effect this, all the intervening ground and the former parados, or back wall of the trench, were levelled. In order to deceive aeroplane observation, however, a dummy parados was constructed of a wooden framework covered with netting and scrim which would not interfere with the fire of the supporting troops but would at the same time throw the all-important shadow in the eye, so to speak, of the aeroplane camera.[1] Not less importance was laid on the maintenance of the front parapet in these gaps than in the localities, and on patrolling them and sniping from them. Machine guns and Lewis guns fired regularly from them; and from them the infantry encouraged the baleful activity of the trench mortars so as to draw a substantial proportion of hostile artillery fire on to the untenanted portions.

A further point of difference was that, owing to greater room than on the confined area at Anzac, the trench systems showed far more marked complexity and depth, with support lines and reserve or subsidiary lines and all-round Strong Points. The long winding communication trenches were also capable of defence and lined with "fire-steps" at intervals

[1] At 3000 ft. aeroplane observers could follow an attack, see bombing fights, state the general conditions of trenches and note tracks; at 2500 ft. could see men massed in trenches; at 2000 ft. wire in good light, overhead traverses and comparative width of trenches; at 1500 ft., dugout entrances, comparative depth of trenches and men making signals; at 1000 ft. could distinguish our men from the enemy, especially by the British round tin helmets.

for the purpose of holding up a flank attack. Each trench line was guarded by more extensive wire entanglements than were possible at Gallipoli, and from each rear line there ran forward emergency overland routes in the open for approach when the communication trenches were under fire or for counter-attack. To facilitate movement by night, these routes were marked by pegs painted white on the side turned from the enemy. Zigzag gaps similarly marked were left in the entanglements.

Again, the mass of materials, timber, iron, revetments and revetting frames, heavy beams for dugouts, stakes, sandbags,. and so forth, was astounding after the poverty of the Peninsula. Unknown at Anzac were the duckwalks at the bottom of the trenches and in the dugouts where, covered with sandbags, they made a rough bunk. There were real tables and chairs in headquarters, borrowed from the deserted houses, and even in the front line system there were carefully screened and protected dwelling huts of solid timber. The machine gun dugouts in particular were roofed with massive baulks. The accommodation generally, though not so luxurious as in the German lines, was of an incomparably higher level of civilisation than the primitive stone-age dwellings at Anzac. Much of the heavier material was manufactured in a sawmill on the Lys controlled by the Division, where civilians, especially women, were employed on the day shifts, and part of the lighter material in the brigade workshops in Armentières. So, too, the concrete blocks used as bursters on the tops of dugouts, with a 12-inch air space, or "cushion," underneath to give protection against high-explosive, were mostly made in another factory under Divisional management.

Similarly the unfailing quantity and variety of rations revealed in the strongest possible light the British capacity for organisation. These were delivered by the Train to the quartermasters' stores in Armentières, where they were made up for the different company and specialist messes in the line. After dark the transport, with the quartermaster-sergeants in attendance, took them along the exposed roads to the mouths of the saps, whence carrying parties man-hauled them or pushed them up the narrow tramways to the kitchens in the trenches. Thus, as far as hardships and privations were concerned, the balance was all in favour of France. On the other hand, there was the added and ever-dreaded danger of gas, which involved the most elaborate precautions in the way of drill, precautionary measures and warning arrangements. Nor did life at Anzac afford preparatory warning of the weight of artillery fire on the Western front.

A very remarkable contrast arose from the continuous development of military technique and the intensive application of science to the military art. This feature made the Gallipoli campaign appear a century behind the warfare in France. It embraced every phase of activity, whether the meticulous care to restrict the use of telephones in the forward area to times of emergency and active operations, or the extensive buried cable systems, or the arrangements for storing water rations and ammunition or the wireless communication between aeroplanes and batteries, or the log-books kept for recording the progress of work, or the organisation of the battalion snipers with their telescopic rifles and armour-piercing bullets to penetrate the enemy's loopholed plates, or the trench code books, whose numbers represented particular messages, and whose key-number was periodically changed. As a particular instance, we may take that of the organisation of intelligence, as being in addition illustrative of the life in the line. Systematic and detailed reports were collated daily by all formations, ensuring continuity of observation from different parts of our positions. This information showing enemy movement, position of active batteries, and so on, was circularised to all concerned and enabled trench intelligence maps to be brought up to date. The following infantry report has been selected as typical of an ordinary quiet day in the trenches. The letters and numbers refer to certain sections and subsections of subjects, thus defined for facility of collation by the staffs of higher formations:—

INTELLIGENCE SUMMARY

Confidential

UNIT—3rd New Zealand Rifle Brigade
TIME—Twenty-four hours ending 6 a.m., 18/7/16
PLACE—Brigade sector, Bois Grenier
MAP REF.—Sheet 36, 1/10,000

A.(1) OPERATIONS
Our machine guns were less active than usual. An enemy working party reported by our patrol was fired upon. Ammunition expended, 1500 rounds.

GENERAL GODLEY INSPECTS TROOPS

AT A FIELD AMBULANCE

An Auckland Battalion on the March

Otago Mounted Rifles

Our patrols operated as usual in No Man's Land. (Report on enemy's wire. See below.)

A.(2) Identification

A man wearing brown cap was seen in front line at I.26.d.0.2.[1]

(Identification from bomb—see G.46 below.)

B.(4) Enemy Front and Support Lines

(a) Wire.—Our patrols examined German wire from I.31.d.3.5 to I.31.c.7.0 and report that it is continuous and generally good. Two parties were seen at work strengthening it at I.31.c.9.2 and I.31.c.8.1. Another patrol attempted to carry out similar work from I.26.c.9.4 to I.32.a.3.4, but was unable to proceed owing to the number of enemy working and covering parties.

The enemy parties signalled to each other by a low whistle that our patrol was in the vicinity.

Five enemy parties were heard working on this front.

Fewer flares than usual were used, some of which rose from No Man's Land.

Covering parties appeared to be extended for fifteen or twenty paces.

(b) Movement and Work.—New work is visible at I.21.c.6.1½. Gap made in parapet here by our artillery two days ago has been filled and covered up.

New work visible at I.21.c.8.4. A concrete work knocked down by our artillery has been replaced.

Very little movement visible in enemy's front line, though working parties were seen at work in rear making a new trench.

They appear to be digging very deep, as the soil is not being built up to form a breastwork, but is being spread out.

B.(6) Snipers' Posts

Station Building I.27.b.2.4 is suspected of being a snipers' post. This building enables the enemy to dominate Rue du Bois Salient.

B.(18) Enemy Activity

Activity below normal.

1 The large lettered squares of maps were divided into numbered squares, each of which was in turn subdivided into 4 smaller squares, a, b, c, d. The sides of these smaller squares again were "ticked" on the decimal system. Pin-point references were obtained by reading from the lower left-hand corner of the smaller square, first along the bottom side, and then up the left side.

C.(24) Movement Behind Enemy's Lines
Haymaking is proceeding as usual at about 1.28.a.0.6.
At 4 p.m. the usual party, consisting of 25 men, passed this point.

D.(33) Searchlights
Enemy searchlight was again in operation on Brigade front.

F.(36) Enemy Shelling
Enemy shells fired into our sector amounted to about 70 during the day.
One shell demolished a snipers' post in our lines, otherwise slight damage.

G.(46) Grenades
A patrol brought in a German stick bomb marked as follows:—

On body   L
                     Vor Gebrauch
                     Spreng Kapsol
                     einsetzent
On handle
                     Carl Spaeter (burnt on)
                     35 (in ink pencil)
                     5½ Sek. (burnt on)
                     10/3/16 (stamped on)[1]

M.(88) Enemy Ruses
A periscope was seen to be thrust up inside a box which shows prominently above the parapet at 1.21.c.7.2.
Enemy are using dummy heads opposite Rue du Bois Salient.

M.(98) Miscellaneous
At 6.45 a.m. two pigeons were seen to fly from behind our lines across to German lines opposite Brigade sector.[2]

K. G. S. Caldwell, Lieut.
For Brigadier-General Commanding 3rd N.Z.(R.)B.

Even more different was life out of the line. Instead of bare hillside bivouacs above the Anzac beaches and in rest gullies, the reserve battalions and the personnel employed behind the trenches lived in comfortable billets of brick and

1 "Before use insert detonator." Spaeter was the maker's name, and the time of the fuse was 5½ seconds. The importance here attached to an ordinary stick bomb indicates recent arrival in France and ignorance of German on the part of the compiler of the report.
2 An ever-recurring item in "intelligence" at this time. The majority of the birds seen, it may be surmised, were not in German service.

mortar. At the outbreak of war Armentières had been a
well-built manufacturing town of some 20,000 inhabitants,
and at this period was still largely intact. It was not till
the spring of the following year that it was systematically
razed by hostile artillery. The few buildings that then
escaped were destroyed during the German offensive in 1918,
when the whole of the sector passed temporarily into enemy
hands. Much of the civil administration was, in accordance
with previous practice, entrusted to the Division. The Sanitary Section undertook responsibility for water supply,
street cleaning, collection and destruction of all refuse and
waste material, the inspection of dairies estaminets and
retail shops where foodstuffs were exposed for sale, the dis-
infection of premises and clothing, and the supervision and
evacuation of cases of infectious diseases among the civil
population. During June, for example, 1,200 tons of refuse
were disposed of, and the equivalent of 100 miles of streets
was swept and cleaned. For the sanitary services thus rendered the Maire of the town paid 40 francs a day. But the
Division did not merely efface from the streets the traces of
occasional bombardment, but looked after the civil wounded
and sick. The appreciation by the local authorities of the work
done in this connection is evidenced in the following letter
to the A.D.M.S. of the Division from the Maire:—

"J'ai bien reçu votre estimée lettre date du 8 courant
m'informant du nombre de malades et blessés civils de
notre ville soignés dans les hôpitaux britanniques.

"J'ai l'honneur de vous addresser l'expression de ma
plus sincère gratitude, ainsi qu'au personnel médical sous
vos ordres, pour les soins devoués que vous avez bien voulu
prodiguer à la population civile éprouvée de notre ville.

"Au nom de la population d'Armentières je vous prie
d'agréer, Monsieur le Colonel, avec mes meilleurs remerci-
ments l'assurance de ma considération la plus distinguée."

Very rarely an aeroplane would drop bombs or a gas
cloud would drift through the outskirts. Shelling was rather
more frequent. The first heavy bombardment was at the end
of May, when a 5.9-in. howitzer, firing 130 rounds with aeroplane observation, demolished the spire of Sacre Cœur church
in Houplines, and other batteries put temporarily out of
working order the power-plant which supplied current to
the pumping-station. Many civilians, especially among the
poorer classes, still remained, and there were open all kinds
of shops estaminets and restaurants. The separate rooms set

aside in the "Au Boeuf" in the Rue de Lille were a favourite gathering place for officers and non-commissioned officers. Even in Houplines some comfortable billets existed, as at Lock House and the Chateau Rose, whose tower, overhanging the inky waters of the Lys, formed an admirable vantage point from which to observe at night the inferno of a bombardment, with gas or smoke waves billowing over the enemy trenches against the lurid glare of the German rockets.

At Pont de Nieppe, the north-western suburb, on the high road to Bailleul, the Divisional baths were located in buildings that once formed part of a textile factory and had been used for bleaching and dyeing. These the Division rented at 1,000 francs per month, and here 1,500 men were bathed a day. Here too 40,000 garments were washed and mended a week by 200 women employed by the Division for this purpose. Practically this was the only source used for issuing underclothing, and while the men bathed, their tunics and trousers were cleaned of vermin. These baths were of inestimable value at all times, and were not least appreciated by the little parties which were sent in turn from the trenches during the activity which was to characterise July. In Armentières itself good swimming baths were installed in the Place Victor Hugo, which 2,000 men visited a day, and in which subsequently the Division held aquatic sports.

Thus there existed a variety of interests, an intermingling with civilians, and a fair share of the amenities if not of the luxuries of peace. Some billets near gun positions came in for spasmodic shelling, but the infantryman, after his period of duty in the trenches, trudging back past Shrapnel Corner to, say, the Breuvert Factory in Barbed Wire Square felt, whether fatalist or cheery optimist, that he had for the time left the war behind him, a mental atmosphere which was unknown and impossible in the safest and most secluded gullies of Anzac.

At the outset, in holding the line the Division followed the method which they had found practiced by the previous garrison. The right brigade subsector, about 2,000 yards in length, was held by the 1st Brigade with 2 battalions in the trenches and 2 in reserve in Armentières. The left subsector, about 4,000 yards in extent, was occupied by the 2nd Brigade with 4 battalions in the line. Its reserve was furnished by a battalion of the 3rd (Rifle) Brigade. The remainder of the Rifle Brigade and the 3 engineer companies constituted Divisional reserve. This inconvenient arrangement was altered in the first week in June. The front was then divided into 2 equal brigade subsectors, each held by 2 battalions. The third battalion of each brigade was in immediate reserve in the subsidiary line, and the fourth battalion in billets in Armentières.

During June, the II. Anzac Corps, comprising the 4th and 5th Australian Divisions, was transferred from Egypt to France, and on the 20th General Godley established his headquarters at Bailleul. The New Zealand Division was at once transferred to his command,[1] the 4th Australian Division replacing it in I. Anzac. For the present, however, the Division remained for both tactical and administrative purposes under General Birdwood's control till the first week in July, when I. Anzac, consisting of the 1st 2nd and 4th Australian Divisions, set out for the battlefield on the Somme. General Godley then took command of the sector. Prior to his departure General Birdwood paid a farewell visit to the New Zealand trenches, as he had made a final tour of their positions on Gallipoli after the commencement of the evacuation. This move of the Australian troops affected the New Zealand Division in another way, as its front was now extended southwards to include the adjoining Bois Grenier subsector. Here, during a heavy hostile bombardment, a brigade of the 2nd Australian Division was relieved on 4th July by the 3rd New Zealand Rifle Brigade. The Divisional artillery at the same time took over the battery positions supporting the new subsector.

All 3 infantry brigades were now in the line, and no formed Divisional reserve was available. The Pioneers were earmarked for the inner Armentières defences, and arrangements were made to form a composite reserve of the Engineer companies and the battalion of each brigade in the town billets. On alarm these would assemble at their respective alarm posts and report to Divisional Headquarters by telephone, or, if the wire were cut, by an officer. During the following week the front was again extended south by the inclusion of the Rue du Bois subsector, held by another Australian brigade. The Rifle Brigade side-stepped south and retaining half of the Bois Grenier subsector took over the whole of the new subsector. The northern half of the Bois Grenier subsector was added to the 1st Brigade area. At the same time the 5th Australian relieved the 4th Australian Division in the southern half of the Corps sector.

1 p. 11.

This extension to a long front of $8\frac{1}{2}$ miles, normally occupied by 2 Divisions, threw a considerable strain both on the fighting troops and on administrative services. Thus the Field Ambulances now manned 5 advanced and 3 main dressing stations, in addition to the Divisional rest station. Each infantry brigade had now 3 battalions in the trenches and 1 in the subsidiary line. The Division was left without infantry reserves, and reliefs in the line were confined for the most part to internal battalion arrangements, companies taking turn in the front and support trenches. This unusually long period of duty in the line without a rest spell in Armentières, added to the trying conditions during July, led to a rather high rate of sickness, which was further aggravated by a measles epidemic. Not least affected by the arduous nature of their duties were the machine gun companies.

The Battle of the Somme commenced on 1st July. With a view to distracting the enemy's attention and retaining his troops in their areas, active minor operations were undertaken along the whole northern front, both previous to and after the outbreak of the storm. In this liveliness the New Zealanders played their full part. Gas and smoke were repeatedly discharged over the German positions with at least occasionally happy results, as on the night 13th/14th August, when it was established that the enemy had manned his parapet in strength and suffered heavy casualties from the gas and the artillery bombardment which accompanied it. The 24th June dates the inception of a marked increase in artillery expenditure, which was maintained thence onwards for 18 days. During this period the expenditure of ammunition by the Divisional batteries rarely fell under 1,500 and frequently exceeded 3,000 shells a day. Not merely the battery positions and observation posts, but also the "tender spots" behind the German line, the large dumps also, as at La Crois au Bois, and the battalion or regimental headquarters, as at the Ferme du Chastel and Ferme des Deux Treilles, were subjected to systematic bombardment. Billets were treated with sudden short salvoes. Every night the Divisional Ammunition Column wagons, in addition to the battery wagons, went to the gunpits. Their work was heavy, as after the expansion of the Divisional sector they supplied no less than 11 miles of front. In the air, activity similarly increased. On 26th June, in the pellucid clearness of the summer evening, 4 German balloons above Quesnoy hung in the sky looking over our area. Above the New Zealand trenches 3 British aeroplanes circled and hovered slowly; and then at a given signal from their leader suddenly darted off in a straight line across the sky toward the enemy balloons. Like lightning, each aeroplane dived at a balloon, and in 2 minutes 3 of these were falling in a mass of red flames, and the fourth was being lowered with frenzied haste. At the sight of the flames and the cigar-shaped streamers of smoke which hung for long in the windless air, the New Zealand sentries, not yet sophisticated, broke into exultant cheers, feeling dimly the incident to be an auspicious omen for those great operations which they knew were on foot somewhere in the near future.

The instructions for activity of all arms were repeated on 9th July. The Corps Commander then laid it down "that it must be clearly understood that greater risk must be incurred and heavier casualties faced than would be profitable under normal conditions of trench warfare." He desired that "all ranks should understand that they had an opportunity of materially assisting the action of our armies in the south, and that special efforts were required of them." Wire-cutting, demolition of parapets, bursts of fire on enemy billets, and raids or gas discharges or dummy raids were to take place nightly. This programme was rigidly adhered to.

Of greatest importance was the series of raids now delivered on the enemy trenches in rapid succession. This species of military enterprise had originated out of the lessons taught by renewed and expensive experience, that no permanent lodgment on a small scale in an enemy's fortified system is, even if possible, worth the inevitable cost. Participants in small raids seldom stayed beyond 15 minutes in the German trenches. The objects of the raids were, while maintaining and developing the offensive spirit in one's own forces, primarily to secure identification from the enemy, to kill or capture the garrisons assaulted, destroy or bring back machine guns and mortars, and weaken his morale. Now there was the added object of retaining his troops. In the stagnant trench warfare, unproductive indeed of large movement but offering extensive scope for resourcefulness and ingenuity, these operations were on both sides conducted with a very high degree of scientific skill and elaborate preparation.

The length of trench to be assaulted was carefully selected and reconnoitred from the ground and the air, and

when opportunity permitted an exact replica was constructed
well in rear for practice by the raiding party. The artillery
plans for careful registration so as to avoid suspicion, for
diversions, such as wire-cutting elsewhere, to detract attention from the real objective, and for protection to the raiders
in the actual attack were worked out with minute thoroughness. All marks of identification were taken off the raiders,
and hands and faces were blackened so as not to show in the
darkness. Bayonets were specially sharpened and dulled. To
light up dugouts, electric torches were often attached to the
rifles, bound on with insulated tape just below the lower
band. Next to the revolver, a favourite weapon was the
knobkerry, carried suspended from the wrist by a stout thong
running through the hole in the handle. Special signals
were used to recall the raiders, and white tapes to guide
them back to the gap in our own wire. To ensure success all
arrangements were completed days previously; but sometimes,
as also in the case of gas, when discharge depended on the
direction and strength of the wind, it was not possible or
desirable to settle the exact zero hour till comparatively
shortly beforehand. In that case notification of the time
selected would be sent over the telephone in such a form
as to rouse no suspicion in the German operators sitting at
their listening apparatus, and occasionally with felicitous
irony, such as in the case of a raid accompanied by bombardment, "Iron rations will be delivered at . . . . ."

To meet similar action on the part of the enemy, elaborate
measures were taken. Plans of our counter-action at salients
and other vulnerable points were formed after careful study
of maps and photographs from the enemy's point of view.
Good wire entanglements, the command of No Man's Land
by patrols, and a sound system of listening posts made a silent
raid in the nature of a surprise all but impracticable. Wire,
above all, was necessary, and wiring was one of the infantryman's most important and dangerous duties. The risks may
be illustrated by a 2nd Wellington experience at the beginning
of July. Sergt. J. Courtney was in command of a wiring
party when hostile machine gun fire was directed at them.
Two men were killed and two wounded. Courtney ordered
the remainder of the party back, he himself carrying one
of the wounded men. The other walked in by himself, but
in ignorance of this Courtney went out again with the
stretcher-bearers to find him. He found the body of one
of the dead men and brought it in. Then finally he went out

to search the ground to ensure that no one was left in No Man's Land. All this was done under continuous heavy machine gun fire, which greatly increased the difficulties of negotiating our own entanglements.

Of hardly less importance was thorough and systematic patrolling. Every night the front was covered by little groups in No Man's Land, and many and diverse were their experiences amid the ditches shellholes ruins and hedges. It was now that Pte. Richard Clark Travis, of 2nd Otago, began to win a name for marked resourcefulness and initiative. Not satisfied with night work, he repeatedly led daylight patrols close up to the enemy's wire. For 40 nights in succession, from dusk to daylight, he spent the whole time in No Man's Land. One of his characteristic actions may be briefly related. One evening, just before he moved out on his nightly mission, an enemy patrol was reported near our wire. Our sentries chanced to be raw recruits. Relieved that no worse befell them, they were allowing the Germans to withdraw undisturbed. Wrathfully Travis picked up the nearest rifle. He went unhesitatingly over the parapet through our wire (not necessarily a difficult feat at that time) and emptied his magazine into the dimly discerned forms of the retreating patrol, one of whom fell.

Where our wire was good, bombardment was necessary to break it and so afforded warning. In the case of an obvious "box" barrage at any point in our trenches, unnecessary loss and demoralisation could be avoided and our infantry could escape destruction by going out into No Man's Land, where also they might be expected to deal more effectively with an attack, or by slipping to a flank. No retrograde movement was allowable, and the garrison detailed to hold the line had to fight it out to the last. The hostile bombarding guns, whose exact positions were generally known by aeroplane photographs, flash-spotting towers, sound-ranging instruments, and other technical inventions, were themselves engaged with high-explosive from the "heavies" or seige howitzers of the Army and Corps artillery set aside for counter-battery work, which was as a rule undertaken by guns employed on this purpose practically exclusively.

Communications between the infantry garrison and the Divisional artillery were vital and were maintained by telephone lamp and rocket, and by close personal touch and mutual understanding between the officers of each arm. Thus, for example, the night lines of the artillery were not necessarily

within the zone allotted for day shooting, but depended
largely on the representations of the infantry brigadier, who
was responsible for determining the question as to which
part of his front the Germans could reasonably hope to rush
by night without previous bombardment. Behind the front,
in suitable places, were the observation posts manned day
and night by artillery personnel, whose scrutiny of the line
never flagged. These posts were in factory chimneys,[1] trees,
rising ground, houses, and so on, all as far as practicable made
proof against weather and direct hits from field artillery.
Beside each was a dugout, proof against direct hits from
"five-nines." Each post was named and marked by a board
bearing its name. Telephone lines, moreover, for maintenance
of which the infantry was responsible, connected battalions
and brigades with supporting artillery. In the same way,
each front-line company was connected with its supporting
battery, though in this case, owing to the proximity of
hostile listening sets, the actual use of the telephone was
restricted to test or actual S.O.S. messages. Brigade and
battery commanders visited the line so many times weekly,
and were directly represented in the trenches by a liaison
officer, who acted as observation officer during the day and
lived at battalion headquarters at night.

In cases of intense bombardment of our lines when observation was good and no indication presented itself of an
infantry advance, it was generally enough to ask for artillery
retaliation. But when No Man's Land and the enemy's
parapet were shrouded in mist or darkness, and when the
circumstances were such that an attack appeared probable,
recourse was had to the S.O.S. signals. These were a call
for immediate assistance from the artillery covering the
attacked or threatened sector. It was not necessary to wait
till the enemy's infantry were actually seen. All our trenches
were numbered or named, and each company and platoon
officer and artillery forward observation officer in the
front line carried a message already written out, with
only his signature to be completed, "S.O.S. Trench 81,"
for example, or its abbreviated name. The company
signaller transmitted it "priority," first to the supporting
battery and then to Battalion Headquarters. Above the
latter's telephone hung a similar form ready for completion
by the insertion of the trench and signature, and on the same
principle as above, the battalion commander would repeat the

---

[1] Some of these swayed alarmingly in any wind.

S.O.S. calls first to the batteries supporting the battalion and then to the infantry Brigade Headquarters.

To test efficiency of signal communications a battalion or company commander could at any time call for a test round by the message, "Test one round," followed by the number of the trench. The time between the acceptance of the message by the signal operator in the trenches and the arrival of the round in the enemy's position was not expected to exceed 30 seconds.

In addition to the telephone and lamp signals as means of communication were the S.O.S. rockets. These were the same throughout a Corps front, but from time to time their nature and colour changed. They were kept on sticks or stands, ready to be fired, at the headquarters of battalions and companies, at every officer's dugout in the front line, and 1 convenient spot at least on each company sector. On an attack they were fired at short intervals till the response of the artillery was unmistakable.

On the appearance of a S.O.S. rocket the gunners at their observation posts would at once clamp a pointer on a graduated and orientated dial in its direction; and thus discovering the position of the locality affected communicate it independently to the batteries. The instant the call for support came to the batteries, whether from their own observers or direct from the infantry, the 18-pounders placed a shrapnel barrage as near our trenches as safety permitted at the rate of 3 rounds per gun per minute, and after 2 minutes crept forward lifting 50 yards at 1-minute intervals at the rate of 2 rounds per gun per minute to the enemy front-line trenches, where the barrage became stationary, and high-explosive was substituted wholly or in part for shrapnel. The howitzers at the same time fired each a round a minute with the object of destroying the enemy's front trench and garrison, or blocking his communications, or bombarding known headquarters. Mortars and machine guns had their action similarly defined.

A like procedure was adopted in cloud gas attacks. The howitzers and trench mortars bombarded the trench from which it was emitted, and the 18-pounders, alert for a possible S.O.S. call, placed a light barrage in front of the enemy's lines to prevent his patrols from crossing No Man's Land. The working of the machine guns was tested by occasional short bursts. With their respirators adjusted, the troops directly

4

affected fired their rifles at a slow rate, while those on the flanks made ready to enfilade an infantry attack.

Immediately prior and subsequent to the beginning of the Somme battle the number of the British raids was increased, and the scale on which they were delivered was enlarged all along the front of the Northern Armies. In the last week of June no fewer than 70 were delivered between Ypres and the northern fringe of the battle area. On the Divisional front one raid had already been delivered by the 2nd Brigade at the extreme northern end of the sector, opposite the village of Frélinghien, which lay down the Lys north-east of Houplines. Early in June suspicions had been aroused in the minds of the Army Staff by a new trench which had crept forward at this point some 800 yards across a German re-entrant and thence diagonally over No Man's Land towards the Lys. On an aeroplane photograph this new work looked exactly like a harbour breakwater, the main trench and the saps connecting them appearing like the wharf side and the town streets. It was accordingly called the Breakwater. It was possible that the new works were designed merely to improve the German positions. But certain indications, such as an increase in local wireless communications, appeared suggestive of hostile preparations, and it was thought probable that the enemy would try to follow up a recent success snatched against the Canadians in the Ypres salient[1] by a similar attack on other Overseas troops— for the identity of the Australians had been discovered—if only to form some estimate of their value. In this neighbourhood there was no specially important tactical feature to attract German attention, but on the other hand the enemy would have an initial advantage from the fact that there was no depth behind our line owing to the proximity of the village of Houplines, and that his right flank was protected by the river. Corps Headquarters considered that the enemy's works might be connected with some plan to capture and include in his line the ruined buildings called Hobbs' Farm, which lay just behind our front trench and which were indeed suspiciously immune from shelling.

Elaborate measures were at once undertaken for strengthening the fortifications and especially the wire round the Farm. Daily progress of the Breakwater was studied on aeroplane photographs, and a raid was organised to discover

1   This attack, 2nd June, was intended to interfere with the arrangements for our Somme offensive.   The lost ground was recovered on 13th June.

TRENCH-CONSTRUCTION

SALVAGE

COMMUNICATION WITH AEROPLANES

the strength and purpose of the new trench. The raiding party of 5 officers and 83 other ranks was composed of selected volunteers from the whole brigade, and was led by Capt. E. B. Alley, of 2nd Otago. Preceded by an intense local bombardment of 20 minutes' duration and protected by a covering barrage, the assault was made during the night 16th/17th June. The party was unlucky in crossing No Man's Land, where 4 officers, including Alley himself, were wounded, and 1 man killed and 5 wounded by shell-fire. The trench was found not yet advanced enough to be garrisoned except by outpost sentries. Half a dozen Germans had already been killed in the bombardment, but the raiders had the satisfaction of bayoneting 2 others. Unfortunately Alley succumbed to his wounds in the morning. The following night a patrol went out to ascertain whether attempts were being made to repair the damage. A large enemy party was detected at work, and was swept by artillery fire. The effect of these operations and subsequent bombardments was to discourage the enemy for the time from pursuing whatever object he had in view in developing the Breakwater.[1] In the light of after events it appears probable that the Germans were credited with a more sinister purpose than they actually entertained.

As an auspicious beginning to the raids delivered in connection with the offensive on the Somme, a highly satisfactory enterprise was carried out by the Rifle Brigade late at night on 25th June. At the same hour the 2nd Australian Division executed a not less successful raid to the south. A party of the 2nd Rifles, consisting of 3 officers and 70 other ranks, under Capt. A. J. Powley, raided the enemy trenches opposite Pont Ballot salient. As on the 16th, several Germans had already been killed in the prelude of artillery fire, but this time the enemy trenches were fully manned. Many were bombed in the darkness of their dugouts, and 29 were killed in the open trench. Nine prisoners, including a warrant officer, were brought back, together with rifles, bayonets, gas helmets, letters and papers. Two sappers attached to the party blew up a gas engine used for pumping, and destroyed the main dugout, which was fitted with electric light. 5 other ranks were wounded by the enemy retaliation, and a German bomb, which a rifleman was carrying homewards, exploded, killing him and wounding 3 others. Powley was later awarded the

1 p. 136.

Military Cross in recognition of his successful leadership, and 2 of his n.c.o.s the Military Medal for marked gallantry.

It was now the turn of the 1st Brigade, and on 1st July a raid was carried out by 1st Wellington on the trenches opposite Pigot's Farm. These marked the junction of the sectors held by 2 German Divisions.[1] The unusually excellent account rendered by the battalion to Brigade Headquarters is reproduced.

1st BN. WELLINGTON REGIMENT

Particulars of Raid carried out on the Night of 1st/2nd July
REFERENCE MAP 36 N.W.4 1/10,000

A raiding party under Capt. A. B. McColl, consisting of 4 officers and 77 other ranks, assaulted the enemy's trenches on the night of the 1st/2nd July at 1.17.a.1½/5½.

The night was dark and the weather fine.

The scouts[2] moved out through the sally port as soon as it was dark, and at 11.45 p.m. two returned and led out the remainder of the raiding party to selected positions in No Man's Land.

The bombardment by the artillery and M.T.Ms. commenced at 12.30 a.m. Six M.T.Ms. were employed solely for cutting wire.

After 20 minutes' bombardment, the artillery firing at the assaulting point lifted and formed a semi-circular barrage.

The scouts went forward and found the wire had been thoroughly cut. They had only to clear the loose wire away. They were not fired on and encountered no opposition.

Where the wire had been cut, a listening sap had come out to the outer edge of the wire, and the centre party had an easy method of entry to the trench along this.

None of the parties met with the slightest resistance. What men were in the trench were cowed by our artillery fire and were crouching in shelters under the parapet. These were either passed up to the prisoner parties or killed if they refused to move.

The raiders remained 8 minutes in the trench, and at a whistle signal withdrew. Without waiting in No Man's Land they returned direct to battalion headquarters.

The artillery ceased fire at 1.24 a.m.

1 The 24th and 50th.
2 It should be added that the scout sergeant, R. C. Potter, guided the raiders with great skill and courage and was the first man to reach the enemy's parapets.

The enemy continued his bombardment until 1.45 a.m.

Telephonic communication was satisfactorily maintained throughout.

Our casualties were:—

1 officer died of wounds.

1 man killed.

9 men wounded.

Of these, one man was killed and four others were wounded by a shell bursting when waiting in No Man's Land. One man was wounded in our trenches after the return of the parties. Four were wounded during the course of the raid.

Capt. A. B. McColl reached our trenches, but returned to help our stretcher-bearers, who had got into difficulties in a ditch not far from our parapet. When getting back over the parapet he was caught by machine gun fire and severely wounded. He died before reaching the dressing station.

Prisoners—Ten prisoners were brought back, two of whom were wounded.

All the enemy that were in the trenches were taken prisoners or killed. It is not known how many were killed, as bombs were used and nobody took account of the dead.

Information Gained.

Entanglements—The entanglements were approximately 35 yards thick and about 4 feet 6 inches high. The wire, which was very strong, with heavy barbs close together, was erected on knife-rests and screw-stakes. Before the bombardment it had been in good order.

Parapet—The parapet was fully 20 feet wide at the base and 6 feet wide at the top. There were no sandbags, and the trenches were revetted with lattice work. There was a very shallow "Borrow Pit," completely clear of wire, in front.

Trenches—There were no dugouts under the parapet, but there were shallow shelters. At one point in the parapet there was a large bomb store with iron doors. Out of these doors three men came, a fourth remaining inside with the doors shut. These doors were blown in by an engineer when the raiders withdrew. In the front trench a pump shaft was found leading from a deep well to a pumping station some distance in rear. The shaft was demolished by an engineer, who followed the pipe line for 10 yards to the rear but could not find a pump. The trench was about 6 feet deep. It was narrow, strongly traversed, and floored with duckboards. There was a traffic trench at the back of the parados, through which about every 20 yards there was an opening to the front line.

PARADOS—The parados was not so high as the parapet. In it were a number of dugouts, several of which had beds. They were all very strongly constructed, with a thick solid roof supported by heavy iron girders. The floor of most of the dugouts was level with the floor of the trench, but a few were a little deeper from the trench level. In all of them it was possible to stand up. They were lighted by electricity, and the doors all faced towards the enemy's rear.

MACHINE GUNS—No machine guns or snipers' positions were found.

THE ENEMY—An officer was taken prisoner but would not cross No Man's Land, and had to be shot. The enemy were evidently expecting to be relieved, for their packs were made up. A number of these, including one belonging to an officer, were brought away, and from them a Corps Intelligence Officer obtained a number of useful papers. On account of the expected relief there was little in the dugouts.

The trench was not heavily held.

OUR ARTILLERY—Our artillery co-operation was very good. The parapet was in places much knocked about, and one dugout was considerably damaged. The parados was hit in many places, much damage having been done.

There were very few dead as the results of our shelling, but what men there were had no fight left in them.

ENEMY'S ARTILLERY—The enemy's reply started 5 minutes after our bombardment had commenced. No. 1 Locality, Central and Port Egal Avenues and Graham's Post suffered a fair amount of damage.

MISCELLANEOUS—No steel helmets were found, but spiked helmets with Prussian and Saxon badges, a quantity of clothing, a number of books, flares, rifles, bayonets, and a pair of field glasses were brought back.

The Division was not, however, to be exempt from the vicissitudes of war, and ill fortune attended the next few ventures. A raid by 2nd Wellington, directed at the trenches near the Frélinghien Brasserie, on the following night, 2nd/3rd July, at 11.30 p.m. was unsuccessful. As soon as ever our bombardment started, the enemy put down on and in front of our parapet a heavy artillery fire which by accident or design fell with special weight on a drain in No Man's Land, where our party lay prior to the moment for moving forward. None the less at the appointed time the raiders advanced to the enemy's entanglements through machine gun fire, which caused further severe casualties. There only a gap of about 6 feet had been cut, and as the raiders dribbled through this and forced their way into the trench, they were bombed in detail by the Germans, who had evacuated their front line and threw their bombs from a close support trench. The artillery plan on this occasion was while shelling the flanks and encircling the position by the customary protective box barrage, to bombard the interior of the position only for the final 10 minutes so as to give the raiders a chance to capture a number of prisoners. Though well conceived, however, this idea actually allowed the enemy time to collect smoke bombs and grenades, and was considered afterwards to have been a mistake. An enemy attempt to follow up the raiders was frustrated without difficulty. More serious, however, was the intense enfilade machine gun fire to which the withdrawal was exposed. But it was carried out with consummate steadiness and skill, and thanks to this the casualties proved less than had been with reason feared. An officer and 11 men were killed and 2 officers and 34 rank and file wounded. In addition, 5 men were missing. Where all behaved with courage, exceptional gallantry was shown by Coy.-Sergt.-Major W. E. Frost, who assisted Lt. R. E. V. Riddiford to cover the withdrawal. Paying no heed to the imminent danger to his own life, Frost twice returned under heavy fire to the German lines through the enemy wire and carried back 2 seriously wounded men who, lying within a few feet of the enemy's parapet, would certainly but for his action have been killed or taken prisoners. Frost was recommended for the V.C. and awarded the D.C.M. and Médaille Militaire.[1] Great devotion to duty was shown also by the regimental stretcher-bearers under Sergt. L. R. Nicholas who remained at their post in the front line under continuous heavy shelling for an hour and a half.

1 Frost died on 27/8/16 as the results of wounds sustained while extricating a wounded horse from a wagon in Armentières.

The Maoris were keenly anxious to emulate these achievements and revive in modern battle the traditions of their
warrior stock.   Fortune, however, was to be unkind.   They
proposed to raid the trenches opposite the locality called Pety
Cury in our left brigade subsector on the night 9th/10th July.
The enterprise was to be "silent" without artillery support but
in combination with a dummy raid on Brune Rue to the
south.   With intense chagrin the Maoris found that a gap cut
previously in the German wire by our artillery was now closed,
and that the entanglements were too dense to permit of
ingress.   Attempting it again on the following night,
10th/11th July, while a diversion was carried out on a flank,
they cleared a gap after some time and deployed silently
inside the wire ready to rush the trench.   But the German
sentries had observed them, and strong German patrols crept
out on either side to cut them off.   The crawling forms of
the enemy were noticed just in time, and the raiders having
no chance against their very superior numbers withdrew
without confusion.   The enemy followed them up with some
deliberation over No Man's Land, wasting his bombs, till he
reached within 70 yards of our trenches.   Once the Maoris
had clambered over our parapet, the garrison's machine guns
and rifles lashed their pursuers, who could now be faintly
discerned, and followed them up with fire as they retreated
in disorder and with casualties to their own trenches.
    The following night, 11th/12th July, a raid by 2nd Otago
at Pont Ballot was also a failure.   The wire was reported
to have not been cut.   On the 13th/14th, while gas was released on the 2nd Brigade subsector, a large raid by 1st Otago
from the 1st Brigade trenches marked the high-water mark
of our reverses.   Assembled in No Man's Land, the raiders were
swept by a tremendous concentration of shrapnel and machine
gun fire which burst out the very instant our bombardment
started.   No regiment was less likely to be disheartened or
deterred from a project by any form of hostile opposition
than the hard-bitten soldiers of Otago.   With their lines
raked by fire, they pressed as far as the enemy's entanglements, and only then, after they had lost three-quarters of
their strength, was the order to withdraw reluctantly given
and as reluctantly obeyed.   By the time that the party
regained our trenches, 4 officers were killed and 4 wounded,
and 50 other ranks killed and over 100 wounded.   Only 6
men indeed returned unhurt out of the original muster.   As
in the case of the 2nd Wellington raid on 2nd/3rd July, such

was the uncanny promptitude and deadly accuracy of the enemy retaliation that it seemed certain that the Germans had acquired information through unguarded conversation either in a town estaminet—for Armentières was not without its German agents—or over the telephone.   The shelling was extended to the batteries and about midnight caused the death of Capt. J. L. H. Turner, commander of the 4th Howitzer Battery.

This disaster was to some extent avenged on the night 14th/15th by a successful raid of the 4th Rifles at the Lille Road Salient.   An excellent track 10 feet wide was cut through the wire by our trench mortars.   The real attack was preceded half an hour previously by a dummy raid on the same spot.   Intense havoc had been wrought by our artillery.   The trenches were completely obliterated.   The remains of several dead were so shattered that it was impossible to procure identification.   The raiders lost only 1 man killed and 2 wounded.   An effort by a German flank party to work round our rear was dispelled by the protecting scouts with bombs, and the enemy fled immediately.

Meanwhile the drain of the deadly struggle to the south was affecting the German garrisons in the same way as it had thinned our own.[1]   It was calculated that since the beginning of the Somme operations 9 of the enemy's battalions had been withdrawn from the Lens-Lille area.   Accordingly a threat against Lille was likely to embarrass him gravely.   With this end in view operations were designed to take place just to the south of the New Zealand sector on 19th and 20th July. The attack was entrusted to the XI. Corps under Lieut.-Gen. Sir R. Haking and carried out at 11 a.m. on 19th July by the 61st Division and the 5th Australian Division.   The result was to fall much short of expectation.   To assist the enterprise by way of diversion, smoke and gas were discharged on the night of the 19th/20th on the New Zealand front, and a violent bombardment, in which the Corps "heavies" co-operated, was directed from 8 p.m. till 11 p.m. on the whole of the enemy's trenches billets and batteries.   In addition, 2 raiding enterprises were carried out simultaneously by the 1st and Rifle Brigades.   1st Auckland found only dead and debris, but on their right a party of 75 men of the 1st Rifles led by Capt. J. R. Cowles was more fortunate. A few Germans had been killed by our artillery, but there remained 35 alive in the 80 yards of trench assaulted. Utterly

1 p. 35.

terrified, they would not leave their dugouts, so they were bombed and shot at leisure and afterwards counted. Numerous articles brought back, including shoulder-straps helmets and letters from the dead, yielded useful identifications. The return was made under heavy shell and machine gun fire, but thanks to Cowles' skilful dispositions, the raiders escaped with only 7 men wounded. At the same time the Germans, as we shall see, also made a raid. The ammunition expended on this night by the Divisional artillery alone in connection with these activities exceeded 12,000 rounds. Assistance was given to the 5th Australian Division in the evacuation of their heavy casualties.

A period of comparative quiescence now followed, due mainly to a shortage of ammunition caused by a stupendous explosion in one of the great northern depots.[1] A final raid was made on 12th August, when Capt. G. C. W. Armstrong and a party of the 3rd (Auckland City) Company of 2nd Auckland captured 2 prisoners and a machine gun with insignificant casualties. The scene was again the Breakwater, and a powerful artillery diversion was made on Frélinghien. The trenches in front of the village, which also were subjected to concentrated shelling, were reported to have been strongly manned. It so happened that at the time of the raid a German patrol was in No Man's Land. All but 1 of the patrol were killed, and he lost his way and wandered into our trenches near by. These identifications were of importance as confirming the presence of the VI. Reserve Corps on this part of the front in place of the XIX. Corps which had been transferred to the Somme.

In addition to the infantry penetrations there were practised on several occasions so-called "dummy raids" when the artillery action, feigning to support an infantry assault, carried out a bombardment and box barrage for the purpose of confusing the enemy, lowering his morale, and inflicting casualties. Not the least successful perhaps was one delivered on the night 14th/15th August on the front line trenches opposite 2 projecting points in our lines called the Railway Salient and the Mushroom, while simultaneously on the right the 18th Divisional Artillery bombarded the enemy's Rue du Bois Salient. In this instance the intention was to make the enemy man his parapet between the 2 points under fire. At a given moment on the conclusion of the bombardment, 2 minutes' rapid 18-pounder fire was poured by both

1 Audruicq.

artilleries into the intervening sector. "Judging by the noise heard," observes the Corps Diary drily, "considerable casualties were caused."

If this offensive and aggressive policy did not fulfil its entire purpose, which indeed it was too much to hope for, it was none the less shown by manifold indications to have imposed an exhausting strain on German resources and to have seriously impaired German nerves. The Army Commander, ever ready to recognise merit, expressed his appreciation of the energy and devotion displayed by calling in person at the various brigade headquarters to express his satisfaction and thanks.

The German raids on the Divisional sector were neither so numerous as our own (4 as against 11), nor did they achieve as substantial success. The first was launched at 1st Auckland in the l'Epinette Salient on 3rd/4th July. An effort made on the same night against the Australians on the right was repulsed by machine gun fire. The assault on the l'Epinette was accompanied by a heavy bombardment from 10 p.m. till 11.45 p.m., and after an interval from midnight to 12.45 a.m. Just prior to the commencement of the bombardment the enemy fortified his nerves by a sing-song in his trenches. On the S.O.S. call our artillery put down a barrage on the enemy parapet and in No Man's Land, but shortly after midnight the raiders rushed through it and made for our trenches. In No Man's Land they were broken up by a listening post of 5 private soldiers who threw no less than 80 Mills Bombs at their adversaries. In the end 1 of our post was killed, 1 crawled back to the trenches severely wounded, and the other 3 were taken prisoners. Examined later, the ground showed signs of a desperate struggle. The efforts of these out-numbered but undaunted men prevented all but a handful of the enemy from entering our trenches. At these a machine gunner threw a bomb, and 1 of the party was wounded and fell into our hands. The rest after a brief show of fighting fled, leaving behind them 2 mobile charges. Apart from the 3 prisoners, our casualties, all inflicted by the bombardment, were 33 men killed and 3 officers and over 60 men wounded. The Divisional artillery fired over 4000 rounds in direct connection with the attack. The German casualties were unknown, but "several were heard to squeal," and in the grey dawn of the following morning, the sentries reported that many killed and wounded were being taken over the enemy parapet. Under this ordeal the Aucklanders' behaviour was stolid and resolute. The commanding officer reported that he believed not a man had left his post without orders.

The second attempt was made on 8th/9th July, further south on the Mushroom just beyond the Lille-Armentières railway. On the whole sector this was the point where the irregular lines of trenches as dug under fire in 1914 most nearly approached each other. Long previous to the Division's arrival mines had been exploded here on both sides. The resultant craters, developed and protruding like bulbous excrescences into No Man's Land, had given its name to the locality. Only 60 yards separated the foremost saps. The spot had already won a notoriety in the Division for unpleasantness and been the scene of episodes that stood out from the monotonous routine of trench warfare. On a quiet afternoon towards the end of May a rifle grenade was fired into our trenches with a note attached: "What time is it, Anzacs?" The appellation in itself did not necessarily imply enemy knowledge that the sector was held by New Zealanders, since they had already obtained identifications from the Australians; and as late as the middle of June a Saxon, who was on reconnaissance and was captured by a 1st Otago patrol, thought that our trenches were held by Indians. On 2nd June the enemy placed a white board 5 feet by 4 feet on their parapet, opposite the Mushroom:—

English defeat at sea
7 cruisers sunk
1 damaged
11 small craft sunk
Hip Hip Hurrah!

This was the first intimation received by the troops in the line of the Battle of Jutland.[1] On receipt of the British official despatch a table was displayed by us showing the respective naval losses. This was left exposed for half an hour, and no shot was fired at it. Shortly after its removal the enemy put up a board on which was written "We beg of you to show again the table of the fleets." At the same time 2 enemy heads were seen under brand-new "porkpie" caps. Another message was then hoisted, "Once more, will you let us see the message again?" This request was not complied with, but on 12th June a placard was displayed

1 31st May 1916.

by us in German, giving details of the sea-battle and the news of the Russian successes won at this time. On this a number of Germans showed themselves taking hasty glances at the notice. They consoled themselves by calling out, somewhat prematurely, that Greece had taken sides with the Fatherland. Some 10 days later the German garrison practised a gas alarm, ringing their bells and blowing their syrens, and a stentorian voice shouted in good English "Gas alarm! Are you going to advance?" and a few minutes later, for his own entertainment, ordered "Advance!" Towards the end of June the Mushroom was the scene of the one and only case in the history of the Division of desertion to the enemy. 10/2719 Pte. W. P. Nimot crept unnoticed from the Mushroom across to the German lines. He was actuated mainly by a feeling of soreness over a recently awarded punishment and by an acute dislike of shell-fire and other dangers incidental to the trenches, but German blood was in his veins. It is worthy of note that later he wrote to the High Commissioner requesting his share of the parcels despatched to New Zealand prisoners in Germany. On the same day and at the same place 1st Wellington received in exchange a German deserter.

By this proximity and by its configuration the salient was marked out as a particularly vulnerable spot in our defences. In the first days of July our Engineers had destroyed a mine tunnel by a camouflet which probably caused the death of German miners and may have furnished an immediate motive for the raid. On 8th July the Mushroom was garrisoned by 1st Canterbury. A fierce bombardment was opened at 9.10 p.m. which lasted for 50 minutes. It completely destroyed the trenches and caused very heavy casualties. One 8-in. and several 5.9-in. unexploded shells were found next morning. At 10.15 p.m. 2 red rockets shot up in the German lines, and the enemy attacked. The first assault was repelled by the survivors in our trenches under Sergt. S. G. Brister. At 10.50 p.m. there was a lull. Soon after 11 p.m., however, the bombardment recommenced, and attacking on both flanks, the enemy by a prodigal use of bombs succeeded in forcing their way in. The German officer in command of the party haughtily summoned Brister to surrender, and when he refused fired at him point-blank with his revolver, wounding him in the face. Simultaneously Brister flung a bomb at the officer and was "certain that he got him." But the garrison, losing heavily, was yard by yard forced down the communication trench till they reached a block. Here they stood at bay and continued to hurl their bombs into the Mushroom.

All the Canterbury officers on the spot had been killed or wounded, and the counter-attack was led forward by Lt. E. H. T. Kibblewhite, a machine gun officer, whose section was posted in rear of the Mushroom. With a mixed party of machine gunners, sappers and infantry he reoccupied the salient in half an hour from the time of the German entry. Flanking parties of the Battalion were sent into No Man's Land to cut off the raiders but without success. Our dead had not been searched nor had the dugouts been ransacked. A man who with 2 dead comrades was pinned under a wooden frame of the trench reported that the Germans had been fully occupied in carrying back their dead and wounded. The sandbags on the parapet indeed were marked with their blood-stains. They secured 3 prisoners. Our casualties were in addition 2 officers and 21 other ranks killed and 3 officers and 90 other ranks wounded. Throughout the attack our artillery bombarded the enemy's position and on his withdrawal concentrated on his communication trenches in order to harass the raiders' return. This activity, however, brought down a fresh storm of shell on our own area, preventing the rescue of the wounded. So the guns were asked to discontinue, and the remainder of the night was spent in excavating the buried, some of whom though shaken were still alive, and in repairing our trenches and opening communications. The breaches in the front line parapet were repaired by dawn.

Just before midnight on the feverish night 19th/20th July, only 500 yards away from the scene of the 1st Rifles' raid,[1] a large enemy party made an attempt on the Rue du Bois salient which was at the time held by the 2nd Rifles. Our artillery fire in connection with our own 2 raids and the more ambitious operations of the XI. Corps was active on the enemy's line throughout the period, and it is not unreasonable to suppose that the Germans suffered casualties before reaching our trenches. The enemy bombardment was of exceptional fury, 8000 shells being flung into the area exclusive of trench mortar projectiles. The whole ground was turned over as if by a volcanic upheaval, and the local features altered so as to be unrecognisable. At the northern end of the salient, called the Dead End, the Germans effected a bare lodgment and captured 3 men out of a listening

1 p. 49.

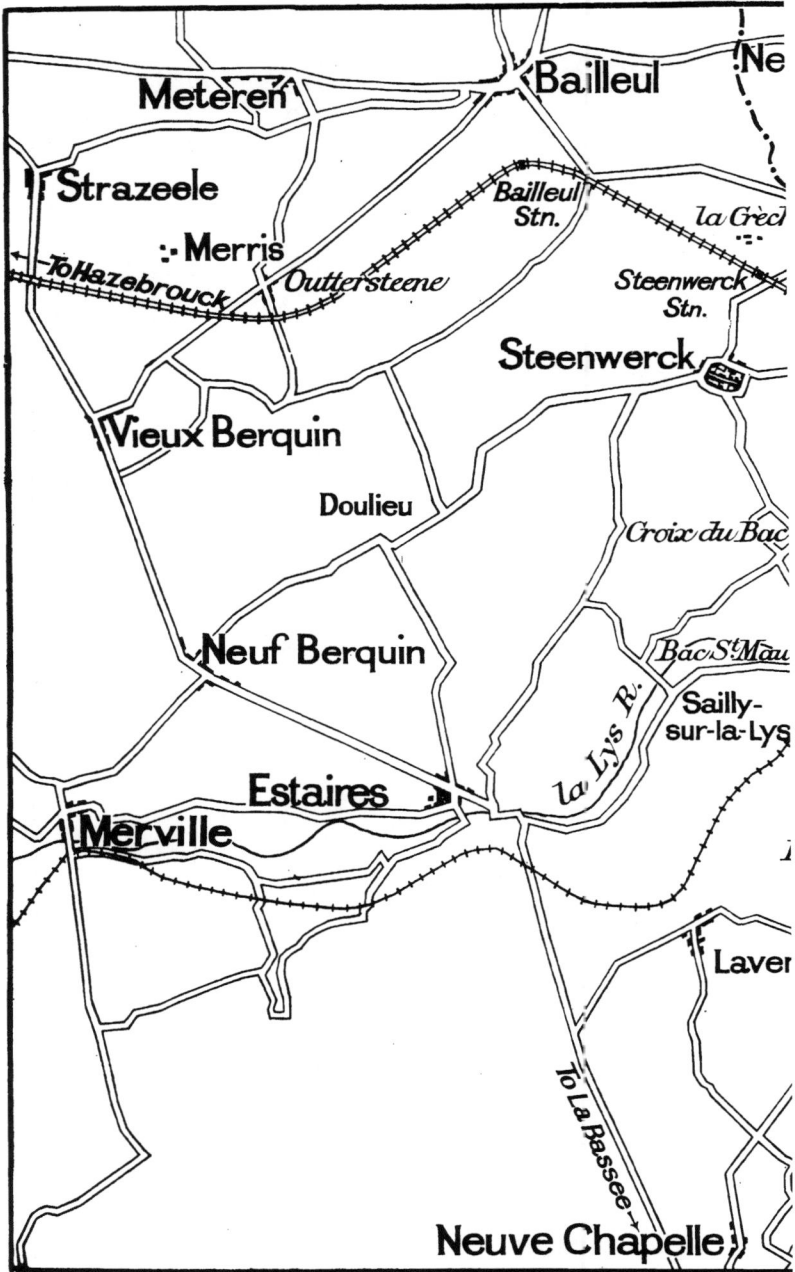

Meteren

Bailleul

Ne

Strazeele

Bailleul
Stn.

la Crèch

Merris

To Hazebrouck

Outtersteene

Steenwerck
Stn.

Steenwerck

Vieux Berquin

Doulieu

Croix du Bac

Neuf Berquin

Bac St Mau

la Lys R.

Sailly-
sur-la-Lys

Estaires

Merville

Laver

To La Bassee

Neuve Chapelle

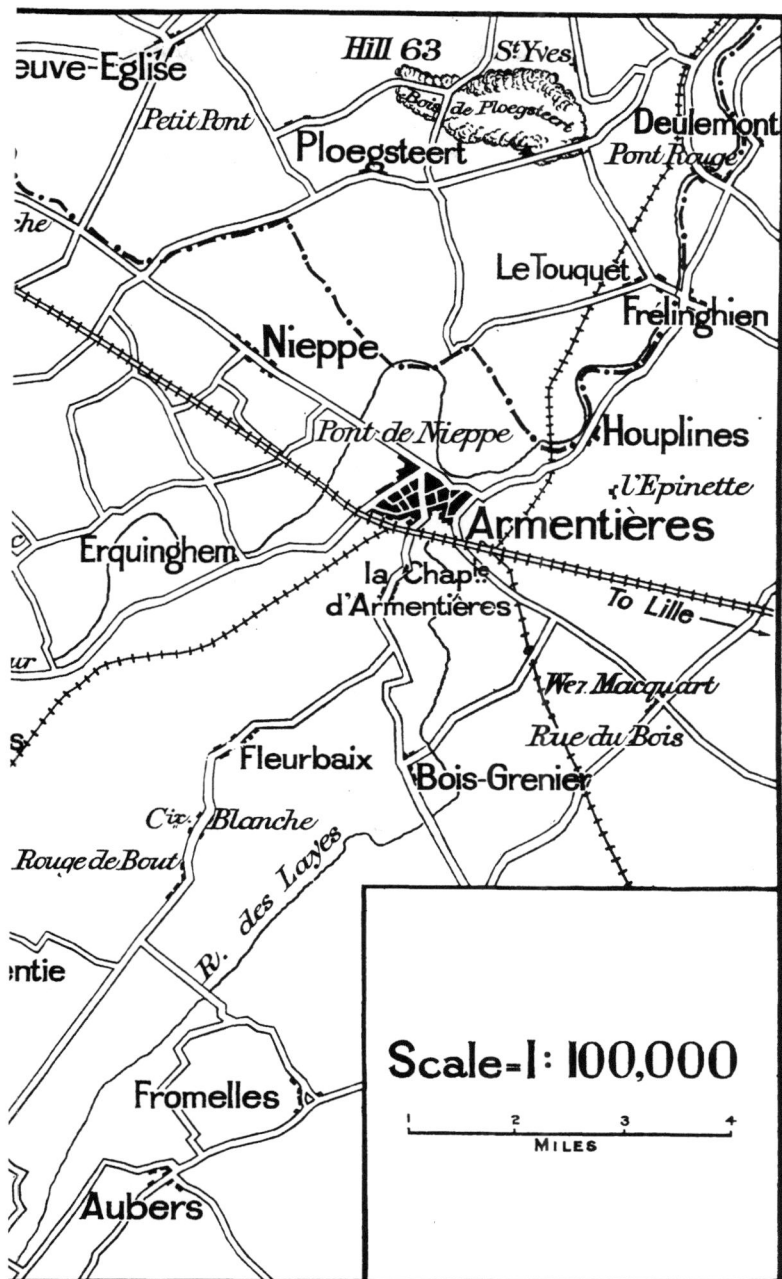

Hill 63   St Yves

Bois de Ploegsteert

euve-Eglise

Petit Pont   Ploegsteert   Deulemont

Pont Rouge

che

Le Touquet

Nieppe   Frelinghien

Pont de Nieppe   Houplines

l'Epinette

Erquinghem   Armentières

la Chap.lle
d'Armentières   To Lille

ur

Wez Macquart

Rue du Bois

Fleurbaix   Bois-Grenier

Cix. Blanche

Rouge de Bout   R. des Layes

ntie

Scale=1: 100,000

1   2   3   4
MILES

Fromelles

Aubers

AND VICINITY   [Copyright

post. They were met at the "stop," where the sap from No Man's Land ran into the trench, and were bombed back, leaving 1 wounded and 2 dead in our hands. At the apex 2 minenwerfer bombs made an enormous crater, which was at first supposed to be a mine, and buried 2 mortars and an officer and 12 men of the 3rd Light Trench Mortar Battery. On the southern tip the attack failed. Under the tornado of shells, trenches and parapets were heaped in mingled confusion, but the riflemen set an example of fortitude and dour resistance which it would have been impossible to surpass. The enemy left behind him 12 mobile charges and a quantity of raiding material. In addition to the 3 prisoners, the total casualties sustained, including those of the machine gunners and mortar battery personnel, amounted to an officer and 16 men killed and 30 men wounded. As retaliation, a specially effective bombardment was delivered on the following evening by howitzers and trench mortars against the enemy position opposite the salient.

The final German effort was nipped smartly in the bud. In the early morning of 28th July a 2nd Wellington listening post near the Lys heard stealthy and suspicious sounds about their wire. A flare revealed a party of 20 Germans some 30 yards away. Without hesitation they were attacked with bombs and driven off, leaving behind them much equipment. So far from obtaining identifications, they betrayed their own by losing one of their party, whose body with the tell-tale numerals on the tunic was brought into our lines.

Throughout this period the enemy's artillery endeavoured to keep pace with our own lavish expenditure of shell. Some days were marked by particular virulence. On 1st July, for example, possibly in retaliation for the bombing of Lille Railway Station by a number of aeroplanes on the previous evening, he shelled the great church of Notre Dame in Armentières with a 5.9-in. naval high-velocity gun. It was new on this front and was surmised to be the one which had attained sinister notoriety at Ypres. It fired from a mounting in a railway loop beyond Pérenchies. 58 rounds were fired from 7.30 a.m. to 10.6 a.m. and 18 rounds from 10.34 a.m. to 11.30 a.m. The first round was a hit, the thirty-sixth brought the spire down, and the fire was throughout extremely accurate. Our heavies retaliated, putting round for round into Comines. Two days later, in

combination with the enemy raid on l'Epinette, after
Houplines had been shelled during the daylight, Armentières
was heavily bombarded after dark with high-explosive up to
10-in. and with incendiary shells. The naval gun was again
active. Many houses were set on fire, the streets damaged,
and several casualties inflicted both among troops and
civilians. The 1st and 2nd Artillery Brigade headquarters
received several direct hits. The quartermaster stores of the
2nd Infantry Brigade Headquarters were burnt to the ground.
The headquarters of the 1st Field Ambulance were demolished
but the patients removed without casualties. The headquarters
of the 4th Rifles were not so fortunate. An 8-in. shell scored a
direct hit on the building, and Major A. E. Wolstenholme, the
Battalion Second-in-Command, and Capt. F. E. Guthrie, the
Regimental Medical Officer, were killed. Every gun in the
Division the Corps and the Army retaliated, the Army heavies
putting round for round into the village of Lambersart,
which lying beyond the ridge was occupied by the Headquarters of the Division opposed to us, and the bombardment
on either side was the heaviest that the New Zealanders had
yet witnessed. As the following days brought no abatement
of the enemy's artillery fire, it was decided not to treat
patients in the 2 Ambulances in the town. This step threw
a greater amount of work on the Divisional Rest Station in
rear and the remaining Ambulance which had charge of it.

In our artillery programme, apart from the unrehearsed
revenge which a harassed battalion or company commander
or on a larger scale an infantry brigadier could always
summon, there were several definite prearranged and frequently varied systems of retaliation. The broad principles
were that such retaliation should follow on the provocation
as soon as possible, that it should be of greater volume, and
delivered with bigger guns, and, if possible, be such as to
connect itself in the enemy's mind with the fire which
provoked it. This last principle was sometimes disputed on
academic grounds, but certainly for the front line garrisons,
when the foundations of their world shook under hostile bombardment, the moral tonic administered by the battering of
their persecutor's own trenches was incomparably more
effective than a shelling of his back areas. Thus as a rule
forward areas suffered for forward areas, billets for billets,
and so on. These retaliations culminated in the so called
Retaliation X for the shelling of Armentières, when all

artillery brigades were called on, and the "heavies," if the bombardment were serious, would shell Lille.

Towards the middle of July this intense activity quietened down, on our side owing to the temporary shortage of ammunition, alluded to above, and on the German side through a similar shortage or a withdrawal of guns. The total ammunition expended by us during the last 10 days of the month did not exceed the average daily consumption of the first week.

By this time our patrols, which included Maori patrols, completely dominated No Man's Land, where their troubles were caused, not by active opposition, but by the searchlights which played along the enemy wire and by the rustling of the grass, which, though the Germans cut it with characteristic thoroughness near their own wire, lay thick in the middle of No Man's Land. Instead of sending out patrols himself, the enemy fired "pineapple" bombs at the points likely to be crossed by us and bombed his own wire. Generally his morale was surprisingly low, and on several occasions our sentries with mingled astonishment and contempt saw a German put his rifle on the parapet and pull the trigger without taking aim, the bullet raising a spurt of dust in No Man's Land or passing high overhead. His machine guns were active and admirably handled as usual, and it was not often that they gave their position away, as by smoke from an overheated gun drifting in the moonlight against a dark background of bushes. Only now and again strong enemy patrols ventured out, and bombing fights ensued, almost invariably to our advantage. Various devices were employed to destroy or capture these hostile patrols, and on 26th July a familiar German booby-trap was utilised with apparent success. A patrol of the 3rd Rifles laid out wires with bombs attached, and withdrew a little distance to await results. First 1 German appeared followed by 12, but their route did not take them in the way of the trap. The L/Cpl. in charge of our patrol therefore shot the leader. His men bombed the rest of the party, and only 3 were seen to escape. Alarmed by the noise, immediately afterwards another German party approached, and one of their number becoming entangled in the trip-wire exploded the bombs. This time not a man was seen to escape. The second explosion brought down a gust of machine gun fire and shrapnel, and our patrol on its way to make investigation was compelled to withdraw. One man, Rflmn. Woods, was wounded and unable to drag himself in,

his absence being discovered only when the patrol returned.
He could not be found that night.   On the following evening
he was searched for by a patrol under Sergt. R. Simmers.
The patrol itself was surprised and heavily bombed by the
enemy who were lying in wait, 1 of our men being killed
and 4 wounded.   Simmers returned the bombing, drove
off the enemy, and continued to advance with the 4 riflemen
remaining.   He located Woods, who was still alive, and
returned with him and all his party and the body of the
dead soldier to our trenches.

During the first week in August the 18th Division came
into the centre sector of the Corps front between the 5th
Australian Division on the right and the New Zealanders on
the left.   The Rifle Brigade was relieved by troops of the
new Division, and the New Zealand front was therefore
contracted to its original length.   In connection with this
re-organisation the 4th Artillery Brigade recovered its 8th
10th and 14th batteries from the respective groups.   Various
British units were now coming up from the Somme fighting,
and several valuable lectures were given on the terrain, the
tactical methods of the opposing armies, questions of supply,
and experience generally in the battle.   Towards the end of
the week orders were received that the Division would be
relieved by the 51st (Highland Territorial) Division, from the
Somme, in order to release it for a period of preparatory
training for battle.   The relief commenced on 13th August,
and was completed on the 18th, when the command of the
sector passed to the Highlanders, and the Division marched
out after a continuous stay of 3 months in the line.

During this period they had sustained 2500 casualties.
25 officers and 350 other ranks had been killed.   70 officers
and 2000 men had been wounded, and 30 men were missing.
Some of these last were in enemy hands, others had been
blown to pieces by explosive or buried irretrievably in trench
cataclysms.   On the 14th, 2 battalions of the Rifle Brigade,
marching back with the newly issued Lewis gun handcarts
to the railhead at Steenwerck, were inspected informally by
H.M. the King.   The infantry entrained there for the
concentration area at Blaringhem.   They were followed by the
batteries who trekked the 27-mile march with their guns via
Estaires, Vieux Berquin and La Motte.

On the 20th the entrainment of the Division was commenced
at Arques and St. Omer for a training area east of Abbeville
where it was to pass under the command of the X. Corps of

the Fourth Army. The concentration in this new area was completed by 22nd August. Headquarters was at Hallencourt, the artillery in billets about Longpré, the 3 infantry brigade areas being Yonville Airaines and Limercourt respectively.

Meanwhile the Divisional Cyclist Company[1] had reached France in July. In accordance with the Army policy, which transferred this unit with the mounted squadron from the control of Divisions to that of Corps, the company was taken on the strength of II. Anzac Corps Headquarters. In the Mounted Regiment, there was 1 New Zealand and 2 Australian squadrons. In the Cyclist Battalion the balance was to be reversed, and reinforcements were drawn on to make 2 New Zealand companies. The command of the battalion was given to Major (later Lt.-Col.) C. H. S. Evans who had organised and trained the New Zealand company from its formation. At the end of August 1 platoon of the battalion was attached to the Division to be used as runners and orderlies in the forthcoming operations.

The Division followed with keen interest the passing into law in New Zealand of the Military Service Act on 1st August. This measure of far-reaching political and historical importance was brought to the notice of all ranks in the following Divisional Routine Order of 13th August: "The New Zealand Government wishes the men of the New Zealand Division to feel that the Military Service Bill just passed by both Houses of Parliament represents the assurance of New Zealand both to the Motherland and to her troops in the field that the obligation to keep the ranks full will be carried out as long as men are available."

During the period under review certain changes in appointments were made which it is convenient here to summarise. On 22nd July Lt.-Col. Pinwill vacated the appointment of G.S.O.1 to take command of a battalion in his old regiment. He was succeeded by Lt.-Col. R. O'H. Livesay, D.S.O., Queen's R.W. Surrey Regiment. About the same date Major Chesney, Brigade Major, 1st Brigade, was invalided and succeeded by Capt. M. H. Jackson (29th Lancers), whose appointment as D.A.Q.M.G. was filled by Lt.-Col. Hamilton, hitherto commanding the Divisional Train. Command of the Train was assumed by Lt.-Col. J. Atkinson, A.S.C. Lt.-Col. H. A. Reid succeeded Lt.-Col. A. R. Young as A.D.V.S., the latter returning sick to New Zealand. Various

---

[1] p. 7.

changes took place in the 2nd Infantry Brigade. Major
Puttick relinquished his appointment as Staff Captain to
become Second-in-Command of the 4th Rifles.[1] His place was
taken by Capt. T. M. Wilkes, N.Z.S.C., who subsequently,
on Major Lampen's becoming sick, was promoted Brigade
Major. In the appointment of Staff Captain he was
succeeded by Capt. Richardson, who transferred from the
same appointment in the 1st Brigade, where the vacant
position was filled by Capt. A. S. Falconer. In the
battalions Lt.-Col. C. H. J. Brown had taken over the
command of 2nd Auckland from Lt.-Col. Alderman on 6th
July, and on arrival in the training area in August, Lt.-Col.
Moore, commanding 2nd Otago, was transferred to the
British Army and was succeeded by Major (now Lt.-Col.) G.
S. Smith, D.S.O.

1   p. 56.

CHAPTER III

THE BATTLE OF THE SOMME, 1916

The expansion of their armies and armament made it at length practicable for the British to undertake, in accordance with the general Allied policy, an offensive campaign on a large scale in the summer of 1916. It was decided that the French should co-operate and that the thrust should be made up the valley of the Somme. In his despatch of 23rd December 1916 the British Commander-in-Chief has defined the objects of the offensive as threefold: to relieve the pressure on Verdun, where the German assault had been designed partly to frustrate the impending blow; to assist the Allies in the other theatres of war by stopping any further transfer of German troops from the Western front; and to wear down the strength of the enemy forces. The British would have preferred a somewhat later date in the summer, which would have permitted of an increase of men and munitions and a period of further training for the new levies, but the continually increasing strain at Verdun forced their hands. It was agreed therefore that the combined attack should be launched not later than the end of June. The British share in the joint operations was committed to the Fourth Army under General Rawlinson. Arrangements were also made for a subsidiary attack on the northern flank of the selected area by troops from General Allenby's Third Army, and a skeleton Reserve Army was formed in rear under General Gough.

Owing to their commanding situation and bare glacis, destitute of cover for assaulting infantry, the enemy positions which confronted the British on the watershed between the Somme and the rivers of South-Western Belgium were in themselves of immense strength and had been converted by unremitting and skilfully directed industry, and by every technical device known to modern military art, into fortifications as nearly impregnable as any in history. Against them, indeed, along a considerable part of the front, British valour was on 1st July to dash itself in vain, for not merely was the subsidiary operation abortive, but in the northern sector of the main blow, from Thiepval to Serre, the assaulting lines withered away under the deadly combination of artillery, machine guns and wire. At the end of the day the Commander-in-Chief made up his mind perforce to cut his losses and not persevere for the moment with the attack in this sector. The 2 northern Corps of the 5 which formed General Rawlinson's command were handed over to General Gough. The latter's augmented Army was directed to act as a pivot on which our advance on the right could swing, and for the meantime to confine itself to a steady and methodical pressure. In the southern half of the British area, however, the first defence system, including trench lines, redoubts, woods, and villages, for a frontage of over 6 miles to a depth of a mile or more, was in our possession by 15th July. Of the second system, which ran along the southern crest of the main ridge from Guillemont through Longueval and the two Bazentins to Pozières, some $3\frac{1}{2}$ miles were captured in the middle of July. For the remainder there ensued a stern and prolonged struggle (the second phase of the battle), in which the British troops, not without being mauled in the process, satisfactorily fulfilled the main object of the offensive. As they strained forward, the role of the Reserve Army became one of more active co-operation. By the second week of September, not merely had the enemy's Second Line been won, but at certain points very considerable penetration had been effected beyond. "Practically the whole of the forward crest of the main ridge from Delville Wood to beyond Pozières was now in our hands."[1] Meanwhile on the right the French had carried their lines by a series of brilliantly conceived and vigorously executed operations to within striking distance of Péronne.

It remained now to develop in a third phase the advantages obtained at the cost of so much blood and labour. Between Morval and Le Sars, behind the last of the enemy's original systems of defence which now faced the victorious British, there had been added since the summer several new lines on the north-eastern slopes of the main ridge. None were, however, of the elaborate nature of those already stormed. Though fresh Bavarian Divisions had been thrown in, incontestable evidence betrayed a weakening of the German morale and an acute strain on his reserves. His guns, though enormously increased, were outweighed by the British artillery: and much was hoped from our as yet untried weapon of the tank. The failure at Verdun, the collapse in

1 Despatch of 31st December, 1916, para. 25.

A BURIAL SERVICE

TRANSPORT MOVING TOWARDS THE LINE

AREA OF THE SOMME BATTLEFIELD (1916)

Italy, the intervention of Roumania, the opening of the offensive in the Balkans, all seemed to presage the waning of Germany's star. Towards the end of August capable military opinion believed that we were approaching a stage when bold and energetic action might yield great and possibly decisive results. Consequently, as General Rawlinson now told his Corps commanders, Sir Douglas Haig was going "all out," with every possible resource in men and engines of war, to bring the Battle of the Somme to a successful and immediate conclusion.

For all the gigantic preparations necessary there was, in view of the lateness of the season, little time to lose. Plans were immediately drawn up for a grand attack at the earliest possible moment, which could not well be before the middle of September, with the aim of overwhelming the enemy at the outset and following up the advantage won with the utmost rapidity and vigour. Once the enemy was driven from his prepared positions into the open, it was hoped to abandon the snail-like progress of trench warfare and employ cavalry on a large scale. The other British Armies to the north were instructed to be prepared to assist in exploiting a decisive success. Preliminary attacks were made in the beginning of September to afford suitable assault positions or to deny observation. For the main operation, arrangements were put in hand for the employment of rested Divisions with their morale at its bloom. Among these it was the privilege of the New Zealand Division to be included.

The New Zealanders, meanwhile, were recuperating from their arduous work on the Lys amid the delectable wooded valleys of the lower Somme. Health improved rapidly, and at no time perhaps were more energy and keenness thrown into the training, which was itself based on the assumption of participation in a renewed offensive on the Somme. In the artillery work, therefore, it was natural that fire discipline should be a paramount feature, and that emphasis should be laid on the principles governing the close barrage. There was fortunately some fair manoeuvre ground, and the drivers, exercised in so-called "refresher" courses in field movements, speedily regained the proficiency which had been in some degree impaired by the prolonged conditions of trench warfare. Guns equipment and harness were minutely overhauled. The Engineers paid particular attention to the construction of Strong Points and to rapid wiring. Specialists in all branches intensified and widened their theoretical knowledge and practical skill. Above all, the infantry were familiarised with the new methods of assault, and great importance was attached to the thorough appreciation by every private soldier of the principles involved and the general scheme of each practice operaticn. The efficacy of these new methods had been proved over and over again, and it was vital to diffuse a complete comprehension of them. The lesson was hammered in, therefore, that infantry, trained to hug the protective curtain of shrapnel, which advanced in front of them and prevented the manning of the enemy's machine guns,would have all the odds in favour of success; that the risk of casualties caused by an occasional short burst must be faced, and that in any case these would be few compared with those to be expected in an unsuccessful attack, or in an attack driven home in the face of effective machine gun fire. So, too, stress was laid on the necessity of absolute punctuality. Experience had already shown that while an assault delivered immediately the artillery fire lifted from the objective was, humanly speaking, assured of victory, the delay of even a fraction of a minute might be fraught with disaster.

By night as well as day, all over the meadowlands and the stubble of the harvest fields, battalions in fighting kit incessantly practised the advance of assault waves in extended formation, the avoidance of crowding, the progress of small columns of supporting troops in rear, and the methods of communication with co-operating aeroplanes.[1] The different objectives were represented by different coloured flags, and the lifts of the creeping barrage by lines of men waving branches to indicate the fall of shrapnel, or by horsemen galloping forward in succesive "bounds" in accordance with a prearranged timetable. The planning and execution of these operations constituted invaluable training.[2]

From these scenes of carefully staged rehearsal the first troops to move up to the front were the Engineers and the Pioneer Battalion. They left on 27th August, and partly on

---

1 Contact patrol work by aeroplanes was designed to keep Headquarters of formations informed as to progress of troops, to report on the enemy's positions, the advance and movement of his immediate reserves and the state of his defences, and to transmit messages from the troops engaged. They were specially marked and carried Klaxon horns and Verey lights. On their part the infantry lit flares at specified times and places in their most advanced positions, and if they carried Klaxon horns sounded them on their own initiative. Brigades and battalions indicated their position and identity to the aeroplane by ground signal sheets and stripes and sent messages by ground signal panel arranged to represent letters. Thus, in a later development, a succession of G's meant "further bombardment required," of N's "short of ammunition," of Z's "held up by wire." The aeroplanes communicated with headquarters of Corps and Divisions by dropping marked maps and written messages. See also footnote, p. 28.

2 It may be noted that during this period of training the Division formally adopted the method of wearing their felt hats with brim horizontal and crown peaked.

foot and partly by train proceeded to the neighbourhood of
Fricourt. Here they were first employed under the Chief
Engineer of the XV. Corps in consolidating the old German
Second Line on the Bazentin Ridge and then, with a view to
the forthcoming attack, in digging west of Delville Wood the
2 communication trenches of Turk Lane and French Lane,
which were to become such famous arteries of the battlefield.
The next arm to follow was the artillery, who, marching by
different routes through 29th and 30th August, concentrated at
Bonnay. The same vile weather which was impeding the
sappers in the reconstruction of the Carlton and Savoy
trenches made the march a trying one for the gunners,
harness and equipment being soaked in the torrential rain.
From Bonnay on 5th September the artillery began to
relieve the 33rd Divisional Artillery, which in accordance
with the artillery policy of the time was not administered
as a separate unit, but had been divided between the 7th and
the 14th Divisional Artillery Groups. It thus came about
that during the Battle of the Somme the C.R.A., New Zealand Division, had in that capacity no actual command.[1]
The 1st and 2nd Brigades were attached to the 14th Divisional Artillery, covering the left Division of the XV. Corps,
and the 3rd and 4th were joined in a group under Lt.-Col.
I. T. Standish and attached to the 7th Divisional Artillery,
covering the centre Division. Batteries were brought
forward by sections each night to Caterpillar Valley and the
reverse slopes by Montauban. They found the emplacements
partly completed, in most cases with splinter-proof head-
cover. The 8th Battery of the 4th Brigade remained for the
moment in reserve. Relief was completed by 6 p.m. on 6th
September. On that same day the gunners experienced a
foretaste of the repeated bombardments to which they were
to be exposed before they were done with "the Somme."
Their positions were searched with 8-in. shells, and one lucky
hit blew up an ammunition dump and destroyed a howitzer.
Before the infantry came into the line, the artillery co-
operated, besides carrying out daily routine fire, in several
minor attacks, in the latter stages of the capture of Ginchy
by the XIV. Corps on the 9th, and in the repulse of the
German counter-attack.

It was not till 2nd September that the infantry began to
move up from their peaceful billets towards the realities of

1 On the senior C.R.A. being wounded, Brig.-Gen. Napier Johnston assumed
command on 1st September of the artillery eventually destined to cover the New
Zealand Division's front and remained in command till relieved on 25th September.

war. On that date the 1st Brigade marched to Airaines, the 2nd to Cavillon, and the 3rd to Le Quesnoy. In beautiful autumn weather, the march continued on the following day, when the 1st Brigade reached Yzeux, the 2nd Picquigny, and the 3rd Vaux-en-Amienois. In this area, still well in rear of the surge of battle, the brigades remained for 4 days, and engaged in manoeuvres over the country-side. The whole district, and particularly the 2nd Brigade area with its splendid remains of the Roman legions, left an abiding impression of picturesque charm and historical interest. The march was resumed on the 7th by side roads to the mean and crowded villages of the Allonville area, and that day, as the battalions breasted the slopes on the tree-shaded roads, the distant throb of the guns, now sinking, now swelling, became audible. The following afternoon they passed through the old British rear defences, the 3rd Brigade to Dernancourt, the 1st and 2nd into the hutted camps about Lavieville of the XV. Corps (Lt.-General H. S. Horne). It was on this day (8th September) that the German Guards and other picked troops hurled themselves against the whole arc of the allied line. All day long heavy artillery action was distinctly heard. In the evening the unbroken ring of gun flashes round the horizon flickered red like continuous sheet lightning, and the menacing rumble of the opposing artilleries exactly resembled thunder. On the battlefield itself the number of guns heard is more circumscribed, the ear more attuned to the German batteries, and the dangers, faced and known, lose their frightfulness. The Lavieville bivouacs were at just that distance when the sounds of the massed and opposing artilleries blend in indistinguishable unison, and are invested with a mysterious and awful impressiveness.[1]

1 In this connexion may be quoted Mr. L. Binyon's too little-known lines:—
THE DISTANT GUNS
Negligently the cart track descends into the valley;
The drench of the rain has passed, and the clover breathes;
Scents are abroad; in the valley a mist whitens
Along the hidden river, where the evening smiles—
The trees are asleep, the shadows are longer and longer,
Melting blue in the tender twilight; above,
In a pallor, barred with lilac and ashen cloud,
Delicate as a spirit, the young moon brightens,
And distantly a bell intones the hour of peace,
Where roofs of the village, gray and red, cluster
In leafy dimness.   Peace, old as the world!
The crickets shrilling in the high wet grass
And gnats clouding upon the frail wild roses
Murmur of you: but hark! like a shudder in the air,
Ominous and alien, knocking on the farther hills
As with airy hammers, the ghosts of terrible sound—
Guns! From afar they are knocking on human hearts
Everywhere over the silent evening country,
Knocking with fear and dark presentiment.   Only
The moon's beauty, where no life nor joy is,
Brightening softly and seeing nothing, has peace.

While the 1st and 2nd Brigades remained for a day here, visited by General Godley at training or on parade, and bathing in the deep willow-fringed waters of the swift-running Ancre, the 3rd Brigade set out on 9th September, marching past the varied scenes of astounding activity along the main road to the Moulin du Vivier and thence by the dry-weather track to Fricourt. On all the slopes tens of thousands of British troops were bivouacked under the eyes of the German balloons. The twinkling of their camp fires at night was like the lights of a great city, and in the morning the smoke from a thousand cookhouses rose up and spread a haze over the hillsides.

On the following day and night the Rifles relieved a brigade of the 55th Division towards Delville Wood and a portion of the 1st Division on the left nearer High Wood. The 1st[1] and 4th Battalions went into the advanced trenches, and the 2nd and 3rd[2] into the old German Second Line (Carlton and Savoy) in rear, where the dugouts were still full of German dead. Brigade Headquarters occupied a cellar in Bazentin-le-Grand.

These rear positions commanded an extensive view of the German trenches on the crest. To the right lies Longueval village and Delville Wood, now at length wholly in British hands. In front, just beyond Carlton trench, the road runs from Longueval to Bazentin, and across the valley to the north the scarred and pock-marked slopes rise up gently to the enemy's positions in the Crest Trench, on the ridge by High Wood. Just over that ridge is the formidable Switch Trench, connecting the German Third and Second Systems, and about three-quarters up is our own front line. Breaking the skyline further to the left are the stark trees of High Wood, from which rises ever and again the black smoke of bursting explosive. This grimly contested wood was now a charnel house, full of sinister memories to the British, and inspiring not less horror in the mind of the German infantryman. "We are actually fighting on the Somme with the English," wrote a Bavarian in September. "You can no longer call it war; it is mere murder. We are at the focal point of the present battle in Foureaux[3] (High) Wood. All my previous experience in this war, the slaughter

1 Major (Temp. Lt.-Col.) J. G. Roache, vice Lt.-Col. Austin, wounded 20th July.
2 Major (Temp. Lt.-Col.) A. E. Winter-Evans, vice Lt.-Col. Cowles, invalided to New Zealand; later in the year appointed to command it.
3 *Foureaux* is the spelling of maps. The Maire of Flers assured us (Sept. 1919) that the correct spelling as given in title deeds and official documents, etc. is *Fourcaults*. *Foureaux* no doubt, however, will persist.

at Ypres, and the battle in the gravel pit at Hulluch, are the
merest child's play compared with this massacre, and that is
much too mild a description. I hardly think they will bring
us into the fight again now, for we are in a very bad way"—
the last pium desiderium is a distinctly human touch.

Pending the day of attack, the Rifle Brigade improved
their trenches and dug a new line through the shellholes in
front, first constructing a chain of posts 100 yards apart and
each 20 yards long, with flank trenches of 5 yards, then connecting these posts together and the whole with the original line.

On the 10th (Sunday), after a joint service by the 2
sister battalions of each regiment, the 1st and 2nd Brigades
marched up to the rear of the battle area. The 1st Brigade
went to Fricourt, the 2nd to Fricourt Wood and Mametz
Wood, where they lay in bivouac among the trees till the
morning of the 12th. On the 11th, at 9 a.m., the command
of the sector passed to the New Zealand Division.

Long ere now the Fourth Army plans had been crys-
tallized. While the French would continue their pressure on
the south, the Reserve Army would attack on the north in
conjunction. An attempt would be made to seize Morval,
Les Boeufs, Flers and Gueudecourt, through which lay the
nearest avenue to the open country beyond. On their capture, the cavalry, supported by the XIV. and XV. Corps, who
would follow up at once in rear, would be pushed through
the outposts. With a flank guard of all arms established
on the general line Morval-Le Transloy, the cavalry would seize
the high ground east of the Péronne road, and establish a line
in country later to become familiar to the New Zealanders,
from Rocquigny through Villers-au-Flos and Riencourt-les-
Bapaume to Bapaume itself. They would moreover assist in
rolling up the enemy's lines to the north-west by operating
against his flank and rear in conjunction with the attack
which would be continued against his front. The cavalry
would not enter the villages, so fire would be maintained on
them. Corps and Divisional Commanders, with whom it lies
to feel the pulse of a battle and turn favourable opportunities to account, were admonished of the need of boldness
and determination.

The XV. Corps was now composed of fresh Divisions with
their fighting spirit at its zenith. All 3 Divisions were to
be put in the line, each on a frontage of about 1000 yards.
This formation was preferable to keeping 1 Division in rear,
as facilitating the more rapid advance of reserve troops with

a view to paralysing the enemy defences and producing panic. On the right was the 14th, in the centre the 41st, and on the left the New Zealand Division. On its left again on the right flank of the III. Corps, the 1st Division had been relieved by the Londoners of the 47th.

In the forthcoming battle the Corps objectives were 4 in number, marked in accordance with custom in different tints on the maps and referred to by these colours; firstly the seizure of the Switch Trench with the intermediate defences on the crest (the Green Line); secondly the establishment of a Brown Line in German trenches on the far slopes; thirdly the passage of the Flers System, the capture of Flers village and the consolidation of a Blue Line in front of it; and lastly the carrying of Gueudecourt and establishment of a protective Red Line beyond it, bending back to the north-west to the junction with the III. Corps, whose advance would still leave the XV. Corps in a marked salient. Flers fell within the zone of the 41st Division, in the centre of the Corps, and Gueudecourt within that of the 14th Division, on the right. In addition to minor trench elements the advance would involve the capture of 3 formidable trench systems, the Switch, the Flers Line, and the Gird Line that protected Gueudecourt. Opposite the New Zealand sector the German positions were held by Bavarians.

The first 3 objectives set before the New Zealand Division, the Green, Brown, and Blue Lines, lay square to its front, but its section of the Red Line, forming as it did the Corps' north-western flank, ran across its front diagonally. The left of the Red Line thus coincided with the left of the Blue in the Abbey road which ran from Flers to Eaucourt l' Abbaye, and the area to be secured in the final advance was roughly triangular. For the actual Red Line, which would mark the limit of advance and cover the exposed left flank of the Corps, there was conveniently situated a strip of high ground which extended back towards a sugar factory halfway between Flers and Ligny Thilloy. Along this high ground lay the important trench called Grove Alley which connected the Flers and Gird systems, and just beyond it was a shallow valley down which the North Road led to the Factory. The ridge on the other side of the depression similarly had a communication trench along its crest called Goose Alley. Both Alleys were to be scenes of epic fighting, but for the present attack the high ground about Grove Alley was selected as the final objective.

For these operations General Russell decided to employ the 2nd and 3rd Brigades, and hold the 1st Brigade in reserve. Two battalions of the 2nd Brigade, who would during the interval relieve the Rifle Brigade and be in the line, would seize the Switch. Passing through them, the Rifle Brigade would capture the remaining objectives. 1 battalion would leave the Green Line for the Brown an hour after zero, 2 battalions the Brown for the Blue Line 2 hours after zero, and 1 battalion the Blue for the attenuated Red Line 4½ hours after zero. Should the fourth objective be reached without undue difficulty, it was intended to exploit success in a northerly direction, with the co-operation of tanks. The Rifle Brigade were accordingly instructed to push out strong offensive patrols and the 2nd Brigade to be prepared to support them.

Stupendous weight of artillery was behind the infantry to neutralise the advantages given by modern warfare to the defence. In addition to overwhelming heavy artillery a field gun was available for every 12 yards of enemy front opposite the New Zealanders. German newspaper critics might growl fiercely in terms like these: "Anyone would think that the object of the French and the English was simply to kill so many Germans every week or every month. They have no tactical ideas; they are simply butchering us." Their soldiers knew, however, that no other alternative was feasible. The experience of Neuve Chapelle, Loos, and Verdun had established firmly the principle of demolishing trenches saps and machine gun emplacements, cutting communications, and in a word destroying the enemy's physical and moral powers of defence by a heavy bombardment preliminary to the operation and continued during the attack up to the time of the arrival of the infantry at each objective. The actual advance of the infantry was covered by stationary and rolling barrages of field guns. Normally the rolling barrage commencing in No Man's Land would move back steadily and evenly at a rate calculated by the infantry advance, lifting, say, 50 yards at a time and halting on certain defined lines for definite periods to enable the infantry to reorganise. The stationary barrage on the other hand remained on the position to be assaulted till joined by the rolling barrage when it lifted at one bound to the next objective. While the heavy guns did counter-battery work, the field howitzers co-operated with the siege howitzers in bombarding objectives in advance of the stationary barrage.

The front held by the Division was, as we have seen, covered by the 14th Divisional Artillery and the 1st and 2nd New Zealand Field Artillery Brigades, the other half of the Divisional artillery assisting the Division on the right. The New Zealand batteries were disposed on the northern slopes of the valley running from Caterpillar Wood to Bernafay Wood as close to the front as could possibly be arranged. Forward positions in the event of success were selected. The initial bombardment commenced on 12th September. Sunken roads and road junctions, headquarters and villages as well as trenches and battery positions were subjected to a steady fire. Particular attention was given to the Switch line and above all to its extensive wire entanglements on the smashing of which the success of the operation largely depended.

On the same day (12th September) the Rifles were relieved by the 2nd Brigade and marched back for a short period of rest to Fricourt and Mametz Woods. 2nd Auckland and 2nd Otago took over the front line, 2nd Canterbury went into support, and 2nd Wellington into reserve. Brigade headquarters was established in a tunnelled dugout built by the Pioneers in Turk Lane, just south of Carlton Trench. The assembly trenches initiated by the Rifle Brigade were extended and further ones constructed. All other preparations were being pushed on with vigour both in front and in rear.

The 14th was a squally day of rain which cleared off towards evening. Throughout the day the enemy shelled the areas of Caterpillar and Marlborough Woods and Bazentin-le-Grand but refrained from harrassing our front trenches. During the daylight the German outposts appeared to have been withdrawn over the crest, and our infantry to their equal astonishment and gratification were able to work openly in No Man's Land, and to complete their jumping-off line and assembly trenches unmolested. The 1st Brigade moved up to Fricourt and Mametz Woods, and after dusk the Rifle Brigade marched up from their bivouacs there to the assembly area in front of the 2 rear battalions of the 2nd Brigade. In accordance with the sound principle already laid down by the General Staff, all battalions sent to the Reserve Camp, as so-called "B Teams," the proportion of officers non-commissioned officers and specialists, who would in the event of heavy casualties serve as a framework on which the renewed unit could be built. Parties were told off for all the heterogeneous duties of the battlefield, to police the trenches, to bury the dead, to salvage abandoned equipment, to act as ammunition carriers for trench mortar sections or machine gunners, to assist the Engineers, to carry up stores from prearranged advanced dumps—ammunition bombs water and tools, in that order of importance.

After darkness the tanks, male and female, crawled forward to their assembly area by Delville Wood. They were still in the first stage of development. Their pace was not more than on an average 33 yards per minute, or 15 yards per minute over badly shelled ground. They carried a crate of pigeons for communication with Headquarters and different coloured flags to denote to the infantry that they were out of action or had arrived at their objective. Their mission was, roughly, to move in front of the infantry, attack certain positions at which particular resistance was expected, and assist the infantry in clearing difficult places if called on. There had been, however, little opportunity of practising co-operation, and it was to be expected that they would act largely as free-lances of the battlefield. The tactical experience of the officers in command was naturally not at this time equal to their gallantry. Of the 4 allotted to the Division, 1 broke down in Longueval.

The hour of attack had been fixed for 6.20 a.m. on the 15th. Before midnight the troops were all in position. Each man was in light fighting order. Two gas helmets were slung over his shoulders. Over 200 rounds of ammunition were contained in his pouches and bandoliers. In his pocket he carried 2 bombs, and behind on his belt were tied the precious sandbags for consolidation. His greatcoat was left with his pack in the regimental dump, but he retained his waterproof sheet with cardigan jacket rolled inside. His waterbottle was filled, and in his haversack was a day's rations and an "iron" ration. Fastened down the centre of every other man's back was a shovel or pick. Each platoon carried so many smoke bombs for rendering enemy dugouts untenable and so many flares for signalling to our contact aeroplanes that, marked by white streamers and a black band under the left plane, would hover over them at prearranged hours on the following day and after dawn on the 16th.

German aeroplanes had noted the tanks and reported them as heavily armoured cars; and on our left a German officer wrote in wrath and despair an unheeded report on the suspicious massing in the British trenches and the inactivity of the German artillery. If the enemy anticipated an attack, he took no counter-measure. Opposite the New Zealand sector he proceeded with the relief of the 3rd and 4th Bavarian Divisions by the stout 6th Bavarian Division from the Argonne and the fibreless 50th from Bois Grenier. His mood appears to have been one of confidence, inspired by the repeated repulses of the British attacks on High Wood. A captured Brigade Order, dated 10th September and relating to the defence of High Wood and its vicinity, stated categorically that the German positions in Crest and Switch Trenches were so strong that they might be relied on to resist the fiercest attack.

In the New Zealand trenches the infantry, trained to the last degree of physical fitness and with the fine edge of morale undulled by exposure to artillery fire, snatched a little sleep. The sentries on duty, without either excitement or the boyish insouciance of the English soldier, but in stern and serene elation of spirit waited for the coming of the dawn and whatsoever fortune might bring them.

By 6 a.m. they had breakfasted, and drunk their rum. A ghostly pallor was now creeping into the sky, and the Otago left could just faintly discern the silhouettes of the gaunt trees in High Wood, whose silence was unbroken by German shells. The watch hand crept slowly and as it were reluctantly toward the appointed time. The weather held out every hope of a fine day.

To the second our guns broke out into thunderous uproar, and to the second the leading infantry waves of Auckland and Otago, with bayonets fixed and rifles sloped, clambered out of their assembly trenches and advanced straight up over the hummocks and between the shellholes. The 8 companies moved abreast in 4 waves about 50 yards behind each other. Each wave was made up of 8 platoons in single rank, some 3 yards separating man from man. The advance was marked by admirable direction pace and alignment. To those watching in the Carlton System the long line of sombre figures was visible for a few moments till obscured by thick clouds of smoke and dust. Trudging up the hill, the men hugged the barrage which lifted 50 yards a minute. They twice knelt down in the shellholes to let it precede, firing as they knelt at the machine guns in Crest Trench. An advanced outpost line called Coffee Trench, which lay in front of the Aucklanders, was crossed in their stride. On reaching Crest Trench more Germans were found

than had been expected.   On the left in front of Otago
some 200 turned and ran over the open for the Switch.
Many of them never reached it, for our Lewis Gun teams,
waiting for the barrage to lift, raked the fugitives with fire.

One machine gun on the Otago sector was, however, most
troublesome.   Sergt. Donald Forrester Brown with another
non-commissioned officer, J. Rodgers, crawled forward at the
utmost risk to their lives to within 30 yards of the
position and then rushed it, killing the crew and capturing
the gun.   Otherwise little resistance was met with all along
Crest Trench.   Sections from rear waves were detailed to
"mop" it up, and the leading troops, with their zest for
killing whetted, swept on without delay to the Switch 250
yards in front.

Just before the Switch, the leading waves of Auckland in
their eagerness overstepped the barrage and suffered casualties.
The troops on the right were advancing in line, but on the left
the Londoners had been delayed, after a premature start,
by the peculiarly bad going in High Wood and by heavy
machine gun fire.   Hence there was a gap beyond the left
of Otago, and the enemy machine guns and rifles enfilading
down from the corner of High Wood tore some holes in the
khaki line.   The tanks, for which predetermined lines had
been left in the barrage, so that they could reach the Switch
5 minutes before the infantry, had been delayed by the
broken ground and had not yet arrived.   As the storming
lines lay under the final halt of the barrage on their objective,
the 2 leading waves and the individuals who had pressed on
in the avenues left for the tanks all wedged into 1 solid
wave, which the instant the barrage lifted—almost before it
had lifted—poured through the smashed entanglements
towards the trench.   Again Sergt. Brown and his comrade
rushed a gun and killed the crew.   The Switch had been
terribly battered and wrecked, but many of the garrison
were still alive.   There were also several machine guns,
but such was the speed of the assault that the enemy was
generally unable to use them, and those on the flank and in
rear were masked by his own troops in the Switch.

A letter written by a soldier, who took part in the
storming of the Switch, to his relatives in New Zealand
affords an interesting record of detailed adventure and
emotional experience:—

"On the 15th September our platoon went over in the
second wave, and I could see the Germans' heads above

the trench firing at us when we got about half way
across.   Even when we joined the first wave I could see
that our ranks were pretty thin.   We lay down and
watched for the third and fourth wave to join us before
rushing them.   The four waves combined made up about
as many as one of the original waves.   While we were
lying down waiting for the rush, Fritz was rattling away
with his machine gun for all he was worth, and for a few
seconds he ripped up the ground about a yard in front
of me.   It gave me a bit of a fright, and I wasted no time
in wriggling back a few yards.   I also yelled out to the
man on my left to get back, but when I looked at his face
I saw that he was dead.   When we stood up and started
to run, their fire slackened off a lot, and soon stopped
altogether.   Half of them put their hands up and ran
towards us; some of them took to their heels, and a few
of the fools kept firing at us.   We all wanted to get
at them with the bayonet, but some of us were faster
than others, and those behind were so anxious to do
something that they started firing at the Huns, at the risk
of hitting their own men in front.   I jumped into the Hun
trench and found that it was so deep that I could not
climb out at the other side, so I pulled a dead Hun into
a sitting position at the side of the trench, stood on his
shoulders, and managed to climb out.   When I think of
it now, it seemed a horrible thing to do, and I am not
quite sure whether he was dead or not, but I did not
notice it in the excitement of the moment.   I was chasing
one fellow and almost had him, but I soon found I was
not too safe, as the fellows behind were firing, so I lay
down, took steady aim, and shot him.   Another poor
beggar came stumbling towards me with a shower of
bullets flying all round him.   I knew that if I let him
come too near me I would stand a good chance of getting
hit by one of our own bullets, as he was drawing a lot
of fire, so I gave him a bullet in the chest when he was
about 15 yards from me.   They are the only two Huns
I can claim to have put out of action, although I may
have killed or wounded more that I did not see.''
While some of the occupants made a poor fight, others,
stouter-hearted, threw bombs and fired rifles till our lines
were atop of them, and then on the greater part of the front,
throwing down their weapons, they held up their hands, and
with calculated presumption called for mercy.   Mercy, how-

ever, was shown only to the Red Cross men and the wounded. Where further resistance was made, the enemy in the trench itself were disposed of after a little point-blank shooting and a short struggle with bombs. The dugouts were cleared similarly. On the right, where the enemy were thicker, the Aucklanders used their bayonets freely. With this weapon Pte. A. R. Johnson showed magnificent courage and agility, killing one after another of the enemy who were throwing bombs at his comrades. It was here that 2nd Lt. A. C. Cooper, already wounded, continued to fire his revolver with great effect at the German bombers. Otago found a Headquarters dugout some 100 yards down the forward slope, and its 6 occupants were bombed. By 6.50 a.m. the Switch was completely in our hands, and its captors looked down on the new country where the greenish-brown fields seemed unscarred and the villages unshattered.

Below them, immediately on their right, lay the houses and kitchen gardens of Flers, and in a straight line, 1000 yards beyond, one got glimpses of Gueudecourt. On their left, about a mile and a quarter to the north-west of Flers, Eaucourt l'Abbaye could be distinguished with the picturesque ruins of the old monastery and the 2 orchard-surrounded farms built of its masonry—all enclosed by a high wall. It lay in the III. Corps front, and from it stretched a road to Ligny Thilloy, on which glasses detected the limbers of German transport. Between these villages in the middle distance lay the solitary group of buildings of the sugar refinery at Factory Corner, close to which the Rifle Brigade would thrust the line, if all went well, later in the day. In the background, the eye travelled over gentle wooded slopes on which the roofs of Ligny Thilloy and Le Barque stood out among the trees.

Close on the heels of the 2nd Brigade battalions came the leading battalion, the 4th, of the Rifle Brigade. It was extended over the whole Divisional sector with 2 companies in front, each occupying 400 yards and each in 4 waves. At the rear of each leading company followed 2 sections detailed to clear any intermediate trenches encountered before reaching the Brown Line. The support companies followed 60 yards in rear. At 7.5 a.m. the leading lines passed through the Switch, singing[1] and in high spirits, and lay down as close as possible to the curtain of fire some 300 yards beyond. There was still no sign of the tanks. When

1 A quite unusual feature but reported on reliable authority.

the barrage lifted and commenced to roll forward, now at a slower rate in view of possible difficulties on this reverse slope, the riflemen followed it for their half-mile journey without experiencing any particular difficulty. By the scheduled hour of 7.50 a.m. they had captured the Brown Line. The Battalion Headquarters moved forward to a sunken road some 150 yards behind, but here came presently under heavy machine gun and rifle fire. The artillery liaison officer was killed, and several of the officers and men killed and wounded. Lt.-Col. Melvill and his staff therefore moved forward into the Brown Line itself. Consolidation and organisation for defence were at once taken in hand. Two machine guns were posted, one in the Brown Line, where it did particularly useful work against the German counter-attack launched during the afternoon, and one in a Strong Point on the left, from which it decimated a party of retreating enemy. Unfortunately, later in the morning, a tank was damaged about the centre of the line and drew heavy fire on the trench. The 4th Battalion casualties during the day were 13 officers and 254 other ranks.

All this time the 2nd and 3rd Battalions of the Rifle Brigade had been advancing immediately behind the 4th Battalion. Till they reached the crest, each section wound its way in Indian file up over the shellholes, each platoon group being separated about 100 yards from its neighbour to minimise the dangers of artillery fire. The 2 battalions were each in depth on a 1-company frontage of 400 yards. One company of the right battalion for a time got in front of the 4th Battalion, but this was remedied without confusion. German heavy artillery laid a barrage in High Wood and along the crest, but the shells kept falling in much the same spots, and a passage through was not difficult for seasoned soldiers.[1] The German field guns presumably were moving back, for there was little or no shrapnel, but with characteristic tenacity an overlooked machine gun in the Switch blazed into activity for a few thrilling moments and caused some casualties before the crew were destroyed. The battalions reached their assembly position in rear of the Brown Line well up to time.

Just after 8 a.m. the barrage moved forward again, though the tanks it was to cover were not up, and 20 minutes later,

[1] The instantaneous fuse, which caused the shell fragments to fly much further, was not yet employed, and the system of "crashes" was yet to be evolved: see p. 320. The Germans never at any time used much shrapnel, and almost invariably burst it too high.

in accordance with the programme, the 2 Rifle Battalions started forward, unaccompanied by a barrage, to fulfil their allotted part in the battle. Their task was first to capture the sector of the great Flers Trench System on the Divisional front, then to carry Fort Trench, which lay towards Flers village, clear the north-west corner of Flers and the line of dugouts in the Abbey Road, and lastly to dig themselves a position from the tip of the village along the rising ground beyond the Abbey Road to the North Road valley and the III. Corps boundary.

On the right the 2nd Battalion did not find much difficulty in Flers Trench, where they captured over 80 prisoners, but as soon as they began to move out of it, a machine gun from the hedges at the corner of the village in front caused several casualties, among whom fell Major A. J. Childs. By short rushes, however, the platoons pushed their way to Flers Support, which was found empty. From there to the Abbey Road the support companies, who now took up the struggle, met stiff fighting. Hidden in the plantations, the road had a sheer 20-feet drop, undetected by our aeroplanes and full of dugouts, and there the Germans resisted stubbornly. Part of the 1st Battalion, which followed in rear, joined in the conflict, and a platoon of the 4th which had been in battalion reserve was sent forward to assist. About 9.30 a.m. the road and plantations on the western half of the village were cleared of the enemy, and the 4th Battalion platoon returned to the Brown Line.

Partly to fill a gap on their right and partly drawn by the magnetism of the village, the 2nd Battalion had swung somewhat into the area of the 41st Division on their right, to whom all Flers, except this north-western corner, had been assigned. These English troops had had less distance to cover in the initial stages of the battle, and for them the Brown Line had coincided with the Flers System where it was contiguous with the village. Thus they were among the houses and saw the Germans retiring in disorder towards Gueudecourt, while the New Zealanders, according to programme, were still mastering Flers and Fort Trenches. At 8.40 a.m. an aeroplane saw a crowd of them following a tank up the main street. Ere the Germans retired, however, they released pigeons with a report of their disaster, and the congested troops of the 41st Division in the village were soon heavily shelled and lost most of their officers. Only a handful penetrated to the Blue Line beyond, till the Brigade Major[1] of their left brigade, a fine fighting soldier, personally collected parties and brought them round to the north-eastern side. Owing to these casualties it was fortunate that the 2nd Rifles was in a position to give substantial assistance in filling up the gap on its right and so securing our hold on Flers. By 10 a.m. it was on the Blue Line in its own area on the New Zealand front and had its right thrown well over into the 41st Division's sector, and covering the village.

On the left, with the 3rd Battalion, progress was much less marked. As no barrage accompanied this stage of the attack, it was most desirable that the wire in front of the Flers System should be found well broken. It was a matter, therefore, of grave anxiety to the 3rd Battalion troops to find themselves confronted by a practically intact barrier of rusty entanglements. Machine guns and rifles chattered from the trench beyond, and it was obvious that their hope of surmounting the barrier of Flers Trench without trouble was doomed to disappointment. No tanks were yet visible. Bombing sections, led by 2nd Lt. R. A. Bennett and others, worked up the communication trenches which ran forward from the Brown Line, and succeeded in putting one machine gun out of action, but all their efforts were unable to force an entry. Other parties, utilising the dead ground on the left, made some progress under cover of supporting machine guns. The 1st Battalion coming up joined in the fighting here as they had joined in the fighting in the village, but the barrier remained unbroken. Attempts at a frontal rush to reach the wire and break it with wire-cutters were effectively checked by the stream of lead pumped from the trench.

But the new British weapon was thus early to prove its value. About 10.30 a.m. the men lying in sullen discomfiture in the shellholes, with their rifles trained on any movement in the Flers Line, became aware of 2 tanks, one of which rolled over to the left boundary by the North Road, while the other smashed the wire and stamped out the machine guns. In their wake followed a party of 10 riflemen and bombers of the 4th Battalion, who had pushed forward to add impetus to the 3rd Battalion's attack. This little party, commanded by Major Pow, coming on top of the dismay inspired by the tank actually captured 100 prisoners. The 3rd Battalion then pushed up through Flers Support to Abbey Road to join the 2nd.

[1] Major Gwyn Thomas.

There now remained the final task of capturing Grove Alley. This objective had been allotted to the 1st Battalion, which till now had constituted the brigade reserve. The fighting in the village and before Flers Trench, in which parties of this battalion had become involved, made reorganisation necessary. When the leading companies therefore reached Abbey Road, they paused for a time under cover of the 2nd Battalion and part of the 3rd, now on or close in rear of the Blue Line, to straighten out their units. It was about 11 a.m. Owing to the delay at the Flers System the progress of operations now lagged behind the timetable, but as there was no covering barrage this mattered little. Advantage was taken of the halt to arrange with a small party of English troops in Flers that these should establish a Strong Point in an isolated German system known as Box and Cox, 300 yards north of the village, so as to furnish a defensive flank.

At about 11.30 a.m. the 2 assaulting companies moved off. On their appearance 200 of the German troops garrisoning Grove Alley turned and fled north-eastwards towards Gueudecourt. Our advance was covered by the fire of the machine guns attached to the 2nd Battalion, which had taken up prearranged positions in Strong Points in the vicinity of the Blue Line. This checked opposition in front, but severe machine gun fire, admirably directed from the Goose Alley ridge beyond the North Road on the left, caused several casualties. Somewhat reduced in numbers by this fire, the 1st Battalion pushed steadily forward and captured the centre of the position without overmuch trouble. Particularly fine qualities of leadership were shown by Coy.-Sergt.-Major G. H. Boles, who, when all the officers and most of the n.c.o.s of his company had been put out of action and the men began to falter under the fire, took command, organised the remnants, and led them forward to the objective. Two guns of a German field battery, one of which was in action, were assaulted by 2nd Lt. J. R. Bongard with a party of 7 men, and the crews bayoneted.

Thus the final objective of the Division, except for a portion on each flank, was in our hands. It was now, however, after midday. The tanks had gone over to the right or had been destroyed. No troops were visible in the 41st Division's Red Line, and even at Box and Cox in the right rear, the party that had undertaken to form the Strong Point had been prevented from carrying out the arrangement.

The left or south end of Grove Alley, which the depleted companies were not strong enough to cover in their assault, was still occupied by the enemy. This force was hemmed in by the 1st Battalion and the 3rd, and no doubt could have been trapped. A more pressing danger, however, lay on the 1st Battalion's unguarded right flank, where large numbers of the enemy were beginning to advance from the north-east, and threatening to cut off the thin line of our troops, stretching out here "into the air." The officer in command in the front line had to make up his mind rapidly. He decided to withdraw steadily to Box and Cox and the Blue Line. Bongard's party destroyed at least one of the field guns.

Generally, in such circumstances, it is the duty of troops that reach an advanced position to hold their ground and facilitate the advance of their comrades on the flanks, but sometimes situations arise which are frankly impossible, and to stay then means useless waste of lives. On this occasion, as a matter of fact, the neighbouring troops were not in a position to effect further progress without an interval of at least some hours, and the tactical correctness of the decision to withdraw, however reluctantly made, was confirmed by the orders received shortly afterwards from Corps, that no advance beyond the Blue Line would be made that day. It was now about 2.30 p.m. The 1st Battalion troops set to work at once to consolidate their line. Of the 2 light trench mortars at their disposal 1 was destroyed by a direct hit. The other took up a defensive position. The right flank round the north-east corner of Flers was drawn further back to protect the village from this direction, and to connect up with the handful of English troops on the right. 2nd Lt. N. L. Macky, who was in command of the 1st Rifles' reserve of 2 platoons, moved forward, engaged the enemy with fire and arrested his advance. Thus, though it was impossible to maintain a hold on the last objective, the Rifle Brigade achieved further progress than the troops on either flank. In the course of the day's operations they had captured over 400 prisoners, 6 machine guns and a mitrailleuse.

To meet the threatened counter-attack on the forward position, the 2nd Brigade was ordered to send up a battalion in support of the Rifle Brigade. General Braithwaite accordingly gave instructions to this effect over the telephone to his reserve battalion, 2nd Wellington, which, previously warned for such action, moved off at once with 5 machine guns. They met a considerable barrage on the Switch and heavy shelling between there and Flers, but advancing in splendid order suffered few casualties. Passing through the western part of the village, the 2 leading companies found that the enemy's attack had been finally smashed by artillery fire and had not developed into a serious danger.[1] After reconnaissance of the Rifles' position they filled up a gap north of the village, where, owing to the necessary overflow into the right Division's front, the line was distinctly thin. As the infantry dug in, they were covered by the tank "H.M.S. Diehard," commanded by a gallant young officer of the Highland Light Infantry. It had already done strenuous service, though none of its adventures so impressed its cheerful crew as the sight of passing Bavarians hurriedly adjusting their respirators, under the impression that the smoke from the exhaust pipe was some novel kind of lethal gas. It now moved forward along the road towards Factory Corner, protecting the digging parties with its broadsides and at the same time firing up the road with its forward gun.

At 3.30 p.m., the enemy reaction seemed to swing against the left flank, where a previous attempt had been crushed by our machine guns. Reports reached Divisional Headquarters of skirmishing lines of enemy north of High Wood and west of Flers. The 2nd Rifles moved a composite party of a company strength across from right to left to meet this new threat, and a third 2nd Wellington company was also rushed up, but this attack, too, failed to materialise.

At about the same time the English troops on the right came up to a level with the New Zealanders in Box and Cox by occupying trenches further to the east, but in accordance with Corps orders and as their right flank was in the air, they withdrew again in the evening to the Blue Line. After their experience in Grove Alley, the riflemen were resolutely determined not to relinquish their grasp on Box and Cox. On the left they were now more or less linked through to the New Zealand sector of the Blue Line. If only troops were brought up to swing the right flank back further, they were confident of maintaining their advanced position. For this purpose, the last 2nd Wellington company was sent up in

---

1 This German attack presented to the New Zealand gunners perhaps their best moving target in France, and even, with the possible exception of the Lone Pine and Chunuk Bair operations on Gallipoli, in the whole war. Forward observation officers, already in Flers Support, observed a force of Germans, about a battalion strong, in close formation in the open. For a moment they were mistaken for our cavalry who were expected to be seen dismounted. When their identity was realised, practically every field gun in the sector opened well-directed fire on them.

the evening, and after its arrival units were largely reorganised, the forward troops of the 2nd Rifles being pulled back to support. In the protection and consolidation of this awkward right flank, conspicuously good work was done by Capt. L. M. Inglis, of the 1st Rifles, and Capt. H. E. McKinnon, of 2nd Wellington.

The position in the evening was that the north-east approaches to the village were barred by the 41st Division troops on the Blue Line, and the north and north-west of the village secured by the 1st Rifles, with the three 2nd Wellington companies, 200 yards in front of the Blue Line and connected back with the 3rd Rifles and the other 2nd Wellington company, who were consolidating the Blue Line on the left of the sector. On their left, again, in the III. Corps area, the 47th Division had been very severely engaged in High Wood and been unable to take their objective in the Flers System. The 3rd Rifles, therefore, who had themselves lost nearly half of their effectives in the fight for Flers Trench, placed machine and Lewis guns to command the North Road valley. A further section of machine guns was sent forward in the evening. Blocks and bombing posts were established in Flers Trench and Flers Support, and a defensive flank was manned in a convenient sap which ran from Abbey Road to Flers Support.[1]

About the Abbey Road, during the afternoon, conspicuous gallantry was shown by Rflmn. J. R. Walter, of the 3rd Battalion, who under direct machine gun fire and heavy shell-fire went into No Man's Land, where he dressed the wounds of 8 men and carried them into shelter.

In the village of Flers itself a systematic search was made during the course of the afternoon. Many cellars and dugouts still contained Germans. Seven prisoners had been taken when a machine gun party, after surrendering, fired point-blank into the clearing party, of whom 3 were killed and 4 wounded. Thenceforward no prisoners were taken. Two machine guns were captured with a vast amount of equipment. As in the Switch and other lines, the dugouts were full of cigars, chocolate, mineral waters and food, with which the victors assuaged their hardships. No civilians were found. Previous to the battle the 400 inhabitants, who had remained in Flers under German control, had been withdrawn eastwards. The big brewery had been some time

1   This was later continued to the main left communication trench forward of the Switch, Fish Alley, which led back to the 4th Battalion in the Brown Line and thence into French Lane.

before stripped of its machinery and converted into Baths. The church had been used as a hospital, and the schools for operations. In the evening the 41st Division was instructed by Corps to appoint an officer specially charged with the defence of the village.

While these events were happening in the front of the battle, in rear there was incessant activity in all branches of the service, above and below ground and in the air. As an instance of the work of Staffs and Signallers, it is interesting to note that for the first 24 hours of the action Divisional Headquarters dealt with 700, and the 2nd Brigade Headquarters with 400 telegrams. The formation of forward dumps, the carrying forward of munitions and food, the supply of water, the extension of roads and approach trenches, the evacuation of wounded, the movement of troops and guns, the development of signal communication, all necessitated urgent and considered effort. The rear battalions of the 2nd Brigade moved up to close support as soon as the Rifle Brigade crossed the Switch. Soon after midday the 1st Brigade also marched up nearer the battle. 1st Canterbury and 1st Wellington occupied the old German Second Line in Carlton and Savoy Trenches, and the remaining battalions went forward from Fricourt Wood to Mametz Wood. Batteries were hauled up over the shellholes to new positions under the Switch, between High and Delville Woods, and to Devil's Valley, some 500 yards north-east of the latter wood.

In the Switch itself, 2nd Auckland and 2nd Otago, with the Engineers' assistance, had, immediately after capture, begun to consolidate a new trench some 70 yards in front, with Strong Points on either flank. They had seen enough of war to realise that the lost Switch would certainly prove a ranging mark for German guns. This assumption proved correct, for an hour and a half after capture a heavy and accurate bombardment was opened on it, which continued throughout the day and night. It was not till the afternoon that the German observers noted the new trench, which thereafter came in for its share. Men were continually being buried, and portions of the trench had to be redug. But by evening it was complete. On account of the shelling, the Switch itself was left severely alone, except for exploration in search of souvenirs. For 2 days after, dazed and ghastly pale Germans, whose pockets were being rifled on the assumption that they were dead, would suddenly come to life in its dugouts. From it the battalions brought forward 4 undamaged German machine guns to the new line. The capture of the Switch had cost Auckland nearly 300 and Otago 400 casualties. The left Otago Company had lost all its officers and had been reduced to 34 men. L.-Sergt. H. Bellamy and Cpl. V. W. Shirley handled these with conspicuous ability.

In their new positions Otago were harassed not only by artillery fire but also by considerable enfilade machine gun fire and sniping, which came from their left, where the troops of the 47th Division, heavily engaged and, it appears, indifferently handled, had failed to reach their objective. These snipers were dealt with by the redoutable Pte. R. C. Travis, whose exploits on the Lys have already been mentioned, and who now went out voluntarily into the open and silenced them. Every effort was made to consolidate and strengthen the position, but the uncertainty of the situation in front of High Wood and the fact that our left was seriously exposed gave grounds for anxiety.   A company of 2nd Canterbury was therefore moved early, before the Germans had been cleared out of High Wood, to fill the dangerous gap on the left. Later in the day also this flank was strengthened by 10 machine guns, and in the evening 1st Canterbury was brought up from Carlton Trench into close support. During the night and the following morning 2nd Canterbury took over the Switch.

It was some days before apprehensions about this exposed flank towards High Wood were finally relieved. Prisoners captured on the 16th from different Regiments stated that a strong German counter-attack was to drive in from the northwest on High Wood before dawn on the 17th. Further Strong Points and machine gun emplacements were therefore established and manned, and the 2 supporting battalions of the 2nd Brigade were moved to assembly trenches in rear. The threatened attack did not actually materialise, and after the position was secured on the left, the garrison of the Switch, in order to minimise casualties from shell-fire, was reduced to a nucleus of 50 men, with numerous machine guns.[1]

The night of 15th/16th September was comparatively quiet. Patrols were sent out well ahead towards Grove Alley and the North Road up to the line of our own protective barrage, which was maintained along the whole front. On the 41st Division's sector it had been hoped that an after-

---

[1]   Till our communication trenches passed the Switch, parties moving over the skyline inevitably attracted fire.

7

noon bombardment of Gueudecourt and the Gird System
might induce the Germans to vacate trenches and village and
thus lead to peaceful penetration, but reconnaissance by patrols
made it clear that the enemy was not to relinquish his hold
so lightly.

A resumption of the general attack by the Fourth Army
had been planned for the morrow (16th September), and
orders had been received in the evening by the Division from
Corps for co-operation with the troops on either flank with
a view to the completion of the objectives of the 15th. At
midnight further instructions were issued that in the event
of success the advantages won on the XV. Corps front
should, in accordance with the general tactical scheme, be
exploited in a northerly direction. In that case, the 41st
Division would make a distinct change of direction, swinging
north-west to capture the Gird System as far as Goose Alley,
and the New Zealand Division similarly inclining to the left
would seize Goose Alley from the Gird to the Flers System.
This second movement, however, was conditional and would not
take place before 1 p.m.

On receipt of the Corps orders the 1st Brigade, which
had remained ready to move at 15 minutes' notice, was
immediately warned for the capture of the Red Line in
Grove Alley and for the possible exploitation. The 2 battalions back in Mametz Wood were set in motion at
once for the area in rear of the Switch as a half-way
resting place. The completion of the fourth objective
was given to 1st Wellington; 1st Auckland and 1st Canterbury were selected for the subsequent conditional
operation, with 1st Otago in reserve. Wellington moved
off at midnight and reached their assembly position west
of Flers before dawn, after a most creditable march in
the darkness, made difficult by lack of guides and absence of
previous reconnaissance. The other 3 battalions of the
brigade moved forward in the forenoon of the 16th, through
a heavy barrage of high-explosive. 1st Canterbury and
1st Auckland, as assaulting troops for the second objective,
assembled to the west of Flers, and Otago, less 1 company
detailed for ration-carrying, dug a new trench for themselves
just in rear of the Brown Line. General Earl Johnston, with
characteristic disregard of danger, established his headquarters on the forward slope of the ridge in the new Switch,
but was later forced by interference from hostile artillery to
seek a less exposed position. As on the 15th, the weather was

ARTILLERY ON THE MARCH

AN EMPLACEMENT

A Gun-Pit in the Somme Battle

warm and bright. The artillery, which had through the night been engaged in wire-cutting, commenced the preparatory bombardment at dawn. Just prior to the 1st Wellington attack, an attempt by 2 enemy companies against our right flank was crushed by rifle fire and that of the 4 machine guns allotted to Wellington, together with the help of a tank which was on its way to co-operate with the troops on the right.

At 9.25 a.m., 1st Wellington attacked with 2 assaulting companies in 4 waves at 35 yards' distance, followed by the 2 supporting companies, each in 2 waves. Though the hostile barrage accompanying the enemy's attack was heavy, and his machine guns on either flank took their toll, the assaulting companies had little difficulty in seizing the lightly manned Grove Alley, from just short of the Flers-Factory Corner Road to the point where it joined the Blue Line. The further section of some 400 yards on the right extending north of the road was not taken. The troops on the right had not succeeded in getting forward, and our men, had they reached it, would have almost certainly found it untenable. As it was, on this right flank enemy bombers for some 10 minutes pushed the line slightly back, till L.-Cpl. E. R. F. Scarfe and his Lewis gun section rushed up and prevented their further advance. He then followed the enemy down the trench, assisting materially in recapturing the lost ground, and continued, although wounded, to work his gun till the situation was cleared up. Pte W. S. Brown then led a small party of bombers to clear a further stretch of trench while a block was being constructed. The battalion took 22 Bavarian prisoners, but the guns destroyed by the 1st Rifles on the previous day had been pulled back under cover of darkness. The captured trench commanded an uninterrupted view of the valley along which ran the North Road to Factory Corner, and, contrary to expectations, it was not found necessary to dig a new line in front of it. Unfortunately, the 41st Division, with a longer distance to go and faced by heavier opposition, so far from being able to capture the Gird System or Gueudecourt itself, made only a little progress north of Flers. The tank accompanying them, which had rendered such good service in the German counterattack, pushed on by itself some 300 yards, when it was struck by a shell and abandoned. Thereupon a platoon of 1st Wellington's right support company was used to reinforce the right flank, while the left support company was withdrawn to battalion reserve. In the early morning aeroplanes had reported Gird to be held lightly, but it was strengthened ere the 41st Division's attack developed. In view of the failure to carry Gueudecourt, the second operation was necessarily cancelled, though notification did not reach the batteries in time to prevent their delivering the barrage. As it turned out, Gueudecourt was not to be captured yet, nor this second objective to be taken till 12 days later.

The 1st Brigade supporting troops destined for this second attack remained where they were till dark, when they began to relieve the Rifle Brigade. 1st Canterbury, in rear of 1st Wellington, occupied the Blue Line, now well consolidated, from Box and Cox to the Abbey Road. Despite the heavy shelling on Flers and its neighbourhood, they also dug and occupied a new sap from Box and Cox to Grove Alley, thus linking up with 1st Wellington. 1st Auckland took over from the 2nd and 3rd Rifles the whole of the Flers Trench System, and secured their left by digging another supporting flank trench connecting Flers Trench and Flers Support. In reserve, 1st Otago relieved the 4th Rifles on the Brown Line. On relief, the 3rd Brigade moved back at dawn on the 17th into Divisional reserve; 2nd Wellington similarly returned to the 2nd Brigade area behind the Switch, having lost 3 officers and over 200 men as the price of their service.

Though the full objectives of the Army had not even now been attained, the success won by the British on these 2 days none the less constituted a notable achievement. "The result of the fighting of the 15th September and following days," wrote the Commander-in-Chief in his despatch, "was a gain more considerable than any which had attended our arms in the course of a single operation since the commencement of the offensive." To the south, the strong position known as the Quadrilateral, east of Ginchy, had held up the attack on Morval and Les Boeufs, and Gueudecourt, as we have seen, was not yet captured. But 2 main lines of trenches had been stormed and the advance pushed a mile forward along a front of over 6 miles. Westwards, the Reserve Army had seized Courcelette and Martinpuich. 3000 prisoners were captured by the Fourth Army. As far as the Division was concerned, it had taken all its objectives and captured 500 prisoners, with 15 machine guns and a mitrailleuse, and 3 mortars. Of these prisoners the 1st Brigade had taken 22, the 2nd Brigade 50, and the 3rd Brigade nearly 450. The losses on the 15th had been approximately: Rifle Brigade, 1,200; 2nd Brigade, 800. The Division was gratified to receive a cordial telegram of congratulation from the Commander and Staff of the Second Army. Sir Henry Rawlinson, the Fourth Army Commander, who wrote similar letters of appreciation to the other troops engaged, sent the following message to the Corps Commander:—"Please convey to all ranks New Zealand Division my congratulations and thanks for their successful attacks on the 15th and 16th September. They showed a fine fighting spirit, and admirable energy and dash." In a covering letter, Sir Henry Horne wrote:—"The Corps Commander has great pleasure in forwarding above, and desires to add his own appreciation of their good work."

In the evening of 16th September the weather broke. Occasional showers fell on the 17th, but by midnight 17th/18th heavy rain set in, which continued without cessation for the rest of the night and the whole of the 18th, dying away in fitful squalls on the morning of the 19th. Now, as later in October, the weather robbed the British of the fruit of their efforts and gave a breathing space to the enemy to prop up his tottering line. Difficulties of communication and movement forced the postponement of operations. A modern army lives by its communications, and in the battle area these were inadequate in number and undermined and pitted by shell-fire. On the New Zealand area there was but the one avenue of approach for limbers, up the Longueval-Flers valley. By day it was commanded by German observation, and by night, naturally enough, heavily shelled. Reinforcements in the camp at Fricourt were employed on the rearward roads, but those nearer to the trenches became bogs of liquid mire. The supply of rations water wire sandbags flares ammunition and other necessities from the great Thistle and Green Dumps on and in rear of the Longueval-Bazentin road presented problems of acute difficulty, and relief was felt when the Engineers reported the 6 wells in Flers safe for drinking and fitted them with windlasses. Limbers had to be replaced by pack animals. Despatch riders from Divisional headquarters, 8 miles from Flers, found the road beyond Pommiers Redoubt impassable for their motor cycles. Signal wires, always subject to breaks by shell-fire and the passage of infantry and guns, were now affected also by the weather, and though Corps took over the responsibility for maintenance up to the Bazentin ridge, an ever increasing strain was imposed on the already over-worked but uncomplaining personnel of the Divisional Signal Company.

The clayey trenches became ditches, everywhere ankle-and in many places knee-deep in viscous mud which clogged every step. Cases of "trench feet" caused anxiety. The task of consolidation and drainage became a hundredfold more onerous. None the less the consolidation of fighting and communication trenches was pushed on despite all diffi-culties, and the Pioneers left an abiding memorial of their stay on the Somme in the magnificently constructed continua-tion of Turk Lane. At the same time the Engineers made dugouts for machine gun crews and medical personnel. In Ferret Trench, near the cross-country track which led down-hill from the Switch to Flers, they excavated, with the assistance of a Tunnelling Company detachment, a deep shell-proof dugout which German skill could not have bettered, and which was destined to serve as advanced brigade head-quarters till the close of the Division's operations.

The advance of the artillery also was seriously impeded by the deep mud. Already on the 15th the 3rd Brigade batteries had moved forward. The 1st followed on the 16th, and the 2nd after the weather had broken. The 10th Battery of the 4th Brigade, moving to Flers before dawn on the 19th, harnessed 20 horses to each gun, and even then, after many hours of labour, reached their positions with only 2 guns. At the pits conditions were almost as wretched as for the soaked, mud-bespattered infantry in the front trenches, and in several instances the depth of water put the guns temporarily out of action. The struggling animals taking up even the curtailed amount of ammunition in the 18-pounder wagon-baskets, strapped to the saddle for the field guns, or in improvised canvas carriers for the howitzers, were terribly overworked.

Throughout this time of ceaseless rain some half-hearted attacks, easily repulsed, were made on Capt. F. K. Turn-bull's company on the right flank of 1st Wellington in Grove Alley. Only at one moment was the situation critical. The block at the extreme right of the position was held by a Lewis gun team. A heavy burst of shelling had put the whole team out of action. At this moment, Pte. W. A. Gray, who had come forward under heavy fire with other volunteers carrying ammunition to the front line, was approaching up the trench. He took over the gun and, with the help of 2 other men, served it for more than 12 hours, effectively preventing an attempted enemy entry. Occasional violent bombardments fell on Flers and our trenches, which were all under observation from the church tower of Le Barque and other vantage points. An intense bombardment was carried out on the evening of the 17th on all the front trenches and on the Switch, more particularly on our left subsector. The shelling continued from 8 p.m. to 3 a.m. on the 18th. In this bombardment Major Fleming Ross, of 1st Wellington, was killed, with many others.[1] No assault, however, followed.

During this period the sector allotted to the Division was divided in depth into 3 areas, the forward one, north of the Switch, occupied by the brigade in the line, the intermediate, from the Switch inclusive to the Longueval-Bazentin Road, for the occupation of the supporting brigade, and the rear area, from the road southwards, for the reserve brigade. As each brigade went into reserve, it incorporated reinforcements from the Fricourt camp and was utilised for work on gun emplacements, roads, and the continually extending railway. During this interval, too, a beginning was made with the relief of the 47th Division in the III. Corps by the 1st Division, and the places of the 14th and 41st Divisions in the XV. Corps were taken by the 21st and 55th Divisions respectively. In preparation for the continuance of the attack on the 18th, which was to be frustrated by atrocious weather, 1st Canterbury handed over the position held at Box and Cox outside the New Zealand area to troops of the 55th Division. On the left, 1st Auckland cleared a breathing space for themselves by bombing some distance up the Flers System.

This left flank was now for some days to be the main scene of the Division's activity. From the Auckland position one looked across the level floor of the shallow narrow valley of the North Road up at the bare slopes of the ridge along which ran the long single trench that between the Gird and Flers Systems was called Goose Alley, and from Flers Trench southwards Drop Alley. At right angles to this trench the 2 lines of the Flers System extended westwards over the ridge. The high ground across the valley commanded the Gird System west of Gueudecourt, and for the forthcoming operations of the Division on the Gird System it was highly

[1] Major J. M. Rose, M.C., commanding the 1st Machine Gun Coy., was severely wounded on the 16th.

important to win a footing on it. The position itself lay in the III. Corps area, and it had been the final task of the 47th Division on the 15th to capture the 600 yards of Flers Support from the North Road to the top of the ridge at the junction of Goose Alley, and thence form a flank down Drop Alley. This aim was, as we have seen, found impossible of realisation owing to the desperate fighting in High Wood. It was now agreed, however, that prior to completing their relief they should make a further effort, and on capture of the position hand over the Flers System temporarily to the New Zealanders to facilitate the arrangements for the attack on the Gird Trenches.

This renewed enterprise was carried out in the early morning of the 18th. The actual trench junction on the ridge was not won, but both the Flers System and Drop Alley were captured up to within 100 yards of this Strong Point. Before midday, in accordance with the arrangements made, 1st Otago troops relieved the London Regiments in Flers Support. The section of Flers Trench itself remained for the moment, owing to difficulty of relief, in the custody of the III. Corps. In the afternoon of the 18th a further effort made by the 47th Division to win the junction and secure touch with the troops in Drop Alley failed. That night (18th/19th September), the 2nd Brigade relieved the 1st under intensely disagreeable conditions of rain and shelling. The 1st Brigade moved back to the reserve area vacated by the Rifle Brigade, which came up to the intermediate area. 2nd Wellington took over the right of the line, 2nd Auckland the left, and 2nd Canterbury and 2nd Otago went into support and reserve in the Flers System and the Brown Line respectively. Up to this date the Division had lost in casualties over 100 officers and 3000 other ranks.

After darkness on the evening of the 19th bombing parties of 2nd Auckland, in co-operation with a III. Corps attack on the left up Flers Trench and Drop Alley, endeavoured to work up Flers Support to the crest and seize the southernmost extremity of Goose Alley. They were supported by 2 Stokes mortars, and the trenches beyond the objectives were barraged by the III. Corps heavies and field artillery. The English troops' attack on the left was unsuccessful, and in a determined German counter-thrust down Drop Alley the ground won on the previous morning was lost. In Flers Support 2nd Auckland made considerable ground towards the crest. In the course of their attack Pte. W. P. Middlemiss, leading a bayonet charge, killed no less than 7 Germans single-handed, bringing the total number of the victims of his bombs or bayonet since our arrival in the battle to 23. The shells of the supporting artillery, however, unfortunately fell among the Auckland stormers. Numerous casualties were sustained, and the continuance of our barrage on the upper part of Flers Support made a prosecution of the attack impossible. Our line, however, had been pushed forward to within 40 yards of Goose Alley. Sergt. W. B. Gilmore, blown off his feet by a German grenade, continued to throw bombs till a block had been made and the position rendered secure. Before dawn on the 20th, 2nd Auckland took over from the British their part of Flers Trench which was held up to within much the same distance of Goose Alley. For the moment, the blocks and bombing posts were consolidated, while the hammer swung back in preparation for a heavier blow. On the same evening of the 19th a small party of 2nd Wellington endeavoured to capture a Strong Point on the right of the line at the junction of the Flers-Factory Corner Road with Grove Alley, but as soon as our light trench mortars opened, a heavy barrage fell plumb on the party, who suffered severe losses and were forced to withdraw.

On the 20th the weather cleared, and observation improved. A long string of German horse ambulances was distinctly visible on the road from Le Barque to Eaucourt l'Abbaye. Our artillery shelled the continual traffic on the Ligny Thilloy road. When they registered on the Thilloy church, a conspicuous Red Cross flag was hoisted on a house east of the village. Our aeroplanes reported great train activity in rear. Taking advantage, like our own gunners, of the better weather conditions and with the observation of balloons and aeroplanes, the German artillery shelled our trench positions and batteries with high-explosive, shrapnel, and lachrymatory gas.

Meanwhile energetic preparations were in progress for a simultaneous repetition of the 2 enterprises at either flank of the line. At 8.30 p.m., 2nd Wellington, in the light of their experience on the previous evening, planned to surprise the enemy by a "silent" attack. They found him, however, in too great strength in No Man's Land, and were unable to make headway. Better fortune attended the larger attack made by 2nd Canterbury against the trench junction on the ridge and the lower end of Goose Alley. Like the Wellington troops on the Factory Road, 2nd Canterbury were to attack without preparatory bombardment. On their left the 1st Black Watch of the 1st Division, who had replaced the Londoners, were simultaneously to recover Drop Alley. The frontage to be assaulted by Canterbury was some 650 yards. The password was "Success." Three companies lined up on the North Road in the darkness, and guided by the wire, crossed the valley and moved stealthily up the hill, from which only an occasional flare or machine gun burst told of occupation. The attackers reached within 50 yards of the trench before being discovered. Immediately a shower of bombs was hurled into the wire, and machine guns spat viciously. Many officers and men fell on the glacis, but the attackers fought their way in, and cleared the position. The Highlanders also successfully moved up Drop Alley and joined hands. Punctually a quarter of an hour after the attack was launched our artillery began to barrage accurately Goose Alley and the Flers Trenches beyond the points defined for capture. The enterprise had achieved its aim, and some 20 prisoners and 4 machine guns were captured. With Engineers' assistance blocks were constructed in Flers Trench and Flers Support beyond Goose Alley.

But the 13th Bavarian Reserve Regiment were too stout-hearted to lose this important position without a struggle. At 10 p.m they launched a strong and resolute counter-assault up the Flers Trenches. The daring and skill of their bombers were equally high, and the little egg-shaped bombs outranged our own and dealt havoc. The handful of Black Watch bombers, who had not yet been reinforced, were driven back down Drop Alley, and the enemy swarmed round and in rear of our left flank. Others pushed us back steadily from the blocks. Assistance was sent from the reserve Canterbury company, and supplies of bombs were carried up by parties of the other battalions, but the fighting continued to rage bitterly. No quarter was asked or given. Now a storm of bombs would kill or maim the defenders, now the tide would flow once more up the bloody trenches amid the dead and mutilated and dying. In this soldiers' battle many gallant deeds were done of which no record survives. Pte. J. D. Ross led a bombing party which finally retook a sap that had changed hands repeatedly during the night and was blocked with dead. Pte. H. Anderson held one flank when all his companions became casualties, then, forced back, reported to a sergeant at another point and continued to do magnificent work. In the end, however, the enemy had won

Drop Alley and parts of the Flers Trenches, and encircling both flanks, threatened to cut off the whole force. Our men were dog-tired and the Bavarians becoming increasingly aggressive.

It was at this juncture that Capt. F. Starnes, the commander of the reserve Canterbury company, arrived. He at once organised the defence for further resistance. He rallied the disheartened and imbued the resolute with fresh fire. He led the counter-attack with unsurpassable determination, and to his personality and leadership eventual success was due. Just before dawn the enemy effort slackened, and his "sturmtruppen" were beaten off. The 1st Black Watch thereupon again moved up Drop Alley, which they took over as far as the junction with Flers Trench. In the morning light it was found that close on 200 dead Germans lay in and about the position, many of whom had fallen in the course of the night.

With the respite brought by the dawn Canterbury toiled throughout the day with pick and shovel to improve their position and field of fire towards the Eaucourt valley, which now lay open to view. Blocks were manned by bombing posts. While thus consolidating they were surprised in the afternoon by a sudden and well-organised fresh attack. This time all 3 approaches were used by the Germans, who pressed up the 2 Flers Lines and along Goose Alley. Fresh troops, about 50 strong in each party, were employed. They were of staunch quality, and once more their bombers were formidable. But Canterbury, though the grim all-night struggle and the hard toil of consolidation had drawn heavily on their moral and physical reserves of strength, clung desperately to their hard-won gains. Forced again by the German bombers to yield first one bay and then another, the left company at length climbed out of the saps and, facing the risk from snipers, crept along the Flers Trench parapet, whence they hurled bombs with deadly results at their assailants. Ultimately these turned to fly over the open, and a bayonet charge, led by Capt. Starnes, drove them with many casualties down the slope. On the hillside they left a machine gun and nearly 100 corpses.

On the right, in Goose Alley, a handful of Aucklanders, under Pte. A. McClennan, coming to Canterbury's assistance, adopted with success the same tactics. Here, too, Cpl. H. J. Pattison, Pte. H. Joll, and other machine gunners displayed characteristic courage, stimulating our hard-pressed infantry and enfilading the enemy. An intrepid

Canterbury sergeant, J. Macdonald, who was killed 10 days later, led repeated bombing attacks, and rushed a German machine gun detachment, jabbing his bayonet the few fatal inches into each man in turn and capturing the gun. Thus, the Goose Alley attack, as that in the Flers System, failed, and pursued by fire, the Germans fled down the shallow trench northwards.

2nd Canterbury took into action 18 officers and 500 men. 7 officers and 80 men were killed, 4 officers were wounded and over 150 men. A half-dozen men were surrounded and made prisoners. Capt. Starnes was recommended for the V.C. and awarded an "immediate" D.S.O. No operation in which the Division took part in the battle called for such tenacity and grim determination on the part of the individual soldier. From this engagement, at least, the German infantry, gallant as it was, could not return "filled with the conviction of its superiority."[1] The successful issue of the struggle, coming as a crown to the New Zealand assistance on the III. Corps flank, elicited the following telegrams of appreciation:—

From the III. Corps Commander:—

"The Lieut.-General Commanding III. Corps has requested the [XV.] Corps Commander to convey to the New Zealand Division his appreciation of the good work done by them on the right of the III. Corps and of the assistance rendered by them to the III. Corps during the last few days."

From the Fourth Army Commander:—

"Please congratulate the New Zealand Division from me on their excellent work in Flers Line and Drop Alley. They deserve every credit for their gallantry and perseverance."

From the XV. Corps Commander:—

"The Corps Commander congratulates Major-General A. H. Russell and the New Zealand Division on the success gained last night (20th/21st inst.) by the 2nd Battalion Canterbury Regiment. The repeated attacks, renewed and delivered with such energy and determination speak highly of the fine fighting qualities displayed by all ranks. The Corps Commander particularly desires to express to Lt.-Col. Stewart his high appreciation of the sound conception of the plan, and to Capt.

1 Sixt von Armin's Report on Experiences of the IV. German Corps during the Somme Battle.

Starnes his admiration of his gallant and courageous leading.''

On the night 21st/22nd September the 3rd Brigade relieved the 2nd Brigade, which moved back to support. The portion of Flers Trench west of the Divisional boundary on the North Road valley was taken over by the 1st Division. Under a spell of good weather the ground rapidly dried. Artillery activity was intensified. The New Zealand batteries that had by now moved up to south of Flers in Devil's Valley were heavily bombarded by explosives and drenched with gas and lachrymatory shell. West of Flers the gun-pits towards the North Road valley were not less exposed. Our own guns, too, were now able to bring ammunition up more freely, and their fire unceasingly burst on the German positions or harassed his communications.

The destructiveness and influence on morale of the British artillery fire were described with remarkable frankness in the German Press, and exercised the rhetoric of war correspondents on either side, but their most highly coloured description does not convey a more effective picture than the temperate and truthful language of this German diary, found near Drop Alley on the 22nd:—

"The enemy understands how to prevent with his terrible barrage the bringing up of building material, and even how to hinder the work itself. The consequence is that our trenches are always ready for an assault on his part. Our artillery, which does occasionally put a heavy barrage on the enemy's trenches at a great expense of ammunition, cannot cause him similar destruction. He can bring his building material up, can repair his trenches as well as build new ones, can bring up rations and ammunition, remove the wounded, &c. The continual barrage on our lines of communication makes it very difficult for us to ration and relieve our troops, to supply water, ammunition, building material, and to evacuate wounded, and causes heavy losses. This and the want of protection from artillery fire and the weather, the lack of hot meals, the continual necessity (owing to aeroplanes) of lying still in the same place, the danger of being buried, the long time the wounded have to remain in the trenches, and chiefly the terrible effect of the medium and heavy artillery fire, controlled by an excellent air service, have a most demoralising effect on the troops. Only with the

greatest difficulty could the men be persuaded to stay in
the trenches under these conditions.''

The improvement of the weather and ground at last permitted the resumption of the delayed offensive. It was again
to be on a grand scale, a French Army moving in co-operation, and the whole of the Fourth Army completing and
extending the operations of the 15th. On the right, the XIV.
Corps was commissioned to capture Morval and Les Boeufs.
On the left, the III. Corps was to take some 300 yards of
Flers Trench from Goose Alley, and then to establish itself
on the high ground westwards, joining up at Courcelette
with the Reserve Army, which would swing its right flank
forward on the following day. The XV. Corps' principal
task was to seize Gird Trench as far west as its junction
with the Gueudecourt—Factory Corner Road and capture
Gueudecourt. In the event of its fall, the 1st Indian Cavalry
Division was to take Ligny Thilloy with a view to threatening
the enemy westwards and in rear. The right Division of the
Corps (the 21st) was to capture the village of Gueudecourt,
the centre (the 55th) to make good a sector of the Gird System
west of it, and the New Zealand Division on the left to take
Factory Corner and establish a line thence over the Goose
Alley Spur to meet Flers Trench a little way above its junction
with Goose Alley. There they would join the right of the
advancing III. Corps. At a conference held on the 19th at
Vivier Mill, a proposal was put forward by General Russell
that his objective should be extended to include the remainder
of the Gird System and Goose Alley to their point of intersection. This, however, was negatived on the grounds that
the artillery necessary could not be spared without unduly
weakening the barrage on the other 2 Divisional sectors
where the main task of the Corps lay; and also that should
the attack on Gueudecourt fail, the New Zealanders would be
left in a most awkward position. The final objective of the
Division, amounting to somewhat over a mile, was not an
entrenched position, but the capture of high ground. The
attack was fixed for the 25th, and the preparatory bombardment commenced on the 24th.

The Division's attack was entrusted to the 1st Brigade,
who came into the line on the night 24th/25th. The Rifle
Brigade, on relief, moved into the intermediate area. Since
coming into the line on the 12th, they had sustained over
1500 casualties, of whom 10 officers and 250 men had been
killed. The 1st Brigade troops were disposed, 1st Canter-

Sergt. D. F. Brown, V.C   [Snapshot

Prisoners carrying wounded

PACKING AMMUNITION

BOX RESPIRATORS

bury right, 1st Auckland centre, and 1st Otago left. 1st Wellington, who had already the capture of Grove Alley to their credit, were held in reserve, west of Flers. The plan of operations was divided into 2 stages. In the first, all 3 battalions would capture Factory Corner and the North Road. Then, after half an hour's interval, 1st Otago would seize that sector of Goose Alley, which extended from the part secured by 2nd Canterbury, and now held by the 1st Division, for some 500 yards up to the Abbey Road, and co-operate with the other 2 battalions in establishing a line of outposts along the high ground from Factory Corner to the III. Corps right in Flers Support.

The assaulting companies of the 3 attacking battalions assembled in Grove Alley. The 1st Canterbury objective amounted to 500 yards, that of 1st Auckland to 750, and that of 1st Otago to 500, excluding the flank which they would form down the Abbey Road to the North Road valley. It was arranged between the 2 Corps that as soon as the New Zealanders were established in their objectives they should take over from the 1st Division the whole of Goose Alley from the Abbey Road down to its junction with the Flers System, and whatever further ground should be gained in Flers Support.

The 25th dawned beautifully fine, and only a few puffs of white cloud broke the steely blue of the sky. Early in the day the enemy bombarded our trenches for 2 hours, causing several casualties, and opened a searching fire with shells of all calibres on the battery positions in Devil's Valley. The gunners of one battery were forced to withdraw, but just prior to their returning to the gun-pits before zero, the bombardment fortunately slackened. In the course of the morning an enterprising feat was performed by 2nd Lt. L. S. Carmichael and a few men of the 13th Battery, which was supporting the troops on the right. They went forward to a captured group of German guns east of Flers and fired 80 rounds of high-explosive at one of our abandoned tanks which was being used as a Strong Point in the German front line some 700 yards away. Most of the shots were direct hits. The tank was rendered useless before the party were obliged to withdraw by a concentrated retaliation which destroyed one of the guns and its detachment.

The moment fixed for the infantry attack was 12.35 p.m. The creeping artillery barrage was excellently steady, and the infantry, leaving their trenches at the appointed time, followed within 25 yards of the bursting shells. At the beginning of the assault, the enemy's artillery fire was not heavy, and though later it intensified with particularly marked violence on Flers, at no time were the advancing lines exposed to any considerable volume. Nor did the German infantry show their wonted resolution.

As 1st Canterbury advanced on Factory Corner, about 60 of the enemy attempted to retire towards the Goose Alley ridge, but were practically exterminated by our machine guns. Considerable anxiety had been felt about the Strong Point, which had twice repulsed 2nd Wellington, at the junction of Grove Alley with the sunken Flers-Factory Corner road. It was subjected, therefore, to a severe bombardment by light trench mortars prior to the assault. Its capture was effected without difficulty. The enemy garrison was found to have suffered heavily, and 2 machine gun crews had been put out of action. The guns themselves, however, were undamaged, and were subsequently used in our line. In an intermediate trench connected with the Strong Point some resistance was offered, but for the most part the enemy ran, not a few falling in our machine gun barrage which, as the infantry approached their goal, lifted on to Gird and Gird Support. All the battalion's objectives were secured without trouble, and among the prisoners captured in the German headquarters at Factory Corner was a battalion staff of the same 13th Bavarian Reserve Regiment, another unit of which had disputed so obstinately with 2nd Canterbury the possession of Goose Alley. The German colonel was wounded, and while being attended to in the advanced dressing station was killed by one of his countrymen's shells. Factory Corner had been an artillery headquarters, and one of the buildings also had been used as an Engineers' dump, so that the quantity of useful war material captured by 1st Canterbury was very considerable. In the centre and left, 1st Auckland and 1st Otago established the line of the Road with very few casualties.

After the pause, 1st Otago, gauging their flank by a signal displayed by the English troops in the southern end of Goose Alley, stormed the spur in an irresistible onrush. They captured 30 Bavarians and 3 machine guns. Under cover of an advanced line of skirmishers, a series of posts was then dug in by 1st Canterbury and 1st Auckland on the high ground from in front of the German cemetery at Factory Corner to

the point where Goose Alley crossed the Abbey Road.[1]
Already, at a few minutes after 1 p.m., and again shortly
afterwards, the Division had received reports from aeroplanes
of a line of flares along this part of the ridge, showing that
our furthest objectives were held in strength. Captured
German officers agreed that the attack had been made with
great dash. They spoke bitterly of their artillery, and said
they were waging the war "on their own." Many were
frankly delighted to be taken prisoners and to be out of the
"Hell on the Somme."

In the afternoon a company of 1st Wellington, in conformity with Corps arrangements, moved up to support the
left of Otago, and took over from the British garrison Flers
Support and the southern sector of Goose Alley. Through
the day, though observation was good, only 10 hostile aeroplanes and 4 balloons had appeared in the sky, and these
at different times. In the evening the Indian cavalry trotted
up to Flers. On their appearance a German balloon above
Le Transloy was lowered in panic haste, and the fitful enemy
artillery woke into precipitate activity. The cavalry's turn,
however, had not yet come. Gueudecourt still resisted capture. Elsewhere the day had been one of success for the
Allied Armies. The French had attained almost all their
objectives. The British had seized Les Boeufs and Morval.
The early fall of Combles was assured.

A certain amount of bombing exchanges took place
between the Wellington sentries and the enemy in Flers
Support, but on the whole the night 25th/26th September
passed quietly. A gap of 500 yards on the 55th Division's
flank to the right of Canterbury was filled by Liverpool
troops, and thence to the other extremity of the New Zealand sector the posts on the ridge were converted into a
continuous line by dawn.

The 26th was another fine day. To make up for the
previous day's curious inertia the Germans sent no less than
18 balloons into the sky, but an aeroplane attack destroyed
one, and the rest were lowered. Observation was exceptionally
good. There was considerable movement from the north-east
of Gueudecourt back to the ridge running to Ligny Thilloy,
and on these excellent targets the 3rd Brigade and other
batteries poured effective fire. It was tantalising to the field
artillery to watch traffic on the Bapaume-Péronne Road, out

1 The 1st Otago left does not appear to have connected in front of Goose Alley
with the new III. Corps posts in Flers Support.

of reach. In the afternoon a German battery was seen retiring at full gallop towards Ligny Thilloy. After darkness
fell, the flashes of another battery between the Butte de
Warlincourt and Le Sars were observed. It was located and
silenced.

Shortly after midday (26th September) heavy shelling in
rear of our front line and on Flers village and the Flers
System seemed to presage an enemy attack and indicate an
attempt to bar the advance of our supports. A brigade of
German infantry was also seen advancing from Ligny Thilloy
and Le Barque in the direction of Factory Corner and of the
55th Division's line on our right. As they took cover for
assembly in the corn and long grass, the artillery supporting
the 55th Division and the "heavies" searched the area, and
on the Germans advancing into the open in extended order,
the guns broke into salvoes of destruction. The attack
withered away, and the fleeing remnants were annihilated by
the 3rd and 4th Artillery Brigades and the English batteries.
By 6 p.m. all was quiet on the right. On the left, the 1st
Wellington company, in co-operation with English troops in
Flers Trench, bombed some distance up Flers Support.

While no movement of importance took place on the
Divisional front on the 26th, welcome progress was being
effected elsewhere. Westwards, the Reserve Army struck before
the enemy had time to recover from the blow dealt him on
the 25th by the Fourth Army, and, swinging into line,
seized Thiepval and the Thiepval Ridge. On the immediate
right, Gueudecourt at last fell. A squadron of cavalry was
sent out to the north-east of its ruins, and it was hoped that
their action might lead to the evacuation of the Gird System
in the neighbourhood and its peaceful occupation. This aim
was not achieved, however, and the necessary full-dress
attack by the 55th and New Zealand Divisions was ordered
for the following day.

For this operation the 4th Battalion of the Rifle Brigade
was put under the tactical command of General Earl Johnston
from the evening of the 26th, and took over Goose Alley and
Flers Support from 1st Wellington. The remainder of the
Rifle Brigade lay in the intermediate area ready to move at
15 minutes' notice. The 2nd Brigade, in reserve, were similarly to be prepared to move on 30 minutes' warning. The
road from Factory Corner to Ligny Thilloy was fixed as the
boundary between the 55th Division and the New Zealanders.
The former would seize the Gird System thence to Gueude-

court. The New Zealand Division would capture a further sector of the system from the road to the northern end of Goose Alley, and, in addition, the rest of Goose Alley down to the Abbey Road, from which point southward the success of the 25th had put it in our possession.

During the night patrols inspected the Gird entanglements, which extended on iron standards in 4 rows. Opposite the right of 1st Canterbury they were found considerably damaged, but 1st Auckland reported the wire in front of their objective to be intact. As on the 25th, the 1st Brigade policy was to employ 3 battalions. The right battalion was ordered to seize the Gird System from the road on the Divisional boundary to the parallel road running to Le Barque. The centre would capture the rest of the line to its junction with Goose Alley. The task of the left battalion was to complete the circle by forming a defensive flank from Gird Support down Goose Alley. In each case the frontage to be assaulted was about 500 yards. The enemy trenches were held by Bavarian Reserve Regiments who had relieved other units of their formation during the night. They had suffered heavy losses in the process and were much "mixed up." They were themselves due for relief on the 27th/28th, and were looking forward to leaving the Somme. Before they left, however, they were still to feel the grit of the New Zealand soldier.

Zero was fixed for 2.15 p.m., but in order to avoid observation the troops were formed up before daylight. The dispositions were the same as on the 25th. 1st Canterbury were on the right and 1st Auckland in the centre; 1st Otago, on their left, assembled 3 assaulting companies in the Abbey Road and 1 company in Goose Alley. 1st Wellington were again in reserve in Grove Alley, and were now completed by the company relieved in Flers Support by the 4th Rifles. The weather on the 27th continued fine, and observation was good. Considerable hostile movement was noted, and effectively engaged, on the Ligny Thilloy slopes, where lay the last German line, and towards the roads and hollows behind Gird Support. About an hour before the assault, a party of 150 Germans, apparently relieved in the trenches and carrying full equipment, elected to make for their back area across the open. The batteries fell on them like lightning, and the survivors scattered. The German artillery, which had been active throughout the night on our rear areas, now devoted more attention to the front trenches, and the reserve battalion in particular suffered punishment.

Our preparatory destructive bombardment had started at 7 a.m., but there was no betraying increase of fire prior to the moment of attack. Then the "heavies" dropped ponderously and devastatingly on the position and searched back quickly for 200 yards. In accordance with programme, the attack was launched 3 minutes after zero. Directly our waves appeared, the enemy field guns opened, but their fire, though heavier than in the last operation, was still inadequate to check the assault. On the right, 1st Canterbury made no pause in Gird Trench, and with the 55th Division troops advancing in line, gained their objective in Gird Support with comparative ease and few casualties. The left company was for a time held up by bombers and machine guns, but the opposition was beaten down by the initiative and dash of L.-Cpl. G. A. Hewitt and other Lewis gunners. Generally the enemy were demoralised. A considerable party flying eastwards were caught at 300 yards' range by our machine guns and mown down. Some 80 prisoners were captured, who said that before they knew it the New Zealanders were on them. Ten minutes prior to the attack, a battalion of a Reserve Division had started forward to reinforce the weak Bavarian garrison in the line. Only 1 company penetrated the barrage, and immediately on its arrival it was annihilated. The German losses were excessive. When the attack started, some of our old friends of the 13th Bavarian Reserve Regiment came up to reinforce, but were blotted out of existence. Gird Trench had not suffered much. Gird Support, however, which might have served as our front line, was in places only 18 inches deep, and elsewhere obliterated. A new trench was therefore dug on the reverse slope of a shallow depression beyond.

The other battalions were less fortunate. The right company of 1st Auckland gained its objective. The left company met a heavy artillery barrage and machine gun fire and was held up by the uncut wire reported on the previous evening. The enemy barrage fell similarly upon the 3 companies of 1st Otago who, preserving their order despite an awkward change of direction, attacked the northern end of Goose Alley. Only a handful of these companies reached the neighbourhood of the junction of Goose and Gird, where their numbers were still further reduced by a converging enemy fire on this deadly salient in our line. As our barrage lifted by stages up Goose Alley the remaining Otago company in its southern end bombed up 300 yards from the Abbey Road as far as the Factory Corner—Eaucourt Road, where a Strong Point was made. The remainder of the sap had been blown to pieces and was little more than a track. No news coming in of the other 3 companies, the Goose Alley company sent out patrols to clear up the situation. These were, however, held up by the machine gun fire from the junction of Gird Trench and Goose Alley. It was becoming apparent that just as the southern junction of Goose Alley with the Flers System had given trouble, so also trouble was to be given at its northern junction with Gird.

As soon as the assaulting battalions moved, the reserve battalion (1st Wellington) had sent one company to Factory Corner and a second to Goose Alley to take the place of the Otago company working northwards. A call was therefore made on this latter Wellington company at 4 p.m. Bombing its way up the shallow continuation of Goose Alley, it carried the line another 400 yards north, establishing posts to within 100 yards of the Gird junction, where men fell, struggling in vain to make further progress. Immediately after dusk a platoon of this Wellington company was sent over the open to the right to occupy Gird Trench east of its junction with Goose Alley and establish connection with the 1st Auckland troops in it. A further Wellington company moved up to the southern part of Goose Alley.

Meanwhile, for Battalion and Brigade Headquarters, the situation on the left long remained obscure. The afternoon was slightly hazy, but enemy movement from Thilloy towards the gullies and roads in front of our positions was repeatedly engaged and several times the good effect of our artillery was observed. Back at brigade headquarters, on the slopes beyond Flers, General Earl Johnston and his Staff strained their eyes to discern signs of movement beyond the spot where our waves had been lost to view. An enemy balloon broke loose and rose to an enormous height in the light-blue vault of heaven. Some German aeroplanes hovered over Ligny Thilloy unenterprisingly. But no news came from the line.

Orders were therefore given in the late afternoon to 1st Wellington to clear up the position at dawn. Only 1 company of the battalion now remained for operations, but it was strengthened by 2 companies of the 4th Rifles, who, as has been noted, were at the disposal of the 1st Brigade, and by 2 sections of light trench mortars. An effort was also made to get the assistance of a tank. In the evening, 1st Wellington Headquarters moved to dugouts in the North Road. The Wellington company and one of the Rifles' companies were warned for the attack. The former were ordered to clear up Goose Alley, and the riflemen the Gird Trenches. Of the other companies of the 4th Rifles, one, as has been said, held the left of the line in Flers Support in touch with the 2nd (British) Brigade, and one was held in brigade reserve in Grove Alley.

At 3 a.m. on the 28th, no definite word having been heard of the tank, the 2 companies moved off, but in addition to the darkness a heavy hostile barrage prevented the Rifles' company from reaching the assembly area, and the operation had to be cancelled. The tank, also, for which a Wellington officer waited some uncomfortable hours at Factory Corner, ''failed to materialise.'' All through the night stretcher-bearers toiled back with the wounded survivors of the attack. On daylight the Rifles' company was sent to strengthen the left of Auckland, where it made some progress by bombs up Gird Support. It was now established that the 2 Gird Trenches and Goose Alley were all held to within 100 yards of their junction and there ''blocked,'' but that the junctions themselves were not in our possession. Wellington were therefore ordered to carry out a fresh attack to secure them.

While preparations, however, were being made for this, a personal reconnaissance by Lt.-Col. Hart cleared up the actual position. It was found that the junction lay in an inconsiderable hollow about 150 yards wide, which formed the top of a shallow valley leading towards the Ligny Thilloy Road north of the point where the Gird System crossed it. This depression was not marked on the map and had not been detected on the aeroplane photographs, but, though of slight extent, its local tactical importance was considerable. It was untenable by either side without the possession of all the high ground which rose some 50 feet on its 3 sides, and formed an incomplete lip to the saucer. Local attacks had already cleared the Gird trenches up to their points of intersection with Goose Alley, but the manning of them would have been costly, and they were commanded by our new positions. For while the Germans still held the northern and most of the western slopes, we were now firmly established on the southern and part of the western lips. Thus the objectives had in effect been gained. The further attack was cancelled, and orders were issued for the construction of trenches to connect our 3 separate lines in Gird Support, Gird Trench, and Goose Alley.

The casualties, especially of Otago, had been severe, and in the late evening General Earl Johnston asked the Division for another battalion. The 2nd Rifles was placed at his disposal to strengthen the left flank, and moved up to the support positions, 2 companies occupying Flers Trench and 2 Flers Support. But if our losses had been grievous, the Germans had been reduced by this succession of deadly blows well nigh to despair. A captured diary had a final uncompleted entry for the 27th, written just before our attack:—

"No relief. Feeling of hopelessness, apathetic, everyone sleeps under heaviest fire—due to exhaustion. No rations, no drink. The whole day heavy fire on the left. We got heavy and H.E. shells. Everything all the same to us. The best thing would be for the British to come. No one worries about us; our relief said to be cancelled. If one wants sleep, aeroplanes will not let us rest. In the present conditions, one no longer thinks. Iron rations, bread, biscuit, all eaten. . . . . ."

During the night 27th/28th September patrols were sent out during an arranged interval in our protective barrage to discover any trace of rearward movement induced by these operations and by the fall of Gueudecourt on the 26th. On the right, a patrol moved 300 yards along the Ligny Thilloy Road without gaining touch with the enemy. On the left flank, a reconnaissance penetrated within 300 yards of Eaucourt l'Abbaye. No enemy was actually encountered, but just to the north of the abbey and in Gird Trench beyond were many flares, indicating the presence of strong forces. On the following day (28th) German working parties could be seen in the clear atmosphere feverishly digging trenches some 800 yards south and east of Ligny Thilloy. At various places behind his lines, north-east of Les Boeufs and at Villers-au-Flos, there were explosions and fires. The 2nd Artillery Brigade engaged large bodies of German infantry coming up to the front line north of Eaucourt l'Abbaye. In the afternoon the 1st Brigade infantry captured an officer and his batman of a battalion of the newly-arrived 6th Bavarian Reserve Division, who had come up to reconnoitre the position. This Division had occupied the trenches just south of Armentières since 1914. Though not marked as assault troops, they had proved stubborn in defence, as the Australians had found in their attack on 19th July. They

had left the northern area in the second week of September,
arrived in Bapaume 2 days previously, and were now commencing to relieve the exhausted troops in the line.

On the night 28th/29th the 1st Infantry Brigade said farewell to the Somme front line trenches and marched back, 2
battalions to Savoy and Carlton Trenches, and 2 to Mametz
Wood. The 2nd Brigade, who took over the line under heavy
shelling, garrisoned the Gird System with 2nd Wellington
on the right and 2nd Auckland on their left; 2nd Otago
occupied Goose Alley, and 2nd Canterbury was placed in
reserve in Grove Alley. All these units were now sadly
reduced in number, and the 2nd Rifles remained on the
extreme left of the line in Flers Trench and Flers Support
under the command of General Braithwaite. The 4th Battalion moved back to join the rest of the brigade in the intermediate area, but its place was taken on the 29th by the
3rd Battalion.

The recent progress made had brought the III. Corps
within striking distance of Eaucourt l'Abbaye, and a further
attack was proposed for 1st October with a view to its
capture. In this attack the New Zealanders on the left flank
of the XV. Corps would co-operate. The 2nd Brigade prepared its plans accordingly. On the night 30th September/
1st October the 3rd Rifles relieved 2nd Wellington on the
right of the line, to enable Wellington to be brought into a
preparatory assembly position on the left in Goose Alley and
Flers Support. Under continued sniping fire, the trenches
commenced by the 1st Brigade to connect Gird Trench with
Gird Support and with Goose Alley were pushed through to
provide the necessary accommodation and communications.
Turk Lane was extended by the indefatigable Maoris. The
enemy persistently shelled Goose Alley and Factory Corner,
where a magnificent well, 125 feet deep with 75 feet of water,
was kept night and day under his shrapnel and indirect
machine gun fire. During the night the 1st and 2nd Artillery Brigades pushed their guns still further up, west of
Flers.

The weather was again heavy and foggy, with slight
drizzling rain, which made visibility poor but screened parties
working in the open. Both sides took full advantage of this.
In the early morning of the 30th the light mist cleared away
for a moment, and the sentries on the left of our line detected
an enemy party of 2 officers and 20 men. The machine
gun officer at the spot, Lt. H. M. Preston, had his guns on

the unsuspecting Germans in a twinkling. Both officers and all but 2 of the enemy were killed.

In the afternoon at the same point a particularly clean piece of work was carried out in Flers Support by a party of the 2nd Rifles under Capt. H. E. Barrowclough. The 47th Division, who had again relieved the 1st Division on the III. Corps right, were holding Flers Trench west of Goose Alley. On the previous evening they had attempted, by bombing up Flers Trench and Flers Support, to extend their hold towards Eaucourt l'Abbaye, but without success. Their task would be materially lightened if the thrust up the Support Line were made by the New Zealanders. The 2nd Rifles' party therefore, in co-operation, forced a way up Flers Support for 250 yards past a German Strong Point which gave some little trouble, and then, in sheer fighting enthusiasm, pressed for another 100 yards beyond their objective towards Eaucourt l'Abbaye. The Londoners progressed equally well, and a connecting sap was dug between the 2 trenches and held as a front line. Our casualties were few.

A rather more ambitious operation, designed to clear the way for the Division's part in the attack to be delivered on 1st October, was allotted to 2nd Canterbury and 2nd Otago. It was the intention that they should capture the northern lip which overhung the depression at the Gird-Goose junction, and thence establish a line in front of Goose Alley down to the Abbey Road. This was, however, cancelled in view of the shortness of time available for preparations and owing to other reasons, and it was decided to take all objectives in the one enterprise.

While the 2nd Brigade battalions prepared their plans at greater leisure for the morrow, the Intelligence personnel were busy ransacking the captured Gird dugouts. In the course of their investigations, Lt. H. Simmonds, of 2nd Wellington, lighted on several German papers which looked important. They were at once forwarded to Brigade Headquarters. The sequel is shown by the following extract from Divisional Routine Orders:—

"The following received from XV. Corps is published for information and is to be communicated to all ranks: (I.) A German Army Order was found by the New Zealand Division in the trenches on 30th September. (II.) The Order, which was of great importance, as it showed the position of the German reserves in the neighbourhood, reached Army Headquarters a few hours after it was picked up. (III.) The Army Commander wishes you to convey to the New Zealand Division his appreciation of the promptitude with which the Order was secured and forwarded to Army Headquarters.''

In its next and final attack the Division was to have on its left the same troops with whom it had co-operated in its first assault 16 days previously.   While the 47th Division would capture Eaucourt l'Abbaye, their right would be secured by an advance of the 2nd Brigade to a line across from the Gird-Goose junction to near the abbey.   Of the 2nd Brigade troops, 2nd Auckland on the right, east of the junction, would not participate.   On their left, 2nd Canterbury, coming up from reserve into the line, would act as pivot for the brigade movement.   2nd Otago, supported by 2nd Wellington, would advance in line with Canterbury on the left flank.   The point of junction between the 2 Divisions was laid down in the neighbourhood of a German Strong Point, some 500 yards north-east of the abbey. This redoubt was a maze of concentric circular trenches, which stood out very prominently on the map and won it the name of The Circus.   From it a newly-dug line, called Circus Trench, ran to Gird on the northern lip of the saucer, and half way, a further branch fighting trench diverged from the Circus Trench to the Abbey Road.   The Circus itself resembled a knot in the long thread of an unnamed communication sap which, like Goose Alley, connected the Gird and Flers Systems.   Canterbury would carry the high ground held by the enemy over the depression at the Gird-Goose junction and seize the Circus Trench as far as the Le Barque-High Wood road.   Otago, followed by Wellington, would cross the intermediate branch trench and capture the rest of the Circus Trench, linking up with the right of the 47th Division.   Of the long communication sap, the section from the Flers System to the Abbey Road fell within the 47th Division's area.   The capture of the part from the Road to The Circus was assigned to the New Zealanders.   The northernmost sector from The Circus to Gird lay outside the scheme of attack.

During the night (30th September/1st October) our forward areas were heavily shelled.   At 7 a.m., on 1st October, in fine weather, our preparatory bombardment commenced all along the positions marked for assault and elsewhere.   In front of Canterbury, 4 light trench mortars made a gap in the wire protecting Gird.   Soon after midday the 2nd Rifles' company was withdrawn from its most westerly positions in Flers Support to enable the artillery to shell the remainder of the trench towards Eaucourt l'Abbaye prior to the advance of the 47th Division.

The hour of attack was 3.15 p.m. It had been decided that not merely should the positions aimed at be smothered with high-explosive, but also that the enemy's defences on the Corps front not included in the day's objectives should be subjected to an intense barrage, of which advantage was to be taken to gain useful ground for forward movement in the future. The fact, however, that the New Zealanders were the only troops of the XV. Corps actually engaged allowed the use of preponderating artillery on their front. Up to the present the Division had been supported by 88 field guns and howitzers; for the forthcoming operation, 180 field guns and howitzers were behind the attack, and the increase of "heavies" corresponded. A detachment of the Special Brigade, R.E., operated on the 2nd Canterbury sector, and installed 36 oil mortars in Gird Trench. These were fired a minute before zero. 6 were a failure, but the remaining 30 projectiles were seen to reach their objective satisfactorily, bursting about 1 second after landing and covering the German trenches with lurid flame and great rings of black smoke. The moral effect, as testified to by an English-speaking prisoner, was terrifying. Our contact aeroplanes came down at zero and hovered over the scene for 2 hours, after which one "was up" till dark. The enemy's artillery replied to our bombardment within a few minutes of zero. A large proportion of his shells was wasted on Flers and at Factory Corner. His barrage was, however, appreciably better organised than hitherto. A high-velocity gun shelled the area between Bazentin and Montauban in rear.

2nd Canterbury had come into the line during the morning and occupied the south-eastern slopes overlooking the saucer depression in which the northern end of Goose Alley joined the Gird System. These slopes sank gradually to the valley below, but on the other side of the saucer the ground rose steeply, with a well-defined terrace on which clustered ragged clumps of bushes. The whole surface of the once grassy slopes was now a churned-up mass of clayey shellholes. From the slopes in our possession which overlooked the hollow, 4 machine guns fired over the heads of the advancing Canterbury infantry at the enemy trenches on the crest and swept the saps and bushes on the terrace opposite.

A few minutes after the attack started a large party of Germans jumped out of Gird Support and began to run back across the open country. They were literally wiped out by our machine guns. 2nd Canterbury attacked with 3 companies, holding 1 in reserve. Of these, the task of the right company was to seize the high ground on the north about Gird Support. The centre company was ordered to occupy the slopes overlooking the saucer from the west and capture the 200 yards of Gird Trench to the point of departure of Circus Trench. The objective of the left company was Circus Trench to the Le Barque road. The right and half the centre company of Canterbury in the hollow were exposed only to a moderate amount of hostile fire and bombs from the barraged trenches immediately in front, but on the hogsback of high open ground further west, the inner flank of Canterbury and the right of Otago were heavily raked by distant machine gun fire from Gird. Despite their losses, however, the left of Canterbury, like the centre and right, completed its task after some bitter fighting. The trenches were found packed with corpses, piled in many places one over the other. One or two loathsome groups in the centre of the position lay burned and half eaten away by the oil. The huddled German dead, not a few of whom carried souvenirs of the Australian attack in July,[1] looked spick and span in uniforms which made the victors appear ragged in comparison. Their physique, however, was strikingly poor, and many of them were mere boys.

The whole lip of the contested depression had now once for all come into our hands. Round its far crest a new trench was dug, which was strengthened by the reserve machine guns. The continuation westwards of Gird was strongly held by Germans, who sniped at and harassed our working parties. They were effectively dealt with by Ptes. R. E. Fairbrother and L. D. McLachlan, who fired their Lewis guns over the shoulders of 2 of their comrades and inflicted many losses. The Canterbury reserve company was not sufficient to fill all the gap in the line caused by their casualties. 2nd Auckland, therefore, extended their left up Gird Support, and an Auckland company went into the line. In the afternoon, an enemy battalion was seen massing in rear, but was scattered by machine gun fire, and no attack developed. The services of a further Auckland company were called on at midnight to strengthen the right flank and

1 p. 49.

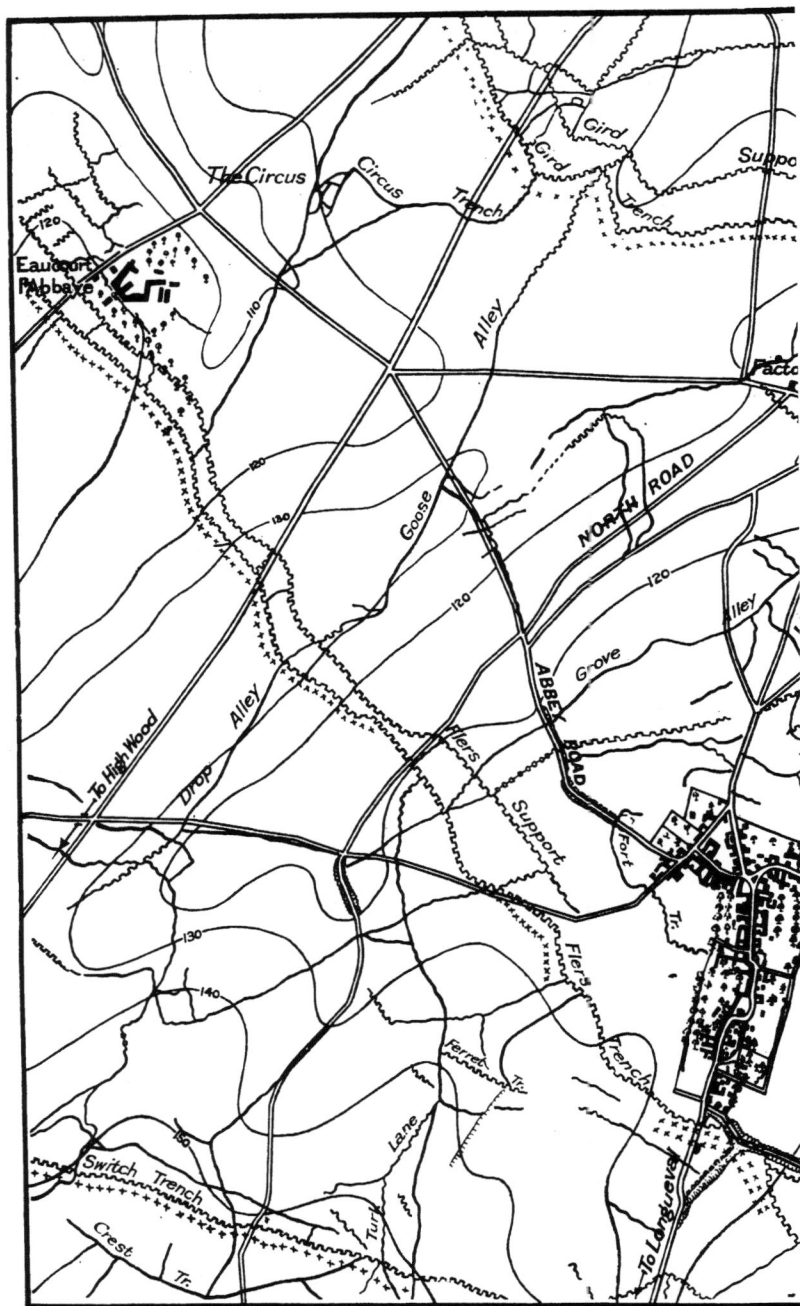

FLERS AND

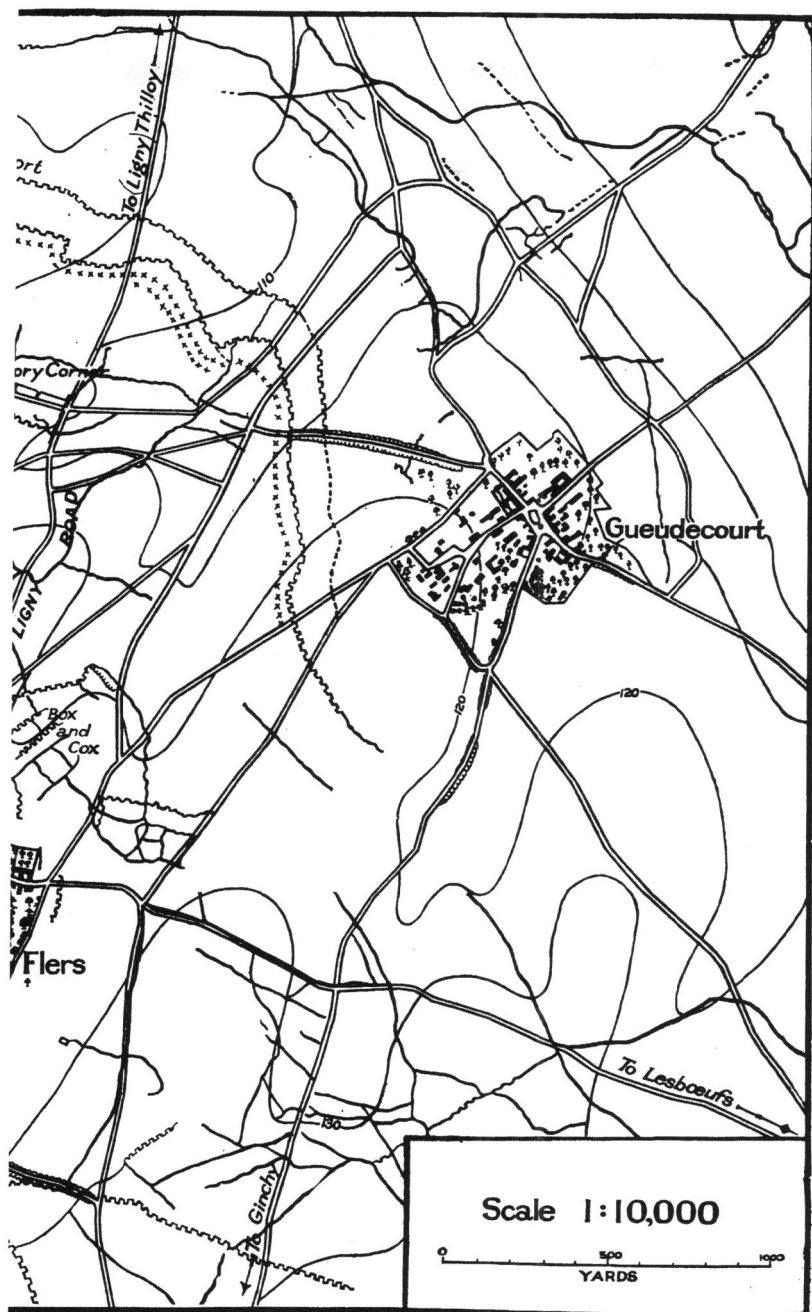

To (Ligny)Thilloy

Gueudecourt

Flers

Box and Cox

LIGNY ROAD

To Ginchy

To Lesbœufs

Scale 1:10,000

0   500   1000

YARDS

centre and to act as supports. A bombing counter-attack began at 11 p.m. down Gird, but the attackers were not of the same calibre as those with whom 2nd Canterbury had last to grapple with, at the other end of Goose Alley. They were easily held, and our light trench mortars, in the bottom of the hollow, enfilading the approaches, intimidated further efforts.

Of the 4 companies of 2nd Otago, the 2 on the right had a difficult manoeuvre to perform, first advancing to their front for about 200 yards, and then executing a double change of direction towards the right. This was carried out, however, in cohesion and order, despite the fire of machine guns, which at once began to play as they moved up the slope. By the time they reached the crest, all the officers and a large proportion of the men in these 2 right companies had fallen. The survivors reached and cleared their sector of Circus Trench, but lacking the guiding control of their officers, pressed on further, overrunning their objective, and moved right up to the protective barrage. It was not till the 2nd Wellington supporting company arrived that the gap thus caused on the Otago right, and further accentuated by the Canterbury casualties, was filled. Capt. L. H. Jardine, who commanded the Wellington company and who had already shown himself possessed of rare soldierly qualities, quickly grasped the situation and disposed his men in little groups to hold the line. The remnants of the Otago companies and a Wellington Lewis gun section, which had followed them, were recalled to the proper objective, and Jardine assumed command of the whole line at this part of the front.

Among the gunners of this Wellington section was Pte. K. D. Barr. He had injured his foot previously, and on the morning of the battle it was painful and swollen, so that he could not wear a boot. It was characteristic of the spirit which imbued the New Zealanders at the end of 2 weeks of fighting, that despite intense discomfort nothing would induce him to stay out of the engagement. He wrapped a sandbag round his foot and limped over the top with his comrades. By a caprice of fortune they had all been killed or wounded, and now it was left to him to carry back the precious gun to Jardine's line.

Lower down the hill and consequently more sheltered than their companions on the right from the Gird machine guns, the Otago left companies attacked the branch of Circus Trench which led to the Abbey Road. As the storm-

9

ing line pressed nearer, they were at one point checked by a machine gun. The same Sergeant Brown whose exploits in the Crest and Switch on 15th September have been noted,[1] once again similarly saved the situation. Single-handed he rushed at the gun and bayoneted the crew. The checked line of skirmishers at once poured breathlessly into the trench. The garrison were killed or fled. Many of them fell victims to the fire of Lewis guns supported on strong and willing shoulders, others to Otago marksmanship with the rifle. It was while sniping coolly at the flying enemy that the heroic Sergeant Brown was killed by long-range machine gun fire. His magnificent conduct throughout the Somme battle and superb daring on all occasions, when unhesitating readiness for self-sacrifice could alone overcome resistance, won the dead soldier the first Victoria Cross which the Division received in France.

In the dense smoke and dust the Otago left had lost touch with the sorely reduced companies on the right, but they advanced, meeting now less opposition, towards their final objective. At the point where they expected to find the redoubt, they came on an insignificant smashed up bit of trench. Could this be the famous Circus? A heavy enemy barrage was falling on the spot and decided their uncertainties. They pressed on to a well-marked ridge some 300 yards ahead across a cutting, whence they formed a line down a road to the north of Eaucourt l'Abbaye. This particular cutting, as it happened, was not marked on the map, and the officers, realising then that they had overshot the mark, believed that they were still further westward at a cutting, which was represented on the map, on the road from Eaucourt to Le Barque.

The position had obvious tactical advantages, and the companies started its consolidation and reported their location, as they believed it to be, by runner to Battalion Headquarters. The message was at once communicated to Brigade. It was with some consternation that General Braithwaite, plotting out the map references, found his troops in a position so much "in the blue" as to invite disaster. He had no option but to order a withdrawal on The Circus. Meanwhile, however, as the smoke and dust cleared away, an opportunity offered itself for taking bearings, and the real position was discovered by the officers on the spot. They were joined by a party of the Londoners about Eaucourt, and a communi-

1 p. 74.

cation trench had now been dug back to The Circus. Permission was therefore obtained to remain on the line occupied.

The leading Wellington companies had joined in the later stages of the fighting and cleared the long German communication trench from The Circus to the Abbey Road. The other companies were sent forward in the evening to replace casualties. The 2 battalions proceeded with the consolidation, which was completed by dawn. A Strong Point was made on the Abbey Road. A hostile bombing attack during the night was repulsed. In the morning it was found that the party of Londoners had been cut off from the rest of their Division, and that Germans were still in their rear and to the east of Eaucourt l'Abbaye. Arrangements were made to supply the party with food. Eaucourt itself was not finally cleared by the English till the evening of the 3rd.

In these operations the 2nd Brigade sent about 250 prisoners to the collecting station at Bernafay Wood. Of these, 2nd Canterbury had taken 50, including a battalion commander and his staff. The remainder were secured on the left. The Wellington losses were light. In the 2 battalions which had borne the brunt of the fighting the casualties worked out evenly: 2nd Canterbury, going into action with 19 officers and 487 men, lost 11 officers and 164 men, 6 officers and 26 men being killed; 2nd Otago attacked with 19 officers and 314 men, and lost 10 officers and 175 men, 4 officers and 33 men being killed.

It had not been anticipated that the 3rd Rifles on the extreme right of the line would move, and they received only short warning that they too were required to deliver a simultaneous local attack at 3.15 p.m. They were ordered to establish a line of Strong Points on high ground some 300 yards in front, in order to support a forward movement by the 21st Division, who had relieved the 55th on the right. Such hurried efforts are apt to result in failure, but the riflemen secured their objective with the loss of an officer and 15 men killed and 55 wounded. Many enemy were killed by fire and bayonet and lay in heaps in the sunken road leading to Ligny Thilloy. A counter-attack, reported by pigeon message to Division, was repulsed.

During the night (1st/2nd October) the troops of the 21st Division were relieved and, as sometimes happens during relief in an advanced portion of the battlefield, the incoming platoons of the 12th Division did not go beyond, or far beyond, the Gird System. Intimation of this was received by the

2nd Brigade Headquarters, and the 3rd Rifles were ordered to verify the information and, if their exposed position made it necessary, to withdraw. The posts were accordingly withdrawn under cover of darkness. On the following morning, however, the 12th Division moved forward to the advanced position won on the previous afternoon, and in conformity the Rifles again stalked their posts in face of enemy snipers and reoccupied them, fortunately with but a few casualties. German snipers had filtered in nearly as far as our vacated line, but these were driven off, and the posts were connected up the following night in pouring rain. Under cover of the darkness and storm a thorough reconnaissance was made of the enemy's new positions by Sergt. A. Shearer. The outposts in front of Gird Support were occupied in the early morning (3rd October) by the Rifles' garrison. An enemy aeroplane flying low failed to locate them, and when the German guns opened it was on the now empty Gird System that their fury fell.

In the evening of 1st October the 1st Rifles were put under General Braithwaite's command to strengthen his depleted forces. They moved up into the support positions, whence platoons were detailed to act as local reserves to the battalions in the line or as carrying parties. Thus no less than 3 Rifle battalions lent their support to the 2nd Brigade at this stage. The 3rd held the right flank, the 2nd the left, and the 1st lay in support.

It was clear that the spell of fine weather was over. Heavy showers fell during the night, and 2nd October was a day of strong wind and tempestuous rain. Continuous shelling was directed at our whole front. Telephonic communication was destroyed between battalions and brigade and between battalions and companies, except where the hollow gave shelter to 2nd Canterbury. There was no observation, and only 1 German aeroplane appeared, which was brought down near Beaulencourt.

On the following night (2nd/3rd), as the 3rd Rifles toiled at their new trenches, the remainder of the Rifle Brigade took over the line. Rain was now falling in torrents, the trenches were knee-deep in mud, and relief was not completed till dawn. The 3rd Battalion extended its left, the 4th Battalion went into the centre, and the 1st took over the left in front of Eaucourt l'Abbaye from 2nd Otago and 2nd Wellington. The 2nd Rifles were withdrawn from the Flers System to Goose and Grove Alleys, 3 companies acting as brigade reserve.

As with the 2nd Brigade, the Rifle battalions were all depleted to an average strength of 380, and on the 1st Brigade's coming forward into the intermediate area, which had now been extended to include the Flers Trench System, 1st Canterbury and 1st Wellington were put under General Fulton's tactical command.

The 2nd Brigade moved back to the reserve area, and after a rest and midday meal went straight on to the tents of Fricourt Camp. The troops were exhausted by the fighting, lack of sleep, and the long march, and to put a finishing touch on their hardships, many men of Otago had lost their greatcoats, which had been dumped prior to their attack and been blown up by shell-fire.

In the forward areas the conditions were now indescribably miserable for the gunners in their flooded pits and the sentries in their ditches, waist-deep with mud. The mere physical strain imposed on runners stretcher-bearers and all whose business it was to move along trenches or over the open was excessively arduous. The endurance of the infantry, however, was not to be much longer tested. In the evening (3rd October) the 41st Division commenced to relieve the forward units. The command passed on the following morning to the new Division.[1] During the relief the enemy artillery was unusually inactive. The weather, however, still remained execrable, and it was through miry trenches and slippery shellholes that the battalions wearily plodded back to the camp at Pommiers Redoubt. There they found enough tarpaulins to give overhead shelter, but the ground was a swamp.

Prominent among their feelings, no doubt, was that sense of relief which found ironical expression even in the austere solemnity of battalion War Diaries. All had experienced continued privations and repeated perils. There were few that had not seen comrades stricken or blown skywards, or had not themselves been face to face with imminent death in manifold forms of horror. Some had been knocked over by concussion, some had been buried in the cataclysm of a trench, some had just in time parried a fierce bayonet thrust. Their nostrils had not yet banished the stench of putrefying corpses, their eyes the ghastly scenes in entanglements saps

1 In accordance with custom the outgoing Machine Gun Company (the 3rd) remained in the line for some time after relief. At 6 a.m. (4th October) the enemy counter-attacked Gird Support. The account of the action, given by the G.O.C. 122nd Infantry Brigade, includes the following passage: "The New Zealand Machine Gun team was of particular assistance. All except one man of the team were hit and the machine gun was at length put out of action. This man, L.-Cpl. [C.O.] Samson, behaved with the greatest gallantry, working his gun to the end."

and shellholes, their ears the detonations of bursting bombs, the roar of mighty projectiles rushing towards them, and the crash, deafening and soul-shattering, as these exploded all around them. The following letter, written by a private soldier immediately after the battle, recorded in an un-affected, manly way, but with unconscious dramatic feeling, incidents to which all could have found parallels in their own experience. A small bombing enterprise had been successful:

"Just as the Lieutenant, who was the last to come back, was getting into our trench, a German machine gun away on the right got to work and just managed to pump five or six bullets into the Lieutenant's back. He lay in the trench in awful pain all the afternoon. It was im-possible to get him down to the dressing station before dark. The trench was not wide enough to get a stretcher along, so that meant walking along the parapet, and that again meant the stretcher-bearers and wounded being riddled with bullets. There was an awful strafe going on all along the line all afternoon, and the village of Flers, just about half a mile at the back of us, was getting it hot and strong from the heavy German guns. As soon as it got dark, volunteers were called to carry the wounded officer down to the dressing station, a half-mile away. I was one of the party of four. We started off about 8 o'clock, and I, for one, never thought we should get to the station. First a huge shell, weighing nearly a ton, would come roaring and screaming through the air. Of course, if one should happen to meet one, there is one con-solation—one would never know anything about it. Well, these shells were dropping all round us, some going over our heads and some falling short, and once we got knocked over by a shell exploding about thirty yards away. The explosion made a hole in the ground large enough to bury a horse in. The four of us got up again, and no one was hurt. I think the officer was unconscious, he never said anything. We moved on again, and at last reached a dressing station, but it was the wrong one, of course. Ours was half a mile away on the other side of the village.

"The village was in an awful state. Buildings blown down in the streets, huge trees cut down half-way up and blown down in the street. One half-tree landed in a shell-hole and looked as if it were going to be set there. The whole sky was lit up by shells exploding. like continuous

lightning.   Half-way through the village a gas shell
exploded, and the fumes were awful. By the time we had
got the officer's gas helmet on, we were nearly choking.
We were not long getting our own helmets on.   We
arrived at the right dressing station at last, more dead
than alive, and handed our man over.''

But at the same time the exhausted troops at Pommiers
Camp were grimly conscious that they had, as they might
have said simply, done their job, that they had not merely
performed the tasks set themselves, but on more than one
occasion rendered effective help to formations on their flanks.
Commencing on a frontage of under 1000 yards, they were
holding at the close a line nearly 3 times as long. In the
great battle of the 15th, and subsequent advance on the 16th,
in which all brigades took part, in the grisly struggle of the
20th in Goose Alley, in the 1st Brigade operations of the 25th
and 27th, and in the final assault by the 2nd Brigade on
1st October, they had achieved all but unbroken success,
captured 5 miles of enemy front line and 5½ miles of
other trenches, and fought their way forward for over
2 miles.   Themselves losing under 20 prisoners, they had
captured nearly 1000 Germans, with many machine guns
and war material. Finally, what only soldiers can appreciate,
they brought out with them their full complement of machine
and Lewis guns. On the other hand, they had sustained 7000
casualties. The bodies of 60 officers and 1500 men were left
in the cemeteries or battlefield graves of the Somme.[1]

In the afternoon of the 4th, Major-General J. P. du Cane,
who had relieved Sir Henry Horne in command of the XV.
Corps, visited the battalions to express his appreciation and
say good-bye. On the departure of the Division from the
battle the Commander-in-Chief sent the following telegram to
the New Zealand Government:—

"The New Zealand Division has fought with the
greatest gallantry in the Somme battle for 23 consecutive
days, carrying out with complete success every task set
and always doing more than was asked of it. The Division has won universal confidence and admiration. No
praise can be too high for such troops.''

In a copy sent to the Fourth Army, the Chief of the
General Staff intimated that: "The Commander-in-Chief
desired to add his warm congratulations to the Division on

1 In October 1918 an opportunity was taken to erect individual crosses and
arrange for a memorial cross near Flers.

the splendid record they had achieved." On forwarding this letter to the Corps, the Fourth Army Commander desired that his congratulations should be conveyed to the New Zealand Division "on the well-deserved praise they have received from the Commander-in-Chief, and his admiration of their gallantry and success."

In addition, he sent later the following tribute:—

"Fourth Army,
October 7th, 1916.

"I desire to express to all ranks of the New Zealand Division my hearty congratulations on the excellent work done during the battle of the Somme.

"On three successive occasions (15th and 25th September and 1st October) they attacked the hostile positions with the greatest gallantry and vigour, capturing in each attack every objective that had been allotted to them. More than this, they gained possession of, and held, several Strong Points in advance of and beyond the furthest objectives that had been allotted to them.

"The endurance and fine fighting spirit of the Division have been beyond praise, and their successes in the Flers neighbourhood will rank high amongst the best achievements of the British Army.

"The control and direction of the Division during the operations have been conducted with skill and precision, whilst the artillery support in establishing the barrage and defeating counter-attacks has been in every way most effective.

"It is a matter of regret to me that this fine Division is leaving the Fourth Army, and I trust that on some future occasion it may again be my good fortune to find them under my command.

"H. RAWLINSON, General,
"Commanding Fourth Army."

The efficiency of the work of the Medical Corps was sufficiently attested in the following memorandum:—

"The D.M.S., Fourth Army, and D.D.M.S., XV. Corps, desire to make known to all ranks of the N.Z.M.C. their appreciation of the work done during the recent operations. The arrangements for evacuation of wounded and the successful way in which the arrangements worked met with their special approbation. Casualty clearing stations report that the treatment of all cases evacuated to them had reached a very high standard, and that no case had been evacuated without having received anti-tetanic serum.''

While the artillery remained in the line, the rest of the Division constituted Corps Reserve for the attack proposed for 5th October. The weather, however, necessitated its post-ponement. On the 6th, Divisional Headquarters moved back to Hallencourt, and the 2nd and 3rd Brigades entrained for the X. Corps area in the lower Somme. The 1st Brigade left Albert on the following day for the same destination. On the 10th and 11th the Division (less artillery) entrained to rejoin II. Anzac.

The sector held by the New Zealanders and now handed over to the 41st Division had been covered at the beginning of September by the 14th Divisional Artillery Group which comprised the 14th Divisional Artillery and the 1st and 2nd New Zealand Artillery Brigades. At the end of September the 14th Divisional Artillery was relieved by the 21st Divisional Artillery. The 3rd and 4th Brigades, which had been attached to the Group covering the front of the Division on the right, were now transferred to the 21st Group. In the middle of October the 21st Divisional Artillery was replaced by the 12th Divisional Artillery, which gave its name for the time being to the Group, now comprising its own brigades, the New Zealand artillery, and certain other elements. The New Zealand batteries supported the numerous attacks made throughout the month of October, and remained exposed to the enemy counter-battery activity in positions which had been pushed distinctly far forward in anticipation of a further advance. On the 5th, for example, a gun of the 3rd Battery was destroyed by a direct hit which blew up the ammunition and killed the detachment, and an 8-in. shell struck an ammunition pit of the 15th Battery, causing the shells to explode and killing an officer and 8 men, in addition to inflicting other casualties.

Towards the end of their stay the weather became de-finitely unpropitious, and constant rain, impeding communica-tions, robbed the British Armies of the full advantages that their achievements might not unreasonably have been ex-pected to yield. No cessation or slackening, however, was made in our bombardment. Day and night, fire continued on the German entrenched positions, batteries, and villages. In view of the hoped-for improvement in weather and the re-sumption of operations, the enemy's approaches were system-

atically shelled.   Dead ground was searched by day, and all
roads and tracks at irregular intervals and at constantly
varied points throughout the night to prevent the bringing
up of supplies and material.   Indications pointed to the possibility of a counter-offensive, and cover for guns and crews
had to be constructed to minimise the danger of loss of gun-
power in case of a hostile preparatory bombardment.   For
this reason, too, the amount of ammunition at the gun positions was augmented, and as the condition of the roads made
wagon transport impossible, the unfortunate animals, now
in miserably poor condition, "packed" it up through the
mud, making more than one trip a day.   After 52 consecutive
days in the battle the New Zealand gunners were relieved on
25th and 26th October by the 1st Australian Divisional
Artillery.   By herculean exertions a few Australian guns
were actually brought up to positions after darkness on the
25th.   Others were bogged on the Flers Road and hauled
back to the wagon lines under cover of mist on the 26th.
The brigades for the most part exchanged guns.   Of those
which had been replaced by the Australians and had to be
dragged to the wagon lines, some sank deep in the mud,
and not all the labour of men and horses could move them.

In this "set-piece" warfare little scope was offered for
spectacular performances by the artillery, but their records
are illuminated by repeated instances of devotion to duty,
as shown, for example, by gun detachments continuing to fire
a barrage under a hail of shells, and of initiative, as in the
handling of captured German guns close to the front trenches
for sniping purposes.   Throughout the battle their action
exemplified the skilful application of a high standard of
technique, and was extolled by the British regiments not
less highly than by their New Zealand comrades.   Yet it may
be doubted whether any feature of their work displayed
greater qualities of resourcefulness and resolution than their
never-interrupted success, despite prolonged conditions of the
utmost difficulty, in bringing up their ammunition over those
forlorn and shelled wastes of mud and craters.   The batteries
had fired approximately 500,000 rounds on the Somme and
sustained over 500 casualties.   The Divisional Ammunition
Column alone had over 70 animals killed and 8 wagons
destroyed by shell-fire.   The 3rd Battery had lost its
gun detachments 3 times during the battle, and had
5 battery commanders casualtied in succession.   The
following message of appreciation was sent by the Com-

mander of the 21st Divisional Artillery Group on his severing connection with the New Zealand gunners:—

"On handing over command of this Artillery Group I wish to convey my thanks and the thanks of the 21st Divisional Artillery to the officers, n.c.o.s, gunners, and drivers of the New Zealand Divisional Artillery for their hearty co-operation during the recent operations and for the splendid work which they have done.

"The difficulties of ammunition supply, which have been great, have been overcome, and the good shooting of the batteries and the successful barrages have been spoken of in most complimentary terms by our infantry.

"Please convey to all ranks under your command my congratulations and best wishes for their future success."

124

CHAPTER IV

WINTER ON THE LYS

By 12th October the Division, less its artillery, was concentrated in the rear area of II. Anzac, Divisional Headquarters at Merris, the 1st Brigade at Estaires, the 2nd at Strazeele, and the 3rd at Outersteene. Corps Headquarters had meantime shifted from La Motte[1] to the town of Bailleul. In the right of the Corps there was now the 5th Australian, and in the centre the 34th Division. The northern sector was no longer held by the 51st Division, which had relieved the New Zealanders in August, for in the following month they had been withdrawn for a second visit to the Somme. At the moment there had been no fresh troops available to take their place. A composite formation, therefore, had been raised by withdrawing 2 Brigade Groups from the other 2 Divisions that completed the Corps. Command had been given to Major-General Franks, of the Second Army Staff, and the formation itself was designated Franks' Force. To avoid drawing on the resources of the Divisions, the Staff, together with the necessary clerks and office equipment, had been provided by the Army and Corps.

Little time was to be given the newly-arrived New Zealanders to rest, refit, and assimilate the reinforcements that came overseas from Sling to make good the wastage incurred at the Somme. On 13th October they began to relieve the 5th Australian Division in the Sailly sector, on the extreme right of the Second Army. There the Division took over the Cordonnerie and Boutillerie subsectors with the 1st and 3rd Brigades. One of the Australian brigades, however, as has been seen, formed part of Franks' Force and occupied the Houplines subsector in front of Armentières. For its relief the 2nd Brigade was detached from the Division and passed under General Franks' command. Accompanied by a medium trench mortar battery, a company of Engineers, a company of Pioneers, a Field Ambulance, and an A.S.C. company, it went up in 'busses from Strazeele and relieved this Australian Brigade Group in the familiar trenches which it had held throughout the summer on the Lys. On the Divisional front

1 p. 21.

proper, the right touched the flank of the XI. Corps of the First Army; its left was separated from Franks' Force by the 34th Division. General Russell's headquarters was established in the township of Sailly-on-the-Lys, some 5 miles up the river and west of Armentières. The 1st Brigade Staff occupied a cross-roads inn at Rouge de Bout, and the 3rd dugouts in the village of Fleurbaix, 3 miles south-west of Armentières on the road to Neuve Chapelle. Among the troops relieved by the 1st Brigade were the II. Anzac Cyclist Battalion, who had been attached to the Australians and in addition to other duties had on occasion garrisoned the trenches. The 5th Australian Artillery remained temporarily in the line, but the rest of the Division now passed once for all from its original Corps to join I. Anzac on the Somme.

The Sailly sector extended for 3 miles in flat pleasantly wooded country before the German positions at Fromelles and on the Aubers Ridge, which guarded the south-western approach to Lille and had looked down on the slaughter of Neuve Chapelle and the XI. Corps repulse in July.[1] The front area was crossed by a network of several sluggish streams and drains running back among the hedgerows to the Lys. The principal of these was the Laies. All were now considerably swollen by the late autumn rains, and broad tracts along their banks were little better than marshes, in which the movement of our patrols was to be much hampered till the frosts of January.

Across these streams ran the continuous breastworks of the front line and the derelict close support line. This latter, though not manned, was maintained in outward repair, and in it men occasionally showed themselves and fires were kindled in order to give the enemy the impression of occupation and to attract shelling. The real support line lay somewhat in rear, in a series of small garrison posts connected laterally by a continuous fire trench. Further again in rear were the series of defended localities, Charred, Windy, Winter's Night Posts and others, that formed the third or subsidiary line of the front system. These were joined by a rudimentary trench, which was in a few places fire-stepped and revetted.

For the protection and maintenance of the whole of this system the Division was responsible, but certain of the posts formed part also of the A.B.C. or G.H.Q. second line, which fell to the charge of the Corps. The village of Fleurbaix was extensively protected by a ring of such redoubts. Mention

[1] p. 49.

has previously been made of the bridgeheads on the Lys at Nouveau Monde, Sailly, and Bac St. Maur, which formed part of the X.Y.Z. or G.H.Q. third line.[1]

In each brigade sector 2 battalions garrisoned the trenches, and 2 were in support in the farms and villages in rear. In accordance with the established principle of defence in depth, and to avoid unnecessary casualties, the front line was held only by outposts with sufficient support of Lewis guns and a few machine guns to ensure the repulse of a hostile attack delivered without bombardment. Not more than 150 men all told manned 1000 yards. The garrisons of the support line were 3 times as strong. Here there were some deep dugouts, electrically ventilated and lighted, each capable of holding a company. Several of the subsidiary line garrisons, again, could boast of a habitation in abandoned farmhouses, but generally the accommodation was inadequate. The relieved Australian battalions had been of weak strength, and the first urgent task was to provide shelter for all the troops in the line. Trench kitchens too had to be made weather-proof before the winter rains set in. To effect these and similar improvements, as well as to replace by training the specialists lost on the Somme, and to familiarise themselves with their new surroundings in and in front of their trenches, the battalions remained temporarily quiescent. Towards the end of the month they were visited by the Premier of New Zealand and Sir Joseph Ward, who attended the presentation by General Plumer of decorations won on the Somme, and with him inspected the troops in reserve and the Pioneer Battalion.

The artillery had not yet rejoined from the Somme, but were already on their 80-mile march northwards. On their arrival (4th November) they rested for one or two days, during which time their guns were overhauled at the Ordnance Workshop at Bailleul and the last of their debilitated horses evacuated. They then (7th November) commenced the relief of the 5th Australian Divisional Artillery. The 2nd Brigade, with a section of the D.A.C., relieved the Australian batteries detached with Franks' Force. On the Divisional front the Australian artillery had been divided into 2 groups, 1 of which supported each brigade subsector, and this policy was now adhered to. The 1st Brigade of the New Zealand Artillery, with the 8th Battery of the 4th Brigade formed the right group, while the 3rd Brigade and the

1 p. 27.

remainder of the 4th Brigade constituted the left group. This artillery support might be confidently expected to be adequate, while the front remained quiet. Should a general hostile attack on a large scale develop, reinforcing positions had been selected and would be occupied by batteries sent forward by Corps, while in the event of local attacks, a prearranged programme was drawn up, in accordance with the usual practice, to ensure the support of the artillery group covering the attacked sector by the group on either flank. Thus on the call "Co-operate Boutillerie," certain batteries both in the Cordonnerie group on the right and in the Bois Grenier group on the left would give assistance by firing on selected targets opposite the Boutillerie subsector.

By the beginning of November the infantry in the line had constructed tolerable accommodation and could turn undisturbed attention to the markedly inaggressive troops of the II. Bavarian Corps opposite.[1] The first attempt to renew acquaintance was not to be crowned with success. Early in the morning of 6th November a small raiding party of 1st Wellington attempted an entry, without artillery support, into a German post known as the Tadpole. A gap in the wire had been cut on the 5th. Stealing across the 100 yards of No Man's Land, however, the party found 4 rows of knife-rests placed just outside the parapet, effectually preventing an entry. At the same hour, 34th Division troops, further on the left, forcing a way in, killed several Germans but secured no prisoners or identifications. To atone for this lack of success, the artillery on all 3 sectors of the Corps front took up the work and pounded the enemy's trenches for 2 half-hour periods, causing satisfactory destruction.

Undiscouraged on their part, the infantry prepared for a fresh and more ambitious enterprise. This was undertaken 10 days later by the 1st Rifles. Some 250 yards opposite their front the German line formed a salient called Turks' Point. By its exposed configuration it was in itself peculiarly suitable for assault, and in addition No Man's Land lent itself to the raiders' purpose. A narrow ditch running right across from parapet to parapet afforded a good line of advance. This ditch was itself crossed at right angles by several parallel ditches, which patrols knew to afford cover and a position for assembly. To one of these, in the mists of a cold wintry evening, Capt. G. K. Gasquoine and 50 men of "C" company, with a few sappers, were guided by

1 The 38th Landwehr Regiment and a portion of the 5th Bavarian Division.

Cpl. O. A. Gillespie across the swamps of No Man's Land. All identifications, as usual, were removed, and the raiders wore British tunics. As a distinguishing mark, 2 strips of white cloth were sewn by 1 end and tucked inside the collar of the coat, 1 strip in front and 1 behind. Field guns and two 6-in. howitzers and a heavy trench mortar battered the objective and vicinity for 20 minutes. Under this fire and covered by a patrol some 10 yards in front, the assaulting party crept up to within 50 yards of the enemy wire. There they sheltered in another ditch and pulled out the free ends of the white cloth strips. On the artillery lifting, Gillespie and other scouts examined the wire and found it demolished. Thereupon the raiders pushed through it. They found the trench, however, knee-deep in water and unoccupied. Parties worked for 100 yards to right and left and down the communication saps. One group, espying dark figures, would challenge "Shell," with rifles and bombs ready to deal death to an enemy patrol, but to their disappointment invariably received the countersign "Hole" from some other members of their party. The most diligent search failed to discover the enemy. The solid concrete dugouts were found flooded and contained neither men nor articles which provided identification. Behind the travel-trench was a sheet of water that extended to both flanks as far as the eye could penetrate in the darkness.

Much the same experience befell a 1st Canterbury party with a small detachment of Engineers, on 21st November, in the trenches opposite the south-western face of the Cordonnerie salient. They attacked also on a very dark evening of a misty day. The artillery bombarded the whole front from the salient known as the Sugar Loaf, opposite our extreme right, northwards to the Tadpole, except the objective itself, which was dealt with by trench mortars. The time laid down for the assault was 7 p.m. At 6.55 p.m. the medium trench mortars twisted and crumpled the wire into heaped-up masses, and at 7 p.m. lifted on to machine gun emplacements in the enemy line. As the raiders went forward, one of them trod on a "blind" mortar bomb, or caught the trip-wire of an enemy mine. In the explosion Capt. E. H. L. Bernau, who led the party, and 12 men were wounded. The others scrambled through the wire and entered the 8-feet deep trench. They found it blocked with knife-rests and empty. Flashing their torches into the dugouts, they could discover neither within their sandbagged walls nor elsewhere any sign of recent occupation. Only a pair of rotting human legs in dirty field-grey trousers protruded from underneath a heap of debris. A large concrete block, which appeared to cover a mine-shaft and which was strongly protected by barbed wire, was blown up by the Engineers. On the same night a patrol found the area between the enemy position known as the Knucklebone and the Laies unoccupied, except by one of those itinerant German "Flareboys" who were detailed to move along empty trenches, lighting rockets and firing occasional rifle shots.

These enterprises were enough to show that the enemy's line was held even more lightly than our own. From this time on till the Division left the sector, not a single night passed without raiders or patrols—for the functions merged —entering his lines, ransacking his quarters, sometimes kidnapping a sentry, sometimes meeting opposition. Nor was this enough to satisfy the bold temperament of the snipers, who ere long ensconsed themselves in his front line parapet and harassed the sentries of his support line. Not a little information was obtained on the habits and dispositions of the enemy. Following on incursions made by 1st Canterbury and the 2nd Rifles, the Corps Commander forwarded the following message of appreciation from General Plumer: "The Army Commander has read your report on the results of reconnaissances carried out by patrols of the New Zealand Division on the night of 7th/8th December. He considers that very good work was carried out by the units concerned, and that useful information has been obtained." In this warfare of silent stalking and reconnaissance in the dark mazes of the enemy's flooded trenches the infantry became exceptionally adept, and when the 3rd Australian Division came into the area, suitably selected officers were sent to give the newly-arrived battalions lessons in the art.

To bombard these waterlogged positions would have been a waste of ammunition, which moreover had been drastically curtailed by the requirements of the Somme battle and by the necessity of accumulating reserves for the spring. But trenches, parapets, machine gun emplacements, mortar positions and wire were daily bombarded by our heavy and medium trench mortars. This was indeed their halcyon period. In carrying their weighty projectiles up the muddy duckboards they had infantry assistance, but the work of building positions, moving the mortars, and firing their

10

300 or 400 rounds a day was excessively laborious. Into their task they threw themselves with an energy and enthusiasm which made it a sport and relaxation. They played havoc with the German trenches. Wire duckboards debris iron timber and on rare occasions a sentry were thrown high into the air. Some projectiles landing in the swamps behind the German line sent up tall tree-shaped geysers of mud and water. The incessant work of Lt. F. J. W. Stallard and the personnel of the medium trench mortars in particular won General Russell's special thanks.

Despite all this mortar activity and our nightly visitations to his lines, the attitude of the harassed enemy remained passive. While our aeroplanes bombed Fromelles and the other centres of activity in rear and reconnoitred his trenches, his airmen very rarely offered themselves as targets to our machine and Lewis gunners. He made little effort to repair his trench parapets and wire. Only very rarely was a nervous patrol to be seen in No Man's Land, and such few raids as he made were not pushed home. It was from the support trenches that his flares rose, and there was a marked absence of rifle fire. The Tadpole and Turks' Point were unheld when patrols reconnoitred them on 22nd and 25th November. On the 26th and 27th his trenches were tested at other points and found empty. A patrol at Corner Fort, on the 28th, was repulsed with casualties,[1] but on the following evening a large sector alongside proved to be unoccupied. It was highly desirable to clear up the situation and establish by extensive reconnaissance and the capture, if possible, of a prisoner, the location of those positions which the enemy actually held. At midnight, therefore, on the night 30th November/1st December the 2 brigades each sent out 6 officers' patrols simultaneously to discover the dispositions of the enemy's advanced troops and report on the position and condition of his wire in rear of his front line. These patrols were instructed not to attempt to force an entry should resistance be encountered, but to avoid aggressiveness, carry out their investigations silently and secretly, and in no case to penetrate to a depth greater than 100 yards. Uncharted points requiring exploration were carefully selected

---

1 When this patrol was ordered to withdraw, Rflmn. N. A. Nicholson did so, but lay on the outer edge of the enemy's wire with another man to cover the movements of his companions. Hearing groans coming from the parapet, he made his way again through the entanglements and discovered a badly wounded comrade. Having dressed his wounds, he decided that in view of their nature it was not advisable to carry the man. He therefore returned to our lines and reported the case to his Company Commander, who at once organised a party with a stretcher. Nicholson guided this party back, and the wounded man was safely recovered.

as their objectives and were clearly defined laterally to obviate collision of parties from adjoining patrols. The commanders were given a free hand as to the length of time they would remain in the enemy's line.

The night was cold and misty when the raiders set out. Of the 1st Brigade parties from 1st Auckland and 1st Wellington, 4 found the positions unoccupied and a stench of fetid water and rotting bodies. In rear of the front trench was abysmal mud, through which some floundered as far as a shell-torn farm near the support line. Of the other 2 parties, 1 was detected in the wire. It was fired on and sustained casualties. The second reached the parapet when they were challenged by a sentry, who called out what seemed to be "New Zealand," and the sound of hurrying feet along the duckboards was followed by ineffective rifle fire.

The right Rifle Brigade patrol from the 3rd Battalion found entry barred by a 20-yard broad entanglement. The centre party from this battalion saw a glare of lights and heard a machine gun fire in the support trench 200 yards in rear. The third was checked at the intended point of entry by a 15-feet wide moat, which contained 6 feet of water and was blocked with wire. Bent, however, on introducing some newly-arrived reinforcements in the party to the interior of the German lines, their leader made a detour over an awkward icy-cold ditch and brought his party to the parapet at another point. Here too the trench was empty. There was no sound of life save the hammering of wire pickets in the distance. Of the 4th Battalion parties, 1 saw in No Man's Land an enemy patrol, which frustrated an attempt at its capture by precipitate withdrawal. The raiders then made for the German lines. They found them occupied. The stretch of intervening trench between communication saps was wired, but at their heads were sentry posts, which were periodically visited by patrols. The centre party found the wire impassable all along its front and the sector strongly manned.

The most interesting adventure befell the left patrol, which reached the enemy's parapet without difficulty. Some 30 yards away a middle-aged German of the 82nd Regiment was keeping an inadequate watch. He was suffering from a cold, and to give himself some protection from the wind he had blocked the trench with a sheet of corrugated iron. His cough betrayed him to the crouching assailants, and they determined to capture him. As the trench in front looked dark and deep, they waited for a German flare to illuminate it before they took the plunge. When the flare went up, the trench was seen to be 9-feet deep and blocked with wire. The officer decided then to work along the parapet, but after crawling a few yards found the enemy wire brought right back to the trench's edge. There was nothing left but to throw a couple of bombs at the unsuspecting German and rush him. The bombs burst suddenly in the silence. The raiders picked a hasty way over the wire, tore the sheet down, and behind it found the sentry lying dead. A second German, badly wounded, was crawling down to the communication trench. Chase was at once given by part of the patrol. Hearing the panting pursuers behind him, the German redoubled his efforts. He just managed to half enter, half fall into a deep dugout with steel doors. Inside it were 3 unwounded men. They made frantic efforts to shut the door. Ere it slammed, 2 bombs were thrown in, and the muffled explosion shook the loose earth down by the raiders' feet. Inside the dugout all 4 must have perished. Meanwhile the rest of the patrol were searching, none too gently, the dead sentry. His greatcoat was tightly buttoned against the damp cold of the night, and he wore a belt which it was found difficult to undo. At the first sound of the bombs a party of Germans had moved up at once from the support trench, and their stick grenades were now falling close, but the patrol secured the necessary identifications before it withdrew.

All the parties were back, without casualties, by 3 a.m. As a result of this highly successful operation the posts held in the enemy's line were largely determined. The 5th Bavarians, opposite the 1st Brigade, had abandoned their front line with the exception of one or two posts in the Sugar Loaf. The Landwehr Brigade, opposite the Rifles, still garrisoned their front with sentry posts at certain places. These Strong Points at the heads of communication trenches and elsewhere were marked down for operations in the future.

A few enemy were seen on the evening of 7th December by a 2nd Rifles party which penetrated the Angle. In order not to frighten the sentries away, the raiders attacked without any artillery or mortar preparation. As they neared, they saw 3 Germans working on the parapet, but these ran away. Somewhere a horn blew an alarm. Our party lobbed a few bombs before them into the trench and made for the parapet. The trench was found much demolished. Bombs were thrown at the intruders from a distance, but no German could be discovered. The sappers blew up a stick-grenade store, and the party returned unscathed through slight enemy retaliation, which, on our rear trenches, took the form of lachrymatory gas.

These raids and nightly visitations by patrols at last goaded the Germans out of their torpor. As the light was fading away in the afternoon of 10th December, a heavy burst of machine gun and rifle fire swept the 1st Rifles' parapets. At the time our men were "standing-to," and our own Lewis guns and rifles answered immediately. The flashes from the enemy trenches died away, and half an hour later everything was still quiet. The night sentries were posted, and the rest of the line "stood down" to draw their tea.

All at once a heavy bombardment set in of mortar pro-jectiles on the front trench and of shrapnel and high-explo-sive shells on the support. The garrison dropped their tea and ran back to the fire-bays. Every man was in position three or four minutes after the first shell landed. In No Man's Land a line of pollarded trees ran along a small ditch to our parapet near a "gap." Alongside the "gap" was a Lewis gun position, manned by 4 private soldiers. A "rum-jar" landed in the bay, severely wounding 3 of the men and knocking the No. 1, Rflmn. W. H. Butler, off the fire-step. The wounded gunners refused to leave their bay, and Butler, though severely shaken, instantly picked up the Lewis gun again and asked them to put up a flare. In its light he saw a small party of Germans fumbling with the wire in front of the "gap." At once he opened fire, but after half a minute the gun, with characteristic obduracy, jammed. The gunner cursed it and furiously strove to set it again in action, but the leading Germans were already beginning to lumber through the wire. A corporal in the next bay shot one through the head. The raiders replied by a shower of bombs. One landed in the corporal's bay, sweeping the men off the fire-step, and another wounded Butler. Then Rflmn. P. H. Gifford, one of the gun team, who had already been severely hit, resumed his place on the fire-step and stood guard over his stricken comrades, continuing to fire at the approaching raiders. The Germans, however, finding their entry was to be opposed, decided that they had had enough, and while their covering bombardment was still falling on each flank and on our support line, they turned and fled. All our machine guns and Lewis guns vindictively swept their retirement, but then ceased to allow the riflemen to pursue. Intent on revenge, these patrols followed the raiders across to their own parapet. In our own wire, opposite Butler's bay, they found a second dead German, riddled by Lewis gun fire, but were unable to capture a live prisoner. The retreat had been too hasty, and all along the trees in the wet grass lay the discarded grenades and dropped helmets of the fleeing raiders. In our own trenches 4 men had been killed and 12 wounded. Gifford, who had been a particularly skilled and fearless Lewis gunner, died of his wounds a few days later.

If the Germans required a lesson in the thorough organisation and daring execution of a raid, it was given to them a week later by the 4th Rifles. Under Capt. W. W. Dove, a large party of 5 officers and 170 men, with a dozen sappers, assembled just before midnight, 17th/18th December, to attack Corner Fort. The necessary gap in the wire was cut by trench mortars previously, and these, with artillery, stood by ready to give support if required. The night was peculiarly dark and foggy. At rare intervals an enemy sentry shot a foolish unaimed bullet across No Man's Land or fired a flare. The raiders were divided into 3 parties. All reached their allotted point of entry. Directly they threw their first bombs, flares shot up along the front line at the Fort and in astonishing profusion from the support line. Heavy machine gun fire opened behind the Angle, but was at once stifled by the watching mortars in our trenches. One party floundered down a communication trench, waist-deep in water, amid floating duckboards. They secured no prisoners, but killed 5 Germans.

The second party, under 2nd Lt. B. Mollison, found the same miserable conditions in Corner Fort, where dummy works of canvas and wood had been sorely battered by our trench mortars. A sentry group of 4 was "done in." From a maze of trenches in rear, which formed a Strong Point, 2 machine guns opened fire, but these were bombed, and the crews were killed. A strenuous effort was made by Rflmn. J. Keys and E. M. Phelan to bring back the guns, but the entanglements and floods surrounding the position were impassable. One was destroyed. This second party also were unfortunate in not being able to secure prisoners, but

they left 20 lifeless Germans prone in the water and mud
or stretched across the wire.

The objective of the third party, which was led by Sergt.
W. McConachy, was the support line. Unlike the front line,
it was found in good condition. The walls were well revetted
with birch branches, the duckwalks wired, and every 20
yards was a good 7-feet high dugout with a porch holding
rifle-racks. Nearly all the occupants, however, had fled. Some
17 showed fight and paid the penalty. This party secured 9
Landwehr prisoners, some in the communication trench, others
in the support line, and 1 in No Man's Land. Meanwhile the
Engineers had blown up a long section of the tramway and
a large pumping-plant. The half-hour allotted for the enterprise had now expired. Across No Man's Land came the
strident blast of a Klaxon horn, blown in our lines as a signal
of recall, and a white rocket rising from our parapet and
bursting into green stars summoned the raiders home. In
addition to the prisoners a mass of papers was brought back.
Of the raiders, only 1 was killed and 4 wounded. The
battalion received congratulatory messages from the Army
and Corps Commanders.

On 20th December, a 1st Auckland raiding party penetrated far behind the German front line, but found no sign
of the enemy. Three nights later the German defence secured
a solitary success, and a disastrous enterprise by the 3rd
Rifles, in bright starlight, was redeemed only by individual
acts of gallantry and self-sacrifice. The enemy allowed the
party to get through his entanglements, when he opened up
a strong fire and threw masses of bombs. 2nd Lt. M.
F. Walsh, cheering his men to the attack, fell mortally
wounded on the parapet. An enemy machine gun was hoisted
on a flank, but Cpl. H. Anderson, a very gallant non-
commissioned officer, with another man, rushed at it unhesitatingly, and flung his bomb so accurately that it killed
the crew and blew the gun into the air. His promptness
saved many lives. On the raiders' withdrawing, after suffering many casualties, Rflmn. J. Hansen, a stretcher-bearer,
tended our wounded for nearly an hour under artillery
machine gun and rifle fire, in the shellholes on the enemy
parapet and between the parapet and wire, till an opportunity offered and they were brought back to our trenches.
There, on its being discovered that 1 wounded man had
been overlooked and was still in the wire, Rflmn. W. D. H.
Milne volunteered to return to his rescue. He had reached

the wounded man and was bringing him back through the enemy entanglements when he was mortally wounded.

Meantime, the stay of the detached 2nd Brigade at Houplines had been comparatively uneventful.   Just after its arrival, President Poincaré motored to Armentières to present medals to the Maire and others of the civil population, but his visit was strictly private, and at his express wish no military honours were paid.   Brigade headquarters was in the Rue des Jésuits in Armentières.   2 battalions, relieved every 8 days, held the front line, 1 occupied the subsidiary line, and 1 was in billets in the town.   For the most part they carried out the normal duties of a trench garrison, harassing the enemy, draining their areas, improving accommodation and trenches, and carrying up the weighty gas cylinders for installation under the front line parapet.[1]   Once or twice the two opposing trenches broke into rifle fire at the flocks of geese passing overhead from the Lys swamps.   On 20th October, following a dummy raid with heavy trench mortars and in co-operation with enterprises on our flanks, a 2nd Canterbury patrol endeavoured to enter the Pont Ballot trenches, but found 2 rows of wire out of the 5 uncut.   Unable to break through these, the patrol moved along for 100 yards, throwing bombs into the trench.   In the right of the sector, Auckland and Canterbury relieved each other, and here, after artillery preparation, a raiding party of the 6th (Hauraki) company of 2nd Auckland, under Lt. C. Hally, in the evening of 3rd November, killed 4 Bavarians and captured 2 prisoners.   They stayed but 5 minutes in the enemy trenches and suffered no casualties.

The left battalion sector lay next the Lys and opposite Frélinghien and the Breakwater,[2] which, in the Division's absence, had been completed and formed now a very strong front line.   This sector was occupied alternately by 2nd Otago and 2nd Wellington.   At ''88,'' one of its ''localities,'' the opposing lines were only 100 yards apart.   Here the British had at an earlier time dug mine galleries, which were now maintained.   With a view to guarding the gallery entrances, we still held ''88,'' though its occupation was made costly by constant German bombardments.   A well-marked 15-feet high bank led from it across No Man's Land to an intricate tangle of earthworks in the enemy line known as the Chicken Run.   This bank was constantly used by both our own and the

1 The gas was actually emitted by personnel of the Special Brigade, R.E.
2 p. 42.

TRENCH MORTAR AMMUNITION

INFANTRY IN BAILLEUL

BRIG.-GEN. C. H. J. BROWN, D.S.O.

BRIG.-GEN. H. HART, C.B., C.M.G., D.S.O

enemy's patrols. North of it lay swampy flats of no considerable breadth to the Lys, and on either side of it several
ditches ran across No Man's Land. Owing to the conformation of the ground, the fall of the water was in the direction of our lines, and the opportunity of flooding the enemy's
trenches was not neglected. One night, after heavy rain,
our Engineers built sandbag dams in 10 of the ditches in
No Man's Land. In the largest of the ditches, which carried
a considerable volume of water, a double dam was erected,
and the water level was raised about 5 feet. Much baling
and pumping of water over the enemy's parapet betrayed
his difficulties, and he had recourse to a raid to destroy the
obstacles. His party reached the block in the ditch, and his
sappers blew up the first dam with a mobile charge. The
second dam, nearer our line and just awash, escaped his
notice, and the destruction of the first did not lower materially the water level.

2nd Otago were holding this line on the evening of 25th
October, when a German party was noticed near our wire
and dispersed by bombs. Half an hour later, our listening
post of 2 men again saw 20 Germans making for the wire.
On their being challenged, a muttered order was given, and
the enemy deployed, making ready to rush the post. Before
these withdrew to give warning, they shot the leader of the
hostile party and threw their bombs. Our Lewis guns then
opened and dispersed the raiders, and later the dead body
was brought in.

Otago was to be less fortunate on 15th November. For
3 days previously a slow continuous trench mortar bombardment had been directed at our wire in front of "88."
A mortar bomb fell every 20 minutes, and in the end
scarcely a vestige of our entanglements remained. In the
evening of the 15th, our front line garrison heard a loud
noise, as of stakes being hammered, in the enemy trenches.
It was just the time for our evening meal, and the fire-bays
were to some extent depleted. No special attention was
paid to the unusual noise. But it was not without purpose.
It was designed to drown any sound of movement made by
a party of German raiders passing over their parapet and
wire, and under its cover the 30 Bavarian "sturm truppen"
formed up in No Man's Land undetected. Without warning,
an intense and most accurate bombardment was opened by
the enemy's "five-nines" and by mortars firing from the
Chicken Run and from the 4 Hallots Farm, known also by

another name. The whole Otago front was affected, but the shelling on Hobbs' Farm and at the Lys were diversions, and the fire fell with special severity on the ill-fated "88." The trenches at its flanks were demolished by a quite exceptionally heavy box barrage by trench mortars, and the communication trench running forward to it was barraged at the support line. Most unfortunately the garrison of "88" did not put up its S.O.S., while the occupants of the Hobbs' Farm trenches did. Thus our artillery response fell east of Hobbs' Farm, and the "sturm truppen" traversed No Man's Land against "88" unmolested. Three parties attacked, the main assault coming down the northern side of the 15-feet bank. About 20 of the garrison had been casualtied in the bombardment, and the remainder, caught disorganised, were unable to prevent the raiders' entry or offer effective resistance. They were overwhelmed, and many were killed by revolver shots. Two men had taken refuge in a small bivouac. The outside one was not completely hidden, and a passing Bavarian blew his brains out over the inside man. On the noise of the revolver shots in "88" our Lewis guns on the flanks and rear opened fire, and a neighbouring section, under Pte. J. W. O'Brien, made a gallant counter-attack. He had been wounded at the outset in the left shoulder and was unable to use his rifle. His post on the parapet had been blown in, but till the limits of the raid were defined he had refused to leave it. He now led his comrades down the trench, hurling bombs passed to him from the rear. But it was too late. Five minutes from the moment of entry, a horn-blast signal was given in the German lines. The Bavarian officer blew his whistle, and the raiders disappeared into No Man's Land as suddenly as they had come. The raid had been admirably planned and was a distinct success for the enemy. The Germans left behind one of their number dead. A heap of unexploded mobile charges at a dummy entrance to our mine galleries indicated that the destruction of the last had been aimed at but frustrated by reason of the darkness, the shortness of time at the raiders' disposal, or some other cause. One of our garrison was taken prisoner, and one missing man was buried in the trenches or killed in No Man's Land. Including the losses of a working party in the vicinity, some 20 men were killed and an officer and 30 men wounded. Our trenches suffered almost irreparable damage.

In retaliation, on the following afternoon, 16th November, our heavy howitzers and guns bombarded Frélinghien and the enemy trenches and rest billets, the German batteries answering by a desultory shelling of Armentières in the evening. Our infantry too sought revenge. At dusk a small Otago raiding party reconnoitred the strong German entanglements, but were unable to discover a gap for entry. For the same reason, success was not vouchsafed to a raid made on 18th November by the Australian company of the II. Anzac Cyclist Battalion, which was attached to the British brigade on the right sector of the Franks' Force area.

On the arrival of the New Zealand artillery from the Somme, the 2nd Field Artillery Brigade had relieved the Australian gunners that supported General Braithwaite's infantry. Shortly afterwards, in accordance with a principle now introduced prescribing a 3 months' tour of duty at Sling for the infantry brigadiers in rotation, General Braithwaite went to England. In command of the 2nd Infantry Brigade he was succeeded by Col. V. S. Smyth, N.Z.S.C. Towards the end of November, the 3rd Australian Division, under Major-General J. Monash, who had been so long and intimately associated with the New Zealanders on the Peninsula, arrived from its base in England and began to relieve Franks' Force. The new Division was, even for Australians, magnificent in physique and morale, but this was their first experience of the trenches, and the line was handed over gradually, half-battalions moving in at a time. On completion of relief, in the first week of December, Franks' Force was broken up. The Corps front was now held by 3 Divisions, the New Zealand on the right, the 34th in the centre, and the 3rd Australian on the left, each with 2 brigades in the line and 1 in reserve. The 2nd Infantry Brigade group rejoined the Division and acted for a month as brigade in reserve. Two battalions went to Estaires, one to Sailly, and 1 to Bac St. Maur. The 2nd Field Artillery Brigade passed under the command of the Australians, whose artillery had not yet arrived. It rejoined the Division towards the end of January.

On 22nd December the Commander-in-Chief inspected the reserve troops of the Corps. Units of the Division, now brought up to and above strength by the continual arrival of reinforcements, were drawn up on the road near Sailly, and Sir Douglas Haig, accompanied by the Corps Commander, rode slowly down the line. After the inspection the troops marched past. Subsequently General Godley issued the following order:—

"The Corps Commander is directed by the Commander-in-Chief to convey to all ranks of the Corps his high apreciation of the appearance and turn-out of the troops that paraded for his inspection to-day. In conveying this message, the Corps Commander wishes to congratulate all concerned on the excellence of the Staff arrangements and to thank officers, n.c.o.s and men for the special effort they had evidently made to show up so favourably under such adverse weather conditions."

After 3 weeks' rest the 2nd Infantry Brigade left their comfortable quarters at Estaires and the other villages on 23rd December, and relieved the 1st Brigade in the Cordonnerie subsector on the right. Christmas was spent as a holiday so far as the duties of the various units permitted. Cordial messages from the King and the New Zealand Ministers were communicated, and every effort was made to give the troops whether in the trenches or in the rear the good cheer associated with this season. Towards the enemy it was not yet a time for peace and goodwill. The artillery undertook a comprehensive and unusually active programme, and were favoured by comparatively good observation. The howitzers fired at selected targets at a slow rate, each shot being carefully observed, while from 7 p.m. till midnight, at regular intervals, the 18-pounders, firing altogether with single salvoes, swept tramways and transport routes. The Germans reserved their retaliation for New Year's Day.

During the month of January the 4th Artillery Brigade was completed by the arrival of the 16th (Howitzer) Battery from England. Shortly afterwards, however, in accordance with instructions which affected the whole British Army, a very drastic change was made in the organisation of the artillery. Experience on the Somme had shown the necessity of massing on an offensive front a much greater proportion of field artillery than that which actually formed part of the Divisions engaged. Thus Divisional Artilleries had frequently been divorced from their Divisions. The reorganisation now brought into effect aimed at preserving a permanent relation between a Divisional Commander and his own artillery, and at the same time establishing a pool of artillery at the disposal of the higher command by the formation from the Divisional artillery of independent brigades. The scheme also involved the universal adoption of the 6-gun battery. The number of the brigades was reduced to 3. Two of these, each consisting of three 6-gun 18-pounder batteries and

one 6-gun howitzer battery, were left under the immediate
command of the Divisional Commander. The third, comprising the same number of batteries and guns, was placed
under the control of the Army Commander and called an
"Army" Brigade. The 4th Brigade was therefore broken
up. Its batteries (the 8th 10th 14th and newly-joined 16th),
losing their individuality, were incorporated in the batteries
of the 1st and 3rd Brigades, and its Headquarters Staff was
split up among the various artillery units. Lt.-Col.
Falla shortly afterwards took over the command of the
D.A.C., vice Lt.-Col. Gard'ner, who received an appointment on the Corps Staff. The 2nd Brigade, detached
at the time with the Australians at Armentières, was designated the "Army" Brigade. To bring it up to establishment
an additional 18-pounder and howitzer battery were required,
and pending its completion it was at the first opportunity
withdrawn into reserve. A portion of the D.A.C. was allotted
as the "Army" Brigade Ammunition Column.

On the first day of the New Year a change was effected
also in the organisation of the 1st and 2nd Infantry Brigades,
with the object of bringing the sister territorial battalions
into the one formation and facilitating administration, especially with regard to the transfer of officers. The 1st Brigade
was reconstituted with the 2 Auckland and the 2 Wellington battalions, and the 2nd Brigade with the 2 Canterbury and the 2 Otago battalions. Such severance of old
associations, cemented by common experience in the trenches
and on the battlefield, must inevitably cause regrets. Just
previously, as we have seen, the 2nd Brigade had relieved
the 1st Brigade in the Cordonnerie subsector, and now, as
1st Canterbury and 1st Otago moved up from reserve to the
front area, their Wellington comrades "turned out" in Sailly
to do them honour, and their band played them through. In
the same month the Rifle Brigade received notification that
H.R.H. the Duke of Connaught had consented to be their
Colonel-in-Chief.

Throughout this period the battalions of the 2 brigades
in the line, during their weekly turn of duty in support,
formed working parties for the necessary maintenance
of the trenches and for wiring. Under cover of the dull
misty weather the infantry and the Pioneers constructed
miles of splendid successive bands of entanglements before
the subsidiary line or rear trenches of the Divisional system,
and it was with no little chagrin that they read, in the spring

of 1918, of the Germans forcing their way through the Portugese garrison with little opposition.

For the brigade in reserve, in addition to normal military training and constant anti-gas drill in the recently issued small box respirators, a comprehensive scheme of recreational training as laid down by the Army was carried out, and competitions were arranged in football, cross-country running and boxing. To organise this training, Lt.-Col. Plugge in January relinquished command of 1st Auckland. Major (now Lt.-Col.) S. S. Allen, the next available senior officer in the regiment, was at the moment absent on duty, and the command of 1st Auckland temporarily devolved on his brother, Major R. C. Allen.[1] The scheme of recreational training, providing for the participation of all ranks in manly exercises, was a welcome change from drill, and proved a valuable benefit to health and morale. With the same object, rest houses for officers and men, canteens, a cinema, and a theatrical troupe were organised by the Division. Musical elocutionary and literary competitions, concerts and lectures were also provided by the New Zealand Y.M.C.A., who began at this time to extend their beneficent activities on a large scale.

In somewhat raw wintry weather, constant efforts were made to preserve the health and increase the comfort of the soldier, and in weekly administrative conferences held at Divisional Headquarters this object was borne steadily in view. In the rear areas, wherever high winds had stripped the leaking roofs of billets, the tiles were repaired, and a constant supply of fresh dry straw was procured. To prevent contamination of the floors and straw by mud, the vicinity was drained, and scrapers and duckboards were provided. In the trenches, efficient draining was of the utmost importance, and formed one of the chief tasks of the Engineers. For this work and for garrison duties, thigh gum boots were issued, and arrangements made whereby each man in the trenches had a dry pair of socks every day. The wagon lines in wet weather were often quagmires, but the animals were protected as much as possible by the construction of brick standings and malthoid roofs. Administrative developments may be illustrated by a reference to the establishment in the Division at this time of an officers' club, a hair-dressing shop, a watch repairing ship, and a printing-press. A survey of the steps taken to eliminate waste in the distribution of

1 p. 150.

equipment clothing and foodstuffs, and in the preservation and useful employment of man-power, though unsuitable for discussion here, would be of profound interest to the student of economics. The efficiency attained was reflected, to take but one example, in the outstanding position which the Division occupied in the statistical lists published regularly by the Corps to show the returns of fat and dripping sent to the base for conversion into glycerine for munitions.[1]

About this time a very remarkable personality was associated with the Division for some weeks, in the person of a fourth-class chaplain well above military years. Daily he might have been seen flying up in a side-car to the trenches, visiting the foremost saps, on more than one occasion narrowly escaping German explosives, and inspiring and endearing himself to all ranks alike by his indomitable fortitude that triumphed over ill-health and by his unaffected manliness and lovable character. That unassuming padre was the Right Rev. A. W. Cleary, Roman Catholic Bishop of Auckland.

The first active operation of the new year was carried out by the 2nd Rifles on 7th January. 2 officers and 80 men, under Capt. J. B. Bennett, accompanied by 4 sappers, made a successful raid on a strongly garrisoned point in the enemy line known as the Lozenge. The raiders entering the trenches were led by Lt. L. I. Manning and 2nd Lt. D. C. Bowler. The 4th 13th and 14th Batteries supported them. Moving forward, as soon as darkness fell, across No Man's Land, they crossed one of the innumerable channels of the country by a specially made bridge. Scouts crawled up and examining the wire found the wide gap made by our mortars still open. The raiders thereupon passed through it in 3 assaulting columns. The borrow-ditch in front of the parapet was wide and 4-feet deep, but it did not suffice to hold them back, and they plunged unhesitatingly through the icy water. The parapet had been demolished and the trench partly filled in by the effect of our mortar and artillery fire. Here and there broken rails of the tramway line running parallel to the front trench stood up on end in air. The 3 parties at once went to their assigned objectives.

Of the right column a blocking party had not gone 30 yards before they met 7 Germans. The corporal in com-

[1] The II. Anzac Medical Officers' Training School, which owed its inception to Col. Begg, was a particularly useful institution, and was copied elsewhere in the British Armies. A Divisional school of instruction in Field Sanitation was opened on 8th January.

mand was wounded by a bomb, and the leading bayonet man killed. Hearing the bomb and a shout for assistance, the main party, who, led by Sergt. R. G. Bates, had been exploring a communication trench, hurried back and attacked the Germans with bombs. The struggle continued for 8 minutes before the enemy was overcome. 8 Germans were killed, 3 held up their hands, and 1 escaped. Beyond the block a machine gun opened fire, but it was silenced by bombs.

The centre party, working down their allotted trench, found a 6-feet high concrete sentry-post dugout with a domed roof, and took the 2 occupants prisoners. Further on were 2 large concrete dugouts, with a winding stairway of wood leading underground. The first was empty, but in the next sparks of fire issued from an iron chimney. Summoned to surrender, 3 Germans crawled out submissively. As their captors were dealing with these, 3 others emerged and tried to escape rearwards. The New Zealand rifles cracked out simultaneously, and the stumbling figures fell headlong against the trench. Terrified by these shots and the rough imperious commands of the raiders, the rest of the occupants refused to leave their shelter. Two mortar bombs were rolled in, and their demolished dwelling became their tomb. From another dugout further prisoners were taken, and 7 other prisoners who showed fight were summarily killed. The left party found the dugouts and machine gun emplacements in their area destroyed by artillery fire, but had the satisfaction of shooting 7 and bombing 3 Germans in the open sap. In all, the raiders found 16 bodies of Germans already killed by artillery fire, and themselves killed a certain 26. 19 prisoners were captured.

On the following day (8th January) the Rifle Brigade was relieved in the Boutillerie subsector by the 1st Brigade The weather now turned much colder. There was a heavy fall of snow and an unusual spell of hard frost, in which temperatures were recorded lower than any experienced since 1884. Snow veiled the shellholes and showed up the Australian dead in No Man's Land still more distinctly.[1] Even with white overalls patrolling became difficult. Enemy guns remained quiescent and enemy patrols inactive except for one brief encounter in front of the 2nd Wellington wire, when they captured one of our patrols. On 24th January the 2nd Brigade in the Cordonnerie subsector

---

1 Many paybooks and identifications were brought in from the dead.

was relieved by the Rifle Brigade. They were not, however, destined to remain long in reserve, for 2 days later the 34th Division on the left of the New Zealanders was suddenly withdrawn from the line, to be held in readiness to counter an anticipated German attack. Thereupon the 3rd Australian Division extended its flank to include their left subsector in Rue de Bois, and the 2nd Brigade set out at a moment's notice on the 10-mile march from Estaires to relieve the right brigade in Bois Grenier.[1] Thus all 3 New Zealand infantry brigades were now in the line. The 3rd Artillery Brigade moved down the river to support the new subsector, and their place was taken by the 2nd (Army) Brigade from Armentières. It was the first occasion on which a New Zealand artillery brigade had carried out a double relief on the same day, and the 3rd Brigade had every reason to congratulate itself on the smoothness and expedition with which the moves were effected.

Active patrolling continued. The action of a small 2nd Rifles' patrol of 14 men, under Cpl. S. F. Hanson, at the end of the month, deserves special notice. Previous reconnaissance had located a German post at the head of one of the enemy's communication trenches, and the patrol set out to capture or destroy the sentries. The frost still continued, and the ground was covered with snow. Clad in white overalls, the patrol lay in ambush in convenient shellholes till the 3-minute preparatory light trench mortar bombardment ceased. Then leaving 4 men on the parapet to safeguard their rear, they rushed the trench. The 7 sentries in the bay were killed. Close by was a large strongly-built dugout with a heavy timber door. It was fitted with bunks, in which were a dozen or more Germans. A revolver shot into its interior brought out 2 prisoners. Bombs were thrown into it, and the remainder of the occupants were presumably killed. Hanson and his men had now been 4 minutes in the trench, and before definite information could be obtained the bombs of hurrying German reinforcements began to fall about them. The leader blew his whistle, and the party withdrew. It was well that they had guarded their exit, for a few enterprising Germans had crawled along the parapet to cut them off. The covering party waited in composure for the enemy, bombed them and killed 2, and highly satisfied with their venture, the patrol returned with

---

1 The infantry reliefs were conducted with exceptional rapidity. Thus 1st Canterbury. receiving warning orders at 1 p.m., had taken over their portion of the front line by 7 p.m.

their 2 prisoners and without a casualty. One of the captives was a Bavarian. The other stated that he belonged to the 11th Regiment, but bore no identifications.

A 1st Wellington party, under 2nd Lt. S. G. Guthrie, M.C., was equally successful in the early morning of 3rd February in the Angle. No Man's Land was slippery with ice, and the raiders, though in white smocks and calico-covered helmets, were visible to our front line sentries all the way across the frozen ditches. The Germans, however, failed to notice them even while they lay cutting the strands of wire that had survived the previous mortar bombardment. The raid was covered by artillery, and machine guns swept the flanks of the Angle. On the raiders' rushing up the parapet they were wildly fired at by 3 sentries in a lean-to shelter protected by wire, but on a bomb being thrown, these at once surrendered to L.-Sergt. W. A. Francis.

The enemy retaliated on the following night with a some-what severe gas shelling of Fleurbaix, in which we incurred 40 casualties, mostly slight, and a week later with one of his equally rare and unsuccessful raids. He selected a small salient in the 4th Rifles' line. His effort was preceded by 2 days' mortar activity on our wire, turning the white level surface into a chaotic mass of black pits, and thus giving indications of his intention. At 9.2 p.m. (8th February) an intense artillery and minenwerfer bombardment opened without warning, and our parapets were swept by machine gun and rifle fire. 5 minutes later 2 green flares shot up from the German trenches. On our front line the fire ceased, but intensified on the support line. Our troops at once stood to arms. Within 4 minutes the counter-attacking platoon and the reserve company were issued with extra bombs, and bombing squads had manned prearranged positions in the communication trenches. The S.O.S. call was sent to the artillery and the signal rocket fired, and instantaneously came the swish of our shrapnel into No Man's Land and the thud of our machine guns. The raiders scattered. A patrol, sent into No Man's Land immed-iately after the bombardment, found no dead but a large number of grenades. Till morning it was not thought that the enemy had crossed our wire, but then it appeared that one or two had entered a disused gap and bombed an old mineshaft. A bag of wire-cutters and bombs had been dis-carded, and there were manifest traces of a hurried with-drawal. The excellence of our infantry dispositions, the

admirable rapidity with which both artillery and machine
guns opened, the slight losses sustained in the bombardment,
and the energy with which the gaps in the wire were at once
filled by ready-made circles of loose tangled wire known as
"gooseberries," all reflected the highest credit on the soldierly
qualities of the defence.

Four nights later a further half-hearted and abortive
effort was made at the head of the "avenue" which separated
the 2 battalions of the 1st Brigade. Opposite the "avenue,"
on the preceding night, one of our officers had just escaped
capture by a German patrol. Our machine gun fire had been
rearranged to command the approaches more effectively. On
this spot, shortly after dark on 12th February, a severe
minenwerfer bombardment was directed, which was maintained with half-hour intervals till midnight. The hostile
minenwerfer were engaged by light trench mortars and
howitzers in accordance with a preconcerted programme.
They persisted, however, and just before midnight the
enemy's artillery co-operated in a full-throated roar, perfectly timed and startling. A listening post brought in warning of the approach of the expected raiders. The S.O.S. call
was given. Some 15 Germans reached the parapet of an
abandoned derelict salient and were at once bombed by a
party of 1st Auckland that worked towards them from the
flank. The raiders withdrew immediately, and suffered some
casualties in No Man's Land from our machine gun fire. The
policy of the thin line of defence once more proved its value,
and despite the severity of the bombardment only a handful
of the garrison were wounded.

Since the first week in January there had been up to this
time continuously frosty weather with occasional falls of
snow. For days on end the ground had been covered by a
white shroud. Round the guns, movement had to be restricted
to avoid the making of tracks, and the difficulty of concealing
positions was increased, for the blast of a firing gun melts
the snow for an area of about 15 or 20 yards, leaving a black
smear in the white very noticeable to observation from the
air, and on which falling snow will not lie for days. This
dry, bracing cold had been most beneficial to health.

With the thaw[1] that set in about the middle of February
the Division began its preparations for a move to a more

1   On the eve of a thaw, to avoid irreparable damage to roads, orders were issued
reducing the use of transport to a minimum, lessening loads by half, and confining
traffic to the pavé highways.   On receipt of a warning telegram, "Prepare Thaw
Restrictions," the C.R.A., C.R.E., and S.S.O. (Senior Supply Officer) established 3
days' reserve forward dumps.

northerly sector, where it would be called on to undertake
active operations in the spring. Already at the beginning
of February representatives of a "New Army" Division, still
in England, (the 57th), had for experience been living with
the New Zealanders in this quiet area, where on 4 days
these had the unprecedented experience of wholly escaping
casualties. On 14th February, an infantry brigade of the
57th Division began a gradual relief of the Rifle battalions.
A similar partial relief of the artillery followed. In the
course of the instruction thus given in familiarising the new-
comers with trench warfare, a 1st Canterbury patrol, accompanied by an officer and n.c.o. of the English troops, had
the misfortune to be ambushed at the apex of the Bridoux
Salient.

After the Rifle Brigade, the relief of the 1st Brigade followed, but before they said farewell to their winter sector, a
last smashing blow was planned against the enemy. It was
to take the form of a full-dress raid, with minute preparation
and overwhelming artillery support. It was to be on a larger
scale than the Division had hitherto undertaken or were
afterwards to undertake. 2nd Auckland was entrusted
with the mission. The time fixed for the raid was dawn on
21st February. The 500 raiders, who were under the command of Major A. G. Mackenzie, D.S.O., were trained intensively, first by sections, then by platoons and by companies
on a replica trench system laid well in rear, cut to a depth
of 6 inches and then disguised by straw from prying aeroplanes. For a fortnight previously the medium trench
mortars were engaged in breaking the wire, nightly re-
erected by the spider-like industry of the enemy. On the
previous evening the 2nd Wellington garrison bridged the
ditches and creeks of No Man's Land, and with memories of
the evacuation from Anzac padded the duckboards in the
front line and the communication trenches with straw, over
which hessian fabric was nailed down.

The plan of the Auckland raiders was to assault the front
line with the Hauraki and Waikato companies in 1 wave,
and the support line with the Auckland and North Auckland
companies in 2 waves. Sixteen sappers were attached.
The mass of artillery supporting the raid included over sixty
18-pounders, over twenty 4.5-in. howitzers, four 60-pounders,
and four 6-in. howitzers. In addition to the light mortars,
1 heavy and 3 batteries of medium mortars were engaged.
A special co-operating programme was arranged for the

BIVOUACS IN PLOEGSTEERT WOOD

BIVOUACS IN PLOEGSTEERT WOOD

VICTIMS OF ENEMY AIRCRAFT

TRAINING FOR "MESSINES"

machine and Lewis guns, the former barraging 300 yards beyond the final objective. Prior to zero our garrison in the vicinity was withdrawn.

At 5.45 a.m. on the appointed morning, mortar projectiles fell with shattering crashes on either flank of the assaulted position. On the position itself our shrapnel lashed the parapet to force the enemy's heads down, lifting after $2\frac{1}{2}$ minutes in accordance with the raiders' movements to the support line, and, after a further $4\frac{1}{2}$ minutes, to form a box barrage. The garrison were standing to arms and lined the fire-steps thickly. The storm of shell played havoc with them. The Aucklanders found the wire well cut, and all were over the parapet and among the demoralised Germans in the front trench by the time that the enemy's barrage fell in response to a multitude of red flares. As soon as ever his guns opened, our heavy howitzers broke into intense counter-battery work, depriving the enemy's fire, which lifted some 20 minutes later from our front to our support line, of much of its vigour and most of its accuracy. On the German second trench the assault was equally successful, though here a more stubborn resistance was shown by the enemy, some of whom fought with bitter fury. The raiders stayed half an hour searching the dugouts, blowing up bomb stores and machine guns, and completing their task of destruction. Then, showing great judgment in passing through the hostile barrage, they returned to our trenches. Nearly 200 Germans had been killed by the artillery and raiders. An officer and 43 men of the 77th and 78th Landwehr Regiments and of a freshly-arrived Bavarian regiment were made prisoners.

Our losses were unfortunately heavy. An officer and 17 men had been killed, and 6 officers and over 70 men wounded. In bringing back the wounded over No Man's Land the stretcher-bearers showed their wonted devotion, but not a few of these casualties were inflicted by enemy shells after the Aucklanders had returned to their own lines. In addition, 60 men were missing. These for the most part belonged to the companies that had assaulted the support line. They had been warned of a derelict trench before the real support trench. The morning chanced to be exceptionally misty and dark. Under these unlooked-for conditions the raiders might have fared better had the hour of attack been later. As it was, in the pall of smoke and dust, and owing to the battered state of the ground, they passed over the derelict trench without noticing it, and taking the real trench for the derelict one, pressed on beyond into our barrage, where they were killed or cut off. Nothing is easier than to lose sense of direction under these circumstances. A wounded officer returning with some prisoners found himself going away from our line towards what appeared to be 2 overturned and derelict German field guns, whereupon the prisoners complaisantly put him right and accompanied him back to our trenches.

Apart from these casualties, the raid had been a conspicuous success. 2nd Auckland received, amid other flattering messages, the congratulations of the Commander-in-Chief, and were later specially inspected by General Plumer. 3000 rounds were fired by the light trench mortar batteries. Two guns burst, and all emplacements were exposed to uninterrupted shell fire, but the staunch personnel stuck to their work with their customary fortitude and determination. The rounds fired by the Divisional Artillery alone exceeded 8000.

After this exploit the 1st Brigade was relieved on the following day by troops of the 57th Division. On 23rd February the artillery completed their relief in the line, and on the 25th the last remaining units of the 2nd Infantry Brigade handed over the Bois Grenier trenches, and the command of the Sailly sector passed to the new Division. The heavy and medium mortar batteries remained in the line pending the return of the 57th Division's batteries from training; similarly, while the Division moved northwards to its new sector, the 2nd (Army) Artillery Brigade remained in rest in the Fleurbaix area, completing its establishment as sections arrived from England, and supporting on occasion raids by the 57th and 3rd Australian Divisions.

Just prior to the relief of the 2nd Infantry Brigade, General Braithwaite had returned to it from Sling.[1] His duties in England were assumed by General Earl Johnston, and in the latter's place Lt.-Col. Brown was appointed Brigadier-General to command the 1st Brigade. Command of 2nd Auckland was assumed by Lt.-Col. S. S. Allen, the appointment of his brother, Major (now Lt.-Col.) R. C. Allen in the 1st Battalion being now confirmed.

On relief by the 57th Division troops, the 3rd Brigade had marched to staging billets at Outtersteene. Thence on 22nd February, crossing the Belgian frontier, they relieved the left brigade of the 25th Division in the IX. Corps area immed-

1   p. 139.

iately north of the Lys. The 1st Brigade took over the right subsector on the 25th. On the following day the 2nd Brigade marched into reserve, and the command passed to the New Zealand Division, whose headquarters were now established at Steenwerck. The 1st and 3rd Artillery Brigades were in position by the end of the month, after the 1st Brigade had supported a successful raid by the 3rd Australians on the trenches east of Armentières. The 25th Division went back for offensive training behind St. Omer. The sector was transferred from the IX. Corps to II. Anzac, whose line now extended from in front of Sailly to St. Yves, a distance of approximately 13 miles. The trenches were necessarily held thinly. On the right, in the Cordonnerie, Boutillerie and Bois Grenier subsectors, was the newly-arrived 57th Division; the central subsectors, Rue de Bois, l'Epinette and Houplines, were held by the 3rd Australian Division; and now the New Zealanders were extending their knowledge of the Lys flats in the subsectors of Le Touquet and Ploegsteert, on the left bank of the river.

In their new positions the trenches were of the poorest description. Accommodation was hopelessly inadequate, and drainage had been neglected. The thaw made conditions doubly uncomfortable. Not merely unoccupied "gaps," but portions of the fire trenches also were under water. The communication trenches were narrow, deep in mud, and all but impassable. There was a humiliating contrast between the massive German entanglements and the scanty shreds of wire in front of our own trenches. The parapet was low and in bad. repair, and the enemy enjoyed marked superiority in sniping. The artillery positions were in a similarly poor condition, and sections of the 4th and 13th Batteries were practically in the open. For the troops in support there were few or no villages to provide billets, but this involved no hardship, for the men were as comfortably and, from a medical point of view, more satisfactorily housed in the many hutted camps about Romarin and elsewhere.

Nor was the welcome given to the Rifle Brigade in these miserable trenches an enviable one, for on the very night (22nd/23rd February) on which they entered the line they were raided by the enemy. The relief of the 4th Battalion had been delayed through the activity of enemy mortars on a section of the front trench at St. Yves Hill. When at length the 25th Division troops had quitted the area, the company commander detailed a platoon to stop the breaches

in the parapet and clear out the debris that blocked the
trench. Despite the fatigue of the march, the men set to
work with a will. They were, however, interfered with by
minenwerfer bombs dropping at odd intervals on the spot.
Cpl. J. McQuillan, of the 3rd Light Trench Mortar Battery,
despite this fire, kept his Stokes in action for 45 minutes,
firing over 100 rounds. About 4 a.m., a deluge of shrapnel
swept the position, and a number of mortar shells exploded
in quick succession. Patience being exhausted, artillery
support was invoked, which silenced the minenwerfer.
The work of clearance continued. At 5.45 a.m., however,
a perfect tornado of shells "rumjars" and "pineapples"
burst afresh on the same section of the line. The
working party was ordered to withdraw, and on either
flank the harassed defenders manned the parapets. An exceptionally heavy fog hung over the swamps, and they could
discern nothing. Nor could the green Verey light of the
S.O.S. signal be seen by the artillery or battalion observers,
and all telephonic communication had already been cut. Thus
no S.O.S. support was given.

After a few minutes of fierce bombardment, the enemy's
fire lifted from the front trench and fell in a circle round
the doomed sector, where the mortars had obliterated wire
and trench, hemming it in and hampering the approach
of supports. At the same moment a body of 200 Germans
rushed forward and forced an entry. The raiders'
hopes of securing a large number of prisoners were not to be
realised. Only the working party was in the battered fire-
bays, and the majority of them had managed to withdraw.
One or two still remained. One of these had been wounded,
and lay outstretched in the bottom of the trench. Some 40
Germans ran over him, and one in passing, taking him for
dead, cut off the shoulder-strap of his greatcoat. Four others
they took prisoners, but the raiders were not stout-hearted
enough to push their assault home.

In 5 minutes, when our men on the flanks, penetrating
the box barrage, got in touch with them, they withdrew without offering resistance, leaving behind them some mobile
charges and many stick grenades. Our rifle fire and bombs
had killed and wounded some of the enemy, and these,
except for one dead man, they took with them, together with
their prisoners. One of these, Rflmn. J. Emmerson, who had
been wounded, escaped, but was again recaptured by a
second party, some 80 strong, of the returning raiders. Near

the enemy wire, Emmerson saw another chance of making a bid for freedom. He tripped up his burly guardian, wrenched himself free, and in a flash, despite his wound, dashed back for our lines. The Germans opened fire and hit him in 2 fresh places, but struggling on he finally succeeded in reaching our lines in extreme exhaustion.

The documents found on the dead German were at once forwarded to the Army Intelligence Staff and established the presence on the Western front of a Division last identified in Roumania. Our casualties, in addition to these 3 prisoners, were 6 men killed and an officer and 20 other ranks wounded. Very considerable damage was done to the already wretched trenches.

Nor were the 1st Brigade to be immune. Just before dawn, on 28th February, the Germans attempted a raid, accompanied by their usual shelling, on a Strong Point known as Glasgow Redoubt, in the 2nd Auckland trenches. Only half a dozen of the enemy, however, reached an empty bay. These were at once bombed out by the occupants of the next bay, and fled, leaving one of their number wounded, who died shortly afterwards. In their retreat they were pursued by fire and suffered further casualties. 10 men of 2nd Auckland lost their lives, and 15 were wounded in the bombardment. A further German attempt, on 9th March, was crushed by artillery.

Snow fell again during the first week of March, rendering the tasks of working parties more arduous. Their strenuous toil, and the labours of the Engineers and Pioneers, had already made a new world of the sector. The wire was stronger, and the trenches were drained and defensible. The enemy snipers, too, were now effectively mastered by the New Zealand marksmen. It was common and inevitable experience in the Army, however, that for good or ill troops should reap what they had not sown, and the labour bestowed on the position was to benefit others. On 13th March, in view of coming events, the Corps front was extended northwards to the road from Wulverghem to Wytschaete. The New Zealand Division side-stepped northwards to relieve part of the 36th (Ulster) Division on the southern flank of the IX. Corps. In consequence of this move, the 57th Division took over the Rue de Bois subsector from the 3rd Australian Division to enable the latter to relieve the New Zealanders in the Le Touquet and Ploegsteert trenches. Each of the 2 southern Divisions thus now manned 4 brigade subsectors

with 2 brigades, holding 1 in reserve, while the New
Zealanders occupied the 3 subsectors of St. Yves, Messines,
and Wulverghem.   These last were now divided into 2
brigade fronts, north and south of the river Douve.   The
1st Brigade on the right in Le Touquet, wholly relieved by
Australians, went into reserve.   The Rifle Brigade side-stepped
to the Douve, and the Wulverghem subsector north of the Douve
was taken over by the 2nd Brigade, who now came into the
line.   In its period of reserve it had been training on the hill-
slopes near Bailleul, and had been reviewed on 9th March,
with the 3rd Australian Division's reserve brigade, by the
Right Hon. Walter Long, Secretary for the Colonies.   The
artillery followed into their new positions shortly afterwards.
Divisional Headquarters remained at Steenwerck.

In their new area the New Zealanders were to remain,
with various minor adjustments, for the 3 months preceding the Messines offensive.   Half the long straggling
Ploegsteert village and the northern part of the Ploegsteert
Forest behind the ruins of St. Yves were still included in the
Divisional area.   This wood had been the scene of bitter
fighting in 1914.   It was thin and except where blocked by
wire entanglements passable for infantry everywhere.   The
dominating features of the country were, on the one hand,
the gaunt ridge crowned by the houses and the ancient and
massive church of Messines, which had been German territory
since November 1914, and which now half-faced and half-
enfiladed our trenches; and on the other hand, behind our
own line, the beautiful tree-clad hill, Rossignol, or Hill 63,
so called from its height in metres.   Instead of the unbroken
flats, with which the Division had been familiar through the
winter, the country behind the front area was markedly
rolling.   The hills themselves produced their characteristic
effect of exhilaration and adventure, and from Hill 63 the
distant view of the great bluff of Kemmel, of the picturesque
Mont des Cats, with its monastery, and of other abrupt and
isolated eminences, steeped in blue haze, was instinct with
romantic beauty.   On the steep southern side of Hill 63,
screened from German observation and inaccessible to hostile
shrapnel, the Army had built on the edge of Ploegsteert
Wood log-houses such as Stafford House and Limavady
Lodge, used as billets for supporting battalions.   And at Hyde
Park Corner, where the road from Ploegsteert to Messines
began to mount the south-eastern shoulder of the hill, deep
shelters, known as the Catacombs, and capable of holding a

weak brigade, were opened by General Plumer in November 1916. That road, on mounting the ridge, came under enemy view, and was of little service to the New Zealanders. More useful was the road which leading from Romarin and adjoining farms, now occupied by Brigade Headquarters, turned to the north near Red Lodge and crossed the western slopes of the hill by a wayside Shrine and the ''White Gates'' of the ruined chateau. Here it joined a cart track that ran across the fields from the hamlet of Le Rossignol back in the direction of Neuve Eglise.

The defence of Hill 63 was of the utmost importance. On its retention depended the safety of the Division's new positions and those of the Australians to the south down to the Lys. It formed the northern pivot of our defences in case of a German ''break-through'' about Fleurbaix. The Armentières system guarded against its being outflanked from the south, and it was from a blow northwards at our lines from the Messines Ridge up to the salient round Ypres, that its secure possession was most likely to be endangered. It was known at this time that the Russian disintegration had enabled the Germans to accumulate on the Western front adequate reserves for offensive action, and it was believed that such action was actually being contemplated, either to forestall the threatened Allied blow or to neutralise it when delivered. Should an offensive be launched, this was the sector of the whole British front considered most likely to be affected. If it were delivered on a grand scale, the exposed positions in the Ypres salient might be found untenable. Should they be abandoned, Hill 63 and the Neuve Eglise ridge in rear furnished a pivot connecting the present first-line system with the second line, of which Kemmel formed the corner-stone. The northern face of the hill, therefore, was already defended by successive lines of trenches and a line of small self-contained redoubts, but a new rear line was dug and fresh wire erected by the 1st Brigade to join the G.H.Q. system and the so-called Wulverghem Switch at the village of that name. Leading features of the defence policy were the carefully-concealed and well-protected machine gun emplacements and the shell-proof cover to protect infantry garrisons during a bombardment. On the subfeature of St. Yves Hill, lying just to the north-east of Ploegsteert Wood in the right brigade subsector, a maze of trenches afforded a striking example of the ill co-ordinated labours of successive tenants and the destructiveness of German artillery.

Apart from the screen afforded by Hill 63, the whole country lay open to the enemy's observation from the ridge. He looked straight down the important road from Neuve Eglise to Wulverghem, so that wheeled traffic was impossible in the daytime, and parties moving up to the trenches had to move at intervals and in single file, hugging the side of the road. A little way up from the village was a gum-boot store, where working parties drew gum-boots for the trenches, and any assembly here at once attracted fire. Our own observation posts on Hill 63, which lies a few feet lower than the Messines Ridge, similarly commanded an extensive view eastwards down the Douve valley and along the southern slopes of the ridge to the Warneton church spires.

Behind the opposing lines the country was on either side covered with hedges and spinneys, and the roads screened by trees. The centre of the Divisional area was marked by the Douve, which running eastwards falls into the Lys at Warneton. In summer it is an insignificant shallow stream, some 10 feet wide, but in the winter rains it rises and becomes a serious obstacle to military operations, especially near the front line trenches, where it floods its banks and at times forms a sheet of water 40 feet wide. Hence at this point there were alternative defensive systems, called respectively Summer and Winter Trenches, those in the flat nearest the stream not being held in the winter months. North of the Douve and directly facing Messines, the ground behind our support line sloped up to the rise of Midland Farm, which, forming a sister bulwark to Hill 63, was of considerable tactical importance and was correspondingly fortified with earthworks and concealed machine guns.

Among the trees and the trenches lay the shattered farms of now exiled Belgian peasants. Most of their names, if ever known, had been forgotten, and they were re-christened by troops in the early days of the war with titles which reflected the humour and the realism of the soldier: Donnington Hall, Mac's Ruin, Dead Cow Farm, Stinking Farm, and so on. These were in the front line company areas; somewhat further back Battalion Headquarters were located in the shacks behind Hill 63 or up the Douve valley, at St. Quentin's Cabaret, for example, or in the concrete quarters under the shell cf La Plus Douve Farm buildings.

Close to La Plus Douve was Ration Farm, where after dusk the battalion limbers came down the hill from "White Gates" with rations stores and letters. It was here that in

Scale =1 : 100,000

0   1   2   3
MILES

Bo...

Vlamertingh...

Poperinghe

To Hazebrouck

Dickebusch

Reninghelst

Westoutre   La Cly...

Boeschepe

Mt Des Cats

Berthen   Mt Rouge   Kemmel

Mt Noir   Locre   Mt Kemmel

To Bailleul   Dranoutre

St Jans
Cappel

To Neuve Egli...

12   MESSINES A...

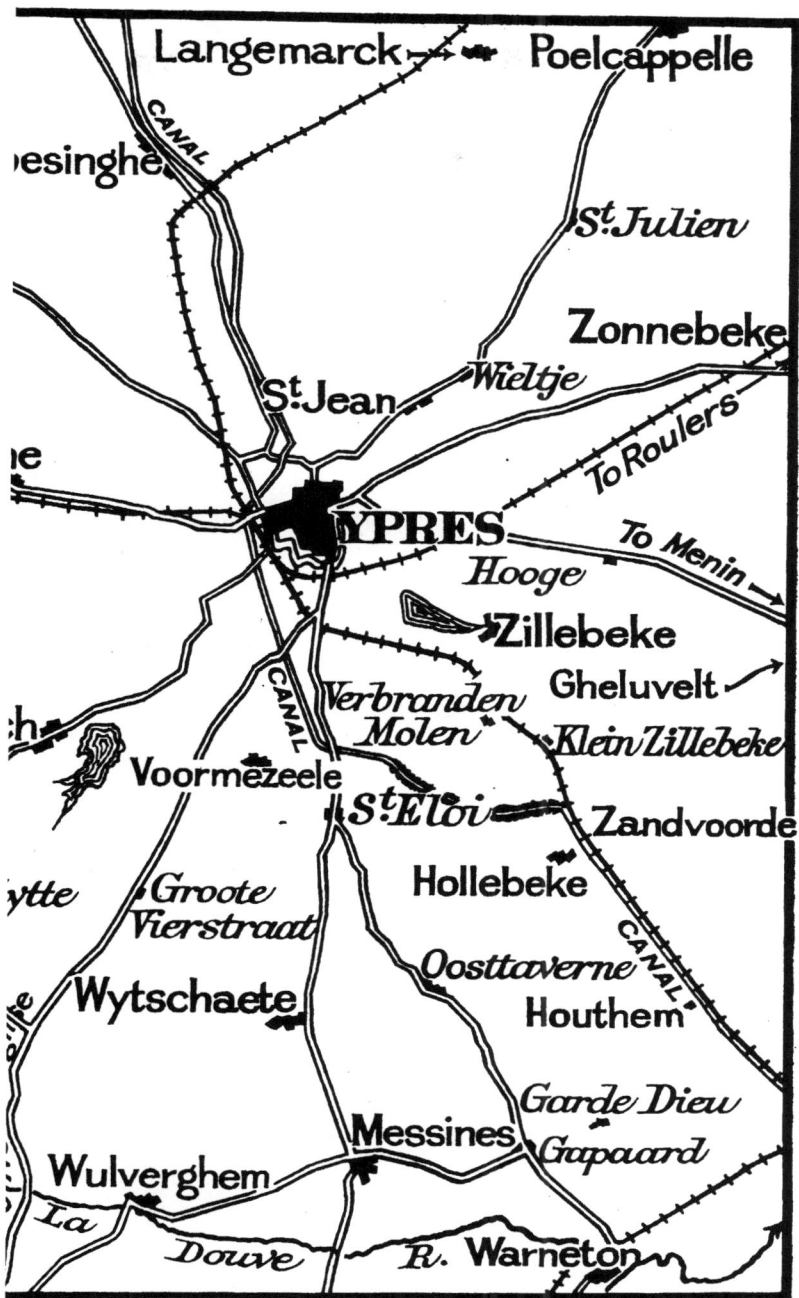

Langemarck — Poelcappelle

esinghe

CANAL

St. Julien

Zonnebeke

St. Jean

Wieltje

To Roulers

e

YPRES

To Menin →

Hooge

Zillebeke

Gheluvelt

Verbranden Molen

Klein Zillebeke

ch

Voormezeele

St. Eloi

Zandvoorde

ytte

Groote Vierstraat

Hollebeke

CANAL

Oosttaverne

Houthem

Wytschaete

Garde Dieu

Messines

Gapaard

Wulverghem

La

Douve

R. Warneton

[Copyright

April a 5.9-in. shell exploded a dump of 100 mortar
bombs, inflicting casualties and causing an enormous crater
in the road. The incident was mentioned in the German
communiqué, which with misplaced indignation protested
against our abuse of the Red Cross flag and justified the
shelling of the supposed dressing-station by the continuous
movement at it and by this explosion. Actually, however,
the dressing-station was a clear 300 yards away. Transport
drivers and carrying parties at the farm were for some days
after exposed to bursts of fire till some fresh provocation
distracted the attention of the enemy artillery elsewhere.

About 1000 yards down stream from these farms
past our front line the larch-fringed Douve entered the
German trenches at La Petite Douve Ferme, where the
enemy line projected sharply into No Man's Land. This
salient was the most advanced and exposed position of the
Messines defences. La Petite Douve was the objective in the
autumn of 1915 of the first of these operations that came to
be known later as trench raids. Owing to the proximity of
the lines about the ruins of the farm, mining operations had
at an early date been started on both sides. The British,
however, had allowed the Douve to flood their shaft at this
particular point, but they maintained activity underground
in the vicinity, and kept a careful scrutiny of German progress, which it was anticipated would break into their own
abandoned works. On 10th January 1917 the expected
happened. The water in our shaft dropped with a sudden
rush 70 to 80 feet, and must at once have flooded the German
galleries and drowned miserably the Silesian miners.
Laboriously and patiently, as was his wont, the German
undertook the Sisyphan work of unwatering. He continued
it for some weeks till he realised that he was vainly pumping
the running water of the Douve. From this point the
German lines bent back northwards to the lower slopes of the
Messines Ridge, which they followed on a level some 15 yards
higher than our own front line. The Steenebeek, a small tributary of the Douve from the north, flowed through No
Man's Land between the opposing trenches, entering our lines
a short distance before it mingled its waters with the larger
stream.

Towards the end of March, on 2 successive days, the
Germans made attempts at the extreme flanks of our line to
secure identifications. At 4 a.m. on the 23rd the 2nd Rifles,
on the right, were suddenly bombarded with a hail of mortar

bombs fired in flights of 6 or 10, swooping down 60 to the minute. The box barrage was picked out after dawn in the snow in a regular line round the position. Three parties attacked our trenches. One that reached the wire was dispersed by bombs and Lewis gun fire, the second was beaten back in No Man's Land by machine gun and rifle fire, and with the help of the 1st 12th and 13th Batteries. The third entered an unoccupied portion where a small working party emptied their rifles at them. Two of the raiders were seen to collapse, but their companions managed to bear them away with them. The fire had been heavy on the support line, where all our casualties were incurred. 4 men were killed and an officer and 9 men wounded. Otherwise the raid was ineffective.

On the following morning, at the same hour, 100 Germans attacked our left flank at the junction of 2nd Otago and the Ulster troops of the 36th Division. An unusually heavy bombardment of artillery and mortars broke all telephonic communication, but the S.O.S. rocket was answered promptly and efficiently by the artillery. The Germans, advancing in single file, were raked by the flank Otago Lewis guns, which cut noticeable gaps in their line. Pressing on, however, with great determination, they reached our wire. At one point they were checked by bombs, but in another they effected an entry and captured one of the garrison. The Otago bombers on the flanks immediately counter-attacked, and after an exchange of bombs drove them out. Conspicuous gallantry was shown also by the Lewis gunners. Remaining at their posts, they did everything possible to prevent an entry and to harass the raiders throughout the bombardment. In one team of 5, for example, 3 were killed and a fourth wounded, but the remaining man worked his gun on the bloodstained sandbags with unflinching resolution. 10 men of Otago were killed and 12 wounded in the bombardment, which did material damage to the trenches. Pools of blood on the enemy side of the parapet showed that the raiders had not gone unscathed.

During the day the enemy bombarded our batteries severely, 300 rounds of high-explosive being fired into the 4th and 13th Batteries' positions. A gun of the 13th Battery was damaged and 500 rounds of 18-pounder ammunition exploded. The 11th Battery suffered similarly the following day, and in the evening the damaged gun-pits were observed and no doubt photographed by a German aeroplane, which descended to within 200 feet over the guns.

At the end of March the weather, which had been milder and showed promise of summer, changed to heavy gales, accompanied by frost snow and hail. The 25th Division had now returned to the II. Anzac area as Army reserve from the Tilques training grounds. Circumstances did not permit of the New Zealand Division's going out as a whole, but the different artillery and infantry brigades went in turn. In the 12 days' training for the forthcoming offensive nothing was left undone to achieve realism. The ground at the training area happened to conform with the actual position to be assaulted, and replicas of the whole German trenches and our assembly ones were cut out a foot deep to scale. In these, battalions and brigades rehearsed the delicate operations of the assembly and attack, and attained an invaluable certainty of purpose. The final full-dress rehearsals were witnessed and criticised by the Second Army Commander and his Staff. A day was also devoted to open warfare manoeuvres. Throughout the infantry training every effort was made to illustrate practically the principles of tactics underlying the recent reorganisation of the platoon into semi-specialised sections of riflemen, Lewis gunners, bombers, and rifle-bombers. The quick and sound appreciation of situations and the initiative shown by subordinate commanders in these operations in the training area were auguries of success on the battlefield which were not to be belied.

On the last day of March, in a heavy fall of snow, the 1st Brigade relieved the Rifle Brigade in the line, and 2 days later the Rifles proceeded on the 3 days' 40-mile march to Tilques. The 1st Field Artillery Brigade went at the same time. In place of the Rifles, a brigade of the 25th Division was lent to General Russell for tactical purposes and for work on the New Zealand Division's front. Shortly afterwards permission was given by Army to the Corps to employ the 25th Division brigades as line garrisons under the proviso that if required they could be withdrawn at short notice into Army reserve. This was taken advantage of to allow the 2nd Infantry Brigade to withdraw from the line preparatory to its following the 3rd to the training area. The 3rd Artillery Brigade went also towards the end of April, and the 2nd (Army) Brigade, after a further temporary attachment to the 57th Division, in the first week of May. On 6th April the 3rd Australian Division extended northwards to embrace the position assigned to it for the impending attack on the ridge, and the 25th Division took over the northern subsector from the vicinity of the Wulverghem-Messines road to the Wulverghem-Wytschaete road. As a result of these moves the contracted New Zealand front now held by the 1st Brigade corresponded roughly with the sector defined for the Division's assembly position.

For the attack, disguised in the memoranda of the time as the Magnum Opus, preparations were already in progress. Several new lines of accomodation were in process of construction. But the area of our assembly trenches was not to be bounded by the front line. Between the front line and enemy trenches on the Messines hillside ran, as has been said, the valley of the little Steenebeek, crossed by the road from Wulverghem to Messines. On this road, between our front trench and the stream, a heavily wired German listening post had been captured and occupied by 2nd Wellington, but a large part of the valley was dead ground, not visible from any point in our trenches. With a view to securing command of observation over it and also to providing a nearer assault position, the construction of a new trench 750 yards long in No Man's Land was desirable. To dig it immediately preceding the attack would court disaster to the assembled troops. In order therefore to familiarise the enemy with it and avoid arousing untimely alertness and aggressiveness, it was resolved to construct the work in good time.

The undertaking was committed to the 2nd Brigade before they left for training. The 1st Brigade garrison cut and taped 7 gaps through the wire, and a party of 2nd Brigade officers, all of whom had been constantly on patrol and knew every detail of the ground intimately, surveyed and pegged out the new trench. On the night of the 13th, covered by a party from 2nd Wellington, who were then holding the line, 500 men of 1st Otago, under command of Major J. Hargest, came up from the reserve area. Such a task required minute elaboration of detail and fine discipline. Each party knew its task. Sentries kept the trenches clear for them. They entered the sap heads at 9 p.m. Splendidly organised and disciplined, without the least noise or confusion, each party went to its position, completed its task by 2.30 a.m., and was clear of the trenches by 3 a.m. When dawn broke, our sentries eyed a long new trench 100 to 180 yards out in No Man's Land.

While Otago dug, arrangements had been made for artillery and machine gun action in case of enemy fire or interference, and the battery commander concerned was present in the front line with the officers commanding the working and covering parties. The silent precision, however, with which the task was carried out raised no alarm in the German trenches. Not a single casualty was incurred, and the unerring judgment of the Divisional Commander, which had discounted predictions of disaster, was amply vindicated. On the following evening the trench was extended, drained to the Steenebeek and connected with our old front line by 2nd Wellington. It was later completed with travel and support trenches in rear.

In face of this new line, the multiplication of communication trenches and similar works elsewhere, and all the various preparations for an attack, manifest both in our front and rear areas, the enemy began to show unmistakable signs of uneasiness. The frequent changes in the dispositions of our troops for the purpose of adjusting frontages and withdrawing brigades for training increased his anxiety to obtain identifications and possible information from prisoners.

During April he attempted 7 organised raids and 5 patrol reconnaissances against the Corps front. An attempt on 30th April on the New Zealanders was crushed by our artillery before it developed, and the enemy was seen to run back over his front parapet and thence to his support line. In the beginning of May he embarked on 2 equally unsuccessful enterprises. Just before dawn on the 5th, a 4th Rifles' patrol, which happened to be out on the Steenebeek, reported a party of 60 Germans advancing along the Wulverghem-Messines road. Our S.O.S. shot up, and the Germans, casting from them their bombs and raiding gear, turned and fled. A few ran forward, but it was to drop into the shelter of the new unoccupied trench, and there a patrol found one dead and captured another. They belonged to the 40th (Saxon) Division, and the prisoner stated that their object was to discover the character of the new trench and ascertain whether the relief movements noticed were connected with the supposed arrival of a Division from Arras. Two days later, under cover of the inevitable bombardment, a raid was made on our new trench. The working party in it withdrew to our front line. Three men, who chose to remain, narrowly escaped being cut off. A fighting patrol sent forward immediately afterwards found the trench clear.

In the front area, apart from these enterprises and the bombardment of our new earthworks in No Man's Land, the enemy's attitude for the remainder of May was surprisingly quiet. Nightly he tried, harassed by our machine and Lewis guns, to repair the destruction caused by our mortars to his front wire. Retaliation by his minenwerfer was rare, and the hillside seemed denuded of snipers. On the back areas, however, his increasing artillery became very active, with persistent shelling of villages, roads, transport lines, dumps, and battery positions.

After dark on 6th May, an exceptionally heavy enemy bombardment, surpassing anything experienced in this area since the autumn of 1915, was opened all along the Second Army front with high-explosive and incendiary shells. The bombardment lasted intermittently throughout the night, at intervals of 3 hours reaching great intensity, particularly over intermediate and back areas of billets and camps. The Divisional casualties exceeded 100, of whom 24 lost their lives; 81 horses were killed in the 1st Battery and other wagon lines. The bombardment was designed undoubtedly to catch the troops whom the enemy had reason to believe were now assembling for the Messines attack, and the extent of the Division's losses shows how serious the effect would have been, had not our attack been in reality postponed. Several huts were burnt, a gum-boot store destroyed, and a shell falling into one of the 1st Rifles' huts destroyed the band instruments and killed 4 of their oldest bandsmen. Another shell struck one of the huts occupied by the 1st Field Company of the Engineers, and the woodwork immediately burst into flames. Sergt.-Major J. Woodhall, assisted by Sergt. J. S. L. Deem, rushed into the burning hut and rescued a badly burnt sapper. Meanwhile Sergt. M. H. Grigg carried out the Orderly Room box containing the men's pay and secret papers. All 3 were severely burnt about the face arms and legs.

In retaliation for this bombardment our heavy artillery fired 2500 rounds, but the enemy shelling was repeated the following night, when fortunately the Division's casualties were few. On the night 7th/8th the bulk of the masses of artillery now concentrating on the Second Army front opened on selected targets in the enemy's hinterland at an intense rate for 5 minutes at 8.45 p.m. and again at 11 p.m. Salutary punishment was inflicted. Strings of ambulance wagons were observed on the roads on the following day, and the lesson was effective.

In the battle of the trench warfare type opportunity for manoeuvre is denied, and there is no sudden clash of the

opposing arms. The positions of the defence are impregnable
to infantry without prolonged artillery preparation. It is
easy to say that the battle is not, properly speaking, initiated
with the swarming of the attacking infantry out of their
assembly trenches. It is more difficult to fix a date marking
a definite commencement. Plans mature, preparations develop,
counter-measures are taken gradually. For our present
purpose we may note that while the general policy had been
long determined and definite preparations in hand weeks
before the beginning of May, the 21st of that month saw the
initiation of the systematic preparatory bombardment of the
enemy's trenches. On that date, therefore, it is convenient
to break the thread of the story. The further activities of
the opposing forces up to the time of the actual infantry
attack may be reserved for a general paragraph dealing with
the initial phases of the battle, which is the subject of the
succeeding chapter.

Certain developments of organisation and changes in appointments may be here briefly reviewed. An additional (Divisional) machine gun company was raised from reinforcements
in England towards the end of 1916, and joined the Division
in February. In the beginning of 1917 an improvised working battalion was formed from surplus personnel in the units
of the Division. The Signal Company establishment was augmented in accordance with G.H.Q. instructions, in view of the
increasing importance attached to artillery communications.
The Sanitary Section was struck off the strength of the
Division and constituted an Army Troops unit, administered
by Corps. A Light Railways Operating Company was formed
in England from men temporarily unfit. It arrived in France
in February and was attached to the Second Army. Of
greater importance was the formation in England of a 4th
Infantry Brigade from the surplus reinforcements sent
monthly from New Zealand. It was raised at the urgent
request of the War Office, anxious to throw the maximum
man-power into the field, on the distinct understanding that
its formation would not involve the provision of additional
reinforcements from New Zealand, and that its personnel
should be utilised, if required, as drafts for the Division. In
the selection of commanders to form the nucleus of the new
units, an opportunity was afforded of promoting officers who
had done good service in the field. Lt.-Col. H. Hart
was appointed to command the new brigade with the rank of
Brigadier-General, the command of 1st Wellington falling

thereupon to Major (now Lt.-Col.) C. F. D. Cook. His Brigade Major was Major T. R. Eastwood who, after doing such good service in the same capacity in the Rifle Brigade, had been forced to relinquish the appointment by sickness, from which he had now recovered. The Brigade Staff Captain was Major H. S. N. Robinson, N.Z.S.C. The battalions were commanded as follows:—

> 3rd Batt. Auckland Regt.—Lt.-Col. D. Blair, M.C.
> 3rd Batt. Wellington Regt.—Lt. Col. W. H. Fletcher
> 3rd Batt. Canterbury Regt.—Lt.-Col. R. A. Row
> 3rd Batt. Otago Regt.—Lt.-Col. D. Colquhoun

Additional units to complete the Brigade Group were formed, including a 4th Machine Gun Company and a 4th Field Ambulance (Major H. J. McLean). Drafts began to be posted at the end of March, and to meet the increased demands for officers likely to be made in the future, a special party of over 100 n.c.o.s and men was selected from the Division and sent to England for training in Cadet colleges. The new brigade trained at Codford. It had the honour of being inspected, with other New Zealand troops, by H. M. the King on 1st May, when the Prime Minister of New Zealand and Sir Joseph Ward were present, and on 10th May by Field-Marshal Viscount French. It proceeded overseas shortly afterwards and arrived at Bailleul at the end of the month. In the spring, also, the 2 composite reserve battalions at Sling of the 4 territorial infantry regiments were expanded into an organisation of 4 battalions, each unit forming a 4th (Reserve) Battalion to the regiment in the field.

In October, Col. Begg was promoted to be D.D.M.S. of II. Anzac, and in his appointment as A.D.M.S., New Zealand Division, was succeeded by Lt.-Col. (now Col.) D. J. McGavin. Lt.-Col. E. J. O'Neill succeeded the latter in command of the New Zealand Stationary Hospital which, leaving Salonica in March 1916 had arrived at Havre in June and been established in Amiens in July. Major (now Lt.-Col.) M. Holmes took over command of No. 1 Field Ambulance. The Divisional Staff sustained a serious loss prior to the Messines operation, when Major Temperley left it for promotion on the Staff of a British Division. He was succeeded as G.S.O. 2 by Captain L. A. Newnham, Middlesex Regiment. In the G.S.O. 3 appointment several changes have to be recorded. Captain Hastings was promoted to fill the Brigade Major's appointment in the Rifle Brigade when Major Eastwood vacated it through sickness, and his place was taken by Major J. E. Duigan, N.Z.S.C., who had been in command of the Tunnelling Company.[1] On Major Duigan's receiving a Staff appointment in the British Army, he was succeeded by Major N. B. W. W. Thoms, N.Z.S.C. Major H. E. Avery, D.S.O., N.Z.S.C., was appointed D.A.Q.M.G. in place of Lt.-Col. N. C. Hamilton, D.S.O., who rejoined the British Army. Lt. S. Cory Wright assumed the duties of Divisional Intelligence Officer in February. On the Brigade Staffs, Capt. T. R. Jackson (General List, British Army) had replaced Capt. M. H. Jackson, who had been wounded on the Somme, and was in turn succeeded as Brigade Major in the 1st Brigade by Major Thoms. The vacant G.S.O. 3 post was now filled by Major W. I. K. Jennings, N.Z.S.C. In the 2nd Brigade, Capt. Richardson and Capt. Wilks had exchanged appointments on the Somme. In the 3rd Brigade, Major Hastings was recalled to India in March. After an interregnum, Capt. R. G. Purdy exchanged his appointment for that of Brigade Major, and was succeeded in the appointment of Staff Captain by Capt. G. C. Dailey.

1 p. 168

CHAPTER V

The Battle of Messines

From the first strategic developments of the war the British Cabinet had regarded as their particular charge the defences which protected the coast line and the approaches to the Channel. The German drive on Calais in the First Battle of Ypres and the second attack in 1915 had been, providentially as it were, frustrated, but the menace of a further thrust was ever present. As it was, the enemy had secured nearly all the ground of tactical importance; and especially in the Ypres salient, commanded as it was by the low ridges to the east, where the German lines hung like an arrested wave ready to topple over and deluge the ruined city, the positions of the British were far from satisfactory. Costly to hold, the feasibility of their continued defence against a third German attack did not present itself as assured to sound military judgment.[1]

Early in 1916 the General Staff had weighed the difficulties involved in the capture of the Ypres ridges and decided that at that stage an attempt would be premature. In the vicinity of the Channel ports, moreover, failure might be attended by momentous consequences. Various preliminary measures, however, and in particular the construction of railways, were taken in hand with a view to the possibility of action at a later date. The development of the submarine campaign from Zeebrugge and Ostend and its crippling effect on the general British effort accentuated attention on the northern sector. A successful attack from this point would rob the enemy of these bases and might not only cut off his troops on the coast, but also compromise his whole position on his right flank. The new armies had been tested in the Somme Battle with satisfactory result, and the postponed operations appeared now feasible. In the Allied conference, therefore, held in November 1916, it was agreed that the main role of the British field forces in 1917 should be an offensive on a large scale in Flanders.

Previous to the main enterprise, however, it was proposed that an attack should be delivered against the salient south of Arras, in which the Germans were now confined by our

---

[1] p. 155.

advance on the Somme. From this earlier operation no great strategical results could be looked for without undue optimism, but besides wiping out the salient it promised useful attrition of the German forces. It might be expected also to preoccupy the enemy's attention ere he realised its conclusion, and thus enable the initial blow of the main attack, the preparations for which could not be concealed, to be delivered before he anticipated it.

The Allies had with reason hoped that the combined offensive planned for all fronts in 1917, the British part in which has been indicated above, would yield decisive and final success. Fate willed, however, otherwise. On the Eastern front, any prospect of effective co-operation was dissipated by the Russian revolution and its aftermath, which were, as events proved, to strengthen the failing powers of the Central Empires and to exert an incalculable influence on the prolongation of the struggle. As the general Allied policy was thus upset, so too in the first months of the new year the British plans underwent considerable alterations. They were largely modified by the German withdrawal to the Hindenburg or Siegfried line, and they were vitally affected by a new plan of attack laid down for the French Army by General Nivelle and accepted by the Allied Governments. To his bold conception of a great break-through from the Aisne heights at the southern pivot of the Hindenburg Line, with the capture of Laon as the first day's objective, all other proposals of operations on the Western front were subordinated. As a preparatory measure to it the British front was extended. General Haig's attack at Arras was to be proceeded with at an earlier date than at first contemplated, and with the additional object of attracting hostile forces from the French front. Nor was this all. The main offensive task of the British was altered from the original plans to the more subsidiary role of co-operation in exploiting the gains to be won by the French. Only in the event of these advantages failing to accrue within a reasonable period would the original proposal of the attack in the north hold good. The work of preparation in Flanders was therefore somewhat restricted owing to the demands for the necessary labour in the south.

In pursuance of these plans the Battle of Arras was fought in the beginning of April by the Third and First British Armies, the former now commanded by the same General Horne under whom as Corps Commander the Divi-

sion had won its first laurels on the Somme. Subsidiary
operations were conducted at the same time by the Fourth
and Fifth Armies threatening the Hindenburg Line. In the
vast preliminary underground operations at Arras substantial
assistance was given by a detachment of the New Zealand
Pioneers, who were despatched thither at the end of 1916,
and by the New Zealand Tunnelling Company. This latter
unit, formed in New Zealand in October 1915, went to the
Arras neighbourhood on arrival in France in March 1916.
The company was originally commanded by Major J. E.
Duigan, N.Z.S.C., and later, on his accepting a Staff appointment, by Capt. (now Major) H. Vickerman. They left an
abiding mark of their work in the New Zealand place-
names given to the subterranean caves and galleries which
they opened up, such as "Nelson," "Blenheim," and "New
Plymouth," and the following letters written prior to the
Battle of Arras indicate the appreciation with which their
services were regarded:—

To Commander Third Army.

I wish to bring to the Army Commander's notice the
excellent work done by the New Zealand Engineers Tunnelling Company during the past twelve months. First
under Major Duigan and now under Captain Vickerman
the work of the company has been excellent. Not only
have the men worked extremely hard and well, but the
excellent relations that have been maintained with the
various Divisions show a first-class organisation. I attach
a copy of a report I have received from the G.O.C. 3rd
Division which expresses clearly the opinion held by the
Divisions in the line of the New Zealand Tunnelling
Company.

A. Haldane,
Lieut.-General, Commanding VI. Corps.

To VI. Corps.

I wish to bring to the notice of the Corps Commander
the excellent work and willing help of the N.Z.E. Tunnelling Company in all their undertakings with the 3rd
Division. All work has been punctually and thoroughly
carried out to my entire satisfaction without a hitch or
difficulty of any kind.

C. J. Deverell,
Major-General, Commanding 3rd Division.

The fruits of the first phase of the Arras operations were
substantial, and Sir Douglas Haig would probably have been

well content to have stopped the offensive at that point. But it was part of the general policy to maintain the pressure while Nivelle's grand attack by 4 French Armies burst out on the Aisne. The French struck on 16th April. Their dream of a break-through was shattered by the German machine guns. It became speedily apparent that the day of rapid and extensive operations in open country was not yet. On 5th May, with the capture of the long plateau north of the Aisne traversed by the Chemin des Dames, the French effort was brought to a conclusion. The Fabian policy of the limited offensive pursued by methodical progress was again endorsed, and Pétain succeeded Nivelle.[1]

The French attack failing in its main objects, Haig's armies were thus released for the originally planned and now delayed attack in the northern theatre. For the purpose of diversion minor operations were continued by the British southern Armies.

Before the principal blow could be delivered in Flanders, it was essential to capture the strongly fortified, if not impregnable, ridge which leaving the southern tip of the Ypres salient stretched south-east past Wytschaete and Messines to the Douve valley. From it the enemy commanded unique observation over the whole of the British lines about Ypres, and from it they were in a position to strike at the flank of any attack originating within the salient further north. It was with the object of removing at once this observation and this menace to the right flank of the main operation that the Battle of Messines was fought. It is not merely connected with but is an integral part of the tremendous Third Battle of Ypres.

While some of the assaulting Divisions were faced by outliers and subsidiary ridges, the New Zealanders lay directly against the main bastion, separated from it only by the shallow valley down which the Steenebeek streamlet ran sluggishly to join the Douve. The Steenebeek was half choked in places by debris or shattered culverts, and had formed small swamps. It was, however, narrow and shallow, measuring from bank to bank some 5 feet. Its bed was soft and muddy, and torn coils of wire had been strung along it by earlier garrisons. Constant reconnaissance had proved that while it might prove an obstacle to tanks it would not

---

1 On the inner history of the French offensive and on the causes of Nivelle's failure much light is thrown in an article by M. Paul Painlevé, who was at the time Minister of War. His statements are summarised in *The Times*, 1st Nov. 1919.

stop assaulting infantry. At the foot of the ridge and again
on the crest the 2 front systems of German defences were
clearly visible. On the top of the ridge, along which the
Armentiéres-Ypres road ran through Messines towards Wytschaete, the skyline was broken by the roofs of the village
of Messines and the medieval masonry of its church. Information obtained from civilian records, refugees, and the survivors of the 1914 fighting was circulated concerning the
deep cellars under the Institution Royale[1] and other features
of military importance in the village. From Hill 63 partial
observation was obtained of the tree-bordered road known as
Huns' Walk, that ran from Messines eastwards towards the
hamlet of Gapaard and the town of Comines, the base of all
German traffic in the area immediately north of the Lys.
Two miles to the east on the reverse slopes of the ridge this
road crossed the first of the enemy's 2 trench systems that
ran from the Lys across the base of the Messines-Wytschaete
salient towards his lines at Ypres. This first system, which
lay just beyond Gapaard and the village of Oosttaverne,
further to the north opposite Wytschaete, was called the
Oosttaverne Line. A mile further back was the Warneton
Line. For the moment the Oosttaverne Line was to be the
limit of our objective.

In addition to the German earthworks on the ridge, concrete abounded everywhere—machine gun emplacements, observation posts and dugouts, and in particular the defence
relied on a number of very substantial Strong Points,
small fortresses of heavily reinforced concrete, each of
which contained 2 or 3 machine guns and a garrison
varying from 15 to 40 soldiers. Half-way up the
hill in front of the New Zealanders were the cellared
ruins of an old inn, "Au Bon Fermier Cabaret," at
the point where the country road from Le Rossignol and
Stinking Farm in our lines meets the main Armentières-Ypres
road from Ploegsteert village and Hyde Park Corner. Further
to the north at the left flank of the Division the road from
Wulverghem, bordered by shell-stricken tree-stumps, ran
straight up the hill to the northern end of the village, and
half-way up the slopes it also was joined by a sunken road
which led from Birthday Farm on the left. At this junction
stood the shattered remains of a mill, the Moulin de l'Hospice,
set on a high knoll and surrounded by a trench. Birthday

1 A Roman Catholic Orphanage for girls. At an earlier date the Mother
Superior had cheerfully assented to and witnessed from behind our lines a British
bombardment of her Institution.

THE TUNNELLING COY. EXPLODE CAPTURED AMMUNITION

AND STACK CAPTURED TIMBER

THE WULVERGHEM-MESSINES ROAD

SHELLS BURSTING ON MESSINES

Farm was just included within the left boundary of the Division's area. The inn, the mill, and the farm, no less than the La Petite Douve Ferme defences, might be expected to form centres of resistance, and specially detailed troops would be required to deal with each.

Pending the delivery of Nivelle's attack on the Aisne, the labour and material available for the Flanders offensive was only such as could be obtained on the spot; but the preparations which had been undertaken since the end of 1916 were developed steadily as far as the means at hand permitted.

"A large railway programme had been commenced. and as soon as it was possible to divert larger supplies northwards, work was pushed on with remarkable speed. Great progress was made with road construction, and certain roads were selected for extension as soon as our objectives could be gained. Forward dumps of material were made for this purpose, and in the days following the 7th June roads were carried forward with great rapidity to Messines, Wytschaete, and Oosttaverne, across country so completely destroyed by shell-fire that it was difficult to trace where the original road had run.

"A special problem arose in connection with the water supply. Pipe lines were taken well forward from existing lakes, from catch-pits constructed on the Kemmel Hills, and from sterilising barges on the Lys. Provision was made for the rapid extension of these lines. By the 15th June they had reached Messines, Wytschaete, and the Dammstrasse, and were supplying water at the rate of between 450,000 and 600,000 gallons daily."[1]

All the while underground there were being actively pursued operations and counter-operations which were to give a special character to the eventual attack.

"The inception of a deep mining offensive on the Second Army front dated from July, 1915, but the proposal to conduct offensive mining on a grand scale was not definitely adopted till January, 1916. From that date onwards, as the necessary labour became available, deep mining for offensive purposes gradually developed, in spite of great difficulties from water-bearing strata and active counter-mining by the enemy.

"In all, twenty-four mines were constructed, four of which were outside the front ultimately selected for our offensive, while one other was lost as the result of a mine

1 Official Despatch.

13

blown up by the enemy. Many of these mines had been completed for twelve months prior to our offensive, and constant and anxious work was needed to ensure their safety. The enemy also had a deep mining system, and was aware of his danger.''[1]

The final progress of the general preparations above ground was expedited by uniformly fine weather. A certain amount of the personnel necessary for the purpose was supplied by the various labour companies, but the bulk was drawn from the infantry. During May the network of broad and narrow gauge railways and trench tramways was developed by extensive ramifications. Ammunition stations, sidings, and forward dumps multiplied. An infinite number of new gun positions was constructed by the New Zealand gunners for the incoming artillery, and heavy and field guns were steadily brought into the area and formed into different groups. In addition to a stupendous mass of field artillery the II. Anzac armament included a 15-in. howitzer, a 12-in. and a 9.2-in. gun, over fifty 60-pounders, six 12-in. howitzers, over thirty 9.2-in., the same number of 8-in., and over a hundred 6-in. howitzers.[2] As early as the middle of May some of the batteries were in forward emplacements under skilfully erected camouflage which merged with the natural grass and foliage, and by midnight 2nd/3rd June all pieces were in their Magnum Opus positions, and the trees which blocked the line of fire had been levelled. Long ere then, too, forward positions had been selected and prepared for guns of all calibres to occupy as soon as the crest was carried. A vast effort, amply repaid, was spent in the extension of the tramway or light railway systems to the battery positions.

The general preparatory bombardment may be dated from 21st May, though already 10 days previously orders had been given for our artillery activity to increase gradually till the end of the month. A systematic study of the enemy's defences by means of direct observation, air photographs, prisoners' statements and other means of information enabled a methodical progressive destruction to be carried out of each feature in turn of his fortifications. The heavy howitzers and long-range guns undertook counter-battery work with balloon and aeroplane observation and made preliminary registrations to cover the approaches and bridges over the Lys and

1   Official Despatch.
2   Four of the new 6-in. trench mortars were also included.

the Ypres-Comines canal. Comines Houthem Warneton Basseville and other villages were subjected to periodical bombardments. All wire visible from ground observation was dealt with by light and medium howitzers, with non-delay fuses and with the closest co-operation of the air service. On the visible wire before the 2 front systems the 18-pounders and trench mortars dealt continual and increasing havoc. Divisions vied in the expenditure of mortar ammunition. On the morning of 3rd June the New Zealand heavy mortars fired no less than 227 rounds and the medium mortars 1950 rounds, a total which may be expected to compare favourably with that achieved by any similar unit in the war. The strong concrete emplacements uncovered on the hillside were first engaged by the heavy howitzers and heavy mortars, and after the concrete was broken the work of destruction was continued by the 6-in. and 4.5-in. howitzers. With the destruction effected in his front line by our mortars the enemy was unable to keep pace. He withdrew the bulk of his garrison to the support line, leaving only such sentry posts as had concrete shelter.

As at the Somme, night firing was employed to prevent the repair of the enemy's defences and to interfere with his communications, and the roads on which no ground observation was possible were also harassed by day. In barraging the roads, a short sharp bombardment was put down at a selected point so as to cause a halt in a column of transport approaching that point. The road in rear was then searched up and down with shrapnel for a space of 1000 yards to catch the blocked column. One of the ingenious features of the artillery policy was to drill the enemy into using certain roads and forming blocks of transport at certain points which he considered safe. These points were left to be dealt with on the nights immediately preceding the attack. Gas was discharged or projected frequently on the La Petite Douve Ferme defences and elsewhere.

Messines itself had been shelled repeatedly and with special violence on 17th and 24th May, when enormous pieces of timber and debris were flung high into the sky, and the whole crest veiled in clouds of smoke that made observation impossible. On 30th May it was again subjected to a concentrated bombardment by Army and Corps heavies both in the morning and evening, and similarly on the "U," "V" and "W" days, preceding the "Z" day of the attack. On these days practice barrages and bombardments were fired by the Corps or Army artillery, partly to force the enemy to disclose his batteries and partly to test our barrage. On 5th June an opportunity was given to effect final improvement in technical points by an Army practice barrage, under cover of which, as we shall see, the 2nd Rifles executed a daring raid in broad daylight.

In the successive bombardments and barrages on Messines the machine guns co-operated actively, firing from localities appreciably distant from their battle positions. On these and on the dugouts in their vicinity, designed to hold spare personnel, reserve ammunition and belt-filling machines, they devoted much labour, which it was very important to disguise. They avoided breaking new soil or piling new earth on the parapets, and all their work was carried out by night, the results being screened before dawn.

This deadly bombardment and counter-battery work, which the enemy endeavoured to hinder with smoke screens, grew in intensity during the 10 days preceding the assault. "Harassing fire" was now directed nightly on railway junctions, unloading points, and all known transport halting places and approaches, special arrangements being made to ensure that there should be no pause between the night firing and the activity which began with daylight. Even now, however, the full weight of artillery was not revealed. Not more than half the total number of guns in action had been disclosed at any one time till "U" day, and even then only three-quarters were to be in action simultaneously till the attack should be launched on "Z" day. For the final 3 days of preparation, the counter-battery work took precedence of the bombardment of the trenches and achieved marked successes. The enemy's field guns were largely destroyed or forced to withdraw to fresh positions in rear, the heavies behind the Comines Canal and a considerable proportion of the field guns behind Warneton. As a result his retaliation in the latter period of the artillery conflict was marked by an absence of field guns, and at the actual outbreak of the battle many of these were in process of moving eastwards. During the last few days before the attack the German counter-battery work also decreased and became erratic. Information was afterwards vouchsafed by a prisoner that on the night 6th/7th June no fewer than 11 guns including 4 heavies were "knocked out" in a single artillery group.

During the earlier part of May, as has been seen,[1] the enemy had endeavoured with limited success to acquire information with regard to the frequent changes of our dispositions and the amount of work in our back areas. The vast preparations later becoming daily more visible could leave him in no doubt, but his infantry remained unenterprising and inaggressive. On the other hand his artillery activity developed. His retaliation to our bombardments at the outset was mostly confined to field guns, but by 20th May his batteries, like his garrisons, had been reinforced, particularly with his useful 5.9-in. howitzers, and while leaving the forward infantry positions completely unmolested, he became increasingly active with gas and explosive on roads and batteries. The evening sky was continually lit up by the glare of our burning dumps. Neuve Eglise and the other villages in rear were violently bombarded from Warneton and from Frélinghien and the German positions south of the Lys, and distant Bailleul was shelled on 3rd and 5th June in the morning and afternoon with heavy long-range guns. The German counter-battery work was directed specially on the batteries on and behind Hill 63. On 5th June English gunners attached to the 1st Brigade Group received unwelcome attention. Their positions were in an open field, and the artificial camouflage, erected over the guns, instead of concealing them, actually attracted notice in aeroplane photographs. The camouflage caught fire, and 13,000 shells and 5 guns were destroyed. It was at this time that a gallant action was performed by Lt. C. T. Gillespie, of the 7th Battery, assisted by Fitter H. Selby and Gunner L. D. Belton. A shell struck a pile of boxed ammunition at the gun-pit, and the boxes caught fire. Gillespie, with these 2 men, taking no heed of the bursting explosive and shrapnel, separated the burning boxes and extinguished the fire.

Though the British held marked ascendancy in the sky, every effort was made by the Germans to utilise their air service at high altitudes, which our squadrons could not patrol, for bombing and reconnaissance. And in the early morning and again in the evening, after our aeroplanes went home, they repeatedly hovered over our line. Thus on 4th June 2 aeroplanes reconnoitred the batteries of the 1st Brigade for some time till chased off by shrapnel. They flew at a height of 300 feet, and the observers could be seen taking photographs. On a Sunday afternoon in April, when the

1 p. 161.

streets were crowded with soldiers and civilians, a bomb fell
on Bailleul from a height of 12,000 feet, causing several
casualties. Early in the morning of 5th June 3 bombs
were dropped on the great Duke of York Siding near the
same town, setting an ammunition train on fire. The train
and the siding dumps burnt all day, and the railway line
and the houses in the vicinity were damaged by the series of
explosions.

In the general preparations the New Zealand Division
played their full part. The expenditure of shells rose
steadily.[1] The multifarious tasks that fell to the Engineers
Pioneers and Infantry included the laying of an elaborate
buried cable system,[2] the excavation of advanced headquarters
dugouts for battalion and brigade headquarters, the construction of signal dugouts, relay-posts for runners and
stretcher-bearers, regimental aid posts and advanced dressing
stations, the tunnelling of new catacombs in Hill 63 for the
accommodation of the Divisional reserves, the formation of
forward dumps, the screening of approaches, the clearing of
obstacles behind our front line, the thinning of the thick
hedgerows in No Man's Land, the preparation of portable
bridges over the Douve and Steenebeek. Above all, the
infantry were engaged in the completion and draining of the
assembly trenches and the arrangements for rapid egress
from them. The sector bore many names reminiscent of
former Canadian occupation, and now, like the Tunnellers at
Arras, the New Zealand battalions christened the new works
in memory of their homes. Thus to Medicine Hat Trail and
Calgary and Toronto Avenues were added Otira Otago and
Auckland Trenches, and the congeries of names significantly
reflected the co-operation of 2 widely separated Dominions
in the Empire's cause.

Nightly reconnaissances were made of the enemy line by
patrols who examined the wire and trenches and occasionally
captured a prisoner from his posts. The work done by the
2nd Rifles in this connection merits special mention. On the
night of 16th May a small party under L.-Cpl. E. E. Islip
could find no Germans. Two night later another party, under
2nd Lt. R. P. Vaughan and including Islip, visited La Petite
Douve Ferme just after midnight. Nearing the position, they

1 Between noon 31st May and noon 7th June the artillery attached to the
Division fired 126,200 rounds of 18-pounder and 33,700 rounds of 4.5-in.
howitzer ammunition.
2 In cable-burying the II. Anzac Cyclist Battalion rendered conspicuously
useful service.

crouched in a shellhole in front of the enemy parapet. Generally the trench was known to be damaged, but opposite the shellhole was a concrete shelter with 2 loopholes. A hissing bomb came flying out of one of these and wounded a member of the patrol. The others immediately scrambled out of the shellhole and charged the trench. There were a dozen Germans in the dugout. When called on to put up their hands they made no move to come out and showed fight. Two bombs were thrown in to make sure. One exploded. All the occupants were killed save 1, and he was wounded To save his life he must get rid of the second bomb. He stooped down for it, secured it, and crawled painfully and hastily up the steps, with one hand holding his side and the other gripping the bomb. Ere he could fling it from him, it exploded. It blew the German to pieces, killed Islip and wounded Vaughan and 3 of his party. As the raiders carried back their casualties, rifle and machine gun fire was opened on them, and 1 further man was wounded.

Under cover of artillery the 2nd Rifles carried out a further enterprise on the night 21st/22nd May on the north edge of the Farm. Some way off, 2 Germans were seen running in from a listening post, but the trenches were found battered and empty. The dugout bombed on the 18th/19th had in the meantime been damaged by our mortars, and the entrance was found blocked by debris. Finally, on the afternoon of "X" day (5th June), the same battalion made a very thorough reconnaissance of the Farm, under cover of the now perfected Army practice barrage. The party, including a few sappers, was commanded by Lt. L. I. Manning. Grenades and rifle fire were directed from the support trench in rear, but the position itself was found deserted. The enemy's most advanced defences had been rendered by our mortars and artillery untenable.[1] 2 dugouts of the 3 which were found to have survived bombardment and were still habitable were now blown up by our party with ammonal. The enterprise was highly successful but was marred by an accident at its close. Three of the party, engrossed in private investigations, did not return with the others, and Manning, disregarding the snipers, went straightway back for them. On his return journey, being short of wind after the double trip, he flung himself for a minute's rest into the shelter of a shellhole, and Capt. S. A. Atkinson,

[1] At midnight, 1st/2nd June, a Stokes (light trench mortar) gas-bomb bombardment was carried out on the Farm by the Special Bde, R.E. It appears probable that its reputation caused us to attach overmuch importance to the Farm.

watching from our parapet, thought he had fallen wounded. With true spirit of comradeship he ran out to help him and was killed by an unlucky shot through the throat. The others returned safely.

Mention should also be made of a particularly valuable reconnaissance over the enemy front system carried out on the evening of 1st June by Major J. Hargest, the Second in Command of 1st Otago, who was rapidly coming into prominence as one of the finest soldiers in the Division. In company with a n.c.o. he explored the German front line and went nearly 200 yards up the communication trench to near the support line, when the enemy's night sentries taking up their posts in the front line behind him made it necessary to withdraw.

In the preliminary instructions issued to the troops, the purpose of the forthcoming attack was veiled as an effort undertaken to compel the enemy to withdraw his reserves from the main battle front at Arras. The aim of the Second Army was to seize the whole 6 miles' length of the ridge from its southern base at St. Yves to its junction with the hills of the salient beyond Wytschaete, to capture as many as possible of the enemy's guns in the vicinity of Oosttaverne and to the north-east of Messines, to consolidate a line which would secure possession of the ridge, and to establish a forward position on which counter-attacks could be met at a safe distance from the crest. The requisite amount of elbow room would be given by the capture of the Oosttaverne Line, and this accordingly was fixed as the final objective. To secure all the fruits of a surprise attack and to effect the capture of guns it was imperative that the attack should be pushed through in 1 day. The troops available for the operations were, from right to left, II. Anzac, the IX. Corps and the X. Corps. In reserve was the XIV. Corps, which had in the Battle of the Somme been on the right of the XV.

Under General Godley's command at the beginning of May were the 57th, the 3rd Australian, the New Zealand and the 25th Divisions. The Corps was reinforced in the middle of the month by the 4th Australian Division from I. Anzac, then forming part of the Fifth Army. The Divisions earmarked for the attack lay approximately in their assembly areas. On the right, from St. Yves to the Douve, the 3rd Australian Division held a frontage of some 2000 yards. The New Zealanders, in the centre, from the Douve to just

north of the Wulverghem-Messines road occupied some 1500
yards. On the left, where II. Anzac were divided from the
IX. Corps at the Wulverghem-Wytschaete road, the frontage
allotted to the 25th Division was still narrower, in view of
the greater distance that lay between them and the crest.
On the Corps front south of the Lys the 57th Division had
extended their positions[1] to the north to include the subsectors
of l'Epinette and Houplines just south of the river, and now
held a frontage of 18,000 yards, formerly garrisoned by 3
Divisions, each with 2 strong brigades in the line. Towards
the end of May, to relieve the Second Army and II. Anzac
of responsibilities outside the active area, the 57th Division
sector right up to the Lys was transferred to the XI. Corps
of the First Army. The defensive front of the Corps, as con-
trasted with the offensive front on which the 3 Divisions
were preparing their spring on Messines, was thus restricted
to the short sector from the Lys to St. Yves, held by the
3rd Australian Division. To relieve its garrison a separate
force of 2 battalions of the already extended 57th Division
was brought up on 3rd June north of the Lys and attached
for tactical purposes to the 3rd Australians.

The tasks laid down for the Corps were the taking of
Messines, the capture of as many guns as possible within the
area of its further advance, and the consolidation of the
southern part of the new British line, which would run from
St. Yves across the slopes of the ridge to meet the Oosttaverne trenches east of Messines and thence along them to
the Corps' northern boundary. The furthermost objective in
the Oosttaverne system, roughly 1 mile forward of the crest,
was known as the Green Line. The position defined as
the reserve line of occupation some 500 yards east of Messines on the eastern and southern slopes back to the Douve
was designated the Black Line. The 3 Divisions, the
3rd Australian on the right, the New Zealand in the centre
and the 25th on the left, would advance abreast to the Black
Line, the New Zealand Division occupying Messines. The
capture of the Green Line was allotted to the 4th Australian
Division, which would pass through the New Zealand and
25th Divisions. The troops entrusted with the establishment
of the Black Line were ordered on reaching it to push out
patrols, to capture the enemy guns and establish posts on a
Black Dotted Line some 300 yards in front, which would act
first as a stepping-stone to the Green Line and then after the

1 p. 153.

4th Australians' advance as a support position to it. While the seizure of the Oosttaverne trenches was committed mainly to the 4th Australians, the occupation of a small triangle of country in front of the 3rd Australians on the Black Line, necessary to round off the right flank from the Green Line back to the projection of the newly won ground about St. Yves, would be carried out by one of the 3rd Australian Division's battalions.

The assaulting positions of the 3rd Australians and the New Zealanders lay in a line, and no difficulty faced the Staff in synchronising their advance. At the left boundary of the New Zealanders, however, an awkward problem presented itself. Here the German trenches bulged out westwards over the Steenebeek valley and up the rising ground on its right bank, where they included the ruins of a large farm called Ontario, from which point they turned again northwards along the IX. Corps' front. As a result of this, the 25th Division's trenches lay 600-800 yards echeloned in rear of the remainder of the Corps' front. So too the German support positions in the upper Steenebeek valley, opposite the 25th Division, enfiladed the passage of the New Zealanders across No Man's Land. To bring all assaulting troops into line, it might have been thought feasible to launch the 25th Division and the northern troops some minutes before the 2 Overseas Divisions, but in that case the enemy barrage would have time to come down on the front line and catch the Australians and New Zealanders in their assembly trenches. It was vital that all along the front as many of the attacking troops as possible should have crossed into the enemy's country before his protective curtain of fire fell. The advance, therefore, must start simultaneously.

This point once settled, arrangements were made that the left flank of the New Zealanders' line, placed so awkwardly in front of the 25th Division at the outset of the attack, should be protected and guided by an enfilade barrage, which would be gradually followed up by the creeping frontal barrage of the 25th Division. Smoke clouds could also, if necessary, be discharged on the slopes of the upper Steenebeek valley, and Ontario Farm would be hurled sky-high by means of our mines which lay under it. The New Zealand left as it advanced would be swung back along the boundary line to ensure a flank defence; and the halts were so arranged that the 25th Division would catch up just short of the Ypres road running along the crest, and thereafter would continue in line. A corresponding manoeuvre was to take place at a later stage on the boundary between the 25th Division and the IX. Corps.

On this rapid crossing of No Man's Land ere the German barrage fell, great emphasis was laid in the Divisional plans, and it was largely with this end in view that the numerous lines of assembly trenches had been constructed. For the same reason the first New Zealand objective was fixed, not at the German front line, where delay might cause congestion in No Man's Land, but at the support line. And the front line trenches had been so battered that serious resistance in them need not be anticipated.

The role allotted to the Division was the storming of Messines, the consolidation of the Black Line within the New Zealanders' boundaries, the establishment of a series of Strong Points on the Black Dotted Line, and the capture of any enemy guns within their area. These objectives fell naturally into 3 phases, firstly the capture of the trenches on the west slope and of the village with the ring of trenches immediately surrounding it, secondly the capture and consolidation of the Black Line, and thirdly the establishment of the Strong Points on the Black Dotted Line and the capture of the guns. The first phase, including as it did the capture of the 2 front systems of defence (the Blue and Brown Lines) and the village, bristled with difficulties and necessitated the employment of 2 brigades which would advance side by side. The second and third phases in the comparatively open country might be left to 1 brigade. For the capture of the crest and the village 2 battalions in each brigade sector would advance side by side and carry the first and second trench systems, and 1 strengthened battalion in each sector would divide the village between them. Half of each battalion would pass through the village to its further ring of defences and half remain to deal with the garrison. In the capture of each successive objective the "leap-frog" principle of advance was to be observed. Separate units were told off for the capture and consolidation of definite positions, and through them would pass fresh troops destined for further objectives.

The 3rd and 2nd Brigades were ordered to carry out the first phase and the 1st Brigade the second and third. Brigade and battalion plans were scrutinised at conferences at Divisional headquarters, which at the end of April had moved to Westhof Farm, near Neuve Eglise. There, on 24th May,

Sir Douglas Haig visited General Russell to express his approval and confidence.

Of the 20 tanks put at the disposal of the Corps, 12 had been allotted to the Division. Their routes and tasks were carefully defined, and special bridges were constructed for their use over the Douve. In addition to the medium and heavy howitzers and guns of the Corps, the Division was directly supported by nineteen 18-pounder batteries and six 4.5-in. howitzer batteries. A field gun was available for every 7 yards of enemy front. The 2nd (Army) Artillery Brigade supported the 25th Division's attack. Special arrangements were made to give the artillery transport increased mobility.

Not the least interesting provision for facilitating the advance of the infantry was the formation of barrages by the machine guns, of which 144 were arranged along the Corps' front to sweep a line 500 yards in front of the advancing bayonets. The New Zealand attack was supported by 56 machine guns, divided for tactical purposes into 3 groups. Each assaulting brigade retained 8 of their guns for direct co-operation. The remainder, with those of the Divisional Company[1] and of the newly arrived 4th Infantry Brigade, were employed under Divisional control. Like the artillery, the machine guns would maintain their normal harassing fire on communications throughout the final night, but at zero they would put down stationary and creeping barrages, lifting by 100 yards at a time as far as the crest of the ridge. On the capture of the trenches on the crest, 2 groups would move forward to the ridge to deal with any hostile attack on the Black Line, and later advance again to support the 4th Australians' attack on the Green Line with similar standing and creeping barrages.

From 1st June the New Zealand lines were held thinly by 1 battalion at a time, and though the area and especially the communication trenches were periodically shelled in retaliation for our bombardments, the troops, well disposed in depth, suffered few casualties. Two battalions were in support on and behind Hill 63. The reserves of officers and specialists forming the "B Teams" that would not be put into the battle had been sent to the Corps Reinforcement Camp at Morbecque. The 1st Infantry Brigade was now on its way back from Tilques, and the bulk of the other 2 brigades were enjoying a few days' rest in concentration areas immediately in rear. They were somewhat

1 p. 163.

harassed by the high-velocity naval guns from the Lille defences, but though sleep was thus broken the fine weathei and the respite from the shell-fire of the trenches were keenly appreciated, and it was with assurance and optimism that all looked forward to the forthcoming venture. Each platoon and section was fully conversant with the role it would be called on to play and had studied the trenches and the terrain of the ridge on the great relief clay model, as large as a tennis court, whose erection exemplified the minute elaboration of the preparations for the battle. On 3rd June the 1st Infantry Brigade relieved the 2nd Brigade in the line.

On the afternoon of the 6th a company of 1st Canterbury were having tea on the slopes of Hill 63 when 3 shells fell without warning in the crowd round the dixies, and 30 men were wounded or killed. No misadventure, how-ever, befell the small advance parties of the assaulting brigades that took over the line from 2nd Auckland. In the late evening their fellows left the concentration areas, and marched up to the trenches by specially pegged and marked overland routes which were employed to avoid con-gestion and shelling on the main roads. A thunderstorm had cleared the sultry air, and the night was cool and fresh. All over the Army front innumerable platoons of the different Divisions were moving at 200 yards' distance from each other. No match was struck to light pipe or cigarette, and high overhead aeroplanes guarded the sky. On the right an Australian brigade was heavily gas shelled. Gas and lachry-matory shells fell also with their characteristic soft explosions in the New Zealand area, especially about Hill 63, where Advanced Divisional Headquarters were obliged to wear gas respirators for 6 hours prior to zero. The infantry suffered less. Few duties are more laborious than groping one's way up dark saps in respirators, but with order and precision the troops filed into the trenches, and thanks to good gas dis-cipline suffered but few casualties.[1] The machine gunners, who had moved to their positions on the previous evening and remained under cover during the day, now completed their emplacements or finally cleared their lines of fire.

Every possible precaution was taken to avoid confusion and disguise the assembly. Telephone communication was absolutely forbidden, and all the code messages reporting completion of assembly, such as that of the Rifle Brigade:

---

[1] The German gas shelling was favoured by a gentle steady easterly wind, owing to which our own proposed gas attack had to be cancelled.

"Working Party will report as ordered at 9 a.m. to-morrow" were sent by runner. Watches were for a last time synchronised with the standard time communicated to Corps from the Eiffel Tower and brought to brigade headquarters by a Divisional Staff Officer. By 2 a.m. (7th June) everyone was in his place in the numbered firebays. The right was in close touch with the extreme left wing of the Australians, which was accommodated north of the Douve to avoid crossing the river in No Man's Land. The liaison officers and n.c.o.s were with flank formations. The Divisional reserves, consisting of the Engineer Field Companies and the Pioneer Battalion, were in the galleries under Hill 63 or in back areas. Shortly afterwards tanks crept up to behind our support line. Underground the tunnellers waited, watch in hand, for the appointed second. The elaborate mechanism was now fully wound up, and the moment of the culminating point of the battle, so long and laboriously prepared for, was fast approaching, when the bayonets of the infantry would complete the work of the artillery and other arms.

In these congested trenches a bombardment would cause destruction and demoralisation. Arrangements had been made, therefore, that enemy shelling of our trenches should be frustrated by prompt and overwhelming counter-battery work. Should such bombardment arise within 30 minutes of zero, a S.O.S. signal would not be answered by our field artillery, in order that there might be no danger of our infantry mistaking retaliatory action for the opening of the barrage. Though our batteries, however, received the usual attention, our forward areas were left unmolested by artillery fire, and shortly after midnight the enemy gas shelling ceased. Fully anticipating our attack, the German Command did not expect it for some days yet, and his intention was to relieve with fresh troops the Divisions on the ridge, sorely tried by our unceasing bombardment. That very night, indeed, reliefs were being carried out on the silent hillside. Opposite the 25th Division the trenches were crowded with incoming and outgoing Saxons and Bavarians. In Messines the infantry exchanges had been completed, and troops of the 40th Division (Saxons) and the 3rd Bavarian Division held the line opposite the New Zealand front. The machine gun reliefs, however, were still in progress and were to be caught in the storm.

Up to the moment of attack our own artillery and machine guns maintained their normal activity without either slackening or intensifying. It was a fine night, lit up in the earlier hours by a full moon. Before the trenches, patrols covered No Man's Land with special vigilance; others examined the bridges over the Steenebeek, and where necessary repaired them, or laid guiding tapes from the bridges to the top of our parapets, or placed duckboards across the front trenches as bridges for the troops in rear. By 3 a.m. the parties in No Man's Land had withdrawn to the trenches, and at that hour the stormers silently fixed bayonets.

The moment of assault was fixed at 10 minutes past 3. The moon had now sunk below the horizon. The morning was dark and misty, but the first streaks of dawn just enabled close objects to be discerned. A minute or two before zero, some machine guns anticipated the barrage, but were fortunately not taken seriously by the enemy. Within a few seconds of the proper time the mines were sprung at Factory Farm, just beyond the right of the Australians, and at Anton's Farm Road, in the centre of their position. On the other flank of the New Zealanders one at Ontario Farm, in reality of lesser dimensions but appearing owing to its proximity even more stupendous, caused the bottom of their trenches to heave and rock, and the volcano of jagged crimson-red flames lit up the forms of our infantry moving over the parapet.

Ten seconds after the explosion of the mines and the opening roar of our artillery and machine gun barrages, the dark hillside under Messines was illuminated by the white rockets and white flares bursting into 2 green stars of the German S.O.S., and the observers on Hill 63 witnessed an astonishingly beautiful display of fireworks stretching away north as far as the eye could see. There were the unseen enemy, now all too certain that the awaited British attack had in the end surprised them.

The German guns had been located by their activity during our barrage feints. The effect of the deluge of gas and high-explosive with which they were drenched at the moment of zero by our heavies was instantaneous. They at once ceased the sporadic shelling of the batteries that had continued through the night, but it was not till 10 minutes later that their barrage fell about No Man's Land. Even then it was thin and irregular, and it was directed at now empty front lines. For, moving forward with the rapidity and ease born of frequent practice at Tilques, all 8 battalions of our 2 assaulting brigades were clear of our

trenches in 7 minutes. Later the hostile barrage extended to
the 1st Brigade trenches in rear without inflicting serious
casualties. It descended with more weight on the 25th Division.
The Douve chanced to mark a boundary between 2 different
German Armies, the Fourth on the north and the Sixth on
the south, and the Australians, who faced the latter, were
hampered by a second heavy barrage of gas.

In view of the tiers of trenches on the hillside it had
been decided to put standing barrages on them from the
outset rather than devote part of the artillery to cover the
infantry across the 200 yards' breadth of No Man's Land.
It was from the German front line onwards that the creeping
18-pounder barrage advanced up the hill, protecting with
its mighty shield the assaulting waves. Up to this date no
barrage had been more scientifically planned, nor was one
even later to be more admirably executed, and it was spoken
of long afterwards by the infantry, ever sufficiently severe
critics, with enthusiasm. Carefully calculated on the probable pace of the waves and their varying progress as they
would be faced by difficulties of ground or points of resistance, It rolled up majestically to the support line, lifting 100
yards every 2 minutes. From there uphill to the trenches
on the crest, It stretched forth Its destructive hand more
slowly, taking 3 minutes to the 100 yards. Through
Messines, in view of the difficulties of mopping up, 11
minutes elapsed from every 100 yards' lift. Once over the
hill and in the open country It again hastened Its stride.
The 18-pounder standing barrage waited for It and then
lifted to the next trench. A standing 4.5-in. howitzer barrage
fell 300 yards ahead of the infantry. The standing barrages
of the medium and heavy howitzers were established on successive trenches and Strong Points within the limits of safety
(400 yards) for the advancing waves.

Till the last possible minute every part of the area
through which the infantry had to pass was kept under fire.
During the lifts there was no perceptible pause. A system
of alternate guns lifting 10 seconds before the remainder, as
well as other technical devices, gave the advancing barrage
unbroken continuity. Normally each gun fired 2 rounds
a minute, but when the barrage reached definite Strong
Points and trenches, it dwelt on these, quickening its rate
to 3 rounds a minute, for 2 or 3 minutes prior to bounding
forward. On the diapason of the artillery the whip-like
crack of the machine gun bullets overhead broke in fiercely.

MESSINES: RESULTS OF BOMBARDMENT

THE RUINS OF MESSINES

TANK GOING INTO ACTION

MESSINES: WOUNDED PRISONERS

As with the artillery, arrangements were made to avoid any cessation of fire. Only half the machine guns fired at each 100 yards' lift, the remainder relaying and "oiling up," so that their roar also was continuous.

For purposes of facilitating intelligence work, the German trenches had been given names beginning with the letter of the map square in which they were located. The New Zealand attack fell mainly in the square U and partly in the square O, and the trenches of the front line system (the Blue Line) were from south to north known as the Ulna Ulcer Uhlan and Oyster Trenches and Supports. Towards these the 2 battalions in each brigade now moved abreast, accompanied by their machine gun detachments. In the Rifle Brigade to the south were the 1st Battalion[1] on the right and the 3rd Battalion on the left, the latter being strengthened by 2 platoons of the 2nd Battalion,[2] which was in brigade reserve. In the 2nd Brigade, 1st Canterbury[3] was on the right and 1st Otago on the left.

In the darkness the men moved steadily and rapidly over the Steenebeek with their rifles carried at the high port across their breasts. The German barrage had not yet fallen, but a few shells dropped in No Man's Land, and by an unlucky mischance 2 of these destroyed the machine gun crews attached to the 1st and 4th Rifles. There was no confusion, no trace of excitement. Officers and n.c.o.s quietly adjusted distances. The 2 platoons of the 1st Rifles detailed to take La Petite Douve Ferme met resistance from isolated groups in the ruins and the sap in rear, but speedily overcame it.

The main attack scrambled through the front line without making a pause and pushed on to the support line, dropping parties to clear up any occupants. As the left company of the 1st Rifles approached Ulna Support, Cpl. H. J. Jeffrey suddenly found himself facing an enemy dugout. He was alone, and a German crouched behind a machine gun which was trained on the Australians in the valley. Jeffrey immediately rushed the gunner, who fled into the dugout. Jeffrey followed, and flinging a bomb into it called on the inmates to surrender. Eight men came out with their hands up. Among them was an officer. Behind his men he made as

1 Major (temp. Lt.-Col.) J. G. Roache, vice Lt.-Col. Austin, wounded 21st March.
2 Major R. St. J. Beere, vice Lt.-Col. A. E. Stewart, sick.
3 Major A. D. Stitt, vice Lt.-Col. Young, on liaison duty.

though to draw his revolver. Jeffrey lunged at him with his
bayonet, and the officer succeeded in escaping. 4 more Germans emerged, and the whole 12 were added to another party
of prisoners going to the rear. In the dugout Jeffrey's bomb
had killed 5 and wounded another. Their victor rejoined his
platoon. In the support line here 40 prisoners and 2
further guns were taken. The 3rd Rifles and 1st Canterbury,
in the centre of the line, seized their first objectives without
noteworthy incident. On the left, the 2 leading companies
of 1st Otago took the German front system with ease, and
each sent a party forward to the Moulin de l'Hospice and to
Birthday Farm. The Mill, which was expected to give
trouble, was surrounded before its machine guns could come
into action and fell with little resistance It yielded 2
machine guns and 20 prisoners. On its capture the 2
light trench mortars which accompanied the storming parties
moved to the left flank to cover Sloping Roof Farm, and
when the attack should have passed that point to proceed
on to the crest. In the second Strong Point at Birthday
Farm on the extreme left, the barrage had not passed an
instant before a machine gun came into action. Our men
had repeatedly practised the tactics to meet such an emergency. A handful of snipers dropped into the shellholes
to hold the attention of the machine gunners, and bombers
and rifle bombers started to rush from shellhole to shellhole
round the flanks, but ere they got to the Farm the work was
done for them. A lucky and somewhat dilatory shell, for the
barrage was now ahead, shrieked low over their heads and
crashed into the Farm. 30 prisoners and 3 machine guns
were captured in and about it. Here too the mortars
were not required, and they moved forward up the left flank.

On the battered and blocked line of dirt timber wire-
netting concrete and dead, which was all that remained of the
once splendid trenches of the front system, the whole attack
had poured so swiftly that the Germans had no opportunity to
resist. They were bombed in their dugouts or bayoneted
within 2 yards of them. There was still remarkably little
hostile artillery fire. The absence of machine gun fire, too,
was noticeable. It had been calculated that there were at
least 10 heavy machine guns besides light machine guns in
the front line system and behind it opposite each of our
brigades, but, as we have seen, the assault surprised the
process of their relief, and a captured machine gun officer
admitted that at the moment of attack his section was in-

operative.   Within 16 minutes and up to schedule time
the front system (the Blue Line) was securely ours.

In the support line of the front system, the 2 leading
companies of each battalion stayed, and after a brief pause
further companies passed through them and up the hill
towards the second system (the Brown Line).   The ascent
was extraordinary difficult.   Vast 15-feet-deep craters with
sheer sides covered the whole slope.   Scarcely a foot of level
ground remained amid the shellholes.   The dawn too had
hardly broken, and the darkness was accentuated by the
smoke of the shells, but the officers checked direction with
their compasses, and in every case the companies reached
their objectives practically correct.

On the Rifle Brigade front the right company of the 1st
Battalion found a machine gun emplacement 200 yards below
the Brown Line wire, with a machine gun and ammunition,
but the personnel had fled.   Pressing forward and jumping
into the trenches the moment the barrage lifted, the company
accounted for the garrison, of whom they took 30 prisoners.
Their objective, Ulcer Reserve, lay about 100 yards further
east than the rest of the Brown Line.   The left company
were fired at from a hedge while still 200 yards from their
goal, but rushed the hedge and bayoneted the Germans in the
roughly fortified shellholes beyond, taking also a handful of
prisoners.   In their sector of trench were 2 concrete dugouts.   One, containing explosives, they later blew up.   From
a loophole in the other a rifle fired down the sap.   Dodging
behind the debris, the riflemen surrounded it, and the 6
occupants surrendered.   In all, the 1st Battalion captured
over 70 prisoners and 4 machine guns.

The 3rd Battalion companies, with the 2 platoons
attached from the 2nd Battalion, reached the neighbourhood
of the Brown Line without opposition, but here they came
under intense fire from a well-posted machine gun on the
edge of Messines.   The officer commanding the company
opposite the gun was killed.   Men fell rapidly, and the line
was checked.   Then L.-Cpl. Samuel Frickleton, although
already slightly wounded, called on his section to follow him
and dashed through our barrage with his men.   Flinging his
bombs at the gun crew, he rushed and bayoneted the survivors and then, still working within our barrage with the
utmost sang-froid, attacked a second gun some 20 yards
away.   He killed the 3 men serving the gun and then
destroyed the remainder of the crew and others, numbering

in all 9, who were still in the dugout. The infantry at
once swept on to the trench. Frickleton, who was later
severely wounded, was awarded the V.C. for the magnificent
courage and leadership which prevented many casualties and
ensured success. In this gallant action Cpl. A. V. Eade was
also prominent. He carried one of the machine guns forward
to engage another gun further on, but was killed while
getting the gun into action. Another member of the party,
Rflmn. C. J. Maubon, a few minutes later when a machine
gun opened fire from the ruins of the inner wall of the Institution Royale, rushed up within the shells of our barrage,
bombed the gunner and destroyed the gun. The 3rd Battalion captured in the Blue and Brown systems nearly 100
prisoners and 3 machine guns. Their casualties in the actual
advance were 21 killed and 75 wounded. Only 9 officers
remained to supervise consolidation. Major A. Digby-Smith
had been severely wounded in the face by shrapnel in No
Man's Land, and suffered in addition from the effects of gas
poisoning, but continued to lead his company till consolidation was well under way.

Meanwhile along the farm road dividing the 2 brigades
a 1st Canterbury party had carried the group of houses at
the Au Bon Fermier Cabaret. Light trench mortars accompanied them to assist in beating down the resistance expected
at this Strong Point, but the Germans, driven back from the
sandbagged entrances, threw up the sponge. From the cellars
Canterbury collected 17 prisoners and 3 machine guns, and
the light trench mortars, in accordance with the pre-arranged
plan, moved over to the left flank. In the further advance on the Brown Line trouble was given by an enemy
machine gun. Two Lewis gunners, L.-Cpl. G. A. Hewitt
and Pte. R. T. Garlick, however, pushed through our
barrage and engaged it. The Germans presently made signs
of surrender, and Hewitt and Garlick went forward to take
them prisoners. As soon as the 2 men emerged into the
open, the machine gunners opened fire and wounded both.
But the Germans reckoned without the determination of their
opponents. Making light of their wounds, Hewitt and
Garlick crawled up a sap and bombed the gun, killing the
whole crew of 6. Then rushing the emplacement they captured the gun and 11 prisoners in the adjoining dugout.

The Otago company detailed to seize the crest trench on
the right of the battalion's sector of the Brown Line gained
their objective without difficulty, Pte. C. A. Fitzpatrick

showing marked gallantry in rushing a machine gun, bayoneting 5 of the crew and capturing the remaining man and the gun. On its left 2 platoons of the remaining company, pending the arrival of the 25th Division, fulfilled their function of safeguarding the flank by occupation of a communication trench which ran diagonally down hill in the direction of Birthday Farm. 1st Otago captured 2 field guns, 3 trench mortars and 9 machine guns, and 6 officers and 150 men. By the evening, shelled erratically but heavily, the battalion had lost 11 officers and over 200 men, of whom 3 officers and 30 men had been killed.

It was now close on 4 a.m. Except on the left, where it was part of the policy to wait till the 25th Division was in line, the second system of trenches (the Brown Line) had fallen, like the first (the Blue Line), up to timetable. The day was now rapidly becoming lighter, and the artillery forward observation officers were already on the foremost positions won, eager to find targets for their guns. The infantry lost not a minute in beginning consolidation. In the front line trench system they dug themselves in some 70 yards above the German defences. On the crest in front of the Rifle Brigade the protective barrage stood somewhat close in, and hence the new trenches were perforce constructed rather closer to the old than was desirable.[1] Before Messines the 2nd Brigade sited their trenches below the German ones, for otherwise they would have been too near the outskirts of the village, which was certain to be shelled, and in addition the German wire, which was still despite the bombardment in fair condition, now served their own purposes. 1st Otago was for a time harassed by machine guns from the ruins of Swayne's Farm on the Wytschaete road, but forthwith a tank came up and, manoeuvring with some difficulty past a large shellhole, crashed into the wall. The wall crumbled before it in a cloud of reddish dust. The roof fell in. The garrison of 30 came out and surrendered.

As soon as the capture of the Brown Line was reported, the 2 machine gun groups, whose part it was to cover further advance, began to move up the hill. Other little parties of Battalion Headquarters and Brigade intelligence personnel and signallers were also picking their way about the slopes in search of suitable headquarters. As these were found, the signallers set out in the shellholes the ground

1 p. 84.

sheets and the 12-feet long strips which indicated their position to the aeroplanes.

The portion of the ridge on which the frontier village of Messines is built is flat, and the ground falls gradually away to the south-east and west. The natural strength of the position was recognised in ancient times and was improved by a fortified enceinte, traces of which still remained in a depression on the western outskirts, now filled with barbed wire. In his scheme of defence of the ridge the German had designed Messines, the southern corner-post of "the Wytschaete bend," to be a fortress capable of all-round resistance. On the north and north-east as well as on the west he had surrounded it with well-constructed and heavily-wired trenches.

A permanent commander (Capt. Thomas) had been appointed for its outer and inner defences. The former consisted of the whole trench system round the town, the latter were based on 5 completed concrete works commanding the lines of the streets and on others still in course of construction. Should the outer defences be broken, the town was to be defended by sectors. Each of the 5 concrete dugouts was a self-contained Strong Point, and as such was to be held to the last until the town should be retaken. Of the 200 odd houses the majority were small cottages with ground floors only, but some were substantially built with 2 floors. Nearly every cellar was converted into a concrete shell-proof dugout. The stronger were used as offices and telephone exchanges and for accommodation. In addition to troops of the reserve battalion, Capt. Thomas could call on certain Pioneers and other forces as an emergency garrison, and these as a distinguishing mark carried a white band on the left arm.[2]

For the storming of these outer defences of Messines on the north south and east (the Yellow Line) and the capture of the village itself, General Fulton employed the 4th Rifles and General Braithwaite 2nd Canterbury. Each battalion was strengthened by a company from the battalion in brigade reserve. The village was divided equally between the 2 battalions, and each had subdivided their half into definite company platoon and section areas, and issued to each man taking part in the operation a detailed map with all the information available about cellars and suspected Strong Points. 2nd Canterbury on the left would seize Oxonian Trench, which extending from the Wytschaete road

2 The German Defence Orders were captured and are held as a New Zealand war trophy.

to Huns' Walk defended the village on the north and north-east from an attack down the ridge. To them was assigned also the capture of a trench line east of the village on the southern side of Huns' Walk from the road to the commencement of the great Unbearable Trench, which was a "switch" between the Messines defences and the Oosttaverne Line. The 4th Rifles would take the southern half of the village and the less strongly developed trenches that continued the circle to the south and south-west round the village back to the Brown Line.

These 2 battalions pressed close behind the leading troops of their brigades. The 4th Rifles, following the 3rd Battalion, was on a 3-company frontage. The right company, in conjunction with a 1st Battalion company, was to take a half-finished trench beyond the Brown Line on the open ground south of the village, and so straighten up the position with the advanced right flank of the 1st Rifles.[1] The centre and left companies had their task in clearing the village. In rear came the remaining 4th Battalion company, which passing through the village would complete the capture of the Yellow Line on the left of the brigade sector due east of the village, and the attached company of the reserve battalion. 2nd Canterbury extended over the whole of the 2nd Brigade area on a 2-company frontage. The first wave was composed of the assaulting platoons that would capture Oxonian Trench. Behind them followed the troops detailed to clear the northern half of Messines, and finally came the supporting platoons of the leading companies. Slightly echeloned in rear of the left companies moved the 2nd Otago company, which would be used, as the 25th Division came abreast, to take the trench known as October Support beyond the Wytschaete road north of the village.

On the capture of the Brown Line an interval of 10 minutes elapsed to allow of the deployment of the 2 assaulting battalions. When the barrage lifted anew, a company of the 1st Rifles and on its left the right company of the 4th Battalion on the open ground south went forward to clear the half-finished trench and straighten up the line, Simultaneously the main assault entered the dust-filled village. In front of the 4th Battalion a few disorganised parties of Germans were visible, who sniping through doorways and shattered windows or throwing bombs from behind walls made some show of resistance. No covering fire was possible

1 p. 189.

from the machine gun attached to the 4th Battalion, for it had been early destroyed, but the close following up of the barrage and the unfaltering precision with which each party moved to its allotted objective overcame the opposition of the snipers and prevented the enemy from getting his numerous machine guns into action. On the whole, much less fighting was encountered than had been looked for, and only here and there, where the Germans largely outnumbered their assailants, did they show stubbornness. Each party cleared the cellars in its area, and when the enemy showed reluctance to leave them drove him out by smoke bombs or destroyed him by light trench mortar bombs. Nor was much difficulty experienced in taking the trenches to the east, where a strong post was pushed well down Unbearable Trench. Capt. Thomas and his Staff in the massive concrete dugouts under the Institution Royale fell into the Rifles' hands. Splendid feats of arms were performed by 2 n.c.o.s, Sergt. J. W. Penrose and L.-Sergt. J. E. Thomson, both of whom fell. With Dunthorne[3] they were recommended for the V.C.

2nd Canterbury met somewhat more opposition both in the village itself and in Oxonian Trench. The leading platoons following close behind the barrage took no part in the systematic mopping-up but pressed steadily through the ruins. The right company was for a time checked by trenches in a small cemetery near the Yellow Line, but when the support platoons came forward, the whole strengthened attack dashed forward with irresistible élan, and the enemy fled. In these trenches a number were killed and 50 prisoners captured. Enemy machine guns in Oxonian Trench failed to hold up the left front company for long, and a post was established in the communication trench, Oxonian Row, which led up from the north-east. Of the left supporting company part was earmarked to clear the northern fringe of the village. The remainder wormed their way round the protective flank barrage, which here was falling a little short, and seized the northern sector of Oxonian Trench. Like the other trenches round the village, Oxonian was meant to repulse an attack from the outside, and its massive entanglements gave no assistance against an interior attack from Messines. Thus by the scheduled time of 5 a.m. the Yellow Line was in our hands and Messines was, if not cleared completely in its northern half, closely invested. Shortly afterwards the con-

3   p. 207.

tact aeroplanes dropped maps at Corps and duplicates at Division showing a line of our flares all along its perimeter.

In the village itself, especially in its northern half, fighting was to smoulder for some short time yet. It was packed with machine guns. 5 were captured just preparing to come into action, and another 5 were rushed from neighbouring vantage points. 2 which fired across the open square it was impossible to rush, and these gave trouble till silenced by rifle grenades. Another gun was posted at a dressing station in violation of the decencies of war but in a commanding position which made approach peculiarly hazardous. None the less, F. White, a Canterbury private, led a party against it, capturing the gun and killing the sacrilegious gunners. He had already earlier in the morning shown conspicuous gallantry. Single-handed he had cleared an enemy dugout and brought up to the light of day no less than 18 prisoners, and elsewhere in the village killed a plucky and aggressive sniper with a well-directed bomb. Nothing could daunt this gallant soldier, who in less strenuous days was the company barber. Turning now against another of the troublesome machine guns he rushed it, bayoneting 5 of the crew, and bringing back the sixth with the gun. Wounded at the end of the day, he was later rewarded by a D.C.M. Actions like his bear fruit. The last centres of resistance fell one after the other, and official confirmation of the capture of the whole village reached Division at 7 a.m. The 4th Rifles captured a field gun for anti-tank defence, 3 machine guns and over 60 prisoners. 2nd Canterbury, faced by large numbers, secured a correspondingly greater haul of prisoners, together with 20 machine guns, 2 trench mortars, 3 anti-tank guns and 4 searchlights.[1]

As at the Strong Points on the western slopes, so too in the village the light trench mortars had been unable to create opportunities for action. On its capture they took up positions covering Unbearable and Oxonian. The bulk of the brigade reserve machine guns were now also pushed forward to obtain direct fire on suitable targets on the reverse slope. The smoke, dust, and dull light to some extent blinded them, but they scattered enemy parties in the hollows to the northeast. Four German machine guns, taken east of the village with an abundant supply of ammunition, were brought into

---

1 No satisfactory evidence supports the improbable statement that the wells in Messines were poisoned with arsenic. The chemical analysis made appears to have been faulty.

action by New Zealand machine gunners under Lt. A. J. M. Manson, who, though wounded, remained with his section.

Meanwhile on the left flank the 25th Division had overcome all difficulties about the Steenebeek valley and pressed up towards the crest, the enfilade barrage which protected the New Zealanders' left flank lifting off before them as they came. When they drew abreast of the diagonal sap in which the 1st Otago troops refused the New Zealand left, the frontal barrage covering these also lifted forward, and Otago rose from their trenches and, in conformity with the 25th Division, swept up to extend in a straight line the position held on the ridge. Through them presently moved the 2nd Otago company attached to 2nd Canterbury. This company passing the now innocuous Swayne's Farm,[1] from which the tank had drawn the sting, crossed the Wytschaete road and captured October Support a few minutes after 5 a.m. 200 yards in front of the trench a new line was dug across the position, and the machine guns of the battalions in rear rapidly took up posts in it.

While the assaulting troops of the 2 leading brigades were thus rounding off their tasks, the reserve battalions, the 2nd Rifles and 2nd Otago, were engaged in consolidating their positions on the western slopes. The 2nd Rifles, who had captured some 15 prisoners with a machine gun and trench mortar overlooked by the leading battalions, dug in between the first and second German systems. As they consolidated, a machine gun opened fire from the outskirts of the village, but a party rushed forward and put its crew out of action. 2nd Otago lay somewhat further down the hill under the shelter of an embankment in the Steenebeek valley. Both battalions were ready at a moment's notice to assist their comrades in Messines or move to any point threatened. Averse to employing more troops than were necessary, the infantry brigadiers were none the less clearly decided that it was far better to use all their effectives and reach the last objectives than to fail to reach them and have troops intact. In accordance with this principle, a company of 2nd Otago was sent forward early in the morning to assist 2nd Canterbury in mopping up Messines and consolidating the trenches in front. As the morning advanced, the rest of the battalion was also largely called on for the consolidation of the new line dug beyond Oxonian Trench. The deep admirably sited

---

1 25th Division troops seem to have made doubly sure of this (?) Farm by a subsequent "capture." A succession of small concrete Strong Points, or "pillboxes," on the Wytschaete road made identification difficult.

trenches in the valley had given effective shelter, but in the exposed positions east of the village 2nd Otago bore their share of casualties and at the close of the day had lost 24 killed and over 100 wounded.

The first act was thus brought to a triumphal conclusion, and the stage was set for the appearance of the 1st Brigade. The position of the Black Line selected for consolidation east of the ridge was on an average some 600 yards in front of the trenches which had been captured and were now being redug by the 2 leading brigades. From the point of junction with the 3rd Australians near Bethleem Farm it followed the contour of the hill over Unbearable Trench and Huns' Walk to the northern boundary, where it swung back slightly westwards along the head of a shallow valley. The line passed just in front of a little wayside shrine, the Chapelle du Voleur, on Huns' Walk, and of the mound of a former windmill called the Blauwen Molen. Further north, just before it bent westwards, it included the fortified buildings at Fanny's Farm.

The two 1st Brigade assaulting battalions left their assembly trenches shortly before 4 a.m. 1st Auckland moved on the right and 1st Wellington on the left. 2 light trench mortars accompanied the former and 3 the latter. Advancing side by side in small columns through the empty front line over the Steenebeek and up the hill, they swerved right and left to avoid confusion or shelling in Messines. The 2nd Brigade paid a tribute to their perfect formation. Just before 5 a.m. they reached the rear of the Brown Line.

At this moment the curtain of fire encircling Messines was still halted in suspense, the furthest arc of the circle waiting for the barrage with the following troops on either side to draw up level and join it in making once more a straight line across the whole Divisional front. On the north we have already marked the approach of the barrage in the advance of the 2nd Otago company over the Wytschaete road. On the southern edge of the village the guns lifted at 5 a.m., and the expectant lines of 1st Auckland immediately followed. Across their front ran the upper section of a well-wired trench called Ungodly. This was unheld, and the company detailed to take it at once established 4 posts in front. Another company passed through them to advance to the Black Line. They knew that they would cross the road from Messines to Basseville. It ran across their front and would be helpful in checking direction. In the smoke and dust their eyes were strained towards it. Before they discerned the road itself, they saw a sight that thrilled their pulses. Through the battle fog appeared a crowd of Germans on a bank intent on dragging something away. In a flash the men realised what that something was. With a cheer and shouts of "Guns" the line broke from its steady walk into a panting run. The straining gunners redoubled their efforts, and a German machine gun from a niche in the bank opened fire. Down in a shellhole dropped the Lewis gunners on our flank and poured in a hot covering fire which silenced the machine gun, while the infantry streamed forward to the road. They jumped down from the near bank. They jabbed their bayonets into the panic-stricken Germans. The 2 guns and the machine gun were captured, and the greater part of the enemy were killed or taken prisoner. Exultantly this right company then pressed on without further adventure to the Black Line. The leading company on the left meantime had skirted above Ungodly and taken Unbearable and the shrine without much difficulty. Both companies without delay proceeded to dig themselves in.

North of the village 1st Wellington had followed close on the 2nd Otago company and in their eagerness not to miss the barrage were in October Support but a second or two behind them. Wellington attacked with 3 companies abreast, the right company swinging out to connect with Auckland once it had rounded Messines. A special platoon under 2nd Lt. A. R. Blennerhassett, detailed to storm Blauwen Molen and the sap leading to it, had a few minutes' sharp fighting at the Mill, but the enemy was rushed by Cpl. J. Fernandez and his men with a determination that ensured the minimum of casualties. It had been an artillery headquarters, and the dugouts were full of Germans, whom they bombed. 3 machine guns, an officer and 26 prisoners were captured, Pte. R. Alexander taking a machine gun and its entire crew single-handed. The right Wellington company did not meet with much opposition, and 2 machine guns and 25 prisoners fell to them. In this company Sergt. R. Corkill commanded the platoon on the right of the battalion sector. He led his men to the objective with great dash and judgment. He was hit in the right eye by a sniper. Though in great pain he remained on duty while touch was gained with Auckland on the right and consolidation well advanced, and he refused to be taken to the aid post till he had collapsed from pain and exhaustion.

Against the centre company a stiff resistance was shown in their task of clearing up a battalion headquarters and attacking stoutly-held enemy posts in the shellholes. A platoon of this company under Lt. R. Wood fought with magnificent courage. Here as elsewhere on the brigade front the enemy barrage was not severe, but the German snipers were marksmen and took heavy toll. Shortly after a charge at and the capture of a machine gun, Woods himself was wounded and his platoon reduced to 12 men, but Sergt. M. Beck, L.-Cpl. C. W. Hansen and the remainder charged the Germans with desperate fury. Unhesitating gallantry on the part of a handful of men in close quarters not infrequently annuls a disadvantage of numbers. It was so to prove in this case. Beck and his men killed a round 50 of the Germans and were mortified to see others escape. To the remaining platoons of the centre company it fell to clear Fanny's Farm and the trench guarding it, where less stubborn resistance was overcome. The total prisoners of this company amounted to 100, and they also shot many of the enemy.

The Wellington company on the left who pushed up the communication trench leading from October Support to Fanny's Farm had also to fight their way. One man in this company, Pte. J. A. Lee, was prominent for fearless gallantry. He tackled single-handed a machine gun near the Wytschaete road and captured the 4 gunners, and later, when the centre company was held up by an enemy post, he worked to its rear and rushed it successfully. In all this struggle the Stokes mortars gave valuable assistance, and here they ejected a machine gun from a concrete emplacement near the Wytschaete road, and silenced with 4 shells another troublesome one at the trench junction near Fanny's Farm. The left company secured 2 machine guns and 40 prisoners. The battalion in all captured 7 machine guns and nearly 200 prisoners, including 5 officers. On this battalion area perhaps more than elsewhere the Germans showed bitter resistance, but generally speaking their morale was high. In later examination the prisoners denounced the lack of support given by their artillery, many stating emphatically that the infantry was sacrificed to save the guns.

The attacking troops were to be on the Black Line at 20 minutes past 5. At 20 minutes past 5 consolidation was being begun, and pigeons were winging their way back with the news of success to the Division lofts at Westhof

Farm. As soon as word was received of the capture of
Messines, the forward group of the barraging machine guns
had come on with remarkable quickness. They were led by
the Divisional Machine Gun Officer, Major R. D. Hardie.
Wounded in the eye and having every reason to believe that
he had lost its use, this splendid officer disdained to leave his
men for treatment, but continued with a skill equal to his
fortitude to direct their fire and remained with them throughout the action. On reaching the intermediate position allotted
on the eastern slope the machine gunners found it right on
the line of the enemy barrage, and so, skilfully led by Lts. B.
Palmes and P. C. Ashby, pushed further forward to their final
objective, arriving in rear of the Black Line some 10 minutes
after the infantry. Heavy casualties had been sustained in
their advance, and on this new line 2 guns were destroyed.
A third gun, with Lt. A. H. Preston, M.C., a conspicuously
fine officer, and 2 of its crew were buried. The other
members of the team, under heavy shell-fire, contrived to
extricate them, and Cpl. H. M. Hopper, using artificial re-
spiration, succeeded in bringing round the 2 men. The
gun was recovered and again brought into action. All efforts
failed to resuscitate Preston. In the task of consolidation, in
which the reserve companies lent a hand, water was soon
reached, and the sides of the trenches fell in, but the shelling
was not yet intense, and the men were in extraordinarily high
spirits. In the morning General Brown paid a visit to his
troops all down the inchoate line.

Equally satisfactory progress had been made by both the
3rd Australians and the 25th Division. The latter, indeed, on
the north dug so far ahead of their objective that they were 300
yards in front of 1st Wellington. The IX. Corps had seized
the German lines to an equal depth, but as their point of
departure had been more to the westward their foremost
troops were still considerably in rear. It was part of the
plan that they should at this juncture advance into line with
II. Anzac. During the 3 hours in which they carried out
this manoeuvre, and while the left wing of the 25th Division
swung up with them, the 3rd Australians and the New
Zealanders pressed on with their consolidation. 300 yards
to the east of the line of digging infantry a protective barrage was maintained, and the Oosttaverne Line was solidly
bombarded. It was at this stage that the New Zealand Division tanks returned to their rendezvous. There had been
6 guns of an anti-tank battery along the crest, but they

2ND LIEUT. S. FRICKLETON, V.C. [*Photo Swaine*

CAPTURED TROPHIES IN BAILLEUL.

15

H.R.H. THE DUKE OF CONNAUGHT INSPECTS TROPHIES

AND VICTORS
(Generals Plumer and Godley in background.   Note fernleaf on General
Russell's armband.)

had been irretrievably damaged by the bombardment and did not come into action. The torn ground, however, had proved impassable to most of the tanks. Others were more fortunate but could not keep pace with the swiftly mounting infantry, who seized the crest without their assistance. A few had reached the ridge, and as at Swayne's Farm, had proved highly useful, though the 2nd Brigade signallers piled expletives on one which had destroyed their wires.

Meanwhile the 2nd Auckland companies who had followed the 2 leading battalions of the 1st Brigade had been halted since 5 a.m. at the Moulin de l'Hospice. Up to this point their casualties had been inconsiderable. At 6.40 a.m. 2 companies started forward to get into position behind the continuous Black Line for the execution of the third phase of the Division's action, the establishment of a Black Dotted Line of posts in front of the Black Line, the capture of the guns and the consolidation of 5 specially selected Strong Points. At the appointed time, 8.40 a.m., the protective barrage lifted and began to creep forward 100 yards every 3 minutes to east of the Black Dotted Line followed closely by the patrols. On the right a 1st Auckland platoon pushed a post 200 yards down Unbearable Trench. The other 4 Strong Points were established further north, each by a platoon of one of the two 2nd Auckland companies. The other company was retained for the moment behind the Black Line. The withdrawal of the German batteries beyond Warneton frustrated any hopes of large captures of artillery, but the platoon on the extreme left captured a field gun. Two of these posts were heavily shelled after noon by our own or the enemy's artillery and had to withdraw temporarily for a short distance.

An hour's protective barrage was put down in front of the posts to cover consolidation. It was not kept on the same line all the time, but throughout swept forwards and backwards up to a depth of 1000 yards, so that the ground in front was completely searched and all enemy movement frustrated. The forward observation officers on the crest were able to some extent to direct it on suitable targets. On its conclusion, patrols of the other company of 2nd Auckland, who had rested behind the Black Line, moved out to reconnoitre the ground as far as the Green Line. All troops operating east of the line of posts had been instructed to do everything in their power to facilitate the advance of the 4th Australians, and it was in this spirit that these patrols carried out their mission. With fine audacity they went right up to within 100 yards of the Green Line, where they found the wire destroyed. The runners despatched back to Brigade Headquarters with the results of this reconnaissance appear one and all to have fallen victims to enemy fire, but the good news was told by word of mouth to the Australians as they passed through the Black Line. During this long but unavoidable pause of several hours, necessary to co-ordinate movement on the whole battlefront, 3 New Zealand and Australian cavalry patrols from the II. Anzac Mounted Regiment, in addition to the Aucklanders, pushed well forward to keep in touch with the enemy. They formed, however, too conspicuous a target to German artillery and machine guns, and were forced to withdraw with the loss of most of their horses.

It was now after midday. In the early morning (7.40 a.m.) the enemy trenches east of Ploegsteert Wood beyond the Douve had been reported by aeroplane to be full of troops, and the fire of a portion of our artillery had been diverted to that quarter, but opposite the Corps front as yet no reaction had been felt. Shortly after noon, however, the enemy had been able to collect and bring forward reserves. Their attack was launched an hour afterwards along the whole of the Corps front and extended also to the north. It was prepared and supported by a marked intensity of hostile shelling all along the ridge, clearly visible to the balloon observers and to the powerful glasses on Kemmel. Our barrage was forthwith ordered down in front of the Black Dotted Line. The strength of the enemy's effectives is not yet known, but 10 successive waves were reported. The 2 remaining companies of 2nd Auckland, held in addition to 2nd Wellington[1] as brigade reserve and engaged in digging communication trenches, were ordered forward to strengthen the defence, and 2nd Wellington was warned for the same movement. The Germans, however, did not get far beyond the Oosttaverne trenches. The thick lines of skirmishers offered unhoped for targets to the New Zealand machine gunners behind the Black Line, and under their fire and the tremendous artillery barrage the attack, as the observers reported, "crumpled up." An aeroplane reconnoitring the position of our posts on the Black Dotted Line at 2 p.m. saw nothing of the attack, and shortly afterwards an artillery forward observation officer in one of the trees at Bethleem Farm was able

1   Major C. H. Weston, vice Lt.-Col. Cunningham, "B" Teams.

to report our infantry moving about freely. The losses of the enemy were probably considerable.

On the definite crushing of this attack all the available guns turned again to their interrupted task of bombarding the Green Line and its entanglements. In the morning an aeroplane had passed along it from Ploegsteert to its northern boundary and reported that at this time it held no concentration of troops. By the afternoon, however, the garrison had been largely increased. The original time fixed for the Australian advance had been extended some days previously by the Army Staff to a time which would be determined on the actual day by the progress of events. At 10.30 a.m. Corps were informed that the new zero would be exactly 12 hours after the opening of the attack. It was thus not till close on 3 p.m. that the protective barrage re-established itself in front of the Black Dotted Line to cover the deployment of the 4th Australians. The gentle easterly breeze did not mitigate appreciably the sultriness of the afternoon.

At 3.10 p.m. the 4th Australians advanced simultaneously with Divisions of the other Corps on the north. The artillery covering the New Zealand and 25th Divisions supported them, and they were accompanied by tanks. Northwards the assault was successful, but east of Messines the machine-like precision with which the earlier stage of the battle was conducted did not characterise either the assault on the Green Line or the holding of the portion taken. Information came in vague and fragmentary, and mounted patrols were again pushed out in the afternoon to supplement it. Between 8 and 9 p.m. the enemy put down a strong barrage, which included 8-in. shell and extended to the New Zealand positions. He followed it up with a series of determined local attacks by the 1st Guards Reserve Division. Under the pressure portions of the Australian line which had reached the Oosttaverne trenches but had not yet consolidated were driven in. There followed not a little confusion in the forward areas and uncertainty at Headquarters due to varying and inconsistent reports—now that all was well, now that the forward troops were retiring and the situation critical. The New Zealand batteries and machine guns answered the S.O.S. signal with the utmost vigour, one machine gun group firing no less than 21,000 rounds. No enemy were observed from the Black Line, and the hourly reports received by the Division from its own brigades made it clear that

the New Zealand positions were secure. General Russell and his
Staff were imperturbable. Some commanders on the Corps
front, however, fearful of the safety of the Black Line, took
the extreme step of shortening the barrage, which entailed
an unfortunate amount of casualties among those Australians
who remained stubbornly in the Ooosttaverne System. Notification of these instructions to the artillery was communicated to Corps Headquarters, who at once took strong action.
The barrages both of field and heavy guns were peremptorily
ordered to be advanced again east of the Green Line; further,
they were to be accentuated at 3 a.m., at which hour the
Australians were instructed to reoccupy the positions. The
remainder of the night was fairly quiet. The Australians
carried out the necessary reformations, and the whole of the
Oosttaverne Line was in their possession by the early forenoon of the 8th.[1]

Meantime in rear of the ridge the administrative and
technical troops had been working at full pressure. As the
last of the New Zealand infantry moved forward, they were
followed by all available men of the Cyclist Battalion, who
were employed to make a rough track for the mounted
troops past Boyle's Farm and over No Man's Land up the
ridge. By extraordinary exertions the tangles of wire were
removed and the shellholes levelled in half an hour, and at
7.30 a.m. the II. Anzac Mounted Regiment patrols, moving at
a smart trot along the winding path and cheered by the
happy wounded, had passed on their errand of reconnaissance
over the hill. The Divisional reserves were engaged in the
opening up of communication trenches, the provision of water
supply, the construction of mule tracks to Messines for the
use of the Packmule Company formed by Division from the
regimental transports, the extension of the tramway system,
and the consolidation of mutually supporting Strong Points
in rear of the new trenches. Where these Strong Points
were invisible to the enemy they were extensively wired, but
on the forward slopes low trip-wire only was erected, to
obviate attracting attention and shelling. At all hours of the day
and night, carrying parties with "Yukon" packs braved the
enemy shelling to take forward ammunition water food and
everything required by the troops in front. Nothing that
the transport officers and battalion quartermasters could do
to ensure the well-being of their fighting comrades was left

1 The disadvantages arising from the independent command of the 4th Australians
in front of the New Zealanders and the 25th Division are of a somewhat technical
nature and need not be discussed here.

undone, and in the fiercest night of shelling only 1 company failed to receive abundant rations and a hot meal. On the first evening the limbers came as far as our old front line; thereafter they ventured right up to the Moulin de l'Hospice. The travelling kitchens were brought up to the Steenebeek valley. The medical staff worked with untiring and inextinguishable devotion in alleviating the sufferings of the wounded, and the chaplains gave Christian burial to the fallen. While engaged in these last solemn rites of the battle-field a shell killed the Rev. J. J. McMenamin, a man of the highest character, unsurpassable courage, and kindly disposition, who showed to perfection that shrewd judgment, tempered by charity, of men and things characteristic of the best type of Roman Catholic priest. On the shell-swept battle-fields many lives were saved and unforgettable examples of energy resourcefulness and fearlessness shown by Capt. J. G. Crawford, of the Medical Corps, the Rev. S. Parr, and many others.

Throughout this time the activity of our artillery never slackened. Continuously and regularly the railways and tramways brought loads of shells to the batteries, thus freeing the roads of ammunition limbers and thereby avoiding those blocks in traffic which had so often hindered movement at the Somme. Soon after the capture of the Black Line a battery of an English brigade attached to the Divisional artillery moved with inspiring élan to the neighbourhood of Messines to render close support to the Australian attack. Other batteries pushed forward to positions previously selected and prepared on Hill 63 or north of the Douve in the shallow hollows about Stinking Farm, and were in action by the evening. On the following day further batteries were to move to the Steenebeek valley. For the first few hours of the battle our gun-positions were practically immune from hostile shelling, but about 9 a.m. fire from Deulemont and Warneton began to fall heavily on Hill 63. No damage was done to the guns, but a dump of 3000 rounds of 18-pounder ammunition was destroyed. On the subsequent days of the battle the gunners were to be seriously inconvenienced by the German observation balloons.

For military students the victory of Messines will remain a classic example of the battle undertaken with limited objectives, characterised by prolonged and recondite preparations, by minute elaboration of detail, and exact definition of tasks. They will not readily exhaust the skill with which each piece of mechanism fitted in with the whole. In the result, the Staff work both of the General and Administrative branches proved of surpassing excellence. The battle had been a gauge of the enemy's ability to stop the British advance under conditions as favourable to him as any army could hope for, with every advantage of ground and preparation. The victory won by General Plumer was complete.

The work of the Division was stamped with the same thoroughness. But Staff work, however excellent in itself, cannot win battles, and the ultimate factor of success is the fighting spirit of the troops. To its high pitch each brigadier has left on record grateful testimony. "I attribute our success," writes one, "to the careful and methodical preparations which were made during the weeks preceding the attack, but above all I attribute it to the magnificent leading of all officers and non-commissioned officers and to the incomparable bravery of our men." This was no perfunctory compliment, but the deliberate judgment of one who weighed every word with care.

All objectives were taken up to time without confusion. Of the prisoners taken, 438, including 11 officers, passed through the Divisional cage.[1] A 5.9-in. howitzer, 10 field guns, 39 machine guns, and 13 trench mortars were captured, with a large amount of war material. As typical of the many messages of congratulation received, the following tribute from General Godley may be quoted:—"Please convey to all ranks of my old Division my sincerest thanks and heartiest congratulations on their successful capture of Messines, which adds another page to their already brilliant record and of which New Zealand will be proud to hear."

The rapidity and sureness of touch with which the Division carried out its tasks were reflected in the lightness of the losses suffered in the attack itself. It had been calculated that the cost of casualties which would be incurred in the capture of the Blue and Brown Lines would be about 30 per cent., and in the Yellow Line about 60 per cent. of the troops engaged. Actually, as instances have shown, the numbers fell much below this estimate. One result of this was that in the forward positions there was considerable congestion of our men. About 4.40 a.m. on the 7th a barrage was placed on the ridge by the German guns and howitzers about Warneton and by the enfilading group of batteries at Quesnoy and Deulemont, south of the Lys. This fire increased considerably about 6 a.m.,

1 The Corps captures amounted to 25 officers and 1600 other ranks.

and in the afternoon had become severe. A single example may suffice to illustrate the conditions. Rflmn. A. Dunthorne, a stretcher-bearer of the 4th Rifles, noticed that an enemy salvo had buried a handful of his comrades. He at once rushed along the trench, and amid thickly falling shells toiled to recover them. He had dug out 2 of the 3 buried men, when another salvo again completely buried them and severely shook and dazed Dunthorne himself. Although the salvoes continued to fall deafeningly on the trench, he worked on and eventually succeeded in extricating and saving the lives of all 3 men. Recommended for the V.C., he received a D.C.M.

Owing to this German fire it became a matter of urgency to minimise losses by withdrawing all but the proportion of troops actually needed for the security of the position. Once the necessary garrison is provided for, the denser an infantry line is, the greater the casualties and demoralisation, and the heavier the labour of taking up supplies and carrying back wounded. Thus the reserve battalion companies attached to the 4th Rifles and 2nd Canterbury, and the working parties sent forward by the reserve battalions rejoined their units in the Steenebeek valley during the evening or night, and 2 companies also of the 4th Rifles were withdrawn to our old front line for salvage purposes and for assistance in the removal of the wounded or burial of the dead.[1] During the morning of the 8th the enemy bombardment recommenced. On the useful shell-trap of Messines village, which the troops knew to avoid and which was shortly afterwards put out of bounds, the German gunners squandered enormous quantities of ammunition.

It was in the course of this shelling during the forenoon that General Brown was killed while talking to General Russell near the Moulin de l'Hospice. Lt.-Col. (now Brig-Gen.) Melvill took over the command of the 1st Brigade, and Major E. Puttick temporarily that of the 4th Rifles, which was later assumed by Major (now Lt.-Col.) J. G. Roache. In General Brown's death the Division lost a splendid New Zealander and a brilliant soldier, whose quiet unassuming manner veiled both intense determination and knowledge of his profession.

On the Green Line being securely established on the morning of the 8th, the situation permitted of a further

1 In view of the uncertainty of the situation after the evening counter-attack, these 2 companies were again sent forward up the hill. It may be noted that some criticism was directed against Corps Headquarters for retaining the whole of the Division east of the Steenebeek during the night 7th/8th. The fault, however, if fault it was, lay with the Army Staff, whose orders yielded to no argument or protest.

thinning of the New Zealand troops on the forward slopes. Orders were issued for the infantry to be disposed in depth, the 1st Brigade taking over the area in front of Messines, the 2nd Brigade moving into support in the German systems on the hillside, and the Rifle Brigade withdrawing 2 battalions to the old British lines and 2 to Hill 63. The various reliefs due to be completed by the evening were delayed by heavy shelling. For some time this was thought to be a prelude to a further infantry attack, and 2 Rifle Brigade battalions were ordered to stand by. The new dispositions were not completely effected till the morning of the 9th, and these relief movements of the 1st Brigade, combined with lateral adjustments of the 4th Australians under a particularly violent storm of shell-fire, created some alarm in the 25th Division that the troops were retiring. A strong patrol, under Lt. A. G. Melles, of 2nd Wellington, did much to clear up the situation.

After relief, the 1st Brigade front, in support of the Australians, was held by 1st Auckland on the right and 2nd Wellington on the left in the Black Line. 2nd Auckland and 1st Wellington took over the areas held by the 4th Rifles and 2nd Canterbury respectively. During the night (8th/9th June) half the machine guns on the Black Line were withdrawn, and others in the forward area were relieved by the 4th Brigade guns which had supported the preparatory barrage. A fine feat of consolidation was carried out during the darkness by 3 companies of 2nd Otago. The German communication trenches were too badly damaged to be serviceable . Working in reliefs, Otago dug a 5½-feet-deep communication trench a distance of over 1000 yards up the ridge connecting our old front line in the valley with October Support.

At 9 a.m. on the 9th the 4th Australian Division assumed command of the whole ridge on their front, as far back as Messines inclusive, and the New Zealand Division, less its artillery, withdrew into Corps reserve. For the time being, the 1st Infantry Brigade and the 56 forward machine guns remained on the ridge, passing under command of the 4th Australian Division, but they were relieved by the Australians in the evening and night 9th/10th June, and thereon marched back to Neuve Eglise. The casualties, light at first, had mounted up. Thus 1st Wellington in the 3 days and nights had lost 2 officers and over 70 men killed and 11 officers and over 300 men wounded. The total losses of the

Division in the battle amounted to 3700, the heaviest burden being borne, as was to be expected, by the 1st Infantry Brigade.

With the transfer of command, Divisional Headquarters had moved to Bailleul and the 2nd Infantry Brigade to a rearward area. The Rifle Brigade remained on Hill 63, mending roads and burying cable. On the 10th they were placed at the tactical disposal of the 4th Australian Division, but moved to Nieppe on the following day and passed again under General Russell's command. The artillery remained in the line supporting the Australians. The 2nd (Army) Brigade on the capture of the Green Line had been attached to a 3rd Australian Division group on the right flank to equalise the number of field batteries along the new front.

One of the results of the Messines victory was to compromise the enemy positions on the defensive front of the Corps from St. Yves southwards to the Lys; and the gravity of the German situation was still further accentuated when, on the afternoon of the 9th, the 2 Australian Divisions began to push strong patrols eastwards. During the night 10th/11th the Australians established a hold on the Uncertain System about La Potterie Farm, which continued the Oosttaverne Line south beyond the original area of the battlefield. Here their posts were now half a mile east of the final objective of the 7th. The Corps were determined to pursue the enemy disintegration, and issued orders on the 11th that patrols should be pushed out energetically all along the front to keep touch with the enemy, and that outposts should be established as far forward as possible. The II. Anzac Mounted Regiment were engaged for the same purpose and showed not less enterprise than the infantry. Coming under shell-fire their patrols dismounted, sent their horses to the rear and pushed forward on foot. The remainder of the regiment attached to the 3rd Australian Division succeeded during the night in establishing a line of posts east of La Potterie Farm.

While continuing this policy of infiltration by strong patrols, General Godley resolved on still more aggressive measures, aiming at the clearance of all the low ground north of the river as far as the village of Basseville. Owing to the sharp turn to the north which the Lys makes at Armentières, this area was in the shape of a long narrow inverted triangle, with its apex pointing south at Frélinghien. It was covered with plantations which sheltered substantial farm houses.

The eastern side of the triangle was formed by the 30-yard broad Lys. Above the river's scrub-covered left bank the ground rose very slightly towards the Armentières-Warneton railway, which lay roughly parallel with the river. Still well within the narrowing confines of the apex flowed the small muddy stream of the Warnave which, running also roughly parallel with the Lys and the railway, joined the river at the village of Pont Rouge half-way down stream from Frélinghien to Basseville. North of the point where this brook cut our front line, the Corps planned that one Division should drive out 1500 yards eastwards and establish a position in front of a series of farms, Loophole Farm, Les Trois Tilleuls, La Truie and Sunken Farms, and thence to the Douve, while another Division should similarly advance north of the Douve and capture Gapaard. The whole frontage involved amounted to some 6000 yards, and in the event of success the apex of the triangle held by the enemy must prove untenable.

Little alteration of gun positions was necessary, and much of the preparatory destructive bombardment had been done, but further wire-cutting in particular was essential, and the relief of the Australian Divisions was deemed desirable. It would not be possible in any case to carry out the operation before 12th June, and to give the troops much wanted rest it was suggested to the Army that it should be undertaken on the 14th. The Corps proposal was approved and the co-operation of the other troops arranged further to the north.

All this defensive sector had been taken over on 10th June from the 57th Division battalions[1] by the 4th New Zealand Infantry Brigade, which had formed part of Corps reserve during the Messines battle. They had been placed under the tactical command of the 3rd Australian Division. For the proposed operation it was arranged that rested troops should relieve the Australians on the 12th. The 25th Division would go into the line north of the Douve, relieving the 4th Australians, and the New Zealanders would take over from the 3rd Australians the right sector, including the advanced posts north-east of St. Yves and the original British line as far as the Warnave. The 4th Brigade, passing now for the first time under the tactical command of the Division, would be confined to the trenches south of the Warnave, where the success of the main operation would facilitate the capture of the enemy's front line system right down to the

[1]   p. 179.

Lys and the establishment of a Strong Point at Pont Rouge. The greater part of the heavy artillery was detailed to the New Zealand sector, where the defences were more highly organised. The preliminary bombardment began on 12th June. Field artillery, whose howitzers used the new instantaneous fuse, and mortars dealt with the wire and the front trench system. Approaches bridges roads and billets were subjected to increasingly active fire. Divisional Headquarters moved forward to Steenwerck, and on the 12th the relieving troops marched up again under the shadow of Hill 63.

Action developed, however, earlier than had been looked for. Prior to the relief on the 12th, a 4th Brigade party had been detailed to bury the dead on the old battlefield, and some time later the snipers in our front line were astonished to see a group of individuals, obviously our own men, with spades on their shoulders moving leisurely in the open about the German positions. On investigation it was found that the burial party had missed their way and borne too much to the south. The 4th Brigade was at once ordered to investigate the situation. Crossing No Man's Land, their patrols occupied without serious opposition the larger portion of the German front line as far south as the railway. Like the 57th Division troops the 4th Brigade garrisoned the line with 2 battalions. Of these, Auckland on the south were more harassed by snipers than Canterbury, and it was clear that the Germans were not yet prepared to relinquish their less exposed positions further distant from our new salient at Messines. The vacated trenches were found to be incomparably superior to the British ones and to be blocked with wire and full of booby-traps. North of the Douve corresponding progress brought the line just west of Gapaard.

Thus the sharp re-entrant from the posts about La Potterie Farm was rounded off, and it was a much greater extent of the old German front system than had been anticipated that was taken over in the late evening (12th June) by 2nd Canterbury[1] and 1st Otago. There had been no time to make communication trenches, and observation balloons overlooked all the approaches. The relief of the front line therefore was delayed till dusk. The 2 support battalions marched up to the Catacombs on Hill 63. Brigade Headquarters moved into a deep dugout in Ploegsteert Wood. The Rifle Brigade were not to take over the rest of the line north of the Warnave till the following evening.

1 Major G. C. Griffiths, vice Lt.-Col. H. Stewart, wounded 7th June.

As soon as Canterbury and Otago had completed their relief, strenuous efforts were made to strengthen the trenches, and patrols were sent forward in the direction of Flattened Farm, Knoll 30, and Les Trois Tilleuls Farm. The Germans, however, were resolved not to be pushed. The worn Bavarian garrisons were being relieved by Prussians who had come from rest in the Lens area and had seen little fighting during the year. Our patrols came under hot rifle fire. The whole of the vacated positions occupied by us were heavily shelled, and the Otago trenches about La Potterie Farm in particular were swept by machine guns in Sunken Farm.

On the 13th the 4th Brigade bit still deeper into the crumbling defences, and by the evening the whole front line system north of the Armentières-Warneton railway was in our hands, together with a large section of the Le Touquet earthworks between the railway and the river. Evidence pointed strongly to further German withdrawal, and it appeared feasible that the tasks set the New Zealanders in the proposed operation might be won after nightfall by active patrol work, which would avoid the set-piece attack under a barrage, with its inevitably higher casualty roll. Enemy rearguards might be looked for, but the enterprise and initiative of platoon commanders and a policy of mutual support and covering fire would, it was hoped, enable small bodies of hardy fighters to move forward from point to point till the final objective was reached.

Orders to this effect were at once issued to the 2nd Brigade, already in position, and to the 3rd Brigade, who were to take over that evening the remainder of the 4th Brigade line north of the Warnave. The heavy artillery was instructed to continue the bombardment of Les Trois Tilleuls, La Truie, and Sunken Farms until 6 p.m., and then to increase their range so as not to shoot within an area 500 yards east of that line and of the old German second system southwards.

In the evening (13th June) the 4th Rifles relieved the rest of 3rd Canterbury, and the 4th Brigade sector was, in accordance with plans, contracted to a 1-battalion frontage south of the Warnave.

It had been General Braithwaite's intention to hold the line with the 2 battalions, 2nd Canterbury and 1st Otago, who had suffered most on the Messines ridge, and to carry out the attack with 1st Canterbury and 2nd Otago. The rapid development of events, however, precluded this, and the 2 tired battalions were called on for a further effort. The

4th Rifles, on their part, had not had time or opportunity for reconnoitring the position by daylight. None the less at nightfall the 3 battalions started out with alacrity on their enterprise. Each was supported by machine guns, and 2nd Canterbury had 4 light trench mortars. No sooner had the troops left their trenches than they were overtaken by an unforeseen mischance of war. Seven enemy aeroplanes flew low overhead and sent a wireless call to the German batteries. An intense bombardment at once followed. The assistance of our heavies was invoked, and shortly afterwards they succeeded in silencing the enemy guns, but not before considerable casualties and confusion had been caused in the attacking troops, especially of the 2nd Brigade, on whom the storm fell with particular violence.

The 4th Rifles pushed on into the darkness, and their parties, led with great skill by Lts. E. A. Winchester and D. C. Armstrong and 2nd Lts. W. J. Organ and A. Bongard, established outposts in the unknown country beyond Loop Hole Farm and Les Trois Tilleuls. One or two posts fell back temporarily under heavy artillery fire but were speedily re-established. An invaluable reconnaissance by Sergt. H. J. Mitchell located the enemy's outposts, and in the early morning of the 14th a patrol under Cpl. T. Wilson coming into contact with an enemy party effected a skilful surprise attack which forced the Germans to withdraw. Wilson then established a line of snipers' posts and succeeded during the day in killing about 12 of the enemy in front of Basseville.

The 2nd Brigade was not to be so fortunate. The heavy shelling which swept their area disorganised and delayed their advance. In the pitch-dark night the number of hedges trees spinneys and copses was baffling and bewildering. The enemy forces proved to be appreciably stronger than had been expected. The 1st Otago parties returned with their mission unfulfilled. 2nd Canterbury made considerable progress. One company, strengthened by 2 platoons of the reserve company, occupied Flattened Farm. Pressing on towards La Truie Farm and the important Unchained Trench, which commanded the ground towards the railway, they were met by very heavy rifle and machine gun fire directed from a strong concrete emplacement. On it the light trench mortars poured in a brief hurricane of fire, and the infantry rushing forward seized it and occupied the trench. The other companies, too, succeeded with extraordinary good fortune in reaching Unchained Trench, which chanced to be held thinly. It was cleared of the enemy and linked up with our possessions about La Potterie. 150 yards in front, however, there were the ruins of an inn at the point where the St. Yves road joined the road from Basseville to Messines. It was called the Au Chasseur Cabaret. From its concrete works a volume of machine gun and rifle fire poured towards Unchained Trench.

The Deulemont and Quesnoy batteries had been, as it happened, that night drenched with gas discharged by the XI. Corps from the old New Zealand sector at Houplines, and in any case could not shoot so near the German positions. Thus the checked patrols were not faced with artillery fire. Though fully recognising the strength of the enemy position, they were determined, as they said afterwards, "to give it a go." The tough resistance already encountered made it certain that the La Truie and Sunken Farms, still 400 or 500 yards away, were inaccessible to troops unsupported by artillery. That gloomy cabaret immediately in front, however, was a more likely proposition. In the darkness and fighting the platoons had become much mixed, but Capt. M. J. Morrison organised the troops on the spot and led them to the attack. The German machine gun fire, however, was too heavy, and the attackers, suffering heavy casualties, could not reach the inn. The dawn was now brightening the sky over Basseville. Disdaining to withdraw on Unchained Trench, the survivors gathered in shell-holes in close proximity to the cabaret and dug a series of small trenches on a low rise (Knoll 30), by a former German observation post. This knoll, commanding the low ground towards the river and Warneton, was of the utmost tactical value, but so long as the enemy held the Cabaret we were unable to derive full advantage from its occupation. Were we to secure the Cabaret as well and be enabled to develop our lines on the knoll, we would dominate the German positions in the flats. The enemy was fully aware of his danger.

In this night attack the 2nd Canterbury casualties were heavy, 75 being sustained in a single company. Though they had failed in their full task, they had appreciably advanced their line, and in their capture of Unchained Trench, however much "a lucky fluke," they had performed a noteworthy achievement. Throughout the 14th their foremost posts were in a very exposed position, and the enemy in the Cabaret made the task of consolidation and the supply of water and rations extremely difficult. On account of the

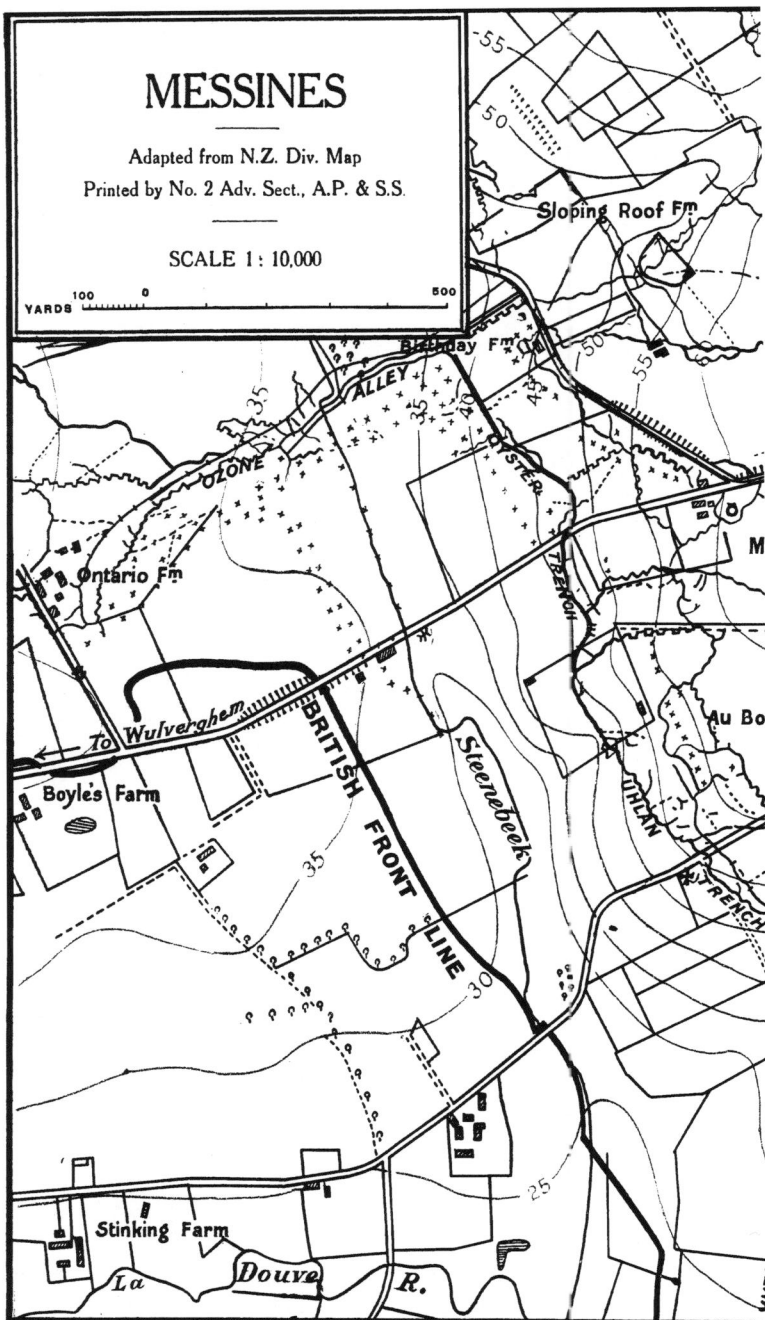

MESSINES

Adapted from N.Z. Div. Map
Printed by No. 2 Adv. Sect., A.P. & S.S.

SCALE 1 : 10,000

YARDS 100   0   500

Sloping Roof Fm

Birthday Fm

ALLEY

OZONE

Ontario Fm

To Wulverghem

BRITISH FRONT LINE

Boyle's Farm

Steenebeek

OYSTER TRENCH

M

Au Bo

ULHAN TRENCH

35

35

35

30

25

Stinking Farm

La   Douve   R.

55

50

50

55

50

55

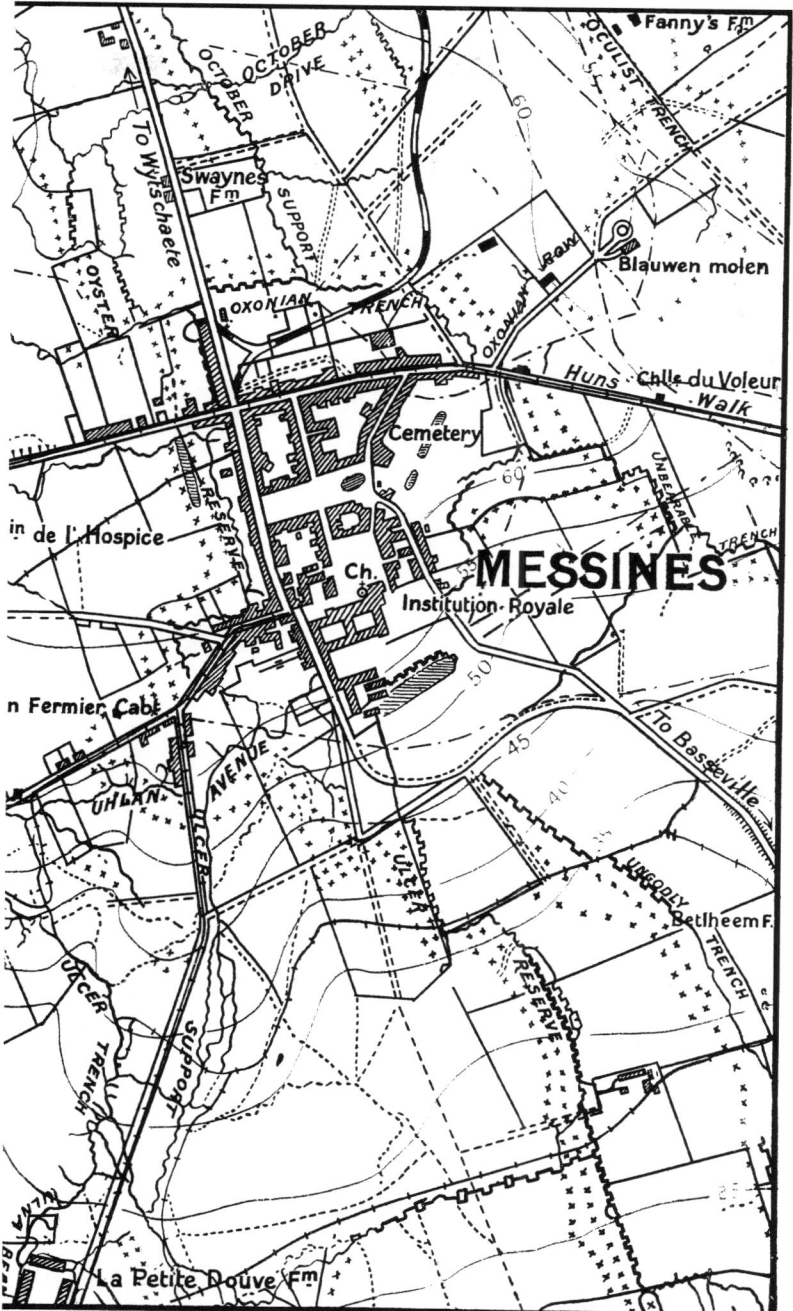

| Copyright

unexpected opposition encountered by the 2nd Brigade in the northern subsector it was necessary to fall back on the original plan of an attack supported by artillery.

It had been hoped that the 2 rested battalions of the 2nd Brigade, 1st Canterbury and 2nd Otago, would be available for carrying out this attack at dawn on the 15th. Army arrangements, however, involving a simultaneous advance by the 25th Division and other troops to the north, laid down the zero hour for the evening of the 14th. Brigade plans had no alternative but to conform. In the absence of communication and assembly trenches it was impossible to bring forward fresh troops, and once again therefore it was necessary to employ the 2 worn battalions in the line, whom it had never been intended to use, and who had already been severely tried on the previous evening. One modification it was possible to make. In view of the casualties which 2nd Canterbury had sustained, the capture of Sunken Farm was now allotted to 1st Otago, who were instructed also to cooperate with the 25th Division in seizing Ferme de la Croix on the Douve. To the fresh call made on them the 2 South Island battalions were to make a splendid response.

No tanks were available, but the artillery assistance was overpowering. The New Zealand Division alone was supported by thirty-two 18-pounders and nine 4.5-in. howitzers; and a 12-in., a 9.2-in., and a 6-in. howitzer were added to the Corps heavy artillery of 7th June. For the most advanced Rifle Brigade posts established on the previous evening, the margin of safety afforded in the proposed heavy artillery bombardment was inadequate. They were temporarily withdrawn. The nearer bridges over the Lys up-stream from Pont Rouge were kept under fire by the field guns, and the more distant below Pont Rouge by the heavies. The Warneton trench system and the batteries at Deulemont and Warneton were severely bombarded. A great fire was already blazing in Deulemont. At somewhat short notice the battery commanders worked out the barrage lines, and at 7.30 p.m. the guns opened. Under this covering fire the 2nd Brigade assaulting lines moved out to attack, and the Rifles reoccupied their posts.

1st Otago this time made no mistake. A platoon under 2nd Lt. A. R. Cockerell carried Sunken Farm and dug in 50 yards east of it. Another party reached Ferme de la Croix on the Douve simultaneously with the 25th Division troops, and others again established a line of posts over half a mile in advance of the Potterie System. The slight losses were mostly due to machine gun fire. 2 men were killed and over 30 wounded.

2nd Canterbury encountered more serious resistance. The concrete shelters in the ruins of the Au Chasseur Cabaret which had foiled their efforts in the early hours of the morning were a tough nut to crack, and a frontal assault threatened to be costly. While strong bombing parties were therefore pushed up the communication trenches leading directly towards the stronghold, others crept up from the flanks along the ditch on the Basseville road and along a disused sap bearing towards the blind side of the Cabaret. As soon as our barrage opened the German machine gunners in the loopholed concrete structure itself and in a communication trench to the south swept the approaches with a traversing stream of lead. Our light trench mortars flung their projectiles at the ruins, and the moment they exhausted their ammunition the bombing parties rushed towards the dark outlines of the building. The garrison of this enemy Strong Point and of the dugouts under the metalled road which led from it to St. Yves mustered close on 150. They put up a stubborn fight, but the 3 machine gun crews were killed. In a further short struggle several Germans were bayoneted and 27 captured. The enemy survivors retreated down the road towards Basseville. As they ran they were seen by the flanking party that had attacked the inn from the north and by the other Canterbury company advancing on the south towards La Truie Farm. At close range their machine guns and Lewis guns mowed down the fugitives. La Truie Farm also was vigorously defended and did not fall at the first thrust. At 9.30 p.m. the contact aeroplane dropped a message at Divisional headquarters that flares had been seen east of the other farms, but that they were doubtful about La Truie Farm. Shortly afterwards, however, it was surrounded, the garrison killed, and a fourth machine gun captured.

Canterbury, thus in possession of all their objectives, were not to be left in undisputed ownership. The enemy was determined to recover the Cabaret and with it the all-important knoll. Forces seen massing in a Sugar Refinery near Basseville, in front of the Rifle Brigade, were dealt with by 18-pounders, and no assault developed. Further to the north, however, an organised counter-attack was delivered almost immediately against 2nd Canterbury by troops of the 22nd Reserve Division. These pressed back along the Messines road and poured up the main communication trench, Unchained Avenue, running to the inn from the east. For 3 nights on end Canterbury had been engaged in arduous consolidation or bitter fighting and had foregone sleep. During the whole of the present attack they had been exposed not only to fire from their immediate front but to a heavy machine gun barrage from the railway. They once more proved, however, the sterling fighting qualities of the New Zealand soldier. Assisted by the indomitable machine gunners, they drove back their assailants with rifle fire and bombs, and on a further enemy machine gun beyond La Truie Farm opening fire to support the counter-attack, they rushed it, killed the crew, and put the gun (making the fifth) out of action. Their General left on record his admiration of these men. "Throughout these operations," he wrote, "they fought with the tenacity and valour which they have always displayed."

Nor had 3rd Auckland, on the 4th Brigade sector south of the Warnave, been idle. On the previous evening they had pushed their way still further among the Strong Points opposite Frélinghien, and now, covered effectively by the trench mortars, they occupied the enemy's support and reserve line along the whole front down to the Lys. For these operations the troops concerned received tributes of appreciation from the Army and Corps Commanders.

After their failure on the Cabaret the Germans attempted no further reaction, and our artillery intensity slackened before midnight. The 25th Division, to the north, had been not less successful and had captured Gapaard and a howitzer. Seventy prisoners lay behind the wire of the Corps cage. Along the whole Army front posts had been successfully pushed forward and the line brought up against the Warneton System.

In the early daylight of 15th June, after considerable hostile shelling throughout the night, Cockerell's platoon in front of Sunken Farm killed 2 German snipers and drove a third from his position. Throughout the day the enemy's reorganised and regrouped batteries bombarded our new line of posts, particularly in the centre of the Divisional front and in the Potterie System. When evening fell he betrayed marked nervousness. His S.O.S. went up repeatedly, and heavy shelling searched the Douve valley. About 10 p.m., in response to a call from our infantry, the artillery retaliated with an intense barrage on his forward positions and with

15 minutes' concentrated and effective bombardment of his batteries. After his shelling ceased, 1st Canterbury and 2nd Otago at last took over the 2nd Brigade front, and the 2nd Rifles relieved the 4th Battalion. On the 16th the New Zealand batteries began to move to the Ploegsteert area immediately in rear of the infantry.

South of the Warnave, 3rd Wellington[1] had relieved 3rd Auckland and were pushing out posts three-quarters of a mile in front. An achievement of one of their patrols well illustrates the spirit of initiative that animated the Division and the good fortune that waits on the brave. On the 15th, in the early afternoon, Lt. T. L. Ward a sergeant and a private crossed the Lys by a plank over a partly destroyed pontoon bridge. Leaving the sergeant to guard the bridge, Ward and the private went along the road into Frélinghien. The place seemed deserted, and in search of adventure they turned, revolvers in hand, through an archway into a factory. In a cellar they found 3 Bavarian pioneers asleep, took them prisoners and came back unchallenged. The Bavarians thoroughly appreciated the humour of the situation. Frélinghien, they pointed out, was held in strength, and the bridge guarded by a machine gun detachment, whose sentries must have been asleep. An attempt to repeat the enterprise on the following evening found the enemy keenly alert along the river.

Active patrolling continued along the slopes between the river and the railway. On the night 17th/18th L.-Cpl. P. Moffitt, of the 2nd Rifles, and a small party reconnoitred the ground on a front of 1500 yards to a depth of 900 yards beyond our outposts and penetrated Pont Rouge, where they established touch with the enemy. It was now manifest that the Germans had evacuated all the north bank of the Lys as far as Basseville, except for posts in Pont Rouge and elsewhere close to the river. By the morning of the 18th our posts were established on the railway along the whole Divisional front. Along the Douve also posts were pushed well forward towards Warneton. Already by the 17th, however, conditions were reverting to the normal atmosphere of trench warfare. A large part of our heavy artillery was under orders to move or was already on the move towards Ypres. On his lost positions the German maintained persistent but erratic shell-fire. Reassured now that our main attack was not being developed eastwards, the enemy's batteries, already

1 Major J. R. Short, vice Lt.-Col. Fletcher, wounded 14th June.

withdrawn prior to our advance against Messines so as to escape capture, were by this time obviously settled down and reorganised into groups. Ploegsteert Wood and our batteries on Hill 63 were repeatedly and violently bombarded by gas and high-explosive. On 2 successive days, for example, the 11th Battery was heavily shelled, lives being lost and guns damaged. The handful of German snipers and a group of machine guns on the railway about Basseville were less aggressive than the enemy airmen. Many of our squadrons, which had been at the disposal of the Second Army, had been withdrawn into reserve in view of employment elsewhere, and the Germans, now with reinforced aircraft, profited by their temporary and local mastery of the air. Emulating the British practice of low flying at a height which rendered them immune from anti-aircraft gun fire, they swooped down on our trenches firing their machine guns at the men in the saps or shellholes, and directing artillery fire. On occasion as many as 18 hovered over our lines at one time, defying the machine and Lewis gun efforts to turn them. They penetrated also inland, repeatedly burning our balloons and bombing Bailleul and back villages.

After the establishment of the posts on the nights of 13th/ 14th and 14th/15th June preparations were made for joining them in a continuous front trench and for constructing a support trench some 400 yards in rear and a subsidiary line some 900 yards in rear of the support. The lines were taped by Lt. C. W. Salmon, D.C.M., during the night 15th/16th, and work was begun in earnest the following evening. In order to augment the necessary personnel for labour on the spot, the 1st and 3rd Battalions of the Rifle Brigade relieved on the 18th the 2nd Battalion in the line. On the 18th also the 1st Brigade took over the line between La Truie Farm and the Douve from the 2nd Brigade, who withdrew into reserve, 2nd Wellington relieving 1st Canterbury on the right and 1st Auckland[1] relieving 2nd Otago on the left. In the combined operations at Messines and before Basseville 12 officers and 250 men of the 2nd Brigade had paid the supreme price. 44 officers and 1100 men had been wounded. 50 men were for the moment unaccounted for. The heaviest casualties had been sustained by 2nd Canterbury, who had lost 16 officers and nearly 500 men.

Opposite our new line of trenches the enemy held War-neton and the Warneton Line strongly, but at this time had

1 Major E. H. Orr, vice Lt.-Col. R. C. Allen, wounded 7th June.

only weak forces in Basseville, in the Sugar Refinery and in the other buildings on the Lys. On 19th June the New Zealand patrols pushed further afield. The dugouts in the abandoned lines showed traces of hasty evacuation. The concrete shelters had been blown up and the wooden bridges over the Lys destroyed. The Rifle Brigade parties were fired at from the Sugar Refinery, but the roofless houses of Pont Rouge were apparently deserted, and in Basseville the 2nd Wellington snipers had Red Indian fighting with German machine gunners.   On the following day (20th June) 1st Brigade patrols entered the Refinery. Indications such as fires and explosions in his back country pointed to the possibility of a withdrawal from Warneton, but till this supposition could be established there was no intention at the moment of undertaking a further advance, which would, without a corresponding movement both northwards and also to the south of the Lys, have merely involved thrusting our troops against the enemy guns.   Patrols were pushed out to the railway, which here bent eastwards towards Warneton, not as permanent posts, but for reconnaissance and observation.

As events turned out, indeed, the Germans so far from withdrawing were preparing to assert their hold on Basseville and the zone in front of the Warneton Line.   The snipers' activity on the railway became more marked.   In the wide No Man's Land between Sunken Farm and Ferme de la Croix on the Douve was a slight ridge some 450 yards west of the railway embankment.   Its reverse slope was dead ground from our lines.   Here, in accordance with the enemy's new policy which favoured a series of isolated trenches in preference to a continuous line, his infantry began to entrench a row of strongly wired posts which, while not forming a marked forward line, would cover Basseville, be connected with the Warneton trenches, and act as an outlying bulwark of that system.   To raid this suspected line of consolidation and destroy his covering and working parties, 2 patrols, each composed of a platoon, were sent shortly after midnight, 21st/22nd June, by the two 1st Brigade battalions in the line, 2nd Wellington and 1st Auckland.

The weather was cold and unsettled.   The way was paved for the operation by a 5 minutes' intense fire by 4 brigades of artillery.   The light trench mortars had brought up ammunition and guns forward of our posts and now bombarded the machine gun emplacements on the railway.   To this fire the enemy made no reply till half an hour later, when 2 green flares were at once answered by heavy shelling of our posts and support trench. The 2nd Wellington patrol, about 40 strong, was led by the same Lt. A. G. Melles whose admirable reconnaissance on 8th June has been noted above. They now entered Basseville, and in fierce close fighting among the buildings and hedges killed some 20 of the enemy. Prominent among the bombers was Cpl. J. D. Fraser, who, though wounded, continued to lead his men with dash and determination, and killed a powerful opponent in a hand-to-hand encounter. The enemy fought grimly. On the way home the patrol caught 2 prisoners, but these refused to cross the railway and were shot. 1 man of the patrol was killed, another wounded and missing, and 16 wounded. Melles showed remarkable qualities of leadership throughout. The other patrol lost its way in the darkness.

In consequence of this lack of success against the posts in the shellholes, it was decided to act on a larger scale and with a barrage on the following night (22nd/23rd June). Zero was fixed at 1 a.m. on the 23rd. The purpose of the enterprise, as on the previous evening, was to prevent the enemy from holding an outpost line between our posts and the railway. There was no idea of occupying the enemy's positions or thrusting our line eastwards. One company of 2nd Wellington attacked on the right, and a company and a half of 1st Auckland on the left. The enemy expected the attack, and his barrage fell at once and inflicted heavy casualties. On our artillery opening, the patrols went forward and confirmed the evidence of the air photographs that the enemy had not yet connected his posts in a continuous line. A 2nd Wellington party came across several Germans in shellholes and under the hedge near the railway. Of these they killed about 17. Another Wellington patrol pushed into Basseville, but found it now occupied strongly. In the centre of Auckland the enemy were holding his wired shellholes in some force, but the area was cleared except along a well-defined bank south of the Douve from Ferme de la Croix to the railway. Here a machine gun concrete dugout and strong wired positions near the Douve proved unassailable. Here, also, for some 50 yards, the railway line was not reached. It was estimated that at least 100 of the enemy were killed. 9 prisoners were captured. 1st Auckland lost about 20 men killed and 2nd Wellington 7 men killed. Almost 100 men in all were wounded. A further advanced post was dug by 1st Auckland nearer the railway, and it was hoped that this area had definitely passed from German control.

In retaliation, on the following day the enemy artillery shelled intermittently throughout the hours of daylight, and at 10 p.m. began an unusually heavy bombardment with high-explosive and gas shells over the whole sector from Hyde Park Corner and Ploegsteert Wood forward to our support line. The left area particularly suffered, and it was fortunate that the relief of the 1st Brigade battalions in the line by 2nd Auckland and 1st Wellington had been completed just previously. A certain number of casualties was caused by the gas.

In the 4th Brigade area 3rd Otago had come into the line on the 22nd for their first experience of the trenches, and on the 24th the 4th and 2nd Battalions of the Rifle Brigade relieved the 3rd and 1st. On the 26th, representatives of all units of the Corps were reviewed in Bailleul by H.R.H. the Duke of Connaught, who inspected the trophies captured in the Battle of Messines. At this function the Rifle Brigade were particularly strongly represented to meet their Colonel-in-Chief.[1]

The enemy artillery still maintained continuous activity on all our back areas. Hill 63 was nightly shelled. Transport and reliefs, unwary enough to be caught at Hyde Park Corner after dark, underwent unenviable experiences The last phase of the battle, however, was now over. Our own artillery had already been denuded of siege batteries despatched to the Fifth Army now in the north. Apart from such heavies as remained, the front was covered by the New Zealand guns and by 2 brigades of the 3rd Australian Division, all of whom had for weeks past borne the strain of arduous exertions and incessant hostile shelling, their casualties, as at the Somme, proving to be heavier before and after an operation than during it. In order to rest the exhausted personnel, the covering field artillery was now reduced on each Divisional front in the Corps to 2 brigades. The Australian batteries, therefore, and the 2nd (Army) Brigade went into reserve. Thenceforward the remaining brigades, whose allotment of ammunition had already been reduced, adopted a less aggressive attitude in order not to provoke the enemy at a time when we had no marked superiority of guns.

1   p. 141.

The Germans rapidly followed suit, and the end of the month became much quieter. Patrol activity, indeed, was maintained both by night and day, and the New Zealand infantry attained their usual complete and unchallenged mastery of No Man's Land.[1] The adventures of these patrols comprise many instances of inspiring courage and fortitude. One example may be quoted. L.-Cpl. G. H. Nielson and Pte. E. Grieve, of 3rd Otago, were at a bridge over the Lys studying the loopholed houses in Frélinghien across the river, when they were fired on by 6 rifles and 2 machine guns from one of the buildings. The corporal was severely wounded in the thigh, and the private pulled him back into a shallow sap. The bitterness of Lt. Ward's exploit[2] may have rankled in German memories, for not merely did the enemy fire a volley of rifle grenades and sweep the parapet with machine guns, but actually called on his field artillery to shell the 2 men in the sap. All this diversified fire, however, could not shake Grieve's resolution. Half-pulling, half-carrying the semi-conscious corporal, he did not rest till he brought him into a place of safety.

Towards the end of June the weather was again cool and unsettled, with days of continuous rain or violent thunderstorms. The decreased activity of the enemy's guns, however, enabled rapid progress to be made with the consolidation of the different fire positions, the construction of communication trenches, and the erection of entanglements. It was a point of honour to leave the position complete ere the forthcoming relief by the 4th Australians, and the Pioneers and every available man of the support battalions were employed from dark till dawn. The relief of the 1st and 3rd Brigades in the line by the Australians was effected on the night 29th/30th June. The rear companies went out by daylight and the front line companies at dusk.

The 4th Brigade and the Pioneers remained temporarily in the line and were attached to the Australians. 3rd Canterbury relieved 3rd Otago on the 30th. The 2nd Brigade also came under Australian command for tactical purposes, and remained in the forward area supplying parties for road-making and cable-burying under Corps arrangements. The 1st Infantry Brigade marched out to De Seule, and the Rifle

1 The Germans scored a success on 26th June. Capt. G. A. Avey, M.C., and Lt. R. Tennant, on a daylight patrol, ran into a strong enemy post. Tennant was killed and Avey taken prisoner. After repeated escapes from his prison camp and recaptures Avey was repatriated to England in December 1918.

2 p. 218.

Brigade to the Berquin area. Divisional Headquarters moved back from Steenwerck to Vieux Berquin. The artillery were relieved at the same time. At the end of the move the 3rd Brigade lost Lt.-Col. Standish, who went to England to supervise training in the New Zealand Artillery Depot. He was succeeded by Lt.-Col. Falla, whose work during the recent operations in command of the D.A.C. had been so signally successful. In his place Major (later Lt.-Col.) H. C. Glendining assumed command of the D.A.C.

2ND LIEUT. L. W. ANDREW, V.C.   [*Photo Wilkinson*

PIONEERS REPAIRING ROADS

INSPECTION BY THE COMMANDER-IN-CHIEF

CHAPTER VI

BASSEVILLE

In pleasant summer weather the respite from the line speedily reinvigorated all ranks. A Divisional gymkhana, and athletic boxing and swimming competitions were interspersed with training in open warfare. On 4th July, in the Bailleul square, representatives of the Division were introduced to H.M. the King, and troops of the 2nd Infantry Brigade lining the Neuve Eglise road cheered him and the Prince of Wales as they drove past on a tour through the Corps area. It was during this period that the enemy's development of night bombing by aeroplanes first made itself appreciably felt. On the British side this feature of aggressive policy in the air had been long established and was a particularly prominent factor in the preparations for the Battle of Messines, but hitherto it had not been actively favoured by the Germans. On the night of 6th/7th July, however, nearly 100 bombs were dropped on Bailleul alone, inflicting many casualties, especially in the tents of a Casualty Clearing Station near the railway. Other bombs fell elsewhere in the back areas, and of these 1 struck the 1st Wellington transport lines, causing the destruction of over 20 animals. The continued bombing and shelling of Bailleul forced Corps Headquarters to move to the less exposed village of Flêtre.

During this interval of "rest" an interesting experience was given to the Rifle Brigade. With the Pioneer Battalion, a company of Engineers, and a company of the Divisional Train, they were attached for over a week to the First French Army in the north on the work of constructing gun positions and making roads. In fighting, other troops might with greater or smaller claims challenge the New Zealand record, but in the use of pick and shovel the "Diggers"[1] were incontestably unsurpassed. General Anthoine, who was later to give his satisfaction tangible expression in a number of decorations, wrote the following letter to Sir Douglas Haig:—"Now that the New Zealand troops are preparing to leave the First French Army, I wish to point out the fine attitude of these men whom you have put at my disposal. Infantry battalions, Pioneers, and Engineers have rivalled

1 A sobriquet of disputed origin, applied also to the Australians.

one another in hard work and fine behaviour. I thank you very heartily for the valuable help they have given to the First Army. I should be grateful if you would let them know my satisfaction." On 12th July the 2nd Brigade completed its task of cable-burying in the forward area about Hill 63 and Messines, and rejoined the Division at the village of Doulieu, which had been one of their staging billets on their first march up to the Armentières trenches a year before.

Two or three days previously the 1st and 3rd Artillery Brigades had reoccupied their old positions about Ploegsteert.[1] On 18th July the infantry began to move forward to relieve the 4th Australian Division. The relief was completed by the 20th, when the 4th New Zealand Brigade, still garrisoning with 1 battalion the right subsector on the Lys, reverted to General Russell's tactical command. The centre was now occupied by the 2nd Brigade with 2nd Otago and 1st Canterbury, and the 1st Brigade took over the left sector on the Douve with 2nd Wellington and 1st Auckland. Each of these 2 brigades held a battalion in close support at Hill 63 and a reserve battalion in huts further in rear. Divisional Headquarters returned to Steenwerck. A few days later the 3rd Brigade replaced an Australian brigade as Divisional reserve.

By this time the storm clouds about Ypres had banked up solidly. The activity of aeroplanes and guns was already marked, and all the countless preparations for the continuance of the battle, to which Messines had been the overture, were approaching completion. A tremendous concentration of troops was gathering in the Ypres flats. South of Arras the Third Army (General Byng) had extended their front over the Fourth and Fifth Armies' area, relieving them for the Flanders offensive. The Fifth Army (General Gough) held the northern part of the old Second Army sector. On its left General Anthoine's Army had relieved the Belgians, and still further north General Rawlinson's Fourth Army occupied the former French sector by the sea. The spear point of the Allied attack was to be the Fifth Army, whose thrust would be covered on the north by an advance of the right wing of the French. At a later stage the Second Army and the Fourth Army were to be used on the flanks to exploit success.

The purpose of these preparations could not be hid from the Germans, whose Press indeed discussed the forthcoming

---

1 On 10th July the 2nd (Army) Bde. set out to join the 1st Div. Art. near Nieuport.

attack at length. Nevertheless it was possible for Haig to take various measures with the object of dissipating the enemy's reserves and artillery and to feint elsewhere, especially in accordance with time-worn British strategy in the direction of Lille, already menaced from the north by our new positions east of Messines. For this reason local attacks were continued, occasionally on a considerable scale, by the Third and First Armies throughout June in the Lens area, and orders were issued for the Second Army to co-operate directly in the Flanders attack by a limited advance on the right flank. The movement, in itself of comparatively little tactical importance, would nevertheless have the effect of stimulating German anxiety for Lille and their communications and of diverting part of the enemy's guns from the troops storming the Ypres ridges northwards. A demonstration would be made threatening a further offensive on the Warneton Line, and a passage of the river Lys would be feinted as a northern counterpart to the converging movement on Lille from the south. The remainder of the Second Army, including the 3rd Australian Division in the left of the II. Anzac line, would advance simultaneously with General Gough's main attack. The New Zealanders, however, on the extreme right flank of the Second Army, would move one or two days previously in order to carry out this feint and incidentally seize ground about Basseville which would secure the Australians' right flank.

During the month II. Anzac had lost to the Fourth and Fifth Armies the bulk of its siege batteries and other heavy pieces, but there was still a formidable weight of artillery to support the proposed operations. In addition to six brigades of 18-pounders and thirty-six light howitzers, it marshalled twelve 60-pounders, one 15-in., four 12-in., six 8-in., and thirty-two 6-in. howitzers. Wire-cutting, counter-battery work and trench bombardment were begun in the middle of July, and from the 20th onwards the artillery programme was accentuated. Night firing was especially intensified. While a quarter of the ammunition allotted for harassing fire was used in daylight, three-quarters were expended in the hours of darkness. One or other of the rear towns or villages, Comines Deulemont or Quesnoy, was daily subjected to a devastating bombardment. With a view to "drilling" the enemy, practice bombardments and barrages were carried out nightly at an hour previous to and also at the exact hour fixed for the attack. The enemy guns retaliated with heavy shelling both on our forward trench system and on Ploegsteert and the back areas. The 4th (Howitzer) and the 11th and 12th Batteries were punished severely, several of their guns being destroyed. Extensive use was made by the enemy of his newly-introduced "mustard" gas.

During the interval that the Division was in reserve, the enemy had again established himself in the shellholes and ditches in front of the railway line north-east of Basseville from which he had been evicted at the end of June. He had heavily wired the hedges. The strength of his position was definitely established by a 2nd Wellington patrol which had a severe bombing fight over his wire on the evening of 21st July, and it was manifest that an attack in this quarter would now require substantial artillery assistance. While this was arranged for, the other necessary preliminaries were expedited. Assembly trenches were dug, posts pushed forward and dumps prepared.

A certain reorganisation of the troops, too, was necessary in connection with the general redistribution of the forces for the Ypres attack, and with the consequent extension of the Division's front northwards which was to follow later.[1] The initial stage was effected on the night 23rd/24th July, when the 4th Brigade took over the right battalion sector of the 2nd Brigade area. Here 3rd Canterbury relieved 2nd Otago. The Divisional front was now held by 3 brigades, those on the flanks with 2 battalions and the centre with 1 battalion in the line. On the following night 3rd Otago relieved 3rd Wellington on the Lys.

Owing to the German withdrawal across the Lys, there now existed between the river and our posts on the railway a wide No Man's Land which, low-lying and exposed to German fire, it was not in our interests to occupy. In the course of the active patrolling carried out over this extensive area by 3rd Otago, one party had a midnight encounter on the river somewhat out of the ordinary. They were in the rushes above the towpath when they observed 4 Germans warily enter a boat on the opposite side of the river. The boat began to push off furtively. Our patrol loosened the pins of its bombs and flung them, and as a direct result of their action or owing to panic-stricken movements of the crew, the boat overturned and sank. Not all the Germans had been killed, for the silence that followed

1 p. 242.

the explosion of the bombs was broken by the sound of frantic splashes of an inexpert swimmer. The patrol could not see him, but they whipped the water with rifle fire, and the splashings ceased.

This energetic patrolling, not only towards the Lys and the 1 remaining bridge opposite Frélinghien but over the whole New Zealand front, in itself heralded the approach of the Division's more aggressive role. This embraced 3 tasks. In the first place, to make the feint against Lille they would establish one or two forward posts commanding the river and dig on its banks isolated trenches intended, not for occupation, but to convey the impression of being designed to cover the construction of bridges and the crossing of the river. Secondly, they aimed at the capture and occupation of Basseville. Lastly, they proposed to raid the enemy's posts north-east of the village among the hedgerows and to advance their line in this neighbourhood. The Allied attack in the north, originally fixed for 25th July, was for various reasons postponed to the 28th. The preliminary operations of the New Zealanders were so timed that their first and second tasks should be carried out on the night 26th/27th and the third operation on the following night. The construction of the posts was assigned to the 4th and 2nd Brigades on the right and in the centre of the line; the capture of Basseville and the clearance of the hedgerows to the 1st Brigade on the left.

The 26th was a warm sunny day. The evening was unusually clear. After dusk, however, without attracting attention, 3rd Otago on the extreme right dug 4 short trenches on the river bank opposite Frélinghien and north-wards to Pont Rouge, and laid, as if for the purpose of directing a night attack, white and noticeable tapes across No Man's Land down to the Frélinghien bridge and the water's edge. On their left, one of the three 3rd Canterbury parties carrying out similar work was equally undisturbed, but the other 2 were to have adventures. One party down stream from Pont Rouge was absorbed in its work when the sentry became aware of a hostile patrol approaching in single file from the direction of Basseville. When the Germans were within 15 yards, 2 flares happened to go up across the river and revealed our working party. The leading German challenged. The Canterbury sergeant at once fired a bullet, and the German fell. The rest of our party opened fire with rifles and grenades, and the enemy

17

ran, some silently, others calling out "Mercy, English."
Another large group of Germans blundered right into the third
Canterbury party still further down stream, but were dispersed
with casualties. In addition to the construction of these
dummy trenches and the laying of the tapes, 2 posts were
established by 3rd Canterbury in Pont Rouge. In the centre
sector similar short trenches were dug and lengths of tape
extended by 1st Canterbury. A forward post was also established near La Grande Haie Farm to cover the right flank
of the 1st Brigade after their capture of Basseville and to
prevent the Germans from crossing the river and taking them
in rear. These operations on the right and centre of the front
were carried out without artillery, and no casualties were
incurred by any of our parties.

For the main operation, the attack on Basseville, on the
1st Brigade front, the commander of 2nd Wellington had
selected the Hawkes Bay company (Capt. W. H. McLean).
It had been sent out for 10 days' training and had come into
the support line on the evening of 25th July. During the
26th its trenches were heavily shelled, and the company lost
4 men killed and 11 wounded. After darkness it completed
final arrangements and moved into its assembly positions for
the assault at 2 a.m. For nights past, as has been noted, the
enemy had been drilled by a preliminary bombardment and
by a practice bombardment and barrage at the actual time
selected for the attack. The first bombardment took place
as usual, and with the second and the barrage Wellington
left their trenches. Their left flank would be exposed to
enemy fire from beyond the Douve and their right to fire
from beyond the Lys, and in front, beyond their objective,
the Warneton Line bristled with machine guns. To cover the
Wellington advance, therefore, it had been arranged that
Australian shrapnel should sweep down the Douve, and that
in addition to the support of the New Zealand artillery the
machine guns should provide a creeping barrage up to the
Warneton Line, in front of Warneton, and sweep the Uncut
Trench System that faced Basseville south of the Lys. When
this machine gun barrage should reach the Warneton Line,
the fire of the bulk of the guns would remain there, but a
few would search forward to catch fugitives or supports
before rejoining the others in their fire on the trench itself.

The Wellington company was divided into 3 parties.
One platoon (2nd Lt. J. S. Hanna) made across the swamps
for the ruined Sugar Refinery that stood somewhat detached

at the south edge of the village. At the outset of the bombardment its garrison of 40 Bavarians had taken refuge in the cellar, and it was captured with ease. Into the cellar incendiary bombs were thrown, causing an explosion of ammunition and effectively destroying the garrison, not one of whom emerged. A post was then dug beyond the Refinery. When day came, it would be in touch with the new 1st Canterbury post on its right.

The second platoon was commanded by a fine fighting n.c.o., Sergt. C. N. Devery. His mission was to clear the village itself. He divided his men into groups of bombers and riflemen on one side and Lewis gunners and rifle grenadiers on the other, and systematically dealt with house after house in the straggling main street. A considerable amount of resistance was offered, but in the end the village was cleared by sheer fighting power, and 2 posts proceeded to dig in east of it, in a position to command the river crossings at the partially wrecked wooden bridges used by the Germans. On the cobbled street or about the buildings were counted 30 German dead.

On the northern extremity of the village, but detached from it, as the Refinery at its other end, was a second factory on the road towards Warneton. Here the third platoon (2nd Lt. W. G. Gibbs) had a brief and hot encounter, and killed 10 Germans in the open. The others fled towards Warneton, pursued by Lewis gun fire. A post here completed the ring round the captured village, and the whole chain was linked up by an intermediate post with our front line to the north. By dawn the posts were dug 4½ feet deep. A section was left in each. To avoid shelling in the daylight, the remainder of the company was withdrawn to the front line. It was most unlikely that the enemy would attack during the day, and at dusk the posts would be doubly manned to meet any counter-stroke in the night.

The expectation of a quiet day proved optimistic. Two hours after the attack, the enemy barrage fell heavily round Basseville and grew in intensity, cutting off the approach of supports. Sergt. Devery's 2 posts in the centre were twice attacked by small bodies approaching down the river bank from Warneton. These were driven off by the men's rifles and Lewis guns. Shortly after daylight, however, a resolute attack was launched by a force then estimated at 250 strong, and later identified as a whole support battalion of the 16th Division. A large detached party moved down the railway on the Wellington left and worked round the northernmost post. They had almost surrounded it. The post moved out to meet them, but the enemy's pressure was overpowering, and to avoid capture our men were forced to withdraw towards the railway. Their retirement was covered by a Lewis gunner, Pte. M. Vestey, who remained alone in the sap. A German platoon from straight opposite tried to rush him, but he dispersed them with casualties. He then turned his attention to the more dangerous party working down the railway from the north along the ditch under the embankment. He forced them to take cover. Seizing the opportunity offered by their check, he ran to the railway line with his gun. Here in a shallow shellhole on the permanent way he once again brought his gun into action. The enemy by this time were advancing in force, and rifles and machine guns blazed at the lonely and intrepid figure on the railway. But only when his last magazine of ammunition was expended did Vestey withdraw. As he dashed for the shelter of the embankment a great gust of fire swept the railway, but he escaped unscathed. "By his coolness and gallantry," says the official record, "he undoubtedly saved the lives of his comrades besides holding up the counter-attack most effectively for some time, and inflicting many casualties on the enemy."

Through this withdrawal of the post on the left Sergt. Devery's posts, already harassed by machine guns from a 2-storied estaminet 100 yards north of the factory on the Warneton road, were now in turn exposed to intense enfilade fire. They were obliged to give ground and move nearer the village. They were determined to die rather than be driven further. Presently an unlooked-for misfortune was added to their trials. Conceivably the occupants of some overlooked cellar, seeing the turn of fortune, resolved to make a bid for freedom. More probably a party of Germans, creeping along the river bank, whose steep declivity had not been fully recognised by us and was not commanded by our posts, succeeded in entering Basseville undetected.[1] At any rate, the posts facing the attacking enemy from Warneton became now exposed also to sniping and machine gun fire which was directed with deadly effect from the roofs and windows of the village in their rear. The posts kept their vow and fought to the last. In the end every man was killed or

1 The notebook of an officer captured on 31st July contained a diagram of dispositions referring probably to this attack. Two strong forces were on either flank, a skirmishing party in the centre.

grievously wounded except Devery himself, who had been the spirit of resistance throughout, and 1 private. By careful stalking they succeeded in making their way through the outskirts of the village and through the hostile barrage back to our line. The southernmost post, now completely in the air, was also compelled to withdraw. By 6 a.m. Basseville was again in the enemy's hands. His signal flares of triumph shot up, and his barrage ceased.

For some reason the Wellington posts were without S.O.S. rockets, and it was some time before it was realised that an attack accompanied the bombardment. By the time the call for a protective barrage reached the artillery, it was too late. One of the machine gun groups, too, considering its task completed, had already withdrawn. As soon, however, as word came of his men's straits, McLean led a counter-attack of 2 platoons up to the railway through the barrage; but it was clear that the moment for their action had passed, and he showed good judgment in not persevering further in a forlorn hope.

The company had lost 4 men killed, 25 wounded, and 9 missing. Despite the ultimate failure, the performance was an extraordinarily gallant feat. It had been believed that the Basseville garrison did not total more than 2 platoons, but, as was corroborated by prisoners' statements, the village was actually held by 2 companies, whose combined effectives numbered at least 200 rifles. This garrison had been completely disposed of by the 130 attackers. They had killed half of them, captured 12, as well as 2 machine guns, and routed the remainder. Even when outflanked, the 44 men in the posts had put up a magnificent fight against overheavy odds. McLean was awarded the M.C., and Devery and Vestey the D.C.M. As it was, however, the bitter fact remained that Basseville, if taken, had been lost.

But it was not intended to leave the enemy in enjoyment of his success, and plans were at once formed for a fresh enterprise. In the meantime the final stage in the operation, the clearing up of the shellholes to the north, was of necessity postponed; and the 1st Canterbury post on the right, which had remained in an exposed position during the 27th, was withdrawn in the evening.

The extent to which the enemy was alarmed by these activities and the feint of crossing the river is not yet known, but the desired symptoms of nervousness were immediately forthcoming. On the following day (28th July) flights of his aeroplanes carried out a prolonged reconnaissance, and our whole area was shelled furiously throughout the afternoon and evening. Just before dusk hostile artillery undertook a violent bombardment of Armentières. At about 9.40 p.m. the shelling on the New Zealand trenches concentrated with special intensity on the left sector of the 1st Brigade held by 1st Auckland. In the right sector at the moment 2nd Wellington was being relieved by 1st Wellington, and the communication trenches were crowded, but fortunately the fire passed just beyond them, falling on the forward posts by the Douve. Telephone lines were at once cut, but our S.O.S. was answered promptly by the batteries and the machine guns. The so-called "normal" rate laid down for machine gun fire at this time was 3000 rounds per gun per hour, but on a S.O.S. call each gun fired 250 rounds a minute for 10 minutes, followed by 20 minutes' "normal" fire. Through this stream of lead and shrapnel 60 German raiders, under cover of their own barrage, made a valiant effort to reach the Auckland posts, garrisoned by the 15th (North Auckland) company. They were successful in driving 1 advanced section back with flammenwerfer. Another moved to its flank to escape the bombardment. The third held firm.

The withdrawal of 1 post was, as often happens in war, magnified into a disaster. The reserve company, which had stood to arms on the first alarm, was sent forward to re-establish the situation. They remained up in front till shortly after midnight, when the posts were all back in position, and then returned to the support line. Auckland, suffering some 60 casualties, got off lightly, considering the violence of the shelling, which continued intermittently till 5.30 a.m. A few men were found to be missing. The Germans left 9 dead and a wounded prisoner in our hands.

At about the same hour retribution was being exacted on the other flank of the Division. There a 3rd Canterbury patrol was lying in wait at a moated farm in front of their lines for one of the German patrols whose tracks in the long grass showed clearly in our aeroplane photographs. They were not to wait in vain. A party of 15 approached them. They opened fire and killed 8, all well-built, soldierly-looking Bavarians.

Rain fell heavily the next day (29th July). An even gentle wind blew over the German lines, and a very large concentration of gas bombs was projected after dark on Frélinghien under highly favourable conditions which allowed the fumes to hang for a considerable time about the billets and dugouts. In the evening 2nd Auckland relieved 1st Auckland by the Douve, and 1st Otago moved into the 1st Canterbury position in the centre of the line.

All the while preparations were being pushed on for the renewed attempt at Basseville. The main attack in the north had again been postponed owing to ''a succession of days of low visibility combined with the difficulties experienced by our Allies in getting their guns into position.''[1] The new date was to be 31st July. As the German anxiety about an advance in the Lys valley was already manifest, and as any local attack now would meet strong resistance and prove costly, General Plumer himself decided that the New Zealanders' co-operation on the extreme right flank of the Second Army's subsidiary attack should not predate the general advance but be simultaneous with it. The feint of crossing the Lys had already been carried out, but the role now allotted to the Division was again, as on the 27th, threefold: the capture and holding of Basseville, the clearance of the hedge system 500 yards to the north of the village combined with an advance of our posts, and the raiding of the enemy's position between our front and the railway on the extreme left towards the Douve.

The 1st Brigade area, from which the attack would debouch, was now held on the right opposite Basseville by 1st Wellington, and on the left up to the Douve by 2nd Auckland, in touch with the Australians. It was arranged, however, that the greater part of the attack should be carried out by the other 2 battalions, who had completed their plans and were more conversant with the terrain. 2nd Wellington, therefore, would complete the enterprise undertaken on the 27th, and capture and hold Basseville. The second operation, the clearing of the hedge system in the centre of the line, was also entrusted to 2nd Wellington. The raid in the northern area was allotted to 1st Auckland. The captured positions would be consolidated by the battalions garrisoning the line. During the day there had been rain, and in the greasy trenches it was no light matter to carry up barbed wire and tools for consolidation, ammunition, mortar bombs, rations and water. The assembly of the incoming troops was similarly laborious. The night, however, was comparatively quiet.

1 Official Despatch.

At 3.50 a.m., 31st July, a roar of artillery fire along the whole 15 miles of the Allied front inaugurated the effort to win the coast, with the Passchendaele ridge as the first main objective. The field artillery directly assisting the New Zealanders was divided into 2 groups. The right group supported the attack on Basseville by a barrage delivered by a gun to every 47 yards of front. Judged by the usual standard this was somewhat thin, but its deadly effect was to be testified to by the prisoners. On the open ground northwards to the Douve the left group had a gun available for every 23 yards. Howitzers bombarded the Strong Points and machine gun emplacements south of the Douve and in the Warneton Line. Barrages were also provided by machine guns, organised like the artillery into 2 groups. The right, supporting the attack on the village, searched the southern bank of the Lys and its trenches, and the treacherous dead ground on the northern bank. The left, protecting the assault on the hedges and the railway, swept the Warneton Line, the open ground to the east, and the Douve valley. Admirably planned, these artillery and machine gun barrages were to prove of invaluable assistance.

The renewed 2nd Wellington attack on Basseville was carried out by the Wellington West Coast company (Capt. McKinnon), assisted by 2 platoons of the Taranaki company, and a handful of Hawkes Bay men who had penetrated the village 4 mornings previously and now volunteered to act as guides. Officers and men were equally eager to avenge their misfortune. In the meantime the German defence had not been idle. Round the west edge of the village they had fortified a series of shellholes, and here stubborn resistance was offered by fresh troops who had just come into the line. The leading Wellington platoon seized the Refinery. Two platoons followed it and worked up the village, one on each side of the main street. The fourth platoon made for the northern factory. The south part of the village and the 2 factories fell easily. The houses of the main street were cleared by bombs and bayonets in half an hour. The dugouts were left full of dead. Beyond the town a few snipers lurked in ditches or behind hedges, but these were killed or fled along the river bank in the direction of Warneton. Into these grey running figures rifles and Lewis guns poured their lead, and many fell to run no further. In an hour's time the whole vicinity was cleared and consolidation already in progress.

INSPECTION BY THE COMMANDER-IN-CHIEF
(Right Hon. W. Churchill in mufti)

BOXING COMPETITION

WATER POLO

Special arrangements had been made to deal with the estaminet on the Warneton road which had proved so troublesome to Devery's men on the 27th, and 2 sections under L.-Cpl. Leslie Wilton Andrew were detailed expressly for the destruction of its occupants. As they moved forward, pushing close behind the barrage, they threatened a machine gun post on the railway line to the north which was holding up our troops on the left. Diverging towards it they captured it, killing several Germans, and then dashing after the barrage picked it up afresh, pushed right into it for their proper objective, and ran towards the estaminet. In it a machine gun fired continuously. Its assailants made a detour round one side. Crouching and worming their way through a patch of thistles, they crept within striking distance of their prey. They flung a shower of bombs and rushed. Some of the Germans fled towards the river, in the wake of our barrage. The others were killed and the gun captured. While the rest of our party withdrew with the gun, Andrew himself and Pte. L. R. Ritchie undertook a reconnaissance towards Warneton as far as our standing barrage permitted. 300 yards along the road, on the very threshold of the village, was a wayside inn, In Der Rooster Cabaret, and in its cellars some of the hunted Germans sought refuge. A machine gun post was in an open trench beside it. The post was rushed, the cellars and adjoining dugouts were thoroughly bombed, and only then did the 2 men turn their faces towards our line. For his leadership and gallantry Andrew was awarded the Victoria Cross.

In the centre meanwhile the Ruahine company on Wellington's left front (Capt. M. Urquhart) had experienced bitter fighting. The general plan of the left machine gun group was on similar lines to that carried out in the former attack. Opening at 400 yards to the west of the Warneton Line, they lifted 100 yards every minute till they reached the trenches. After dwelling on them for a few minutes, 16 guns searched forward 100 yards per minute to the outskirts of Warneton to their extreme range. Here they were ordered to maintain a protective barrage till shortly after 4.30 a.m., when they would shorten their fire to unite with that of the remainder of their group on the trenches. 4 machine guns enfiladed down the Douve valley for 10 minutes and then lifted to the outskirts of Warneton.

The Ruahine company attacked with 2 platoons, keeping a third in reserve. The fourth platoon was used to dig an advanced company headquarters. The task of the right party under Lt. H. R. Biss was to establish a post on the railway line. As they neared it they came under heavy fire from 2 machine guns in the embankment. Several of the party fell, and the remainder were forced to take cover in the shellholes. They worked their way forward from one shellhole to another as far as the edge of a glacis, devoid of a vestige of cover. No further progress was possible, and fire was exchanged with the Germans on the railway. It was at this moment that L.-Cpl. Andrew's men approached on their way towards the estaminet. Lt. Biss' party saw them, and the Germans saw them, and wavered. Biss observed them looking behind—a tell-tale sign. In an instant he shouted to his men strung out in the shellholes to follow, and the whole party rose to their feet and dashed at the embankment. Their determination was not to be in vain, and while Andrew's men dealt with the one gun, they captured the other, killing its crew. Biss, who had been wounded in the charge, stayed to see consolidation well under way and then reported the events of the morning to his company and battalion commanders before making his way to the dressing station.

The second platoon (2nd Lt. C. S. Brown) had the difficult task of clearing the hedgerows. After a 5 minutes' bombardment by the light trench mortars and under cover of close Lewis gun and machine gun fire from the flanks, the platoon left its trenches. It was divided into 3 parties. Two of these were practically annihilated by the Prussians' rifle fire from behind the hedge. Brown himself was wounded. The third party was led by Sergt. S. C. Foot, one of those splendid n.c.o.s that the type of manhood in the Division produced in inexhaustible profusion. It reached its objective but was fired at from the railway and on each flank and obliged to fall back. The Germans had just relieved the former garrison and had been in the position for only 3 hours. They were not less uneasy than the party that had confronted Biss, and the loss of the machine guns down the railway line decided them. They began to steal away. Foot was not the man to be content to let them go so lightly. He immediately sent one of his men, Pte. A. Stumbles, to work round one flank, and he himself ran to the other. Both were expert marksmen. They steadied their breath and fired coolly. In a few seconds 8 Germans pitched forward, each with a bullet in his head. The other 24 held up their hands and surrendered. One of the prisoners was an officer, and he vouchsafed the information that the company headquarters was in a concrete dugout not far away. Foot and his men hurried there to capture the company commander. They found, however, only his servant, a young lad of 18. The commander himself had found urgent business at battalion headquarters at the beginning of our bombardment. The rest of the hedge system was cleared without difficulty and a machine gun captured. The advanced posts were established and consolidated with the help of the support company.

The 1st Auckland[1] raiders by the Douve were drawn from the 15th (North Auckland) company (Capt. J. G. Coates), which had its own revenge to seek for its trials of a few nights previously. They had since been taken out of the line for a night's rest. They attacked in 4 parties, and were followed as a second wave by a party of 2nd Auckland, who were made responsible for the construction and garrisoning of the new posts. The Germans had strongly organised their shellholes, roofed them with timber and matting and on top spread a 6-in. layer of earth to provide some protection from splinters. Over the earth thistles and grasses had been strewn, and in the long grass the positions proved most difficult to locate. A small hole gave entrance to each at the rear, and loopholes commanded the approach. In these shellholes the right party had a brief encounter on its objective, but the bulk of the garrison ran, and those who remained and fought were killed. One was taken prisoner. The second party's experience was similar. They killed nearly 50 and captured a prisoner and a machine gun. The third party was also successful in inflicting casualties. The platoon on the left, faced by intense fire from 3 machine guns and by a heavy mortar bombardment, were unable to make much progress. This check prevented the 2 parties in the centre from reaching the embankment, but the raid had achieved its purpose. Some 80 Germans were killed, 12 were taken prisoners, and 2 machine guns captured.

Under cover of these operations a forward series of posts, about 500 yards in front of our main position, was consolidated by parties of the 2nd Auckland garrison on a line with the new 2nd Wellington posts on their right. These last were now in process of being cut forward at intervals from a long

1 Now commanded by Lt.-Col. Alderman rejoined from Sling, pp. 60, 219.

drain which lay in front of Basseville across the Warneton road.   The 2 Taranaki platoons were digging in near the Refinery as immediate supports and as wardens of the Lys crossings.   The post safeguarding the right flank, which 1st Canterbury had put out on the 27th, was now re-established by 1st Otago.   At 5.30 a.m. our contact aeroplanes looked down on a line of flares along the whole length of the allotted objective.

The Germans lost no time in directing intense shelling on Basseville and our new line to the east and north of it. Machine guns from the In Der Rooster Cabaret and from positions south of the river swept and enfiladed the advanced posts and the approaches from our old front line to Basseville.   Under cover of continuous bombardment 3 efforts were made at the recapture of the village, one in the early morning, one in the afternoon, and one in the evening.   All were repulsed.

Shortly after dawn the first counter-attack was delivered at the centre of our line by local reserves from Warneton approaching between the river and road.   They were observed concentrating at the In Der Rooster Cabaret.   The mistake of the 27th was not repeated on this occasion.   The S.O.S. green Verey lights, and rifle grenade signals, bursting into 2 red and 2 white balls, were at once fired and taken up by the rocket-post sentries in rear, whose gold and silver rain rockets had scarce died away when shrapnel and machine gun fire lashed the attackers.   A few came on with great tenacity but fell to the Lewis guns and rifles of the posts.

The afternoon attack aimed at the post on the right.   All our officers here had been killed or wounded, but the command of the post was in very competent hands.   The light trench mortar officer, Lt. R. K. Nichol, who had covered the attack on the hedgerows, had moved his guns to Basseville to assist in its defence.   Shortly afterwards his mortars had been put out of action by shell-fire, and Nichol readily obtained the company commander's permission to take command of the infantry post.   About 50 Germans assembled in the dead ground under the river bank, and sneaked along it, endeavouring to come in behind our front line.   Nichol collected about 10 men and was reinforced by a small 1st Wellington party under Sergt. W. A. Wasley.   Biding his opportunity he charged the enemy. With a cheer and a volley of bombs the little party demoralised the surprised Germans. 13 were bayoneted and 20 shot, and the rest fled.

The attack in the evening was a repetition of the morning one, delivered with larger effectives and pushed home with a determination to which our men paid generous tribute. Rain had set in, and in the heavy drizzle the observation posts saw the Germans again massing at the Cabaret. Throughout the operations Wellington had used their rifles with masterly confidence and effect. They were now to give a final exhibition of their skill. Decimated by the barrage, groups of Germans pressed on to within 100 yards of our posts, where Lewis guns and rifles vied with one another in picking them off. The attack dwindled away, and we remained in complete posesion of our objectives. In the late evening the posts were taken over by 1st Wellington in pouring rain which had already reduced trenches and posts to muddy ditches and greatly impeded work and movement.

In these operations 1st Auckland lost only 2 men killed and some 20 other casualties. The 2nd Wellington losses were inevitably heavier. An officer and 26 other ranks were killed or died of wounds, and 4 officers and 100 other ranks wounded. They had, however, the satisfaction of triumphing over their previous ill-fortune by an operation abounding, as the former one did also, in incidents of courage and self-sacrifice, but crowned with success. It was indeed one of the most brilliant minor operations which the Division executed. While all ranks insisted on laying stress on the magnificent co-operation of the artillery and machine guns, 2nd Wellington had full reason to be proud of their own courage skill and success. One further instance of devotion to duty may be quoted in the conduct of Pte. J. E. Ryan, a company runner. The other runners in the company were killed or wounded, and Ryan was for 20 hours incessantly engaged in making his way under fire from his company commander back to battalion headquarters or forward to the posts east of Basseville. Dangers and exertions alike he accepted with coolness and cheerfulness, and not yet satisfied with his arduous duty, when in the evening the relieving company wanted guides, Ryan was the first man to volunteer.

In their captured material 2nd Wellington included 5 machine guns and 2 trench mortars, and took an officer, a warrant officer and 40 men prisoners. Capt. McKinnon was awarded a bar to his M.C., Capt. Urquhart a M.C., and Ryan and Foot D.C.Ms. The regimental doctor, Capt. H. M. Goldstein, and Urquhart's sergeant-major. W. McKean, received for conspicuously fine work a M.C. and a D.C.M. respectively.

Immediately across the Douve the 3rd Australians had been equally successful in capturing the enemy's line of posts along the road from Warneton to Gapaard. In the north, the left wing of the Second Army had pushed astride the Ypres-Comines canal, and Hollebeke and Klein Zillebeke were after 3 years' interval once more in British hands. Still farther north the grand offensive of the Fifth Army was falling short of expectations.

After the failure of his counter-attacks on the New Zealand front the enemy resigned himself to the loss of Basseville and confined his activities to heavy shelling, under which the 1st Wellington posts suffered severely.[1] No infantry attack developed, however, and no opportunity was given to test our strong machine gun protective barrage covering the approaches from Warneton. On the evening of 1st August, as a further[2] step to the approaching prolongation of the Division's front northwards, the 2rd Brigade took over from the 1st Brigade their right battalion front, including Basseville. In the following evening the trenches on the south bank of the Douve were handed over by the 1st Brigade to the Rifle Brigade, and during the night 3rd/4th the Rifle Brigade relieved a battalion of the 3rd Australian Division north of the Douve. In the interval which had elapsed since their last visit to the trenches the Rifle Brigade had lost General Fulton, who had gone to Sling for his period of duty. General Earl Johnston, whom he relieved there, took over on rejoining the Division, the command not of his old 1st Brigade, now commanded by General Melvill,[3] but of the Rifle Brigade. These changes of areas prepared the way for an extension of the Corps front a mile northwards on 8th August, when the 4th Australians relieved the remainder of the 3rd and took over the southern extremity of the IX. Corps line.

The Divisional front was now held by 3 brigades, the 4th on the Lys, the 2nd round Basseville, and the 3rd astride the Douve. Each brigade had 2 battalions in the line. The 1st Brigade was in Divisional reserve. Strenuous efforts were at once made to strengthen the defences and organisa-

---

1   Among other casualties to be deplored was the death of Major A. E. Horwood, M.C., R.N.Z.A., commander of the 7th Battery.

2   p. 228.

3   p. 207.

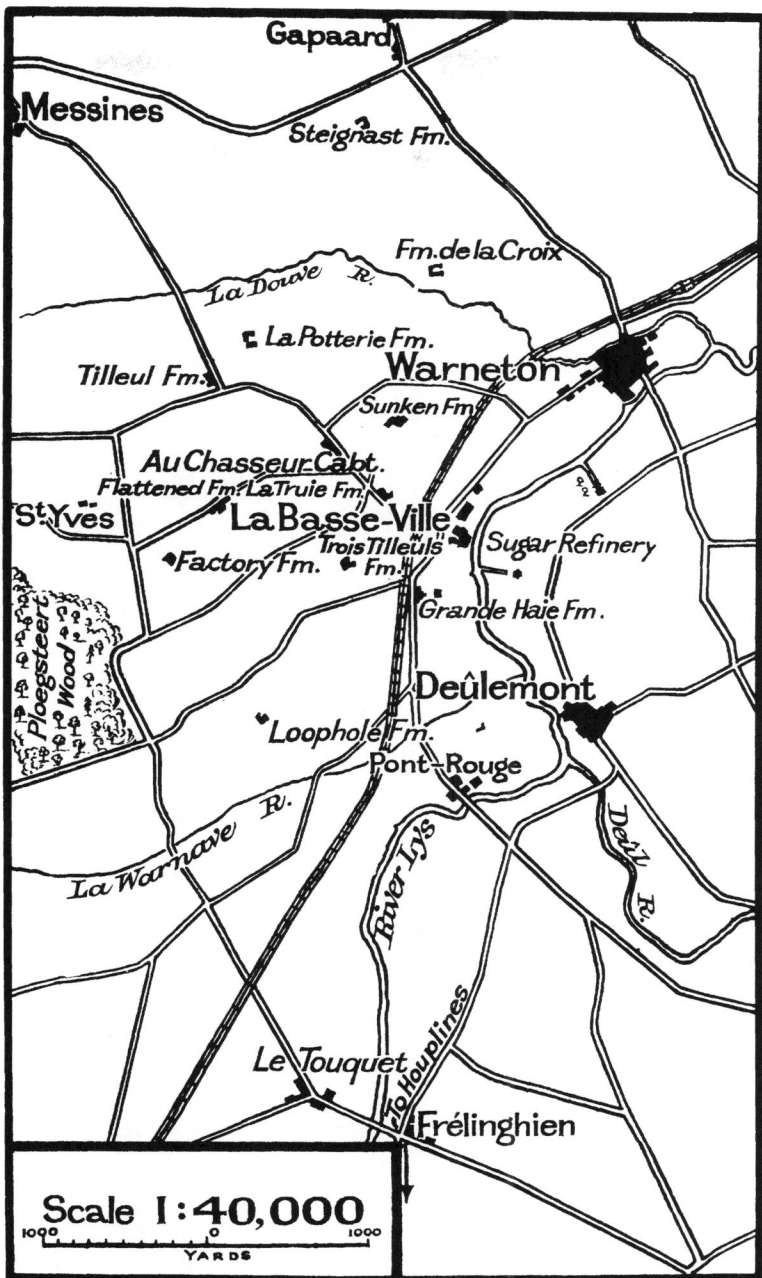

Gapaard

Messines

Steignast Fm.

Fm. de la Croix

La Douve R.

La Potterie Fm.

Tilleul Fm.

Warneton

Sunken Fm.

Au Chasseur Cabt.

Flattened Fm. La Truie Fm.

St Yves

La Basse-Ville

Trois Tilleuls Fm.

Factory Fm.

Sugar Refinery

Grande Haie Fm.

Ploegsteert Wood

Deûlemont

Loophole Fm.

Pont-Rouge

Deûl. R.

La Warnave R.

River Lys

Le Touquet

To Houplines

Frélinghien

Scale 1:40,000

1000   0   1000
YARDS

LA BASSE-VILLE

18

A MOTOR AMBULANCE

TRANSPORT LEAVING FOR THE LINE

tion of the whole area.[1] Wire was the first essential, for it was an established principle that the heaviest counter-attack is likely to fail if the defence is well-wired, whereas the feeblest counter-attack has a chance if wire is poor or non-existent. The posts in front of Basseville, the front line, and the support line were swathed with entanglements. Much of the wire was erected by the Pioneers, who under intensely disagreeable conditions showed all their wonted cheerfulness and unsurpassed ability at work of this nature. In one night, for example, they put up 800 yards of "double-apron" wire north-east of Basseville.

The infantry were fully occupied in building a continuous front line and communication trenches. This front line itself was covered by detached posts and by groups thrown as far forward as the river Lys and including Basseville. The main line of defence, however, was the support line. Owing to the flat and low-lying nature of the country it was not possible to make habitable "bivvies" in either the support or the front line, and the troops garrisoning them were withdrawn, after a 4 days' tour of duty, to the more comfortable dugouts of the subsidiary line. Much work was necessary throughout, and especially north of the Douve on the new battalion sector which ran up to Steignast Farm, east of Messines. Here there were no communication trenches and practically no fire trenches. The front line posts themselves lay in converted shellholes on high ground about an isolated windmill on the road from Warneton to Gapaard, and formed a marked salient with the enemy on 3 sides. These posts and the rear trenches generally were alike waist-deep in mud.

While visiting these outposts in the early morning of 7th August, General Earl Johnston was killed instantaneously by a sniper's bullet. Trained in the British Army, a man of commanding presence and wide experience, he had rendered invaluable services to the New Zealand Force since its formation in New Zealand, and throughout its campaigns in Egypt Gallipoli and France. His death was felt moreover as a personal loss by all who were aware of his manly character and robust straightforwardness.[2] He was succeeded in command of the Rifle Brigade by Lt.-Col. (now Brig.-General) R. Young. The command of 1st Canterbury was bestowed on Lt.-Col. King, whose vacated appointment

1 A change of command in the Engineers may be noted here. Lt.-Col. Pridham, in July was recalled to the British Army and succeeded as C.R.E. by Lt.-Col. H. L Bingay, R.E.
2 An excellent memoir appears in the Stonyhurst Magazine, Vol. XIV. No. 213.

in the Pioneer Battalion was filled by Major (now Lt.-Col.) C. G. Saxby, D.S.O. General Young was not to hold his new post for long. Two days later, near the spot where his predecessor had met his death, he was seriously wounded by a sniper. The command of the brigade was given temporarily to Lt.-Col. A. E. Stewart of the 2nd Rifles.

The work of consolidation was very much hampered by the wretched weather conditions of the first part of August, which were at the moment affecting so disastrously Sir Douglas Haig's plans further north. Day after day rain fell continuously. The sector, already largely water-logged, became a muddy and deplorable swamp, worse than "the Somme." The conditions in the trenches were miserable. Carrying parties and stretcher-bearers preferred to risk enemy fire and did much of their work in the open. Thus when an exploding 5.9-in. shell fell on the 2nd Canterbury front line at dawn on 15th August and grievously wounded Capt. Morrison, whose fine work at the Au Chasseur Cabaret was noted in the preceding chapter, his stretcher-bearers carried him overland to the dressing station, where he died. All the way the little party was escorted by 2 German aeroplanes, who flying at a low height refrained from firing. Forethought and care could not prevent the men in the trenches from living and sleeping in wet clothes. The rate of sickness increased correspondingly.

In addition to this wastage many casualties were caused by the German artillery, which maintained abnormal activity. Armentières Nieppe and Ploegsteert, and all our back areas, were continuously and heavily shelled. The last remaining civilians, who had endured so much, were at last constrained to evacuate their reeling houses. The baths at Nieppe were destroyed by shell-fire, and the Division temporarily deprived of their immense benefit to comfort health and morale. On our posts and front areas, commanded by the towering observation posts in the Warneton buildings, the shelling raged persistently, and in the first fortnight in August from this cause alone the Division lost the equivalent of a battalion. Gas fell for the most part in the back areas and about the batteries and round Hyde Park Corner and Hill 63, compelling on several occasions the wearing of respirators by reliefs marching up to the trenches or by men working at the quartermasters' stores or wagon lines some miles in rear.

The enemy aeroplanes continued by day to harass the forward troops and battery positions and by night to bomb the rear villages, considerably increasing the frequency of their visits and widening the radius of their operations. On 9th August the 2nd Infantry Brigade Headquarters lost several horses, and on the 11th the 1st Machine Gun Company and 2nd Wellington stables were wrecked and nearly 100 animals destroyed. Our own guns were even more aggressive than the German. Warneton Deulemont and other villages were reduced to heaps of ruined roofless walls, gaps in which revealed the more substantial concrete dugouts which they screened. Co-operation was given to the attacks in the north, particularly to that of 16th August on Langemarck, by artillery and machine gun barrages and violent counter-battery activity. Frélinghien also was on that date drenched in gas and liquid oil.

While about Basseville both artilleries remained active, there was now little infantry fighting. Both sides were engrossed in consolidation. A single effort at a raid by the Germans was summarily repulsed. Our patrols, however, were continually active towards Warneton, along the Lys and down the Douve valley, where some encounters took place with enemy parties. Over the Lys the enemy made no attempt to throw bridges or force a crossing, and aggressive sniping by our patrols denied him the right of moving freely in front of his own lines on the southern bank. Towards the end of the month a notable achievement was performed by a 3rd Wellington[1] party under the leadership of Sergt. S. S. Pennefather. In the afternoon Pennefather had swum across the Lys and reconnoitred the enemy positions. Crossing again in the evening for further exploration he found 2 rafts hidden among the rushes below the enemy bank. One he cut adrift, the other he converted, by means of German signalling wire, into a ferry. When darkness fell, he led a party of 7 men to the river. 4 were left on the tow rope to guard the passage and cover the return. The other 3 he took with him. Penetrating into the enemy's country the party heard talking, and spied a group of Germans in a shellhole. They crept towards it but were noticed, and the enemy threw stick-bombs and opened rifle fire. Pennefather received a serious wound in the wrist, but in the excitement of the moment scarcely felt the pain. He and his men flung their bombs and rushed. Four dim figures rose up from the shellhole, making off into the darkness.

---

[1] Major (now Lt.-Col.) Weston had taken over command from Major Short on 19th August.

Two were killed; the others escaped. In the bottom of the shellhole was found a fifth badly wounded German. No papers were on the dead, so the party collected the enemy rifles and lifted their wounded prisoner to carry him to our lines. He died, however, on the way. The party recrossed the river on the ferry without further misadventure. For this enterprise Pennefather received the coveted D.C.M.

In the intensity of the enemy's artillery fire there was a marked decrease in the last 10 days of the month, due to the withdrawal of guns for his defence in the north. The number of active positions recorded by Sound Rangers and Flash Spotters dropped very suddenly, and the result was reflected in the Corps casualty roll:—

Week ending	August 2	1329 total casualties
,, ,,	August 9	919 ,, ,,
,, ,,	August 16	752 ,, ,,
,, ,,	August 23	631 ,, ,,
,, ,,	August 30	212 ,, ,,

With his reduced groups, however, counter-battery work was continued persistently even in the latter part of the month, and several New Zealand guns were destroyed, but in the trenches and forward area conditions were becoming normal as early as 17th August, when the 2nd Brigade was relieved in the centre of the line by the 1st Brigade and withdrew into reserve. On the 21st it began to move to the La Motte area. The rest of the Division was not to be long in following it. Arrangements were already under way for the 8th Division to take over the right and centre subsectors and for the 3rd Australians to occupy the Rifle Brigade subsector on the Douve. The latter move began on the 22nd. Owing to the proximity and activity of the enemy opposite the Windmill on the Warneton-Gapaard road, the Rifle Brigade had experienced the utmost difficulty in the construction of their front line, but the ground was of particular tactical importance, and it was essential that our grip of it should be strengthened. By untiring efforts the work had been completed. The posts were now connected with each other and the whole with the support line, and movement under cover was possible throughout the entire subsector.

During the 21 days that the Rifle Brigade had been in the line it had sustained casualties not less heavy than those of a serious engagement. 5 officers had been killed, 14 wounded, and 1 was missing,[1] and the casualties among other ranks amounted to 60 killed, 350 wounded, and 2 missing. On relief by the Australians the brigade moved to the La Crèche area in tactical support to the 57th Division, who were holding the familiar trenches about Fleurbaix. The 8th Division completed the reliefs of the 1st Brigade on the 27th and of the 4th Brigade on the 31st. As these 2 brigades were withdrawn, they marched back to the Corps rear area. After their 3 months in the trenches the 4th Brigade, burdened with full packs, blankets, steel helmets, and other accoutrements, were severely tried by the 17-mile march.

From these staging billets the Division, less the artillery and the Rifle Brigade, proceeded by train at the end of the month to the Second Army reserve area at Lumbres in the Aa valley west of St. Omer. Units were accompanied by their travelling kitchens and water carts, but the remainder of the transport trekked by road. The last of the artillery moved out of the line on 6th September and rested for a few days in the neighbourhood of Morbecque, whence they presently rejoined the Division. The Rifle Brigade was left in the forward area for work on cable communications under the orders of the Second Army. At the end of August the 4th Australian Division was relieved by IX. Corps troops and transferred to I. Anzac. Thereupon II. Anzac Headquarters handed over the command of their sector to the VIII. Corps and moved to Lumbres.

1 Captain W. A. Gray, M.C., 3rd Battalion, captured after being wounded 6th August.

CHAPTER VII

Gravenstafel and the Bellevue Spur

The tactical skill shown by the British infantry at Arras and Messines, and especially the devastating effects of the British artillery, led to various modifications in the German principles of defence. These had hitherto been based on the contesting of every yard of ground. The enemy had filled his trenches with troops and machine guns. On the other hand, once driven from a position he had rarely made a serious effort to retake it. This close succession of strongly-manned trenches in the forward zone had in the end proved equally wasteful and ineffective. The Flanders battle saw the introduction of tactics designed mainly to neutralise our artillery preparation.

The main features of the new policy were the comparative lightness of the front-zone garrison, increased depth of defences, and the maintenance of powerful reserves used for counter-attack. These last were stationed close behind the battle and were employed both to effect immediate local reaction and also, after a somewhat longer interval but before the assaulting troops could reorganise and consolidate, to launch previously prepared counter-strokes on a large scale. This policy of "elastic" defence was likely to yield limited areas of ground, but it promised to conserve man-power and prove expensive to the attack. Entanglements were used lavishly, and a notable feature was the construction of concrete block-houses or machine gun posts arranged chequerwise or in echelon for mutual support. These had already been encountered at Messines and were at once necessitated by and well adapted to the waterlogged marshes of Flanders, where the construction of deep dugouts was generally impossible. Upon them, by reason partly of their shape, partly of the unpleasant nature of their contents, the unerring humour of the English soldier had bestowed the name of "pillboxes."

The policy was worked out in practice with considerable technical ability, and at the outset caused no little perplexity to our attacking infantry and Staff. Gradually, however, the necessary modifications in our infantry artillery and machine gun tactics were evolved, and all the lessons gained by experience were communicated to the formations resting and training behind the line.

The enemy's defence was at once more mobile and indeterminate, and left the attack more ignorant of his dispositions and probable counter-action. Assaulting troops could no longer be certain where they would meet the enemy's advanced troops, whether in front of or behind or in his trench systems, nor could they tell on what portion of the front his previously prepared, as distinct from his local, counter-stroke would fall. In order to be able to fight the enemy wherever encountered between our starting point and objective, and to have fresh and organised troops in hand to meet counter-attacks wherever they might fall, it was necessary that our own formations should be more flexible, under closer control and capable of greater freedom of manoeuvre than the old "waves."

A solution was found in a formation of small columns or "worms." These were covered by one or two lines designed to draw the enemy's fire, engage him, locate his defences, and generally discharge the functions of an advanced guard protecting a main body. By this screen freedom of manoeuvre was secured for the attacking columns. Similarly, the "moppers-up" following behind the columns now dealt with areas instead of trench lines. Musketry and ground reconnaissance regained values somewhat obscured in recent battles, and the handling of reserves to meet enemy counterattacks was of paramount importance. Fighting was assuming a much more open nature. Trench warfare and trench-to-trench assaults were becoming things of the past.

It was on these new features of attack that the New Zealanders in the Lumbres area now concentrated their attention. A certain amount of training was done in open manoeuvre and wood fighting, but for the most part all arms studied the principle and rehearsed the practice of the new methods of advance over areas defended by scattered concrete fortresses. In their spare hours the New Zealanders gave much assistance in harvesting the crops.

During this period of training an impressive and memorable review of the 1st 2nd and 4th Infantry Brigades and other units of the Division was held in beautiful weather by Sir Douglas Haig, accompanied by the Right Hon. Winston

Churchill. The troops were first inspected in line of battalions in close column of companies, and then marched past with splendid steadiness in columns of platoons in line.

Meanwhile the 3rd Brigade battalions were engaged under I. Anzac and the X. Corps in burying cable in the rear areas of the Ypres battlefield. The Cyclist Battalion was employed on similar tasks. Working frequently under shell-fire and in gas respirators they completed all tasks set them with despatch and thoroughness. Lt.-General Morland, of the X. Corps, wrote to General Godley:—

"It is difficult for me adequately to express to you my gratitude for the splendid work of the 1st, 2nd, 3rd, and 4th Battalions, New Zealand (Rifle) Brigade, and the II. Anzac Cyclists in burying cable on my Corps front during the last 3 weeks. Their achievement in digging over 13,000 yards of cable trench, laying the cable and banking it from 3 to 4 feet is an extraordinary one. The keenness that they displayed is universally admired, and their skill is acknowledged to be an example to any troops. Will you please tell these gallant men how much, while I deplore the casualties they suffered, I appreciate both their valuable work and their soldierly spirit."

A similar tribute was paid by the very able chief of the Second Army Staff, Major-General C. H. Harington, and the Army Commander found time in the insistent pressure of work following the battle of 20th September to issue the following order:—

"The Army Commander wishes to place on record his appreciation of the work done by the 3rd New Zealand (Rifle) Brigade in burying cable to assist in yesterday's operations. The success of the operations was in a great measure due to the good communications established, to attain which results the 3rd New Zealand (Rifle) Brigade played such an important part."

In the momentous operations, known as the Third Battle of Ypres, the comparative success of the initial engagement on 31st July had not been maintained in the second attack, delivered, after a delay due to unpropitious weather, on 16th August. Especially on the southern flank, where the road from Ypres to Menin crossed the ridge, meagre results had been effected at heavy cost. It was thought that more progress might be achieved by an extension of the attack further to the south. The Fifth Army already had its hands full, so this area about the Menin Road was transferred in the beginning of September to the Second Army, and General Plumer was ordered to carry the crest-line in a self-contained operation. It was too strong a position to win in a blind rush, and the Second Army attack was delayed till 20th September to allow time for the satisfactory completion of characteristically thorough preparations, which included the extensive burying of cable by the Rifle Brigade mentioned above. The result was a substantial victory. To the north the Fifth Army achieved no less welcome success. The advance was resumed on 26th September, when I. Anzac carried the remainder of Polygon Wood, and English Divisions captured Zonnebeke and pushed out along the Ypres-Wieltje-Passchendaele road towards Gravenstafel Ridge. This road was soon to be printed indelibly on the minds of the New Zealanders.

For the Division was already on the march from the Lumbres training area towards Ypres. The artillery had moved forward previously to the Hazebrouck area. On 24th September General Godley had received warning that II. Anzac would relieve the V. Corps in the northern sector of the extended Second Army front and would carry out operations in the near future. On this occasion there were to be no long rehearsals as at Messines. Six days only were available in which the Corps would march up to Ypres, relieve the troops in the line, and plan and carry out an offensive in an area and on a front that were unknown both to the Corps Staff and to the Divisions. The 49th and 66th Divisions were added to the New Zealand Division and 3rd Australian Division under General Godley's command to bring the Corps up to adequate strength. The 2 English Divisions were for the time left in rest and training, but the 3rd Australians and the New Zealanders had been warned for an immediate movement towards Ypres. On 25th September Divisional Headquarters moved to Hazebrouck, and the 1st and 2nd Brigade Groups to Renescure. The 4th Brigade, who were further west in the training area, marched up into the vacated billets about Lumbres. On the 26th the 1st and 2nd Brigades reached Wallon Cappel and the 4th Brigade Renescure. The weather was swelteringly hot, the hard roads dusty, and though the troops were in splendid fettle they were severely tested by these long marches of 20 miles and over a day. Divisional Headquarters and the 1st and 2nd Brigades moved on the following day (27th September) to Watou, some 5 miles west of Poperinghe, and the 4th Brigade reached a staging area north of Hazebrouck. On the 28th II. Anzac, with Headquarters just north of Poperinghe, took over from the V. Corps the command of the latter's 2 Divisions in the line, the 3rd Division on the right and the 59th on the left, on the front between Zonnebeke and St. Julien, east and north-east of Ypres. The Second Army then once again extended its area northwards to include this new sector.

Arrangements had been made to relieve the 3rd Division by the 3rd Australian Division and the 59th Division by the New Zealanders. On the right of the new Corps sector was I. Anzac (General Birdwood), on the left in the Fifth Army was the XVIII. Corps. The 2nd Brigade was sent up on lorries from Watou at short notice on the 28th to be in support to the 59th Division as a preparatory step to the taking over of the whole Divisional front. 2nd Canterbury[1] and 2nd Otago went into the old German front line trenches at Wieltje, and the two 1st Battalions into a reserve area north of Ypres. In the same evening sections of the 1st[2] and 3rd Artillery Brigades, now also concentrated in the Poperinghe area, trekked up to commence the relief of the 42nd Divisional Artillery on the right Division sector, taking over their guns. Throughout the night our batteries were heavily shelled.

The infantry reliefs in the left Division sector began the following evening (29th September). 2nd Canterbury and 2nd Otago went into the front trenches, some 4 miles in front of the original British line, of the left brigade of the 59th Division, and on the following night (30th September/ 1st October) 1st Canterbury and 1st Otago took over the forward posts on the right subsector in bright moonlight and under fitful bursts of machine gun fire. At the same time 2nd Wellington moved forward to the old German front line. The 2nd Brigade, with all 4 battalions in the line, passed temporarily under command of the 59th Division. The Australians were moving into the right Division sector simultaneously, and on the nights 30th September/1st October and 1st/2nd October the New Zealand gunners, relieved by the 3rd Australian Divisional Artillery, moved northwards into the St. Jean sector in support to and to the great satisfaction of their infantry.

1   Major (temp. Lt.-Col.) O. H. Mead, vice Lt.-Col. Griffiths, on duty to England.

2   Lt.-Col. J. A. Ballard, R.F.A., vice Lt.-Col. Symon, on duty to England.

Throughout the short period spent by the gunners in the positions now handed over to the Australians they had been heavily shelled, and 4 howitzers of the 15th Battery had been destroyed. In the northern sector no time was wasted in reconnoitring and occupying new advanced positions from which in the forthcoming operation barrages might be placed beyond the furthest objectives and the enemy's most distant batteries be engaged. A section of each battery was in action in new forward positions by dawn on 1st October and the remainder by the following morning. The batteries of both brigades were formed into a group under the temporary command of Lt.-Col. Falla, General Napier Johnston taking command of the larger group covering the whole front in which the New Zealand group was included. The New Zealand guns were the most advanced and, except for necessary registration, carried out no firing.

On 1st October the command of the St. Jean sector was taken over by the New Zealanders. On the same day the 4th Brigade, which had meantime arrived at Watou, and the remainder of the 1st Brigade moved up by traffic-encumbered roads to the reserve positions in the old front lines and northern outskirts of Ypres. The 4th Brigade lay on the right, the 1st on the left. Each disposed 2 battalions in the old British and German front lines as reserves to the 2nd Brigade. Both rear Brigade headquarters were located at Wieltje. Forward divisional headquarters was established on the Yser canal bank north of Ypres.

The area taken over by II. Anzac from the V. Corps was in the shape of a corridor about 17 miles long. Some 2 miles broad across its front, it contracted towards the rear to under a mile. In this confined area road communications were highly inadequate. Westwards of Poperinghe there was but one good road to Watou, and this lay wholly in the area of the XVIII. Corps on the left. Towards the battlefront the only serviceable route was the main road to Ypres through Vlamertinghe. Poperinghe formed not only the base for all the communications of II. Anzac, but also the centre for most of the XVIII. Corps traffic to the north and part of the traffic of I. Anzac to the south. On this meagre line of communications it was no inconsiderable task to cope with the continual movement of relieving troops and the unceasing stream of motor lorries and transport loaded with material for the forward area. East of Ypres the tracks were deplorable, and all available labour was employed on their maintenance and improvement. Every augmentation of technical troops, however, in the front zone involved a corresponding increase in the traffic on the already congested approaches in rear. In the case of the roads generally, as also in that of the light and broad gauge railways, the conflicting interests of construction and supply needed to be reconciled with the utmost care. The actual front line of the Corps lay roughly along the road from Zonnebeke to Langemarck, falling just short of the road on the extreme right but gradually drawing further eastwards from it as one went towards the north. On the right the Corps was separated from I. Anzac by a line which was at the moment just south of the Ypres-Roulers railway, but was shortly afterwards marked by the railway itself. The left boundary coincided with the Army Boundary on a line drawn roughly parallel to and some 1200 yards to the north of the road running from Wieltje to Gravenstafel.

As a result of the 2 successful attacks on 20th and 26th September the British front in the battle now constituted a marked salient. Its right rested on the high ground about the Menin Road, whence it trended north-east in front of Polygon Wood. In the neighbourhood of Zonnebeke it began to curve inwards but lay still well to the east of St. Julien and Langemarck, whence it bent back with a decided sharpness to the point of junction with the French in front of Houthoulst Forest. With the Fifth Army thus in complete possession of the Langemack Ridge and the Second Army firmly established on the southern extremity of the main Passchendaele Ridge, the way was now open for a direct attack from the I. Anzac position in the centre on the Broodseinde portion of the main ridge east of Zonnebeke, and for the outflanking of the enemy's position in the Houthoulst Forest. This third phase of the battle would be conducted by a series of bounds, each bound constituting a separate operation and following on its predecessor after an interval of several days. In view of the advanced season, preparations were being pushed forward with the utmost rapidity for the resumption of our offensive on 4th October.

The heights at Broodseinde, the objective of the first operation, would be seized by I. Anzac in the centre of the Second Army line. Their right flank would be covered by operations on the southern curve of the salient, their left by an advance of II. Anzac. Further to the north the Fifth Army would conform by striking out along their sector up

General Russell inspecting 1st Canterbury

Water Bottles

ENTRAINING FOR "YPRES"

AN EARLY MORNING SCENE

to and beyond Poelcapelle. The whole front affected amounted to some 7 miles. The necessary alterations of troops had been rapidly effected, and the fresh Divisions such as the New Zealanders were now familiarising themselves with their assaulting positions.

From the main ridge, on whose plateau in front of II. Anzac lay the shattered houses of Passchendaele, various small subsidiary spurs run out north-westwards, separated from each other by the headwaters of the sluggish streams characteristic of this part of Flanders. Two such spurs faced the New Zealand Division, one immediately confronting their trenches, the other in echelon northwards behind it. The nearer and more southerly one of these rose just over the small stream of the Hanebeek, which lay immediately beyond our front line. It was called the Gravenstafel Spur. Soon after it projected from the Passchendaele Ridge its even crest was broken by an isolated almost imperceptible rise called Abraham Heights; thereafter it fell gradually towards the ruins of Gravenstafel and Korek, and beyond them to the plains. As the Hanebeek drained the slopes which faced the New Zealanders, so its reverse slopes to the north were drained by another stream which in its upper part was called the Ravebeek but presently, after receiving some small tributary channels, the Stroombeek. On the other side of its valley, standing further back and further to the north from the New Zealand lines, was the second spur which jutted out from the main Passchendaele ridge. This was the Bellevue Spur. These 2 low hills were to be the scenes of the New Zealanders' engagements in the final stages of the Ypres Battle. The Gravenstafel Spur was to be carried in the forthcoming attack. The turn of the Bellevue Spur would come later.

Through constant artillery fire and bad weather both the Hanebeek and the Ravebeek-Stroombeek had lost all semblance of running streams. Their channels were marked by broad quagmires that were pockmarked by deep shellholes full of mud and water. Their crossing might be difficult even to infantry and was insuperable to tanks. Soon after the Gravenstafel road passed it, the course of the Hanebeek turned westwards through our positions, and similarly the Stroombeek, between the Gravenstafel and Bellevue ridges, rounded the former spur in a north-westerly direction and percolated, rather than flowed, into the XVIII. Corps area on the left.

19

The country, dismal and war-scarred to a degree exceeding even the desolation of the Somme, could with difficulty be imagined to have ever served the purpose of peaceful civilisation. Here and there were stunted remains of copses: here and there levelled heaps of bricks and stones on the spurs and in the valleys told of farms and villages. Thus, between our posts and the Hanebeek, one could with difficulty trace the ruins of Dochy Farm and Riverside. On the edge of the stream groups of pillboxes represented the scattered buildings of Otto Farm, and up the hillside untidy heaps amid the shellholes marked the sites of Boethoek, Van Meulen and Wimbledon. Further to the north-west, where the ridge fell away from Gravenstafel village to the flats towards the Stroombeek, were the ruins of the little hamlet of Boetleer. In the Stroombeek valley there had been substantial farmers' houses. Waterloo Farm and Calgary Grange lay on the reverse slopes of the Gravenstafel Spur; and just over the Stroombeek, where it entered the area of the troops on the north, was Kronprinz Farm. From it a country road ran back, beyond the Division's left boundary, to Albatross Farm and to a nest of dugouts called Winzig, which directly faced the 48th Division on our left. In the vicinity of most of these houses and at all points of importance the Germans had constructed numerous pillboxes. The last local feature of importance was the road which roughly divided the Divisional sector and ran north-east from Wieltje over the Gravenstafel Spur down into the Ravebeek valley, whence it mounted the Bellevue Spur towards the main ridge a little north of Passchendaele.

For the next attack the Corps' final objective corresponded approximately with the old British line in 1914. It ran from near the intersection of the Ypres-Roulers railway with the great enemy Zonnebeke-Staden system, along the eastern slopes of the Gravenstafel Spur to Kronprinz Farm. The 3rd Australian Division would carry out the attack on the right and the New Zealanders on the left. A brigade from each of the 49th and 66th Divisions was brought up into Corps reserve. The ground was, as we have seen, unsuitable for the employment of tanks, but the Corps had adequate artillery.

The frontage of the Division was some 2000 yards and the depth of its proposed advance over the ridge about 1000 yards. The furthest objective line was called the Blue Line. Just beyond the Gravenstafel crest on the forward slopes overlooking the Stroombeek valley a support position was

marked on the map as the Blue Dotted Line. The first
objective (the Red Line), which fell just short of Gravenstafel village, lay on the near side of the hill. General
Russell's plan was to attack with 2 brigades, the 4th on
the right against Abraham Heights and the 1st on the left
over the lower slopes beyond Korek. The frontage of the 4th
Brigade, which was faced by the more difficult task, was some
800, that of the 1st Brigade some 1200 yards.

It was agreed that each assaulting brigade should use 2
battalions to reach the Red Line, and "leap-frog" them with
2 others who would pass over the crest and down the
further side to the Blue. The 2nd Brigade, at present holding the line, would be withdrawn into Divisional reserve
prior to operations. The Rifle Brigade, which arrived at
Poperinghe from Vieux Berquin on 3rd October, was employed under Corps direction on cable-burying, road construction, and the digging of emplacements for the heavy artillery.
Their machine gun company, however, was taken over by
the Division for co-operation in the forthcoming attack.

In the first days of October, though the nights turned
noticeably colder, the days were still warm and the weather
favourable. The British guns remained normally active. In
every phase of the Ypres Battle our artillery programme was
altered to mystify the enemy as to the moment of launching
the next blow. The previous attack had been preceded by a
24-hours' intense bombardment. For the forthcoming operation severe preliminary bombardment was dispensed with,
and the hurricane fire reserved for zero. Two-thirds of the
ammunition allotted for harassing fire on roads and
approaches were expended by night, and special precautions
were taken to avoid any slackening at dawn. On misty days,
when night conditions were reproduced, the amount of
ammunition fired by day was correspondingly increased.
Practice barrages were carried out daily. The enemy artillery fire, particularly on the roads, was little less active than
our own. Long-range pieces shelled Poperinghe. On either
side the use of bombing aeroplanes for dispersing and
harassing the great congestion of troops and material in the
battle area became an increasingly marked feature of the
struggle. The Engineers toiled at the construction of duck-
board-tracks across the waste of shellholes and at the repair
of the cratered roads. In the line of fortified shellholes the
2nd Brigade carried out active patrolling about the Hanebeek
swamps and at Dochy Farm, where they found and killed a

small party of Germans. Early in the morning of 1st
October a strong German patrol attacked a 1st Canterbury
advanced post in a shellhole. The post was held by a Lewis gun
team under L.-Cpl. R. H. Halligan. After a few rounds the
gun jammed, and Halligan and his 3 men leaving the
shellhole attacked the enemy with bombs, killing 4 and
driving the remainder to flight. From the dead important
identifications were secured. At the beginning of our evening
barrage on the 2nd two or three elderly Prussians wandered
into our lines.

On the evening of 2nd October, under good weather conditions, the 4th and 1st Brigades moved up from Ypres to
take over the trenches. Each brigade disposed 2 battalions in the front line in considerable depth, 2 companies
being echeloned back for a distance of 500 yards and the rear
2 companies for a further distance of 500 to 800 yards.
The 2 supporting battalions took over the old British and
German front lines. The 4th Brigade front was held by 3rd
Auckland on the right and 3rd Otago on the left, with 3rd
Canterbury and 3rd Wellington in support. Each of these
supporting battalions left half their personnel behind to move
forward on the following day. The 1st Brigade took over
the front positions with 1st Wellington[1] on the right and 1st
Auckland on the left, and placed in support behind the
former battalion 2nd Auckland, and behind the latter 2nd
Wellington. The 2nd Brigade Machine Gun Company remained in the line. Two battalions (1st Canterbury and 1st
Otago) of the 2nd Brigade were left in the forward area as
reserve troops for the 4th and 1st Brigades respectively in
case of counter-attack. The remainder of the 2nd Brigade
moved back into Divisional Reserve.

3rd October was again a fine day and favoured
reconnaissance of our approaches to the line and of the
German country. The enemy's artillery was comparatively
inactive, responding but feebly to our practice barrage. The
last touches were put to our plans and preparations, and
dumps were moved forward without molestation. In the
absence of regular and continuous trenches it was necessary
that the assembly of the assaulting troops should be done on
taped lines. During the afternoon stakes were placed along
the lines selected, and as soon as darkness fell tapes were
laid out parallel to the objective to ensure proper direction
at the outset. They were placed also along the routes of

1 Major H. Holderness, vice Lt.-Col. Cook, invalided.

approach to all the different lines on which the troops would deploy. The front line of tapes was laid some 200 yards behind the outposts, partly to secure immunity from observation, partly to provide a satisfactorily straight "jumping-off" line, and partly to enable the barrage, which it was the practice to start 150 yards in front of the infantry, to fall across the whole of No Man's Land and deal with machine gun posts that might have, as the phrase was, "cuddled up" to our line. Some 40 yards behind was the tape line for the supporting companies, and some 1000 yards in rear was the first tape line of the supporting battalions. The outposts for the moment remained out before the taped lines to give protection against enemy patrols, while the supporting companies and the rear battalions moved up in the darkness to their positions. Little opportunity had been given for elaborate study or prolonged conferences, but such was the rapid appreciation and understanding of the plans by the men that everyone knew the general points of his task. This was the first engagement of the 4th Brigade as a corporate unit, and all ranks were bent on rivalling in the classic battleground of Ypres the achievements of the older brigades at Gallipoli, the Somme, Messines, and elsewhere. Not the mud and cheerless conditions nor the intermittent shelling nor previous experience of battle could shake the hearts of the attacking soldiers.

The weather just held up. It was a dark night but exceptionally quiet. Lulled by the absence of a preparatory bombardment, the enemy calculated on our not yet being ready to deliver the next stroke, and he had himself every reason for avoiding heavy artillery activity. For he was, on his part, moving troops up over the Hanebeek for a dawn attack. A Reserve Division had been brought up to thrust astride the Ypres-Roulers railway, and a Guards Division lay ready to follow it and consolidate the positions won. The attack was to be extended southwards by other Divisions, and the final objectives included Zonnebeke and Polygon Wood. His men were therefore silently deploying out opposite our own, and it was vital to him not to have their assembly disorganised by the British artillery.

The New Zealand companies were guided forward to their positions without noise or confusion. A platoon from each battalion in the posts was extended at 25 yards' interval to show the alignment. During this assembly the enemy, masking his own designs by a maintenance of normal machine gun activity, caused several casualties. Our own movements, however, passed completely unnoticed, and the guiding platoons rejoined their companies. The men were not overloaded. The battalions for the Red Line carried 120 rounds of ammunition and the attackers of the Blue Line 170. One Mills grenade had been found sufficient for the present form of fighting. The men were heated, however, by the march and by the construction of their shallow trenches. Now, as they knelt down on the oozy soil in such protection as these shelters and shellholes afforded, a clammy drizzle began to fall, and a strong westerly wind chilled them to the bone. Shortly before zero the forward posts quietly withdrew into battalion reserve.

Everything remained normal on the New Zealand front. On the right, opposite the Australians, the Germans appeared nervous and repeatedly fired flares bursting into clusters of yellow lights. There at 5.30 a.m. his guns opened a strong bombardment which gradually worked down on to the New Zealand front. The shells fell in the unoccupied area just in rear of the support companies, and casualties were few; but there was a general feeling of relief when at 6 a.m. precisely our own guns opened.

It was still dark and misty, but the drizzle had temporarily ceased. The intensity of the barrage, specially designed to deal with the new defence tactics of the Germans, satisfied the most exacting. Exclusive of the heavy and medium howitzers the Division was supported by a hundred and eighty 18-pounders and sixty 4.5-in. howitzers. Super-heavy guns and howitzers engaged special points, and there were 4 distinct artillery barrages in addition to a machine gun barrage, to take the assaulting columns forward, break up counter-attacks, and protect the infantry on the captured objectives. They covered a depth of 1000 yards. Nearest the advancing lines was the creeping shrapnel barrage of the field guns; beyond it a stationary curtain of fire was provided by the light howitzers and a proportion of the field guns. At increasing distances from the advancing infantry a third barrage was given by the 6-in. howitzers and a fourth by 60-pounders, 8-in. and 9.2-in. howitzers.

A vivid picture is given of the work of the guns in the following letter of a New Zealand artilleryman :—

"Those who heard it say it was tremendous, the din, but we in the pit heard it not at all, or only in a subconscious way, to be remembered afterwards, heard nothing but the vicious whanging of our own guns, nothing but the jerk of the breach as it opened and the snap as it closed again, nothing but the clang of falling "empties" and the rattle of the live shells as the No. 4 jammed them on, nothing but the ticking of the watch covering the interval between the rounds and the No. 1's voice: ' Thirty more left! Elevate five minutes! Drop one hundred!' then the watch's ticking again till he opened his mouth once more, and before the 'Fire!' had hardly left it, the spiteful tonguing of the gun, her rattle and quiver as she settled down, and the hiss of the buffer coming home.

"Normally our old 'B' gun is the pick of the bunch, but the whang she got the day before had put her on edge, and she behaved not nearly as sweetly as usual. Still, we were lucky to have her going at all, for that was more than we thought possible at first. The firing lever slipped occasionally, and No. 3 swore bitterly; the 'bubble' developed tricks, and his curses became deeper, the range-drum jumped at each shot like a nervous maid, and the trail stuck like a mule in the Flanders mud. But when the buffer on the run-up stopped within a few inches of home each time, I, too, felt that language was needed. As the range lengthened and her nose pointed further skyward the brute got worse, and between sticking trail and sticking buffer, the sweat came down in streams, blinding my eyes and tasting salt to my tongue; but we got there with the best, neither skipped nor lagged behind. Of the two, that last is the greater crime, for a late shot in the lifting barrage often means death to many of our fellows."

The shrapnel of the creeping barrage lashed the appointed line 150 yards in front of the foremost tape except opposite a small re-entrant on the left brigade subsector, where it fell 50 yards westward. At this point, with a long first bound it picked up the rest of the barrage, which then rolled forward slowly in a straight line all along the Divisional front, lifting 50 yards every 3 minutes with certain pauses up towards the Red Line. The object of the frequent practice barrages had been to mystify the enemy as to the delivery of the actual attack, and it had been calculated that the artillery barrage in itself might not betray the movement of our infantry. In order, therefore, to preserve the effect of surprise as long as possible, the 3 groups of 60 machine guns detailed for barrage work did not open fire with the artillery but waited for 5 minutes. The Germans, however, were not to be deceived. In a few moments their machine gun barrage opened, with special intensity on our left flank.   Four minutes after zero a heavy machine gun barrage was placed on the Zonnebeke-Langemarck Road, and a few moments later on the same spot there fell an artillery barrage which tore gaps in the 2nd Wellington lines then crossing it.   This barrage remained heavy for some 30 minutes, after which it became more scattered.   Throughout the attack the assaulting battalions were not greatly harassed by hostile artillery fire.   In response to variously coloured lights fired from the pillboxes the German guns continually shortened range as our advance progressed.   Their barrage, however, was ill-managed and fell always just in rear of our leading battalions.

Meanwhile these units allotted for the capture of the Red Line were pressing down towards the reedy channel of the Hanebeek.   Each battalion was on a 2-company frontage. They moved in sections in single file covered by a screen in extended order like beaters.   The formation, in itself suitable for dealing with the enemy pillboxes, was also adapted to the nature of the ground, where the little ridges between the lips of the shell-craters provided the sole tracks for advance. The assaulting infantry had not gone more than 200 yards when they came on the first lines of the enemy which were to have carried out the attack anticipated some 10 minutes by our own.   Another 200 yards in rear was the second, but both lines had been decimated by our artillery fire.   On the 1st Auckland front alone were about 500 corpses, and generally along the whole line every shellhole held 1 to 4 dead Germans.   Few wore steel helmets, and only here and there was a bayonet fixed.   Some of the survivors fought pluckily with rifle fire, but when it came to bayonet work and close quarters, neither physically nor morally were they a match for their assailants.   In the I. Anzac dressing stations and casualty clearing stations the proportion of prisoners suffering from bayonet wounds was noted as unusually high.   The majority of the Germans surrendered readily.

More determined resistance was offered to the 4th Brigade by the occupants of the pillboxes, whose morale had not suffered from our artillery.   Dochy Farm and Riverside were occupied with ease, but about 100 yards from the Hanebeek and the pillboxes about Otto Farm heavy machine gun and rifle fire broke on the advancing lines.   These works also, however, were not to give much trouble. As 3rd Auckland rushed forward towards the group of the Farm pillboxes in their sector, the garrison of 15 came out with hands up, leaving 4 dead and 4 machine guns. In the larger group on the other side of the Farm a 3rd Otago party, led with consummate gallantry by Pte. D. Mackenzie, mopped up 35 prisoners and 4 machine guns.

It was known that the Hanebeek was a quagmire of shell-holes full of water. The barrage had been arranged, therefore, to halt here so as to cover the crossing. As it was, the men picked their way through the shellholes without overmuch difficulty, and the rear waves coming up and halting here for our curtain of fire to lift suffered somewhat heavily from the enemy barrage which was naturally placed at this spot. Moreover, a sickly grey daylight was now in the sky. The leading troops became dim targets for the machine guns on the bare terraces of the Gravenstafel hill, and when the barrage at length lifted, they lost no time in pressing closely (some 40 yards) after it.

On the right, 3rd Auckland beat down by rifle and Lewis gun fire opposition at pillboxes on the sites of various ruined farms, and captured their garrisons and 3 machine guns. On their left 3rd Otago pushed past the important works at Van Meulen, leaving them to be dealt with by a specially appointed party, who captured here a machine gun and 50 prisoners. As the battalions made steadily up-hill for the Red Line, the shells of our heavier guns and howitzers were now passing high over head on to the reverse slopes, but the 18-pounder fire fell in a sheer unbroken curtain in front. Near the crest, smoke shells, fired by the left hand gun of each battery, fell suddenly amid the shrapnel and continued for 5 minutes. At that pre-arranged signal the infantry knew that the protective barrage was being formed and that they were on the Red Line. Both battalions reached it up to time-table.

Here the barrage halted 150 yards in front for an hour, and both battalions pushed out strong parties to clear dugouts and pillboxes in their immediate front. The enemy machine gunners and infantry who did not at once surrender were shot. These pillboxes were particularly close to 3rd Auckland, whose parties here captured 8 machine guns. Opposite 3rd Otago the protective barrage was placed beyond Gravenstafel, and a company cleared the pillboxes and other concrete shelters by the ruins and captured 100 prisoners. All the forward parties, on completing their mission of clearing the area up to the ''Red Protector,'' where our covering barrage continued, withdrew to the Red Line to help in the consolidation already under way. 3rd Otago in all captured 200 prisoners and 8 machine guns, and 3rd Auckland a corresponding number of prisoners and 15 machine guns.

On the lower slopes northwards and on the flats towards the Stroombeek the 1st Brigade had similarly reached their objective. In this area the battalions detailed for the capture of the first objective were 1st Wellington on the right and 1st Auckland on the left.   1st Wellington, like the two 4th Brigade battalions, had to cross the Hanebeek just before it turned sharply westwards.

Beyond the Hanebeek 1st Auckland diverged, as we shall see, too far north, and the left Wellington company keeping in touch with them had stiff fighting at the pillboxes at Boetleer, which had resisted the Fifth Army's right wing on 26th September and were now included in the Auckland objectives. The whole brigade front was thus covered by Wellington who, with splendid examples of bravery shewn by Capt. J. Keir, Lt. E. L. Malone and 2nd Lt. L. M. Dixon, overcame the resistance offered at Boetleer and elsewhere.   Rapid progress was time and again thwarted by German machine guns. Against one, Sergt. K. A. Goldingham, bidding one of his men engage the gun with rifle grenades, rushed alone from the flank and bayoneted the crew of 4.   Pte. D. Jones, when his company was checked, dashed forward alone under heavy shell-fire and killed the whole gun crew and other enemy, in all 12 men, single-handed.   Pte. T. Geange, a Lewis gunner, whose gun was out of action, was in a section which with another was held up by an enemy machine gun.   For a time no one could see its position.   At last locating it, Geange rushed forward against the post, armed only with his revolver. His fine example led another man to follow him.   Both were wounded, the second man dying later, but their bold action provided a chance for the rest of the section to dash forward, and the gun was immediately captured and the crew killed. By similar gallant feats on the part of individuals and by skilful concerted movements 1st Wellington pushed on steadily to the Red Line, successfully clearing the entire brigade area. On the crest the right company were met by heavy machine gun fire from 2 dugouts in front of the ruins of Korek. These were about 120 yards beyond the Red Line, but it was essential to silence their fire in order to push on consolidation

The Ypres Canal

OTTO FARM   [*Photo by Capt. S. Cory Wright*

THE CAPITOL

without interruption. 3rd Otago were similarly inconvenienced, and parties from both battalions, led by Sergt. F. E. Chappell and others, pressed on into our own barrage and rushing towards the pillboxes threw bomb after bomb into the entrances. Of these pillboxes one was of considerable size. It appeared to be full of Germans, and to be a place of importance. The Wellington n.c.o., Cpl. A. Paterson, who captured it, entered its doorway to reconnoitre. The outer chamber was a scene of horror. It literally dripped and ran with the blood of 30 dead Germans who lay mangled and mutilated by our bombs. There was an inner recess where a German officer and some men, most of whom were wounded, had taken refuge. As Paterson entered, the officer set fire to a mass of papers with some incendiary material. The flames seized the wood-work and fittings, which at once leapt into a blaze. Paterson was forced to withdraw, and the Germans alive or dead were incinerated. The dugout burned all the morning.

1st Auckland on the left beyond the Hanebeek were faced from the outset with heavy fighting. Under a blast of machine gun fire from Aviatik Farm and the shellholes the first line of the attack withered away. Most effective help was given by the light trench mortars. Unfortunately one of these was destroyed early in the morning, but the other, admirably handled, came time after time to the assistance of the infantry. Some 200 yards in front of the tape line, at Dear House and Aviatik Farm, were groups of pillboxes. Auckland's right was held up for a few moments by machine gun fire from Dear House, but the leading platoon surrounded the pillbox and captured guns and crews. Similarly, after a shower of bombs, Aviatik Farm fell to 2nd Lt. C. F. Seaward's platoon, and the successful attackers were able to pick up the barrage before the Red Line.

In a line with these concrete structures was a further group at Winzig, just off the Auckland front on the extreme right of the XVIII. Corps. Machine guns from here played on Auckland's left and threatened to arrest progress. Partly attracted by the magnetism which fire exerts over brave troops, and with a view to protecting their flank, partly perhaps owing to the confusion in the darkness or to a desire to maintain touch with the troops on the left, themselves swinging towards the north, 1st Auckland gradually diverged on to the front of the 48th Division, where they captured in turn Winzig, Albatross Farm, and Winchester, with over 200 prisoners, and carried the Red Line in front. The 48th Division troops had suffered heavy casualties under the distant machine gun fire, which also harassed Auckland, from the Bellevue Spur down the Stroombeek valley. They were not at the moment able to fill the line. Auckland therefore stayed where they were. A troublesome machine gun in front was silenced by the remaining light trench mortar, and the infantry consolidated with their usual rapidity. The original Auckland objective was captured by the left company of 1st Wellington.

Thus there was for a time a considerable gap in the centre of the Red Line, and the two 1st Wellington companies were faced with the manifestly impossible task of consolidating the whole front. This gap was filled first by the Wellington company in support and later in the day also by the reserve company. By 10 a.m., however, the right Auckland company had moved across into the New Zealand area to already constructed trenches. Along the whole of the Red Line, as soon as the immediate front was cleared, every man worked with a will at consolidation. Down in the Stroombeek flats 1st Auckland soon struck water, but on the slopes the other battalions found good soil, and by the time that the barrage moved forward, though the line was not yet connected, the different posts were 4 or 5 feet under cover.

While this consolidation was in progress, the remaining battalions of the 2 brigades, which with their attached sections of machine guns had left their assembly positions at zero, passed through the Red Line in splendid order and assembled under the barrage on the Red Protector. From south to north this line was formed by 3rd Canterbury and 3rd Wellington in the 4th Brigade area, and 2nd Auckland and 2nd Wellington on the 1st Brigade front. Their assembly was complete a few minutes after 8 a.m. It was their task to develop the advance over Abraham Heights and the continuation of the crest northwards down the eastern slopes. On these they would establish first the intermediate objective (the Blue Dotted Line), and then the final objective (the Blue Line). The light trench mortars which had co-operated in the attack on the Red Line now joined these battalions, and the machine guns took up positions in front of the Red Line to move with the infantry to the crest and the Blue Dotted Line, where they could cover our advance down the far slopes by engaging enemy machine guns on the Bellevue Spur over the Ravebeek.

At 8.10 a.m. the barrage lifted to move forward by bounds of 50 yards every 4 minutes. It maintained irreproachable density and accuracy. The troops at once met resistance in the shellholes, and as soon as ever the extended wave of beaters crossed the crest, machine gun fire beat against them in a steady driving hail from the main ridge and from Bellevue Spur. A pre-arranged smoke screen was formed by our artillery along these commanding positions, and this and the dull light to some extent blinded the Germans' observation, but their machine guns took a toll of casualties. The hostile artillery fell mostly on the western slopes of the spur and on the Hanebeek valley.

As the troops pressed down the eastern face towards the Ravebeek, centres of resistance had to be overcome all along the line. On the extreme right 3rd Canterbury was held up temporarily by 2 pillboxes in Berlin Wood. These resisted a slapdash attempt to rush them by bombs, but fell before a little model set-piece attack by 2 platoons. A machine gun and 17 Germans were taken. The total captures of this battalion were 8 machine guns and 86 prisoners. When nearing the crest, 3rd Wellington similarly met obstinate fighting about 2 well-concealed pillboxes which had not been marked on the map. A frontal assault was frustrated, but 2nd Lt. F. C. Cornwall directed the survivors into 2 parties, which worked from shellhole to shellhole round each flank and bombed the enemy position from the rear. There was another check for 20 minutes round a group of pillboxes on the site of the farm known as Berlin, but the ubiquitous light trench mortars delivered a short hurricane bombardment, and the place was rushed. On the north side of the Gravenstafel road, a joint attack by 3rd Wellington and 2nd Auckland captured a German Battalion Headquarters in the group of pillboxes at Waterloo, which were a week later to witness such tragic scenes. 3rd Wellington secured 8 machine guns and 150 prisoners. By 9.30 a.m. the moppers-up of both 4th Brigade battalions had cleared all the nests, and their front troops were in full possession of the Blue Dotted and Blue Lines.

In the 1st Brigade sector 2nd Auckland and 2nd Wellington breasted the slopes at Korek and reached their final objectives with equal punctuality. The former battalion on the right had to cross an intense machine gun barrage on the lower slopes of the spur and lost all its senior officers. The infantry pressed forward through the danger zone as speedily as the barrage would allow, and trench mortar personnel, slinging their weapons like Lewis guns, advanced scarcely less quickly. On the 2nd Auckland front in particular, the one mortar's co-operation with the infantry was again invaluable through the rapidity with which the team came into action and the demoralising effect of their bombs on the German machine gunners.

On approaching the pillboxes amid the chaotic jumble of brick heaps that had been Korek, our lines were checked by deadly machine gun fire at close range. The Germans were here in force. Within a few minutes the mortar placed a barrage all round the spot, and the garrison of 80 came out and surrendered. As our screen neared the Blue Line, another enemy machine gun fired short rapid bursts. The mortar dropped a few rounds about it, and the crew came forward with their hands up. Just beyond the objective a third gun came into action. Five rounds were fired at it. The Germans waved a rag in token of surrender. The mortar ceased fire. Then the enemy, instead of coming forward, began to run back. A few well-placed shots shepherded them, and they turned and came in. The group of ruins at Calgary Grange fell to a combined attack of Aucklanders and Wellingtons. In their advance 2nd Auckland captured altogether 9 machine guns and 200 prisoners.

In the low country on the extreme left 2nd Wellington, though troubled by distant machine gun fire, met at first comparatively little fighting. Like 1st Auckland on the Red Line, but to much lesser extent, 2nd Wellington also encroached on the XVIII. Corps front, but the 3 platoons which so erred were, on their arrival at the Blue Line, at once brought across to the New Zealand area. Only when the Wellington screen was approaching the Stroombeek did they encounter signs that their further progress would be obstinately resisted. On the far bank the featureless waste was broken by a group of ill-defined concrete blockhouses well hidden in the ruins of Kronprinz Farm. They were covered by a wired trench in front, and here the Germans defended themselves with resolution. The platoon commander was wounded, but under the same Sergt. Foot, who had distinguished himself at Basseville[1] and whose work now won a bar to his D.C.M., our men gradually forced their way nearer and nearer, and at length rose with a yell and went in with the bayonet. Not less than 7 machine guns and 39 prisoners were captured here, and the saps were left full of dead.

---

[1] p. 238.

Marked gallantry won D.C.M.s for Sergts. M. Ward and C. E. Menzies. The one led his company forward with splendid leadership after all the company officers had become casualties. The other was a Lewis gun sergeant. Wounded early in the day he refused to withdraw. During consolidation he placed a captured machine gun in position, visiting his men under heavy machine gun fire and himself kept in action one of his guns when its crew were destroyed.

The dugouts at Kronprinz Farm had formed a battalion headquarters, and the papers and plans captured in the orderly room yielded valuable information. The total captures claimed by 2nd Wellington were 10 machine guns and 213 prisoners.

At Kronprinz Farm the left flank of the Division was joined by the 48th Division, whose line northwards fell somewhat short of the final objective. On the right flank, the 3rd Australians after severe fighting had seized the whole of their Blue Line well up to schedule time. Observers in the contact aeroplanes, patrolling with great difficulty in the high wind and rain, marked on their map the line of our red flares all along the II. Anzac objective.

To cover the consolidation the various barrages continued for varying periods after the capture of the Blue Line. The shrapnel curtain fell 200 yards in front on the Ravebeek and on the road which ran along its valley at the foot of the Bellevue Spur past the ruins of Peter Pan and Yetta Houses towards Adler Farm. 200 yards further on, our 4.5-in. howitzers and some 18-pounders bombarded the trench elements along the lower slope which were swept also by our machine guns. The 6-in. howitzers' line was 800 yards, and that of the heavier pieces, 8-in. and 9.2-in. howitzers and 60-pounders, 1000 yards away from the Blue Line, on the pillboxes on the top of Bellevue Spur. The smoke screen was similarly retained for nearly 2 hours. The heavier and more distinct barrages remained stationary for a quarter of an hour and then progressed along the eastern slopes of Bellevue Spur for 45 minutes, reopening fire later at definite times and for definite periods. The machine gun barrage ceased as the howitzers lifted, but the near shrapnel curtain maintained its protection for a further period of 3 hours, when it also gradually died away.

By that time not only the troops on the Red, but those also on the Blue Line were under cover. Our foremost trenches were not greatly harassed by enemy artillery, which

20

played rather on the reverse slopes of the Gravenstafel Spur and on the batteries. The 1st Artillery Brigade guns in particular were severely punished, 5 being put out of action. Throughout the day our batteries were also shelled by a high-velocity naval gun which did considerable damage and inflicted many casualties. On the forward slopes it was the activity of the enemy's snipers and machine guns which accelerated the task of consolidation. The Bellevue Spur pillboxes looked down commandingly across the whole valley back to Korek. The Blue Line was constructed like the Red as a continuous trench and not merely as a line of posts. It was consolidated and held in such a manner and in such strength as to ensure the repulse of counter-attacks before it, and to secure a good starting-point for the next stage of our attack. 300 yards in rear of the Blue Line on the forward slopes beyond the crest, a line of shellhole posts was constructed on the Blue Dotted Line which would gradually be connected and act as support positions. On this line some battalions had kept their leading companies, leap-frogging the supporting companies through to the Blue; others, having made both it and the Blue successive objectives for the same troops, occupied it with their reserves. Behind the crest the Red Line, with a fine field of fire along its length, was now continuous and capable of a stout defence as a reserve position. As soon as the Blue Line battalions had passed through them, parties of 1st Wellington commenced communication trenches forward over the crest. With the additional task of consolidating the Red Line on 1st Auckland's front, they were unable at the time to accomplish much. By dusk, however, the garrisons of both Red and Blue Lines in particular could be well satisfied with their positions. Between the 3 lines, posts were arranged chequerwise at suitable places.

The Battle of Broodseinde was a signal success for the British arms. It is true that the Armies' objectives were not fully secured, and that certain portions of the ground won, as at Polderhoek Chateau on the extreme right flank of the attack, were regained by German counter-strokes. It was, too, a disappointment that the plans formed for immediate exploitation of our success had to be abandoned, owing to a check on the Fifth Army's left, though it appears doubtful whether much further progress would have been actually realised. It was in conformity with these plans that 2nd

Wellington pushed out towards Adler Farm and established posts which were later withdrawn. On the other hand, in the centre of the Second Army front, General Birdwood's Australians and some British troops had thrust the line well over the main Passchendaele-Broodseinde ridge, 9000 yards of which were now held in front of Noordemdhoek Molenaarelsthoek and Broodseinde. Unusually heavy casualties had been inflicted on the enemy, and over 5000 prisoners captured.

Of these the New Zealand Division provided no less than 1159, drawn from 4 different Divisions.[1] In the day's operations it captured also 60 machine guns and a large quantity of war material, which included some maps and documents of the highest value for our Intelligence Staff. The Gravenstafel Spur gave excellent observation on to the north end of the Passchendaele Ridge and formed a strong buttress on which to bend the line back from the ridge, should the General Staff consider it advisable to break off the battle. The first essay in the new methods of warfare went even more smoothly than was expected, and the value of the training at Lumbres was proved.

Though heavy, the price paid for these successes could not, in view of the magnitude of the results, be regarded as excessive. The 1st Brigade lost 12 officers and 180 men killed, with 700 other casualties. 1st Auckland paid severely for trespassing into the Stroombeek valley, and under machine gun fire from Yetta Houses suffered more heavily than the other battalions. By the time of their relief 7 officers, including Major A. G. Mahan, were killed and 4 wounded; over 50 other ranks were killed and 200 wounded. In the 4th Brigade over 600 had been wounded; 10 officers and 120 men had been killed. The severest losses in the brigade had fallen on 3rd Wellington. The artillery had come off cheaply, losing 2 officers and 6 men killed and 4 officers and 19 men wounded.

Two reasons accounted for the heavy German casualties. In the first place, captured documents showed that the High Command had reviewed their new policy of elastic defence, which had been practised throughout the whole of the Ypres operations, and condemned it as not merely costly and entailing an enormous strain on reserves, but also tactically unsatisfactory. They had resolved to revert to their former principle of holding the front line in strength with not less

1 The majority of these were from the 20th German Division, which this day lost two-thirds of its effectives. This Division included the notorious 77th Infantry Regiment, which in 1914 was responsible for the atrocities at Malines: see also p. 367.

than half a regiment in the foremost trenches in its sector. In some units on the battlefield this plan had actually been put into practice. In the second place, our artillery fell with dire havoc among the unprotected troops lying in assembly for the attack which our own assault anticipated by so brief an interval. Prisoners differed as to whether the exact time fixed was 6.10 or 6.20 a.m., but all accounts agree that the enemy forces were deployed on their lines ready to advance when our barrage fell on them and annihilated them.

The coincidence of the 2 attacks, the enemy's losses, and the successful British advance entailed a confusion in his plans and a disorganisation both among his artillery and infantry which ensured quiescence for the next few days. His shelling was continued, but was light and scattered. All along the Second Army front, in different local counter-attacks, the lack of cohesion, no less than the mixture of units for thickening up the line, clearly betrayed his straits.

No grand counter-attack developed on the New Zealand front. Some isolated attempts were indeed made, but on receipt of early warning, given by S.O.S. signals or the long brown streamers of the smoke bombs dropped by our special counter-attack aeroplane, were at once checked by our artillery. Thus, shortly after midday on 4th October, some 200 of the enemy assaulted east of Kronprinz Farm. The 2nd Wellington sentries fired the red-over-green-over-yellow S.O.S. rockets, and our batteries smote the attack ere it developed. About 4.30 p.m., again, enemy advancing from Passchendaele were scattered by our artillery and machine gun barrage. To provide against eventualities the reserve company was moved forward, and 1st Otago was brought up to near the brigade headquarters in Capricorn Keep. Later in the afternoon about 300 enemy were seen assembling in shellhole positions at Peter Pan and along the lower slopes of Bellevue. The artillery barrage invoked could not have been placed more happily. It smashed up the attack completely. The 2nd Auckland sentries on the Blue Line could observe the dead lying where they fell and the wounded crawling laboriously back up the hill. Further small attacks after dark were repulsed with artillery, machine gun, Lewis gun, and rifle fire, and served only to swell the enemy's casualty roll.

Dry weather had prevailed during the earlier part of the day, and the evacuation of wounded proceeded smoothly. Early in the afternoon, however, heavy rain set in and speedily converted the whole area into a quaking morass. It had not been found possible to push the dumps as far forward as had been intended. Over the almost impassable surface the mules became bogged, and one was actually drowned in the Hanebeek. The labours of the carrying parties were correspondingly aggravated. Under these disadvantages the last of our wounded, with a few exceptions still in the aid posts, were carried back to the dressing stations, and food and munitions were brought to the wet, tired, muddied but cheerful men in front. The movement forward of guns and heavy material proved of surpassing difficulty. At the earliest possible moment the Engineers and Pioneers were set to work on the construction of a tramway system, the repair of the Gravenstafel road, the laying of mule tracks, and the extension of duckboard tracks for the infantry. It was necessary, too, to provide landmarks in the featureless waste of mud and shellholes. Every 25 yards a line of posts painted white on our side blazed the track beyond the point where the duckboards ended, and noticeboards, giving the names of all farm sites and places of importance shown on the map, were to prove invaluable. Throughout the night rain fell intermittently. Without opposition the infantry patrolled the miasmatic pools of the Ravebeek and Stroombeek and the ruins of Fleet Cottage.

The 5th dawned grey and dismal, and chilly rain fell all but continuously during the day. The mud and water in the forward trenches reached almost to the men's knees. The enemy's artillery activity was desultory, and evidence pointed strongly to a withdrawal of his guns as a result of our advance or counter-battery work. On the Bellevue Spur stretcher-bearers with a Red Cross flag were moving about the saps collecting their casualties.

Advantage was taken of this quietness to complete the dispositions of our forward troops, arranged with a view to minimising losses, ensuring depth of defence and facilitating the approaching relief by the 49th Division. Troops from the Blue took over the Red Line, and the bulk of the support battalions, thus relieved, consolidated new positions further in rear. The 1st Auckland companies still in the XVIII. Corps area moved back in the late evening (5th October) to behind 2nd Auckland on the Red Line. Shortly afterwards a brigade of the 49th Division came to relieve both forward brigades on the New Zealand sector. That evening the 2nd Brigade travelled back by lorries to the Winnezeele

area beyond Watou. The 1st and 4th Brigades on completing their relief moved to the old British and German
front lines and thence on 6th October to the northern outskirts of Ypres. On the latter date the 4th Brigade left by
lorries for the reserve area at Eecke. The 1st Brigade
remained in the battle area, with headquarters at Poperinghe,
to take over from the Rifle Brigade the duties of the working
brigade engaged under Corps control. On the 6th the
command of the sector passed to the incoming Division, and
General Russell's Headquarters moved back to Watou. The
artillery remained in the line, and the New Zealand C.R.A.
continued to command the field artillery on the 49th Divisional front. The Engineers Pioneers and various medical
units were also left under the G.O.C. 49th Division. At the
same time in the southern half of the Corps sector the 3rd
Australians made way for the 66th Division.

Long ere now it had become but too clear that the
strategic aims of the Ypres offensive were incapable of
realisation. Delayed at the outset, the Allied attack had
encountered improved methods of resistance ably planned
and practised by a brave and skilful enemy and, above all,
had been attended by uniformly unfavourable weather, which
making each blow disjointed neutralised the finest qualities
of the attacking armies. It was already a matter of uncertainty
whether even the completion of the immediate tactical objective, the capture of the remainder of the ridge, would be
possible before winter put a stop to operations. Added to
these difficulties in the field, general policy was thrown out
of gear by one of those divergent plans which, receiving
sanction in high quarters, periodically allured optimistic
minds with its promise of rapid victory. It was now
seriously contemplated to weaken the Franco-British sector
by the despatch of troops for the purpose of exploiting the
Italian successes against Austria. Even after this scheme was
hamstrung, the whole question of preserving an aggressive
policy at Ypres had gravely to be weighed. Continuance of
wet weather would make the task gigantic, and the German
reserves released from Russia were accumulating beyond the
Rhine. It was possible now for Sir Douglas Haig to break
off the battle in a fairly satisfactory position. On the other
hand, the continuance of pressure in the north would assist
the forthcoming French blow on the Aisne. The capture of
the ridge would to some extent tranquilise public opinion,

BOGGED

FIELD GUNS IN SHELLHOLES

FUNERAL OF LT.-COL. G. A. KING

AN ANTI-TANK GUN

secure the positions already won, rob the enemy of his observation over our lines and gun positions, and yield a fuller command over the German country about Roulers and Thourout. Moreover, the enemy losses had been severe. Indications pointed to a sensible decline in his morale. For the moment his artillery was considerably disorganised.

In the end it was decided to persevere and deliver the next blow on 9th October. The state of confusion in the enemy forces appeared to offer a considerable chance of exploitation of success. Arrangements were therefore made for the concentration of cavalry, including the I. and II. Anzac Mounted Regiments, in forward areas, and for the rapid entrainment of lightly equipped infantry brigades of reserve Divisions, should an opportunity occur for pursuit. In this connection certain of the New Zealand troops in the reserve area moved to positions of closer proximity to the railway, and the Corps Staff prepared a timetable for 2 brigades of the New Zealanders and of the 3rd Australians, which would enable them to be entrained at short notice and detrained at Hell Fire Corner east of Ypres to press the German retreat.

But from 5th October the weather continued unfavourable, hindering alike the work of consolidation and the advance of the guns, and making the ground still more unsuitable for movement. The exploitation scheme was cancelled, and instead a further deliberate stroke was ordered for the 12th. On the II. Anzac front this would be delivered as on the 4th by the 3rd Australians and the New Zealanders who would relieve the 66th and 49th Divisions after their attack on the 9th. For the New Zealand attack General Russell selected the 2nd and 3rd Brigades, the latter of whom had, as has been noted, handed over its tasks under the Corps Engineers to the 1st Brigade. The 4th Brigade would be used as Divisional reserve.

The main purpose of the attack delivered on the 9th was to swing up the Allied left. In the extreme north the French and the British XIV. Corps carried all before them up to their final objectives in the outskirts of the Houthoulst Forest, and the line was driven well eastwards north of Poelcapelle. South of that point success was considerably less marked. The XVIII. Corps on the left of II. Anzac made little progress. South of the railway I. Anzac, who formed the pivot of the main attack, captured Nieuwemolen and their first objective on the main ridge. On the II. Anzac front the objective of the 66th and 49th Divisions had been the Bellevue Spur and the high ground that lay opposite Bellevue, south of the Ravebeek. Part of the troops, delayed by the miserable conditions of a 4-mile march through quagmires in rain and inky-black darkness, did not reach their assembly in time. The 66th Division on the right carried Keerselaarhoek and made good progress, but becoming exposed to enfilade fire from Bellevue, which the 49th did not succeed in capturing, were ultimately obliged to fall back. In the evening the troops lay on their first objective some 500 yards in advance of their starting point. The southern Division's right rested on the railway east of Keerselaarhoek on the lower slopes of the main ridge. Thence the position ran north past a mutilated copse, known as Augustus Wood, down the slopes to the Ravebeek. The 49th Division met them in the valley at Marsh Bottom and continued the line along the bottom of the Bellevue slopes above the Ravebeek just beyond the farm ruins at Peter Pan and Yetta Houses to the XVIII. Corps boundary east of Adler Farm. Small pockets were established further up the Bellevue slopes on the western edge of Wolf Copse, Wolf Farm and a cemetery on the northern boundary. Casualties had been heavy, and conditions imposed extreme hardship.

The relief, if it could be called a relief, of the exhausted troops began on 10th October. The 3rd Australians moved into the right sector, and the New Zealanders, filing over the Gravenstafel ridge, crossed the Ravebeek-Stroombeek valley to the general line Marsh Bottom—Peter Pan—Yetta Houses. Somewhat severe shelling was experienced on the march-up. One or two advanced posts of the 49th Division lay only 150 yards from the German lines on Bellevue Spur, but in view of the forthcoming attack and the necessary barrage arrangements, no advantage was to be gained by taking over a series of isolated half-determined posts on the heights. As it was, the front line was much confused, and the 4th Rifles, for instance, relieved elements of no less than 6 battalions. The 2nd Brigade took over the right subsector, establishing their headquarters at the Capitol, a redoubt west of the Hanebeek valley. The Rifle Brigade in the left subsector made their headquarters well forward at Korek. Each brigade was disposed in great depth on a 1-battalion frontage. 2nd Otago, with 2 companies of 2nd Canterbury, held the 2nd Brigade front, and the 4th Rifles the northern area. The command of the whole Divisional sector passed on the following morning (11th October), and Divisional Headquarters took up their former position on the Yser Canal. Engineers Pioneers and medical units together with the artillery of the outgoing Division remained in the line, and an infantry brigade was placed at General Russell's disposal pending the arrival of the reserve (4th) New Zealand brigade.

In the artillery preparation for the attack on the 12th the prominent factors were intense counter-battery work and the so-called "isolating" fire directed on advanced enemy Strong Points. As the German artillery constantly shifted their positions, no effort was spared first to locate active batteries in the morning, and then to destroy them in the afternoon. The enemy's communication trenches were blocked by knocking in lengths of 10 yards. It was necessary to bombard by heavy artillery his wire entanglements, machine gun emplacements, pillboxes, telephone exchanges and observation posts, but it is interesting to note a growing insistence, at this time, on the principle that terrain should not be reduced to such crater condition as might unduly hamper our movement and communications after the attack. Practice assault barrages were fired, and series of shrapnel and gas barrages, preceded by high-explosive storms, were passed over the hostile shellhole system and dugouts for the purpose of inflicting losses and reducing morale. Bivouacs hutments and likely places of assembly were bombarded by day and night with sudden short violent bursts of concentrated fire.

The fulfillment of all these tasks demanded enormous supplies of ammunition. In the case of the majority of the gun positions, the state of the forward roads was such as to preclude the use of mechanical transport. Pack animals were largely employed. Conditions were so adverse that the Staff sanctioned and gave authority for a reduction of rates of fire, should the task of replenishing dumps be found insoluble. But the artillery, knowing how much the infantry depended on their efforts, worked with an energy and enthusiasm to which no finer tribute can be paid than the mere statement of the fact that no gun had to diminish its rate of fire for shortage of ammunition.

Even more serious, however, than the ammunition question was the problem of moving the guns forward. A gun was considered to be in action when it was prepared to open fire on S.O.S. lines either by map or registration, and had 200 rounds dumped at its position. It was now laid down

that not more than one-third of the guns should be out of
action at any one time, owing to moving forward; and in the
shortness of the time available, this provision, sound in itself,
added to the gunners' difficulties. Positions were prepared
beforehand, and ammunition was taken forward and protected from the rain. During the night 9th/10th October
one or two sections were hauled forward with the utmost
difficulty. It took 5 hours of daylight on the 10th to
bring forward a single gun of the 1st Battery and another of
the 13th. In the afternoon 2 howitzers of the 15th were
bogged beyond St. Julien, and the teams and men trying to
extricate them were subjected to heavy shelling. The
locality was bombarded through the night, and coming forward
again before dawn on the 11th the gunners found the road
blocked with dead horses, dead men and destroyed vehicles.
By almost superhuman efforts the howitzers were dragged to
the new pits by 7.30 a.m., and by the afternoon eight 18-
pounders and 4.5-in. howitzers were well forward, but with a
lamentable deficiency of stable platforms. The heavies were
faced with even greater difficulties.

The object of the forthcoming attack on 12th October was
to renew and extend the effort of the 9th. The Fifth Army
would again push forward on the left of the battle front.
The whole of the Second Army attack would be delivered by
Australians and New Zealanders. Its aim was to strengthen
our hold on the main ridge by the capture of Passchendaele
village and of the Goudberg Spur to the north. The main
attack on the Second Army front would be carried out by II.
Anzac. As their northern flank would be safeguarded by the
XVIII. Corps advancing some 2000 yards, so on the south a
brigade of I. Anzac would secure their right by connecting
the new line with the positions already won over the crest of
the main ridge southwards. The II. Anzac plan allotted the
capture of Passchendaele to the 3rd Australians and that
of the Goudberg Spur to the New Zealanders. The furthest
depth of advance was some 2500 yards. On the New Zealand
sector each brigade frontage was about 750 yards. Each
of the 2 attacking brigades was given full disposal of its
machine gun company. The other 3 companies were
employed for barrage work. The artillery and machine gun
barrages were arranged on lines similar to those adopted on
the 4th, and the artillery received instructions to be prepared
to move batteries forward, after the final objective was gained,
with a view to barraging the enemy's country from 1000 to

2000 yards beyond Passchendaele. The Division had the direct support of a hundred and forty-four 18-pounders and forty-eight 4.5-in. howitzers.

Owing to the failure on the 9th the Divisional plans previously drawn up had to be largely recast. The shortness of the time available for preparations and reconnaissance, and the indefiniteness of the information obtained from the relieved Division added to the Staff's difficulties. Hurried measures had to be taken for the selection of headquarters and medical posts and stations, the extension of signal communications, planked roadways and duckboard tracks, the bridging of streams and morasses, and the taping of approach routes. In particular, there was insufficient time to deal with the fields of barbed wire on the Bellevue Spur. Their formidable nature was even now insufficiently realised by the outgoing Division. The trenches themselves, forming part of the once strong Zonnebeke-Staden line, had been destroyed by our artillery, but since the 9th the entanglements, especially round the Strong Points and pillboxes, had been assiduously strengthened. They were closely reconnoitred on the night of the relief (10th/11th October) by a 2nd Otago patrol under Sergt. Travis, and their strength could be gauged from the Gravenstafel ridge. The 2nd Infantry Brigade Headquarters secured some assistance from the heavy artillery, but the damage done was small. For all these reasons a postponement of the attack would have been welcomed, but the decision did not rest with the Division or with the Corps. The Army's orders had been issued, and Divisions were but pawns in the tremendous game played over these Flanders swamps and ridges.

In the early morning of the 11th the enemy artillery shelled the forward areas with some intensity.[1] Thereafter the day passed quietly enough. Final conferences were held, and liaison was established with the 3rd Australians on the right and with the 9th Division (XVIII. Corps) on the left. Every possible effort also was made to clear the forward area of the British wounded who had fallen on the 9th and still lay famished and untended on the battlefield. Their stretcher cases crowded the regimental aid posts. Many more lay in the shellholes in front. All wounded found were fed, and as far as preparations for the attack could permit were carried back to the dressing stations. Those that could not be brought back were dressed in the muddy shellholes. On the morning

of the 12th many of these unfortunate men were still lying
upon the battlefield, and not a few had meantime died of
exposure in the wet and cold weather.

The forming-up lines were taped well in rear of our posts
to ensure that the leading waves should start level and in
line with the 9th Division troops on their left, and that the
creeping barrage should open on all points held by the enemy
close to our positions. The principles that governed the siting
of the foremost tape line were, on the one hand, that it should
be not less than 150 yards from the opening barrage line,
and on the other, not more than would allow the infantry to
close up under the barrage before it lifted. In the evening
(11th October) the 4th Brigade detrained at Ypres and
relieved the reserve brigade of the 49th Division, placing its
2 foremost battalions in the old British and German front
lines on either side of the Wieltje-Gravenstafel road.

The afternoon and evening of the 11th were cold and
bleak. The skies were an unrelieved grey, and the desolate
landscape of mud, marsh, shellholes and bald ridge took on
an even more inhospitable and forbidding appearance. At
dusk the assaulting brigades struggled up to their positions.
Shelling was normal, and the troops were spared the gas which
incommoded the Australians, but the ground, especially in
the valleys, was extremely heavy and in many places flooded.
At every step men sank over their ankles and frequently up
to their knees in the mud. It was not difficult to understand
how the English troops on the 9th had failed to reach their
positions in time. In such country, even on prepared tracks,
a mile an hour was good progress for formed troops, but
over the mud of the forward area it was necessary to allow
a period of 4 hours for each mile. At 2 a.m. a drizzle
started and added to their discomfort. Five crossings made
of cocoa-nut matting had been laid over the Ravebeek by
the 1st Field Company of the New Zealand Engineers.
Much assisted by these, the leading troops reached their positions well up to time, with the second battalion closed up on
the heels of the leading one on the eastern bank.

In an attack on a comparatively narrow front, experience
had shown the advantages of giving each of a series of objectives to a single battalion. This principle was now adhered
to. On the north, from front to rear, the Rifle Brigade battalions were the 4th the 2nd[1] the 3rd and the 1st. The 2nd
Battalion was to seize the first objective (the Red Line)

1   Capt. W. G. Bishop, vice Lt.-Col. Pow, "B" Teams.

beyond the Bellevue defences; the 3rd Battalion the next objective (the Blue Line) at the point where the spur abutted on the main ridge, from the Ravebeek on the south over to the upper valley of the Paddebeek on the north; and the 1st Battalion the final objectives (the Green Dotted and Green Lines) on the Goudberg Spur. The 4th Battalion, holding the line, was marked as brigade reserve and, by a somewhat unusual manoeuvre, was to follow each assaulting battalion to its goal. Eventually it was intended to form a support in rear of the final objective and assist in smashing a counter-attack.

The 2nd Brigade on the right aimed equally at taking each objective with 1 battalion and leap-frogging the next through, but adopted a different plan for the capture of its first objective and the employment of its reserves. The leading battalion, 2nd Otago, would be used to carry the Red line; the next, 1st Otago, would pass through them to the Blue Line; and leap-frogging them in turn would come 1st Canterbury, charged with the capture of the final objective. 1st Canterbury was strengthened by 1 company of the reserve battalion, 2nd Canterbury. Of the other 2nd Canterbury companies, 2 were temporarily lent to 2nd Otago and 1 to 1st Otago as local reserves. These 3 companies, however, were to be employed only in the event of necessity, and it was intended that on the Otago battalions' taking their objectives they should pass again under Lt.-Col. Mead's orders and consolidate a line about Meetcheele. There they would help 1st Canterbury to break up any counter-attack on the 2nd Brigade front, or, if necessary, support the Australians with 1 company in the capture of Passchendaele.

The Rifle Brigade had benefited neither by the training nor rest which had fallen to the others at Lumbres. For the last 6 weeks it had been constantly exposed to shell-fire, to marches averaging 7 miles a day, and to the arduous conditions accompanying night work in forward areas. After digging over 50,000 yards of cable 7 feet deep, they were not in a state to make a sustained effort or to undergo a prolonged strain. The 2nd Brigade were considerably fresher. Nevertheless it was remembered afterwards that the feeling of buoyant confidence, which usually inspired the New Zealanders on the eve of an attack, was on this occasion lower pitched. They were insensibly affected by their exposure to miserable weather in undrained shellholes, the sight of the unbroken wire, and the knowledge of the previous failure. None the less, every man steeled his heart and, checking dispiriting speculation, grimly determined to do his duty.

Winter time had been introduced on 8th October, and the zero hour for the next action of the battle on Friday, 12th October, was 5.25 a.m. Throughout the night the enemy's nervousness and apprehension of an attack had been shown by a multitude of flares, and about 5 a.m. he opened a fairly heavy bombardment of the assembly area, occasioning unfortunate casualties. It was a particularly unkind blow of fortune that these were heavy in the Stokes trench mortar personnel, and that the small amount of ammunition which it had been found possible to bring forward was now destroyed. As the troops waited under the rain, there were few whose thoughts in these last moments did not revert to the barbed wire and the pillboxes, and whose prayers were not fervent for an overwhelming barrage, sufficient of itself to blast a passage through the thicket of wire, or to spread such an efficient shield before them that they could cut their way through by hand with the minimum of aimed hostile fire.

But when at length the guns opened, it was at once apparent that the infantry must rely on their own efforts. Faced by insuperable difficulties a not inconsiderable proportion of the artillery had been unable to reach forward positions. Other guns had been knocked out by the enemy's artillery, and time had not permitted of their being replaced.[1] The general absence of stable platforms and the oozy morass of the guns' positions, into which the trails sank after a few rounds, affected their accuracy, and the consequent necessity of frequent relaying diminished the density of the fire. Not only was the barrage weak and "patchy," but there was a limited amount of short shooting, which was scarcely avoidable under the circumstances and which fell as far back as our support lines. As the barrage moved up the hill towards the pillboxes, where above all it was vital to increase in strength, it became on the contrary still more ragged and could hardly be distinguished at all by the observers at Korek. On the Bellevue Spur the howitzers flung their projectiles in profusion, but without that shattering destructiveness which it was their function to accomplish, for in the semi-liquid mud a large proportion of the shells buried them-

1   On the 11th the C.R.A. had reported that effective artillery support could not be depended upon.

selves deep, failing to explode, or on explosion sending up harmless geysers that added mud showers to the descending rain.

As soon as the British guns opened, the enemy artillery fell again, without marked increase, on the forward assembly lines and back to Waterloo. On the western slopes of Gravenstafel it was somewhat heavier, and the rear battalions suffered. Much more serious to the leading troops were the enemy machine gun barrages which their crews, effectively protected against our weak artillery fire, placed forthwith along the front of the hillside. In addition to these barrages the upper valley of the Ravebeek was swept by fire from the trenches by Crest Farm on the main ridge in front of Passchendaele. The hill slopes were also covered by immediately effective enfilade fire from the Source Trench system which continued the Bellevue defences northwards on the high ground into the XVIII. Corps area. Special evidence is given of the admirable order alignment distances and intervals, in which the assaulting battalions, despite the fire and the nature of the shell-torn country, advanced to the attack. Men dropped steadily, but at the outset the progress was satisfactory. Shortly after leaving the starting point, part of the 2nd Rifles were held up by an enemy Strong Point, but a gallant act by C.S.M. J. W. Voyle, who unaccompanied worked to the flank and killing 3 Germans captured 2 and a machine gun, enabled the advance to proceed. The first wounded brought back word that all was going well.

About 6 a.m. a strong wind set up, and the drizzle turned to heavy rain which, after a brief respite in the morning, was to fall continuously throughout the day and add to the miseries of defeat and wounds. Owing to this heavy rain and mist, observation from the rear was difficult even after full daylight. As the leading riflemen drew further up the lower slopes, the intensity of the machine gun fire grew heavier. On these cratered and sodden hillsides a quick rush forward or a charge at the deadly guns was utterly impossible. Under the stream of lead the attack must either be wiped out or effect slow progress by bounds from shellhole to shellhole. The number of machine guns in the pillboxes along the crest seemed to be reinforced, and particularly severe grazing fire was directed at the Rifles from a forward position half-way up the ridge opposite the 2nd Brigade on the right.

As the pace slackened and the forward ranks grew thinner, the rear battalions pressed up to fill the gaps in front of them.

21

Thus the storming line was no longer composed of the original battalion but received accretions from the troops following. The different units became speedily intermingled, and it was a composite party of the 2nd 3rd and 4th Rifles, together with some Scotsmen of the 9th Division, that Sergt. A. K. Coley of the 4th Battalion led to the capture of the cemetery on the extreme left. Here, after stark fighting, the party killed 20 Germans and captured 3 prisoners and 3 machine guns. They dug themselves in on this position, of great tactical importance for both Divisions, and established posts 150 yards eastwards.

In the centre also of the Rifle Brigade attack, elements penetrated beyond Wolf Farm and to the edge of Wolf Copse. Parties of Germans could now be seen retreating without arms over the sky line. The machine gun fire, however, so far from slackening, accentuated as our barrage passed beyond the crest, and all attempts to force a way through the wire instantly brought down annihilating fire from the inaccessible pillboxes beyond. No better fortune appeared to attend the 2nd Brigade on the right struggling up from Marsh Bottom, for in the pillbox which raked their own advance the riflemen could observe a strong party of Germans firing at the Otago men in the wire about the Gravenstafel road.

The Rifles' casualties were already heavy. In the 3rd Battalion, Lt.-Col. Winter-Evans and practically the whole of his Headquarters had fallen. About 8 a.m. Lt.-Col. Puttick arrived at Wolf Farm. Grasping the situation, he ordered the troops of the 3 leading battalions to dig in. The 1st Battalion was not yet engaged, but where the others had failed it was thought costly and futile to throw it in also. When it should come up, it would be better policy for it to dig a support position in rear. From 9 a.m. the enemy infantry regained courage, and during the rest of the morning formed parties, some with light machine guns, were observed advancing back over the crest all along the ridge. These were discerned also by the artillery and infantry observers at Korek, and gun fire directed on them. Two enemy machine guns were planted on the roofs of the pillboxes on the summit, and many men were visible both on the top of the concrete and in the neighbouring saps.

Any movement on the unsheltered face of the hill brought instant and deadly fire, and the Rifle battalions sustained further severe losses as they dug themselves in among the

THE RUNNER

SIGNALLERS LAYING WIRE FROM BRIGADE H.Q.

YPRES

A PILLBOX

shellholes from the cemetery along the hillside down towards
Marsh Bottom. On their right, between them and the 2nd
Brigade, there had been from the outset a gap, due partly
to flooded and impassable marshes, partly to an effort to
swing past or outflank a pillbox. Into this gap Puttick
had pushed 2 of his platoons with a view to bringing Lewis
gun and rifle fire on the enemy machine guns which harassed
the 2nd Brigade. Their action lessened the intensity of the
German fire but could not develop sufficient volume to silence
it and allow the Otago infantry to advance. Nor were their
numbers adequate to bridge the full extent of the gap. Over
the whole front, indeed, it was doubtful if the Rifles' line
mustered now more than 500 bayonets. As they scrambled from
crater to crater, splashed by shell-bursts and floundering
over the slippery and treacherous slope, the semi-liquid mud
had not merely plastered the troops from head to foot, but
had also clogged rifles and Lewis guns. Now that they
were checked, their first thought was to clean their weapons
and render them serviceable to meet a counter-attack or kill
any of the enemy that exposed themselves in the crest saps.

The 1st Battalion, meantime, unconscious that the leading
troops were held up, crossed the Stroombeek under distant
snipers' fire. As they approached the Peter Pan—Yetta
Houses line, molestation from snipers and machine gun fire
became acute, and it was obvious that all was not well in
front. On finding the 3 leading battalions arrested, they
dug, as Puttick suggested, a support line 150 yards in rear
of the road which ran from Wolf Farm to the cemetery.

Astride the Gravenstafel road and in Marsh Bottom the
2nd Brigade, after heroic efforts, were similarly baffled. 2nd
Otago had speedily found that the enemy was holding his
front system in considerable strength. Under a torrent of
rifle and machine gun fire they pressed on to the entanglements. They found them here 25 yards, here 50 yards wide,
and altogether unbreached. Only where the sunken Gravenstafel road ran up the hill was there a lane. It proved a
veritable lane of death, for the men who, on seeing their
comrades foiled by the wire barrier, made in desperation and
knowledge of their peril for the open passage on the road, were
one and all mown down by the cunningly-sited machine guns
which commanded this trap from either side. Rifle grenades and
Lewis guns were used with effect on the machine guns in the
shellholes outside the blockhouses, and under this covering
protection 2nd Otago fought desperately to break through

the wire and reach the pillboxes before the barrage, such as it was, lifted from them. Among these brave men Major W. W. Turner showed surpassing bravery. He cut his way through the first belt of wire before being riddled with bullets. The two 2nd Canterbury companies attached to the battalion were soon involved, and both Capt. E. J. Fawcett and Capt. C. R. Rawlings, who commanded them, were severely wounded in endeavouring to work round the flanks.

1st Otago, who followed, were not destined to see the Blue Line. They pushed into the gap left by the heavy casualties, and with the survivors of the leading troops, officers and men tried to crawl under the wire. Several succeeded in cutting a passage through the first band of entanglements and a few also through the second belt, just beyond which were the pillboxes, surrounded for the most part by an interior ring of wire. 2nd Lt. J. J. Bishop and 2nd Lt. N. F. Watson actually reached the aperture of one pillbox and were in the act of throwing a bomb inside it when they were killed. In the left company of 1st Otago every officer was killed or wounded, and out of 140 only 28 men remained. With these Sergt. E. C. H. Jacobs showed undaunted initiative by endeavouring to work round towards the north and assault the pillboxes from a flank where it was thought possible that the wire might permit of progress. He and his men reached Wolf Copse, but there, like the Rifle Brigade, found further advance completely arrested. The reserve company of 1st Otago suffered as severely. All the officers but one were killed or wounded. In helping him Sergt. T. A. Bunbury showed qualities of leadership that on a happier field would have been likely to yield complete success.

On the right company front in the marshes down by the Ravebeek, where our lines joined those of the Australians, were 2 pillboxes that were equally active with those on the hill but less completely fortified by entanglements. As it was, the obstacles of wire mud and enemy fire were formidable enough to daunt the stoutest-hearted. Here, however, the gallantry and readiness for self-sacrifice which strewed the slopes above with the bodies of brave men were to show what, even without artillery support, a New Zealand attack could accomplish under the most adverse conditions and against the greatest odds. 2nd. Lt. A. R. Cockerell led his platoon from one muddied crater to another against these blockhouses and the trench connecting them, half the party alternately

covering the advance of the other with rifle grenades. Under
this fire some of the Germans in the trench sought the
shelter of the concrete. The others surrendered. While the
embrasures in the pillboxes commanded their approach, the
attackers were bound to lose heavily, but at last, holding the
garrison in front with Lewis gun fire, Cockerell himself and a
handful worked round the rear and secured the entrances.
Threatened with annihilation by bombs the trapped occupants,
some 80 in all, did not hesitate to surrender. They were
sent to the rear. Cockerell himself after hand to hand
fighting, in which he had bayoneted several Germans, had by
miraculous good fortune come through unscratched, but of his
platoon only one man was now left. Him he despatched to
battalion headquarters at Waterloo for urgent reinforcements, but saw him killed on the way. Fortunately some
Australians now appeared, and with them Cockerell garrisoned
the pillboxes. Of the conditions in the Ravebeek valley some
idea is given by the fact that 5 of the Australians sent
back with messages to Otago headquarters were shot in the
attempt. This feat of arms, which under any circumstances
would have been brilliant, stood out on this calamitous day
all the more conspicuously. Cockerell's initiative leadership
and courage won him an ''immediate'' D.S.O.

While he was thus storming the pillboxes in the swamps,
1st Canterbury had crossed the Ravebeek and joined the other
2 battalions on the hillside. Shortly after the attack
opened, an unlucky shell had burst disastrously on their
Headquarters then moving up the road. Lt.-Col. King and
the Regimental Sergeant-Major were killed, and the Adjutant
and nearly all the rest of the Staff wounded. Later in
the day a detachment of his old Pioneers came up for
King's body. On his death Major D. Dobson, M.C., had
assumed command, but was almost immediately afterwards
wounded by a sniper, and command fell to a subaltern (Lt.
A. C. C. Hunter), until Major Stitt came up from the rear.
Undiscouraged by the failure of the other battalions, 1st
Canterbury in turn faced the machine guns and made for the
wire. The bravery and determination of their efforts as of the
leading troops, said the official report, were magnificent.
They were also in vain. The Bellevue snipers and machine
guns picked off any man that exposed himself, showing
marked quickness in distinguishing officers.

Every unit in the 2nd Brigade had now flung itself at
the enemy position. In the end here, as on the Rifle Brigade

subsector, the company commanders ordered their men to dig in where they lay, close under the wire on the ridge, and about Laamkeek in the Ravebeek flats. Runners were sent back with reports on the situation to Waterloo where all 4 battalions had their headquarters. Throughout the day communications were to be at all times difficult owing to weather mud and hostile fire. It was found impossible to establish forward brigade stations, and the only medium of communication with the attacking companies was by runners, whose casualties exceeded on this day the even normally high rate inevitable through the nature of their duties. On this occasion the runners brought back the pencilled and muddied message-forms safely. Lt.-Col. Smith went forward to try to reorganise the attack, but on reaching the hill-side was quickly satisfied that nothing which courage and self-sacrifice could accomplish had been left undone, and that further efforts at the moment were predestined to failure. Snipers made his return to Waterloo difficult and dangerous, and Lt.-Col. Charters, who with his intelligence officer attempted later to make an independent reconnaissance, was forced to abandon the attempt after his companion had been wounded.

Some of the barraging machine gun units, whose duty it was after the capture of the first objective to provide covering fire for the further advance from the Bellevue Spur, had by now come forward. Although puzzled by the volume of hostile fire, they had continued to push well up the slopes before they grasped that the New Zealanders' habitual success, taken for granted on this occasion also, had not been realised.[1] The remainder were reorganised in time on the forward slopes of the Gravenstafel ridge, whence they fired on to the Bellevue defences over the heads of our infantry.

Some time elapsed before news of the check reached the 2nd Brigade headquarters. The Brigade Major, Major Richardson, was sent forward without delay to discuss the position personally with the commanding officers at Waterloo. He had scarcely arrived and been acquainted with the general blackness of the situation when a message came through for him on the telephone. It was of disconcerting tenor. There arise occasions in war when a General has to steel his heart and in view of the larger situation call on exhausted and weakened troops for renewed efforts against what locally seems impossible. He does not know their particular difficulties, but

1 In much the same way 2nd Lt. A. Bongard's signal party, who were laying lines to the proposed Rifle Brigade forward station, reached the front line and were extricated only with difficulty and thanks to Bongard's coolness and skill.

he knows of the progress effected elsewhere, with its possibilities of reaction in their favour, and it is his function to discount the effect local failure may have exercised on morale, and turn reverse into success by further stern pressure. Such was the situation now. While the New Zealanders were completely held up, the right wing of the 3rd Australians had crossed their first objective successfully and penetrated to their second; and on the northern flank, elements of the 9th Division had actually reached their final objective north of Goudberg Copse. The Corps ordered therefore the suspension of the attack for the moment and its renewal at 3 p.m. Divisional Headquarters had accordingly arranged for the barrage to be brought back to the Red Line and issued instructions in compliance with Corps orders. Two battalions of the reserve brigade were to move to the western slopes of Gravenstafel Spur, now comparatively free from shelling, and the 2 leading brigades were to take instant measures to reorganise with a view to renewing the attack in the afternoon. The final objective for the day was limited to the original second line (the Blue). The advance on the Goudberg Spur must be postponed. It was suggested that the pillboxes might be carried by an attack from the north-west by the Rifle Brigade, while a holding attack was delivered from the south-west by 2 companies of the 2nd Brigade, the whole of the remainder pressing forward with 2 battalions abreast on each side of the Gravenstafel road.

Had the plan offered the slightest prospect of success, none would have welcomed it more cheerily or striven more whole-heartedly for its realisation than the experienced soldiers who now, with the more limited but more intimate knowledge of "the men on the spot," discussed the position in the candle-lit dugout at Waterloo. They were unanimous, however, in urging its abandonment. Casualties were heavy, particularly in officers, and the troops were exhausted. The wire was still unbroken, and on the one hand our men were too near it to permit of bombardment, while on the other it was impossible to bring the intermingled units back for reorganisation in daylight under full view of the enemy snipers and machine gunners. Their first representations in this direction were disregarded. All possible measures of reorganisation were proceeded with. The 4 battalion commanders, fully satisfied of the hopelessness of the task, made ready to accompany their men and share their fate in the certain extinction of the brigade. Similar measures were taken by the Rifle Brigade.

By the early afternoon, however, although in the north the Guards and English county Divisions reached their objectives, the general situation on the right wing of the battle was profoundly modified. The left of the 9th Division had made little progress, and the small parties of Scotsmen on the right flank who had penetrated to their final objective were captured or killed or obliged to fall back. On the south the left brigade of the Australians, faced by much the same obstacles as the New Zealanders, had been similarly checked. The right brigade had swept on triumphantly to the second objective below Crest Farm, but becoming exposed by our failure at Bellevue Spur to extremely heavy enfilade and reverse fire from that direction, and with their right flank also in the air, owing to a check to the I. Anzac brigade, were forced to withdraw. Under these altered circumstances, the renewal of the attack by the New Zealand brigades was definitely abandoned, as was another project, for some time entertained, of utilising the Rifle Brigade alone in a turning movement from the north-west.

The decision to cancel the attack was arrived at too late to interfere with the artillery programme, and at 3 p.m. the barrage recommenced. It was now considerably better than in the morning, but had little effect on the well-protected machine guns. It was all but inevitable that some of the 18-pounders and howitzers should fire short, and one shell landed with devastating effect on a Rifle Brigade forward post of 18 men in the centre of the position. The survivors were withdrawn to the main line. As it happened, however, this barrage fell on 3 parties of Germans assembling for a counter-attack. Two suffered severely, and refused to face the open. The third, in the northern sector, was to some extent protected by the dead and broken ground used to cover their assembly and succeeded in rushing one of our forward posts east of the cemetery. Any further advance that may have been intended was checked by Lewis gun and rifle fire.

Thus amid unceasing rain, continual machine gun fire and desultory shelling the curtain falls on the ill-fated attack on Bellevue. It was the Division's one failure on a large scale, and it is difficult to describe the troops' mortification and chagrin. It would be incorrect to say that their losses and hardships did not for the moment affect their spirits, but officers and men alike of the battered brigades were generally anxious and expressed a wish to make another attempt, after renewed bombardment of the wire, to atone for their non-success and to complete their work before the Division should be relieved. After experiences like those just undergone, none but troops of the finest calibre are capable of such determination. Their wish, however, was not to be realised. But if the sense of failure rankled, there was no secret shame arising from any suspicion that where they had failed other troops might have succeeded, or that they had fallen one iota short of their most exacting conception of duty. They had indeed done everything possible and impossible. They had poured out their blood like water. The bodies of 40 officers and 600 men lay in swathes about the wire and along the Gravenstafel road. The 2nd Brigade had lost 1500 men, the 3rd Brigade 1200. About 20 wounded who had fallen in shellholes beyond the first belt of wire were taken prisoners. The artillery alone had again suffered lightly. 100 Germans were captured, including a battalion commander.

As the obstacles were overwhelming, so the causes of failure are easy of analysis. Among the circumstances under which the attack was launched, notice has been made of the absence of adequate reconnaissance, the lack of time to make preparation, and the troops' physical exhaustion and want of assurance of success. These factors, however, were not to influence appreciably the course of events. Nor was the morale of the enemy infantry such that, had close quarters been reached, success could have been doubted. Some fled, the remainder made no effort to emerge from their trenches and pillboxes, assume the offensive and drive downhill their tired assailants, clinging by their eyebrows, as it were, under the wire. The attempted counter-attacks were not pushed home. The reasons for our failure lay rather in the inevitable weakness of our artillery barrage, the nature of the ground, the strength of the machine gun resistance from the pillboxes, and above all in the unbroken wire entanglements. In the earlier stages of the Ypres battle the greater distance of our objectives and the severity of our preliminary bombardment had caused the enemy in conformity with his general change of tactics to withdraw his heavy machine guns further in rear.[1] Mainly on account of the failure of this new policy and also because our later attacks were marked by comparative shortness of objective and by a decrease in the intensity and duration of our artillery preparation, he had reverted to his former practice of a stronger system of defence generally in his forward area and of massing machine guns in

1 p. 248.

and close behind the front line. On this occasion both machine guns and pillboxes had been practically undamaged by our artillery. Neither the deep mud, however, nor the pillboxes, nor the machine guns, nor weakness of supporting artillery would even conjointly, as Cockerell's attack in the marshes demonstrated, have held our attack. The direct cause of failure was the wide unbroken entanglements against which infantry resourcefulness and fortitude broke in vain.[1]

In the evening the difficult task of reorganisation was carried out with a remarkable precision and orderliness which reflected the highest credit on subordinate officers and the many n.c.o.s who now commanded platoons and companies. As in view of a future attack it would be necessary to bombard the ridge anew, the bulk of our troops were withdrawn to the lower slopes of the hill a short distance in advance of the line from which they had started at dawn. A series of posts was retained further up the slopes. A firm hold was maintained especially on the cemetery, whence the line ran through Wolf Farm to Peter Pan. Each brigade distributed 2 battalions in the front area as far back as the Stroombeek, the line running, from right to left, 1st Otago, 2nd Otago, 1st Rifles, 2nd Rifles. The 2nd Brigade posted the 2 Canterbury battalions on either side of the Wieltje road on the forward slopes of Gravenstafel Spur. The Rifle Brigade held the northern declivities beyond Korek with 1 battalion and placed the other in reserve nearer the Hanebeek. The 4th Brigade battalions withdrew again from the western slopes of the Gravenstafel ridge to the rear. Shortly after 10 p.m. the redistribution of troops in the battle area was complete. The line was now held continuously except for the gap between the 2 brigades. It was filled on the following day by 2 companies of 2nd Canterbury.

---

1 The following extracts from the private diary of a senior and experienced officer are of interest:—

October 11th—We all hope for the best to-morrow, but I do not feel as confident as usual. Things are being rushed too much. The weather is rotten, the roads very bad, and the objectives have not been properly bombarded. However, we will hope for the best.

October 12th—To-day has been a very bad day for us. We were hung up a very short way from the starting point. The situation is not yet very clear, but it is almost certain our men came up against a lot of pillboxes, concrete and ferro-concrete constructions, very strong and with machine guns. No guns can smash them up except with much concentrated fire. They are very small and strong and hard to hit. They are arranged chequerwise and form a very stiff obstacle. My opinion is that the senior generals who direct these operations are not conversant with the conditions, mud, cold, rain and no shelter for the men. Finally, the Germans are not so played out as they make out. All our attacks recently lack preparation, and the whole history of the war is that when thorough preparation is not made, we fail. . . . You cannot afford to take liberties with the Germans. Exhausted men struggling through mud cannot compete against dry men with machine guns in ferro-concrete boxes waiting for them.

The night was dark and squally, without a break in the continuous rain. The appalling conditions restricted infantry hostility on both sides. Our untiring artillery began to shell Bellevue Spur, but otherwise the night was quiet and no S.O.S. was asked for. Rations and water were taken forward without much molestation from machine gun fire. The enemy was also engrossed in reorganising his defences and removing his wounded.

This last problem involved on our side extraordinary difficulties. Even before the attack, dressing stations and regimental aid posts as well as the battlefield itself were crowded with the wounded of the 49th Division. Our own casualties very speedily added to this congestion. No duck-board track existed forward of Gravenstafel Spur, and in the broken state of the country, made still more difficult by the wretched weather, 6 and sometimes 8 men were required for a single stretcher-case. During 12th October, 400 men of the 4th Brigade had been detailed to clear the aid posts but were able to evacuate only a portion, whose places were at once refilled. Every possible shelter was given to the wounded. When the regimental aid post at Kronprinz Farm was already over-crowded, further stretcher-cases were brought into the 2 dugouts, each 12 feet by 10 feet, which formed 2 battalion headquarters. By the evening these 2 rooms held no less than 56 men, consisting of the staffs of the 2 battalion headquarters, doctors and medical orderlies, and wounded. Outside dozens of stretcher-cases lay in the cold driving rain and hail. Without sleep and snatching food at odd moments the regimental medical officers toiled unre-mittingly and uncomplainingly. Even more lamentable were the conditions at Waterloo. Both places were spasmodically shelled, and it was worse than useless to bring further hundreds of wounded men off the battlefield to already con-gested localities from which for the moment it was impossible to evacuate them. In the Medical Corps casualties were abnormally heavy, 13 trained men being killed and over 70 being wounded in the 4 Ambulances.

On the 13th the brigades employed every available man of their support battalions who, though themselves worn with strain and want of sleep, repeatedly while light lasted traversed the unimaginable 3-mile journey back to the dressing-station at Spree Farm. They made also urgent representations for additional assistance in carrying down the wounded. As a result, 1200 men of the 4th Brigade and parties of Army

Service Corps and artillery personnel were despatched to the
forward area, but even then the Division alone was not
equal to clearing the field.   Assistance was invoked from Corps
who ordered the 49th Division to place their reserve brigade at
the New Zealanders' disposal.   A battalion of this brigade
came into the forward battle area.

On the stricken hill-slopes themselves there was throughout
the day an informal truce.   Our stretcher-bearers worked
without interruption right up to the wire which had been
lapped by the furthest wave of our attack.   The enemy also
continued to remove his own wounded.   Snipers on both sides
dealt instantly with any one not carrying a stretcher, but
the bearers did their work without molestation, and the
German marksmen and gunners who looked down on the rows
of our 200 stretcher cases at Waterloo fired no shot there.
By the afternoon of the 14th all surviving wounded had been
evacuated.

On the same day II. Anzac received notice that it would
be presently relieved by the Canadian Corps.   It was decided
that pending relief the 3rd Australian and New Zealand
Divisions should stay in the line.[1]   Immediate steps were
taken to relieve the 2nd and 3rd Brigades by the 4th Brigade.
3rd Auckland and 3rd Otago moved up during the afternoon by small parties to behind Gravenstafel Spur, and by
10.30 p.m. were holding the front line with the other battalions of the brigade in support positions north and east of
the Hanebeek.   The 2nd Brigade went into support west of
the Hanebeek, the 3rd Brigade into reserve in and about the
old British and German front lines.   Half their machine gun
companies remained to strengthen the forward defences.

On 15th October a spell of good weather set in, and with
it our artillery commenced systematic bombardment and wire-
cutting on all Strong Points, especially on Bellevue Spur and
the slopes about Meetcheele that connected it with the main
ridge.   Passchendaele itself, which overlooked so many of
our artillery positions, was given over to destruction by the
heavies, and kept by night and day under the fire of the
lesser howitzers and 18-pounders to prevent alike repair and
observation.   Vigorous counter-battery work, gas shelling,
and harassing fire on the German approaches were again in
full swing on the whole front.   While the heavies bombarded
the actual dugouts on the Bellevue Spur and its wire, the

1   A brigade of the 49th Division moved on the 15th into tactical support to the
numerically weaker 3rd Australians.

Divisional artillery had the special charge of "isolating" the occupants of the pillboxes. It was their function to keep the occupied areas under continual bursts of shell-fire, deluge them with gas, and cut off communications. In view of the proximity of our forward posts to the zone bombarded by the heavies, they were at first withdrawn half an hour before dawn and then re-established at dusk. The positions were specially marked to be readily recognisable, and every precaution was taken to conceal this movement from the enemy, whose erratic shelling showed that he was still ignorant of their actual locations. Eventually, however, in Marsh Bottom and the Ravebeek valley the forward posts were maintained continuously, as being less exposed to danger from our heavies than had been anticipated, and as occupying a much drier site than the "day" positions further down the valley, where in the most solid ground water was struck at less than 2 feet below the surface.

On the 16th the Rifle Brigade entrained for Lumbres and the 2nd Brigade moved back to the reserve area. The latter was relieved in the support zone by the 1st Brigade, now released from Corps employment. In response to our artillery activity that of the enemy was every day increasingly aggressive. His guns had naturally not been disorganised by our abortive action on the 12th to the same extent as in previous attacks. Hence the artillery duel was more quickly resumed. He strove untiringly to destroy our batteries and prevent our guns being moved forward. Our heavies about Spree Farm were subjected to violent shelling, and three 9.2-in. howitzers were destroyed. The infantry positions on Gravenstafel Ridge and further east suffered considerably, but there was now little machine gun or rifle fire. Behind the Ridge, our battery positions, tracks and cross-roads were periodically shelled with high-explosive and mustard gas. The German air service was extremely active. Many large flights crossed and recrossed our lines. Bombing aeroplanes repeatedly visited Abraham Heights and Waterloo, and low-flying planes harassed the troops in the shellholes and on the roads, and reconnoitred our positions at dusk and dawn and throughout the day. Our own artillery remained active, but patrols found the wire on Bellevue still practically intact.

The sector passed on the 18th from II. Anzac to the Canadian Corps, who assumed for the time command of such portions of the II. Anzac Divisions as remained in the area.

II. Anzac Headquarters moved back to Hazebrouck. On the following evening the 1st Infantry Brigade took over the forward area from the 4th Brigade, which went into support. The Canadian advanced guards were now all about Ypres, and the withdrawal of the Division followed apace. The 2nd Brigade went to Lumbres on 21st October. The 4th Brigade, which in the second phase of the Division's operations, from the 11th to the 22nd, had sustained 400 casualties, followed it on the 22nd. A proportion of the transport accompanied units by rail. The remainder was formed into transport groups and went by road. The command of the Divisional sector passed to the 3rd Canadian Division on the 23rd, and that night the 1st Brigade was relieved in the line and moved back into support. On the 24th it passed into reserve, and on the 25th entrained at Ypres and Dickebusch for Lumbres. With the exception of the artillery and 1 company of Field Engineers employed by Corps, the whole of the Division was now already concentrated in or on the way to the training area. It is noteworthy that, despite all obstacles, on no occasion had any task set the Engineers been left uncompleted.

The failure of the 12th October definitely crushed any lingering hopes of carrying the remainder of the ridge before the winter. The capture of Passchendaele, however, and the adjacent part of the ridge northwards would relieve the artillery from direct observation, and a maintenance of activity here was desirable in view of the impending French offensive on the Aisne and of the intended British surprise attack in the vicinity of Cambrai, for which preparations were already afoot. The next general blow in the Ypres front was delivered on the 26th. The objectives now set the Canadians were less ambitious than those of the 12th. Their right flank was successful, but their left was again checked on the Bellevue Spur. Fresh troops attacked it in the afternoon and carried it. On the left of the splendid Canadian achievements, the Fifth Army made some progress against disheartening difficulties. After an interval of 4 days the Canadians made their next bound. They gained nearly all their objectives, capturing the Crest Farm positions and reaching the outskirts of Passchendaele. Its ruins and pill-boxes with the greater part of the Goudberg Spur fell on 6th November, 3 weeks after the Australians and New Zealanders had aimed at their capture, together with the occupation of the whole of the intervening ground, in a single operation. Further efforts to extend our hold on the main

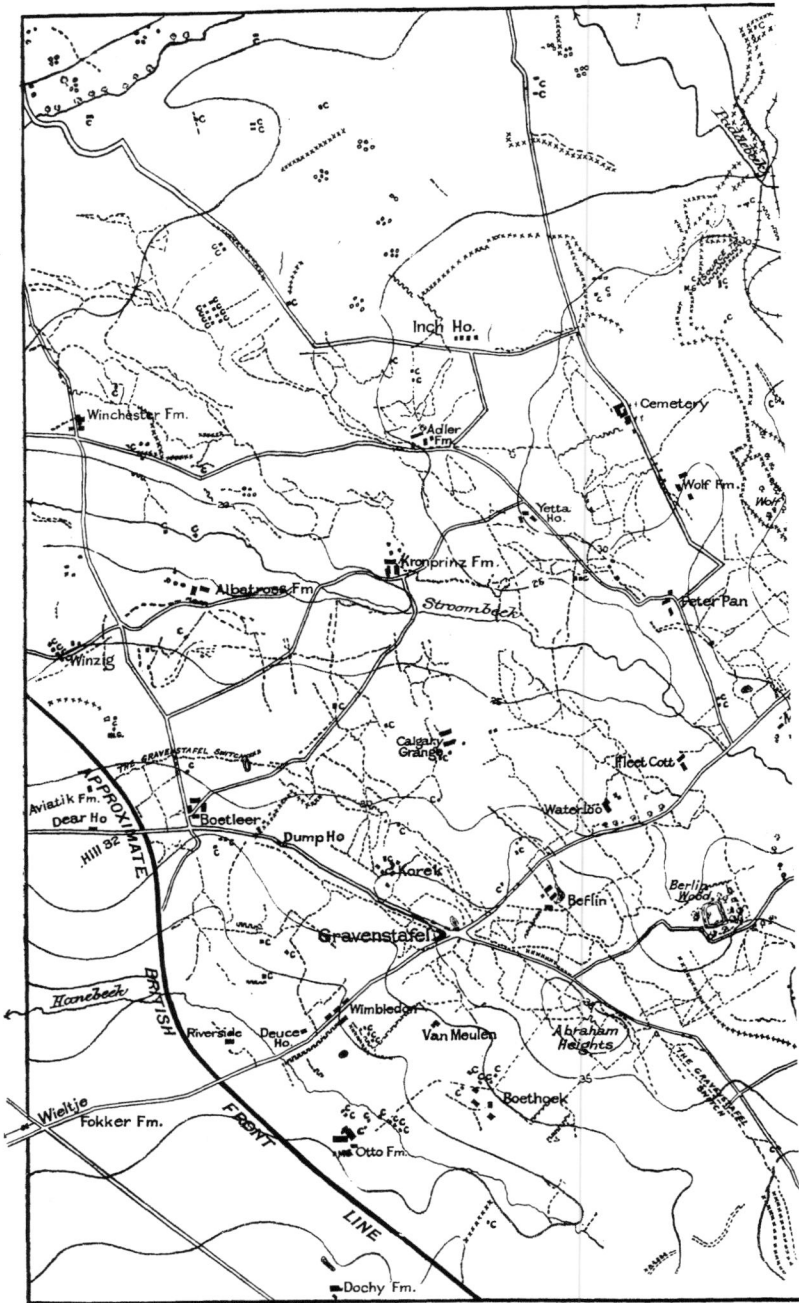

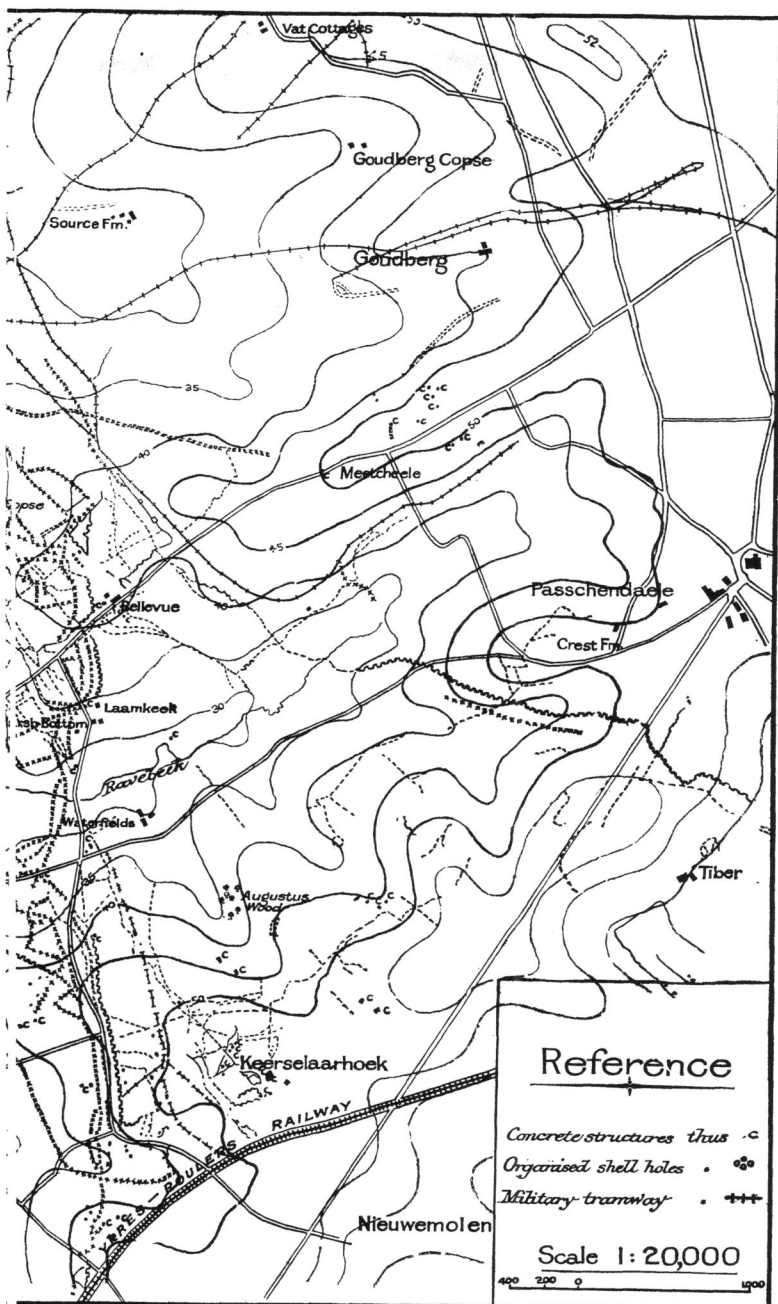

Vat Cottages

Goudberg Copse

Source Fm.

Goudberg

52

Meetcheele

Bellevue

Passchendaele

Crest Fm.

Laamkeek

Bottom

Ravebeek

Waterfields

Tiber

Augustus
Wood

Keerselaarhoek

RAILWAY

YPRES ROULERS

Nieuwemolen

Reference

Concrete structures thus   ·c

Organised shell holes   · °o°

Military tramway   · +++

Scale 1: 20,000

400   200   0   1000

ridge achieved little success, and the greatest and bloodiest battle in history died away.[1]

Despite every effort, despite colossal expenditure of lives and munitions, neither the coast line with its promise of strategic possibilities nor even the whole ridge had been secured. The number of British casualties had been unprecedented. The enemy had justification for his paeans of satisfaction. On the other hand, the strong fibre of the British stock withstood the strain, and morale and determination remained generally unimpoverished. Assurance was theirs that failure was due not to inferior generalship or equipment or fighting qualities, but to the mud and weather and unpropitious elements. Moreover, though on the surface Germany appeared unshaken, though no tangible gains, commensurate with our losses, rewarded the British effort, yet a profounder scrutiny of the enemy's position and a larger outlook made for confidence. In addition to the efforts of our Allies elsewhere and to the disintegrating effects on the civil population of the blockade and our propaganda, the enemy's field forces were being ceaselessly exposed by the British armies to a grinding process of attrition. Germany fought magnificently, but her man-power and her spiritual and material resources were being sapped and drained with a cumulative effect, which was not to be fully alleviated by the release of her troops from Russia. Ypres of 1917, and the Somme of 1916, were not isolated self-contained episodes with little or no bearing on the subsequent evolution of the drama. Directly and powerfully their influence was to be felt in the dénouement of 1918.

1 For the co-operation of the New Zealand artillery with the Canadians see foot-note, p. 298.

22

CHAPTER VIII

WINTER AT YPRES

Warning notice was received from the Army on 4th November that the Corps would presently relieve I. Anzac in the area south of the Ypres-Roulers railway which had formed the boundary between the 2 Corps in the attack on Passchendaele. On General Birdwood's right the X. Corps were being withdrawn to rest, and part of their line also was added to the new front. The 3rd Australian Division was marked for transference to I. Anzac, leaving the Corps composed of the 49th 66th and New Zealand Divisions, with various Corps troops. On 8th November, after a period of training and rest marked by cold and wet weather, the first 2 Divisions set out towards Ypres to relieve the 2nd and 1st Australians on the right and left of the I. Anzac front respectively. Corps Headquarters moved from Hazebrouck to the village of Abeele, south-west of Poperinghe.

The New Zealanders began to entrain 4 days later, and on the 13th the 4th Brigade marched up to the left subsector of the 21st Division in that part of the X. Corps area which was now included in the II. Anzac front. The Rifle Brigade followed into the right subsector the next evening, and on 16th November the command of the whole Divisional front passed to the New Zealanders. Divisional Headquarters were established in the hutted Anzac Camp at Chateau Segard, about 2 miles south-west of Ypres, and the headquarters of the 2 brigades in the trenches occupied deep dugouts in Hooge Crater. The 2nd Brigade was held in support. The 1st was placed under Corps control as working troops, to be used at the moment mainly for cable-burying. The artillery brigades, after supporting the Canadian attacks, had only on the night 2nd/3rd November been withdrawn from their positions behind Gravenstafel to the vicinity of Hazebrouck.[1] There they remained for the time, but Div-

[1] The assistance given by the New Zealand batteries to the Canadians is acknowledged in the following letter from the C.R.A., 3rd Canadian Division. "Now that the New Zealand Artillery are leaving my command, I wish to place on record my appreciation of the high standard of efficiency maintained by them while they were assisting to cover the offensive operations of the 3rd Canadian Division. In spite of the difficulties of bad weather and almost impassable roads, they kept their guns in action and their ammunition dumps filled with a regularity which would have been impossible without a high standard of discipline energy and efficiency. I should be glad if you would convey my thanks to all officers, n.c.o.s, gunners and drivers of the N.Z. Divisional Artillery for their gallant and faithful work in trying circumstances." On the night 31st Oct./1st Nov. the 15th Battery lost 20 horses from aeroplane bombs.

isional Artillery Headquarters accompanied the Division and assumed control of the 3 English (Army) brigades which covered the Divisional sector.

The northern limit of the Corps front was at the pillboxes called Tiber, 1000 yards south of Passchendaele and a mile south-east of Marsh Bottom, where a month previously the New Zealanders had suffered their tragic reverse. Thence it extended for $4\frac{1}{2}$ miles south along the vital key position of Broodseinde Ridge and in front of Polygon Wood to the stream of the Reutelbeek which, rising on the slopes of the main ridge north of the Menin Road, flowed, or rather oozed, first eastwards and then south-eastwards to the Lys at Menin. Of this front the Division occupied the right sector of about a mile and a half. Their line was marked in the north by a pronounced salient at the In de Ster Cabaret between the ruins of Noordemhoek and Reutel. Beyond Reutel it trended back south-westwards, falling to the marshes of a stream that rose in the Polygon Wood and was called the Polygonebeek. This stream joined the Reutelbeek in extensive flats about 500 yards in front of our positions. From the south bank of the Polygonebeek the line, still bending to the south-west, mounted the forward slopes of Cameron Covert, which we held with a series of posts, and then descended again towards the Reutelbeek. Here at its southern boundary it joined the IX. Corps trenches at a point less than a mile short of the famous and terrible Menin Road.

In front of the Division the Germans held a line of posts in and about the copses known from north to south as Joiners' Wood, Journal Wood, Judge Copse, and largest, if not most important, of all, Juniper Wood. They had advanced positions also in the outskirts and cemetery of Reutel. Their main defences, however, lay along the high ground 1000 yards further east at Becelaere. Owing to the western trend of our line south of the Reutelbeek they enfiladed our positions at Cameron Covert and Reutel. The whole country recalled memories of the unequal but stubbornly contested struggle of 1914, when the sacrifices of the old Army made Cameron Covert, Black Watch Corner, Hooge, Westhoek, Polygon and Glencorse Woods for ever consecrated ground. It was further hallowed by magnificent instances of Australian gallantry in its recent recapture in September.

Polygon Wood, with its racehorse training track, lay about a mile behind the front line. On the north-eastern edge of the destroyed wood was a very prominent artificial mound called the Butte de Polygon, originally constructed in connection with the musketry training of the Belgian infantry in the Ypres barracks and now honeycombed with German dugouts.[1] Just west of Polygon Wood the ground fell away to a smaller copse whose name, Nonneboschen, or the Nuns' Wood, told of long abandoned convents of which no trace now survived. Between these woods and the Westhoek Ridge, whose outliers dominated the flats beyond Ypres, rose the head waters of a sister stream to that same Hanebeek which the New Zealanders forded to capture Abraham Heights, called by the same name,[2] and eventually mingling its waters with the other in the neighbourhood of St. Julien.

Never a picturesque country, it now presented an aspect of desolation that seemed devoid of affinity with either man or nature. Every yard was a yawning shellhole. The trees were lopped by explosive, and of the young saplings in the spinneys not a single trace survived. The basins of the Hanebeek and other streams, choked by the walls of shell craters and by dead mules, were noisome and repellent morasses. Derelict and abandoned limbers littered the sides of the corduroy roads, and innumerable ugly tanks, knocked out by artillery or bogged in the mud, were strewn over the wastes. Only when snow mantled the landscape did it present to one looking eastwards from the Westhoek Ridge a mournful beauty of its own. In winter nights of hard frost and full moon, the Butte, scintillating with a million diamonds, evoked memories of snowy ranges thousands of miles away Over the whole battlefield shells and war material of all descriptions lay in profusion, and one of the most pressing duties that faced the Corps was the organisation of a definite salvage scheme. Reserve units were systematically employed, and the Division alone saved several hundred thousand pounds' worth of Government property. The need of economy, indeed, accentuated as it was by the shortage of shipping, was now being inculcated with increasing emphasis in every branch of the administrative services. Much could be effected by a thorough system of salvage, and the appeal for individual effort painted on the Corps motor lorries ''What have you salved to-day?'' was but one method of driving the principle home.

Patrols at once reconnoitred No Man's Land and the enemy positions. As a rule they met no Germans and

1 Apparently disused since about 1870. Lately purchased by the Australian Government and converted after the Armistice, by the labour of German prisoners, into a memorial of the 5th Australian Division.
2 In the case of both streams the maps are inconsistent in spelling.

returned safely, but on 21st November a 3rd Auckland patrol came within close range of machine guns, and several men were hit. Fortunately most of the wounds were light, but one man was seriously disabled. Unable to move, he was carried by Pte. K. Campbell, himself wounded, all the 300 yards back to our lines. The general attitude of the enemy's infantry was not aggressive, but his artillery activity was still above normal. On the very evening on which the Division assumed command, a wireless message was intercepted which gave indications of a German gas bombardment to be delivered at midnight along the Corps front. Time allowed adequate warning to be given, and more damage was caused by explosive shells in the back areas than by the gas bombardment, which lasted from 11 p.m. till 1.30 a.m. Two nights later there was an encounter between an enemy patrol and a 3rd Wellington post a little south of the In de Ster Cabaret. Our sentries had just been exchanged, and the men relieved were sitting, quietly smoking, at the rear of the dugout. It was about 9.30 p.m., and the night was quiet. Suddenly by the light of a flare one of the smokers saw, about 15 yards away, a strong German patrol, with their unmistakable caps and helmets. He at once jumped up to snatch his rifle. A bomb exploded harmlessly at his feet. The other men in the shelter ran out, and the whole party opened rapid rifle fire which dispersed the enemy.

Similar patrol enterprises and local raids by the enemy must be expected here as elsewhere, and the probability of their occurrence occasioned no misgiving. Serious consideration, however, had to be paid to the possibility of an attack on a large scale on this all-important sector of the front. Our communications and gun positions were exposed and congested, and our defence lines far from being satisfactorily organised. The enemy possessed concealed ground for assembly of counter-attacking Divisions and had a mass of artillery already in position and registered. It was well within the range of possibility that he might launch a surprise offensive on the whole or part of the Corps front, extending also to the areas of the neighbouring Corps. Such an attack might have a limited objective in the recovery of the high ground from the Menin Road at Clapham Junction along Broodseinde to Passchendaele, or, as a preliminary to a renewed effort to capture the coastal ports, might aim at deeper penetration and at the defeat of the troops committed to the defence of the Ypres salient. On the north of the

Corps sector the loss of the Broodseinde Ridge would make our positions at Passchendaele untenable. Owing to their situation, however, the New Zealanders were more concerned with the southern portion of the Corps line. A local attack here was possible on the In de Ster Cabaret, whose possession would give the enemy a footing on the plateau and yield observation, but the acute danger was at the extreme south. There owing to the failures in the Ypres battle[1] our lines swung, as we have seen, sharply back, and there the capture of the high ground southwards in the IX. Corps area between the Reutelbeek and Clapham Junction would immediately threaten our positions and communications.

To meet such hostile action the general policy had already been laid down in the beginning of November, but the Australians had had little opportunity for translating the paper scheme into wire and trenches. The necessary work was now vigorously taken in hand. The Army defence system had been defined immediately east of Ypres. Beyond it the Corps zone was planned in depth with the object of providing supporting points to stop or localise a breach of the Divisional defences in front, and of affording a line to cover the assembly of Corps and Divisional reserves, or, at the worst, should the Reutel-Broodseinde-Passchendaele Ridge fail, of furnishing a fresh line of defence. Further in front, the siting and consolidation of the defensive systems of the Divisions in the line were pushed on with the utmost possible despatch. They comprised 3 lines of trenches. The front line was in the nature of an outpost system. It consisted at first of groups of shellhole posts placed at selected points as inconspicuously as possible with enfilade machine gun and Lewis gun fire covering the gaps. These posts were intended to be linked together eventually to facilitate lateral movement and mask the localities actually held. Some 200 to 400 yards in rear a support line was sited with continuous lateral communication and with organ-ised localities covering the gaps of the front line. About half a mile behind the support trench the third Divisional line was organised as a reserve position. The whole scheme, in which could be traced "open warfare" principles of defence, was based on a policy of depth, with successive lines of trenches, supplemented by the liberal employment of groups of machine and Lewis guns echeloned in rear of each other, the object being to effect economy of man-power

1   p. 270.

by an organisation of sufficient flexibility to ensure the repulse of all hostile attacks. In view of the awkward situation southwards, where the enemy were in a position of great advantage for an attack on the IX. Corps from the south-east up the spurs which ran parallel to the Menin Road, the Divisional reserve line and the Corps system were specially sited to secure the left flank of the neighbouring Corps. Close reserve troops also were earmarked to refuse this flank, if need be, or to execute an immediate counter-attack in a southerly direction outside the II. Anzac area. Unfortunately the high ground at this southern boundary was narrow, and the Corps and Divisional systems overlapped. Towards the end of February, after the Division was withdrawn, the enemy did seriously propose a limited offensive here, but it was frustrated by violent artillery counter-preparation.

In addition to depth of lines and impenetrability of wire, successful defence against a surprise attack depended on the morale and vigilance of the troops; on their training and confidence in their weapons, particularly rifles, Lewis guns, and machine guns; on the initiative and leadership of subordinative commanders, especially in the execution of local counter-attacks and provision of mutual support; and finally on the excellence of the arrangements made for the rapid deployment of local reserves. Accommodation was arranged east of Ypres for at least 6 battalions of each Division holding the line. It was a point of honour with Divisions that they should hold their defensive system against heavy and continuous attack without inconveniencing Corps by an appeal for assistance which might upset the plans of the Higher Command. The same principle applied in a less degree to the smaller units. Troops were therefore so disposed in the forward areas that a proportion was always available for immediate counter-attack on the front line; a platoon in each company, a company in each battalion, and a battalion in each brigade. These were kept stationed not further back than the reserve line, and were held entirely distinct from the garrisons of the support line who would not leave their positions for this purpose. The company and platoon counter-attacked on their own initiative, and the battalion in brigade reserve under orders of the brigadier. either with or without artillery preparation, according to circumstances. The reserve brigade at the disposal of Division was used in case of need for deliberate counter-attack after artillery preparation and under an artillery barrage.

Specially designed to form the framework of this system of defence was the tactical organisation of the Divisional machine guns. They too were so arranged in depth as to provide 3 belts of fire covering the area from No Man's Land right back to the Corps system. In the protection of the front line the infantry were assisted primarily by their Lewis guns, but also by the direct fire of "silent" machine guns, carefully concealed in or about the front line, and opening only in an emergency, and by indirect fire from machine guns further in rear, which formed a barrage across the front and engaged specially important approaches. Close co-operation was arranged between machine guns and Lewis guns, both for the repulse of an infantry assault and against enemy aircraft. To prevent reconnaissance and aggressiveness on the part of the German airmen over our foremost positions, a line of Lewis guns was placed between 100 and 500 yards from the front line and not more than 500 yards apart. In rear was a second line of machine and Lewis guns not more than 800 yards apart, and from 500 to 1500 yards from the front line. The policy of anti-aircraft defence aimed at engaging aeroplanes flying under 3000 feet with direct fire when seen to be within range, and barraging a definite area by night when direct fire could not be used. Lewis or Hotchkiss guns were similarly mounted to protect battery positions, transport lines and back areas. On more than one occasion the New Zealand light trench mortars also were used with conspicuous success. Only a week after the Division went into the trenches, one of the mortars blew off the wing of a low flying hostile aeroplane and forced a crippled descent into the German lines. 2 of the 3 field artillery brigades were emplaced primarily with a view to defence of the front and support trenches, while the positions of 1 brigade were sited to cover the Divisional reserve line. At this period the heavies were employed almost exclusively on counter-battery work.

In their defence policy the Division had not merely to face the possibility of an enemy attack at some time in the future on the IX. Corps area beyond their right flank. Owing to the sharp re-entrant of our line at this point they were also already actually exposed to continuous and pressing discomfort caused by enfilade fire from the south. Just beyond the Divisional boundary a well-marked spur ran eastward like a finger from the edge of the general plateau down to the flats. On the north its sides drained into the

Reutelbeek, and on the south to the corresponding valley of the Scherriabeek. These 2 streams divided by the spur wound round its eastern end and united in the flats. Beyond the Scherriabeek the ground rose again to Gheluvelt on the Menin Road. The British line had been arrested at the edge of the plateau, and the spur remained in German possession. From it the enemy not only enfiladed our forward trenches about Cameron Covert and Reutel, but fully commanded and incessantly harassed the whole of our approaches to this sector of the front. On it were perched the piled ruins of Polderhoek Chateau and groups of pillboxes which occupied sites of the attached buildings amid the shattered trees of the once luxuriant and beautiful pleasances. The Ypres Battle had seen 3 assaults delivered on the spur, and the Chateau had been temporarily won, but only to be lost again to German counter-attacks.

For the satisfactory occupation of the Division's sector, it was highly desirable that a fresh effort should be made to capture the Polderhoek Spur. A combined attack on it and on Gheluvelt had been contemplated as one of various local operations designed to continue our offensive during the winter, to add depth to our defence along the Army front, and to facilitate the initial phases of a resumed offensive on a large scale in the spring. Eventually, however, the scope of the operation was confined to the Polderhoek Spur alone. The area affected was about 400 yards wide, and an advance of some 600 yards would carry the line as far down its forward slope as was necessary to deprive the enemy of his commanding and enfilading position. Further examination also showed that, owing to the height of the spur and general configuration of the ground, the new lines proposed about the Chateau would not to a like degree be exposed to similar enfilade fire from the Gheluvelt Spur on the south. Though the Chateau lay opposite the IX. Corps front, it was the II. Anzac troops who specially suffered, and it was fitting that they should strike the blow for its capture. The Corps therefore submitted a proposal to the Army that the New Zealanders, immediately affected, should carry out the attack and, on the conclusion of the operation, hand over the territory won to the IX. Corps.

Two alternative lines of attack offered themselves. The Chateau might be carried from the flank and rear by troops advancing from the Anzac positions across the Reutelbeek, or, secondly, a frontal assault could be delivered straight down the spur from the IX. Corps position on the plateau. The former alternative was naturally at first considered, as involving no change of dispositions, but various factors compelled its abandonment. Deadly fire would rake the Reutelbeek valley from the direction of Becelaere and the positions in Juniper Wood. There would also be difficulty in slewing our own guns round from the north to obtain a barrage which at the best would have to be in enfilade. There was no satisfactory assembly position, and above all the Reutelbeek itself was practically unfordable. The deep, all but continuous shellholes which replaced its stream formed an obstacle from 20 to 30 feet wide, and from the left bank stretched an extensive black morass of soft mud, into which patrols sank to their knees within 100 yards from our advanced posts in Cameron Covert. For these reasons recourse was had to the second alternative, which offered several advantages. Assembly trenches were available directly opposite and in close proximity to the Chateau. A frontal barrage could be obtained. The IX. Corps heavies could carry out the preparatory bombardment, and the tell-tale registration by a large number of new guns could be avoided.

These proposals were sanctioned by the Army. The New Zealand attack was entrusted to the 2nd Brigade, and on the evening of 25th November during a snow-storm 2nd Canterbury, with a section of machine guns, took over from the IX. Corps troops the front opposite the Chateau from the Scherriabeek to the Reutelbeek. The command of the sector and the artillery brigade covering it was assumed by the New Zealand Division on the following day. The necessary additional assembly trenches could fortunately be disguised as a continuation of the support system already in process of energetic construction on the New Zealand front north of the Reutelbeek. and these were dug in the sandy soil without delay.

The first heavy artillery concentration shoot on the Chateau and the pillboxes about it was carried out on 28th November. To avoid enemy retaliation, the bulk of our garrison, both opposite the Chateau itself and north of the Reutelbeek, was withdrawn before daylight. Several hits were scored on the ruins, and the 4th Brigade observers to the north could see large numbers of Germans rush out of the cellars into the open to escape the concussion caused by our super-heavies' shells. Enemy stretcher-bearers under the

SERGT. H. J. NICHOLAS, V.C., M.M.   [*Photo H. H. Clifford*

HOOGE

A SNOW-COVERED BATTLEFIELD

THE BUTTE DE POLYGON, SEPT. 1919

[Photo Capt. S Cory Wright

Red Cross flag were busy all the afternoon carrying the wounded down towards Red Cross wagons visible on the Becelaere road. An artillery demonstration was also made on the German system north of Becelaere. The hostile batteries retaliated heavily, particularly in the vicinity of the Butte and at Cameron Covert, where our vacated posts were completely "blown in." On the 29th enemy howitzers destroyed a pillbox which formed the Canterbury regimental aid post and was assumed to be battalion headquarters, inflicting casualties. Our bombardments were repeated on the 30th. The destruction of the wire entanglements strung among the tree-stumps was also taken in hand by howitzers using instantaneous fuses, and the success of their work was established by Canterbury patrols. Our single duckboard approach, known as "E" track, was improved and extended. Engineering material and ammunition were stealthily accumulated in the trenches. The garrison of the Chateau was confidently aggressive. Both on the 26th and 30th they attempted small raids which were completely repulsed. They had, however, no suspicion of the impending attack and exposed themselves injudiciously about the spur to our snipers.

The date of the attack was fixed for 3rd December. Two battalions, 1st Canterbury (Lt.-Col. Mead[1]) and 1st Otago (Major W. F. Tracey, M.C.[2]) were considered adequate for the task, and their companies were in addition reduced to the strength of 100 all ranks. The selected personnel, who included a large proportion of reinforcements without previous experience of battle, rehearsed the operation behind Ypres on ground laid out to scale, with the buildings and pillboxes numbered as on the map and represented by heaps of material. Parties were also sent up to reconnoitre and observe the ground from the 2nd Canterbury lines and from Cameron Covert. The leading waves of the attacking companies moved into the line on the evening of 1st December, and the remainder of the battalions on the following day. The support companies took over the front line. The attacking companies were placed in the rear trenches to familiarise them with their assembly positions, avoid daylight movement and secure them a night's rest. On relief, 2nd Canterbury, who had fulfilled their part and would not be called on further, moved out of the line. The role of reserve was given to 2nd Otago.

---

1 vice Lt.-Col. King, killed 12th Oct. Lt.-Col. Stewart had meantime resumed command of 2nd Canterbury. See also p. 330.

2 vice Lt.-Col. Charters at advanced brigade headquarters with General Braithwaite.

It had been a matter of consideration whether the enterprise should be carried out in combination with the attack to be delivered east of Passchendaele by Corps to the north. The tactical objects in view, however, bore no correlation, and in addition the zero hours selected were different. For whereas the II. and VIII. Corps proposed to attack at dawn, the New Zealand assault was fixed for noon. In the end, therefore, it was decided that the 2 operations should be executed independently. It was hoped that the obvious disadvantages of a daylight attack would be more than neutralised by the surprise effect of an assault delivered at a moment when the enemy would least anticipate it, and when he might be expected to be taking shelter underground from the daily heavy artillery storm with which he was now being familiarised at this hour. Extensive smoke barrages would be employed to blind his troops on the Becelaere positions and on the Gheluvelt Spur, and they would in addition be subjected to a heavy concentration of gas and the fire of field artillery, 6-in. howitzers, machine guns and trench mortars. An immediate preliminary bombardment might, on account of their proximity to the targets, be dangerous to the congested troops in our line, and at the same time would reduce the potent effect of surprise. It was therefore dispensed with. At one and the same moment the barraging guns would open and the infantry would rush to the assault.

Three field artillery brigades were allotted for co-operation. One barrage of 18-pounders would immediately precede the infantry; 150 yards in front of it would be another fired by 18-pounders and 4.5-in. howitzers. Our artillery activity would embrace either flank. On the right, field artillery of the IX. Corps would extend the covering barrage southwards and sweep Gheluvelt, the railway line, the Menin Road, and the Scherriabeek valley. Opposite the New Zealanders' proper front to the north of the Reutelbeek, the enemy's occupied shellholes and emplacements would be similarly kept under fire. From that direction 2 machine gun barrages were arranged to deal with the German trenches and approaches and with the loopholes on the northern side of the Chateau. In addition to light mortars, 5 of the new 6-in. medium trench mortars were also placed in position at Reutel to neutralise, by gas shells, machine guns operating from the vicinity of Juniper Wood; and personnel of the 2nd and 3rd Rifles, who now garrisoned the Divisional sector, toiled to carry up the massy projectiles $2\frac{1}{2}$ miles through the mud.

The actual plan of attack was simple. It would be made by 2 companies in each battalion advancing abreast in 2 waves. The first wave would carry the line to an intermediate objective beyond the Chateau, and the second, following 50 yards behind, would then "leap-frog" through, and push on to a final objective, some 300 yards further, sufficiently far down the eastern slope to give observation of the flats. After the assaulting troops crossed No Man's Land, the support company waiting in the trenches on each battalion front would occupy the present front line to meet counterattacks. The reserve company would be kept well in rear to relieve the victors in the captured line. Eight machine guns co-operated directly in the attack. Of these, 2 were in position in the front trench, 2 in the support line, and 2 were allotted to each battalion for the purpose of providing covering fire during consolidation and of engaging enemy counter-thrusts. The Chateau itself fell within the area of 1st Otago on the left, but 1st Canterbury were faced with a series of strong pillboxes, including those at the stables and at the Manager's House which was suspected to be connected by a tunnel with the Chateau.[1] For coping with these, 1st Canterbury were given the assistance of 2 light trench mortars. From the outset of the attack, Canterbury would form a defensive flank on the south overlooking the Scherriabeek valley and facing Gheluvelt. Definite parties had been allotted to and practised in the attack and mopping-up of each pillbox and dugout. To others was assigned the duty of taking up posts at each angle of the Chateau and of watching for concealed outlets, while the eviction of the enemy was in progress.

At the beginning of December the weather was bright and frosty with a cold biting wind, against which, however, the trenches gave protection. The right boundary of our front line, on the small rise which formed the lip of the plateau, was marked by a conspicuous tower-like pillbox called Jericho. Beyond it the ground began to fall to the Scherriabeek. The left flank was similarly delimited by another old German shelter in the cellar of a demolished house, known as Joppa. Behind this rise the ground fell gradually towards a desolate expanse of shellholes, broken only by the cluster of dreary pillboxes at Veldhoek. Through them the duckboard track

1 Subsequent investigation showed that no such tunnels existed.

ran past battalion headquarters at the pillbox known as the Tower and led up the slopes of the main ridge to the Menin Road.   The Road itself lay, scarcely distinguishable, to the south.   It ran diagonally away from our sector towards Gheluvelt, so that at Veldhoek it was only 500 yards distant, but at the front line was separated from our trenches by the Scherriabeek valley and a full 1000 yards of battered country.

In the trenches every precaution was taken to avoid a premature betrayal of the surprise.   When enemy aeroplanes patrolled over Jericho in the morning of 3rd December, our men lay still in the bottom of the saps or took cover under the corrugated iron of their rough shelters.   No exposure over the parapet or loud talking was permitted.   The Chateau itself, where incautious Germans still fell victims to our snipers, was only some 200 yards distant, and there were enemy shellhole positions still nearer.   For this reason our artillery barrage was arranged to fall close to our own front line. The attacking waves assembled in the support line, leaving in the front trench a few Lewis gunners and snipers till close on zero to maintain "normality."   Each man was in the lightest possible fighting order.   His greatcoat was dumped under a guard in the assembly trench, but he carried his waterproof, and in addition to his fighting kit and invaluable leather jerkin, he took with him in his mess tin a soup square and a tin of solidified alcohol.

The precaution taken to assemble the troops in the support line proved a wise one, for even there on the opening of the barrage 1 battery dropped unwelcome shells, causing heavy casualties among the attackers just emerging into the open, especially in the left company of Otago.   Undismayed, however, the first wave pushed on, crossed our front line, and were rapidly among the wilderness of tree-stumps where the wire was found demolished.   Our hopes of catching the enemy off his guard were doomed to disappointment.   The fear of our heavies' daily forenoon bombardment had not driven the garrison into underground refuge.   His pillboxes were occupied as usual, and his sentries were normally vigilant. Almost as soon as our artillery opened, his machine guns cracked vociferously, both from the pillboxes about the Chateau and from the Gheluvelt Ridge.   A few moments later his artillery put down an intense barrage on the duck-board track and about Veldhoek, but the proximity of the opposing trenches, which had in part compelled the abandonment of our preliminary heavy bombardment, so too now

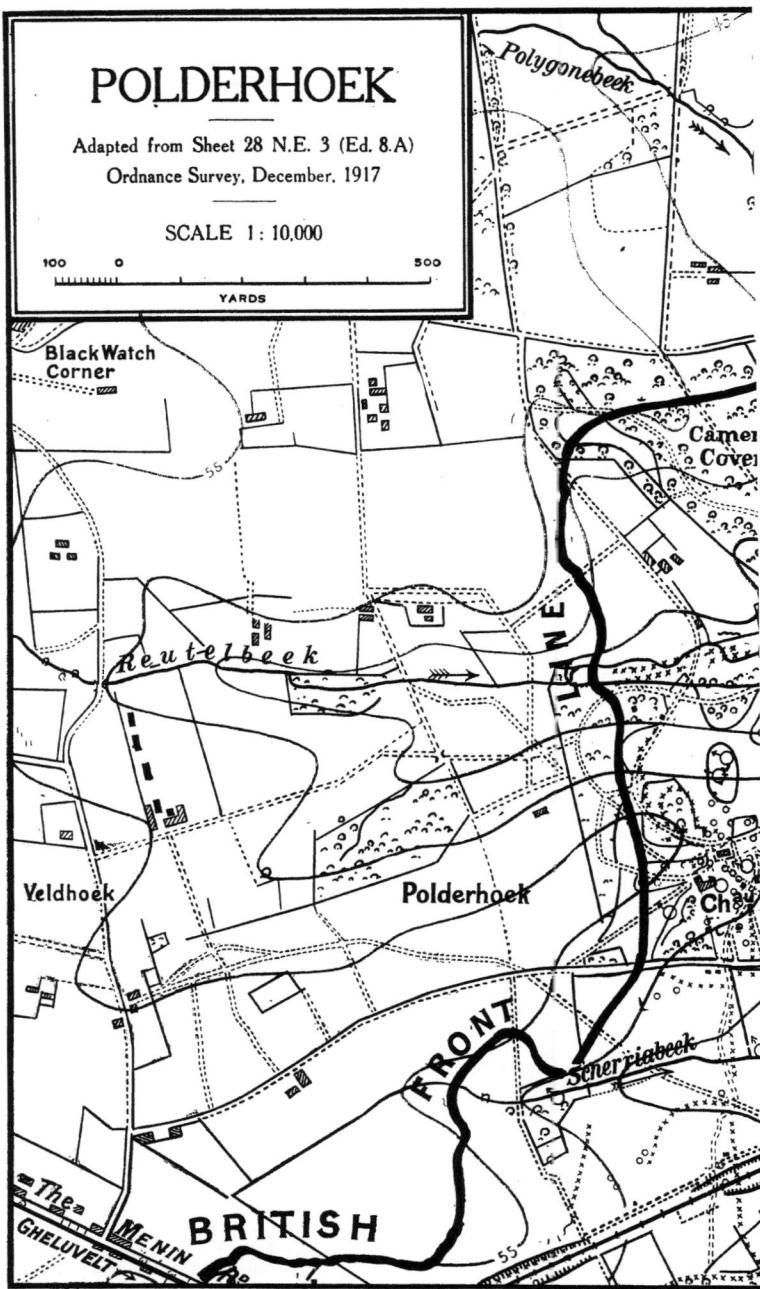

POLDERHOEK

Adapted from Sheet 28 N.E. 3 (Ed. 8.A)
Ordnance Survey, December, 1917

SCALE 1 : 10,000

100   0   500

YARDS

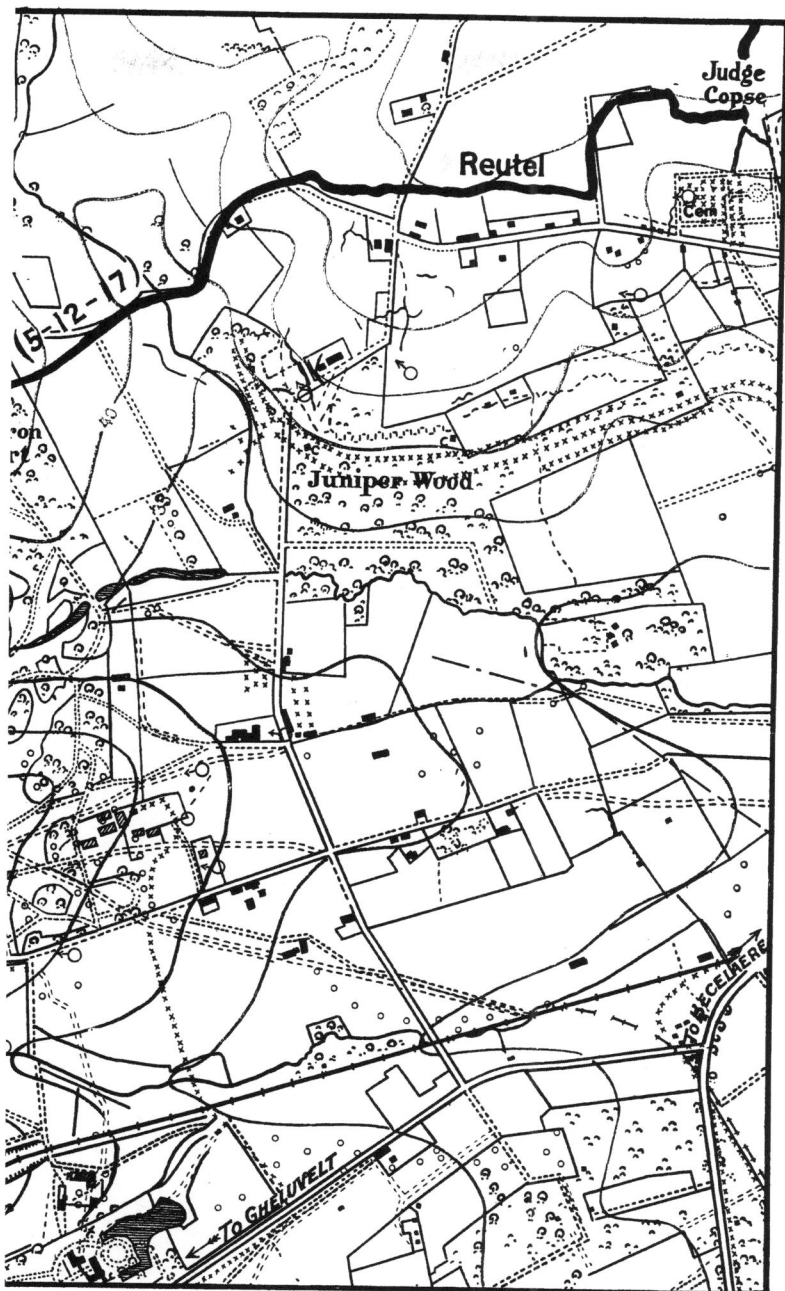

Judge
Copse

Reutel

Cem

(5—12—17)

Juniper Wood

TO BECELAERE

TO GHELUVELT

prevented his shelling our assembly position with appreciable weight.

The right 1st Canterbury company was faced at the outset by a ruined pillbox and dugout, from which a machine gun poured a stream of lead that threatened to hold up the line. Seeing the check, the company commander, Capt. G. H. Gray, rushed the position with a handful of his men and captured the gun and 8 prisoners. The work of this 12th (Nelson) company was of an extremely high order. They, more than the others, were exposed to the blast of machine gun fire from the Gheluvelt Ridge. For in that direction our plans had miscarried. A strong west wind dissipated and rendered useless our protective smoke barrage, and all our artillery activity was powerless to subdue the well-posted and well-protected Gheluvelt machine guns. Their fire indeed became steadily more intense. None the less, though the Nelson company suffered severely from this enfilade fire and were met by strong opposition in front, they continued to fight their way forward. As they advanced, they threw out sections to form the defensive flank and deal with the enemy on the southern slopes. Nor were these little posts ineffective. Their rifles and Lewis guns inflicted heavy casualties, and one Lewis gun had the satisfaction of engaging and putting out of action an enemy machine gun.

It was but fitting that the good work of the company should be crowned by a heroic action which was recognised by the award of a Victoria Cross. An enemy Strong Point garrisoned by 16 Germans with a machine gun offered stubborn resistance. The section commander and several of the men attacking it were killed. Then Pte. Henry James Nicholas, M M., rushed forward, followed at about 25 yards by the remainder of the section. A moment's hesitation would have cost him his life, but he was on the parapet before the Germans realised it. Firing point-blank at the German platoon commander he shot him dead, and then instantly leapt down among the remainder. Those nearest him he bayoneted. At the others further up the sap he flung with deadly effect his own bombs and the German bombs lying about him. He thus killed the whole of the garrison, except 4. These were wounded, and these he took prisoners. The machine gun remained in our hands. After winning the V.C., Nicholas, who was in every respect a particularly fine soldier and man, remained with his company till his death,[1] setting

---

1 p. 551.

23

always an invaluable example of steadfastness and faithfulness.

Shortly beyond this point, however, the dwindling numbers of the company were definitely held up by an exceedingly strong pillbox, which equally frustrated the attempts of the left Canterbury company. First 2 sections, and then a full platoon were sent up from the support company to assist, but were unable to make impression. To take their place in the weakened line about Jericho the reserve company was now brought up through a heavy barrage at Veldhoek.

Meantime on the left 1st Otago received valuable support from the Rifle Brigade machine guns, which repeatedly dispersed hostile parties on the Becelaere road. The medium mortars, too, fired no less than 850 rounds, drawing on themselves intense retaliation by shells of all calibres, which destroyed 1 mortar and damaged another. Nor were Otago raked to the same extent as Canterbury by the devastating flank fire from Gheluvelt. They made at first good progress and captured a pillbox, but from the Chateau came an overwhelming barrage of machine gun fire, which effectively held them up on the same line as Canterbury, about 150 yards short of their first objective. As with Canterbury, supports were sent up, their places in our old front line being taken by the reserve company. Neither individual nor concerted attempts at outflanking the enemy positions availed anything. Three of our machine guns had been put out of action and heavy casualties inflicted on the personnel.

Both battalions had now lost half of their effectives, including many officers and senior n.c.o.s, and once progress was arrested, the lack of battle experience on the part of many of the men was not without result. The strength of the undamaged pillboxes and the tremendous volume of fire which beat against the confined area of assault had proved insuperable. Only some 30 prisoners had been taken. The decimated stormers had no alternative but to dig in. For the moment at least there was no hope of taking their objective or even securing the Chateau, but the ground actually won was of great value, yielding as it did full command of the Scherriabeek valley. Thanks to this advantage of observation, the concentration of an enemy force after midday in the upper part of the valley between Polderhoek and Gheluvelt was immediately detected. A light trench mortar was moved to Jericho, rapid fire was opened, and the enemy fled, discarding rifles and equipment. Full requital was now exacted by the Nelson company, and few of the retreating Germans reached Gheluvelt. The enemy attack never developed, and the German stretcher-bearers coming down from the Menin Road under the Red Cross flag were busy at the spot for some hours afterwards.

In the evening strong enemy reinforcements came up to the Chateau, some of whom were caught by our Lewis guns. General Braithwaite had urged a further effort after dark, and suggested an enveloping movement from the Reutelbeek slopes, but the arrival of these reinforcements, together with the continued alertness of the enemy and the activity of his machine guns did not favour surprise. Moreover, even after darkness fell, the situation about the left flank was still uncertain. Again, the only troops available for a repetition of the attack were the reserve companies and some elements of the support companies, whose advance would leave our positions unguarded against any possible awkward development on the left. Later in the night this position towards the Reutelbeek was cleared up, largely through fearless reconnaissance by Pte. G. Gilbert, M.M., but a full moon now rode in the sky, and the advantage of the darkness was lost. Our wounded lay thick where they had fallen, but the terrible experiences on the Bellevue Spur were not to be repeated. During the night the stretcher-bearers, with their usual devoted courage, searched the shellholes among the trees, still under heavy machine gun fire, and cleared the whole area by dawn.

In the morning of 4th December enemy forces mustering on the eastern and south-eastern declivities of the spur were driven back in disorder by our artillery towards Becelaere, and a very heavy toll was taken by our snipers on individuals about the Chateau, who appeared astonishingly unconscious of our proximity. Throughout the day hostile artillery raged on our new positions and on the approaches from Veldhoek. After dark the assaulting troops were relieved by the other companies, and the work of consolidation was completed. A strong line was constructed with characteristic energy and thoroughness by a company of the Maori Pioneers under Major P. H. Buck, D.S.O. The garrison connected the advanced posts into a continuous line, and deepened to a proper depth 2 communication trenches to our old position, commenced the previous evening. Patrols worked to within 50 yards of the Chateau and saw a German relief in progress.

At dawn on the 5th a party of about 80 Germans, who

had assembled during the night, endeavoured to surprise our left flank. Penetrating to within 30 yards of our position, they bombed and destroyed the Lewis gun there, but the Otago section commander lost not a moment in replacing it with another. Under its fire and that of the infantry rifles the attackers lost at least half their numbers. When our men were later questioned as to why they had not put up the S.O.S. signal, they admitted that they had not thought of it. They had, they said, been too busy with their rifles and bombs to remember about a S.O.S. signal. Despite the reverse they had experienced on the 3rd, there was evidently plenty of fighting spirit left in these men.

Following on these repeated repulses of his infantry counter-attacks, the enemy had recourse to his artillery, and with balloon observation in the beautifully clear frosty air carried out a systematic bombardment of the whole area, causing grievous damage to our trenches and inflicting casualties. This bombardment, as was later confirmed by prisoners, was intended to be followed by an attack about 5 p.m. But our guns, which in response to messages for counter-battery work had already been extremely active throughout the day, now redoubled their rate of fire and crushed the assembling enemy before the attack could develop. Thereupon the volume of the German artillery fire waned. Our blocked trenches were then cleared and repaired, and the wounded were evacuated.

In the evening the position was handed over to IX. Corps troops, and the 2nd Brigade battalions withdrew to reserve. The advance won, though of distinct advantage to the local garrison, would not effect an appreciable improvement with regard to the exposed slopes of Cameron Covert, Reutel, and Polygon Wood, where protection from the Polderhoek fire would have to be won by the labour of the spade. Nor were the IX. Corps long to look down from the spur on the Scherriabeek valley. The ground captured was recovered by the Germans 9 days afterwards.

On the Divisional front north of the Reutelbeek the system of holding the line with 2 brigades had been modified toward the end of November, with a view to presevation of man-power and to a frequent rotation of reliefs. It was now held by 1 brigade, reinforced with 1 battalion from the Corps working brigade. Headquarters were transferred from Hooge Crater to the Butte, to which buried cable was extended without delay. Shortly afterwards, however, the Corps front was reorganised on a 2-Division basis, and the 66th Division was withdrawn to form a Corps reserve. This readjustment involved at the beginning of December an extension of the Divisional front to the north for a further 500 yards east of Molenaarelsthoek, and the reversion to a garrison of 2 brigades. Of these, 1 held the short southern flank in Cameron Covert between the Reutelbeek and the Polygonebeek with 1 battalion, maintaining 3 in reserve. The other brigade held the northern subsectors of Reutel Judge and Noordemdhoek with 3 battalions in the line. A brigade would pass 6 days in the subsector on the left, 6 days in the right subsector, where the former support battalion would hold the line, and 6 days in reserve.

The artillery zones were correspondingly readjusted. The 1st and 3rd Field Artillery Brigades had come into the line a few days previously, replacing 2 of the English brigades. They had been followed by the 2nd (Army) Brigade, which had been relieved by French artillery on 20th November, after a long sojourn under constant counter-battery work from the German large-calibre guns in the sand-dunes on the coast.[1] In the first days of January the remaining English brigade was to be withdrawn and the front covered by purely New Zealand artillery. With artillery support an attempted enemy raid before dawn on Christmas Day, aiming at the demolition of one of our pillboxes, was repulsed. A 2nd Otago patrol under Pte. H. Boreham engaged the raiders outside our parapet with bombs, pursued them and captured a loquacious and informative prisoner. In the following afternoon too (26th December) the batteries co-operated with 1st Canterbury's fire and bombs in crushing a further assault. Preceded by a heavy and prolonged bombardment, this attack had as its object the recapture of a remarkable square crater which had been excavated by the Germans for the construction of a large pillbox, and had been included in our line some days previously. An attempt to enter a 4th Rifles' post at Joiners' Avenue on the night 1st/2nd January was easily driven off, Cpl. A. Adamson greatly distinguishing himself. The body of a dead raider was found in No Man's Land.

Up to the end of 1917 the elaboration of our defensive arrangements had been subordinated to preparations for a resumption of the offensive. By that time, however, it had become apparent that the Russian collapse was to be followed

1 p. 226.

by a German drive on the Western front in the spring. The augmentation of the German forces, together with our unsatisfactory position with regard to man-power and the probability that America would not be able in the near future to put large forces in the field, involved the consequence that for a period of 5 or 6 months the enemy would be in numerical preponderance on the Western front. This situation vitally affected the British policy. At an Army conference held on 9th December General Rawlinson[1] intimated to his Corps commanders that the resumption of the Flanders offensive was no longer feasible, and that our immediate future policy was the strengthening and, where necessary, the revision of our defence systems with a view to making them capable of withstanding a heavy and sustained hostile attack. The carrying out of this policy formed the basis of the Division's activities for the remainder of their stay on the Ypres ridges. It was the first occasion since its arrival in France that a defence scheme was drawn up in real and serious anticipation of an enemy attack on a large scale.

In view of the reduction of material caused by the submarine campaign and of labour by the loss of man-power in the Battle of Ypres, the necessary economy in the construction of defences could best be achieved by a continuity of policy and by resisting the temptation to multiply unnecessarily the lines of trenches in the forward areas. It was laid down as a general policy that Divisions in the line should construct and maintain not more than 3 lines. The New Zealanders had taken over their area under the disadvantages of battle conditions. The trenches had been either shellhole posts or untraversed and unrevetted ditches. Tracks and tramways had not been developed, and above all there was a woeful lack of wire. A systematic policy of construction had been drawn up immediately on our entering the line. Divisional H.Q. had undertaken to employ reserves in the extension of tramways and duckboard tracks, in the construction and wiring of the reserve line, and of a switch portion of the reserve line, and in the opening of such communication trenches in rear of the support line as were necessary. The brigades in the trenches would wire and improve the 2 front lines and maintain all communication trenches forward of the second.

Owing to the strongly marked flank position of the sector there had been a tendency for all lines of communication

1   p. 327.

constructed during the battle to run parallel to the refused southern flank, and the lack of communications running at right angles was already felt. To communication trenches, however, in view of the vast amount of more important work, no great attention would be paid. Only on the forward slopes, where the enemy enjoyed direct observation, would they be constructed, and there wide and unrevetted and as inconspicuous as possible. Behind the crest, duckboard tracks must suffice, with room left for deployment in case of shellfire at the points where they passed through our entanglements. Later, as labour would become available, it was proposed that protection against splinters should be afforded by sinking these tracks and constructing banks alongside. Of the other work undertaken, priority of importance was assigned to wiring, drainage, the construction of localities, and the accommodation of troops, in that order. Wire was, indeed, in view of the possibility of an enemy counter-attack, absolutely essential. As it was, odd German ration-carriers and patrols, losing their way in No Man's Land, frequently penetrated within our area, to be made not unwilling prisoners.

By the end of December immense improvement had been effected in all respects. North of the Polygonebeek the front line was protected by 2 rows of nearly continuous "double-apron" wire, and substantial progress had been made in the erection of 3 continuous belts before the support and reserve lines. Posts and occupied pillboxes, converted to our own use by alterations in the concrete, were protected by wire on their front flanks and rear. In addition entanglements were erected running diagonally to the enemy lines of advance in such a way as to break up his troops, lead them on to our garrisons, but interfere as little as possible with the deployment of our own counter-attacking troops. In the same proportion as this work developed, it received increasing attention from the enemy's artillery. Considerable maintenance parties had to be set aside for the exclusive purpose of repairing the gaps in the wire caused by his shells.

In the trenches the improvements were no less marked. An advance of the line in the middle of December reduced the sharpness of the In de Ster Cabaret salient and allowed wider observation of the approaches from Becelaere. The front line was strengthened by traverses, and was made continuous, and drained forward into several shallow gullies which fell towards the enemy. Its "localities" were revetted by material brought up with great exertion over ice or mud by the support battalions. As a result of well-directed and assiduous labour in the support line, the strong Papanui Switch, and the reserve line, as well as in the Corps system, the series of blue-coloured trenches in being rapidly extended across the Engineers' maps. Only on the Cameron Covert slopes south of the Polygonebeek, where the enormous marshes of the overflowing Reutelbeek and Polygonebeek made an impassable No Man's Land of nearly 800 yards, was the front line left in the post system; and here too a strongly wired support line guarded against irruption from Polderhoek. All this solid work was in the end to prove useless owing to a necessary withdrawal from this area in the spring.[1]

Behind the Divisional system multifarious tasks were allotted to technical troops and the reserve infantry brigades. The light railway was with splendid and successful audacity brought up to within half a mile of the Butte, alleviating the labours of and reducing distances for carrying and working parties. Tunnellers increased existing underground accommodation in the great shell-proof electrically-lit underground dugouts. Additional hutments were constructed east of Ypres to bring units near their work, and in rear of Ypres the draining of camps, the erection of Nissen huts, baths, and drying stores for gumboots, the repair of roads, the construction of stables and horsestandings,[2] the building of protective walls against aeroplane bombs, and a thousand other tasks claimed continuous attention. The Train companies were utilised to the fullest extent in conveyance of engineer stores and road material.

The artillery, too, had to make much necessary provision for the winter in the construction of platforms and cover for the guns, and of shellproof protection for battery commanders' and observation posts, as well as for personnel and ammunition, which near the guns was stacked in small dumps about 25 yards apart and separated by traverses. Certain guns were brought far forward and concealed under the brow of the crest to deal with enemy tanks. Elaborate arrangements were made for the defence of the sector by artillery in depth covering narrowing zones. Reserve positions were constructed for the heavy artillery in case of a withdrawal. The consumption of material by a single New Zealand Field Company

---

1 p. 378.

2 Bricks rubble and debris could be taken from destroyed towns and villages only for certain specified services. Uninhabited houses in good order or slightly damaged could not be used.

allotted to the supervision of this task indicates the scale on which these defensive measures were executed. In a single fortnight they used nearly 800 trucks of material, comprising fascines, sleepers, slabs, concrete blocks, cement, shingle, sand, reinforcing rods, sandbags, duckwalks, and iron dugout segments. Their work elicited warm commendation from the Army and Corps Commanders.

All this work was pushed on under generally adverse conditions. In December a series of snow-storms and frosts made the labour of digging the hard earth at once costly in tools and excessively arduous. On the icy duckboard tracks carrying and working parties, moving in single file, slipped and stumbled, and splinters from the enemy's high-explosive shells flew incredible distances. Even more difficult were conditions during the period of rainy weather, which starting in January lasted with scarcely a break till the first week in February.[1] Parapets fell in, despite carefully made berms, and drains became choked. Under cover of fog or occasional sleety storms, trenches were drained into No Man's Land. Thus L.-Cpl. W. G. Bowers of the 3rd Rifles in broad daylight and in full view of the enemy's positions 150 yards distant worked for an hour and a half on 16th January in No Man's Land in front of Judge subsector. Many bays, however, remained waist-deep in mud, and by the middle of January large tracts lay under water. In the muddy wastes of the Reutelbeek patrols endured extreme hardships. For preserving the health of the troops in the line, minute arrangements were made by provision of gum-boots, of hot food and hot drinks, and of camphor treatment as a precaution against "trench feet."

Following on a decrease of our own harassing fire in January the violence of the enemy's shelling also abated, and his groups at Waterdamhoek Dadizeele and Terhand, though maintaining activity on our wire and the Butte and his old pillboxes, paid more particular attention to the roads and tracks and battery positions further in rear. On Christmas Day they had carried out well-organised and particularly severe counter-battery work.[2] There was an inevitably steady and accumulating roll of casualties in the front trenches, but our losses were still more severe on the unsheltered tracks and at the dumps.

1 On the edge of the Ypres Moat, where the two famous white swans, impervious to the cold, still remained, some N.Z. Engineers had built themselves, during the frost, bivouacs on a small island. They woke one morning to find themselves, owing to the unexpected thaw, marooned. They were rescued by means of the pontoons.
2 Contrast p. 140.

About the beginning of February the enemy began
definitely to imitate our policy of an irregular series of sharp
brief "shell-storms" on cross-roads and other known centres
of activity. Rations for the front line troops were for this
reason not infrequently delayed.   In one of these concentrated local bombardments as early as December, the 2nd
Otago limbers were caught at the transport-head at Wattle
Dump. Twenty 5.9-in. shells were hurled at the dump in a
few minutes, and in addition to other casualties in men and
animals, Otago lost 3 company-quartermaster-sergeants
of whom 1 was killed and 2 wounded.   On these rear
tracks many valuable lives were lost.   Major V. Rogers,
D.S.O., O.C. 5th Battery, was killed on Jabber Track near
Railway Wood. Capt. L. S. Serpell, M.C., the Regimental
Medical Officer of 1st Canterbury, with the orderly-room
sergeant and other members of the Headquarters staff were
killed at Jargon Cross Roads, a place of particularly evil
associations, behind Glencorse Wood. Near Wattle Dump
Major R. D. Hardie, D.S.O., Divisional Machine Gun Officer,
was severely wounded.

To these rear areas, and the battery positions, and
especially to the wagon lines and camps west of Ypres,
Gothas also paid continual attention.   In clear frosty
nights the sky was often asound with the low-pitched drone
of enemy aircraft and stabbed with the shafts of our searchlights.   The Division, however, never again experienced such
misfortune from the air as it had suffered in the autumn,[1]
and the casualties in men and animals that were incurred in
January and were to be incurred in March were due, not to
bombs, but to high-velocity long-range guns.[2] About this time
the use of aircraft and balloons for propaganda purposes was
stimulated on both sides, and on several occasions the
insidious "Gazette des Ardennes" and pedantic and ineffective
declamations in laboured English fell about our batteries and
trenches.

In view of our preponderating artillery, the Germans in
their front system refrained from organising their shellhole
posts into a continuous line.[3] Their wire was generally formidable, but gaps existed, and through these from time to
time individual Germans, failing in the dark to locate the
isolated posts, wandered into No Man's Land and were

1 p. 245.
2 On 10th Jan. the artillery brigades and the D.A.C. lost 40 men killed and
wounded and 18 horses killed.
3 pp. 220, 248.

rounded up before our lines. Towards the end of January opportunities given the 2nd Brigade of inflicting heavier losses were taken advantage of with avidity. The evening of the 19th was lit by clear moonlight, and relieving Germans coming too far forward were discovered by Lewis gunners and snipers who poured in fire which loud groans indicated to be effective. Two nights later the enemy repeated his mistake, and a whole platoon with their packs up moved right across the front of one of the 2nd Otago posts at Reutel. Our sentries opened fire, and the Germans dispersed. A patrol was immediately sent out and shot one man whom they found crouching behind a mound. His identifications were brought in together with a dozen boxes of explosives and a machine gun, which the party had dropped in No Man's Land.

Later in the night the Germans sought revenge in the same vicinity. A sharp trench mortar bombardment prepared the way for their infantry. Otago stood at once to arms and had not long to wait before 4 enemy parties, about 100 strong in all, appeared in No Man's Land. Our S.O.S. rocket was fired, and before it burnt out the artillery shrapnel fell on the invaders. They threw a shower of bombs, but most fell short, and the affair was over in a few minutes. The barrage, the deadly machine gun fire, and the weapons of the garrison were too much for the Germans to face. Only 1 man got through our wire and none into the trench. A patrol sent out later found 7 dead in front of our entanglements and great pools of blood where wounded men had fallen.

As a result of these successes 2nd Otago forgot cold and mud and wet. Their sentries waited with their rifles trained on the enemy parapet, and the unwary German who exposed himself either in the trench system or by running from a pillbox on its bombardment by our howitzers could deem himself fortunate if he saw the Fatherland from the windows of a Red Cross train. Otago's patience was to be well rewarded ere they left the trenches. On a bright moonlight night their rifles and Lewis guns secured many victims in a relieving company of the enemy. A raid by about 20 Germans on the 1st Rifles' position on the evening of 2nd February was dealt with equally drastically. The Germans had succeeded in rushing a listening post and wounding all 4 occupants. They then bombed our front line and opened fire with revolvers. Cpl. J. G. Hart's section repelled them, and under cover of his men's fire Hart dashed forward, bombed the enemy and prevented them from obtaining any identifications from our wounded men in the listening post.   Four enemy dead were left entangled in our wire.

At the end of January the Army redistributed the Corps areas.   The II Anzac front was "side-stepped" southwards to include the positions hitherto held by the IX. Corps, beyond whom in turn, it may be noted, lay I. Anzac (now the Australian Corps[1]), guarding Messines.   The 20th and 37th Divisions, formerly under the IX. Corps, now passed under General Godley's command.   Early in February this extended line was reduced by the transfer of half the left sector of the old front to the VIII. Corps on the north.   The new Corps front was reconstructed on a 2-Division basis.   On the south the 20th Division troops replaced the New Zealand garrison in Cameron Covert, and the New Zealanders similarly side-stepped north, up to the new Corps boundary, taking over the Broodseinde Ridge from the 66th Division, for whom the 49th had made way in the middle of January. Relieved thus partly by the VIII. Corps and partly by the New Zealanders, the 66th Division was withdrawn for transfer to the Fifth Army.

The New Zealand Division, which had originally been on the right of the Corps front, now found itself on the left flank.   This readjustment involved a redistribution of infantry brigade frontages. The right brigade front now comprised the Reutel and Judge subsectors.   Noordhemhoek, hitherto held with Reutel and Judge, was now attached to Broodseinde as the charge of the left brigade.   Each brigade occupied the line with 2 battalions, holding 1 in close support, and 1 in deep dugouts in reserve.   The front system taken over on the Broodseinde Ridge was still only a line of posts just beyond the crest.   The shallowness of our position left us with but an insecure hold on this all-important high ground. Without delay our posts were advanced some little distance, and work was started on the construction of a continuous line, preparatory to our pushing still further forward down the slope to give us greater depth and to command wider observation over the Keiberg valley.   The continuous line would then serve as a support position near the crest.   The northern brigade staff lived in grandiose pillboxes, known as Potsdam, on the Ypres-Roulers railway. The staff of the right brigade shared the Butte dugouts with its left battalion H.Q.

1   p. 328.

Towards the end of the previous year, shortly after the Polderhoek operations, General Braithwaite had been compelled by a breakdown in health, overtaxed by volcanic energy, to say farewell to his brigade and to sever long and fruitful association with the New Zealand forces. The qualities of enthusiasm and mastery over detail which he had shown as General Godley's Chief of Staff in New Zealand and on Gallipoli stamped also his command of fighting troops. Never sparing himself, he demanded a high standard of duty from his subordinates, and appreciated results rather than the effort which made for them. A professional soldier, adjutant in turn of a regular battalion in the British Army and of Sandhurst, he was intolerant of slackness or indecision, and could rend an offender with blunt expression of dissatisfaction. Hardly less marked characteristics were an intense pride in his brigade, a keen sense of humour, a faculty for the creation of bon-mots, speedily retailed with relish throughout the Division, a warmness of heart, and an untiring activity in promoting the advancement and interests of all under his command. Few men were better known throughout the Force. Not seeking popularity he achieved it, and genuine affection survived his departure.

After an interval the vacated appointment was given in the first week of February to General Hart, whose 4th Brigade had, as we shall see, ceased to exist. Their new brigadier, however, was not to command the South Island battalions for long. In the second week of February they went in due course of relief into the right subsector of the line, with brigade headquarters at the Butte. Always a magnet for hostile gas as for high-explosive, special measures were adopted by the brigade gas officer to ensure that its anti-gas defences were satisfactory. On the windless night of 18th/19th February it was heavily bombarded with mustard gas shells. The gas alarms were blown, the weighted blankets at the doorways lowered on their rollers, and all other precautions taken. No ill effects were noticed that night, but on the following day, when the heat of the sun melted the frozen ground, the gas gradually and imperceptibly filtered through the open doorway and filled the Butte. The whole Headquarters of the brigade and of 2nd Canterbury, who chanced to be the left battalion in the line, were poisoned and had to be evacuated. The total casualties amounted to 14 officers and over 160 men, fortunately only a few cases proving fatal.

General Hart's evacuation was followed by a reshuffling
of commands. General Fulton had returned to the Rifle
Brigade from Sling in November. He had been succeeded
in the English appointment by General Young, now happily
recovered from his wound. In December the latter was in
turn succeeded by General Melvill, and on returning to
France had taken command of the 1st Brigade. He was now
transferred to the 2nd Brigade, and General Melvill was
recalled to his old command. The duties at Sling could wait
for General Hart's convalescence.

Neither Ayrton Fans nor Vermoral Sprayers could cleanse
the polluted Butte, and General Young occupied fresh headquarters in dugouts further back at Westhoek. Some little
time afterwards Capt. Falconer was appointed Brigade Major
of the 2nd Brigade in place of Major Richardson. The
appointment of Staff Captain held by Capt. H. Holderness,
who had succeeded Capt. Wilkes in September on the latter's
proceeding to England for a course of training with the
R.F.C., was now filled by Major J. E. Barton, N.Z.S.C.

In General Young's 2nd Brigade, 2nd Canterbury held at
the moment the northern Judge subsector. Reutel was garrisoned by 1st Otago, whose advanced posts lay on the fringe
of Juniper Wood. The shattered wood itself extended over
the miry slopes falling towards the Polygonebeek, and continued in a straggling plantation down the Reutelbeek valley.
Through its northern extremity near the Otago line had run
a German defence system, and here a pillbox by the enemy
trench and a disabled British tank, which the enemy had
included in his defences, still formed one of his advanced
Strong Points. A well-defined track led back from the tank
to the pillbox. Amid the mangled tree-stumps both stood
out conspicuously to direct observation and were prominent
also in aeroplane photographs. They had long been marked
for a raid when the ground should have recovered from the
rains.

As early as 17th January the 6th Battery had fired 40
rounds in the afternoon at the tank and adjoining sector of
the old trench, now largely destroyed, which ran from the
pillbox toward the Reutelbeek. Immediately afterwards,
under cover of a mist, which succeeded a heavy fall of snow
turning at midday to rain, a 2nd Rifles patrol of 4 men under
Sergt. W. B. Bowles, went out to investigate results. Under
distant machine gun fire from the Polderhoek Spur and direct
rifle fire from a post 50 yards down the German trench the

BRIG.-GEN. C. W. MELVILL, C.B., C.M.G., D.S.O.

BRIG.-GEN. R. YOUNG, C.B., C.M.G., D.S.O.

AN ARTILLERY OBSERVATION POST

GUNPITS NEAR WESTHOEK

patrol reconnoitred and entered the Strong Point. The shooting had been splendidly accurate. The sides of the tank were smashed. Twelve dead Germans were found inside with a number of dead and dying in the slush outside. It was impossible to bring back any of the wounded, but shoulder-straps and discs yielded the necessary identifications, and with these and a machine gun the patrol returned safely.

The Strong Point was again bombarded on 26th January, and a daylight patrol of 2nd Otago found the dead still lying there. The entanglements round the tank were broken, and there was but a little crescent wire round the pillbox. The latter itself was undamaged, and a ladder beside it suggested that its roof was still used for observation. As the patrol felt its way nearer, they were spied by a sentry in the trench. He gave a loud shout of alarm. Twenty Germans doubled out from the pillbox. The patrol withdrew under their fire. At the same time 7 flares bursting into 2 green lights were shot up from behind the pillbox or through a hole in its roof, and shortly afterwards 2 enemy aeroplanes flew over the position.

By the middle of February the ground, although still wet, presented reasonably firm going. A Division freshly arrived from Russia and adept in methods of fraternisation was believed to be opposite the Corps front. A suitable welcome had been given in a concentrated bombardment fired by the Corps artillery at the beginning of the month. To establish its definite location identifications were wanted, and the Strong Point at the tank was selected for the purpose. It was arranged that 1st Otago should raid it a few days after relieving their sister battalion on 15th February.

2nd Otago, however, were not to leave the line without a trophy of their own. Some 50 yards from their front line, between the wood and the brick heaps that marked the site of Reutel, a German post was pushed out in Reutel Cemetery on the night of 14th/15th February. Fresh earth and snipers' plates were noticed in the morning by an Otago observer, Pte. A. Macdonald. He pointed them out to Sergt. B. W. Crosker, and the two determined that the enemy should pay for his presumption. They crawled out from the Otago trenches in full view of the Germans and reconnoitred the new post. They found it held by 5 occupants. They shot the n.c.o. in command and brought back the other 4 as prisoners. These proved to be Bavarians, the Division from the East having taken over a sector further north. The

Rifle Brigade on the left, too, were not inactive, and a 3rd Battalion patrol, under Sergt. J. W. Clayson, actually penetrated over 900 yards into the enemy's territory. A German party sought to intercept their return, but was beaten off by covering Lewis guns.

On coming into the line 1st Otago scouts lost no time in reconnoitring the Strong Point and established the fact that the tank was occupied at night. A party of 30 raiders, under 2nd Lt. W. O'Connell, was selected from the 4th (Otago) Company. They were given special training at the brigade school.

The raid was carried out at 3.30 a.m. on 21st February. With a view to diverting the enemy's attention and causing him losses, his trenches and dugouts at other neighbouring points were bombarded by 18-pounders, 4.5-in. howitzers, and medium trench mortars. Light mortars provided the barrage for the raid. By 3.30 a.m., O'Connell and his men were crouching in shellholes some 30 yards in front of our parapet. As the light mortars opened, they moved forward in separate parties. It was not their purpose to attack frontally from the north but to work round from the west. Rain had fallen heavily during the night, and No Man's Land was a squelching quagmire. Through this the parties pushed to within 130 yards of the bursting mortar bombs and then knelt, waiting for the barrage to cease.

The moment the mortars' fire died away they splashed forward over the slippery ground, leaving a Lewis gun to safeguard their flank towards the Polygonebeek. The tank was soon surrounded and its 6 occupants accounted for. Two were killed and the others, who again proved to be Bavarians, were captured. The track to the pillbox, some 70 yards distant, was a mere bog full of treacherous shellholes. Struggling through the deep mud its attackers were only 30 yards away when the specified 7 minutes allotted for the enterprise expired, and the green recall flare shot into the sky. Before withdrawing, the disappointed section flung its bombs in a salvo at the pillbox. Only one member of the whole party was slightly wounded through a splinter from one of our light trench mortar bombs.

During the following evening (22nd February) the 2nd Brigade front was taken over by troops of the 49th Division. On the same night the Rifle Brigade executed, without casualties, the carefully prepared plan for strengthening the left of the Divisional sector by advancing their lines a further distance of 200 yards beyond the crest, so as to overlook satisfactorily the Keiberg valley. They were relieved the following evening. On the 24th the 49th Division assumed responsibility for the sector. The New Zealanders' casualties for the winter months had amounted to 3000, of whom 19 officers and over 450 men had lost their lives.[1] The comparatively high wastage was chiefly due to the great numbers of troops employed on working and carrying in the forward areas, and to the lack of communication trenches and shell-proof cover at the beginning of the period.

By the evening of 24th February the relieved units of the Division had been conveyed by train into the Corps reserve area about Staple, west of Hazebrouck, with Divisional headquarters at Renescure. The 1st Infantry Brigade, the 1st and 3rd Field Companies, and the Pioneer Battalion were left in the forward area for employment on the Corps defence system. The 2nd (Army) Brigade was relieved on 25th February and ceased to be controlled by the Division. The other 2 artillery brigades remained in the line, the 1st Brigade coming under the orders of the 49th Division on the left, and the 3rd Brigade, after a short interval at the wagon lines, under those of the 37th Division, who had previously relieved the 20th Division astride the Menin Road.

Certain important features of organisation must be here briefly summarised. On General Plumer's going to Italy in November, General Rawlinson handed over the Fourth Army area to the XV. Corps and assumed command of the Second Army. His Fourth Army Headquarters ceased to exist as an independent unit and was absorbed in Second Army Headquarters. In December the Second Army was designated the Fourth Army and retained that name under General Birdwood's temporary command, which followed General Rawlinson's appointment to Versailles in February. In March General Plumer returned from Italy and restored its former title.

By the end of 1917 all the Australian Divisions had been transferred to I. Anzac, and Australasia in II. Anzac was represented only by the 1 Division of New Zealanders,

1   As given in monthly states:—

			KILLED Off.	KILLED O. Rs.	WOUNDED Off.	WOUNDED O. Rs.	MISSING Off.	MISSING O. Rs.
November	....	....	3	128	21	474	—	4
December*	....	....	11	110	40	953	—	84
January	....	....	2	97	14	489	—	1
February	....	....	3	98	33	345	—	—
Total	....	....	19	433	108	2261	—	89

*Includes attack on Polderhoek Chateau.

the Corps Mounted Regiment, and the Cyclist Battalion.　On 1st January the former Corps was redesignated the Australian Corps and the latter the XXII. Corps.　To replace the Australian Cyclist Company,[1] a third New Zealand company was formed from men of long infantry service in the Division, and the battalion, now completely a New Zealand unit, changed its name with the Corps and became the XXII. Corps Cyclist Battalion.[2]

In the New Zealand Force itself an important reorganisation was now necessary, for it had become apparent that the maintenance of 4 infantry brigades exposed to the wastage of battle was no longer feasible.　The formation of the 4th Brigade had been sanctioned by the New Zealand Government with express reservations.[3]　By this time the unexpected strain of 3 years' warfare under modern conditions was felt by all the combatants.　The British authorities had been constrained to disband formations and adopt the Continental organisation of 3 instead of 4 battalions in an infantry brigade.　It was possible for the New Zealand administration to follow the same policy and maintain 4 brigades of 3 battalions, which the uninterrupted flow of reinforcements was adequate to keep up to establishment strength.　On the grounds, however, of efficiency and simplicity of organisation it was preferable to adhere to the normal 3-brigades establishment, although the New Zealand brigades, unlike the corresponding British units, would consist each of the unreduced number of 4 battalions.

The 4th Brigade therefore with its affiliated units, relieved in the line by the 1st Brigade in January and thenceforward utilised as Corps employment troops, ceased to exist as from 7th February, and its personnel was drawn on to bring the Division up to strength.　It was not the policy to increase the Division beyond establishment, and there consequently remained a considerable surplus. This was formed into a New Zealand Entrenching Group of 3 battalions. Command of the group, originally given to Lt.-Col. A. E. Stewart, was shortly afterwards taken by Lt.-Col. G. Mitchell, D.S.O.　The battalions were organised as follows:—

1st N.Z. (Inf. Brigade) Entrenching Bn., Capt. G. Dittmer, M.C.
2nd N.Z. (Inf. Brigade) Entrenching Bn., Capt. J. F. Tonkin.
3rd N.Z. (Rifle Brigade) Entrenching Bn., Capt. S. J. E. Closey, M.C.

1　p. 59.
2　p. 601.
3　p. 163.

The Group became a reservoir for the Division, receiving from the New Zealand Reinforcement Wing at Corps Headquarters drafts not merely of infantry but of all branches of the service, as certified to be trained satisfactorily. It thus largely superseded the Etaples Base. It was also available for employment under Corps.[1]

Up to this time the New Zealand Machine Gun Corps had consisted of a Mounted Section in Palestine, the 1st 2nd 3rd and 4th Companies allotted to the respective infantry brigades, the 5th (Divisional) Company and the 6th (Reserve) Company at Grantham.[2] On arrival at the Staple training area a Divisional Machine Gun Battalion was formed. The 5 companies in France were now reorganised into 4 companies (Auckland Canterbury Otago and Wellington), and their administration passed from brigade commanders. Lt.-Col. Blair was given command of the new battalion. In September the Pakeha Company of the Pioneer Battalion, in which all the Europeans had been previously incorporated, had been disbanded, and the unit, now consisting wholly of Maoris, had been designated the New Zealand Maori (Pioneer) Battalion. In February the heavy and 3 medium trench mortar batteries were reorganised into two 6-in. Newton batteries.

In addition to the changes of appointments mentioned in the course of the narrative, certain others have still to be recorded. On the Divisional "G" Staff all 3 appointments had changed hands. Lt.-Col. Livesay, whose work was G.S.O.1 had been marked by consummate finish and qualities at once brilliant and solid, now left the Division, with which he had been associated since before the Battle of the Somme, for duties with the American Army. He was succeeded by Lt.-Col. H. M. Wilson, D.S.O., (British) Rifle Brigade. Capt. Newnham, G.S.O.2, had been wounded in October and succeeded by Major Eastwood, the vacant appointment of Brigade Major in the 4th Brigade being filled by Major R. Logan, N.Z.S.C. Major Jennings, G.S.O.3, had become Brigade Major of the 1st Brigade in place of Major Thoms, wounded at Gravenstafel, and his post was filled first by Major Barton and subsequently by Major D. E. Bremner, N.Z.S.C.[3] Major W. L. Robinson, N.Z.S.C., had been appointed D.A.A.G. vice Major Chesney in August. In the

1 The Group followed the Division to the IV. Corps area in the spring, 1918, was reorganised into 2 battalions at the end of August, and disbanded in October.
2 p. 19.
3 p. 324.

artillery, Major Daltry relinquished in December the appointment of Staff Captain for work of national importance in England and was succeeded by Capt. W. G. Stevens, R.N.Z.A. Lt.-Col. Symon returned to his brigade in December.[1] In March, on Lt.-Col. Sykes' rejoining the British Army, Lt.-Col. Falla assumed command of the 2nd (Army) Brigade, being succeeded in the 3rd Brigade by Major (now Lt.-Col.) R. S. McQuarrie, M.C.

On the infantry brigade Staffs Capt. Falconer's[2] vacated appointment as Staff Captain in the 1st Brigade was filled by Capt. D. S. Chisholm, who had previously succeeded Major H. S. N. Robinson in the same capacity in the 4th Brigade. In the battalions, Lt.-Col. Cunningham exchanged command of 2nd Wellington in January for that of the reserve battalion and was succeeded by Major (now Lt.-Col.) J. L. Short. On the breaking up of the 4th Brigade, Lt.-Col. Row assumed command of 1st Canterbury, held temporarily by Lt.-Col. Mead. Through ill-health, Lt.-Col. Smith relinquished command of 2nd Otago in November to take command of the reserve battalion, and was succeeded first by Major (now Lt.-Col.) J. B. McClymont, and on the latter's evacuation through sickness by Lt.-Col. Colquhoun, of the disbanded 3rd Battalion. In the Rifle Brigade the 3rd Battalion was now commanded by Lt.-Col. E. Puttick, in succession to Lt.-Col. Winter-Evans,[3] and the 4th Battalion by Lt.-Col. R. St. J. Beere (Reserve Battalion), who exchanged duties with Lt.-Col. Roache in December. Lt.-Col. G. Craig was now in command of No. 1 Field Ambulance vice Lt.-Col. Holmes, who had been invalided in September. Mention should be made, too, of the specially selected party of 12 officers and 25 other ranks who left the Division during this period for a secret mission which eventually took them over the Mesopotamian frontier into the wilds of Persia and the Caucasus and to the shores of the Caspian.

1   p. 252, footnote.
2   p. 324.
3   p. 284.

CHAPTER IX

THE GERMAN OFFENSIVE, 1918

The collapse of Russia had not merely saved the Central Powers from defeat in 1917, but held out to them a promise of positive success in 1918, with the realisation of their most ambitious hopes. The German Command was quick to appreciate the wholly changed situation. Masses of men and artillery had been released and the latter reinforced by vast quantities of captured armament. Once again Germany had recovered numerical superiority and that initiative which sne had lost since Verdun. Cards had been dealt her such as she had not dared to hope for. She had little hesitation as to how she would play them. It was on the Western front, and not in the subsidiary theatres of war on the Mediterranean and in the East, that the main issue of the war would be decided. An additional reason for an early offensive in France lay in America's intervention. The submarine campaign promised no effective hindrance to the crossing of American reinforcements, and it was apparent that did Germany not attack speedily, she would once again be outnumbered in the field and thrown back on the defensive by her enemies. Within her own borders, moreover, the Allied blockade and propaganda were not sterile, and there was doubt and uncertainty, even in high quarters. For these reasons it was imperative for Germany to strike with all her might while the golden opportunity lasted. Conscious of their strength, the generals at a secret session of the Reichstag in February promised the elated deputies a complete victory in the autumn.

Their plans were boldly conceived. When General Rawlinson met his Corps Commanders in December and reviewed the possible alternatives open to the enemy, he had directed particular attention to the Cambrai front. As the point of junction between the French and British Armies, and as familiar to the enemy through former occupation, it might be expected to appear specially attractive. On the other hand, Rawlinson pointed out that no objectives of far-reaching tactical importance such as the central ridges about Arras or Ypres seemed to be within reasonable grasp. The German plan, however, was more ambitious than their opponents

believed. Its aim was final and decisive success by complete
defeat of the Allied Armies. The attack was designed first to
separate them by an overwhelming blow at this very point of
junction, which in February 1918 was 30 miles further south
of Cambrai than in December, then to roll the British Army
right back on the coast and immobilise it there, and finally
to turn on the French. Before America could put her levies
in the field the Germans hoped that the catastrophes of the
Armies and the demoralisation of the civil populations would
compel the Allied Governments to accept a strong peace.
Ludendorff's Staff appears to have believed that the close
of the first day's fighting would see the British across the
Somme, and the second day in general retreat down its lower
valley. On the third day the pivot of the British line at
Arras would fall, and before fresh reserves from the south
could restore the situation, Haig's troops would be isolated
and in disastrous retreat towards a precarious bridgehead on
the Channel.

The German Staff had profited by the British tactics of
secret assembly, absence of prolonged preparatory bombardment,
and other features of our surprise attack at Cambrai, and had
developed and perfected them by practice in Russia and
Italy. Hitherto, with the partial exception of the Cambrai
operation, the offensives on the Western front had been
limited by the highly technical but rigid barrage, carried
forward by which the assaulting infantry advanced with
little or no impetus of its own. It was the weakness of these
tactics that they restricted the personal influence of commanders. Condemning them as narrow and sterile, Ludendorff replaced them by others calculated to yield more decisive results. Commanders, he laid down, were to command.
Free play must be allowed for the fullest independence and
tactical skill of subordinate leaders. The foremost infantry
were to advance as long as possible and should be reinforced
or "leap-frogged through" only when it became absolutely
necessary. Attacking Divisions must be prepared not merely
to pass the enemy artillery positions, but to press on the
offensive for many miles and for several days. A feature
which was to exercise immense importance was the insistence
on the principle that reserves should not be thrown into the
battle at points where the attack had been held up by centres
of resistance and where unnecessary sacrifice was involved.
They were to be used at points where the attack was still in
movement, with a view to breaking down the enemy's re-

sistance in the neighbouring sector by rolling it up from flank and rear. Hardly less important than this principle of infiltration was the novel application of machine guns, hitherto mainly regarded as defensive weapons, to the attack. The very framework of the new policy was the bold use of the light machine gun in the van of the advancing infantry and its employment on the basis of what had been conceived as infantry, rather than of machine gun, tactics.

Throughout the winter months the enemy's preponderance of forces enabled him to release a large number of his Divisions from trench duties. They were assiduously and intensively trained in the use of signal flares to indicate breaches in our line, in other features of the new methods of attack and in open warfare movements. They attained a very great technical proficiency. Their morale was of the highest. By the middle of March 46 fresh German Divisions were accumulated on the Western front, making a total of 192. Of these more than half lay opposite the British sector, and on the eve of the battle over 70 were massed against the Fifth and Third Armies. On the opening day of the attack, designated in felicitous encouragement to his soldiers as Michael's Day,[1] Ludendorff was to hurl against a front of 50 miles a force of splendidly trained soldiers, approximately equal in numbers to the entire population of New Zealand.

In anticipation of the German attack, the British Command in December had deliberately exchanged its offensive for a defensive policy. The change was reflected in the proportion of raids delivered by either side. Hitherto the number of the British raids had largely exceeded that of the German. Now twice as many were carried out on the British front by the enemy as by us, though the balance of successes was conspicuously in our favour. Immense efforts to improve defences were made along the whole line of 125 miles, extended since January down to the Oise, where Gough's Fifth Army, released from Flanders, replaced the French.

In gauging the point where the attack would be launched, the British Command had to consider 3 main possible courses of action open to the enemy. In the first place, the old attempt might be renewed in Flanders with the object of securing the Channel ports, immediately threatening England and severing direct communication with France. Again, an

---

1 "Michael" was a favourite German personification of the nation's armed manhood, of somewhat wider significance than, and without the characteristic irony of the English "Tommy."

attack might be delivered in the central sector about Béthune with the primary purpose of breaking lateral communication, and with a secondary aim similar to, but on a larger scale than an operation in Flanders. Thirdly, they must consider the possibilities of that offensive in the south which Rawlinson had discussed, and which would have as its goal the separation of the French and British Armies with the capture of the railway centre at Amiens as a first objective. In the north and centre, where our hold of the Ypres and central ridges about Arras was shallow, little or no territory could be yielded, but in this southern portion of the line the area of the old battlefields might, if necessity constrained, be given up without serious consequences. Here also it was easier to bring up French reinforcements. Till indication of the enemy's plan developed, Sir Douglas Haig disposed his forces in accordance with these factors.

At the beginning of the year hostile activity continued, notably at Ypres. The enemy's ammunition and supply dumps had been augmented, and rail and road communications had been improved along the whole front. By the end of February, however, indications pointed unmistakably to the probability that the enemy's initial attempt would be made in the southern sector. While therefore the northern Armies were left sufficiently strong to meet emergencies, more than half the British effectives, together with the whole of the cavalry, were now at the disposal of the Fifth and Third Armies. Plans were drawn up with special regard to the reinforcement of this front by reserve Divisions from the rest of the British area. Owing to the great bend in the Allied line south of the Oise the German concentration menaced in almost equal degree the French front on the Aisne. Detailed arrangements, therefore, were made with the French for mutual support should the need arise.

Though the threatened fronts were strengthened as much as possible, the defence could not be regarded as thoroughly satisfactory. On the north, General Byng's Third Army, consisting from right to left of the V., IV., VI., and XVII. Corps, disposed 1 Division to nearly 3 miles of front, while General Gough's Fifth Army on the south, composed from right to left of the III., XVIII., XIX., and VII. Corps, had only 1 Division to 4 miles. On the other hand, it was hoped that the southernmost 10 miles on the Fifth Army front would be protected by the Oise marshes. Special measures were taken to construct a strong bridgehead at Péronne to cover the Somme crossings. In his defensive preparations Haig was hampered by the War Office's decision to retain large forces in England as a safeguard against the doubtful threat of invasion. Three zones of defence were, however, under construction. The third and final zone was in skeleton only. Nor was labour available to construct systems further in rear than on the average 4 to 5 miles behind the forward line of outposts. The 2 front systems were, however, strongly fortified, and the Staff, underestimating the German danger, believed them adequate to withstand the shock.

Against these thinly held and inadequately organised defences the German attack burst with unexpected power after a few hours of violently severe bombardment on the morning of 21st March. At least 60 Divisions were employed on a front of slightly over 50 miles. The British Intelligence Staff had predicted the launching of the attack on 20th or 21st March. Strenuous artillery counter-preparation had been carried out, and the garrisons of the different systems were all at their posts. Covered by a dense fog, the enemy troops were enabled to reach within a few yards of our positions before they came under infantry fire. Our S.O.S. signals were masked in the fog, all communications were cut, and information of the attack reached our artillery and machine gun commanders late. The protective barrages were in consequence delayed, and in frequent instances came down in rear of the assaulting Germans. In any case, all fire was largely masked by the fog. The swamps of the Oise, which it had been hoped would protect the extreme right flank, proved owing to unusually dry weather no serious obstacle.

In accordance with their new tactics the Germans drove with special strength on certain selected points and forced their way into our positions by sheer weight of numbers. Obstinate resistance inflicted extremely heavy losses and prevented that immediate and deep break-through on which Ludendorff had counted, but by the evening of the 21st the enemy had crossed the foremost defensive zone and penetrated into the second, before which the British Command had hoped definitely to arrest his progress. His furthest point of penetration was between 4 and 5 miles on the thinly-manned extreme right south-west of St. Quentin, and here, on the 22nd, the outnumbered and hard-pressed III. Corps, which had exhausted all local reserves, was thrown back behind its third and final defensive zone. The centre opposite St. Quentin was ordered to conform by withdrawing to the east bank of the Somme. The 2 northern Corps of the Fifth Army remained for the night east of the river, holding the important Péronne bridgehead and the third zone northwards to the Army boundary. The Third Army, repeatedly repulsing attacks, still clung desperately to its position in the rear trenches of the second belt, but during the night its right and centre were also brought back to the third zone.

On the morning of the 23rd, reluctant to accept battle with tired troops in the undeveloped Péronne bridgehead, General Gough took the "momentous" decision to abandon it and fall back west of the Somme. Thus his northern (VII.) Corps, crossing the river and retiring further, exposed the flank of the withdrawing V. Corps of the Third Army, and created a gap between the Armies. This gap the Germans exploited with remarkable swiftness, forcing the V. Corps back to the ridges immediately south-east of Bapaume. By the evening of the 23rd Ludendorff had advanced only 9 miles, reaching the objectives originally planned for the 21st, and our line was not yet broken. The British, however, had lost, besides other heavy casualties, 25,000 prisoners and 400 guns. The men, who had fought magnificently, were now exhausted, and over a large part of the front they were now behind all existing defence systems. British reserves alone could not save the situation, and on the 23rd arrangements were made with the French, for the moment released from anxiety about Champagne, to take over the Fifth Army front south of the Somme.

At the junction of the Fifth and Third Armies the enemy pressure still continued on the 24th. Measures were taken to strengthen the VII. Corps, and the V. and IV. Corps on its left were ordered to fall back to a line across the old Somme battlefield west of Bapaume. This general line was taken up by midnight 24th/25th, but the withdrawal involved a loss of touch between the V. and IV. Corps which was eventually to affect the movements of the New Zealand Division. On the rest of the Fifth Army front the Somme was still held for some 8 miles south of Péronne, but beyond that point the enemy had made rapid progress and was in a position to threaten Noyon, which, with Nesle, fell into his hands on the following day.

The further developments south of the Somme, the attempt to sever the French and British Armies by an attack from Nesle, the advance of the Germans beyond Roye, the stand by General Carey's mixed force in the outer Amiens defences, the intervention of French reserves, the supersession of General Gough by General Rawlinson, the British resumption of command as far south as the Luce valley, the belated German effort at the Paris-Amiens railway, the final establishment of a stable Allied front in the first days of April, and with it the close of the German offensive on the Somme— all these are subject matter of a larger history which can be studied nowhere better, despite inevitable reticences, than in the Commander-in-Chief's admirably lucid Despatch. It was with the right wing and the centre of the Third Army north of the river that the New Zealanders were summoned to play their part.

By the evening of the first day it was clear that the German attack involved practically the whole of Ludendorff's mass of manoeuvre. It was therefore "at once necessary and possible" to collect reserve Divisions from the rest of the front and hurry them to the Somme. In view of the vital importance of the First Army's position in the centre, its greater proximity to the battlefield and the distinct possibility of its becoming implicated, reinforcements were drawn principally from General Plumer's Second Army further north. Among the troops so called on was the New Zealand Division.

Their period of rest and training in the Staple area was favoured by exceptionally fine weather, under which health and general fitness rapidly recovered from the strain of the winter. A comprehensive scheme of recreational training utilised the men's characteristic fondness of and aptitude for sports and competitions, with the object of promoting physical vigour, developing the fighting spirit, stimulating mental as well as physical alertness and restoring the vitality inevitably affected by a long period in the trenches. In the general military training it is interesting to note that stress was laid on the use of infantry weapons in combination with machine guns and light mortars, and on the development of the initiative and power of leadership of section and platoon commanders, especially as regards use of ground, direction and control of fire, and quickness of decision in dealing with all the varied situations which arise in battle. Rehearsals were made of deliberate fire-covered withdrawals from advanced positions both by day and by night, and of taking over in obscure situations defences held by a mixture of various and disorganised units. Suggestive, too, was the insistence given to emphasising in talks to the men the marked superiority, now long and indisputably established, of the New Zealand soldier over the enemy in any kind of fighting. It had been intended that each infantry brigade should have a training period of 4 weeks, 1 brigade at a time remaining in the forward area for work on the Corps defence system. Musketry was practised on the ranges at Moulle beyond St. Omer. By the middle of March rest and training had reforged the Division into a weapon of sterling quality.

In view of the expected offensive, arrangements had been made for rapid movement in case of emergency to the Ypres ridges. On 21st March, however, when the German attack broke out on the Somme, orders were received that the Division would pass from Corps into Army reserve and be held ready to entrain for the south after midnight 22nd/23rd March. Provision was made for the relief of the artillery from the line and for the concentration in the Divisional area of the 4 battalions training on the rifle ranges at Moulle. On the 22nd the Division was marked for transfer to the Third Army and ordered to commence entrainment on the afternoon of the 24th. On that date the various units in the Staple area marched to the stations at Cassel and Caestre. The Rifle Brigade[1] group, with the Headquarters and 2 companies of the Engineers and with the Pioneer Battalion, all then in the forward area at Ypres, concentrated at Hopoutre, near Poperinghe. The artillery, completing their relief behind Westhoek Ridge on 23rd March, entrained on the 25th at Caestre Godewaersvelde and Hopoutre. The rate of entraining was somewhat retarded owing to the destruction of a railway bridge near St. Pol by hostile action, and consequent disorganisation of the railway system. Caestre was bombed by aeroplanes, but no hitch marred the general arrangements. The Division for the remainder of its history was not again to form part of the XXII. Corps.

By this time the British Staff anticipated an extension of the attack to the northern flank about Arras. It was at first intended, therefore, that the Division should on arrival in the Third Army area come under the command of the XVII. Corps on General Byng's left. The time for this German move, however, had not yet come, and owing to urgent need of further reserves on the Fifth Army front this order was changed on the 24th. The Division was then diverted further south to the Bray area on the Somme, where it would be in general reserve and be prepared to move at 4 hours' notice. It was allotted meantime to the VII. Corps

1 Lt.-Col. A. E. Stewart, vice Brig.-Gen. Fulton, on leave.

RESERVES, MARCH 1918

A FRONT LINE TRENCH, 1918

ARTILLERY TEAMS UNDER COVER

IN ACTION NEAR COLINCAMPS

on the left of the Fifth Army, and General Russell on arrival established his headquarters with the VII. Corps Commander at Corbie.

By the evening of the 24th, however, the immediate danger on the VII. Corps front had been averted by vigorous counter-attacks delivered by the fresh Divisions sent to its support. Accordingly in the early morning of the 25th the New Zealanders were earmarked as G.H.Q. reserves and their destined concentration area moved further north up the Ancre valley to Mericourt l'Abbé, Morlancourt and Dernancourt, places familiar to most New Zealanders who had participated in the Somme Battle of 1916. The railway line east of Amiens had been cut by bombs. It was arranged therefore that the troops should detrain at various stations between Amiens and Picquigny. Thence they would be brought forward, if practicable by busses, as far as Pont Noyelles, some 6 miles from Amiens on the Albert road, where they would be within easy reach of their destination. Divisional Headquarters moved during the afternoon to Ribemont on the Ancre. On this day (25th March) General Byng assumed command of all troops north of the Somme, and the Division thus passed, as originally projected, under the control of the Third Army.

A more important change in organisation was being made elsewhere. By this time the gravity of the situation overpowered reluctance to face the delicate problems involved in the creation of that one supreme command of both French and British Armies on the Western front for which the Advisory Council at Versailles had been a makeshift. Clemenceau and Pétain, Lord Milner, Sir Henry Wilson, and Haig met that day at Doullens and took the preliminary measures for the appointment of Foch as Generalissimo of the Allied forces.

On this day of the 25th, while this momentous decision was being arrived at in Doullens, and while the New Zealand trains were emptying their personnel in the disorganised stations west of Amiens, the German pressure on the right wing of the Third Army had not been relaxed. The VII. Corps had disputed the north bank of the Somme with gallantry and success, but to their north the V. Corps Divisions, out of touch with each other, had begun to fall back independently towards the Ancre. The seriousness of the situation may be gauged by the following message issued by Corps Headquarters at 5.45 p.m. to the 63rd (Royal Naval) Division, which during the day had beaten off a succession of attacks:—

25

"If you are forced back over the Ancre you must secure the crossings between Authuille and Beaucourt. Send back parties if possible to make sure of these crossings beforehand. The 2nd Division is being forced back at Beaumont-Hamel and is practically non-existent. The 2nd Division have been asked to hold the crossings between Hamel and Beaucourt, but G.O.C. does not think this will be possible. It is very important that your left flank should not be turned. Cyclists are being sent to hold the crossings between Aveluy and Beaucourt, but these will not arrive for some time. Retain your hold on the Pozières-Thiepval ridge if you possibly can."

The northern troops of the V. Corps, however, fell back and crossed the Ancre at Beaumont-Hamel. On their left beyond the gap the IV. Corps right was similarly being forced westwards. The 42nd and 62nd Divisions, which had been released by General Horne and for 2 days had been attached to other Corps of the Third Army, were now sent to the IV. Corps with the hope that under their cover the exhausted front line Divisions could be withdrawn at nightfall and reassembled, first at Puisieux-au-Mont and Bucquoy, and later at Hébuterne Gommecourt and Fonquevillers. The insistent drive of the Germans proved, however, too powerful, and the Third Army was obliged to withdraw its centre as well as its right to the Ancre.

Orders were thereupon issued for the V. Corps to hold the western bank of the Ancre, from Albert (inclusive) up to Hamel (inclusive). The 12th Division would be withdrawn from the VII. Corps for this purpose and come under the orders of the V. Corps, whose exhausted Divisions would then reform on the line Bouzincourt-Engelbelmer. On the right the VII. Corps were to withdraw at once to the line Bray-Albert, conforming with the V. Corps and securing the retirement of the Fifth Army south of the Somme. The IV. Corps on the left would similarly fall back from its positions east of Logeast Wood and Achiet-le-Petit to the line Puisieux-Bucquoy-Ablainzeville-Boyelles, where its left would be in touch with the VI. Corps. Meantime the personnel of the Third Army Musketry School was placed at the disposal of the IV. Corps, who with it and fragments of the 19th and 25th Divisions strove desperately to cover the Ancre crossings in the gap on its southern flank.

In this gap hostile patrols had already crossed the river north of Miraumont and were rapidly moving towards Serre, of sinister memory,[1] and Puisieux. During the night (25th/26th March) they were to reach these villages, and advance parties to push beyond under cover of smoke barrages into Hébuterne and Colincamps. On the following morning (the 26th) Logeast Wood and Achiet-le-Petit were to be in German hands, and an aeroplane was to look down on strong parties moving towards Beaumont-Hamel, whose capture illuminated so signally the record of the last days of the Somme Battle in 1916.

Elsewhere on the Third Army front the position on the 25th was satisfactory, but this ever-widening gap between the V. and IV. Corps was fraught with menacing possibilities. To fill it, a further call was made on the jealously guarded reserves. At 10 p.m. General Russell received orders from the Third Army to move with all speed by Hédauville and establish a line between Hamel and Puisieux. At the former place the New Zealand right would overlap the 12th Division of the V. Corps, and at the latter their left secure touch with the 62nd Division of the IV. Corps. The New Zealand Division itself was allotted to the IV. Corps (Lt.-Gen. Sir G. M. Harper, K.C.B., D.S.O.). At the same time the 4th Australian Brigade, so long associated with the New Zealanders on Gallipoli, was detached from its Division, now also in the rear of the battle, and allotted to the 62nd Division with orders to secure Hébuterne and extend the IV. Corps flank southwards.

At this hour (10 p.m., 25th March) the bulk of the New Zealand troops was still west of Amiens. The tremendous strain on transport had made it impossible to provide an adequate number of lorries. Packs blankets and greatcoats had to be left under guard at the detraining stations. Ammunition up to 220 rounds a man had been issued, and to the machine and Lewis gun teams as much as they could carry. In light fighting order the leading troops had set out briskly towards the front, along dusty roads congested with military transport and with labour units, stragglers, and refugees streaming westwards. As yet only the 3 Infantry Brigade Headquarters, with portions of 1st Auckland and of 1st and 2nd Canterbury and the Machine Gun Battalion Headquarters, had reached their destination in the deserted Ribemont area. To such troops as had arrived and were now sleeping in their equipment, orders were hurriedly issued to march immedi-

---

[1] p. 61. Serre was attacked again by us on 11th November 1916 without success. It was evacuated by the enemy on 24th January 1917 in the preliminary stages of his withdrawal.

ately and independently to Hédauville. Arrangements were
made with the lorry-regulating station at Pont Noyelles to
divert thither the other units as they came forward. Brigadiers and officers commanding battalions were summoned
forthwith to Hédauville. In the early morning of the 26th
some of the outlying New Zealand units on the Ancre just
escaped the enemy advance. To Ville-sous-Corbie, for example,
a certain amount of equipment had been brought forward in
lorries on the previous day. It was too bulky to be packed
on the first line transport. A small portion was loaded on a
lorry happening to pass through the village just prior to its
capture. The rest fell into German hands.

Divisional Headquarters reached Hédauville at 1.30 a.m.
(Tuesday, 26th March). Part of the Machine Gun Battalion
had already arrived. In the early hours of the morning it
was followed by the 1st Rifles, who had marched the 10-mile
journey from Pont Noyelles in the dark. The infantry
brigadiers on horseback or by motor arrived shortly afterwards, and at a conference held before dawn the general
plan of action was settled. The unfortunate delay in concentration, due to the absence of lorries, would make it
necessary to send battalions forward, as soon as they arrived,
in improvised brigades, irrespective of the brigades to which
they properly belonged. The 1st Rifles were to move at
6 a.m., and passing Mailly-Maillet[1] would occupy an outpost
position on the Engelbelmer-Auchonvillers ridge in order to
get in touch with the V. Corps left and secure the right flank
of the main New Zealand advance towards Hamel and Serre.
The main operation would be carried out by the 1st and 2nd
Brigade battalions, whose arrival might be looked for in the
early forenoon. No cavalry patrols were available. Information was most fragmentary, but it was hoped that General
Young's "2nd Brigade" on the right would occupy Hamel,
gaining touch there with the left of the V. Corps, and thence
take up a line just to the west of the deep ravines about
Beaumont-Hamel. On the left, General Melvill's "1st
Brigade" would primarily secure a line about the road which
runs northwards from Beaumont-Hamel to Hébuterne, and
then swing its left further east to Serre, extending it to
secure touch with the IV. Corps right, still believed to be in
Puisieux. In conjunction with this second movement the
"2nd Brigade," pivoting on Hamel, would similarly swing its
left forward east of Beaumont-Hamel. In accordance with

---

[1] Corps Headquarters had moved the previous day from this village to Marieux.

instructions issued by Corps at 2 a.m., the troops were ordered to push the enemy back over this ground should he be encountered. If he were met in greatly superior numbers, his advance was to be checked, and the brigades were to manoeuvre so as to gain and hold as a second line the important high ground from Colincamps to Hébuterne. For this purpose the "3rd Brigade" would on their arrival extend northwards the outpost position held by their 1st Battalion.

Little time was given the 1st Rifles for elaborate preparations, and it was already 6.30 a.m. before their leading companies, with 2 sections of machine guns, moved from Hédauville up the open slopes north-east towards Mailly-Maillet. The cultivated fields, the villages and the woods made Picardy appear "a very pleasant country" after the wastes of Ypres. The Rifles were protected by a company as an advanced guard. This screen, moving to the east of Mailly-Maillet at 10 a.m., soon came in contact with the enemy. With Lewis gun and rifle fire its centre platoon drove back German patrols seen 500 yards east of Auchonvillers Wood. The left platoon pushed along the northern slopes from Auchonvillers up the road which leads to Hébuterne. About 1000 yards north of Auchonvillers this road meets the road from Serre to Mailly-Maillet, and at the crossroads stood a refinery for the manufacture of sugar from the beet grown in the neighbourhood. The left platoon found the enemy already in considerable force on the sunken Hébuterne road, south of the refinery, and moving forward with entire assurance. Lining the open ditches they hotly engaged him and arrested his progress.

Fresh enemy forces, about 2 companies strong, now appeared north of the refinery on the road to Hébuterne, and close on 11 a.m. other considerable bodies were seen marching straight westwards along the road from Serre. Two advanced sections, under Rflmn. A. L. Sturmey and C. A. Tucker, held their ground against an overwhelmingly superior force, till the latter reached within 20 yards, then falling back skilfully on to the main platoon position. Sturmey alone killed 14 Germans, including 2 officers, and Tucker's Lewis gun section accounted for at least 90. But against the German numbers the thin screen could hardly have held its ground. At an opportune moment, however, the left platoon of the 2 companies detailed to occupy the outpost position came along the crest. The platoon commander, 2nd Lt. H. A. Mackenzie, had not pre-

viously been under fire, but he handled his men with great
skill and dash, and the situation was temporarily saved.

By 11 a.m. the 2 companies of the 1st Rifles occupied
the Auchonvillers ridge, the remaining company being held in
reserve while the position was consolidated. Patrols, immediately pushed out, found the villages of Mertinsart and
Mesnil to the south-east in possession of troops of the 12th
Division. Elements of the 2nd Division were located astride
the road from Hamel to Auchonvillers. The position of these
troops was reported correctly by the 2nd Division to the
V. Corps, but they were in no condition now to withstand
further pressure.

During all this time the 2 Rifle platoons on our extreme
left, fighting with great determination, held up every effort
of the superior enemy to advance from the sunken road.
Their flank, however, was absolutely in the air, and the
pressure from enemy moving southwards from the unoccupied
country about Hébuterne became severe. Heavy machine
gun and rifle fire from the commanding ground to the north
was increasingly and ominously enfilade. Half the reserve
company were therefore sent forward shortly after 1 p.m.,
and with the remnants of some British troops prolonged and
swung back the left flank to a knoll of apple trees south-west
of the refinery. Somewhat later the remainder of the advancd
guard company, whose work was now accomplished, together
with the other half of the reserve company, were collected
and also sent to this left flank. By this time, however, the
"2nd Brigade" had come up and were moving through, and
the Rifles' task was fulfilled. It only remained for them to
swing up, after the "1st Brigade's" advance, the left flank
from Apple Tree Knoll.

Meanwhile, from 6 a.m., further troops had begun to
arrive at Hédauville. These were 1st and 2nd Auckland, 1st and
2nd Canterbury,[1] and 3 companies of the 2nd Rifles[2], together
with 2 machine gun companies, all of whom had overcome
the difficulties of a march in the dark over unknown roads,
where traffic-control personnel was non-existent. During the
forenoon 3 companies of the 8th Battalion Tank Corps,
amounting to 150 men with 60 Lewis guns, were attached
to the Division. 1 company was allotted to the "2nd
Brigade," and 2 to the "1st Brigade" on the exposed flank.
Arrangements were made with the V. Corps for the 2nd

1 Lt.-Col. Mead, vice Lt.-Col. H. Stewart, in command of Brigade Transport and "B Teams."
2 Major J. Pow, D.S.O., vice Lt.-Col. A. E. Stewart, acting as Brigadier.

Divisional Artillery, or such of it as remained, to cover the New Zealand front pending the arrival of the New Zealand batteries.

With the shortest possible pause for the receipt of orders, for a meal, for the issue of shovels and picks, the insertion of detonators in grenades, and other hurried preparations, General Young's "brigade," consisting of the 1st and 2nd Canterbury Battalions and a machine gun company, moved out of Hédauville at noon to occupy the line of the ridge overlooking the Ancre from Hamel northwards. Behind a protective screen the platoons moved at 100 yards' distance, 2nd Canterbury leading the way. On arrival at Mailly-Maillet, in consequence of the enemy forces in the sunken road, a 2nd Canterbury company was detached to occupy a position near the Apple Trees and so protect the left flank during subsequent advance.

Deploying from the village shortly after 2 p.m., 1st Canterbury on the right and 2nd Canterbury on the left passed through the 1st Rifles' outpost line and moved forward to their objective. 1st Canterbury met some slight shell-fire, but with only a few casualties reached a line west of Hamel. The village itself they found held by elements of the 63rd and 12th Divisions, with whom they established touch. From their new positions they looked down on the Ancre valley about Thiepval. It was full of enemy movement. Directly opposite their front, however, it was manifest that the Germans had not yet crossed the river.

Further north, vigorously exploiting the gap between the V. and IV. Corps, the 4th German Division had by now passed Beaumont-Hamel, and occupied in strength a rise beyond it on the north-west, crowned by a single tree and called One Tree Hill. Already on the western outskirts of Auchonvillers 2nd Canterbury had met machine gun and artillery fire, which, though slight, had compelled deployment into section formations. East of the village artillery fire was distinctly more heavy, and from One Tree Hill on their left and from the ridges in front toward Beaumont-Hamel machine gun fire became troublesome. Our own machine guns, however, taken off the limbers behind Mailly-Maillet, had been rushed up to the high ground and were providing strong covering fire. The enemy immediately confronting us was not present in force, and our objective near the Beaumont-Hamel ravines was reached without heavy opposition. In the evening a German machine gun post was rushed by 2nd Lieut. J.

Sinclair with his company sergeant-major, D. M. G. Mackay, and L.-Cpl. M. I. Anderson. Shooting and bombing the team they captured 2 prisoners and brought back the gun. It was disconcerting to find that the enemy had already passed the line which the brigade was to occupy when conforming with the second movement of the "1st Brigade" further north towards Serre. Till the "1st Brigade" came up, any movement on the left flank would be at best premature. For the moment the Canterbury Battalions turned their attention to consolidating the positions won.

In and about the left of our line were handfuls of very weary troops of all brigades of the 2nd Division, about 80 men in all. These were withdrawn in the evening. General Young's "brigade" had been just in time to forestall the enemy in occupation of what had been the 1916 British front line before the Battle of the Somme. Crossing about Beaumont-Hamel the enemy had penetrated part of the old trench systems, but was not yet in sufficient strength to prevent the South Islanders from taking up their position. Numerous hostile parties were visible, but there was no indication of an impending organised attack. Only 1 small German patrol, about 12 in number, blundered on our outposts southwest of Beaumont-Hamel. In addition to the casualties inflicted on the enemy, 1 man and a light machine gun were captured. The Germans moved about with surprising audacity, and our machine guns and snipers secured many targets. Further in rear and out of range, considerable formed bodies were marching westwards, whom our artillery was not yet in position to engage. The 1916 trenches were still in fairly good order, with valuable belts in places of our old wire.

During the forenoon the IV. Corps Divisions north of the gap had fallen back behind Puisieux and now held a line in the old 1916 German trenches from Star Wood through Box and Fork Woods to the east of Bucquoy. Nearer at hand the position had improved. A battery of the 2nd Divisional Artillery galloping into action during the morning had, over open sights, silenced the German machine guns in Colincamps Cemetery, and the village had been later cleared by 14 of our new light fast tanks, the so-called whippets, which now for the first time proved their value. This was not yet known, however, at Mailly-Maillet. What was known was that the Australian Brigade was not expected to reach Hébuterne till the late afternoon, and that on all the featureless terrain of gentle ridge and valley, where little cover other than the old trench systems was available against the German machine guns, the enemy were already in strength well to the west of Serre. They held the road which ran along the high ground from Auchonvillers past the refinery towards Hébuterne, and were in force on the crest about the ruins of the large tree-encircled La Signy Farm, which lay just east of the road, midway between the 2 villages. Here the Germans had penetrated about a mile into our old 1916 trenches. It was already more than doubtful if General Melvill's "brigade" could reach Serre, and the position on the left flank towards Colincamps and Hébuterne was thoroughly unsatisfactory.

General Melvill's force, composed of the 1st and 2nd Auckland Battalions, the 2nd Rifles, and a machine gun company, had followed at a short interval the "2nd Brigade" to Mailly-Maillet. On General Melvill's arrival the situation was put before him, and he saw at once that a modification of his plan was necessary. It was still hoped, indeed, that despite meagre artillery support it might be possible to reach Serre and establish touch with the Divisions on the north at Puisieux, but arrangements were now made to swing our left flank considerably back so as to drive in the enemy from the vicinity of Colincamps. As a result of necessary deliberations, the "1st Brigade" attack astride the Serre Road did not develop till 5.30 p.m. 1st Auckland then advanced on the south of the Serre Road, the 2nd Rifles on the north, and 2nd Auckland followed in support. As 1st Auckland reached the northern end of the 1st Rifles' outpost line at the orchard on the Auchonvillers ridge, an enemy aeroplane flew low over their heads, and a certain amount of artillery fire followed. More serious were the enemy machine guns, which at once opened. Throwing off their fatigue in presence of the enemy, the 2 attacking 1st Auckland companies thrust forward vigorously along their 1500 yards' front. At the price of fairly heavy casualties they drove the Germans back out of the sunken road, capturing 3 machine guns. They then pushed some 300 yards beyond, where their right lay slightly behind the left flank of 2nd Canterbury. Serre was obviously out of the question. On the left also, where violent resistance was encountered, the 1st Auckland line lay for the time behind that of the 2nd Rifles. A stream of machine gun fire continued throughout the evening from the Serre Road, but after dark the left company advanced east along the road a further

300 yards. There they stormed a Strong Point, capturing 8 machine guns and 40 prisoners, and gaining touch with the 2nd Rifles. Particularly gallant work was done by Capt. H. R. Vercoe.

North of the Serre Road the 2nd Rifles advanced abreast with 1st Auckland, with the object of reaching the Serheb Road, which runs north-west from Serre. Two companies were in the front line, while another company acted as a left flank guard towards the north. The explosions of a blazing ammunition dump between the refinery and the Hébuterne Road forced a detour, but the billowing smoke screened our advance from a machine gun at the cross-roads and from 2 others in a trench parallel to the Serre Road and adjoining it on the north.

On the riflemen emerging from the smoke the machine guns opened fire. The leading platoon of the right company (Capt. W. J. Organ), on reaching the Hébuterne Road, paused a minute to assemble under cover of the road bank, and then, led by L.-Cpl. R. Ellmers and Rflmn. E. H. Dodd, dashed into the trench. 2 guns and 2 wounded prisoners were captured. The remaining 40 Germans retreated to trenches south of the Serre Road, whence in turn they were evicted by our snipers, leaving 5 unwounded prisoners in our hands. We captured also the Orderly Room records of one battalion, with a narrative of its actions since 21st March, and casualty rolls which showed that up to the 26th the unit had suffered 50% casualties. Pushing forward after the final advance of 1st Auckland, 2nd Lt. F. W. Parry actually reached a trench 1000 yards east of the refinery at the southern extremity of an important and commanding hedgerow which ran south from La Signy Farm and of which more will be said hereafter. Thence the company's line swung round north-westwards to the point (Euston Junction) where the road from Colincamps joined the Hébuterne Road. Further advance was barred, not so much by heavy cross machine gun fire from One Tree Hill southwards and from La Signy Farm northwards, as by the fact that the company was already far in advance of its flanks. Two attempts by the enemy to rush our trenches were checked. In the evening, after dispositions were made for the night, a German motor car crept up quietly and without lights on the Serre Road and stopped somewhat short of our furthest post. A lieutenant jumped out and walked up the road alone. Sergt. G. F. Webster and his 3 men in the post all fired at him, and killed him.

A Stray Prisoner in Courcelles

Prisoners, 30th March 1918

PART OF THE MATERIAL CAPTURED 30TH MARCH 1918

CAPTURED MACHINE GUN IN ACTION NEAR LA SIGNY FARM

Meanwhile the left company, somewhat less enterprisingly handled, had cleared the Hébuterne Road up to Euston Junction. From that point the flank guard took up a position along the Colincamps Road. In all, the 2nd Rifles captured 37 prisoners and 4 machine guns. They had lost 9 men killed and 35 wounded, all except 2 of the casualties being caused by machine gun fire. Invaluable assistance was given on this left flank by the light tanks which had cleared Colincamps during the morning.

By nightfall, as a result of these operations, in which the Division had sustained altogether 150 casualties, mostly walking cases, our foremost troops occupied a strong and practically continuous line from just west of Hamel to north of the Serre Road. The southern portion of the gap between the V. and IV. Corps was definitely closed. On the "2nd Brigade" front observation was particularly good. North of the Serre Road the enemy held the high ground and overlooked us, but the time was not yet ripe for further action, and General Russell issued orders forbidding an attack till the general situation cleared itself. Consolidation was pushed on unmolested, and touch maintained by patrols with the enemy in front.

If, however, the establishment of the "2nd" and "1st Brigade" line in the evening of the 26th gave no cause at the moment for apprehension about the Division's right flank, the position was very different with regard to the gap about Hébuterne. Late in the afternoon the 4th Australian Brigade attached to the 62nd Division had passed through the village and formed a line round its eastern edge. But between them and the New Zealand left above Euston Junction, the northern portion of the gap, amounting to about a mile and a half, was still unfilled, and the company swung back towards Colincamps barely saved the 2nd Rifles from envelopment. It was vital to fill this gap with the least possible delay. During the afternoon further troops of the Division had marched into Hédauville. These comprised the Pioneer Battalion, 2 companies of Engineers, a company of the Machine Gun Battalion, a light trench mortar battery, and further infantry battalions. The 3rd Rifles (less 1 company) arrived at 3 p.m. from Pont Noyelles, and 2nd Wellington at 5 p.m. from Amiens. 2nd Otago followed at 7.30 p.m., and 1st Wellington[1] and 1st Otago[2] at 9 p.m. The Divisional

---

1 Major W. F. Narbey, vice Lt.-Col. Cook, sick.
2 Major Hargest, vice Lt.-Col. Charters, wounded (gas) in February.

Artillery, the remaining 3rd Rifles company, the 4th Rifles, a company of the Machine Gun Battalion, a company of the Engineers, and 2 light trench mortar batteries were still on the march.

The whole concentration of the isolated units from their different detraining stations had been characterised no less by masterly Staff work on the part of the Division than by the splendid response made by the men. As a rule the marching of the Division was not above criticism. The troops had been 2 nights without sleep and were tired and footsore, but at this critical juncture there was not a man but put forth his sternest effort on the forced march. Most battalions covered over 20 miles, and among them they had not lost half a dozen men. Thus, to take a single instance, 1st Otago, after travelling all night and day, detrained on the evening of the 25th at Hangest, 11 miles down the Somme valley from Amiens. Marching through Piequigny, it rested for the night in derelict lorries on the roadside. At 6.30 a.m. on the 26th it was again on the move and tramped steadily a further 16 miles through Amiens, Pont Noyelles, Franvillers to Hédauville. Not a man fell out the whole way. The 2nd Field Company of the Engineers, marching with full packs 23 miles between 11 a.m. and 10 p.m., similarly did not lose a single man.

As soon as the gap between the New Zealand line and the Australians was reported to the Division, the more rested troops, comprising the 3 companies of the 3rd Rifles, 2nd Wellington and 2nd Otago, with a machine gun company, were formed into a composite brigade under Lt.-Col. A. E. Stewart, with orders to extend the line northwards up the Hébuterne Road. The Divisional reserves were now reduced to 1st Wellington and 1st Otago till the 4th Rifles arrived about midnight.

At 1 a.m. on the 27th this force marched through Mailly-Maillet and reached Colincamps at 4 a.m. Here, in much the same way as the 1st Rifles had covered the Canterburys at Auchonvillers, 2nd Otago was thrown out in a screen east of the village and behind the left of the 2nd Rifles on the road to Euston Junction to protect the advance of 2nd Wellington and the 3rd Rifles. While Otago moved into position, these rested in the shelter of the buildings for some 10 minutes, and then with the first glimmer of dawn moved forward. They were covered by advanced and flank guards. 2nd Wellington was on the right and the 3rd Rifles on the left towards Hébuterne.

There was no shelling, but machine gun fire was at once encountered, and the troops deployed into skirmishing order. On the north the 3rd Rifles advancing rapidly pushed back the German advanced posts, and by 6.30 a.m. gained touch with the Australians south of Hébuterne. The splendid dash with which the Rifles moved had its due reward. The enemy, in considerably superior numbers, were apparently taken by surprise. They at once decamped, leaving behind them much equipment and entrenching material. Only at 1 point did they attempt resistance. They called on a section of riflemen commanded by L.-Cpl. J. N. O'Donnell to surrender. O'Donnell's reply was an immediate charge with the bayonet, which drove the enemy back with heavy losses. From the position won, L.-Cpl. W. G. Bowers made a notable single-handed effort. He pushed forward alone down a sap to locate 2 enemy believed to be wounded. Instead of these he encountered 12 Germans, armed and unhurt. He at once attacked them. He was wounded but succeeded in capturing 2 prisoners and dispersing the remainder. 2nd Wellington ran right in the teeth of the machine guns firing from near La Signy Farm, and after securing 42 prisoners and a machine gun, in whose capture Capt. Melles, 2nd Lt. J. T. Thomas, and 3 platoons of the Wellington West Coast company did particularly fine work, they were obliged to dig in 400 yards short of the Hébuterne Road, which formed their objective. Touch was, however, maintained with the 3rd Rifles on the left and secured with the 2nd Rifles on the right at Euston. By 9 a.m. there was no gap left for German infiltration, and any further hostile advance would be purchased at a heavy price.

Meanwhile on the "2nd" and "1st Brigade" fronts the night had passed quietly except for an assault on the British troops south of Hamel, which was repulsed by a counter-attack. Beyond them again, owing to an unfortunate misunderstanding, the VII. Corps had abandoned the Bray Line. The German vanguards were pressing towards Albert and reaching positions from which they were to turn the left flank of the Fifth Army on the following day. But no effort had been made against the New Zealand front. Advantage was taken of the enemy's inactivity to reorganise the brigades and restore units to their proper formations. 2nd Auckland relieved the 2nd Rifles north of the Serre Road. During or

shortly after the relief Auckland appears to have pulled back
from the very marked salient about the hedgerow where the
2nd Rifles had established their outposts on the previous
evening. The complacent announcement in German ''intelligence,'' captured later on 30th March, of the peaceful recovery of this important high ground completely mystified the
Divisional Staff, who did not at the time know that it had
ever been in our possession. It was regained only at the cost
of hard fighting.[1] On relief, the 2nd Rifles was brought into
General Melvill's reserve at Mailly-Maillet as a preliminary
step to its replacement by 1st Wellington, when it was
to move first as Divisional reserve to Courcelles and later
as Rifle Brigade reserve behind its own brigade front at
Colincamps. In the early morning (27th March) 1st Otago
relieved the 1st Rifles on their 3000 yards' support line
behind the Canterburys. It was proposed that on relief
the 1st Rifles should go to Colincamps as Divisional reserve,
but in view of the enemy pressure about Hamel they were
temporarily detained as brigade reserve by General Young
at Engelbelmer.

With dawn on the 27th the enemy endeavoured to resume
his advance and extend the Serre gap southwards. After the
rude checks of the previous evening, infiltration methods were
abandoned in favour of violent assaults. His artillery was
moved up and was to be consistently active throughout the
day on Mailly-Maillet Courcelles Hédauville and Colincamps.
For all their recent marching and fighting the Germans were
not yet exhausted. Attack followed attack, for beaten back
at one point the enemy's infantry was remorselessly launched
at another. At 6 a.m., while the 3rd Rifles were driving the
Germans before them south of Hébuterne, strong enemy forces
mustering about the Serre Road were scattered by our artillery fire. It was not till noon that the enemy's first infantry
effort developed. It was accompanied by heavy artillery
and machine gun fire and directed at the 2nd Auckland
positions north of the Serre Road. In the bombardment,
2 Auckland officers and 3 men were killed. The attack
was beaten off by the 15th (North Auckland) Company,
which, despite severe casualties, remained unshaken by
2 further attempts later in the afternoon. 1st Auckland
put a company as reserve at its sister battalion's service, but
this assistance was not required. The only gain made by the
Germans was a short stretch of communication trench, which

1 pp. 361 sqq.

was recaptured after dark. In the course of these attacks about the Serre Road, concentrations of the enemy massing in the old British trenches were severely punished by the 2nd Divisional Artillery.

A somewhat heavier blow was delivered shortly afterwards on the 1st and 2nd Canterbury lines in the south. About 9 a.m. the enemy had begun to shell our front lines, at first lightly, but by noon his bombardment was of considerable weight and extended as far back as Mailly-Maillet. Half an hour afterwards his infantry, which had assembled in the quarries and deep ravines south of Beaumont-Hamel, advanced in small groups over the open and up old communication trenches towards the Canterbury positions. The attack penetrated within bombing distance but was successfully repulsed by rifle and machine gun fire, and the enemy retired to his trenches, leaving 30 dead and 2 light machine guns in No Man's Land. In the afternoon General Young extended his right to assist the English brigade on that flank in restoring a somewhat obscure situation.

The next attack was launched on the other flank at Hébuterne in the afternoon. Very large bodies of hostile infantry had been observed in the morning in close formation about a grove of poplars a mile down the Puisieux Road.[1] They had been thrown into utter disorganisation by our machine gunners. Now from the same direction a battalion endeavoured to envelop Hébuterne. The greater weight of the blow fell on the Australians, but New Zealand rifles and Lewis guns co-operated in its repulse. Some time afterwards odd men could be seen crawling back on the ridge in a manner strikingly reminiscent of the Turks' retreat over Chunuk Bair,[2] and, like the Turks, they were harassed by machine gun fire. A later attempt in the afternoon was similarly beaten back, though not without difficulty. During these afternoon attacks some forward guns of the Wellington Machine Gun Company had a quarter of an hour's crowded experiences. One gun stopped dead, at a few yards' range, an ugly attempt to rush it. A second was forced to withdraw 50 yards to avoid being enveloped. A third was attacked by a strong and determined party. Ten of these were killed, but the team itself had casualties, and the firer was wounded. The gun was captured by the enemy. Then a party of 2nd Wellington came to the assistance of the survivors, and together they counter-attacked, recaptured

1 See Map No. 12.   2 10th August 1915.

the lost gun, took in addition a light machine gun from the Germans and killed or put to flight their assailants.

Foiled at each flank as on the Serre Road, the enemy struck at 7 p.m. at the 2nd Wellington position, 1500 yards long, midway between the refinery and Hébuterne. Here he scored his only success. The reserve company counter-attacked, killing about 80 and capturing 5 machine guns, but could not restore the situation over the whole battalion front. The left company had been forced back 500 yards from the Hébuterne Road. During their withdrawal, one machine gun team on the northern flank was left much exposed. Prudence dictated their falling back some little distance to conform, but prudence in war can be a positive defect. A Rifles' n.c.o., Cpl. J. Dean, came over from the 3rd Battalion line and promised that "if the team would stick it out, he with his Lewis gun team and platoon would do so also." It was agreed to "stick it out." When later in the evening heavy rifle fire ensued from 150 yards in front, this team opened fire to let the enemy know the way was barred. In their uncertainty as to the general position in front, however, they fired high, and when subsequently a party of 40 men passed along 100 yards before the gun position, they could not in the uncertain moonlight distinguish whether they were friend or foe. The party moved away to the left and were presently lost to view. Dean not merely kept his word nobly, but later in the night himself led a section forward and rushed an enemy machine gun which was enfilading his flank, killing the crew and putting the gun out of action. In the course of the day 2nd Wellington had lost 4 officers and 70 men casualtied.

Into the gap caused by Wellington's withdrawal the Germans swarmed, occupying securely the line of the road and pushing some posts west of it. The 3rd Rifles, however, swung back and strengthened their right flank with their last company, which now arrived opportunely on the battlefield.

Similar attacks elsewhere on the Corps front were mostly frustrated. At Rossignol Wood, however, which lying between Hébuterne and Bucquoy was later to become so familiar to the New Zealanders, the enemy penetrated into its eastern outskirts, and further north he captured Ablainzeville and Ayette. Beyond the right boundary, Hamel, which had been definitely assigned to the V. Corps, was lost, and the 2nd Brigade reinforced their right flank and extended it southwards to assist the hard-pressed troops in this quarter

In all his attacks the enemy had incurred heavy losses, and additional casualties were inflicted throughout the day on large bodies of his troops in rear. Our machine gunners, indeed, were thoroughly and keenly enjoying themselves. During the afternoon German artillery teams attempting to bring up ammunition to a battery west of Serre were dispersed with casualties. A pair of guns engaged 2 companies of the enemy in column of route at a range of 700 yards, literally mowing them down, so that stretcher-bearers were busy moving in the vicinity for 3 hours afterwards. Another body of the enemy in mass formation, about 700 strong, was engaged at somewhat longer range. With the second burst of fire about 50 were seen to fall. A long burst was therefore fired plumb into the mass; great numbers fell, the remainder breaking and taking cover in shellholes and undulations. In this one instance 300 casualties at a conservative estimate were inflicted, and the ground was observed to be littered with bodies. At another point in the battlefield, 12 enemy machine gun crews attempted to move over the open towards their front trenches. Bursts were fired on each of the teams, some of which were entirely knocked out. The survivors abandoned their guns and ran back. In repeated attempts made to recover the guns many more casualties were inflicted. Enemy prisoners later testified to the powerful effect of our machine guns in checking their attacks. Such admirable targets could not be expected to continue, and every opportunity was sought to make hay while the sun shone.

In the forenoon of the 27th the anxiously awaited New Zealand batteries, which had detrained west of Amiens on the previous day, began to arrive, and by noon four 18-pounder batteries and a 4.5-in. howitzer battery had concentrated at Hédauville. Their officers rode off at once to reconnoitre positions about Mailly-Maillet, and the guns went into action without delay. Practically all batteries were in position by nightfall. The 2nd Divisional Artillery was then withdrawn.

The considerable movement opposite the New Zealand front, testified to alike by ground and air observation, and the use of smoke screens, covering the deployment of machine gun companies, made it appear very probable that the enemy would renew his attacks in the morning of the 28th. The utmost advantage was therefore taken of the lull that followed the enemy check. A reserve line of trenches was decided on by Corps, and on the Divisional sector every man available, Engineers, Pioneers, and all 3 light trench mortar batteries, for whom Stokes ammunition became available only on the 28th, were employed on its construction. This so-called Purple Line ran in rear of Mailly-Maillet Colincamps and Hébuterne. Its northern portion was the more important, and on it work was primarily concentrated. The line was designed in the first instance to hold 2 infantry battalions and a machine gun company. Orders were given that it should be completed by 5 a.m. on the 28th. 2nd Otago was withdrawn from its former outpost line in front of Colincamps into Divisional reserve to garrison this portion, assist in its construction, and secure touch with the second Australian position behind Hébuterne. Here the battalion stayed till the 29th, when it exchanged places with the 1st Rifles at Engelbelmer, thus completing the reorganisation of the brigades. The Engineers were already beginning their resourceful explorations of the great catacombs under Mailly-Maillet, which had formed a refuge for the inhabitants in 1870 and now promised to afford shell-proof cover for reserve battalions. In the evening (27th March) Divisional Headquarters moved from Hédauville to a more central position at Bus-les-Artois.

During the night (27th/28th March) the 1st and 2nd Brigades improved their positions. The batteries fired bursts on likely concentration areas about Serre. The expected general attack did not materialise. As soon as dawn broke our artillery registered all along the front, and during the day did some splendid shooting, which no one enjoyed more than the infantry in the line. The vigour and efficacy of the fire was proved by the markedly more cautious attitude of the enemy across the Ancre. For the most part only small groups were visible except on 1 occasion when 2 brigades moved to the Ancre from the neighbourhood of Serre. The New Zealand batteries swept the area for over an hour, and the German columns were not seen again. Though the enemy artillery was decidedly heavier, the whole situation on the Corps front was more stable, and General Harper took the opportunity of thanking his troops in the following message:

"The Corps Commander congratulates the 42nd, 62nd, and New Zealand Divisions and the 4th Australian Brigade on their magnificent behaviour during the last few days' fighting. Numerous heavy attacks by the enemy have been completely repulsed with heavy loss and the capture of prisoners and machine guns. He heartily thanks the

troops for their courage and endurance and is confident
that they will continue to hold the line against all
attacks.''

2nd Wellington had found it impossible to retrieve the
gap on their left. They were relieved during the night by
the 4th Rifles, the last infantry battalion to reach Hédauville.
With the morning (28th March) the New Zealand infantry
prepared to strike back. The first enterprise was undertaken by the newly arrived 4th Rifles with the object of
filling the gap on the Hébuterne Road. They had every
reason for immediate action. Apart from their lack of touch
with the 3rd Rifles, their position was commanded by enemy
observation from his line about the Road, and was swept by
the direct fire of a large number of machine guns already in
position. At 5 a.m. a platoon of the right company advanced
against machine gun fire and reached some old gun-pits
west of the Road. Its commander, 2nd Lt. G. Malcolm,
was killed during the operation after gallant hand-to-hand
fighting against heavy odds. Two hours later a bombing
section of the left company drove the enemy back 50 yards
along a sap which afforded direct approach from the Road to
our line, and killed a number of Germans equal to their own
strength. With these efforts the 4th Battalion advance was
momentarily checked.

The left company of the 3rd[1] Battalion immediately south
of the Australian positions at Hébuterne now took up the
action. Beside the Road, 500 yards south of the nearest
houses of Hébuterne, were large quarries secured by the
Germans on the 26th. Shortly before noon the left company
of the 3rd Rifles, under Capt. H. C. Meikle, attacked these
and captured them with slight loss. The enemy offered no
resistance, but retired hurriedly, leaving a large quantity of
arms and equipment. The position won was of the utmost
value, commanding observation up to 3000 yards to the south-
east. Among the German dead it was interesting to find
individuals not only of the 4th Division, but also of that
20th Division, which the New Zealanders had battered so
cruelly at Gravenstafel.[2] The 20th and 4th Divisions had
alternated with each other as front line and support troops
since the opening of the offensive on 21st March.

After the non-success of the morning attacks, which left the
line still well to the west of the high ground at the Hébuterne

1 Major (now Lt.-Col.) P. H. Bell, vice Lt.-Col. Puttick, wounded on 27th.
2 p. 271.

Road, the Rifle Brigade somewhat hurriedly planned a fresh
attempt on a larger scale for the afternoon. The 4th Battalion were again to make a bid for the Road with the object
of depriving the enemy of its commanding position and of
establishing touch with the 3rd Battalion. The latter would
conform by extending its line southwards. The sky had been
overcast all day, and as the men moved out at 4 p.m. heavy
rain was beginning to fall. The 3rd Rifles reached their
objective after some resistance. The 4th Battalion attack was
launched by 2 companies under the covering fire of the
1st Brigade batteries. It at once encountered intense machine
gun opposition. Of the left company, the 2 northern platoons
reached the Road with 2 officers and 12 other ranks.
They were fiercely resisted by a party of 50 Germans, but
drove them off, capturing 6 machine guns and 2 Lewis guns,
and establishing touch with the 3rd Battalion. The 2
remaining platoons, however, were definitely held up, and
thus the left platoons were exposed on their southern flank
and isolated from the remainder of their unit. They safeguarded themselves for the moment by digging a flank
trench, but sharp fighting was to ensue on the days following
before this gap was filled.

The right company, covered by enfilade fire from the 2nd
Auckland Lewis guns, reached the line of the Road from
Euston Junction for 100 yards northwards, repaying 2nd
Auckland by materially improving the situation on their left.
Further north, also, where the enemy was in considerable
strength, they did not quite reach their objective, but pushed
a post close up to some prominent stacks of timber beside the
Road. Though the aim of the operation was not completely
achieved, the post at the "Woodstacks" would be a thorn in
the flesh of the enemy at La Signy Farm and would facilitate
a further attempt.

No effort was made by the enemy this day against the
well-established line of the 2nd Brigade, but against
2nd Auckland repeated strong bombing attacks were launched
from La Signy Farm and down the Serre Road. Two of these
in particular were pushed with great determination in the
afternoon, after heavy artillery and machine gun fire. They
were all repulsed with slight loss to the garrison and severe
casualties to the attackers. In one of these a New Zealand
machine gun was captured, but the gun team obtaining
bombs pursued the Germans, recovered the gun and killed
most of the raiders. A last attempt was made by the enemy

at 10 p.m., under cover of a particularly heavy machine gun barrage, when some of his troops moved over the open as well as up the saps. They were beaten off and left several dead in our hands. Further north the Germans penetrated deeper into Rossignol Wood. These local attacks and other operations of a larger nature elsewhere, similarly repulsed, were undertaken in conjunction with the grand attack at Arras and on the Scarpe, whereby Ludendorff sought to punch out the narrowing salient into which his advance southward was now confined. His decisive failure on the whole battlefield was a severe blow to German ambitions.

The artillery supporting the Division was now reorganised, and General Napier Johnston assumed command of the brigades covering the front. In addition to the 1st and 3rd Brigades these consisted of the 25th Divisional Artillery, 1 "Army" brigade, and 3 R.G.A. brigades with a 60-pounder battery. Our harassing fire became continually more active. During the day (28th) there had also been a marked increase in enemy artillery as well as machine gun fire. The 1st Canterbury trenches had been pounded from close range. In the evening an unlucky 5.9-in. shell secured a direct hit on the cellar which was the Rifle Brigade headquarters in Colincamps. The whole place was wrecked, and the occupants completely buried. Major Purdy was killed, and Capt. Dailey, with the signal and intelligence officers, was wounded. General Fulton, who had arrived back on the 27th, succumbed later to the effects of concussion. General Fulton was the third and last of the New Zealand brigadiers to fall in action. A New Zealander by birth, he had held a commission in the Indian Army. Brusque, masterful, punctilious with regard to details, conscientious and capable, with some marked antipathies, among which was included a particularly keen dislike of strong language, he had ever been keenly sensitive to his men's sufferings and casualties. He had been associated for almost his entire service during the war with the Rifle Brigade, first as battalion commander and then as brigadier. Its interests were intensely dear to him, and it was largely due to his unflagging effort that the Rifles early attained an efficiency not surpassed by either of the other brigades. The casualties in the Colincamps headquarters amounted in all to 2 officers killed and 3 wounded and 9 men killed and 11 wounded. Lt.-Col. (now Brig.-General) A. E. Stewart assumed command of the brigade. Major Logan (later succeeded by Major P. W. Skelly, N.Z.S.C.) became Brigade

Major, Lt. (now Capt.) E. Zeisler was appointed Staff Captain. On the following morning Brigade Headquarters moved from their very unhealthy position in Colincamps to the schoolroom at Courcelles.

The situation on the right of the New Zealanders was improved during the night 28th/29th by the 2nd Division's taking over the elements of its own troops and of the 12th Division, and assuming command of the sector from west of Hamel southwards. Capt. C. G. Hayter, too, of the machine gun company attached to the 2nd Brigade, gave the tired 2nd Division machine gunners assistance in digging in their guns and forming dumps of ammunition and rations. Some personnel also was left to strengthen the teams and ensure the guns' being kept in a fighting condition. On our own front, posts had been pushed out wherever possible 100 yards into No Man's Land. Orders were issued, however, by a higher authority that all communication trenches leading out from our line towards the enemy were to be fillled in for at least 50 yards, and the posts therefore were subsequently withdrawn.

In the early morning of the 29th the 4th Rifle companies made a fresh effort to connect their positions and close the gap in our line between La Signy Farm and Hébuterne. Very bitter fighting ensued with superior enemy forces, on whom heavy casualties were inflicted. A bombing section cleared 200 yards of trench towards a communication sap which ran to the Red Hut at the junction of the La Signy Farm track with the Hébuterne Road. No substantial improvement, however, was effected. Further south, another bombing attack delivered by the enemy against 2nd Auckland was again repulsed. The rest of the day passed quietly.

The Corps was now in process of losing its exhausted 19th 25th 41st and 51st Divisions, and the 37th Division was marching up to take their place. Rain, which had fallen almost continuously since the 28th, streamed in a steady downpour during the night 29th/30th. There was no enemy action on the Divisional front, and the 2nd Rifles[1] relieved the 3rd between the Quarries and Hébuterne undisturbed. To the north the German completed his capture of Rossignol Wood. There was little or no shelling, but as one battalion diary puts it tersely, "the weather was very bad and conditions bloody." The trenches rapidly became ditches of that peculiarly clogging mud, made by wet chalky clay,

1   Major Pow, vice Lt.-Col. (now Brig.-Gen.) A. E. Stewart.

which had been not the least marked characteristic of the
Somme Battle in 1916. Draining was vigorously taken in
hand, and timber was salvaged to make trench floors in the
worst places, but there were no regular duckboards. A large
number of cases of trench-feet was avoided by constant
changes of socks, whale oil treatment and other preventive
measures. Greatcoats and packs had been left at the detraining stations, and though some men had secured oilskin jackets
from deserted camps on the way up, the continued exposure
was beginning to tell on others. A passing tribute must be
paid to the courage and resourcefulness of the N.Z. Y.M.C.A.
personnel, who pushed their hospitable quarters well into
shelled areas at Mailly-Maillet and elsewhere.

Observation improved during the morning of the 30th, and
enemy movement across the Ancre north of Thiepval and a
large amount of transport on the Albert-Bapaume Road were
dispersed by our artillery. The 11th Battery fired on 2
British howitzers in use by the enemy, obtaining a direct hit
and exploding ammunition.

In the afternoon 2nd Auckland and the 4th Rifles carried
out a joint operation with a view to improving their overlooked position north of the Serre Road. Opposite them the
enemy occupied a spur which was the highest ground in the
vicinity and commanded a most extensive view eastwards. On
it, prior to the German withdrawal in 1917, had been situated
the British artillery observation posts. Along its crest lay
the hedge, which had been reached at its southern end by
the 2nd Rifles on the 26th. A very prominent feature of the
landscape, this hedge ran for 1000 yards from the Serre
Road in a north-westerly direction on our side of La
Signy Farm to the Hébuterne Road just short of the Red
Hut. Behind it lay a small system of dugouts. From the
trench alongside it snipers and machine guns maintained
an active fire on our lines and inflicted casualties. General
Melvill had personally reconnoitred the country north of
the Serre Road on the 29th and had suggested to Divisional Headquarters the capture of the crest south and west
of the Farm. 1st Wellington, who had relieved 1st Auckland
during the night 28th/29th south of the Serre Road, would
co-operate with 2nd Auckland by advancing in conformity.
The 4th Rifles on the left would continue the line to the
Hébuterne Road, capturing the rest of the Road northwards
and establishing connection with the 2nd Rifles on the
extreme left.

The morning of the 30th, Easter Sunday, was very quiet, and the details of the operation were threshed out at Mailly-Maillet without interference from hostile activity. The attack was launched at 2 p.m. under an artillery barrage provided by 3 brigades of field artillery. A battery of 4.5-in. howitzers bombarded La Signy Farm, and 2 batteries the Strong Point at the Red Hut, lifting after 3 minutes to a line east of the Farm. 2 batteries of 6-in. howitzers barraged a line still further east, and 2 batteries of 60-pounders searched and swept the Serre Road. The barrage directly covering the attack rested for 2 minutes short of the objective and for 2 minutes on the objective, then lifted 200 yards and searched forward for 500 yards, when it gradually died away, our final S.O.S. line being arranged 100 yards beyond our line of consolidation along the hedge.

The German positions were occupied chiefly by the 20th Division, but also by remnants of several other units which had become confused in the course of their advance. All were now tired and short of supplies. For the last few days they had been living mostly on captured British "dry rations," and these had been by this time consumed. As soon as our barrage opened, at least 100 Germans retired from their trenches south of the Serre Road towards Beaumont-Hamel and were vigorously engaged by the rifles and Lewis guns of 1st Otago, who had relieved 2nd Canterbury on the previous evening.[1] This withdrawal was orderly. The Germans moved along a trench towards Beaumont-Hamel in single file. After most of his men had withdrawn, an officer standing on high ground, just out of reach of our infantry weapons, observed our advance through his glasses. Other parties ran in disorder down the Serre Road, and these were raked by the fire of the machine guns attached to the 2nd Brigade. The machine gunners had been cheated during the preceding days of good targets. Now happily unharassed by enemy artillery, they made good use of their opportunities, silencing at the same time German machine guns which opened flanking fire on the 1st Brigade attack.

The 1st Wellington right company stood fast, the centre and left companies advanced their line with complete success over the heavy ground to the required distance of 500 yards, from One Tree Hill on the right to the southernmost point of the hedge just above the Serre Road. One strongly-established Strong Point fell only at the third assault, renewed

1 2nd Otago relieved 1st Canterbury on the night 30th/31st March.

after 2 failures, of a party under Sergt. R. Hatton. Lt. F. E. Ashby's platoon on the left flank were faced by a strongly held position containing some 40 or 50 men and 6 machine guns, but after a storm of bombs Ashby led his men in a final rush which stormed the position and captured the guns. 25 prisoners were taken. Wellington were now nearly 1000 yards east of the refinery, with an uninterrupted view along the valleys south and west of Serre. In all 74 prisoners and 22 machine guns were captured. About 60 German dead were counted on the position. The battalion lost 20 men killed and 2 officers and over 50 men wounded. During consolidation, the enemy attempted to bring a machine gun into action at close range. The movement was noticed by Sergt. M. Macaskill, who immediately rushed the gun, putting it out of action and killing the crew.

In the centre of the attack 2 companies of 2nd Auckland, protected also by heavy machine gun fire, closely followed the barrage towards the hedgerow. The right company attacked in 2 waves at 50 yards' distance, the left partly over the open and partly up a communication trench which formed the dividing line between the companies. The surprise was complete. Many of the enemy were found lying down with their equipment off, and in 7 minutes, except for a post in the centre of the position and a Strong Point on the Serre Road, the whole objective was in Auckland's hands, and the dugout system behind the hedge cleared. Sergt. W. A. Procter rushing a machine gun post killed 3 of the crew and captured the gun. Fighting was not heavy except in the communication trench, where a platoon of Waikato men encountered deadly machine gun fire and lost 18 men killed, most of them being shot through the head. A machine gun on the enemy's side of the hedge was stalked by snipers and put out of action.

The post in the centre was speedily dealt with. But for the moment the redoubt on the Serre Road prevented touch being gained with 1st Wellington, and the attacking troops here ran short of bombs. Thereupon the light trench mortars came to their assistance. Cpl. G. L. Stuart, of the 1st Battery, collected all available ammunition and brought his mortar well forward to obtain direct observation. At 5 p.m. his preparations were complete. A few well-placed shots were fired, and the 40 survivors of the garrison surrendered.

On the left the 4th Rifles had been faced by very hard fighting, and the Aucklanders were unable to report satisfactory connection till the evening. Touch was maintained for the time by a sap on our side of the main trench by the hedgerow, but in the trench itself, north of the Auckland flank, there was still at 11 p.m. a pocket of Germans. The whole Auckland objective, however, was gained. Four platoons of 2nd Wellington[1] were put at Auckland's disposal for carrying purposes and as battalion reserve.

The trench held several good concrete dugouts. Though muddy, it was found to be strongly consolidated with a double row of wire. The field of fire averaged 500 to 1000 yards. While we thus commanded observation over the enemy's country, the cover of the hedge, though necessarily a mark for his artillery, together with the configuration of the ground, would enable our own troops to proceed overland in the daylight to the front line. Though the further sector of the trench which ran from the captured position along the line of trees towards La Signy Farm was full of enemy, Auckland were confident that in this quarter they could hold a German attack. A more dangerous point was on the right where the enemy might assemble in a depression near the Serre Road. Arrangements were accordingly made for this neighbourhood to be dealt with by artillery periodically during the hours of darkness. From 6 p.m. onwards the enemy shelled the area violently. The 1st Brigade troops were by this time tired. Heavy demands had been made during the last few days on their physical endurance and fighting spirit. Nothing, however, could shake their soldierly morale and resolution, well illustrated, for example, by the evening report of the left Auckland company commander: "We are connected with Rifle Brigade, but the Hun still holds about 150 yards in straight line along trees as shown in attached sketch. We have a strong bombing post in trench to prevent them entering further, and as soon as you can send up a sufficient supply of bombs I will organise a bombing attack and clear the remainder of the trench. I have not sufficient bombs to do that yet. I have strengthened both flanks, and I think the position well held. Am sending out patrols every hour and listening-posts in front of trees. We want more S.A.A." After a visit on the following day the Brigade Major reported that "the operation has left our men in excellent spirits with absolute confidence in themselves and their leaders, and eager to go on and push the enemy back again."

1 Now under the command of Major F. K. Turnbull, M.C., pending the resumption of command by Lt.-Col. Cunningham. 6th April The Bn. relieved 2nd Auckland on the night 31st March/1st April.

During the night (30th/31st March) heavy rain fell. The German pocket was to be cleared, but not by Auckland. The patrols, sent out, duly captured an enemy sergeant-major and a private and directed Lewis gun fire on enemy heard cutting wire about the Serre Road as a preliminary to a counter-attack. These were dispersed, and the attack did not develop. On the left an enemy patrol of 6 was fired on by Lewis guns, 5 being killed. German posts in one or two communication saps were withdrawn, and there were no further signs of the enemy at close quarters. The night remained quiet, and there was now little shelling.

In this strikingly successful enterprise 2nd Auckland lost only 12 men killed in addition to the 18 who had given their lives in the capture of the central communication trench. 7 officers and 75 other ranks had been wounded. These last were evacuated during the attack to the regimental aid post at the refinery. The Germans had lost severely. In a single trench enfiladed by one of our machine guns the retreating enemy had been mown down, and not less than 60 dead lay along its muddy bottom. 140 German corpses were counted in the trench under the hedge, and 156 prisoners had been captured. The war material taken included 42 machine guns, a Lewis gun, 2 mortars, 3 bicycles and a signalling lamp and apparatus.

On the left of the attack persistent ill fortune, through no fault of their own, again dogged the 4th Rifles. Their main assault, like that of Auckland, was delivered by 2 companies, each strengthened by a platoon from the 3rd Battalion. The isolated party on the left, who were in touch with the 2nd Battalion, co-operated by bombing their way forward to establish connection. Very strong hostile resistance with bombs and machine gun fire from the crest of La Signy Farm was encountered all along the front. Part of the right company attained their objective. The remainder reached the flank of the ''Woodstacks'' just short of the Hébuterne Road, where the enemy were in great numbers, and after exhausting their bombs held a precarious position in the adjacent shellholes. The left company met very strong resistance. They drove the enemy back some distance and captured over 20 prisoners, but after stiff hand to hand fighting were obliged to dig in. The bombing attacks of the isolated party met also determined opposition, and they were unable to make much headway.

No higher tribute can be paid to the indomitable fighting spirit of the Rifles than to say that despite these checks they grimly set about preparing to renew their thrust.   As soon as darkness fell, the left company was replaced by a fresh company, and the 2nd Battalion, extending their flank, relieved the isolated platoons.   The first position cleared was on the right.   There, anticipating Auckland's night enterprise, a platoon of the 3rd Battalion moved shortly before midnight through Auckland and bombed its way northwards up the trench along the hedge.   Two prisoners were taken. From the new line a communication trench ran back westwards towards the "Woodstacks."   Down it patrols were sent out immediately, and the fruit of the increasing pressure of the day's struggle was at length gathered.   For the enemy's heart had failed him.   Under cover of the darkness he fell back from his position.   Our patrols found his posts about the "Woodstacks" evacuated.   The right company thereupon moved forward and occupied the remainder of the crest to the point where the La Signy Farm track leaves the Hébuterne Road.   When dawn came, 10 enemy machine guns and many dead were found lying in the area won. Before daylight, too, the left company had pushed their way further forward without resistance to the top of the ridge, where a half-hearted effort by German rearguards was summarily overwhelmed.   During these operations the 4th Battalion had lost 3 officers and 50 men killed and 5 officers and 140 men wounded.

Meantime the 2nd Rifles on their extended southern flank had carried out a brilliant minor operation.   Capt. Barrowclough with 2 platoons struck eastwards and southwards to clear up the gap on their right flank and gain the crest. The party proceeded first along one of the many saps leading up the rise.   On reaching a hedge which ran due east from the Road north of La Signy Farm they possibly made some noise.   The Germans fired 2 star shells.   Our party was not, however, detected, and the enemy machine guns did not open.   After a minute's pause, Barrowclough's men crept nearer to take the German position from the flank. On the first shot being fired as a signal, every man doubled forward and opened rapid fire, enfilading the German position.   L/Cpl. Grover with his Lewis gun poured in a hot fire on a German machine gun crew and within a few seconds killed every man.   In utter panic the Germans fled without more ado, and when pressed further offered little resistance.

In this pursuit Rflmn. J. G. Scaife had laid down his rifle to throw bombs when he was suddenly surprised by the appearance of a German at his side. Without a moment's hesitation he went for his enemy with bare fists, but his knock-out blow was anticipated by a comrade who put a bullet through the German's heart. At the cost of only 2 men wounded, 1 of whom later died, Barrowclough's party had completed the recovery of the whole of the important position lost on the 27th and considerably improved our hold on it. They had killed many Germans, captured 22 prisoners with 16 machine guns, and put the rest to flight.

The effect of these different but co-ordinated operations was both local and general. 250 German dead were actually counted on the front attacked, and doubtless others lay beyond. Wounded were seen to go back in streams. Including evacuations through casualty clearing stations, the number of prisoners taken, chiefly from the infamous 77th Inf. Regt.,[1] was 3 officers and close on 300 other ranks. So heavy were the 20th Division's losses that it was withdrawn from the line and eventually disbanded. In addition, 15 mortars and 110 machine guns[2] were captured. Our own tactical position was completely altered by our advance. Instead of being as hitherto broken and overlooked, the line now ran continuously from One Tree Hill along the whole ridge to the Quarries and lying throughout on the crest, afforded excellent observation over the enemy's position while denying him command over our own. "The infantry," notes an artillery brigade diary at this time, "have the enemy well under hand." The Division received among other telegrams of appreciation a highly prized message of congratulation from General Plumer.

Care must be taken not to overestimate the general moral effect of this success. In conjunction, however, with the stiffening resistance all along the front and with the gallant and remunerative enterprises carried out by the Australians at Hébuterne and by the 32nd Division 6 miles north at Ayette a few days later, it was unquestionably opportune and acceptable to the British Staff after days of unrelieved if stubbornly resisted reverses. It helped, too, to demonstrate to the German Army that north of the Somme the British line had become established. Resigned to his defeat,

---

1 p. 271.
2 The average allotment of machine guns in a German battalion was at this time 25.

the enemy made no immediate effort to reoccupy the important positions lost.

Heavy rain and thunderstorms alternated throughout the 31st, and the day was spent in consolidation and in burying the dead. As soon as the weather cleared, the pressure on the enemy was continued. On 1st April a 1st Otago patrol rushed a trench north-west of Beaumont-Hamel, and 1st Wellington captured 5 prisoners and a wounded officer south of the Serre Road. West of La Signy Farm, following on particularly fearless reconnaissance and daylight patrolling by L/Cpl. R. McMurray, the 1st and 2nd Rifles became increasingly aggressive. A German post was rushed, and its occupants killed or captured. A post of our own was established in its place, and another one pushed forward north of the Farm. On the following day (2nd April) a fighting patrol of the 2nd Rifles killed all the occupants of one sap and had a bitter fight, honours remaining equal, with a second post. The next night (3rd/4th April) in the continuous rain the New Zealand posts thrust themselves all round the Farm and 150 yards to the east.

Protected by this outpost line and reassured by the organisation of the Purple system, of the switch line between Colincamps and Mailly-Maillet, and of other rear defences, all now in an advanced state of completion,[1] the Division could at length release the Lewis gun companies of the British Tank Battalion, reorganise its front generally, and withdraw 1 infantry brigade into reserve. Already on the night 2nd/3rd April the Australians, now under the 37th Division which had relieved the 62nd, had extended their flank 500 yards south of the Quarries so as to completely cover Hébuterne and reduce the very long front held by the New Zealanders. The 1st Brigade in the centre was therefore on 4th/5th April withdrawn into reserve, and the Rifle Brigade took over their subsector, holding now a front of 3200 yards. The 3rd Battalion was placed on the right to the south of the Serre Road, the 4th in the centre at La Signy Farm, and the 1st on the left.

Scarcely was the relief complete when the enemy started a heavy bombardment that was to cover his final effort on a large scale on the northern sector of the Somme battle. On the previous day (4th April) he had purchased successes south of the Somme with heavy casualties. Now in a last

1 The medium trench mortar batteries arriving on 1st April at Bus-les-Artois from a course at the Army Mortar School commenced to dig their defensive positions on 3rd April.

attempt to open the road to Amiens he flung 10 Divisions at the British positions between Dernancourt and Bucquoy and supported their assault by a heavy bombardment continued throughout the day over the Army front.   The whole Third Army line, however, was now firm, and the German infantry tired by their exertions.   Nowhere except at Bucquoy, where he captured the eastern and larger half of the village, did he achieve any result even approximately commensurate with his sacrifices.   At Rossignol Wood a dawn attack by the 37th Division, in which New Zealand batteries co-operated, though not achieving its full objectives, resulted in the capture of nearly 200 Germans, and the disorganisation of his assembly.[1]

On the New Zealand front the German bombardment began at 5 a.m. and continued with intense severity for 3 hours without cessation, extending as far back as Bus-les-Artois and Bertrancourt.   Courcelles and Colincamps were shelled by guns of all calibres up to 12-in.   It was perhaps the severest bombardment that the Division as a whole experienced during the war.   Many fresh German batteries had been brought in for the purpose, and still more guns were to be in action by noon.   All communications were cut.   Soon after 8 a.m. a regiment of the 26th German Division attacked the Rifle Brigade with the object of penetrating as far as Colincamps, now over a mile behind our front line.   The first attack was completely repulsed after reaching within 30 yards of our trenches.   At 10 a.m. it was repeated in great force and succeeded in overwhelming the small 4th Rifles' garrison of 14 men in the most advanced sap to the east of La Signy Farm and in recapturing the Farm itself.   Endeavouring to use the Farm as a pivot and under the cover of heavy mortar fire the enemy pushed many parties up the old saps towards our front line, but our forward posts established in advance of it inflicted severe casualties on the attackers and effectually stopped them.   At no other point did the Germans make progress..   The Farm and trenches in the vicinity were kept under constant fire by our artillery, light trench mortars and machine guns.   In this attack the 4th Rifles had 1 officer and 25 men killed and 1 officer and 46 men wounded.

The 1st Rifles who repulsed determined attacks had 79 casualties, 2 officers and 26 men being killed and 1 officer and 50 men being wounded.   When the enemy's preparatory

---

1 Five of our tanks assisting in this attack stuck in the old wide trenches in this area, and were abandoned. They formed targets for shelling throughout the summer.

27

bombardment fell with extreme severity on the front line, Capt. K. R. J. Saxon, M.C., pushed the garrison forward between the main line and the advanced posts, and his skilful dispositions and personal coolness greatly contributed to the enemy's repulse. Of the advanced posts 1 section formed a salient, and was garrisoned by a platoon under 2nd Lt. J. A. McL. Roy. He and his men broke up all attacks over the open. Then when the Germans endeavoured to approach our posts by an old communication trench, Roy placed a Lewis gun to enfilade it, led a bombing party well beyond our wire to meet the enemy, and forced them back. Many of the attackers clinging to the trench were killed, and those who tried to break from it were cut down by the Lewis gun. At another point in the line Rflmn. R. C. Shannon, a member of a Lewis gun team, had his gun put out of action. Although wounded he immediately attached himself to a post guarding a sap up which fully 100 of the enemy were pushing their way with great determination. Shannon jumped out of the trench, ran over the open to the edge of the sap and commenced bombing vigorously at close range. The German officer who was leading was killed with 2 of his men. 5 others were wounded. The remainder scattered, losing heavily under our Lewis gun fire. By noon all was quiet on the Rifle Brigade front. The commander of the centre company of the 1st Battalion who reported:— "We have beaten off two attacks by the Hun and are wanting him to put in a third," was not to have his wish gratified.

After dusk the 3rd Battalion south of the Serre Road actually advanced their line some 150 yards to improve their field of fire and widen their footing on the high ground. Our machine guns had again had splendid targets, and a captured officer gave them the chief credit for the enemy's failure. A German private made prisoner later near La Signy Farm had the following reflections in his diary:—

"Principally our failure was due to machine gun fire from the flanks. The losses are very great. Many comrades find a hero's death, others writhe in their wounds. Many wounded are lying in the open. At night the battalion retires to its starting point. During the day we are withdrawn to battalion headquarters, but here also we are under fairly heavy fire. Thank God we are now relieved."

Reliable estimates put the enemy casualties opposite the

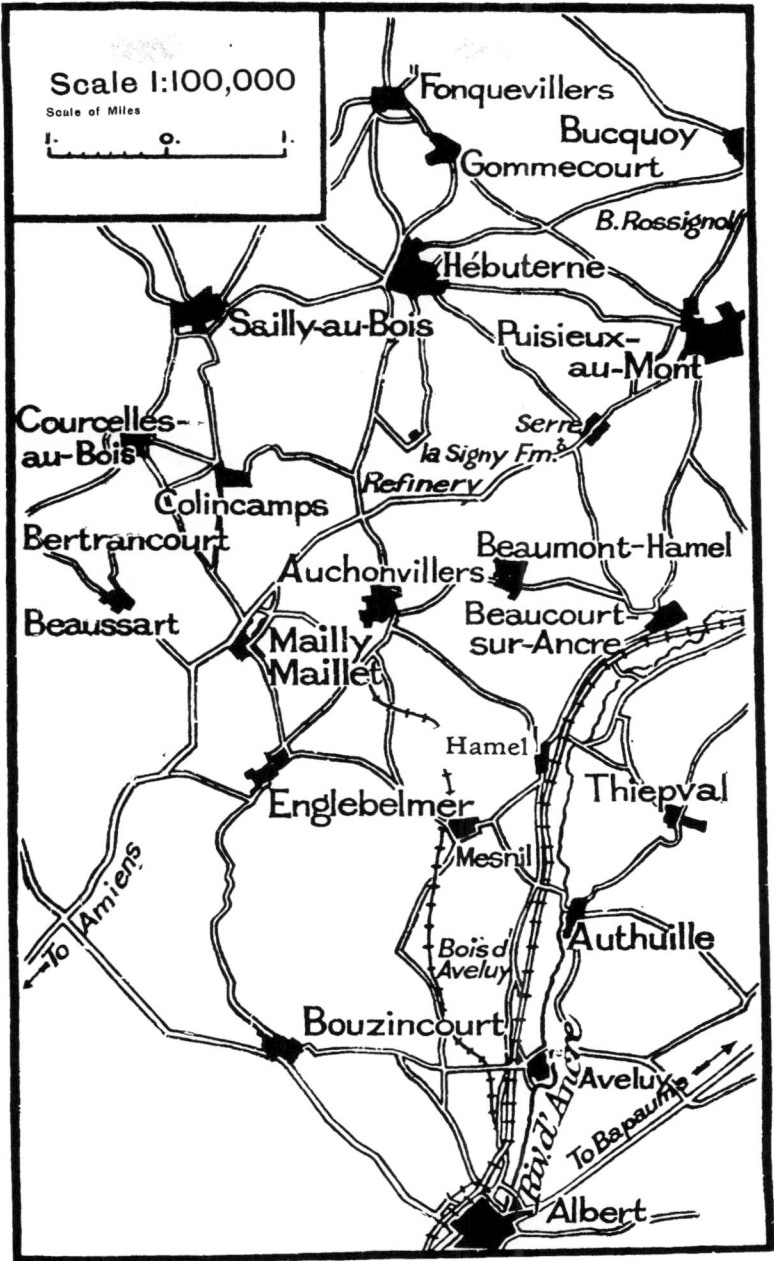

Scale 1:100,000

Scale of Miles

Fonquevillers

Bucquoy

Gommecourt

B. Rossignol

Hébuterne

Sailly-au-Bois

Puisieux-
au-Mont

Courcelles-
au-Bois

Serre

la Signy Fm.

Refinery

Colincamps

Beaumont-Hamel

Bertrancourt

Auchonvillers

Beaussart

Mailly
Maillet

Beaucourt-
sur-Ancre

Hamel

Englebelmer

Thiepval

To Amiens

Mesnil

Bois d'
Aveluy

Authuille

Bouzincourt

R. d'Ancre

Aveluy

To Bapaume

Albert

THE UPPER ANCRE

BRIG.-GEN. A. E. STEWART, C.M.G., D.S.O.

THE MAIN STREET, HÉBUTERNE

Rifles' front as not less than 500. 2 prisoners were captured.

On the 2nd Brigade front another enemy Division was to have advanced simultaneously with the attack on the north, but was disorganised by the weight of our artillery response. It was not till the afternoon that the attack developed, and then it achieved nothing. A mere handful of German infantry worked up a communication trench, just over the boundary, of the British brigade to the south. They were seen and were at once attacked by the right post of 1st Canterbury under L/Cpl. W. White. The whole party was accounted for. 1 was killed and 9 taken prisoners. This was not to be end of the 2nd Brigade successes on 5th April, for their Lewis guns shot down an enemy aeroplane which descended east of Engelbelmer, both the pilot and observer being captured by the troops on the right.

On the 6th the 3rd Rifles again advanced their lines south of the Serre Road, when the enemy put up a S.O.S. and our support and reserve areas were heavily shelled.[1] In the evening 2 companies of enemy infantry were seen moving against the same spot in artillery formation, and another body, estimated at 2 companies, was observed to be massed in their communication trenches. A heavy artillery barrage was put down by us which annihilated the attempted counter-attack. During the day the 25th Divisional Artillery was withdrawn and replaced by 2 (Army) brigades. The batteries continued to bombard the enemy's positions, expending on an average 700 rounds per battery per day, and to harass his working parties now engaged in consolidation. Infantry activity, however, slackened, and conditions were rapidly reverting to trench warfare. During the afternoon rain had begun to fall heavily, and in dismal weather the battle for the moment stood still over the whole Somme front.

After colossal losses the first German offensive of 1918 had ended in a qualified success for the enemy. Immense and important territories had been won, and the strength of the Allied forces had been materially weakened. The German still possessed both initiative and numerical superiority. At the outset 32 British Divisions had been overwhelmed by 64 German, and by the end of March our 46 Divisions of infantry and 3 of cavalry were faced by more than 80. It was

---

1 In this bombardment Major Pow was wounded and the command of the 2nd Battalion assumed by Major (later Lt.-Col.) L. H. Jardine, M.C., previously transferred from the Wellington Regiment to the Rifle Brigade. Pow was promoted Lt.-Col. on Lt.-Col. Roache's evacuation in May to N.Z. through sickness, p. 388.

certain that the enemy had not abandoned his project. Extensive and successive lines of defence were constructed by us, and every possible precaution was taken to resist him. One further effort indeed was to be made on the Somme battlefront, but, temporarily checked, the enemy looked elsewhere. Undertaking enterprises as diversions to preserve the initiative, prevent a counter-stroke on his exposed southern flank, and dissipate Foch's reserves, he was tempted by unexpected successes into heavy commitments and an expenditure of forces on a scale antagonistic to his proper strategy and leading to his undoing. For the time the second Battle of the Somme was at an end, and the pointer of the German offensive had swung northwards to the Lys.

We may now briefly review the action of the Division. After 2 sleepless nights, a fatiguing train journey and forced marches, it had been in consequence of a changed situation diverted from its pre-arranged assembly areas and with marked skill concentrated at Hédauville. Without delay, unit by unit, it had marched into the battle and closed the gap on the Ancre. Not content with that, it had struck back and won an admirably strong position overlooking the German lines. It had constructed formidably-wired reserve trenches through which only a grand assault could hope to break. Artillery, machine guns and mortars had been handled with consummate boldness and efficiency, and despite exhaustion and exposure the men in the trenches were throughout cheerful and confident. It is not too much to say that they eagerly awaited an enemy attack, assured of their power to repel it with their machine and Lewis guns and rifles. When they attacked, here and there they had bitter fighting and were foiled, but generally they smote the enemy irresistibly.

General Birdwood signified his approbation of his old troops' performance in the following message to General Russell:—"My hearty congratulations to you and your Division on the magnificently fine work which you have been doing." With proved success the feeling of superiority grew. Every diary notes the high spirits of the troops and their intense appreciation of the opportunities given of hitting the enemy hard and avenging Bellevue. In barring the German advance the Division had paid an inevitable price, but by no means an unduly heavy one. 30 officers and 500 men had given their lives, 100 officers and 1700 men had been wounded, and some 60 were missing; 127 machine guns, 5 trench mortars and much other booty had been taken,

and 429 prisoners had been captured. The measured terms
of General Harper's congratulatory message convey a
soldier's appreciation of the work of both commanders and
men :—

"The Corps Commander desires to congratulate the
New Zealand Division on their fine record since coming
into the line in the Corps. By a brilliantly-executed
attack they captured a large number of prisoners and
machine guns. They have held their ground successfully
against numerous attacks and have caused the enemy very
severe losses. The organisation of their troops for the
defence of their line has been extremely well carried out."

Not only had the British Divisions, which withstood the
brunt of the storm, fought their unequal contest, as Germany
herself testified, with the utmost gallantry, but the civil
populations also of the Allied countries had shown almost
universally commendable steadiness of nerves. America increased her recruiting and strained every sinew to expedite
the despatch of her troops. France displayed the same quiet
heroism with which she had withstood earlier perils. In
Britain the troubled waves of industrial strife at once sub-
sided, and the workers cheerfully gave up their holidays to
replenish stores and munitions. The limit of military age
was raised to 50. Within a month 350,000 of those home
forces, for whom Haig had hitherto pleaded in vain, were
sent overseas. In New Zealand and the other Dominions,
where owing to distance the full gravity of the situation was
not generally appreciated, there was no lack of spontaneous
declarations of steadfast resolution. On 9th April the
Governor-General of New Zealand sent to Sir Douglas Haig
a message which breathed fervid loyalty and was worded with
simple and fine solemnity :—

"At the present time, when the Armies of the Empire
are engaged in the most deadly struggle in which British
citizens have ever been called upon to take part, the
Government and the people of New Zealand desire to
express most intense admiration for the heroism of our
soldiers and the utmost confidence in the officers and men
of the British forces, as well as the forces of our Allies.
Though the furthest of the Dominions from the scene of
operations and one of the smallest, in this hour of the nation's
trial New Zealand is heart and soul with Britain and the
other dependencies of the Crown, and nothing will be left

undone to support our fighting men and assist in bringing about the decisive victory and permanent peace which we all earnestly desire.''

The Commander-in-Chief replied on the following day:—

"The message from the Government and people of New Zealand has been duly appreciated by all ranks of the British Armies in France. The Empire is proud of the part which New Zealand is playing in this war, and no troops could have fought more gallantly than the New Zealand Division.''

In the new battle of the Lys where Ludendorff, frustrated on the Somme, sought a diversion by attacking the denuded Flanders front and attracting Foch's reserves as a preliminary to a fresh thrust past Amiens to the sea, New Zealand troops were also to be involved. The 2nd (Army) Brigade of the artillery, after enjoying a brief respite from the line in March, had left the XXII. Corps on 6th April, and on the following day had taken over Australian guns in positions on the Ploegsteert front covering the 25th Division. Two English field artillery batteries, the 84th and 85th, completed the group, which was commanded by Lt.-Col. Falla. On 9th April, when the German attack broke through at Fleurbaix, all was quiet on the Ploegsteert sector, but early next morning the Sixth German Army's blow was taken up by the Fourth German Army northwards. A very heavy bombardment with gas and high-explosive shell was followed by an assault in thickish fog and by a rapid advance. At 6 a.m. orders were received for the batteries to be withdrawn to Wulverghem. The 84th Battery was surrounded early in the morning, but the English gunners fired all their ammunition, blew up their guns and, covering the movement with their anti-aircraft Lewis guns, effected a most gallant withdrawal. The 85th Battery on Hill 63 saved all their guns and passed under the command of their own brigade. The New Zealand 18-pounder batteries similarly withdrew safely and were in action again by noon.

Teams coming for the howitzers of the 6th Battery (Major R. Miles, R.N.Z.A.,) about Hyde Park Corner missed their guide. In any case, however, the guns were sunk deep in winter mud and could not have been shifted from the pits. Orders were thereupon issued for the battery to fight to the last round but to refrain from destroying the guns till they found the enemy round them. Rallying the infantry in trenches in the vicinity and shortening ranges, Miles' battery

had by 11 a.m. exhausted all the ammunition of 3 howitzers.
A fourth with its crew had been put out of action by enemy
shelling. The remaining 2 were nearly out of ammunition.
By this time, though our lines still held northwards at St.
Yves, the enemy on the south was through Ploegsteert village
and in the little larch wood, which, well known to all New
Zealanders, covered the flats from Ploegsteert village towards
the Shrine on Hill 63. Machine guns were enfilading the
road from Ploegsteert to Hyde Park Corner, and German
artillery flares were going up from a house in the village.

By superhuman exertions and with the assistance of some
Australian Pioneers 1 gun was brought out on to the Messines
road above Hyde Park Corner and turned against Ploegsteert and the machine guns. With its second round it
demolished the house from which the artillery flares were
rising. Then, silencing the machine gun fire, it enabled the
infantry to recapture part of the village. In a daring reconnaissance Miles himself was wounded by a sniper; 2nd Lt. S.
J. Henrys held on till ammunition was exhausted. He then
guarded the howitzers with his Lewis guns till all hope of a
counter-attack was gone and there was imminent risk of
capture. Only then did the gunners fall back after rendering
their pieces useless. The New Zealander 18-pounder batteries
did not leave their new Wulverghem positions till they fired
every round, and then pulled back according to orders along
the road to Dranoutre.

In the early hours of 14th April Neuve Eglise and its
important ridge fell into German possession. The 2nd Brigade
batteries, including the 6th Howitzer Battery, which had
been re-equipped with new guns, engaged the enemy's
position west of the village. On his advancing in the
evening they continued their withdrawal behind Kemmel
and fought an exemplary rearguard action, the 2nd
and 9th Batteries covering the movement of the 5th, and then
the 9th covering the movement of the 2nd. A forward
section of howitzers remained firing at the slopes south-west
of Neuve Eglise till 3 a.m.

On the 15th, in conformity again with the general movement, the brigade fell back south-west of Scherpenberg.
When on the 19th the French took over the British front in
this neighbourhood the artillery was left for the moment in
the line, where it maintained its harassing fire and shelled
the farms that sheltered German headquarters.

On 23rd April the brigade was advised that they would withdraw to the wagon lines that evening, and that responsibility for answering S.O.S. calls would cease at 7 p.m.   The batteries set about getting rid of their ammunition at likely farms and approaches.   In the early afternoon, however, the enemy started a heavy bombardment, which continued for 2 hours on all battery areas, roads and approaches.   At 7 p.m. it was repeated on an even more violent scale.   S.O.S. signals rose from our front line.   Responsibility for answering these had now ceased, but all batteries that had any ammunition left responded vigorously.   The 5th Battery, which had on several occasions been particularly heavily shelled during the battle, now again came under concentrated fire.   2 officers were killed and 5 men wounded.   Teams were kept in a sunken road waiting for the bombardment to die down.   The 2nd 6th and 9th Batteries "got clear" about 8 p.m., but the 5th not till 11 p.m.

On the following day the brigade moved to the Staple area behind Hazebrouck which the Division had left a month previously.   There they came under the orders of the 1st Australian Division.   Two days later (26th April) they went into the line on the 1st Australian front south-east of Hazebrouck, where Australian infantry and New Zealand gunners, working with great sympathy and mutual understanding, caused heavy casualties to the enemy.   One notable achievement undertaken by the brigade was the salving of part of a large dump of 15,000 rounds of 18-pounder ammunition at Strazeele in the beginning of May.   The dump was only some 500 yards from the German outposts.   This dangerous enterprise was persevered in till stopped on orders from higher authority.   On 16th May the brigade left the Hazebrouck area, and after 4 days' trek joined the New Zealand Division in Picardy.

In the Lys battle other New Zealand troops, too, were to play a humble share and lay down their lives.   On 10th April, while the enemy's northern forces carried Ploegsteert and reached the crest of the Messines Ridge, his Sixth Army had taken Estaires.   Crossing the Lys between that town and Armentières, they had immediately forced the evacuation of Armentières and pressed the British line back north of Steenwerck over country every hectare of which was familiar to the New Zealanders.   On the following day (11th April) the German vanguards carried Neuf Berquin and Merville, and for tactical reasons our troops were withdrawn from Nieppe and Hill 63 to positions east of Neuve Eglise and Wulverghem. On the vital sector south of the Lys the approach of reinforcements checked the hostile advance.

Northwards, however, driving in on 12th April with strong forces between Neuf Berquin and Steenwerck, the enemy pressed very rapidly forward, created a gap on the IX. Corps front south-west of Bailleul and threatened not merely Meteren, but the important railway centre of Hazebrouck. Most fortunately his pressure at Neuve Eglise was this day held, but towards Hazebrouck and Meteren the situation speedily became critical.

No formed reserves were available beyond a brigade of the 33rd Division (Major-General R. J. Pinney). These were strengthened by a body of cyclists and a pioneer battalion. Schools also and reinforcement camps were drained of their personnel in order to fill the gap.   In response to an urgent telephone message from the Second Army, General Godley made every effort to give the IX. Corps ''as much support in as short a time as possible.''

To replace troops sent to the Somme, the XXII. Corps Mounted Regiment and Cyclist Battalion had been formed towards the end of March into a composite battalion and put at the disposal of the 49th Division now holding the whole Corps front.   Under that Division, when the Lys battle opened, they were occupying the Shrewsbury Forest sector before the famous Hill 60 south-east of Ypres.   On 12th April the Otago Mounted Rifles Squadron and one of the cyclist companies had just been relieved from the trenches. These were increased by drafts from the Corps Reinforcement Wing and added to General Pinney's force.   The rest of the composite unit was earmarked as further reserves on their relief.

Of the Entrenching Battalions the 1st and 3rd had already at the end of March been sent to the Somme, but the 2nd was still at Abeele.   It too had been organised for offensive action and provided with 12 Lewis guns from labour units, and now in the afternoon of the 12th, augmented by details of the Corps Reinforcement Wing to a strength of 1100, it was rushed[1] partly by busses, partly by forced marches to Meteren to construct and garrison a line behind the village. These various reinforcements filled the gap that night.   On the following morning 2 companies of the Entrenching Battalion were sent to strengthen weakened English units.

---

1 It was given 24 hours' warning notice and received definite orders 1½ hours beforehand.

The resistance and self-sacrifice displayed on the following day all along the front allowed the 1st Australian Division to detrain undisturbed and march east of the Nieppe Forest and so save the Hazebrouck railway. About Bailleul, however, the German pressure continued. Neuve Eglise fell in the early hours of the 14th, Bailleul on the 15th, Meteren on the 16th. In our withdrawal from the last place 2 companies of the 2nd Entrenching Battalion, now in the front line, were involved. Though 60% of the men were new drafts, they held their ground with tenacity till they found the enemy round both flanks. The left company fought its way back, Sergt. W. P. Morrin, M.M., inspiring his platoon which was surrounded on 3 sides by the enemy. The right company nearer Meteren held on too long and lost 100 prisoners, a number which by far exceeded the greatest aggregate total captured by the Germans in any one action from the Division.

Ludendorff now seemed within measurable distance of bending the British left on to a line from Arras along the Aa to the sea. Attacking north of Ypres, and at Béthune and Kemmel, his troops, exhausted or raw, failed to show the skill in infiltration that marked the March attack, and were repulsed. In the defeat of the attacks on the Meteren reserve line on 17th April the 2nd Entrenching Battalion played a small but useful role. Part of the battalion was relieved by French infantry that night, and the remainder later by the Australians.

This fighting at Meteren did not exhaust the services of the battalion. By 25th April our garrisons in the Ypres salient had been withdrawn in successive voluntary stages as far as Zillebeke, and the XXII. Corps front was now directly affected by the German offensive. The battalion had received orders and was making its final preparations for entraining at Poperinghe to rejoin its group in the south, when the great enemy attack developed on the 25th. They were sent up into support, again under General Pinney, behind Dickebusch. They came into action on 8th May, when they assisted in repelling an enemy assault launched by 2 Divisions and in preparing the way for a British counter-attack which re-captured a position lost beyond their flank. In this action conspicuously fine work was done by Lt. J. M. C. McLeod, M.C., who, when the line on his right was broken, swung up his left flank and drove back the enemy by enfilade machine gun fire. Relieved on 11th May by French troops, the 2nd Entrenching Battalion was thanked by General Godley,

General Pinney and other officers for their services, and then entrained for the south.

We must now turn back to the remainder of the composite battalion of the Mounted Regiment and the Cyclists who were holding Shrewsbury Forest on 12th April. They were relieved that evening. Reorganised as mounted units and ordered to be in readiness to move at half an hour's notice, they were sent forward in the early hours of the 13th, in view of the pressure at Neuve Eglise, to establish a defensive line on Kemmel. The subsequent German advance rapidly exposed their position to severe shelling, in which several lives were lost before French cavalry relieved our men on 18th April. During the attack on the 25th they, like the 2nd Entrenching Battalion, were again called on and despatched to close a gap near Vierstraat north-west of Wytschaete. Here they took up a defensive position astride the Vierstraat road, and here, subjected for several days to heavy shelling, cyclists and mounted men stopped all attempts of the enemy to advance. They were relieved on 1st May. During the operations the Cyclist Battalion casualties amounted to 5 officers and 100 men.

It is convenient to allude here to the action of the XXII. Corps in the Battle of the Marne in July, when the early triumphs of the last German offensive, undertaken on the Aisne in May like the Lys attack in April with a view to dissipating the central reserves prior to a fresh attempt to separate the Allied Armies, were converted by enemy strategical blunders and by Foch's genius into the victory which marked the turning of the tide. For the Generalissimo's counter-thrust Sir Douglas Haig had not merely released the French troops in Flanders but had also sent 4 Divisions under General Godley's command.

The latter took with him his XXII. Corps Headquarters which with the 51st and 62nd Divisions arrived in the Ardre Valley on 19th July. By forced marches and passing through an Italian Corps on the Montagne de Reims, the British Divisions at once engaged in the battle amid the standing crops and coppices overhung by steep thickly-wooded spurs on each side of the valley. The Mounted Troops rendered excellent service on patrols and advanced reconnaissances during the later phases of the operations. In the Cyclist Battalion preparations had been long in progress to celebrate in peaceful festivity the second anniversary of their formation as a battalion, (22nd July) but an opportunity was given them of commemorating and adding lustre to it by battle. Attached

to a 62nd Division brigade, which was weakened after days of
continuous fighting, they captured on 23rd July the village of
Marfaux and a ridge 400 yards beyond, one of the 3
great *points d'appui* in the valley.   "The Cyclist Battalion
fought as infantry," says the official narrative, "and proved
both gallant and efficient."   During the operations the
battalion captured 100 prisoners and 9 machine guns and
recovered many French and English machine guns and a
battery of 75s.   They rescued also several famished York-
shire prisoners who had reached the village during an
unsuccessful attack made by the 62nd Division 3 days
previously.   General Berthelot of the Fifth French Army
signalised his appreciation of the Corps' achievements in an
eloquent Order of the Day, and of the Cyclists' performance
by the reward of a richly-embroidered fanion, presented later
to Lt.-Col. Evans at Epernay during the Peace Celebrations
in 1919.

NOTE.—Ludendorff's Memoirs make it clear that the Somme attack was in April
definitely abandoned in favour of the Flanders offensive.   The latter was to have been
resumed in August.   Some of the remarks in this narrative on the German plans
accordingly require modification.

CHAPTER X

FROM HÉBUTERNE TO PUISIEUX-AU-MONT

In the first week of April the VII. Corps was relieved
on the Somme by the Australian Corps, and certain changes
in the distribution of forces northward followed. The V.
Corps extending their left took over 1200 yards of the New
Zealand sector. On 12th/13th April the 4th Australian
Brigade included in their area another 500 yards of the high
ground about the Hébuterne road. The 2 New Zealand
infantry brigades, therefore, in the line now held a frontage
of a little over 4000 yards. On the 25th, however, the
Australians were withdrawn, and the Division side-stepped
northwards, occupying now a somewhat longer front from
One Tree Hill to the east of Hébuterne. On their left the
centre of the Corps front was held by the 42nd, and the left
sector by the 37th Division.

In front of Hébuterne the depth of our defences was limited
to a quarter of a mile between the front line and the support
system which ran through the centre of the village. With a
view to improvement, a company of 1st Wellington on 4th
May undertook an operation astride the road to Puisieux-au-
Mont in conjunction with troops of the 42nd Division on the
left. 16 medium and 8 light trench mortars together
with machine guns gave immediate support to the attack, and
the Corps heavies bombarded the rear areas and carried out
counter-battery work. For 3 days previously ostentatious
registration had been carried out by 8-in. howitzers on
selected targets in Rossignol Wood and at La Signy Farm, and
a considerable number of casualties had been reported by

1 From 20th to 29th April the 2 medium trench mortar batteries were active daily,
expending a total of 377 rounds. On several occasions casualties had been seen. On
one occasion a trench mortar bomb, or possibly an artillery shell, landed close to an
enemy two-horsed wagon bringing trench mortar ammunition at dusk up the Serre
road. The horses bolted. The Germans firing salvoes of rifle grenades on the road
in front of them stopped them near their own front line. Our men, who by this
time saw what was happening, in their turn fired rifle grenades behind the horses and
stampeded them again towards our trenches. The enemy now turned rifle and
machine gun fire on his lost animals, but only grazed them. The horses themselves
madly leapt our front trench across the road; the wagon stuck in it. Our garrison
cut the traces and sent the horses galloping on towards our support line by exploding
a Mills bomb behind them. There they were safely caught. A similar incident
happened at the same spot earlier in the summer. On the present occasion, owing
to some misunderstanding over the telephone, the Divisional Intelligence Officer was
sent post-haste to the line to "examine" our prisoners.

prisoners. At the moment of attack, very effective diversions
were provided by 2 brigades of field artillery.   The feint
at La Signy Farm achieved its purpose, and on that "tender"
locality practically all the enemy barrage fell.   The infantry
enterprise was only partially successful, owing to a lack of
co-operation between the attacking troops of the 2 Divisions
and to enemy machine gun fire.   As Wellington neared their
objective, Cpl. A. Bradley was severely wounded, a bomb
blowing his foot off.   Repressing any indication of pain, he
urged his men forward, and refused to be assisted to our
trenches.   As he crawled back with his rifle, he encountered 2
Germans attempting to return to their lines and shot them.
The majority of the Wellington party reached the final
objective and captured 10 prisoners.   Exposed, however, to
enfilade machine gun fire from both flanks as well as to
showers of bombs, they were in an untenable position, and
after losing 5 men killed and 18 wounded, 2 of whom died,
the company was compelled shortly after midnight to withdraw to an intermediate trench about 200 yards in front of
our old positions.   The result, though falling short of expectations, shortened our line and added further depth to the
Hébuterne defences.

Against the anticipated renewal of the German offensive,
nothing was now left to chance.   For miles in selected rear
positions, battalions of labour troops and Chinese dug line
after line of splendidly sited and wired trenches, and in all
the forward areas the most careful arrangements were made
for defence and counter-attack dispositions, for signal communications, for the construction of shell-proof headquarters,
machine gun emplacements and advanced dressing stations,
for the digging of tank-traps at selected points on the roads,
and for artillery action to deal with enemy tanks or
infantry effecting a breach.   Certain areas were laid down
well forward in which silent batteries were placed with the
object of escaping enemy counter-battery work and engaging
attacking infantry at close range.   The rest of our field
artillery were drawn well back, and gunners felt the need of
technical devices to give increased range.   The 2nd (Army)
Brigade came into the line on 21st May.[1]   At that time the
Divisional artillery was still extremely active, daily expending
between 5000 and 10,000 rounds, but at the end of May,
after the launching of the German offensive in the south,
this high rate of consumption was reduced to 3500.   The

1 p. 876.

mortars, however, including the 6-in. Newtons, all close up behind the front lines, maintained their steady bombardment of enemy Strong Points and machine gun positions with great effect. A favourite pastime was to ferret an enemy party out of a Strong Point or dugout with trench mortar bombs, and then, as they dispersed, to shoot them down with rifle or machine gun fire.

After his check in April the enemy's artillery activity had rapidly slackened and, except for periodical perfectly timed and intensely heavy "shell-storms," became indeed abnormally quiet. Only in the 2 days preceding his Aisne offensive did he seek to create a diversion all along the Third Army front by violent counter-battery work, heavy bombardment of trenches, active shelling of rear areas with high-velocity guns, and by gas concentrations on villages. Very light casualties were inflicted in the New Zealand sector. Nor were his infantry more aggressive. His patrols were rarely seen in No Man's Land, and a few attempted raids were repulsed, the dead being left before our trenches. An especially determined raid of over 60 men in 4 parties, preceded by a hurricane bombardment, was made against the 1st Rifles near La Signy Farm on 2nd May. It was a complete and costly failure, thanks largely to the leadership of Sergt. R. McMurray, whose conduct won him a bar to his D.C.M. The enemy secured a solitary success near One Tree Hill on 7th May, capturing in a silent raid a Lewis gun and 5 riflemen from an advanced post in front of our line.

Two other successes were due, not to action against our lines, but to an excess of venturesomeness on the part of our own patrols. On 26th April, at 1 a.m., 2nd Lt. J. T. Thomas, led a patrol of six 2nd Wellington men into German positions north of La Signy Farm. Thomas was a conspicuously dashing and bold officer, and his party penetrated deep into the enemy country. The sound of distant rifle fire and bombing reached the Wellington sentries in the front line, and it was clear that something was amiss. Further patrols were sent out then and later without avail. It transpired afterwards that Thomas' party was surrounded by a strong body of enemy. Five of his men were wounded, and Thomas saved their lives by a reluctant but necessary surrender. On 21st May a 1st Wellington patrol attacked a strong enemy party in No Man's Land. The issue remained in favour of the Germans. The patrol secured a prisoner but lost an officer and a sergeant (killed) and a private (captured).

28

This inaggressive attitude of the enemy and a marked approximation to open warfare methods in a fluid and elastic disposition of front line garrisons lent themselves to vigorous and aggressive raids and patrol enterprises on our part. No Man's Land was a maze of old British and German trenches which afforded admirable cover, and in the exceptionally fine weather the ground was hard and dry. Many of these exploits were performed by our patrols, not at night, but in broad daylight, in full view of their delighted comrades and with a wholesome effect on the morale of recently joined reinforcements. Not infrequently a German sentry or two were kidnapped without a struggle, asleep or writing letters, delousing themselves, or at a peaceful meal, and there was nothing to show their commander the reason of their disappearance. More often some had to be killed, or the raiders had to fight. But our continual aggressiveness and the repeated instances of the destruction or total disappearance of the German sentry posts must have called for disagreeable explanations on the part of company commanders opposite. For these minor patrol enterprises were almost invariably successful and were usually carried out without loss to our parties. Their surprising immunity was due partly to their own skill and dash, partly to waning enemy morale. As a result, prisoners and identifications were obtained in a steady stream 3 or 4 times a week. Battalions vied in bold adventures. A few instances may be quoted.

1st Auckland with artillery and trench mortar bombardment raided south of the Serre road on the sultry afternoon of 15th May and secured a machine gun and 2 prisoners. Three days later, north of La Signy Farm, a 1st Otago party under Sergt. P. McGregor, frustrated by wire in their original project, moved to a flank and penetrated 750 yards from our line into German territory. Waiting till the enemy should have had breakfast and relaxed vigilance, they then selected a small shelter, lifted up the waterproof sheet that protected its interior from rain or sun, and collected 4 sleeping Germans, whom they brought back in full daylight. In the early hours of 20th May a 3rd Rifles' party under 2nd Lt. M. Macdonald, after a first check from machine gun fire, immediately afterwards very gallantly attacked for the second time a machine gun post east of Hébuterne occupied by a garrison of 30 men and 2 machine guns. Losing 4 men wounded, they killed 7, captured 3, drove the rest to flight and brought in the machine guns. On the next day another patrol of the same battalion under Sergt. W. Meteven, M.M., captured 2 prisoners, and the 4th Rifles did the same. On 24th May Meteven with 2 comrades crossed No Man's Land, again in broad daylight, and entered an enemy post 500 yards from our line. Of the 2 occupants 1 was shot, and the other taken prisoner. On the shot being fired, some 20 Germans in a trench 30 yards away were alarmed and rushed our patrol. Meteven bade his men withdraw and seeing that it was impossible to get his prisoner with him, shot him. He then threw 2 bombs among the advancing enemy and emptied his revolver at short range into them, inflicting several casualties and securing his own withdrawal. In the beginning of June a small 2nd Otago[2] party under Sergt. J. Scott took 5 prisoners some 500 yards from our front line and brought them safely in.

But by common consent the palm in these freebooting forays was awarded to the trained "gang"[1] of Sergt. R. C. Travis, of 2nd Otago. Two of their exploits in May may be recorded. Their battalion happened to be out of the line, but hearing that identifications were urgently wanted in connection with an expected enemy attack, Travis at once volunteered to obtain them. His party left our lines east of Hébuterne on 14th May, a little after 7 p.m., in broad daylight. Working down a sap and making skilful use of ground, they reached unobserved a suspected enemy post. The post was rushed, and the garrison completely surprised. The officer in command showed fight and had to be shot. His 6 men were taken prisoners. The commotion in the post roused the occupants of a neighbouring trench who hurried to their comrades' assistance. Travis covered our withdrawal with the utmost coolness and dexterity, emptying his revolver at the infuriated enemy. Their excitement did not make for steady marksmanship, and 2 of the prisoners were shot. The other 4 were brought in safely to give important information.

On the last day of the month, north of La Signy Farm, Travis used much the same methods. With 2 of his men he crawled along an old sap towards an enemy post and reached within 25 yards of his objective. Here, cautiously raising a periscope, the little party could see 2 men watching our lines from the post. The question of approaching them was difficult, for the trench was filled breast-high with wire.

1 Sergt. A. Swainson, Ptes. A. D. D. Clydesdale (later killed), R. V. Conway, H. Melvill, N. Thomson.
2 Lt.-Col. McClymont, vice Lt.-Col. Colquhoun, seconded for duty on a transport at the end of March.

Under the very noses of the unsuspecting enemy the 3
scouts wormed themselves out of the sap and crawled through
the grass to within 10 yards of the sentries. Then with one
accord they sprang to their feet and rushed them. The
sentries were overpowered at once and surrendered. Close by
was a dugout. It was investigated and found to contain 9
Germans, one of whom was an officer. In a scuffle 3 were shot
and 3, including the officer, taken prisoner, but the rest
escaped. Travis and his men hustled their captives off over
No Man's Land before reinforcements could arrive. They
were just in time. The German garrison was heard padding
along the hard dry trench, and their fire forced captors and
captives into the sap. Taking advantage of this movement,
one of the prisoners darted back, but was wounded or killed
by covering fire from our trench. The officer and the other
man were brought in without loss. Half an hour later the
Otago Lewis guns got further targets in a small enemy party
headed by 2 officers who, revolvers in hand, were seen to
re-enter the raided post.

On 7th June the Division was relieved by the 42nd Division.
The artillery remained in the line. Divisional Headquarters
moved to Pas-en-Artois and later to Authie. The infantry
brigade groups occupied tents or were billeted in villages.
One brigade in turn garrisoned the Purple Line.[1] The 3
weeks' period in reserve was favoured by dry sunny weather.
The country side, unlike the undulating featureless terrain on
the edge of the Somme battlefield at La Signy and Hébuterne,
offered a richly picturesque landscape of deep valleys, green
woods and clean prosperous villages. The wheat crop had
not yet ripened, but rich fields of rye and clover extended on
every side; and in the forward areas east of the Purple
Line the spring work of the farmers was not lost, for the
Division cut the crops for them and carted them back in
military wagons.

The epidemic known popularly as Spanish Influenza, then
ravaging Europe and the contending armies, had but a
passing, if temporarily serious, effect on the general health
of the troops. The Brigade Horse Shows, which had been
held by the brigades when in reserve, were now succeeded
by a Divisional Horse Show, and by Divisional Tournaments,
Boxing Competitions and Band Contests. A final visit was
paid at this time by the Prime Minister of New Zealand,
attended by Sir Joseph Ward. The proportion of hardy

1 p. 356

experienced soldiers now in the ranks was very considerable, and the hours devoted to military exercises could be appreciably reduced. The policy of training was still largely based on the tactics of an active defence, and just as the infantry brigades in Divisional reserve had practised the launching of a counter-attack from the Purple System, so similar schemes were now executed from the reserve Corps system (the Red Line.) There was, however, growing evidence of a conviction, emanating from the High Command and permeating down to all formations, that the anxious period, during which the Allies' main concern was the preservation of an unbroken line, was, if not actually over, rapidly passing. There was already an eager anticipation of the time when reinforcements and America's Armies would produce a numerical equality and restore the initiative. The training in "open warfare" attack and in the close co-operation between battalions and mobile batteries or sections of batteries, temporarily withdrawn for the purpose from the Purple Line, was no less important than novel, and was to prove incalculably valuable sooner than the participants yet realised.

The more important changes of appointments made since the beginning of the year and not noticed previously may be here reviewed. Lt.-Col. H. G. Reid, D.S.O., after rendering admirably efficient service to the Division since its formation, rejoined the British Army. He was succeeded by Major (now Lt.-Col) Avery, whose appointment as D.A.Q.M.G. was filled by Capt A. S. Muir. Shortly afterwards Lt. (Temporary Major) C. I. Gossage was appointed D.A.D.O.S. vice Lt.-Col. Herbert, who received promotion in a British Corps. In the artillery Lt.-Col. Symon went in June for his turn of duty to command the N.Z.F.A. Depot in England and was succeeded in command of the 1st Brigade by Lt.-Col. Standish, whom he replaced in the English appointment. An anticipatory reference may be made to Major Richmond's taking command of the 9th Battery in August. In the appointment of Brigade Major he was then succeeded by Major R. Miles, D.S.O., M.C. Lt.-Col. Cook died in England on 2nd May and was succeeded in command of 1st Wellington by Lt.-Col. H. Holderness. His brother, Capt. H. Holderness, was appointed in April Staff Captain of the 1st Brigade vice Capt. H. Chisholm, who had vacated the appointment through sickness. Major Skelley, wounded in May and later succumbing to his injuries, was succeeded as Brigade Major in the Rifle Brigade by Major Bremner, whose appointment as

G. S. O. 3 was filled by Capt. O. Opie, R.N.Z.A. Lt.-Col.
Mead, Canterbury Regiment, assumed command of the 3rd
(Reserve) Battalion, vice Lt.-Col. Griffiths, who succeeded
Lt.-Col. J. A. Mackenzie in control of the N.Z. Command
Depot, the latter taking command of the N.Z. Base Depot,
which Lt.-Col. Mitchell had relinquished in March. On
Lt.-Col. Roache's being invalided in May to New Zealand
Lt.-Col. Puttick succeeded to the command of the 5th
(Reserve) Battalion, Rifle Brigade.

The Division went into the line again at the beginning of
July in the centre of the Corps front. The command of the sector
passed from the 57th Division on 2nd July. Headquarters
were transferred from Authie to Couin. The front was
covered by the 1st and 3rd and the 2nd (Army) Artillery
Brigades. The Machine Gun Battalion had 3 companies
disposed in definite positions in the line with 1 company in
mobile reserve. To the north the 37th Division faced Bucquoy.
The former New Zealand sector in front of La Signy Farm
was occupied by the 42nd Division. The 57th and 62nd[1]
Divisions were now in Corps reserve.

The new Divisional sector ran southwards from the south-
east tip of Biez Wood, which lay south-west of Bucquoy, along
the north of Rossignol Wood to east of Hébuterne. A mile
northwards from Hébuterne were the shattered remains
of the village of Gommecourt, whose defences had
broken the subsidiary British attack of 1st July 1916,
and which was occupied by us on 27th February 1917
in the preliminary stages of the German retreat. Now,
owing to the trend of our line to the north-east, it lay at a
greater distance from our outposts than Hébuterne itself.
Both villages stood on high ground, and from their ridges
one could overlook the wastes of the Somme battlefield as
far as Flers of 1916 memory, some 8 miles to the east, and
see the smoke of distant German trains in whose windows, on
a bright afternoon, the western sun's rays were brilliantly
reflected. The Gommecourt ridge, on whose forward slopes
lay the Park and the wood surrounding the village, was a
particularly important tactical feature. Its possession was
essential for the safety of the New Zealanders and the
Division on their left, and it formed a pivot on which counter-
attacks must hinge. It was accordingly formidably protected.
The ground was everywhere covered with rusty wire and

1 Shortly afterwards transferred to the XXII. Corps for operations on the
Marne. p. 379.

DERELICT TANK IN N.Z. TRENCHES BEFORE ROSSIGNOL WOOD

TAKING WATER TO THE FRONT LINE (ROSSIGNOL WOOD)

THE PRIME MINISTER OF NEW ZEALAND WITH A MACHINE GUN COY.
(Mr. Massey accompanied by the Right Hon. Sir Joseph Ward)

HIGH-EXPLOSIVE (NEAR GOMMECOURT)

pitted with old shellholes, overgrown with thistles. In the network of German lines about Gommecourt were many admirable deep dugouts.

The Division found the organisation of the defences in the new sector satisfactorily far developed. Every advantage had been taken of the naturally strong positions to fortify the 2 Divisional systems, the forward (Green) and the reserve (Purple). But though the defences were generally strong, and though we commanded observation over large tracts of the enemy's hinterland, there were none the less several weaknesses in the sector. The effect of the gap between the V. and IV. Corps troops in the March retreat had, as we have seen,[1] allowed the Germans to drive in deeply towards Hébuterne and occupy the high ground immediately east of it. Thus had arisen the inadequate depth in front of the village which 1st Wellington had endeavoured to rectify in May. On the left of the Divisional front about Rossignol Wood also the tactical situation was highly unsatisfactory. The entry into the Wood effected by the 37th Division on 5th April had subsequently been relinquished. Between it and Biez Wood our left battalion occupied a salient over half a mile deep on a front of about 1500 yards narrowing at the base to some 600 yards. In this salient the 2 front line companies lay at right angles to each other, one looking south-west towards Rossignol Wood, the other south-east towards Fork Wood, where, protected by outposts in front, lay the German main defences. A shallow valley divided the New Zealanders from the 37th Division northwards and gave the enemy a possible approach to Biez Wood and a copse beside it, called Square Wood, neither of which was wired or garrisoned. This avenue was safeguarded by powerful machine gun protection, and beyond our front trenches a chain of infantry posts overlooked both this valley and a side valley, down which towards the main valley ran a sunken road, parallel to our trenches and lined by the dugouts of the enemy's outposts about Fork Wood. These New Zealand posts, however, could only be visited by night and were precariously exposed to envelopment.

Even more serious was the proximity of Rossignol Wood. Here the Germans themselves occupied a salient which might prove a trap to its occupants if we ever assumed the offensive. But as the wood covered 20 acres and sloped downhill from the point where it abutted on our lines, it provided the enemy

1 pp. 336 sqq.

with exceptional cover in which he could mass forces. A sudden short advance from it would penetrate deep into our positions, cut off all the troops in our salient between Rossignol and Biez Woods and secure the important Salmon Point Ridge, only some 700 yards from the edge of the wood. The enemy's position in Rossignol Wood might certainly be made unpleasant by artillery attention, but the situation could be materially improved only by an operation which would effect greater depth in our defences east of Hébuterne and give us at least the high western edge of the wood.

Active measures were accordingly at once undertaken with a view to achieving these objects, and the next 6 weeks were to see the application of an unrelaxed pressure on the enemy, which, though overshadowed by the great battles of the autumn, yet exemplified in a striking manner the principles of an aggressive defence and the fine fighting qualities of the New Zealand soldier.

The first operations were aimed at deepening our defences east of Hébuterne. They were carried out by the Rifle Brigade south of the Puisieux Road during the night 5th/6th July. In the afternoon of the 5th, the 2nd and 3rd Battalion patrols had found that the enemy was abandoning his outposts along the bottom of the forward slopes immediately east of Hébuterne. During the night the battalions pushed up the various communication trenches and connected them across the face of the spur. Throughout the following days, partly by pressure partly by peaceful penetration, they won a further 200 yards. Progress beyond was impeded not so much by booby-traps as by masses of wire that choked the trenches. On the 8th, however, a 2nd Rifles' party of 14 men, under the battalion scout officer, 2nd Lt. T. A. Snelling, who had been foiled on 6 previous occasions, now on the seventh attempt crossed this wire and surprised an enemy garrison post of 10 men, 3 of whom were killed, Snelling himself shooting 2 sentries with his revolver. A prisoner was captured and gave much valuable information.

So much was gained, but the Rifles were not satisfied. With a view to carrying the actual crest, crossed by the old German front line of 1916, and to securing observation over the enemy's dispositions, a more ambitious programme on both sides of the road was arranged for 15th July. In the intervening period wire-cutting and destruction of enemy posts were systematically carried out by the artillery under cover of a general shoot along the whole Divisional front.

By day and night patrols explored No Man's Land with its old saps and wire, located enemy posts and reported the progress of the wire-cutting. While engaged on these missions, L.-Cpl. J. Sillifant, of the 4th Rifles, established himself in a sniping position deep in No Man's Land and killed 10 Germans. On the 15th everything was in readiness for the Rifle Brigade enterprise.

It was to be executed by the 1st and 4th[1] Battalions, then in the line. Supporting fire was to be given by enfilading machine guns of both the New Zealand and 42nd Divisions, by light trench mortars bombarding sap junctions and emplacements, by 6-in. Newton trench mortars creating a diversion on the pillboxes in Rossignol Wood, and by 3 field artillery brigades. Two batteries of 6-in. howitzers were to engage somewhat more distant systems, and it was arranged that 5 minutes after zero counter-battery guns should deal with the enemy's artillery. A carefully co-ordinated barrage scheme for the field artillery aimed at inducing the garrison of the trenches marked for assault to seek the shelter of their dugouts, thus enabling our infantry to effect a surprise entry. The batteries were to carry out a 7 minutes' bombardment at a slow rate on certain enemy support trenches called Ford and Jena, on the 1st Battalion front, and on their somewhat ill-defined continuation northwards opposite the 4th Battalion, and then shorten range, and fire at an intense rate for 3 minutes on the actual objective. At zero they would lift forward again to Ford and Jena, on which their fire would remain for a period of 30 minutes. The hour of attack was fixed for 4 p.m. A code message, "Wet Wicket," had been arranged if weather conditions were unsuitable, but the afternoon proved fine.

North of the Puisieux Road the 4th Battalion positions lay in the British and German trenches of 1916 and the intervening No Man's Land. The great Nameless and Nameless Support trenches, which had beaten back the opening attack in July 1916, now ran at right angles to the opposing systems and were used as communication trenches. In addition to these was another sap parallel to them and called Snuff Alley. The 4th Battalion attack was carried out by 2½ platoons of "A" Company. Up Nameless and Nameless Support it was planned to send, in each, 2 attacking sections, followed by 2 sections in support, and 2 sections up the smaller Snuff Alley. Pushing forward 150 yards, the

---

1 Major Barrowclough, vice Lt.-Col. Beere. on leave.

patrols would establish blocks in the trenches and carry a connecting sap which constituted part of the enemy front line, and which could be readily extended to meet our own more advanced positions on the left. The front affected was some 600 yards. The plan of the 1st Battalion south of the road was on similar lines, but as their front amounted to about 1000 yards, they employed 2 companies ("A" and "B"). Unlike the 4th Battalion, they had a clear-cut objective in Fusilier Trench.

For some minutes before zero sections of the attacking companies filtered into our front line. As soon as the field artillery shortened to deliver the 3 minutes' intense bombardment on Fusilier and the intermediate sap north of the Road, the men moved out from our trenches and with a last cheery word to the garrison worked up close to the barrage. At zero, when the guns lifted, they made a swift determined rush up the saps. The 4th Battalion had a certain amount of bombing in the maze of cross-trenches, but overpowering this resistance not merely reached their objective but pushed 100 yards further, capturing 8 prisoners and 7 machine guns. The company lost 2 men killed and 6 wounded.

In the 1st Battalion objective in Fusilier the bulk of the garrison fled in disorder, some escaping down the communication trenches and leaping madly from one sap to another, others running over the open to their death. But in the centre and on each flank, groups of staunch veterans fought a good fight. Within 12 minutes, indeed, 1 white Verey light was fired, low down towards our front line, signifying the capture of part of the position, but it was not till after an hour that the whole long trench was thoroughly cleared. Here, also, exploitation patrols were pushed forward to Jena and Ford, off which the protective barrage had now lifted. Rflmn. B. Radcliffe worked down the connecting sap and found the enemy apparently endeavouring to organise a counter-attack. He threw a bomb, which surprised them. One or two fell, the remainder fled. Radcliffe, following up the advantage, succeeded in catching and bayoneting 2 of the party. An excellent reconnaissance enabled his comrades to move forward without casualties and occupy Jena and Ford. In these 2 trenches the two 1st Battalion companies established posts at a distance of from 200 to 500 yards in advance of the originally proposed line, and the Rifles' outposts now stood close to that line of battered poplar trees on the Puisieux Road which had seemed so distant when the enemy's attack assembled there in March.[1] An officer and 14 men had been slightly wounded. 28 dead were counted in the German trenches; 24 prisoners and 10 machine guns were captured.

In these operations it was instructive to note the recrudescence of "open-warfare" fighting. The advances made since 5th July marked the beginning on our side of the bold daylight movements of scouts and patrols employed to drive in the enemy posts. For the moment their function was to form a screen for the purpose of covering the consolidation of our new lines. Soon this was to be extended to continuous protection throughout a deep advance. The artillery shooting at opportunity targets, and at targets reported by the infantry, and the general co-operation between the 2 arms had proved conspicuously successful. Four days previously the 6th Battery had been heavily shelled, a gun-pit set alight, and the fire extinguished and lives saved only by the gallantry of 2nd Lt. E. F. Tyson. The battery now excelled in their retribution. By the infantry exceptional courage and great initiative had been shown throughout, as they were to be shown too in the operations in which the 1st and 2nd Brigades were shortly to be engaged. Not more than 250 men had been employed, and it was with humorous satisfaction that the Rifles read in the current German Intelligence Summary, which was later captured, of the attack having been launched with a force of from 800 to 1200 men.

Elated by these actions, which gained invaluable ground and observation, the 2 Rifle battalions, despite heavy rain, pushed deeper into the enemy's defences during the night. The 4th Battalion sent in a fresh company, who worked down Nameless and Nameless Support trenches in 2 isolated parties. At a given signal these then rushed to a further and important cross-trench called Owl, and there established communication. One of the parties was strongly attacked by the enemy, who outranged our own bombs. L.-Cpl. H. Baker rushed forward with the bayonet to close quarters. He killed 1 of the enemy and put the rest to flight. 5 of our men were wounded in the 2 parties, 12 Germans were killed, and a machine gun and 2 mortars captured. 5 successive bombing assaults during the night were frustrated.

On the 1st Rifles' right the southern sector of Jena was held by the enemy in force. Jena had been part of the old outer defences of Hébuterne, and opposite the junction

[1] p. 353.

between the 42nd and the New Zealand Divisions it turned
westwards towards those Quarries which lay south of the
village on the road towards La Signy Farm and were already
so familiar to the New Zealanders.[1] The 1st Rifles arranged in
the evening with the Lancashire troops of the 42nd Division
to clear mutually the whole of Jena as far as the Quarries
during the hours of darkness. In both areas, however, the
enemy fought stiffly, progress was slow, and the attackers
decided that the work would be easier on the following
morning.

An enemy counter-stroke anticipated them. A heavy
bombardment on Jena at 3 a.m. (16th July) was followed by
a resolute thrust made by strong forces on our posts in the
captured sector. The 2 right posts of the Rifles were
temporarily withdrawn nearer to the original objective about
Fusilier. One wounded man fell into German hands. Now
the New Zealand light mortars took up the challenge. They
furiously bombarded the reinstated garrison of Jena. Having
arranged to hold the enemy's attention from the front, the
infantry, led by 2nd Lt. W. Henning, bayoneted and bombed
their way down the contested sap and finally evicted the
Germans. They followed the sullenly retreating enemy some
250 yards further south. In the grey dawn a post composed
of a light machine gun crew and 12 bombers was destroyed,
and the other sentries eventually broke and fled. The
wounded rifleman had been taken by the Germans with 3
of their own wounded to a distant dugout which, owing to our
advance, was now in No Man's Land. After dark in the
next night he gathered strength to climb out of the dugout
and crawl back to our lines. In their enthusiasm the 1st
Rifles cleared part of the sector allotted to the Lancashire
troops and handed it over to them. The latter captured the
remainder of Jena during the day. Other troops of the 42nd
Division at the same time reoccupied La Signy Farm and the
ground to the east of it, lost on 5th April.[2] Blocks were then
established in the multitudinous saps leading back to the
next enemy line, which, by a curious coincidence, bore a name
connected with one of the most interesting episodes of early
New Zealand history—Jean Bart.[3] In this subsidiary opera-

[1] p. 357.
[2] p. 369.
[3] In 1839 the *Jean Bart*, a French whaler, touched at the Chatham Islands.
She was boarded by Maoris, on whose threatening attitude the crew slipped the cable,
killing such of the natives as were on board, and battening down the hatches on
others below deck. These last secured arms and offered resistance. The whalers later
took to the boats and were foundered. The Maoris forced their way on deck and
though out of sight of land sailed the ship home where she went ashore and was
broken up or burnt.

tion Henning and his men captured 2 machine guns and killed 20 of the enemy. The 1st Rifles lost 3 men killed and 10 wounded. Subsequently activity was confined to aggressive patrolling, which caused the enemy to withdraw again his forward zone.

The German version of this attack is inaccurate and interesting:—"At 4.30 a.m., after heavy artillery and T.M. fire, the enemy renewed his attack with overwhelming forces. After heavy fighting he succeeded in again penetrating Jena, and into the positions of "B" Company. The southern half of the next battalion sector was slightly withdrawn on account of the seriously threatened flank. The attempts of the enemy to advance further on the 16th were repulsed, and several English prisoners were taken during the counter-attack, but they again fell into the hands of the enemy."

After the success of his brigade General Stewart had the misfortune to be wounded by a sniper while going round the new trenches on the 17th. Lt.-Col. Austin temporarily took command pending General Hart's arrival from Sling on the 22nd.

On the other flank, at Rossignol Wood, similar measures were being adopted to improve our position. The wood was in the shape of a rough square, with a smaller square attached to its right-hand top corner. A series of trenches ran through the main wood, and in the smaller square about 100 yards inside the trees was a system of pillboxes. Reconnoitring patrols had already worked round the approaches to the wood and through the edge of the wood. On 9th July, two 1st Wellington officers, with Pte. C. J. Dallard, were exploring the wood about 11 a.m. They were attacked with bombs from one of the pillboxes. Both officers were severely wounded, and Dallard slightly. He carried one officer 60 yards back to safety and returned to rescue the other, who was lying within 15 yards of the enemy post. In face of a further shower of bombs, in which he was again wounded in 3 places, he got to within 10 yards of the officer, but found him dead He then retraced his way to the first officer, and notwithstanding his own wounds carried him to within 30 yards of our lines, when a party went over the parapet and brought in both the wounded officer and his rescuer The result of further reconnaissances made it clear that if we could establish a foothold in the smaller square we could prevent the massing of the enemy in the wood and render much more difficult any attempt to cut our lines by capture of the Salmon Point Ridge.

On the night of 12th/13th July 1st Canterbury[1] raided enemy posts in front of the wood, captured a prisoner and secured a more suitable jumping-off place for the enterprise. It was planned for the evening of the 15th, to follow the Rifle Brigade's operation in the afternoon of the same day further south. Under cover of a light mortar and machine gun barrage and supported by howitzers and 11 Newton mortars, the 2 Canterbury battalions attacked from its 2 sides the northern corner of the smaller square. From the 2nd Canterbury trench in the salient towards Biez Wood 3 parties rushed impetuously over the open and, without suffering a single casualty, were on their allotted objective on the north-eastern fringe of the wood before the enemy's heavy barrage of machine gun fire fell. 1st Canterbury, who had the main task of penetrating the wood from the north-west, encountered fairly heavy machine gun fire, but with complete success established their posts on their objective. A 1st Canterbury officer was killed and 3 men wounded, but the whole position aimed at was secured and consolidated. A large part of the enemy salient was cut off, and the menace to the left brigade subsector removed.

There was not a man in our trenches but was conscious of a sense of adventure, and of confidence that these operations would not be allowed to die out tamely. The enemy had similiar premonitions. The garrison of his wired pillboxes, 100 yards in front of 1st Canterbury in the wood, were very alert. An attempt to destroy the largest pillbox with light trench mortars on 17th July failed owing to misfires. But further occupation was to be won without fighting. About midnight, 19th/20th July, when the line was occupied by the Otago battalions, there was a loud explosion in the wood. A 2nd Otago reconnoitring party, sent out to investigate the cause, reported that the largest pillbox had been destroyed, and that there was no sign of enemy in the small square. Further patrols, pushed out by both battalions after daylight, had penetrated by noon the whole of the wood and had found it evacuated. Larger forces were then sent forward, and in case the withdrawal might prove to be of considerable depth, the troop of Otago Mounted Rifles now attached to the Division was despatched to a position of readiness west of Fonquevillers. A mobile battery also was

[1] Major Stitt, vice Lt.-Col. Row, on leave.

put at General Young's disposal. Clearing the wood, the covering patrols found the trenches blocked by wire and booby-traps. They pushed into the open, but came under heavy machine gun fire. 300 yards beyond the dip where the wood ended, Moa and Shag trenches on the rising ground were held strongly, and a bombardment by our light mortars, in close attendance on the patrols, failed to force withdrawal and brought down a concentrated retaliation by 5.9-in. howitzers.

As it was clear that the Germans had no intention of being pushed further, blocks were inserted in the saps leading to Moa and Shag. The time had obviously not yet come for the employment of the mounted troops and mobile battery. With considerable trouble from machine-gun fire directed from about Fork Wood, communication was established with our advanced posts on the left overlooking the side valley and the sunken road, which the enemy still held in force. Losses were slight, and about 20 enemy were killed. A mortar and one or two machine guns were captured.

The 1st Brigade had on the 17th relieved the Rifle Brigade on the right subsector. As soon as the news of the evacuation of Rossignol Wood reached them, the 2 front line battalions began to move forward. 1st Auckland, on the left, nearer the wood, cleared Duck Swan and Owl trenches after heavy fighting, but were checked in Hawk by very fierce resistance. They captured 3 prisoners and 2 machine guns and a mortar. Before 2nd Wellington on the right the enemy posts ran, leaving a machine gun behind them, and 2nd Wellington reached the Chasseur Hedge beyond Jean Bart, near the old 1916 British front line. On the following day (21st July) Auckland made further progress, and in the night 21st/22nd July repulsed a strong infantry assault following on an hour's bombardment.

On the left brigade front observation was limited by the rise on which the Germans clung to Moa and Shag, and our proximity to the heavily-shelled Rossignol Wood was not wholly satisfactory. On the right, however, we now enjoyed immediate observation over the falling slopes about La Louvière Farm, 1000 yards south of Rossignol Wood, and towards Serre and Puisieux. To take full advantage of this, a section of the 2nd Battery moved up in the afternoon to a sniping position on the outskirts of Hébuterne. The general result of the operation was to wipe out the remainder of the German salient and shorten and improve our line. The

29

following letter was received from the Third Army Commander:—

To G.O.C. IV. Army Corps.

I would ask you to convey to the G.O.C. New Zealand Division my sincere appreciation of the operations of that Division which has led to the evacuation of Rossignol Wood and the adjoining trenches by the enemy.

This operation, lasting over several days, has achieved a result which has reduced the extent of our front line and placed the enemy in an extremely difficult position.

That this result has been obtained with few casualties and without check is due to persistent enterprise and skilful leading on the part of commanders.

The Division is to be warmly congratulated on its spirit and initiative, and I desire that all ranks should be informed of these few words of commendation and gratitude.

J. BYNG, General,

Third Army.

22.7.18.

The whole of the captured area, and in particular the vicinity of Rossignol Wood, continued to be raked and searched by hostile artillery. It was obviously desirable for the 2nd Brigade to push out further from the shell-trap of the wood and at the same time secure a better field of fire and wider observation over the Puisieux valley. They improved their positions on the 22nd, and patrols closely watching movement in Moa and Shag shot 3 German sentries at their posts. But the enemy's new trenches were heavily wired and too formidable to be rushed without organised preparation. An attack was planned for 23rd July, and the 1st Brigade on the right agreed to advance their line in conformity. Drenching rain on that day necessitated a postponement till the 24th, indicated by the code message, "Stumps drawn." Then too the morning was cloudy and threatening, but shortly after noon the sky cleared, and the ground dried under a freshening wind. With a view to surprising the enemy no initial bombardment was made. Corps heavy artillery, however, carried out a deliberate shelling of the trenches and area generally. Each of the 2 Otago battalions employed its 10th (North Otago) Company. The hour selected for the attack was 5 p.m. As the troops waited in the front line, the 2nd Otago chaplain, the Rev. D. C. Herron, went round all his men distributing the so-called "buckshee" cigarettes. During the attack and afterwards his personal supervision of the stretcher-bearers was to be instrumental in getting in all our wounded.

The saps running to the enemy trenches were full of tangled wire, and one in particular in front of 2nd Otago on the right was made absolutely impassable by a block of massive entanglements. In broad daylight, shortly before the attack, Sergt. Travis crawled out with 2 Stokes mortar bombs and, disregarding the close proximity of the enemy posts, reached the block of wire. There he waited coolly till a minute before 5 p.m. He then blew up the wire block with the bombs and cleared a passage for the attack. On the stroke of 5 p.m. the silent artillery spoke. The 1st and 3rd Brigades bombarded enemy positions in the neighbourhood. The 37th Divisional Artillery created a diversion by shelling Bucquoy and putting down in that locality an extensive smoke barrage which a favouring wind blew over the German rear defences. The actual attack was carried out under a bombardment by light trench mortars, which fired at a rapid rate for 1 minute and then lifted beyond the objective.

The surprise aimed at was complete. The garrison was on the point of being relieved, and they had already strapped on their backs their greatcoats and valises. They were at the moment consuming an evening meal of hot coffee and black bread. Before they had time to fight, their ferocious attackers had scrambled over the blocks in the communication trenches and were among them. Only 2 machine guns on the right were alert. In their fire the right of 2nd Otago was checked, and the success of the whole operation imperiled.

Sergt. Travis had lit a cigarette and was watching the left of the attack when he heard near by the venomous crack of the German machine guns, that none knew better than he. He turned his head and saw the check. He leapt from his block, revolver in each hand, and rushed straight for the position. With rapid and unerring fire he killed the 7 men of the crews and captured the guns. At this moment a German officer and 3 men came running round a bend in the trench towards the assaulted portion and saw Travis and the dead gunners. They hesitated a moment and then charged him, but against that cool brain and steady hand hesitation was fatal. As they came at him down the open sap Travis shot all 4. When the attacking party rushed the trench, and they rushed the instant that the machine guns were silent, they found Travis reloading his revolvers, a line of corpses lying huddled about his feet.

Elsewhere there was not much resistance. In the centre of Shag another machine gun caused trouble to 1st Otago, shooting an officer and his runner, but when parties from each flank began to converge on them the crew fled, abandoning their gun. A strong patrol, pushed southwards by 2nd Otago into Slug Street, cleared the trench as far as Hawk, and taking 2 machine gun crews in flank with rifle fire, wiped them out and captured the guns. 1st Otago secured 2 machine guns and 2 prisoners, and 2nd Otago 4 prisoners, 6 machine guns, and a trench mortar. Many Germans were killed. Over 60 dead, including 2 officers, were counted in the 2nd Otago area alone, half being killed by shell and mortar fire and half by infantry weapons.

As had been arranged, 1st Auckland thrust forward their left simultaneously. Their parties crossed the block in Hawk, where the German resistance had been so strong 4 days previously, and pressing on another 500 yards carried 3 further barriers, after stiff fighting at each. They were eventually stopped by a strong block with a clear enfilade fire of 40 yards. A flank party secured touch with 2nd Otago, and incidentally captured en route a machine gun. In the main attack conspicuous determination had been shown by Sergt. Reginald Stanley Judson. 2nd Wellington similarly moved forward a short distance on the right.

The general result of these 4 days' operations was that on a 4000 yards' front the Division advanced their line to an average depth of between 500 and 1500 yards. The enemy at the moment showed no sign of intention to counter-attack. In the evening a German machine gun in the southern section of Slug was silenced by a trench mortar. But the hostile barrage put down, within 15 minutes of our attack, on the wood and adjoining trenches was continued through the night. Fortunately most of the shells fell in rear of the new front line, but 2nd Otago, who had lost only 1 man killed and 1 wounded in the actual assault, now had 9 men killed and an officer and 20 men wounded.

Among the papers captured by the 1st Brigade was an officer's diary. Together with moralisations about the Staff, not peculiar to the German company officer, it provided an interesting outlook, from the enemy point of view, on the recent struggle. A short extract may be given:—

SERGT. R. C. TRAVIS, V.C., D.C.M., M.M. [*Snapshot*

ON THE BATTLEFIELD NEAR PUISIEUX

THE RUINS OF PUISIEUX

PIONEERS AT PUISIEUX (21ST AUGUST 1918)

July 15/17.—Three active days. Tommy attacked the 180th I.R. and got into the front lines. Of course that handful of men in front could not hold him. In theory and from a deep dugout it is easy enough to carry on the war, but in practice——! Since then a good deal of fire has been on our positions.

16.—There were 2 bombardments of Puisieux. It was astonishing what he threw into that place. At night, ordinary harassing fire.

17.—Enemy fired on our trench junction in Rossignol Wood. One shell landed a yard from my shelter, so I cleared out. We had two wounded; and no wonder, with all that stuff flying about all day. Am reading "Lord Nelson's Last Love." My men have to work hard in comparison with the food they get. Our new offensive at Rheims has begun. 18,000 prisoners—but they talk about local fighting! I only hope bigger results will follow, and after them peace.

18.—Every morning a Tommy plane comes over, called by us the Trench Inspector, and drops 2 bombs on Puisieux. To-night we relieve and go to the main line of resistance in Rossignol Wood, which is now hardly recognisable since the end of June. Before that it was all green, and now nothing but stumps.

19.—Hardly into my dugout when I hear the wood is to be evacuated, and I have to shift. Sweated like a pig fixing a cover on my new shelter with my batman.

20.—4.30 p.m. Tommy rolls up the trench of the 180th I.R. and takes the front trench. I make a counter-attack and have 2 killed and 7 wounded. Some men of the 12th Company are missing. Again the people behind have made a mess of things. The blowing up of the dugouts in Rossignol Wood warned Tommy of our withdrawal, and he is pushing forward patrols. I am running about all night, and people behind us are talking about all sorts of things.[1]

21.—Early to-day the Assault Detachment were to push forward. After getting 2 men killed they withdrew. Will the German never learn common-sense? We have lost our best men, and what we have left are such that we cannot rely on them. It makes a man sick to see the good men sinking fast. A lance-corporal of the 180th I.R. who was lying out wounded was fetched in by us. You should have

---

1 Doubtless rumours based on the decision to withdraw on a large scale.

seen his thankful face. I hope I will be treated the same if I get hit. All night I was running round and got no sleep. On my right is a bad corner, and Pioneers are wiring both that and the trench. We are continuously on the watch, with one man of the post with rifle at the port and the other with a bomb ready in his hand.[1]

22.—At 5 a.m. the Assault Detachment of the 111th Division tried to roll up the trench, but the first men were cut down, and it came to nothing. Another Assault Section tried at midday, but came home again. In the evening I relieved the men who had been continuously on sentry.

23.—At 1 a.m. I came in to find that the lost trenches are to be recaptured. The 9th Coy. has to put a machine gun at the trench junction in the valley, where it is over-looked from both flanks and gets bad machine gun fire. O.C. and I, with 2 machine gunners, are to go down the C.T. at 3.30 p.m. Under cover of an artillery shoot I cut through about 30 yards of wire. Twice the shells are very close, and I have to pull back a little. Then we go down the trench like a patrol and reach the trench junction, which is under fire from 3 sides. There we must leave the sentries to their fate. Thus, after 4 years of war, men in a deep dugout lay down the law, how the outposts are to be held and how the garrison is to repulse patrols. This is all very fine, but a handful of men cannot hold back a powerful enemy who has already "done in" 2 companies and killed and wounded half of a third. Nobody has been up here to look at the situation. The men are done to death. I am relieving them every night to allow them a little sleep. I hear I'm recommended for a decoration, but don't care much about it. We were again bombarded at night, and one landed on the parapet of Coy. Headquarters.

24.—Our contact plane was over to-day. Everything O.K. We are promised some recognition. The battalion is to receive 1200 litres of beer. I am in better spirits. Yesterday I felt very down.

Here the diary ends. Shortly after 5 p.m., with many maps and documents, it was captured in the company headquarters.

Moa and Shag were admirable trenches. They contained a number of dugouts and small "elephant" iron shelters, and

1   This sentence certainly betrays nervousness.

were in good order and in better sanitary condition than was customary for front line German trenches. In this position the 2nd Brigade had again pushed themselves into a salient where they aggressively threatened both flanks of the enemy, and enjoyed direct observation over Puisieux. The enemy had voluntarily resigned Rossignol Wood, but on the high ground beyond its eastern edge he had calculated to dominate our lines. He made preparations therefore to recapture the important positions wrested from him.

At dawn on the 25th his aeroplanes reconnoitred our lines with marked vigilance. An hour's intense bombardment in the morning caused several casualties, despite excellent consolidation on the previous day. Desultory fire was continued throughout the day. At 6.45 p.m. his gun fire burst out afresh with concentrated vigour and was accompanied by heavy machine gun fire. It was an awkward moment for the defence. Reliefs were in progress both in the right brigade area, where 1st Wellington were replacing 1st Auckland, and on the left, where the Rifle Brigade were taking over the whole of the 2nd Brigade positions. The incoming troops were already up the communcation trenches. As a counter-attack appeared imminent, the garrison stood to arms, and the relieving companies took up the best positions available to resist the enemy onset. A few minutes afterwards 2 hostile aeroplanes flew menacingly low over our lines, and the first signs were observed of the enemy infantry. Long lines of helmets became clearly visible above the sides of the several communication trenches over half a mile of front. Up 5 of these saps there now pushed parties, each consisting of about 25 men, but in Slug Street there was a full company. Each party comprised machine gunners, bombers, and snipers. Further massing noticed later in the sunken road northwards was dispersed by artillery fire.

The Germans, staunch fighters and well led, came rapidly forward. Nearing our positions, they crept up flinging stick bombs, or jumped out of the communication trenches and began to run swiftly and strongly towards the unwired garrison. As soon as ever they appeared, the Otago Lewis guns and rifles opened steady fire, and 2nd Otago put up the S.O.S. which was promptly answered by the batteries of the 2nd and 3rd Artillery Brigades covering the sector. Of the smaller parties not a man reached our position. The survivors in the open wavered and ran for the protection of the saps, just as our barrage burst on them, preventing

our infantry's pursuit but taking deadly toll of the bunched
"field-greys." Otago raked the saps with rifle grenades.

At Slug Street, however, by force of numbers the enemy
made temporary headway. In the bombardment a German
shell had here destroyed 2nd Otago's bombs at the block.
Under the pressure our post was forced back, and its
commander, 2nd Lt. E. J. Beechey, fighting to the last
against overpowering odds, was killed by a bayonet thrust.
The Germans followed down the Street, reached our front line
at the junction of the 2 brigades, and penetrated towards
the support line. Here, however, they had no longer a mere
post to deal with, but the garrisons of both 1st Auckland and
2nd Otago. They were immediately counter-attacked by the
reserve Otago platoons. A 1st Auckland Corporal (A.S.
Webster), with 2 men, seeing 12 enemy coming down a sap
towards him, rushed at them. Himself securing their machine
gun and killing 2 of the gunners with bombs he drove the
remainder right into Otago's hands. The same Sergt. Judson,
of Auckland, whose prowess on the previous day has been
noted, was again conspicuous in the defence. Hearing to his
left continuous bomb-explosions along Slug Street, he went
over to make personal investigation. He found 6 Otago
survivors. After reorganising them he fought his way
forward alone to the front line where he found Beechey dead
at his post. He then returned to the little group of shaken
Otago sentries of whom in accordance with orders he took
command. During the following night on 2 separate
occasions he crawled forward into No Man's Land and
dispersed German parties with bombs.

With the arrival of our reserves the attack was finally shattered. Working along from both flanks our parties re-occupied
the junction of our front line and Slug Street, and the enemy
were trapped. Every German who had entered our lines was
accounted for. 37 were killed and nearly 30 taken prisoners.
Only then did the 2 enemy aeroplanes which, imperturbably
disregarding our machine gun fire, had hovered over the wood
and valley, fly disconsolate homewards. Of the Germans who
fled down Slug Street and the other trenches eastwards many
must have been caught in our artillery barrage which was
by this time very heavy. Within half an hour of the
opening of the attack our line was completely re-established.
Of the prisoners secured most were already wounded, and
several were killed by the enemy's heavy retaliatory fire
which followed his repulse, but 18 eventually reached the

Divisional Cage. 2nd Otago, on whom the weight of the blow chiefly fell, had lost 2 officers and 6 men killed and 1 officer and 40 men wounded. The resolution shown by our men in this affair and the admirable initiative of the different counter-attacking parties formed a model of a local counter-attack action, and as such the Corps Staff caused a description with explanatory plans to be circularised to all units. Our success won also a further appreciative recognition from General Byng:—

G.O.C. IV. Army Corps.   No. g 12/296

Reference IV. Corps No. 18/1/4/G dated 26th July, 1918. The repulse of this enemy raid with such heavy loss to the raiders reflects the greatest credit on all ranks of the garrison.

The initiative shown by leaders and men in rallying and surrounding those of the enemy who had entered our line at Slug Street is an object lesson in readiness and resource.

J. BYNG, General,
29.7.18.   Third Army.

The success was marred by one deplorable disaster. In the morning bombardment of 2nd Otago's position Travis went along his trench encouraging his men with his usual cheerfulness and sang-froid under the heavy shell-fire. A fragment struck and killed him. Few individual men had slain so many Germans. Of impeccable behaviour, strong opinions but quiet and unassuming demeanour, Travis had been the hero of numberless instances of exceptional and inspiring gallantry, and had so far cheated Death in several hairbreadth escapes. The news of his end occasioned genuine sorrow throughout the Division. It has been given to few to merit and win as illustrious an epitaph as is contained in his own battalion diary: "July 26th. Sergt. R. C. Travis buried with full military honours at the Cemetery at Couin at 8 p.m. Brig.-General Young, 2nd Brigade Staff, and the officers and men of the battalion attended. The death of Sergt. Travis cast a gloom over the whole battalion. Only those who have been with us for any length of time can realise what a loss his death means to us. He left New Zealand with the Main Body and had never missed an operation. He went over the top 15 times and always did magnificent work. He won the D.C.M., M.M., (Belgian) Croix de Guerre, and has been recommended for the V.C.[1] His name will live in the

[1] Awarded, Gazette 27th September.

records of the Battalion as a glorious example of heroism and
devotion to duty.''

After this attack had been repulsed, the incoming troops
completed the relief. This spell in the trenches was to be
marked by continual shelling and for the first 3 days by
torrential rain, which turned the trenches into knee-deep
channels of mud. One slight modification was made in our
positions. Our exposed line at the Chasseur Hedge was withdrawn to Jean Bart on 27th July, and the 2 deep dugouts and
over 40 boxes of enemy trench mortar ammunition in it were
blown up by the Engineers under cover of an artillery
''crash'' in the neighbourhood. The Engineers pushed on
with the construction of a new reserve line, for which timber
and other materials were brought up through Hébuterne.
These technical troops had ever their share of the dangers
incidental to war. A single everyday illustration must suffice.
On the evening of 24th July a party under Cpl. J. Q. Adams
was accompanying a wagon proceeding to an advanced dump.
In the battered streets of Hébuterne they ran into a shell-
storm. One shell struck the wagon, wounding the driver, 3
of the party, and the 2 horses. The horses bolted, but
became entangled in a belt of wire, close by. Though the
shelling was heavy, Adams ran to them, caught them, and
extricated them from the wire. He then collected his party
and delivered his material at the appointed place.

Certain American personnel of the 80th Division, U.S.
Army, had been for some time attached to the Division for
training purposes, and now a battalion of the 317th Regiment
was distributed in platoons among the different units in the line.
Under the unusually trying conditions of weather and shelling, which the Rifle Brigade considered the worst experienced
since October 1917, these Americans created a most favourable impression by their modesty cheerfulness and fine
morale. They represented the cream of American manhood,
and their temperament and enthusiasm recalled the fervour
of 1914-15, yet undulled by habitude and vicissitude.

On the afternoon of 7th August, in an interval of fair
weather, 2nd Lt. J. A. McL. Roy, M.C., 1st Rifles, with Rflmn.
A. H. Perry, rushed an enemy post in front of Shag, under
cover of a light trench mortar barrage, and brought in 2
prisoners. Roy then went out again and discovered 2 more
of the enemy endeavouring to mount a machine gun. These
also he took prisoners and brought to our trenches. He then
made a third journey to the enemy post to secure the gun.

By this time the enemy was apprised that something was amiss, and a German officer and 6 men were moving up a communication trench towards the post to investigate. They were driven off, however, by Perry's fire, and the trophy was safely carried back to our trenches. After darkness, a 4th Rifles' patrol of an officer and 4 men was suddenly engaged by 30 enemy and forced to retire. On arrival in our trenches the officer was found to be missing. Cpl. R. T. Crosbie and Rflmn. C. V. Murray immediately turned back to find him. He was discovered to be severely wounded and unconscious. On being lifted, he groaned loudly, thus giving the alarm to the Germans, who attacked our party. While Crosbie bandaged him, Murray held the enemy at bay with bombs, and finally the two carried back the officer to our lines, saving his life and preventing the enemy from securing identifications.

These continued successes achieved by the Division during July and early August had brought the fighting spirit of all arms to an extremely high pitch, as a single quotation from the 2nd Wellington diary will indicate. Their front line had been troubled by an enemy machine gun post. "Wellington West Coast Company planned to take the post to-morrow morning, but Ruahine attempted same task on the quiet this afternoon and failed, much to the disgust of West Coast Company, as it spoiled their plans. Men in excellent spirits."

While our infantry for the moment stayed their hand, the British heavy artillery, now augmented to an unprecedented scale, gave the enemy no respite. They bombarded his dumps about Puisieux and Achiet-le-Petit, and his roads between Pusieux Bucquoy and Serre, without intermission, and our infantry garrisons could not but listen in awed fascination to the terrible purr of great shells moving high overhead in an unbroken stream for a quarter or even half an hour at a time. That in itself was an overwhelming indication of the organised power of Britain.

The extent to which the enemy withdrawal from Rossignol Wood was premeditated is, in absence of German documents, naturally obscure. It appears certain, however, that it was principally due to or largely expedited by the New Zealanders' pressure. His troops had been pinned in a salient the retention of which, once its use for offensive operations was negatived, presented no advantages, and was made increasingly costly by our artillery fire and infantry aggressiveness. The subsequent withdrawal, however, towards Puisieux in August, now to be considered, was not due to local pressure. It was undertaken in accordance with the enemy's general policy which underlay similar movements elsewhere and which, forced on the German Command by the collapse of their offensive, was now made a matter of urgency by their defeat in the Battle of Amiens (8th-12th August). To economise man-power and build up reserves, Ludendorff, now definitely on the defensive, decided to straighten and shorten his line by withdrawing from such awkward salients as at Serre.

Already in the first week of August the enemy's outposts had begun to retire on the Lys salient about the Division's old rest areas at Vieux Berquin, and on the night 13th/14th August, after leaving booby-traps and filling dugouts with mustard gas and ineffectively mining them, he began to fall back from the network of trenches west of Serre. The right of the movement pivoted on Bucquoy, and here any forward movement on the part of our patrols would meet greater resistance. At the moment, the 2nd Brigade held the right subsector of the Divisional front in Jena Ford Nameless Hawk and Owl trenches, partly in the British, partly in the German defences of 1916. On their left the 1st Brigade occupied the trenches east of Rossignol Wood, carried on 24th July. In the right of the 2nd Brigade front the 1st Battalion, 317th Regiment, U.S.A., had relieved 1st Canterbury and been in turn succeeded by the 2nd Battalion of the American Regiment on the 11th. On its left was 1st Otago.[1] The 1st Brigade battalions from south to north were 2nd Wellington and 1st Auckland. Reports had already been received of demolitions in Albert and of abnormal movement about Bapaume, and a careful watch had been kept for evidence of withdrawal opposite the Divisional front. Patrols especially had been active by day and night to keep in touch with the enemy.

During the night 13th/14th August active patrolling was carried out as usual, and as late as 2 a.m. enemy posts were encountered. Normal machine gun and rifle fire continued. At 6 a.m., however, one of the enemy's forward posts opposite 1st Otago was found unoccupied. Further parties were at once sent out, and by 7.30 a.m. his withdrawal was established all along the front. Otago and the Americans immediately sent out patrols, following them up with stronger bodies, which before 8 a.m. had passed once for all the Chasseur Hedge and La Louvière Farm and penetrated Hair Alley.

1 Major J. Hargest, vice Lt.-Col. Charters, on leave.

Little opposition was encountered, and by 9 a.m. these battalions had crossed the old British military railway by Star Wood and had reached Box Wood and a trench line on high ground called Kaiser's Lane, some 600 yards north-west and parallel to the sunken road running from Serre to Puisieux. Here, shortly after 10 a.m., friendly greetings were waved them by an aeroplane observer. By noon American patrols were approaching Serre, and Otago scouts Puisieux. Some 20 prisoners were captured.

During the morning a policy had been laid down by the Division restraining undue impetuosity. The enemy was to be followed up by patrols supported by stronger bodies, but was not to be attacked. Stress was laid on the necessity of liaison with the troops on either flank and of a lateral as well as a rearward system of communication of intelligence. The news of the German withdrawal opposite the 2nd Brigade had been at once communicated both to the 42nd Division troops on the right and to the left New Zealand brigade, and the 37th Division on the north beyond them. In case of further advance brigade boundaries were defined, Puisieux being included in the area of the 2nd Brigade.

In the afternoon, sacrificing swiftness for sureness, the 42nd Division made at length a start and gained touch with the Americans' supporting troops by establishing patrols along the old British front line in Mark Luke and John Copses. On the left, however, the 1st Brigade had immediately pushed forward with the primary object of establishing a line from Box Wood to Fork Wood. By 11 a.m., after fine work by a bombing party under 2nd Lt. R. V. Hollis, which drove 3 German machine gun sections before them, 2nd Wellington had reached their objective, and overcoming some opposition gained touch with 1st Otago in Box Wood. The 1st Auckland patrols met stubborn resistance in the sap leading to the enemy's positions about Fork Wood, and it was manifest that considerable German forces still held the strong Crayfish System which ran from Puisieux northwards through Fork Wood and over Biez Wood Valley towards Bucquoy. Still nearer the pivot about Bucquoy, where the enemy's garrisons were not reduced, the 37th Division's patrols could make even less impression. Under covering mortar and machine gun fire Auckland by 3 p.m. had established themselves between German posts in part of Crayfish Trench south of Fork Wood, and had won a precarious footing on the fringe of the wood itself. The part of the trench between them and Wellington was, however, strongly held by the enemy. Wellington strove hard to co-operate by threatening the German rear from the south. They made their pressure felt and captured 8 prisoners. Touch was secured at 7 p.m. between the 2 battalions. At 9.30 p.m. after 2 minutes' bombardment by light mortars and artillery, Auckland patrols now went overland to the northern sector of Crayfish Trench, and 2nd Wellington moved up Crayfish Support. The position south of Fork Wood was thus rendered satisfactory. Throughout the afternoon enemy aeroplanes flew low over the 1st Brigade lines, and dropped flares over our patrols to direct the German artillery.

The 2nd Brigade, in the centre of the advance, was by this time well ahead, and under the threat of their movement our aeroplanes could see explosions behind Serre. While their main forces consolidated and reorganised in Kaiser's Lane, patrols had in the afternoon passed beyond Serre and had reached the Serre-Puisieux road and the outskirts of Puisieux, capturing some 30 prisoners. The enemy's policy was singularly undetermined. He shelled Puisieux about 6 p.m., while still occupied by his infantry, and his rearguards were still in force between Serre and Puisieux. 2nd Canterbury[1] came up from the rear to push through the leading battalions with fresh vigour. One of their companies made good the road at 6 p.m., but their numbers were unable to overcome the resistance eastwards. Two further companies were sent forward, and a few minutes before 8 p.m. these advanced in lines of sections at 100 yards' interval along the whole brigade front. Alarmed at their approach the enemy sent up S.O.S. signals, and a short but intensely heavy hostile barrage fell along the west side of the road just in front of the advancing sections. It lasted only 5 minutes. No casualties were caused, and the dust and smoke actually helped Canterbury by screening their advance. With covering fire from 8 trench mortars they crossed the trench system immediately east of the road, and beating down considerable opposition, reached a line a quarter of a mile east of Serre and of the road. Their left touched the outskirts of Puisieux, and patrols operated in front towards the next trench system, which ran along the Beaucourt-Puisieux road. Both flanks were refused. With comparatively slight casualties Canterbury had captured an officer and 35 prisoners, 3 machine guns and 1 minenwerfer.

1 Major N. R. Wilson, vice Lt.-Col. Stewart acting for General Young, on leave.

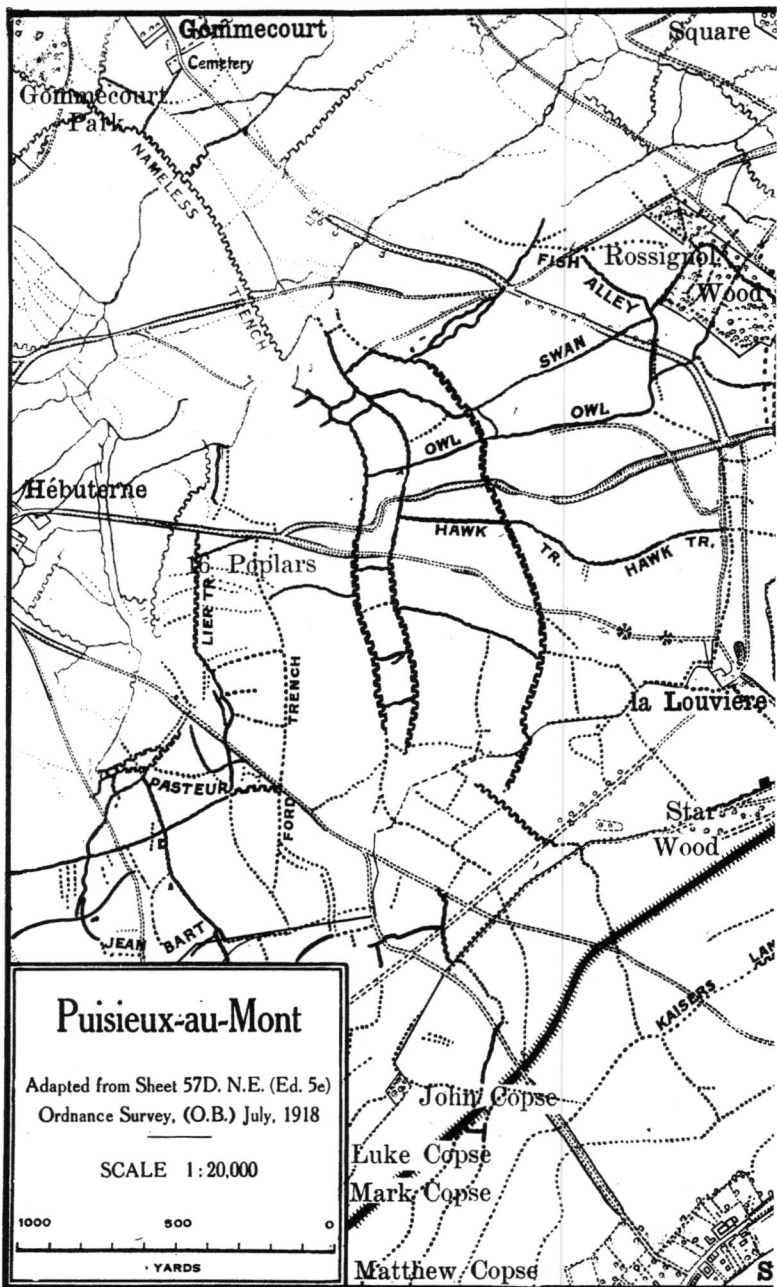

Puisieux-au-Mont

Adapted from Sheet 57D. N.E. (Ed. 5e)
Ordnance Survey, (O.B.) July, 1918

SCALE 1:20,000

1000 ⋅ 500 ⋅ 0
⋅ YARDS

Gommecourt

Square

Cemetery

Gommecourt Park

Fish

ALLEY

Rossignol Wood

NAMELESS TRENCH

SWAN

OWL

OWL

OWL

Hébuterne

HAWK

TR.

HAWK TR.

Poplars

LIER TR.

TRENCH

la Louvière

FORD

PASTEUR

JEAN BART

Star Wood

KAISER'S LANE

John Copse

Luke Copse

Mark Copse

Matthew Copse

S

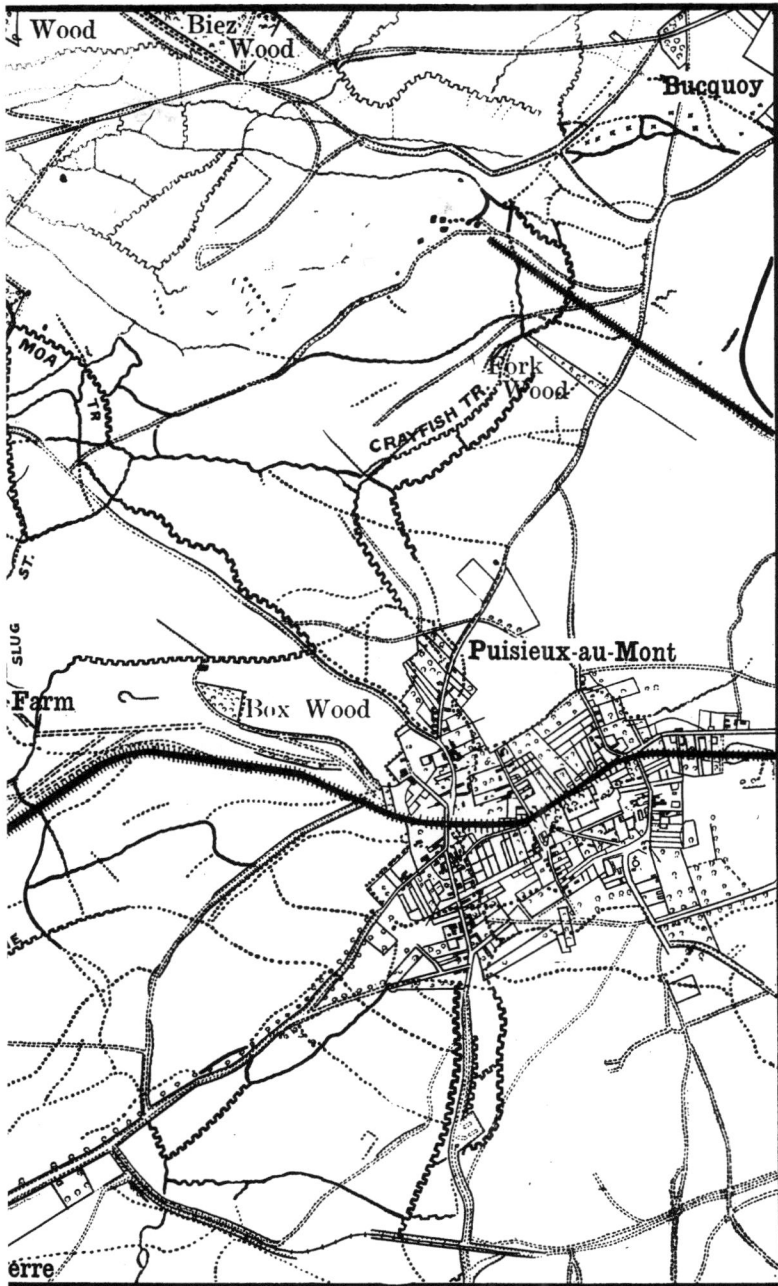

Wood

Biez
Wood

Bucquoy

MOA

TR

CRAYFISH TR.

Fork
Wood

ST.

SLUG

Puisieux-au-Mont

Farm

Box Wood

erre

Arrangements were made without delay to push forward telephone communication and establish advanced dumps of ammunition grenades and water. Throughout the day our artillery fired with noticeably good results on movement and machine guns reported by the forward observation officers and the infantry. During the afternoon and evening they moved advanced gun sections east of Hébuterne. The Engineers were putting the roads forward from Gommecourt and Hébuterne into a condition fit for wheeled traffic, and by the evening the Rossignol Wood road was in order.

The night (14th/15th August) passed uneventfully. The Americans and 1st Otago relieved 2nd Canterbury between Serre and Puisieux, and at dawn both New Zealand brigades struck afresh. 1st Auckland improved their position before Fork Wood, and south of the wood secured a footing in the Puisieux-Bucquoy road, capturing 4 prisoners. 2nd Wellington sent a small patrol to the northern outskirts of Puisieux, where some 40 enemy tried to surround it. The patrol leader was wounded but contrived to withdraw his men without further casualties. An attempt by 2 enemy companies to drive the Auckland posts from the Bucquoy road was indifferently managed and came to nothing. The resistance, however, on the 1st Brigade front and northwards made it clear that no movement beyond the excellent position already won could be effected without artillery support and a corresponding advance by the 37th Division.

The opposition offered the 2nd Brigade was less tenacious, and the Americans and 1st Otago pushed steadily forward. Otago carried the main German trench south of Puisieux on the Beaucourt road, holding practically the whole of the brigade front, while the Americans swung over the Serre ridge, passing through its ruins and forming a defensive flank facing south pending the arrival of the troops on the right. During the day these came forward, captured Pendant Copse, 1000 yards south-east of Serre, and established touch at the southern limit of the trench system on the Beaucourt road. By the evening the 2nd Brigade line lay along this road and the trench west of it, and thence round the western outskirts of Puisieux to join the 1st Brigade right at Box Wood.

2nd Otago then relieved the Americans on the right of the line. 1st Otago patrols scoured the western half of Puisieux without finding the enemy, but in view of the sharpness of the salient in which the 2nd Brigade position now lay, it was decided to make no further advance till the 1st Brigade came forward. During the night the 42nd Division established further posts on the road to Beaucourt. From midnight till 2 a.m. the enemy shelled empty Puisieux with 5.9-in. howitzers and then apparently reoccupied it. Possibly in connection with this movement, a hostile party of 2 officers and 15 men attempted to enter the trench south of Puisieux in the early hours of 16th August. They suffered lamentably under 1st Otago's rifle and Lewis gun fire, the whole party being killed except 6, who were taken prisoners. An hour afterwards the 1st Otago patrols entered Puisieux and found German posts now established about the church.

The situation of one of these posts was so far forward in the western outskirts as to invite capture. A platoon under 2nd Lt. R. E. Fyfe formed up in the trenches south of the village, and Lewis guns were placed in our new line west of the village to cover their advance with enfilade fire, and neutralise any machine guns in the enemy's post. At a given signal the Lewis guns opened, searching the slopes and ruins some 25 yards in front of Fyfe's advance, and the platoon rushed. About 20 of the enemy ran at once and were killed or wounded by the Lewis gun fire. Three light machine guns just managed to come into action, and the rest of their crews threw a handful of bombs, but such was the dash of the attack that Fyfe and his men reached the trench without a casualty. Twelve Germans were killed. The guns and 7 prisoners were captured. Otago posts were then placed through the western part of the village. The captured Germans said, rightly enough, that the impetus of the attack, combined with the tremendous volume of covering fire from the Lewis guns, was too much for them and that they did not have a chance to fight.

This brilliant little feat rounded off the highly satisfactory operations of the previous days. It won General Russell's congratulations and was commended by General Byng in the following message:—

"A very successful instance of initiative. In keeping with the fine record the New Zealand Division has maintained in this Army. Please congratulate the 1st Battalion Otago Regiment on the result."

On the 1st Brigade front in the same morning, 16th August, arrangements were completed with the 37th Division for a 4 hours' bombardment that afternoon by heavy artillery and Newton mortars on the enemy's wire and trenches between Fork Wood and the southern Barricades in Bucquoy.

At 6.15 p.m. the Royal Fusiliers closed in on the outskirts of Bucquoy, carried the northern limits of the continuation of Crayfish above Fork Wood and established posts astride the Puisieux-Bucquoy road opposite their front. At the same time 1st Auckland under cover of a light trench mortar barrage cleared Fork Wood and Crayfish as far as the Divisional boundary at the railway siding in the valley, and in conjunction with 2nd Wellington developed their line of outposts on the Bucquoy road. A section under Sergt. Judson in a dash at the enemy's machine gun positions captured without loss an officer, 16 men and 2 guns.[1] An illuminating commentary on the Division's activities during the last 5 weeks is afforded by the fact that forward sections of our batteries had been by now advanced beyond Gommecourt and our former front line to the neighbourhood of the 16 Poplars.

On 17th August the day passed quietly on the whole front, and the relief of 2nd Otago on the Serre ridge by the 3rd Battalion of the 317th Regiment, U.S.A., was completed without interruption. At dawn on the 18th, however, supported by a considerable weight of artillery a strong local attack was launched at the newly established 1st Otago posts in Puisieux. A detachment of "Sturm Truppen" was brought up specially from Douai, and the total number of the assaulting force exceeded 100. Reconnaissance, however, had been at fault or their orders indefinite. Otago had taken considerable trouble to disguise their posts in the ruins, and the attackers failing to notice them rushed beyond them. Halting in perplexity, they lined a bank which chanced to be directly enfiladed by our Lewis gun and rifle fire. There they furnished the easiest of targets, and the bodies of 2 officers and 30 men were later counted at the foot of the bank. An Otago mopping-up party going out afterwards captured an officer and 13 men, including some of the "assault" troops, and 3 machine guns. Otago's only casualties were due to the enemy shelling which killed 1 man and wounded another.

On 17th August the American detachments in the Divisional back area had been withdrawn to rejoin their units, and in the afternoon of the 18th the 3rd Battalion of the 317th Regiment, in the line, followed. In the evening the 2nd Brigade front was taken over by the Rifle Brigade.

It was not the New Zealanders' nature to suspend their progress at this stage. All looked forward to further

1 Judson was awarded the D.C.M. for his exploits on 24th and 25th July and the M.M. for his gallantry on this occasion. A still greater honour was in store for him, p. 447.

conquests. The artillery was steadily moving forward, and on the 18th there were 2 guns of the 2nd Battery in the valley about John Copse, and 2 howitzers of the 6th Battery by the quarries south of Rossignol Wood. The infantry patrols were aggressively feeling their way for fresh advances. Bigger movements, however, as yet unknown to them, were on foot. Already on 14th August the Divisional commanders in the Corps had received secret and personal warning that their troops would take part in large operations impending immediately along the front of the Third Army.

CHAPTER XI

THE BATTLE OF BAPAUME

By their ultimate failure in the Second Battle of the Marne the Germans had been definitely thrown back on the defensive. Instead of crushing the Allies, their utmost hope was now to secure a stalemate, in which they might find compensation in the East. Their immediate task was to rebuild shattered Divisions, accumulate fresh reserves to replace those expended in the spring, and shorten their line by the elimination of awkward salients. The High Command accordingly had begun to contemplate an orderly evacuation of the salients on the Lys and at Amiens. The Allies on their side had now left behind them that critical period between March and August when their efforts were confined mainly to the holding of the offensive and to the construction of railways and defences. The initiative had been once more restored to them. By the end of July the British Armies had again been welded into an effective striking weapon, and the arrival of reinforcements and the expansion of the American Armies enabled Foch in his turn to pass from the small local and isolated offensive actions of the summer to larger, though still limited, attacks, as a stage towards comprehensive and co-ordinated strategical operations on a grand scale.

On 23rd July, when the success of his counter-offensive on the Marne was assured, Foch convoked a conference of the French British and American Commanders. He asked them to prepare plans for local limited offensives on their respective fronts, with the general aim of freeing rail communications. Should the first semi-independent attacks prove successful, it was hoped that subsequently the French and Americans might converge on the Meuse railways, and the British move towards the St. Quentin-Cambrai line which protected the Maubeuge railway system, thus threatening directly the enemy's communications in Champagne and indirectly his communications in Flanders.

In selecting the stage for the British preliminary operation, Haig, after considering the possibility of action in the Lys salient, decided to strike east of Amiens with the object of

freeing the Paris railway. The British Fourth and the
French First Armies attacked on 8th August, and with the
co-operation of the French Third Army on the 9th not
merely effected the liberation of the Amiens-Paris railway,
but also deprived the Germans of the use of the Roye-Péronne
railway. In addition, the French on the Oise captured the
Lassigny massif, which, if the Germans proposed to fall back
on Bapaume, was the obvious southern pivot of their
shortened line. In view of the unexpected ease with which
these successes were achieved, the Allied Command definitely
made up their minds to increase the pressure. Ludendorff's
and Hindenburg's memoirs well reflect the consternation inspired in the minds of the German Staff by the issue of the
Battle of Amiens.

As a result of this operation, the first stage of our offensive, the enemy was faced with the possibility of having to
seek a line of resistance further east than Bapaume. He
was also urgently and instantly compelled to expedite his
withdrawal from his positions about Serre, where, as a result
of Rawlinson's advance south of the Somme, he was being
confined into a dangerous salient. He no doubt meditated an
orderly movement as in the early months of 1917. Foch and
Haig did not, however, mean to let him go so lightly, but
to force on him a disorganised retreat. Moreover, in the
Amiens area his troops had by this time been heavily reinforced, and there the wire and trenches of the old Somme
battlefield would make a continuance of our attack costly.
For these reasons, therefore, Haig broke off the battle on
the Fourth Army front and transferred it to the Bapaume
sector north of the river, with the object of turning the line
of the old Somme defences from the north and of preventing
the enemy's destruction of road and rail communications in
his withdrawal on Bapaume.

Several circumstances promised success to a rapid and
vigorous attack, and in particular here again, as at Amiens,
conditions favoured the tactical factor of surprise and the
mechanical factor of the tank, two basic principles in the
evolved science of the offensive. The enemy appeared to have
no premonition of an attack here on a large scale. The
ground, which he had yielded in 1917, was only to a small
degree shell-torn and could be traversed by tanks without
difficulty. Moreover, holding the high plateau about Bucquoy
and Gommecourt we now possessed not only commanding
observation but a position of deployment from which an

outflanking attack could be delivered to the south-east in place of the frontal assault of 1916.

The initial stage of the Third Army attack was fixed for 21st August. The objective aimed at for that day was the Albert-Arras railway. The 22nd would see the Fourth Army conform on the right by the capture of Albert and by the passage of the lower valley of the Ancre, while the Third Army brought forward troops and guns into position for the main blow. This would be delivered on 23rd August by the Third Army and by the left wing of the Fourth north of the Somme, while the remainder of the Fourth south of the river would advance to establish a protecting flank. Should success crown these operations, the whole of both Armies would press forward to exploit it. For this purpose, the 1st Cavalry Division was placed at General Byng's disposal. If all went well and the enemy were driven eastwards on the shelter of the Hindenburg Line, the First Army would at a later stage attack on the north with a view to turning it and compelling a further retreat.

General Byng's plans may be summarised as follows. The opening assault of the Third Army on 21st August would be made on a front of about 9 miles by the IV. and VI. Corps in the centre and on the left of his line, their right flank being covered by the left division of the V. Corps which held the right sector. The principal attack to be delivered on the 23rd in co-operation with the Fourth Army would be carried out by all 3 Corps.

The IV. Corps had at its disposal 6 brigades of heavy and 15 brigades of field artillery. The front was now held from right to left by the 42nd, the New Zealand, and the 37th Divisions. The 5th and the 63rd (Royal Naval) Divisions were in reserve. The IV. Corps plans for the 21st laid down 2 stages of the attack. First, the left Division, the 37th, would assault and capture the slopes east of Bucquoy and Ablainzeville. Thereafter, the reserve Divisions, the 5th Division on the right and the 63rd Division on the left, with a battalion of tanks, would pass through the 37th and push forward to the line Irles-Bihucourt beyond the Albert-Arras railway. In the day's programme the 42nd and New Zealand Divisions in the right and centre of the Corps line would co-operate by swinging forward the right flank. In the first stage, they would support the main attack by artillery and machine gun fire, and by advancing in con-formity with the 37th Division to a "Blue" Line on the eastern outskirts of Puisieux and the high ground southwards beyond Serre overlooking the Ancre. In the next stage, as the 5th and 63rd Divisions advanced on the railway, it was their task to conform by refusing the Corps flank north and north-west of Miraumont. In this second stage the New Zealand advance would be in a valley overlooked on both sides by high ground. On the north the slopes were to be carried frontally by the 5th Division. The southern spur, on whose crest was the Beauregard Dovecot,[1] long a ranging mark for our artillery, was to be carried obliquely by the 42nd Division. The New Zealand frontage would be gradually squeezed out by the south-eastern trend of the general move-ment towards Bapaume. General Russell was warned there-fore that his troops would probably be called upon to exploit the successes hoped for in the attack of the 23rd. The New Zealand officers accordingly lost no time in studying the map of the country east of the railway and north of Bapaume.

The inestimably valuable asset of surprise, which, generally impossible of achievement in siege operations, had been reintroduced by the British at Cambrai, November 1917, and developed by the Germans, had contributed in no small degree to Rawlinson's success on 8th August.[2] The utmost efforts were now made to achieve secrecy. The ostensible reason assigned for the concentration of troops in the Third Army area was the provision against a possible riposte in the Arras neighbourhood made with a view to easing the pressure south of Amiens. A much greater measure of reticence than usual was observed in giving information to subordinate commanders and the troops. The issue of bombs, the calling-in of packs and greatcoats, and other preparations were sufficient evidence of an impending "stunt," but it was not till the morning of the 21st when the roar of artillery, somewhat muffled by the fog, broke out in the east, that the men of the reserve brigades knew definitely that the battle in which they were to be engaged had commenced.

Similarly every possible precaution was taken to deceive the enemy. Operations were continued by Rawlinson south of the Somme, and on 18th August the Tenth French Army struck on the Aisne, securing results of tactical importance in themselves and attracting a further quota of Ludendorff's

1 Evacuated by the enemy together with Puisieux Miraumont and Serre in February 1917, see Map No 4.
2 Prior to their attack the Fourth Army issued an admirable memo under the title "Keep your mouth shut," which was by order pasted in the soldiers' pay-books. The elaborate feints then carried out, training operations behind the Lys front, etc., are well known.

rapidly waning reserves. Our reinforcing batteries were carefully concealed in woods and villages till the last possible moment, and were forbidden to fire a single round from their new positions. No increase of work on roads, no fresh hospital signs were permitted. Movement by the concentrated battalions was restricted during daylight to a minimum. Every advantage was taken of cover from observation from the air. Undue fire activity, however, against hostile aeroplanes was forbidden, as being likely to suggest the presence of an unusual number of troops in our intermediate and back areas.

The 5th Division was partly accommodated in the New Zealanders' area, and the 2nd Infantry Brigade, in reserve, moved further back to make room for them. Concentration proceeded smoothly under the cover of darkness. During the nights 18th/19th and 19th/20th August the 3rd Artillery Brigade moved north to cover the 37th Division, leaving the New Zealand front supported by the 1st and 2nd (Army) Brigades. At midnight 20th/21st August General Russell established advanced headquarters in the outskirts of Fonquevillers.

For the limited task which the Division was called upon to discharge at the outset in the valley east of Puisieux, the employment of 1 infantry brigade would be adequate, thus preserving the other 2 intact for exploitation after the attack on the 23rd. The Rifle Brigade, therefore, which had on 18th August relieved the 2nd Brigade in the right subsector, now after nightfall on the 19th took over in addition the 1st Brigade area north of Puisieux. On the evening of 20th August they held the whole Divisional line, on a frontage of some 2800 yards, with 3 companies of the 3rd Battalion south of Puisieux and behind the southern part of the village, and with 2 companies of the 4th Battalion northwards to the junction of the old railway siding with the Puisieux-Bucquoy road north-east of Fork Wood. These 2 battalions were ordered to carry out the attack. The 2nd Battalion was in support and the 1st in reserve. Battalions were compulsorily reduced to a strength of 640. In addition to the artillery, 6 medium trench mortars and the greater part of 2 machine gun companies were placed at General Hart's disposal.

The task of the Rifle Brigade was throughout closely co-ordinated with that of the 42nd Division, and with it dependent on the progress of the main blow on the left. At zero, 4.55 a.m. on 21st August, in conformity with the 37th Division on their left the Rifle Battalions would attack Puisieux and press eastwards to their sector of the Blue Line. As soon as the 5th Division secured an intermediate position (the Brown Line), which they were timed to reach shortly after 7.30 a.m., and from which they would launch their attack on Achiet-le-Petit, the Rifles were to advance about 1000 yards down the valley, refusing their right flank in conformity with the 42nd Division.   At a still later stage, shortly before 9 a.m., when it was estimated that the 5th Division would have effected the capture of Achiet-le-Petit, the 42nd Division would attack the Dovecot crest, and the Rifles' patrols make a further advance down the valley north of the Dovecot, for the purpose of establishing liaison and clearing the ground as far as the Ancre.   In this third movement, beginning at 9 a.m., the Rifles' work would have dwindled to filling a comparatively narrow gap, and the fire of the 2 New Zealand artillery brigades, as well as of the supporting machine guns, would be employed almost exclusively to assist the 42nd Division in carrying the high ground about the Dovecot.

General Hart's plans were that both his front line battalions should effect the first task, namely the capture of the Blue Line immediately east of Puisieux, and that, as his left battalion was squeezed out by the southward movement of the troops on the left, the 2 further steps necessary to clear the remaining triangular area should be carried out by the right battalion only.   1 section of light mortars was given to the left battalion and 2 to the right.   Anxiety was felt on the score of water.   There was a scarcity of wells in the forward area, and water was still being carried from Sailly Hébuterne and Fonquevillers.   The right battalion parties, therefore, detailed for the more distant objectives, were provided with an extra water bottle.   All ranks carried 24 hours' rations in addition to the iron ration.

The night was unusually quiet, and the men had their hot meal and rum at 3 a.m. in comfort.   By the hour of attack the sun had risen, but, as on 21st March and 8th August, there was a heavy blanket of fog which prevented observation beyond 100 yards and completely blinded aeroplanes.   The barrage on the Rifles' front provided by the 1st and 2nd (Army) Artillery Brigades came down at zero on an opening line in advance of our trenches, but stayed there 10 minutes in order to allow the barrage for the 37th Division, who had a longer distance to cover, to come abreast. It then advanced by lifts of 100 yards every 4 minutes. Half the ammunition was the deadly 106 non-delay fuse, and extensive use was made of smoke. The barrage fell with greater intensity on the trench elements east of Puisieux, and here especially the Newton mortars co-operated. Five minutes after it opened, the assaulting troops crept up to its edge and advanced on both sides of Puisieux and just inside the outskirts.

The surprise so studiously aimed at was completely realised. The enemy's artillery was particularly inactive, and after the development of the attack the fog masked his machine guns. On reaching the eastern side of the village the inner flank companies of the 2 Rifle battalions extended to meet each other, and specially detailed parties cleared it up, taking over 80 prisoners. The left company of the 4th Rifles had some fighting on the eastern outskirts, where a Lewis gun section under Cpl. N. C. Neilson captured 2 machine gun positions with guns and a dozen gunners. In and about the village the 4th Rifles with insignificant losses[1] captured in all over 100 prisoners with 12 machine guns and 3 mortars.

On their right the 3rd Rifles moved some few minutes later, as the 42nd Division's plans necessitated, with a platoon specially earmarked for assistance in carrying a 140-metre contour hill on the southern slope. In the open valley south of Puisieux the right company encountered light machine gun fire when approaching the shell-damaged road that here formed the Blue Line, but covered by the fog was able to rush the guns before they could be effectively used. They captured 4 guns, killing the crews. From immediately in front, however, beyond the objective there came now fairly heavy fire which it was essential to silence without delay. On this point of resistance they pushed forward. They found it to lie in another damaged sunken road a further 100 yards ahead, and here about 6 a.m. they captured a fifth gun, the bulk of its crew succeeding in withdrawing under the fog. Patrols were sent out 150 yards and connected up their positions in the shellholes. The centre company captured 3 light machine guns and 15 prisoners. The majority of the prisoners fell to Rflmn. C. W. Batty and J. Lowe. These 2 men, with a third companion who was killed, noticing that a strong machine gun post was holding up a portion of the advance, dashed forward to rush it. Bombing the post, they followed up their bombs and captured the machine guns

---

[1] 17 other ranks wounded, 3 of whom remained with the Bn.

and the garrison of an officer and 10 other ranks. Thus by 6 a.m. Puisieux was taken, and the 2 battalions were established on and beyond the first objective. A section of our machine guns at once came forward to the vicinity of the Blue Line to open fire on the southern spurs of the valley, which from now on were also harassed by field artillery. At 7.30 a.m. our artillery fire on the New Zealand front was stopped in order to give free scope to the Rifles' patrols.

Before this time, however, the remaining company of the 3rd Battalion had crossed the Blue Line to establish touch with the 5th Division, whose right was known to have passed through the 4th Battalion, but whose Verey signals on the Brown Line it would be impossible to see in the fog. 500 yards eastwards of the first objective a temporary line was formed. Patrols were sent forward and gained touch about 8 a.m. with the 5th Division. The advance was then resumed. 6 machine guns and 33 prisoners were captured from machine gun nests. Owing to the fog, which also impeded operations elsewhere, there appears to have been a certain amount of natural confusion in the valley. Rflmn. A. Dalzell, who was detailed to establish liaison with a flank, found that the area between his unit and the next was still in enemy possession. Single-handed he bombed a number of dugouts and captured 5 prisoners. He also located a machine gun in action, and taking 3 men with him he rushed the post and captured the gun. An artillery forward observation officer, 2nd Lt. R. M. Blackwell, M.M., took 15 lost German prisoners. Another, 2nd Lt. W. N. Sievers, with his telephonist, captured 7 prisoners, and with a handful of infantry appears actually to have passed behind the German outposts and reached the vicinity of the Dovecot. Sievers located a large enemy force massing for attack and without delay brought artillery fire to bear on them, which dispersed them. In the fog the left platoons of the Rifles overran the second objective. About 10.30 a.m. the fog cleared, and the riflemen found that they were ahead of the flank troops and on a bare spur immediately overlooking the railway. The position offered no cover from the intense fire of the machine guns about the Ancre. They therefore fell back and occupied a line nearly a mile beyond Puisieux, but somewhat in rear of their objective, where they prolonged and refused the 5th Division's flank. The right platoons, who in the fog had moved somewhat independently, had made less rapid progress in conformity with the 42nd Division's advance along the spur to the

A BATTERY MOVING THROUGH ACHIET-LE-PETIT

GRÉVILLERS CHURCH

SERGT. S. FORSYTH, V.C.   [Photo Swaine

2ND LIEUT. R. S. JUDSON, V.C., D.C.M., M.M.

south. By noon they were connected with the 2 left platoons, whose line they continued across the valley.

The right flank of the 5th Division was meeting trouble in approaching their final objective, and the Rifles' platoons for the moment combined consolidation with vigorous patrolling. Towards evening the New Zealand line was further advanced and strengthened by a platoon from one of the companies in rear. Patrols were pushed out to the railway in the Ancre valley and the whole of the ground was cleared. During the day the 3rd Battalion had captured over 100 prisoners, with several machine guns, and the total bag of the brigade was 8 officers and 227 other ranks. On the right the 42nd Division also reached their objective and captured, after considerable fighting, the important ground at the Beauregard Dovecot.

In the afternoon (21st August) the 2nd (Army) Artillery Brigade moved to the western edges of Puisieux to deal with enemy concentration near Loupart Wood, and during the night, 21st/22nd August, the 1st and 3rd Artillery Brigades came up to the south-eastern and north-eastern outskirts of Puisieux respectively. The 3rd Brigade passed under the orders of the 42nd Division, and the 1st and 2nd (Army) Brigades were held in readiness to support either the 5th or 42nd Division on the following day.

In the early morning of 22nd August heavy machine gun fire developed on the 3rd Rifles' patrols, and about 5 a.m. the enemy launched with a fresh Division, the 52nd, a strong counter-attack from Miraumont on the Dovecot. It was accompanied by heavy shelling on the New Zealand batteries, which sustained several casualties. The troops on the right were forced back, and the enemy came forward quickly to occupy the crest trenches about the Dovecot. These overlooked our positions. The right Rifles' platoon formed a defensive flank along the lower slopes. L.-Cpl. R. Milne rushed forward 150 yards to the crest with his Lewis gun team and opened fire on a flanking party of Germans, killing 12, wounding about 8, and taking 5 prisoners and 4 machine guns. This quick decision and vigorous action saved the commanding positions in our immediate vicinity and freed us from any danger in front. Worse was yet to befall the Germans, for the light was now clearing, and their assaulting waves came under the intense fire of our machine guns, which inflicted very heavy losses. It was estimated that 400 were killed. Some 300, in seeking to avoid the fire, were driven into the arms of and made prisoners by the 5th Division. The main German attack, however, recovered the Dovecot and the important trench along the slopes eastwards down to the railway, thus preventing the New Zealand batteries moving forward down the valley.

Shortly after 10.30 a.m. these were ordered to put down a 2 hours' bombardment on the Dovecot. Following upon this the remaining 3 platoons of the 3rd Rifles' support company, which had provided 1 platoon for strengthening the line on the previous evening, now passed through our screen of posts to establish a more advanced outpost line. This they formed on the lower slopes overlooking the railway, beyond the point where their comrades had been surprised when the fog cleared on the morning of the 21st. Patrols of the 42nd Division similarly reoccupied the Dovecot and its spur, but their hold was insecure, and the enemy again wrested it from them. The weather was very hot. It was the warmest day of the year yet experienced, and the anticipated difficulties with the water supply in the Puisieux area were fully realised.

By the evening of 22nd August, although Irles and Bihucourt and the railway itself along no inconsiderable sector of the front still remained in enemy possession, the IV. Corps none the less was in a satisfactory position to play its part in the great attack planned for the morning of the 23rd. For this operation General Harper assigned the following roles to his Divisions. The 37th Division in the north, relieving the 63rd, would capture Bihucourt, the 5th Division would seize Irles, and the New Zealand and 42nd Divisions prolong and protect their right flank. A preliminary operation would be carried out during the night by the 42nd Division with the New Zealanders' co-operation, for the purpose of recapturing the Dovecot and denying the enemy all ground opposite our right flank west of the railway in the Ancre valley. In the main attack in the forenoon the New Zealand Division would co-operate in the advance of the 5th and 37th Divisions by stepping outside the apex of the triangle originally assigned to it, and by clearing and occupying the branch of the Ancre valley which lies north of Miraumont.

For these new operations the 1st Rifles[1] were brought into the line on the evening of 22nd August to relieve the 3rd[2]. In the preliminary attack the front affected was some 500

---

1   Major N. F. Shepherd, vice Lt.-Col. Austin, "B" Teams.
2   Since 20th August the 3rd Battalion had lost 3 officers and 13 other ranks killed, and 2 officers and 35 other ranks wounded.

yards on the lower slopes of the spur, and it was intended to use only 1 company. Late in the evening, however, the frontage was extended another 700 yards across the valley northwards to secure satisfactory touch with the 5th Division. The change of plan made it necessary to employ 2 companies. The New Zealand artillery were earmarked for the attack on the Dovecot, and the Rifles were supported by an artillery brigade of the 5th Division.

The night attack was made at 2.30 a.m. in bright moonlight, with the air full of the hum of our bombing aeroplanes. On the exposed slopes it was vital that the assembly of our troops should not be detected. No talking or smoking was allowed, and the 2 companies stole quietly to their assembly position. They reached it in good time, and at zero, under an extremely accurate barrage, pushed forward up the slopes and down the valley towards the railway. Our machine guns enfiladed the long trench running from west to east along the slopes under the Dovecot. Little opposition was encountered, and the companies reached their objectives successfully, the left resting some 400 yards short of the railway and the right swinging back its flank to conform with the 42nd Division, who retook the Dovecot.

On the cessation of the barrage, hostile machine gun fire at once broke out from beyond the railway, and the left company suffered. Our machine guns and light trench mortars were sent forward to strengthen the line. At 9.20 a.m. a weak enemy force counter-attacked the right company in a series of small enterprises lasting over an hour and a half. L.-Cpl. G. Hunter, who was in a shellhole in advance of our line, stood his ground and killed 4 of the enemy, though he had to expose himself to secure aim. The Germans brought heavy machine gun fire to bear on the post. Hunter was slightly wounded 3 times, but still held his ground. Elsewhere the enemy were repelled without much difficulty, and when they withdrew were caught in the barrage which supported our further movement at 11 a.m. From then the same 2 companies of the 1st Rifles again advanced on a front of 1000 yards in conformity with the 5th Division on the left, to capture the whole of the valley north of Miraumont, including the railway. For this operation the 1st and 3rd Artillery Brigades had been placed at the disposal of the 5th Division, and the 1st Rifles' barrage was now provided by the 2nd (Army) Brigade. The opening barrage line was fixed with precision, thanks to an admirably rapid and

31

accurate reconnaissance carried out by the battalion scout sergeant, C. R. Wilson, who under continual fire from enemy machine guns and snipers located the exact position of all the new advanced posts on the forward slopes and in the valley.

Each company advanced with 2 platoons. The right company followed the barrage closely. The left pivoted on the right, coming up in echelon and conforming with the movements of the 5th Division. A good deal of opposition was encountered by both companies, especially from the machine guns on the terraced and still wooded slopes of the ridge behind which lay Irles, but all objectives were seized and the line pushed 500 yards forward. The right company secured 20, the left company over 70 prisoners with a heavy mortar and 7 machine guns. A few enemy machine gun nests, though surrounded, held out until nearly dark. Patrols scoured the front and maintained touch with the 5th Division. In the day's fighting the 1st Rifles had an officer and 6 men killed, and 4 officers and 39 men wounded. As a result of this operation, the line of the 42nd and New Zealand Divisions, pivoting on the Dovecot, swung round to face southwards, and a defensive right flank was formed north of Miraumont for the further advance of the Corps. In the evening the 42nd Division extended their front northwards, taking over the New Zealanders' area. The whole Rifle Brigade moved back north of Puisieux and concentrated the next morning east of Bucquoy. Their part in the battle was for the moment over.

During the afternoon, 23rd August, the 2nd (Army) Artillery Brigade moved into the valley east of Puisieux, and in the evening, when German observation from Miraumont was obscured, the other brigades also pushed forward. The Corps heavy artillery had begun systematically to bombard Bapaume and Thilloy. The fire of the enemy's batteries, extremely active during the morning, had diminished considerably, and many of his guns had been withdrawn east of Bapaume.

For the grand attack had won no inconsiderable success. The 37th Division held all but the Factory in Bihucourt, and the 5th Division had reached the western outskirts of Irles. Though in the afternoon the 42nd Division had failed to occupy Miraumont and the high ground between Miraumont and Pys, substantial progress had been achieved by the Fourth Army and by the other Corps of the Third. The attack was now astride the Arras Road and menacing Bapaume from the north-west. The whole south-easterly direction of the movement, which took the heavily wired and strong Le Transloy-Loupart system[1] and the other Bapaume defence systems from the flank, facilitated exploitation, and no effort was spared to take advantage of the enemy's disorganisation. Ludendorff's methods in March had widened tactical conceptions, and the lessons then taught were not forgotten. During the day the Commander-in-Chief issued a special message that all ranks must act with the greatest boldness. Divisions were to be given distant objectives which each must reach independently of its neighbour, even if for the time being its flanks were exposed. Reinforcements were to be directed on points where troops were gaining ground and not where they were checked.

The Corps plans for further advance were drawn up and communicated as rapidly as possible. The 5th Division had sent forward a brigade with the object of capturing Loupart Wood and Grévillers, but these troops had met strong resistance, and their position was obscure. The moment was ripe to throw in the New Zealanders. The 5th Division was ordered to form a defensive flank on the right from Irles to Loupart Wood. On the left the 37th was instructed to capture Biefvillers. In the centre the New Zealand Division were to complete the capture of Loupart Wood, seize Grévillers, and pass on towards Bapaume.[2]

This New Zealand attack would be divided into 2 stages. One infantry brigade, supported by 2 mobile field artillery brigades and tanks, would safeguard the right flank by capturing Loupart Wood and Grévillers and advancing 500 yards beyond. A second infantry brigade following in support would push through the first objective to Bapaume and the high ground east of it, its advance covered by 1 mobile field artillery brigade and tanks. Bapaume was believed to be held lightly.

From the outset of the battle the 1st and 2nd New Zealand Infantry Brigades had been held in readiness to exploit success on any part of the Corps front, and from the afternoon of 23rd August they had been prepared to move at an hour's notice. The 2 brigades now marched forward to concentration areas east and south-east of Bucquoy respectively. They were in the lightest fighting order. Valises greatcoats and blankets had been dumped. Brigade pack-trains accompanied the troops, and transport was brought up

---

1 For description see Haig's Despatch, 19th June 1917, para. 2.
2 Grévillers and Loupart Wood were occupied by the British in the middle of March, Bapaume on 17th March, during the German retreat in 1917.

to be utilised to the fullest extent. Some discomfort was caused by gas shelling and by a few rounds fired by high-velocity guns, but otherwise the concentration area was quiet. Rain, however, began to fall about 10 p.m. Between 11 p.m. and midnight 23rd/24th August General Russell, now in advanced headquarters between Bucquoy and Achiet-le-Petit, dictated his orders to Generals Melvill and Young. The 1st Brigade would carry out the initial task, and the 2nd Brigade following them at 2 hours' interval was to pass through them on Bapaume. Battalion commanders awaited the brigadiers' return at the respective brigade headquarters and received the plans of the attack shortly after midnight.

A number of heavy tanks and of the lighter and speedier "whippets" would assist each brigade. A troop of Scots Greys was also attached for duty to the Brigade Head-quarters. Late in the evening orders had been issued for the 1st and 3rd Artillery Brigades (the latter now returning from the 42nd Division to General Napier Johnston's control) to move northwards from the Puisieux valley to a valley south-west of Achiet-le-Petit by 3 a.m. Further to support the attack an English (Army) brigade was attached to the Division. It and the 1st Artillery Brigade were placed at General Melvill's disposal, the 2nd (Army) Brigade at General Young's, and the 3rd kept in Divisional reserve in a position of readiness. It was hoped that it would be possible to provide a barrage which, owing to uncertainty as to the position of the advanced 5th Division brigade, would fall on the far sides of the wood and village, but it was still indefinite as to whether the guns could be in position in time.

At 1.30 a.m. (24th August) the 1st Infantry Brigade began to move forward skirting the north edge of Achiet-le-Petit to its assembly area on a road half a mile east of the Albert-Arras railway south of Achiet-le-Grand. Precise information as to the exact location of the front line could not be obtained, and the North Island battalions took the precaution of throwing out advanced guards and screens of scouts. Bihucourt was being shelled with some severity, but for the most part hostile artillery was inactive. A nervous enemy post south of Bihucourt was putting up many flares. The sky was overcast, however, and the waning moon gave little light, so that the assembly was completed without detection. On the way the battalions were notified that it was now possible to put down a barrage which would lift 200 yards every 8 minutes.

The 1st Brigade placed 1st Wellington[1] on the right and 2nd Auckland on the left of its line, with 2nd Wellington in support to cover the junction between the leading battalions, and 1st Auckland in reserve. 8 large tanks were available to assist the attack, 6 going to Loupart Wood, and 2 to Grévillers. Whippets were to assist in the northern outskirts of the village. A section of machine guns was given to each attacking battalion, while the remainder would be used to provide direct overhead fire. The enemy defence relied on a few light guns and field mortars with numerous machine gun posts scattered in well-concealed positions.

The attack began at 4.15 a.m. It was still dark. It had in the end been found impossible to provide artillery support, and the machine gun fire in itself did not suffice to alarm the enemy. Some considerable distance was covered before he realised that an assault was in progress, and then the darkness and morning mist protected his assailants who crossed the open ground with light loss. No reconnaissance had been possible, but the leading troops moved straight on their objectives. The 2 attacking companies of 1st Wellington passed beyond the screen of the 5th Division in Loupart Wood, and were enormously helped by gaining contact with the enemy and penetrating beyond his first machine guns in the darkness. As soon, however, as the day broke, the improved visibility, while making the going easier, favoured the defence. The concealed machine guns were troublesome, and the large closely-set trees proved an impassable obstacle to the tanks, who arrived late. Very shortly Wellington were in difficulties. Sergt. H. H. Thomason and Cpl. J. R. Blake each led a section of bombers against a machine gun, killing the crew and capturing the gun. Sergt. W. Murray with a runner put a third out of action, killing the crew of 5. Others were similarly destroyed, and the advance resumed only to be checked by a fresh series of posts. The reserve company and later a company from 2nd Wellington also had to be called on. Two extra tanks were sent forward. By 8.30 a.m. tanks and cavalry patrols reported that the wood was surrounded, but it was not till noon that it was completely cleared. 1st Wellington then established posts on its southern and eastern edges with a company in support in the open ground behind it. Several prisoners had been captured, including 26 who with a machine gun fell to 2nd Lt. G. A. Barton's

1 Major (Temp. Lt.-Col.) W. F. Narbey, vice Lt.-Col. Holderness, sick.

platoon. Our casualties had not so far been severe. 1st
Wellington had lost an officer and 17 other ranks killed and 2
officers and 44 other ranks wounded. But the fact that they
had taken 8 hours to accomplish but a part of their mission,
showed clearly the difficulty with which the advance would
have to contend in attacking machine gun nests without an
artillery barrage.

The 2 leading companies of 2nd Auckland at first met
little opposition. The enemy post on the left flank, which
had been so active in firing flares, opened machine gun fire
and threatened to cause delay. The left platoon was hung
up, the remainder of the line continued to advance, and a
section of the supporting company worked round the post
from the rear and charged it with cold steel. Thereupon the
Germans hastily surrendered. Two 77-mm. guns were
captured and several machine guns surprised with their crews.
The western outskirts of Grévillers were reached with few
casualties. At the borders of the village the right front company swung out round either side, and the support company
passing between proceeded to mop it up. A 2nd Wellington
company also coming forward swept in through the surrounding plantations and cleared the southern part. By 7 a.m. the
village was definitely ours. The German garrison was taken
completely by surprise, and some even were interrupted at
breakfast. But if the village itself proved easy to capture,
considerable difficulty was to be experienced on the flanks.
On the north the 37th Division had made a fine advance
towards Sapignies, but its right had met trouble on the outskirts of Bihucourt, at the Factory and in a triangle of
railways, and had been unable to push down the road towards
Biefvillers. On this road were old British cantonments from
which a heavy fire was directed on the left Auckland company
as soon as it passed over the rise and came under observation.
With the assistance of tanks, however, the huts were cleared,
and with this footing on the road a further 2nd Wellington
company crossed it and pushed on to the high ground beyond
it to the north. This movement considerably relieved
apprehension about the left pending the arrival of the 2nd
Brigade. Posts were accordingly pushed forward for 500
yards east of Grévillers in the direction of Avesnes-les-
Bapaume.

On the south fringe of Grévillers, however, the investing
troops of 2nd Auckland had a sharp brush with enemy
machine guns and were also greatly impeded by the inability

of 1st Wellington to overcome the resistance about Loupart
Wood.   South of the wood and of the village itself lay the
Grévillers sector of the very formidable Le Transloy-Loupart
system which, forming part of the Bapaume defences, crossed
the Albert Road and then turned north-west past Achiet-Le-
Petit to Bucquoy.   At this point the trenches ran west and
faced the 1st Brigade.   They were strongly held by machine
guns and infantry, and fire from them and from advanced
posts in pits and sunken roads was intense.   It was therefore
with relief that the Auckland men saw the approach of 2
tanks with whose co-operation they might hope to beat down
the enemy resistance.

Conspicuously fine work had already in the course of the
2nd Auckland advance been done by Sergeant Samuel Forsyth,
New Zealand Engineers, who was attached in accordance with
the prevailing custom to an infantry battalion on probation
for a commission.   His magnificent efforts now to overcome
the check were to win him a Victoria Cross.   The official
record runs as follows:—

"On nearing the objective his company came under
heavy machine gun fire.   Through Sergt. Forsyth's dashing
leadership and total disregard of danger, three machine
gun positions were rushed and the crews taken prisoners
before they could inflict many casualties on our troops.

During subsequent advance his company came under
heavy fire from several machine guns, two of which he
located by a daring reconnaissance.   In his endeavour to
gain support from a tank he was wounded, but after
having his wound bandaged, he again got in touch with
the tank, which in the face of very heavy fire from machine
guns and anti-tank guns he endeavoured to lead with
magnificent coolness to a favourable position.   The tank,
however, was put out of action.

Sergt. Forsyth then organised the tank crew and
several of his men into a section and led them to a
position where the machine guns could be outflanked.
Always under heavy fire, he directed them into positions
which brought about a retirement of the enemy machine
guns and enabled the advance to continue.   This gallant
n.c.o. was at that moment killed by a sniper.

From the commencement of the attack until the time of
his death, Sergt. Forsyth's courage and coolness, combined
with great power of initiative, proved an invaluable
incentive to all who were with him, and he undoubtedly

saved many casualties among his comrades.''

The other tank was also destroyed, but thanks largely to Forsyth's heroism the high ground about the village passed securely into our possession. Making every use of cover the right Auckland company pushed forward. Sergt. O. E. Burton, M.M., although wounded, led his platoon with undiminished dash and with his men captured 6 machine guns. By 8 a.m. the company had worked well over the intervening space towards the wood. Their right reached a Crucifix on a sunken road running to Warlencourt-Eaucourt and secured touch with 1st Wellington. In acting as emergency runner and in rescuing wounded, an Auckland cook, Pte. R. Fairweather, showed brilliant qualities of courage and energy. Further advance was held up by large numbers of snipers and by machine guns, which from concealed emplacements in the scrub as well as in the trenches swept the open ground and the sunken road. Shortly before 9 a.m. General Melvill, not yet cognisant of the difficulties, instructed the 2 battalions to advance south of the wood beyond the original objective, and capture the Le Transloy-Loupart trenches. Attempts at frontal assault, however, proved vain, and we were not yet in a position to outflank it.

The capture of Grévillers yielded the first of those hauls of prisoners guns and war material, which were to characterise the advance of the next 3 months. 2nd Auckland, in the course of the day, took some 350[1] prisoners, and with the 2nd Wellington company captured in the village two 77-mm. guns, 3 dozen machine guns, 6 mortars, 3 G.S. wagons, a horse with saddle and bridle, and in addition three 8-in. howitzers, from each of which the breach had been removed. The skill and resolution shown by 2nd Auckland during this 2000 yards' advance were thus satisfactorily rewarded.

General Young's battalions had moved forward shortly after 4 a.m. across the railway south-east of Achiet-le-Petit. Here they halted in readiness to follow the 1st Brigade, as soon as Loupart Wood and Grévillers were captured, with a view to fulfilling their task on the high ground beyond Bapaume in touch with the VI. Corps troops on the north. By 8 a.m. it was obvious that the progress of the 1st Brigade as of the 37th Division was meeting greater obstacles than had been anticipated. In view of this check General Young had to consider whether he should maintain his brigade intact for their original purpose or use it to help the hard-pressed

1   A large number of these were sent to the 37th Divisional Cage.

BAPAUME

ARTILLERY MOVING FORWARD

A BATTERY CROSSING THE ARRAS-ALBERT RAILWAY

1st Brigade. Reluctantly but undoubtedly soundly, as subsequent events proved, he decided that he must now throw it
into the struggle, partly to protect the exposed left flank at
Grévillers by the capture of Biefvillers for the 37th Division,
and partly to increase the pressure on the resolute German
defence in front of Bapaume. At 8.30 a.m. therefore he
ordered the 2nd Brigade to move forward, clear Biefvillers
and continue the advance on Bapaume. Certain changes in
dispositions made necessary by the development of the action
were effected at the last moment. The leading troops were
now 2nd Otago[1] on the right and 2nd Canterbury[2] on the left.
They were accompanied by 5 large tanks and 10 whippets.
Little opposition was met till they reached Grévillers and
Biefvillers. At Grévillers the 3 attacking companies of 2nd
Otago deployed from artillery formation into extended order.
As soon as the lines were clear of the village, the machine gun
fire from the Le Transloy-Loupart trenches in front by the
Albert Road, which had checked the 1st Brigade, caused heavy
casualties. The tanks were unable to render much assistance,
being damaged by hostile fire or getting into difficulties. C.S.M.
W. Deuchrass noticed one in trouble and heard the crew inside
calling for help. The tank was drawing heavy fire from
artillery and from anti-tank and machine guns, but Deuchrass
went forward and liberated the imprisoned inmates by
bursting the door open with a crowbar. The front line being
thus arrested, the reserve Otago company was sent forward,
and thereupon the reinforced troops occupied a considerable
stretch of the switch system, which ran from the Le Transloy-
Loupart line north-westwards between Grévillers and Biefvillers towards Bihucourt and which by the direction of our
attack was being taken from the flank. A patrol pushed down
these trenches for 1000 yards towards the Albert Road but
was resisted with excessive stubbornness. Elsewhere by 10
a.m. Otago's progress was definitely checked. They had lost
3 officers and 15 men killed and 3 officers and 90 men wounded.

On the left of the 2nd Brigade attack, the 2nd Canterbury
advance was to a lesser degree exposed to fire from organised
trench defences, and at first the 3 attacking companies progressed smoothly and rapidly. They were supported by 3
sections of tanks. Their first objective was to clear Biefvillers. This proved unexpectedly easy, for as soon as the

1 Lt.-Col. W. S. Pennycook, vice Lt.-Col. McClymont proceeding to the 3rd
(Reserve) Battalion, vice Lt.-Col. Smith appointed 2nd in Command of the 4th
(Reserve) Brigade, Sling Camp.
2 Major Wilson, vice Lt.-Col. Stewart, on leave.

German became aware of the threatening envelopment, he evacuated the village. Canterbury occupied it shortly after 9 a.m., followed by some elements of 2nd Auckland and 2nd Wellington. Only an isolated company of 37th Division troops was yet up on the immediate left, and Canterbury consequently swung their flank well round north of Biefvillers till the 37th Division should be in stronger force. The remainder of the battalion, in face of an increasing volume of machine gun fire, pressed forward in the direction of Bapaume.

As soon, however, as the patrols and tanks appeared on the open crest line south-east of Biefvillers, an intense artillery barrage was put down by the Germans. Four of the tanks were destroyed almost immediately, and the right company was raked by the machine guns which had checked the 1st Brigade and were now harassing 2nd Otago. On the left, east of the village, 2nd Canterbury succeeded in making good the falling slopes, broken by steep banks, chalk pits and dugouts, and their patrols reached the sunken road running north from Avesnes-les-Bapaume. Already high-explosive shells were falling thickly into Biefvillers, and some few shells also on the slopes in front. Nearing the sunken road, the patrols encountered storms of machine gun fire. Movement now attracted an instant stream of bullets, and the duties of the n.c.o.s and privates commanding sections demanded qualities of stern resolution. One instance may serve to show how the call was answered. Pte. W. C. Adams, after his section commander was killed, took command and handled his men confidently with equal skill and determination, eventually establishing a post close to the enemy's line. The Germans made repeated attempts to isolate it, but were consistently thwarted.

During the forenoon our field artillery had come into position east of the railway south of Achiet-le-Grand. Forward observation officers had located the enemy posts, and our batteries shelled them fiercely. Our own machine guns actively co-operated, but the deep defence zone of the enemy on the eastern edges of Avesnes-les-Bapaume and towards the Albert Road was extremely formidable. It was only with the utmost exertion and at the cost of fairly heavy casualties that by noon Canterbury patrols and some Otago men also reached Avesnes-les-Bapaume. In their advance 2nd Canterbury captured 41 prisoners. These belonged to the 44th Reserve Division, who were fresh from reserve and had been thrown into the line to defend Bapaume and relieve the shattered remnants of the 52nd, 111th, 5th Bavarian, 2nd Guards, and other exhausted Divisions.

With the movement on the flanks checked, the forward posts of 2nd Otago and 2nd Canterbury about Avesnes were in a most exposed situation. The enemy presently began to filter round their flanks in a near bend of the sunken road and through the buildings. Colonel Pennycook came forward very gallantly with his adjutant to make a personal reconnaissance with a view to turning the enemy resistance. Both were, however, almost immediately killed by snipers. Two Otago Lewis gunners, L.-Cpl. A. Grant and Pte. C. Sims, the only remaining members of their crew, held out desperately, although outflanked, and inflicted severe losses on the enemy, falling back only when their ammunition was exhausted. Heavy enfilade fire had already forced the Canterbury posts on the road to withdraw somewhat uphill, and at 1 p.m. under cover of a bombardment and machine gun fire the enemy attacked the whole 2nd Brigade line in front of Biefvillers from the direction of Favreuil and the vacated road. Along the greater part of the front the attack was stopped by Lewis gun and rifle fire, but the enemy regained complete command of Avesnes, and a few prisoners remained in his hands. At 4 p.m. the situation was again "normal." Throughout the struggle particularly fine work had been done at this part of our line by a section of light trench mortars under 2nd Lt. C. O. Pratt.

In the afternoon a redistribution of the troops about the right flank was ordered by the Corps so as to strengthen the line for the further advance of the 2nd Brigade on Bapaume. It was intended that the 5th Division should take over Loupart Wood, and that the 1st New Zealand Brigade should "side-slip" eastwards to a front extending from the eastern edge of the wood to the Achiet-le-Grand—Bapaume railway. They were instructed also to make every effort to win the Le Transloy-Loupart trenches and the Albert Road. In face of intense machine gun and artillery fire about the Crucifix, the reorganisation itself proved impracticable during daylight. Nor did attempts of the 1st Brigade to secure better touch with the South Island battalions on their left achieve satisfactory results. All the enemy trenches south of Grévillers between the Crucifix and the Albert Road were full of men, and considerable movement seemed to presage a counterattack. Artillery support was asked and given, and no enemy action developed.

The 63rd Division had meantime moved up to an advanced concentration area east of Achiet-le-Petit. In the afternoon they were ordered at short notice to pass through the 5th Division, who now held Irles, and attack Le Barque and Thilloy. The 1st Brigade was instructed to conform by a corresponding advance across the Albert Road west of Bapaume. Two companies of 2nd Wellington therefore moved forward to leap-frog through their sister battalion and 2nd Auckland. The 63rd Division attack was, however, cancelled by a subordinate commander less than half an hour before zero. Notification of the change of plan did not reach the 1st Brigade till the 2nd Wellington movement had started.[1] One company was warned in time by troops of the 63rd Division. The other captured a machine gun nest south-east of Grévillers on the new brigade boundary and were fortunate in not having become seriously involved when ordered to discontinue. The 1st Brigade positions, therefore, remained substantially unaltered. As soon as the protecting darkness permitted, it was arranged that 2nd Wellington and 1st Auckland should relieve the 2 forward battalions on the readjusted front. Prior to the relief, strong covering parties and patrols were sent forward, and in an audacious enterprise on the Le Transloy-Loupart trenches 1st Wellington captured 23 prisoners and 6 machine guns.

At the end of the day (24th August) the New Zealand outposts rested about 2½ miles north of the scene of the Division's fighting on the Somme 2 years previously. Half a dozen field guns, 3 heavy pieces, many machine guns and 400 prisoners had been taken. During the day the Fourth and Third Armies had made great progress. On the IV. Corps front the 42nd Division on the right had at length carried Miraumont and Pys, and on the left flank the 37th had advanced between Biefvillers and Sapignies. General Harper thanked his troops in the following message to his Divisional Commanders:—

"The Corps Commander wishes to convey to all ranks under your command his thanks for their work during the past three days and to congratulate them on their success, which could only have been attained by great fighting capacity and endurance."

In the evening orders were issued for the attack to be resumed next morning (25th August) along the whole of the

1 2nd Wellington Bn. Hdqrs. received notice of the cancellation half an hour after zero.

Corps front in conformity with the general advance. The 37th Division was instructed to carry the high ground towards Sapignies and to take over Biefvillers from the New Zealanders, thus releasing the whole force of the 2nd New Zealand Brigade for the thrust round the northern edge of Bapaume. From Bapaume 4 great highways run, 1 southwest to Albert, 1 south-east to Péronne, 1 eastwards towards Cambrai, and 1 northwards towards Arras. As a first objective the 2nd Brigade were to reach Avesnes and the near edge of the Monument Wood, on the Arras Road west of Favreuil. Some of our tanks, advancing well beyond the infantry, had operated here during the afternoon and had found the German line held strongly with machine guns. On the right the 1st Brigade were to co-operate in a renewed 63rd Division attack south of Bapaume. Provided that the preliminary operations proved successful, it was hoped to envelop Bapaume by passing beyond it on each flank and to establish the line Riencourt-les-Bapaume—Bancourt—Beugnâtre.

A full share of the burden of this further movement was laid on the 2nd Brigade north of the town. The line of advance of the 1st Brigade, however, would be through the houses and streets, where, in face of opposition, progress would be costly, if not impossible. The 1st Brigade therefore were ordered not to press home their attack against determined resistance, beyond the employment of fighting patrols, but to await the envelopment of the town from the flanks. Their elbow-room clear of the town was extremely limited. If resistance developed and a gradual enveloping movement proved necessary, their attack must be secondary and dependent on the measure of success achieved by the Division on their right, with whom, rather than with the South Island brigade north of the town, their work must be co-ordinated. For the 2nd Brigade operation a company of whippets was made available. The 1st Artillery Brigade, with a British (Army) brigade, was moving forward to a position behind Grévillers for close support, and they also came under General Young's orders. Forward sections of artillery were detailed to destroy machine gun nests.

The hour of attack along the front was fixed for 5 a.m. South of Bapaume the 63rd Division carried the Le Transloy-Loupart line. Their right made further progress and cleared Le Barque. The left wing was, however, unable to take Ligny Thilloy and Thilloy, and nearer Bapaume could make little headway against fierce machine gun fire. In face of it also the 2 North Island battalions seized part of the Grévillers sector of the Le Transloy-Loupart line and made a little progress towards the Albert Road, which was reached by the right battalion, but could win no further. For the remainder of the day they confined themselves to active patrol work.

On the other side of the town a hard day's fighting was to fall to the 2nd Brigade. During the previous afternoon a flight of German aeroplanes had observed and bombed the concentration areas near Achiet-le-Petit, where the two 2nd Brigade reserve battalions and the incoming 63rd Division troops were massed. The results of their reconnaissance were not long in declaring themselves. The batteries of the 2nd (Army) Brigade in the vicinity were subjected to a severe gas bombardment, and now during the night the enemy drenched the approaches to his rearguard positions with gas and high-explosive. Through this bombardment, fortunately with very light casualties, the 2 assaulting battalions, 1st Canterbury on the right and 1st Otago on the left, under a clear moonlit sky, occasionally obscured by slight mists, moved up to their positions of assembly behind 2nd Canterbury on the Biefvillers slopes.

Before them the ridge dropped gently to the hamlet of Avesnes and to the sunken road where the Germans had been in force the previous afternoon. On the far side of the valley the ground rose steeply at first over a high tree-clad bank and then more gradually towards the great Arras Road. On Otago's left a cross-country track from Biefvillers to Favreuil cut the main road on the high ground at right angles. At the cross-roads there stands in a little enclosure a commemorative pillar of the Battle of Bapaume in 1870. From this monument the wide spinney which, half a mile nearer Bapaume, juts out from the Favreuil Wood towards the high road takes its name of Monument Wood. All about the spinney and the high ground in its vicinity Otago might reasonably expect to meet with opposition.

In the late hours of the night the mist had become denser, and combined with the dust of the enemy's shelling, which about 4 a.m. increased in violence, afforded again an invaluable screen. The 8 tanks allotted were late, but the barrage advancing evenly 100 yards in 3 minutes was of gratifying weight and accuracy. The enemy offered stubborn resistance, but at 7 a.m. 1st Canterbury reached their objective in the

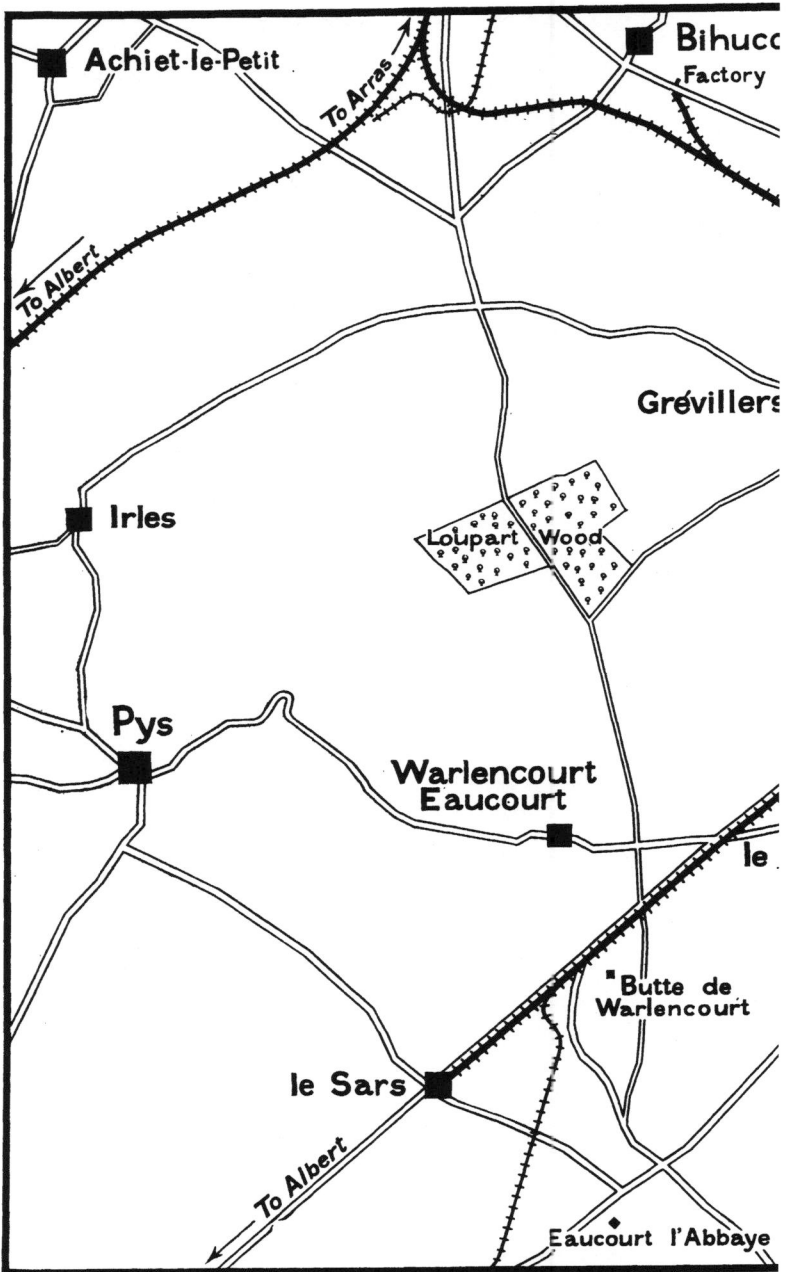

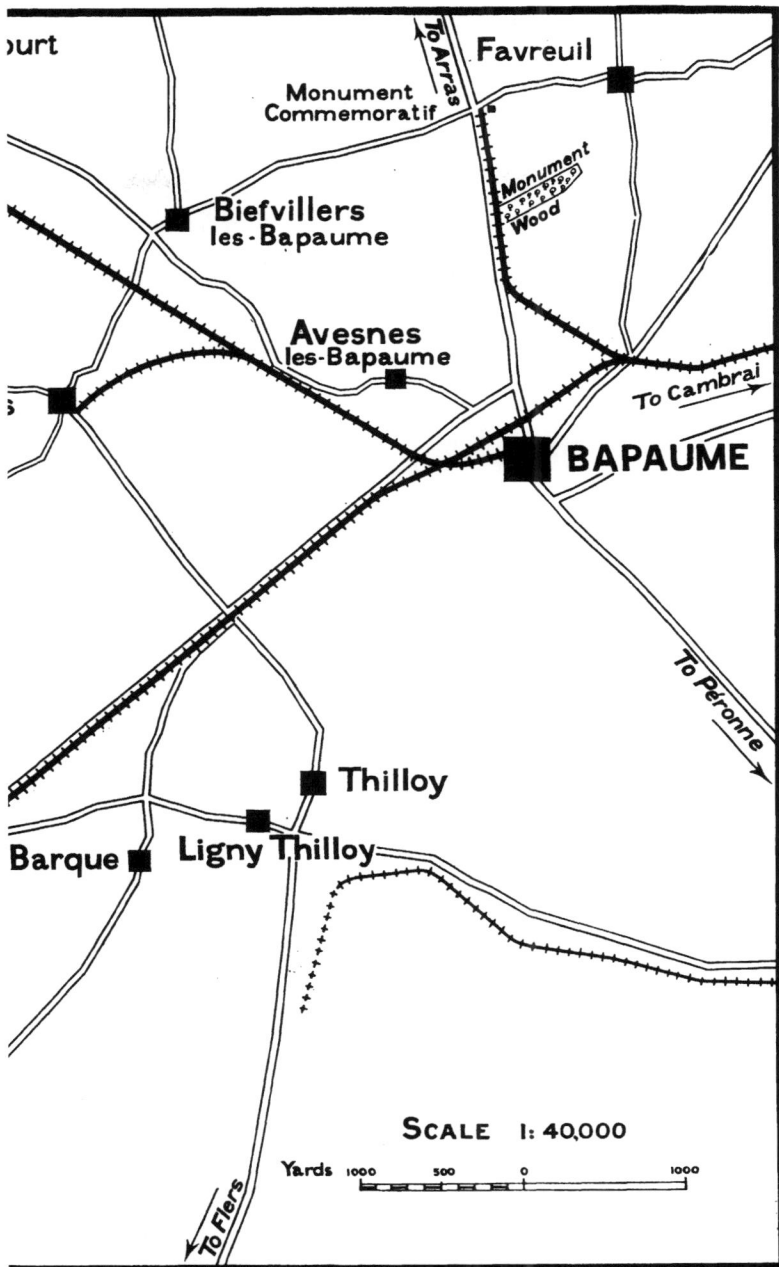

To Arras

Favreuil

Monument
Commemoratif

Monument
Wood

Biefvillers
les-Bapaume

Avesnes
les-Bapaume

To Cambrai

BAPAUME

To Péronne

Thilloy

Barque

Ligny Thilloy

SCALE 1: 40,000

Yards 1000   500   0   1000

To Flers

triangle of broken country beyond Avesnes, their right resting on the Albert and their left on the Arras Road. Before consolidation could be effected, the mist lifted with unforgettable suddenness, ''and there was bright sunshine.'' One or two of our men who had pressed too far forward were captured. The enemy machine guns in the north-western outskirts of Bapaume redoubled activity. There was, however, abundance of natural cover, and 1st Canterbury completed their task with a total loss of 6 officers and 60 men. During the attack a German ambulance section, with part of its equipment, surrendered voluntarily, and a handful of enemy came in under a white flag, asserting that their comrades only awaited an opportunity for doing likewise. In clearing Avesnes and its outskirts the battalion secured 150 prisoners.

On their left 1st Otago, from the valley onwards, met intense machine gun fire. In the mist their advanced screen constantly stumbled unexpectedly on improvised Strong Points. Before one of these, 2nd Lt. Fyfe,[1] with a section, was challenged by an officer and summoned to surrender. He replied by shooting the officer and by storming the position. While fighting and outflanking these posts, a certain number of platoons lost direction, and ere the assaulting line reached the Arras Road there were several gaps. The hostile fire from the vicinity of the Road and from Monument Wood never slackened, and about 7 a.m. it appeared ominously probable that our advance would be held up. It was one of those anxious moments which sooner or later befall every battalion in a prolonged experience of war. Nor were prospects improved when the tanks at length arrived and engaged our own men with misplaced energy from the rear. This misconception cleared up, the tanks rendered yeoman service. Four indeed were put out of action in front of Monument Wood, and most of the others did not long survive the clearing of the mist, but their support, added to Otago's persistence, cleared the stubbornly contested position. Shortly before 9 a.m. Otago was on the line of their first objective on the Arras Road. Beyond this, the barrage having been lost, no further progress was practicable. A heap of dead, 150 prisoners, and 18 machine guns attested the severity of the fighting. Touch was obtained with the 37th Division troops on the left, who were equally arrested, but there was a distinct gap between the right and 1st Can-

1   p. 412.

32

terbury. The Otago companies themselves were somewhat widely separated. 2nd Canterbury was therefore moved forward into close support, and a company was allotted to Otago as immediate reserves.

During the early afternoon there was heavy gas shelling in the rear areas, and enemy aeroplanes were active, dropping small bombs and firing their machine guns on the Otago posts about the Arras Road and towards Favreuil. Ground machine gun fire and sniping, however, diminished considerably, and small parties of Otago were able to work 200 yards into Monument Wood.

In view of this check the IV. Corps asked the Third Army that the VI. Corps might turn Favreuil from the north. The VI. Corps were accordingly instructed to co-operate by pushing down east of Favreuil, while the IV. Corps troops made a fresh effort in the afternoon. It was decided that 1st Otago should consummate their attack under a barrage at 6.30 p.m. It would be made in conjunction with the 37th Division, who would capture the northern half of Favreuil. Otago would thrust their right forward over the Road near a cemetery north of Bapaume; their centre would carry Monument Wood; the left, in close touch with the 37th Division, would capture the southern half of Favreuil and the trench system round its south-eastern edge. Nor would this exhaust the 2nd Brigade effort. For 2nd Canterbury, recovering the company attached to Otago's reserves, would follow up the attacking battalion, pass through it, and exploit success by securing high ground north of Bapaume and pushing patrols towards Bapaume itself. Should the enemy retreat, touch was to be maintained with him by fighting patrols, and the line Bancourt-Beugnâtre established for the night. Meantime a heavy bombardment was put down on Favreuil.

During the afternoon the enemy had begun to set fire to his dumps, but he was also planning a counter-attack with the remaining effectives of the tired 111th Division to recover the important ground lost at the Arras Road. The stroke was timed to take place shortly after the hour fixed for our operation. The assaulting troops were seen by our aeroplanes, who bombed and machine-gunned them mercilessly. They were in addition caught in our barrage falling at 6.30 p.m. 200 yards east of the Arras Road. The bulk of the force was dispersed with serious losses, and the remainder rendered too demoralised either to attack themselves or to resist our onset.

Only on the right, at the Cemetery, was strong resistance encountered. A whole company was required to clear it, and later in the evening the enemy attempted to filter back into it, but was repulsed with 2nd Canterbury help. In the Monument Wood, however, and the southern part of Favreuil, though a temporary withdrawal of the troops on the left caused brief anxiety, opposition proved considerably less formidable than Otago had anticipated. The battalion's task was fulfilled to the letter, and the troops fully recompensed for their trying time in the morning. In the village and the trenches just to the east of it 118 prisoners were captured, including a battalion commander and his staff. Large dumps of S.A.A., shells and engineering plant, a field gun, 4 anti-tank rifles, 4 mortars, 40 machine guns, 4 telephones, and signal apparatus fell into our possession. Casualties in the evening attack were extremely light, but during the day Otago had lost 7 officers and 211 men. In the northern part of the village the 37th Division met tougher resistance and succeeded in securing their objective only by a fresh effort after dark.

The evening had been sultry, with heavy masses of black clouds hanging like a pall over doomed Bapaume. About 9.30 p.m. a violent thunderstorm burst from the overcharged sky, and after the long spell of fine weather rain fell practically all night. It was intensely dark. Hostile artillery remained active. Under these acutely disagreeable conditions 2nd Canterbury pushed 3 companies through the Otago outposts to exploit success. Little opposition was met with. A fresh line of outposts was established on the Favreuil Road, and our patrols approached the Bapaume-Beugnâtre Road. It was held strongly, but by midnight one or two of the Canterbury patrols were close to and on the Road with a flank facing south. At least 10 Germans were killed and 20 wounded, 6 machine guns, 2 mortars and 22 prisoners taken. Towards Bapaume, however, patrols encountered fierce resistance. Here every evidence pointed to a stiffening of the enemy's defence. Large parties were digging trenches. The number of machine guns in action appeared illimitable. During the attacks on the 24th and 25th, 2nd Canterbury had lost 2 officers and 50 men killed, and 7 officers and 50 men wounded.

As a result of the day's fighting the 2nd Brigade had taken over 400 prisoners at a cost of under 300 casualties. The brigade was to hold for 2 days longer the position won

in this last highly successful enterprise, but their part in the
Bapaume Battle was now played. During the night (25th/
26th August), the 1st Brigade extended their left to the railway line, relieving part of the 1st Canterbury troops, and the
Rifle Brigade was already on the way up to take over the left
subsector from the 2nd Brigade and continue the advance on
the following day.

In the Third Army plans for 26th August, the V.
Corps on the right proposed to maintain pressure towards
Flers, and the VI. Corps on the north to clear the ground
about Mory and gain a position in the old British reserve
line of the previous year. On the IV. Corps front the 63rd
Division on the right would capture or contain Thilloy, and
advance eastwards in the direction of Riencourt-les-Bapaume
on the Péronne Road. In the centre the New Zealanders,
now ahead of the flank troops, would make a fresh bid for
Bapaume and the high ground east of it. On their left the
5th Division, relieving the 37th during the night, would
attack towards Beugnâtre.

General Russell's purpose was that the 1st Brigade should
conform with the movement of the 63rd Division on Thilloy.
No frontal assault would be made on Bapaume, but patrols
would ascertain whether enemy resistance had weakened. In
that event the 1st Brigade would co-operate in the mopping-
up of the town. Touch in any case must be maintained with
the right flank of the Rifle Brigade. On the north of the
town, with greater room for manoeuvre, the task of the
Rifles was more important. They were ordered to advance
in co-operation with the 5th Division from the Beugnâtre
Road, cross the railway and the Cambrai Road, and seize the
high ground towards Bancourt. If possible they would also
penetrate Bapaume from the north.

The Rifle Brigade found the roads choked with traffic,
and the battalions moved in open "artillery" formation over
the fields, now drenched by the heavy rain. About 10 p.m.
on 25th August they reached their appointed concentration
area behind Grévillers and Biefvillers. It had not yet been
possible to issue detailed orders. In the thick darkness the
battalion commanders had no little trouble in finding advanced brigade headquarters. General Hart arrived at
1.30 a.m. and issued verbal instructions. It was believed that
the Beugnâtre Road was held by the 2nd Brigade, and that
enemy resistance would not prove formidable except perhaps
at St. Aubyn, the northern suburb of Bapaume.

LIEUT. J. G. GRANT, V.C.

A WELLINGTON POST BEFORE BAPAUME

PRISONERS (BATTLE OF BAPAUME)

MATERIAL CAPTURED (BATTLE OF BAPAUME)

The operations were to be carried out by 3 battalions, on a frontage of 2500 yards, the 3rd Rifles on the right, the 2nd[1] in the centre, the 4th on the left. The left and centre would advance to the high ground, south of Beugnâtre, the village itself falling within the 5th Division's area. The right battalion would carry St. Aubyn, and passing along the northern outskirts of Bapaume itself, would fling a flank round the town's eastern approaches over the Cambrai Road.

An hour after midnight, 25th/26th August, the Rifle battalions moved off to their position of deployment in rear of the 2nd Brigade line. There they found a disagreeable surprise in the enemy retention of the greater part of the Beugnâtre Road. In the early morning the rain cleared off, and at 6.30 a.m. the attack was launched in ideal weather. It was not supported by tanks or barrage, but a battery of New Zealand artillery was allotted to each battalion, together with a section of machine guns and light trench mortars. In the centre of the 4th Rifles' front, Capt. D. W. McClurg rushed the sunken road with 2 platoons, capturing many machine guns and killing or making prisoners the garrison. At the very outset the left company of the 4th Battalion met considerable resistance. Well supported, however, by the covering fire of the attached battery, within half an hour it had joined up with McClurg and established posts along the tree-lined Beugnâtre Road facing the old aerodrome. A counter-attack made by about 2 companies and debouching from Beugnâtre was successfully repelled. McClurg took command of both companies, the company on his left having lost all its officers, and superintended their consolidation in front of the Road.

In the centre the 2nd Rifles "directed." 1 company covered the whole front with patrols, 2 followed in support, and 1 was in reserve. The patrols reached and crossed the Beugnâtre Road, taking an abandoned field gun, 3 machine guns, and a handful of prisoners, but heavy fire from the village held up further advance. Meanwhile nearer St. Aubyn the right support company had advanced with tremendous impetus, and presently found both flanks in the air owing to the arrest of the patrols on its left and to a check sustained by the 3rd Battalion on its right. Heavy sniping and intense machine gun fire not only from Beugnâtre but from the woodstacks and the lofty St. Aubyn buildings, which commanded a wide view of the country, compelled it to dig

1 Major J. Murphy, vice Lt.-Col. Jardine, on leave.

in and await advance on its flanks. As it was, the machine
guns in the upper storeys of the houses were able to reach
the bottom of the company's shallow trenches. This machine
gun opposition fell naturally with still greater weight on the
3rd Battalion, whose 2 attacking companies strove to work
round the northern outskirts of Bapaume and crush the
strongly protected and fully garrisoned centres of resistance.
With the utmost difficulty their fighting patrols, dribbling
forward and "scuppering" the German machine gun nests,
contrived to reach the Beugnâtre Road. The railway remained
still in front of them. Similar difficulties had confronted the
other troops of the Corps, and by 10 a.m. the advance was
suspended all along the front.

Bapaume and the high ground north-east of it towards the
Cambrai Road had been subjected by us to heavy bombardment, which it was reasonably thought must weaken the
enemy's power of resistance. As the 2nd Brigade, checked in
the morning of the previous day, had effected a brilliant
recovery in the evening, so now too General Hart suggested
that the commanding officers should meet at the 2nd Battalion
headquarters in the centre of the line and discuss the
situation with a view to a resumption of the attack. Lt.-Col.
Bell arrived safely, but Lt.-Col. Beere of the 4th Battalion
was wounded on the way. It was agreed that no further
advance without artillery assistance was practicable. Should
it be possible, however, to provide a barrage, the battalion
commanders recommended that the centre of the line should
strike again in the afternoon with the purpose of securing
some three-quarters of a mile along the Cambrai Road from a
point 500 yards east of Bapaume. The left of the line would
conform, but the time was not yet ripe for any considerable
movement on the right, where the enemy's defences about
Bapaume bristled with machine guns. After consultation with
General Russell, the brigadier approved of this plan and
gave orders (3.30 p.m.) over the telephone for a renewed
advance at 6 p.m. under an artillery barrage. The 5th
Division was to co-operate on the left and capture Beugnâtre.

The 2nd Battalion company commanders were at once
summoned to headquarters, where the plan of attack was
explained to them. The battalion commander could not at the
moment withdraw and utilise the right support company
which was pinned to its trenches before St. Aubyn. The
reserve company was therefore to be brought up into support.
The original left support company would attack on the right

and the original patrol company on their left.   A company of the 1st Battalion was allotted as reserves.

From this conference the 2nd Battalion company commanders hastened with all despatch to their own headquarters some 2000 yards forward, whither they instantly summoned their platoon commanders.   Less than 20 minutes remained before the opening of the barrage.   Brief orders were issued, but time did not permit of certain desirable changes in the machine gun positions or of anything but the baldest explanation to the rank and file.   Such over-hurried preliminaries do not augur success.

Punctually to time the promised barrage fell and began its march of 100 yards every 4 minutes.   If the infantry had previously in the day been impressed by the dropping of S.A.A. boxes by parachutes from the aeroplanes, it was now the turn of the low-flying observers to admire the rapidity with which the riflemen shook themselves out into attacking formations.   But from the outset there was an inevitable lack of cohesion between the 2 companies.   At first they swept everything before them.   The railway line, which was halfway to the objective, was reached with but a handful of casualties. Heavy opposition, however, developed on the right flank from Bapaume, and the left flank was harassed by continuous long-range fire from the ground east of Beugnâtre and from the village itself, which the 5th Division did not eventually clear till late in the evening.   Serious casualties were sustained. The right company lost all its officers, and a large gap was torn in the line between it and the left company.   None the less their advance cleared St. Aubyn.   Beyond that point only a few sections managed to progress, and thus as the left company (Capt. W. J. Organ, M.C.) struggled towards the objective, very troublesome machine gun fire began to harass their right rear.   The left company, however, and some men of the right reached the Cambrai Road.   A dozen prisoners were captured.

There was no abatement, however, of the machine gun opposition, and presently a strong party of Germans lining the walls of some brickyards on the Cambrai Road made our position untenable by close-range fire.   Enfilading the line, they forced a withdrawal.   The Rifles fell back slowly some 500 yards to the line of the railway.   Here they stood firm.   On the left the 4th Rifles formed a protective flank, maintaining touch with the 5th Division.   On the right the 3rd Battalion patrols were able to push their way somewhat further forward towards the northern outskirts of Bapaume. By nightfall the line ran from Gun Spur north-east of Bapaume along the railway back to St. Aubyn. The total advance from the morning's position amounted to approximately 1000 yards on a front of about 2500. The Beugnâtre Road was left now well behind, and Bapaume was directly menaced from the north. During the day the 2nd Rifles, on whom the brunt of the fighting fell, lost 6 officers killed or died of wounds and 40 men killed. 1 man had been captured on the Cambrai Road. 6 officers and 126 men had been wounded.

Meanwhile south of the town the 1st Brigade and the 63rd Division had been unable to effect much progress against an extremely strong defence. As the result of their side-slip northwards during the night,[1] the 1st Brigade were not now, except on their right, immediately confronted by the westerly section of the Le Transloy-Loupart system, which opposite the greater part of their line lay south of the Albert Road. But having taken over the positions after nightfall, they had little knowledge of their front and were in addition very much handicapped by uncertainty as to the zero hour of the 63rd Division's attack. The wires to brigade headquarters were cut by shell-fire. During a reconnaissance in the night (25th/26th August) Lt. R. V. Hollis of 2nd Wellington ran right into 4 Germans. He attacked them single-handed, killing 2 with his revolver and closed with the other 2. One he knocked down with his fist, and the other after an attempt to club him with a rifle fled. Hollis collected a couple of his men at once and returned to the scene of his encounter, but found the ground clear except for the dead Germans.

In general conformity[2] with the 63rd Division's movement, the right battalion (2nd Wellington) made an attempt to get forward in daylight (26th August) and effected a slight advance. In the evening they tried again, but hostile machine gun fire was still overpowering. A company of 1st Auckland moved up to help them, and 1 small bombing section under Sergt. Judson, some of whose exploits have been noted previously, pressed through the checked line and rushing forward under intensely heavy fire captured a machine gun in a German sap. While his men consolidated, Judson proceeded 200 yards alone up the sap, bombing 2 machine gun crews before him. Jumping out of the trench, he ran ahead of the enemy. Then, standing on the parapet, he ordered the

[1] p. 442.
[2] Owing to their uncertainty as to the 63rd Division's "zero," 2nd Wellington attacked at the same hour (6.30 a.m.) as the Rifle Brigade.

party consisting of 2 officers and about 10 men to surrender. They instantly fired on him, but he threw a bomb and jumped down among them. He killed 2, put the rest to flight and so captured the 2 machine guns. This prompt and gallant action, which won Judson the V.C., saved many lives and enabled the advance to continue for some little way further.

A somewhat light artillery barrage, however, had completely failed to neutralise the machine gun posts about Thilloy, and the main attack of the 63rd Division made no material progress. From the commencement of the operations a total of no less than 20 German Divisions had been identified by contact on the Third Army front, and the Thilloy sector was now heavily reinforced. In addition, the New Zealand patrols were severely harassed by machine gun fire from Bapaume. In the end, to conform with the general line, our advanced posts were withdrawn on the Albert Road. A proposed renewal of the attack in the late evening was abandoned. The 1st Brigade indeed remained in a position where progress on their right was an essential preliminary to their getting forward. Splendid as was Judson's exploit, not much could be expected from bombing alone. During the night 26th/27th August 1st Auckland took over the 2nd Wellington line and became responsible for the whole brigade front.

At the close of the 26th the order of battle on the Corps front was, from right to left, the 63rd, the New Zealand, and the 5th Divisions in the line. In reserve, the 42nd Division was on the right and the 37th on the left. The vital importance of cutting the German communications by obtaining command of the Péronne and Cambrai Roads was keenly felt. In conformity with a general advance along the Army front, the IV. Corps ordered the 63rd Division to make a further attack on Thilloy on the 27th. The New Zealanders would continue to encircle Bapaume, and the 5th Division move with them on the left. Bapaume and the roads eastward were heavily bombarded. Some of the New Zealanders' Newton mortars were now in position on the town's north-western edge, and in this bombardment they, together with the howitzer batteries, co-operated. In view, however, of the enemy's strength, it was not desired that the 5th and the New Zealand Divisions should force a costly assault. If it should be found necessary, a full-dress attack with a wide encircling movement would be arranged, but this must take a little time. The 63rd Division's attack on the 27th accomplished little. As a preparatory measure, therefore, to the encircling movement, the 1st Brigade, who had during the day made some advance beyond the Albert Road, took over in the evening the front of the Rifle Brigade up to the cemetery on the Arras Road, thus entirely covering Bapaume and leaving the Rifles free for movement north of the town. During the night 27th/28th August the 63rd Division after a further vain effort at Thilloy was relieved by the 42nd Division.

In view of the resistance encountered, plans for formal attack were indefinitely postponed in favour of the policy of maintaining strong pressure by patrols and of taking immediate advantage of any sign of weakening. The Third Army warned the V. and IV. Corps to be prepared for the possibility of the enemy's evacuation of Bapaume through the night. The artillery continued to bombard the place and sweep it with barrages, and barrage plans were drawn up for a "local" attack on the town by 1st Wellington.[1] Further siege batteries were placed at the Corps' disposal. Just as Rawlinson had discontinued his attack in the south, so now it was no part of the High Command's purpose to ram their heads against a brick wall. There were other vulnerable sectors in the German line. Arrangements were continued for the construction of reserve lines in the event of continued resistance or of a counter-thrust. But the hard-pressed German had no such purpose. As our Staff surmised, it was his intention to hold Bapaume only for such time as would suffice to cover his retirement on the Hindenburg Line. When the progress made in the Battle of the Scarpe (begun 26th August) proved a menace to its northern pivot, he hesitated no longer.

The 28th had been a dull day with light showers. But in the evening the weather cleared, and the night was fine with a starry sky. The enemy artillery which had been active throughout the day was appreciably quieter. In the early morning (29th August) the German flares about the western faubourgs became less numerous, and his machine guns noticeably less aggressive. And at last there was silence. As soon as ever these hopeful indications were observed, both brigades at once pushed forward fighting patrols which occupied St. Aubyn railway station and the town's suburbs. By 8.30 a.m. a company (Capt. H. C. Meikle, M.C.) of the 3rd. Rifles had entered the northern part of Bapaume,

---

1 General Russell had promised a flag bearing the word "Bapaume" to the battalion which captured the town.

and 1st Auckland had reached a factory 1000 yards beyond the Albert Road.   Shortly afterwards our artillery was finally called off the town, and fighting patrols of 1st Wellington had passed through it and were pressing after the German rearguards.   In the centre of the Rifle Brigade line the 2nd Battalion early reached the Cambrai Road, and their leading patrols were just in time to see the last of the enemy disappear over the ridge towards Bancourt.   Half a dozen howitzers and several abandoned machine guns fell into our possession.   Only a few prisoners were taken.   Losses were very slight, and the 2nd Rifles, confident of taking Bancourt, were anxious to push on.   This was not, however, permitted till the flanks should be up in line.   For on the left, east of Favreuil, strong opposition was encountered by the 4th Rifles in the railway siding and no appreciable advance made, and as it was, the 2nd Rifles began to be considerably troubled by machine gun fire from Fremicourt sweeping down the Cambrai Road.

By 4 p.m. the flank battalions had come forward into line, and the 1st Brigade had reached a point over a mile down the Péronne Road.   Shortly after 6 p.m. we held securely the German trench system south and south-west of Bapaume to the Péronne Road and thence to the Sugar Factory on the Cambrai Road whence the line continued to the north-east. The flank Divisions had made equal progress, and the hitherto sternly defended positions at Ligny Thilloy and Thilloy had now been yielded without opposition.   On this line touch was again established with strong enemy rearguards, amply furnished with machine guns.   Our new positions were being swept with shrapnel, and whippets operating in the angle between the Cambrai and Péronne Roads drew the fire of the enemy heavy artillery.   The advance was temporarily discontinued, the troops took breath, and arrangements were made to press the pursuit together with the rest of the Army at dawn on the morrow (30th August).

If resistance proved slight, a distant goal was set the Divisions of the IV. Corps in the line Ytres-Bertincourt-Vélu, but as a primary objective the 42nd Division on the right would seize Riencourt, the New Zealanders in the centre Bancourt and Fremicourt, and the 5th Division on the left Beugny.   In the evening General Russell accordingly issued orders for the 1st Brigade on the right to take Bancourt and the Rifles on the left to carry Fremicourt.   Both brigades would advance to a ridge which rose 800 yards east of the villages.

The infantry were to be supported by harassing machine
gun fire specially directed on the trenches in front of the
villages and co-ordinated with the advance of the artillery
barrage. The barrage would be provided by all 3 New
Zealand artillery brigades as far as the Cambrai Road, when
the 2nd (Army) Brigade would cease, in order to come into
Divisional reserve and be ready to move forward at instant
notice.

On the north the Rifle Brigade front amounted to 1000
yards and could be covered by 1 battalion. Warning orders
were given the 1st Rifles[1] in the late evening. On definite
information being received from the brigade at 1 a.m., the
necessary instructions were issued to the company commanders
already assembled at battalion headquarters. Expected
guides from the leading troops failed to turn up, and the
battalion moved off from their reserve position at 3 a.m.,
guided by their officers' compasses to their assembly area
between the railway and the Cambrai Road. The company
which had been in reserve to the 2nd Battalion[2] was made the
left attacking company. Two of its platoons chanced to be
engaged in "carrying" and found it impossible to assemble
in time to advance with the rest of the battalion
at 5 a.m.. It was only with the utmost effort and
thanks to the energy displayed by Sergt. W. L. Free
that they were able to follow the attack some 25 minutes
after the barrage and reach the position for the final assault.

From the outset it was clear that the operation was to be
no "walk-over." On the Cambrai Road just west of Fremicourt was an old British camp that had been used as rest
billets for German troops in reserve. As protection against
splinters from aeroplane bombs, the huts had been surrounded
by the customary thick earthen walls. Over these several
machine guns now fired at the 1st Rifles' screen. They were
cowed, however, by the barrage and circumvented by an
outflanking movement on the part of each company. On
the other side of the road a large camouflaged Strong Point
containing 3 machine guns was rushed without casualties by
the left company. The Rifles were in touch with each flank,
and the 5th Division troops on the left, accompanied by a
tank, were making splendid progress. But Fremicourt itself
presented an awkward problem. Our heavy howitzers had
not yet lifted from its western edge, and their fire, while

1 Lt.-Col. Austin resumed duty this day.
2. p. 445.

effectually subduing the German garrison, prevented direct ingress. Instead therefore of going right through, each company skirted the village for some little distance. They then sent in parties to mop up the opposition which yielded rapidly.

The right company thereupon pressed forward to the crest, beyond which it encountered hot machine gun fire from the right flank. The 1st Brigade had not yet moved to the crest, but had dug in along a subsidiary spur with their left some 300 yards in rear of the Rifles' right, which was consequently exposed. The left company had special anxieties of its own. The 5th Division, harassed by fire from Beugny, drew in its right to overcome it, and left a gap. To reduce it, the left company extended their outer flank and had considerable fighting with a pocket of enemy in their left rear, at the dump and railway line to the north-east of Fremicourt. There they captured 50 prisoners. This flank lost the barrage, but the other half of the company took the full objective, and presently the left flank followed. Fremicourt had been cleared by 6.30 a.m. By 8 a.m. the whole line was on their objective. In an effort to secure touch with the 5th Division the left flank was flung out 300 yards into the latter's area. Thence it swung back in a wide circle round the east of Fremicourt to the railway cutting beside the Cambrai Road, halfway between Fremicourt and Beugny.

Meanwhile the support company in rear, which had been subjected to a very unpleasant 10 minutes' "crash" from the German guns and had throughout its advance been troubled by machine gun fire from Bancourt, had reached the Cambrai Road at 5.40 a.m. Our heavies were then still on Fremicourt. Three platoons were diverted along the Road towards Beugny. Dodging the heavies' shells, 2 passed into Fremicourt. The third moved to assist the left company. It took up a position in support 100 yards south of the Fremicourt cemetery at the eastern edge of the village. Here it was joined by the fourth platoon, which had worked through gardens and buildings from the south.

These 2 platoons in Fremicourt completed its mopping up. 7 officers and 110 other ranks in all were taken prisoners in it, Cpl. E. Sheldrake and a section of 5 men accounting for 5 officers and 76 other ranks. The parties of the attacking companies thereupon moved forward to the outpost line, and the support company's platoons extended the second line by the cemetery.

The reserve company on reaching the Cambrai Road was ordered to send 1 platoon to assist the left company north and east of the village. The remainder waiting by the roadside were mistaken by our tanks for Prussian infantry. There ensued some natural altercation till a diversion was provided by some German machine guns on the western outskirts of the village, which had not come into action against the forward companies and had not been detected. Riflemen and tanks forgot their differences and co-operated in clearing up the enemy nests.

The 1st Rifles captured in all 402 prisoners including a battalion commander and his staff. Their losses were 4 officers wounded, 20 other ranks killed, and about 100 wounded.

The 1st Brigade on a wider front attacked their objective with 2 battalions. The capture of Bancourt itself fell to 2nd Auckland,[1] but 1st Wellington[2] advancing on the left would if necessary co-operate with 2nd Auckland in carrying the village. The 2 battalions took up their positions in saps and in a sunken cross-country track about the Péronne Road. On arrival 2nd Auckland at once got in touch with the 42nd Division, whose attack on Riencourt would safeguard their otherwise exposed right. The 42nd Division troops unfortunately had received their orders late. They informed Major Sinel that they would not be in a position to attack until 6 a.m. Auckland, therefore, was compelled to wait for them. Wellington, less exposed, attacked as arranged at the same time (5 a.m.) as the Rifles.

As soon as our barrage started, enemy shelling fell heavily on the approaches to Bancourt and on the sunken road where 2nd Auckland headquarters were established. The regimental medical officer and the majority of his orderlies became casualties, and the lives of several wounded were saved only through the exertions of the Rev. C. J. H. Dobson, who immediately took charge of the situation, established an aid post, organised stretcher parties, and himself under intense fire and with few facilities attended to the cases requiring immediate dressing. Fortunately for Wellington the resistance in Bancourt was dealt with by 2 boldly-handled tanks, and at first despite hostile shelling they made rapid progress beyond the line of the village towards the crest. As they mounted the slope, 1 platoon was arrested by a hostile machine gun. Pte. G. J. Scothern rushed forward with a

---

1   Major W. C. Sinel, vice Lt.-Col. S. S. Allen, wounded on 24th.
2   Major Turnbull, vice Lt.-Col. Narbey, wounded on 24th.

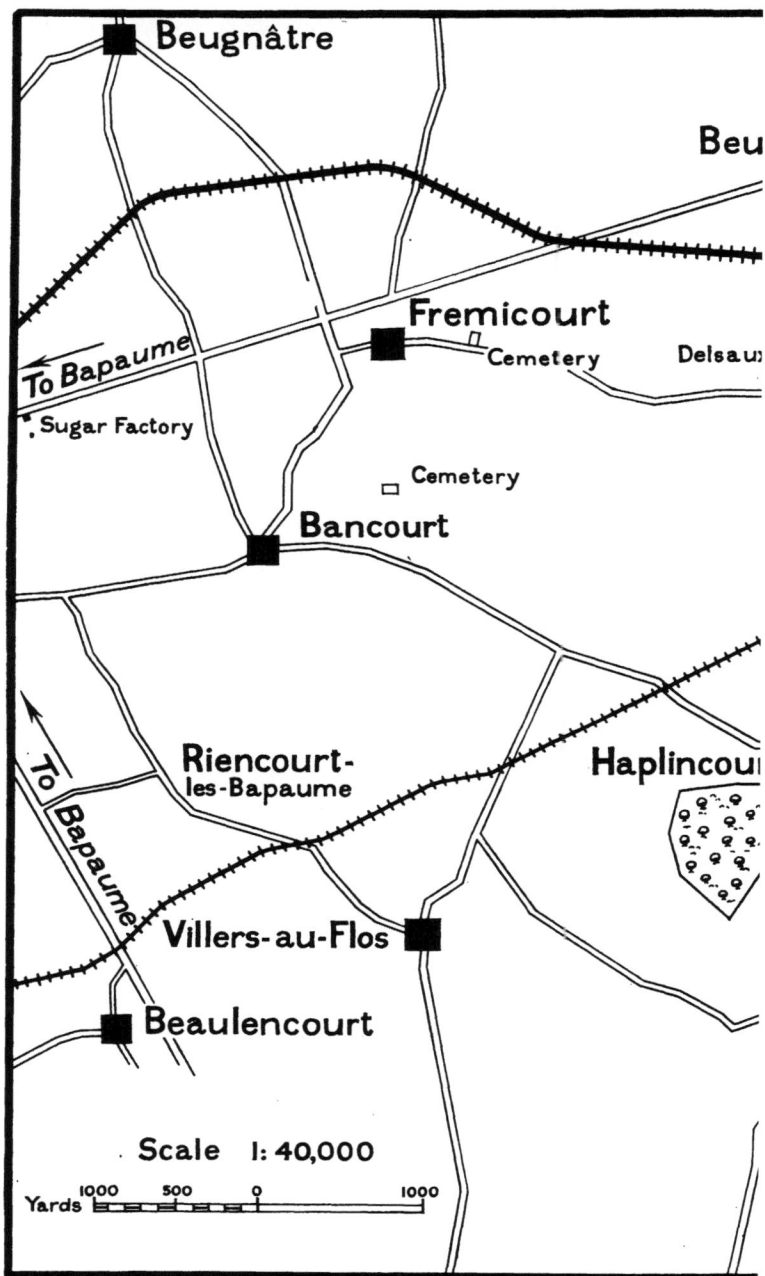

Beugnâtre

Beu

Fremicourt

To Bapaume

Cemetery

Delsau

. Sugar Factory

Cemetery

Bancourt

Riencourt-
les-Bapaume

Haplincou

To Bapaume

Villers-au-Flos

Beaulencourt

Scale 1: 40,000

Yards 1000 500 0 1000

HAPL

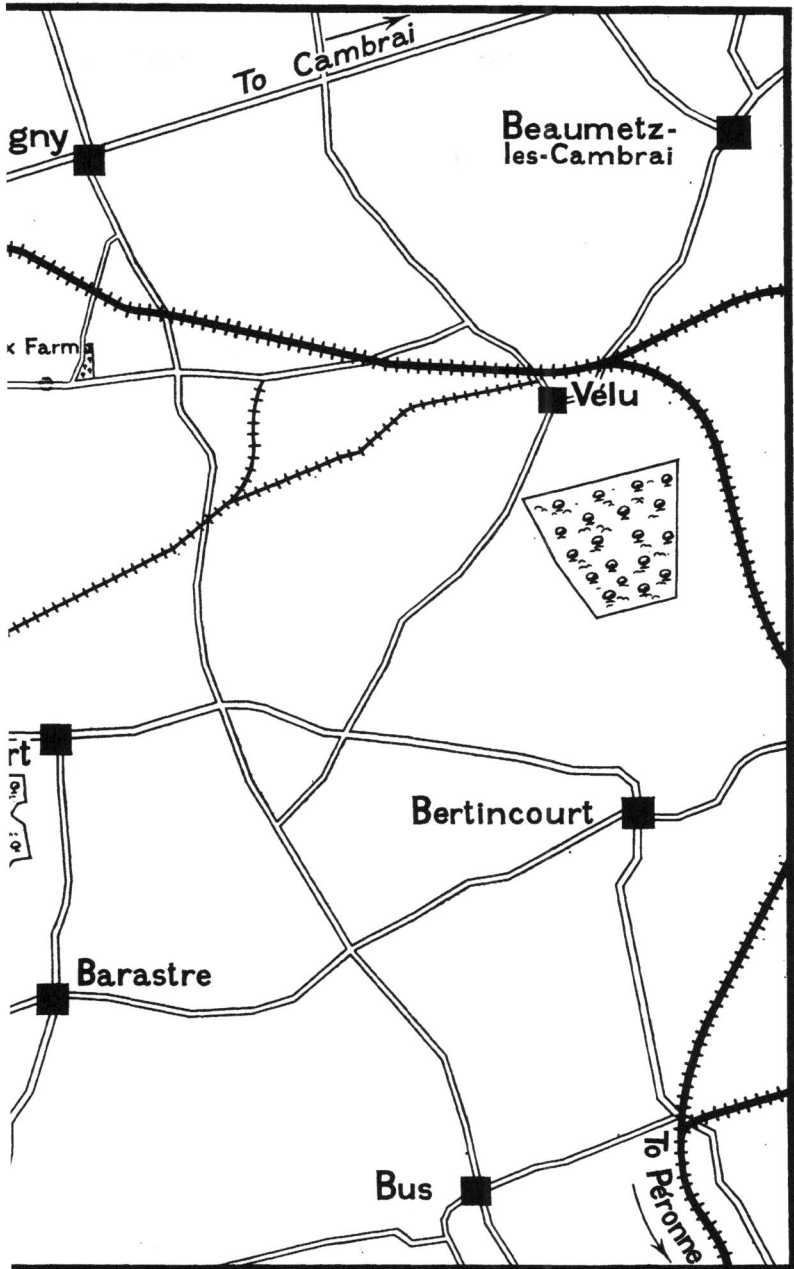

To Cambrai

gny

Beaumetz-
les-Cambrai

x Farm

Vélu

Bertincourt

Barastre

Bus

To Péronne

Lewis gun and from an exposed position engaged the enemy, thus allowing the hostile gun to be rushed. Other machine guns, however, on the right of the ridge, not menaced themselves by an infantry advance, forced Wellington, as we have seen, to establish a line on a subsidiary spur in rear of their objective. One of the tanks moved towards Haplincourt but was put out of action. During consolidation Scothern crept forward and by skilful handling of his gun kept hostile fire down until his platoon had dug in. His gun was immediately afterwards knocked out, but as soon as dusk fell he went into No Man's Land and secured a German gun which he brought into action. Conspicuous devotion to duty was now shown also by Pte. T. M. E. Richmond, the No. 1 of a Wellington Lewis gun crew. Twice left alone on the gun through casualties, he remained at his isolated and important post, on the second occasion for 12 hours without relief.

The 42nd Division moved shortly before 6 a.m. and 2nd Auckland with them. It was now broad daylight with no protecting mist. Raked by fire from the village of Beaulencourt further down the Péronne Road, which had resisted the V. Corps' attack, the 42nd Division was unable to take Riencourt, and this check in turn exposed the right of Auckland. Intense machine gun fire raged from the village itself and the coppices round it, and though artillery support was obtained it failed to neutralise the machine guns. For the moment it was out of the question for Auckland's right flank to attempt to advance over the open slopes north of Riencourt, and consequently a defensive flank was formed well up the ridge pending the fall of the village. Even the establishment of this foothold on the high ground was a creditable performance. The left company advanced rapidly, clearing Bancourt by 8 a.m. and gaining touch with 1st Wellington. In mopping up, Auckland was helped by 2 companies of the 2nd Rifles who came forward and secured 34 prisoners. In this strenuous day Auckland lost an officer and 17 men killed and 8 officers and 112 men wounded. One wounded man was missing. The places of the officers were taken effectively by Sergt. L. Thomas, M.M., Sergt. H. M. Morris, Cpl. L. G. North, L/Cpl. G. C. Ford, and others.

The general advance effected by the 3 battalions amounted to a mile and a quarter. Parties of the enemy digging in east of Bancourt during the morning were heavily shelled by our artillery. Others could be seen moving back towards Villers-au-Flos at noon, but till Riencourt fell the

New Zealanders could make no further move. On the left too the 5th Division had cleared the old British trenches west of Beugny but had been unable to capture the village, and as a result the 1st Rifles' position was not satisfactory. Sustained rifle and machine gun fire from Beugny caused casualties, and the line was thin. Soon after midday the enemy counter-attacked. He succeeded in driving the 1st Rifles' right flank and a post on the left off the crest. In the afternoon no improvement took place on the flanks, and both the Rifle companies were obliged to withdraw their remaining posts. They established themselves in a trench line about 300 yards below the crest. Here they were sufficiently clear of the enemy edge of Fremicourt, and a hostile bombardment on the village at 4.30 p.m. passed idly over their heads. The remaining 3 platoons of the reserve company and a section of Vickers guns were sent up the Cambrai Road towards Beugny to strengthen the left flank, and a company of the 3rd Rifles was attached in reserve.

Meanwhile on the right flank the 42nd Division planned a further attack shortly after 7 p.m. on Riencourt. To destroy the machine gun nests the 3rd New Zealand Battery ran a gun in the afternoon up the Péronne Road within 900 yards of Riencourt, and engaged them over open sights. The attack was preceded by a 2 hours' bombardment. As the 42nd Division advanced, the 1st Brigade's right flank swung forward in conformity. No machine gun fire was directed at them now from Riencourt, and the enemy appeared to be shelling it. 2nd Auckland had no difficulty in moving up another 500 yards. But though Riencourt was clear, a tremendous volume of machine gun fire from Beaulencourt swept the 42nd Division's flank, and they failed to enter the village. A further attempt after darkness proved successful.

During the night 30th/31st August[1] and early next morning the New Zealand batteries moved to the valleys north-east of Bapaume, and constant harassing fire was maintained on German approaches. At about 5 a.m. on the 31st the enemy heavily barraged our front line, and following on a reconnaissance by three or four of his tanks[2] he made a strong counter-attack half an hour later. S.O.S. signals were fired, but were at first masked by poor visibility. Later the light cleared, and the enemy infantry were engaged not merely

1 The 63rd Division, less artillery, marched during the night from the IV. Corps area on transfer to the XVII. Corps.

2 The German tank was a heavily armoured clumsy box on small caterpillar wheels, carrying one 5-cm. gun and 6 machine guns.

by rifle and machine gun fire, but also over open sights by the forward sections of the 1st Artillery Brigade batteries. One or two posts in the centre of the line before the 7th Battery (Major H. G. Wilding, D.S.O.) were driven in about 300 yards, but Wilding held his ground and continued a devastating fire, under which the Germans recoiled. By the cemetery the support company of the 1st Rifles stood fast and strengthened their flank with additional Lewis guns at the southern end of the village. The enemy tanks came forward towards the cemetery, but though heavily fired on made no attack and turned in the direction of Haplincourt Wood, which was forthwith shelled by the Corps heavies. As they withdrew, the enemy machine gunners, who had not been warned about the tanks' reconnaissance, mistook them for British tanks, and hotly engaged them with armour-piercing ammunition. Under this fire some of the tank personnel appear to have lost their heads, and 2 tanks ran into a bank and became ditched. These fell into our hands later on 2nd September. They bore ample evidence of the effect of German armour-piercing ammunition.

On the left of the Rifles, in view of the gap towards the 5th Division, all possible measures had been taken during the night to strengthen the thin line. Daylight revealed that the precautions adopted were more than justified. Two strong enemy parties had infiltrated through behind our line, possibly working down the railway through the railway yard and the dumps, and were now in our rear. Both parties were about 50 strong. The first was taken prisoner by vigorous enterprise on the part of Sergt. A. J. Cunningham, M.M., who, while reconnoitring the front, was surprised by the sight of the Germans. He at once went to a neighbouring platoon and asked for a section. Dividing them into 2 parties, he charged the enemy and captured 46 prisoners, with very few casualties. The other was wiped out by our machine gun and infantry fire, in which the 5th Division co-operated, only half a dozen prisoners remaining. By 7 a.m. the Rifles' posts on the right were restored to the position on the slopes lost at daybreak, and the 1st Brigade also pushed forward again shortly afterwards and were now able to swing their refused right to join the 42nd Division east of Riencourt.

It was obviously desirable to retake the portion of the actual crest lost on the 30th, and also, now that the 42nd Division held Riencourt and protected the right flank, to extend our footing on the high ground for the purpose of securing wider observation. Preparations were pressed forward to that end. The 5th Division on the left were to cooperate. Reconnaissance, however, established that the crest line was held too strongly to be taken without artillery. A conference was held at advanced Divisional headquarters, now at Grévillers. The operation, in which both brigades would take part, was fixed for the following morning (1st September), under an artillery barrage. In accordance with these plans, the 1st Rifles' reserve and support companies passed at 4.55 a.m. through the outpost line. By 5.30 a.m. they had carried their objective, and their centre was beyond it. They secured 70 prisoners of the 23rd (Saxon) Division, together with the usual haul of mortars and machine guns. Later in the morning the right of the 5th Division, which had been unable to attack at zero, pushed forward as far as was possible in the day time, and in the evening, under cover of darkness, it dribbled up into line. At the close of the the day the Rifles' casualties were 84, of whom the greater number were lightly wounded cases.

The 1st Brigade, who were faced by the 44th (Reserve) Division, were not to gain their objective with the same uneventful smoothness. In close touch with the Rifles on its left, 1st Wellington attacked with 3 companies in line. In command of one of the platoons was a Sergt. John Gilroy Grant, who throughout the 2 days' previous fighting had displayed coolness determination and valour of the highest order. On nearing the crest his company threatened to be hung up by a line of 5 enemy machine guns. Under point-blank fire, however, it rushed forward. When some 20 yards from the guns Grant, closely followed by L.-Cpl. C. T. Hill, dashed ahead of his platoon at the centre post. No one but the panic-stricken German at the gun could tell how the fire missed him. He leapt into the post, demoralising the gunners. His men were close on his heels. The instant they were on the parapet he rushed the post on the left in the same manner, and cleared first it and then the next one, and the company quickly occupied the remainder. Grant was awarded the V.C. and Hill the D.C.M. The other companies did not encounter very determined resistance. One platoon was taken by surprise by a hostile machine gun at close range. L.-Cpl. W. E. Ball immediately engaged the machine gun, and by skilful manoeuvring beat down its fire and forced it out of its position. The platoon then moved forward successfully. The whole position was gained and established well up to

time. It had been intended to push patrols forward towards
the Haplincourt Road, but intense machine gun fire from that
direction made all movement impossible. Small sections of
trenches were dug in touch with one another along the
crest.

This fire from the Haplincourt Road and from huts on
the roadside had seriously inconvenienced the advance of the
3 companies of 2nd Auckland who incurred more casualties
from it than in clearing their objective. No touch was yet
obtained with the 42nd Division. A foreshadowed German
counter-attack was stifled by our artillery action. The enemy
gun-fire slackened considerably. The snipers in the Haplincourt Road huts were temporarily dislodged by one of the
2 tanks put at Auckland's disposal[1], and the battalion proceeded to consolidate their position. During the day the
1st Brigade captured 100 prisoners and 7 machine guns.

The tank having fulfilled its mission departed, and ere
long the German snipers and machine guns returned to the
huts. 2nd Auckland, though toiling manfully, were not yet
under cover, and from the huts machine gun fire became very
heavy on their centre. Mortars in a sunken road in front
pounded destructively on the same sector. Anti-tank gun fire
from the direction of Villers-au-Flos also raked these exposed
forward slopes. Movement and consolidation became alike
impossible, and after suffering severely the survivors, too
weak to attack the enemy, even if attack were feasible, were
forced to withdraw behind the crest. On this misfortune being
reported, orders were issued for an immediate re-establish-
ment of the line before the 2nd Brigade, relieving the front
line troops in the evening, took over the position. The
assistance of a 2nd Wellington company was put at Auckland's disposal. The project was, however, eventually abandoned, and General Young expressed himself as satisfied with
the position as it was. During the day Auckland had lost 3
officers and 31 men killed, and 104 men wounded. 1 man
had been taken prisoner.

While this minor action was being effected on
the IV. Corps front, operations of greater importance
were in progress elsewhere in the final phases of the
Battle of Bapaume. By 27th August the enemy, threatened
by the progress of the Third Army, had fallen back on the
whole of his front in the south between the Oise and the
Somme. Roye Nesle and Noyon had been recaptured. In

1 The other broke down behind Bancourt owing to engine trouble.

brilliant operations begun on 30th/31st August the Australians had stormed Mont St. Quentin, and on 1st September
captured Péronne. On the left of the Third Army we were
in possession of Vaulx-Vraucourt Longatte Bullecourt and
Hendecourt. The second stage of the British offensive was
now closed.

The battle had been no facile triumph. The enemy had
indeed been retiring, but his movements had up till this time
been conducted in a great measure deliberately, with marked
skill and in good order. His rearguards had offered fight on
positions carefully selected to give the greatest scope to well-
placed machine guns supported by field artillery. The successive lines occupied were independently organised and
sufficiently far behind one another to prevent troops who had
carried the first from overrunning the second with their
initial impetus. The villages and broken commanding ground
chosen as centres of resistance were in themselves
formidable. The machine gun positions were sited up to
1500 yards, and in such spots as afforded no covered approach
either from the front or flanks. Unoccupied intervals were
left merely as traps. Moreover, each centre of resistance was
sited for all-round defence. The destruction or capitulation
of one did not materially facilitate the task of our units on
either side, for, while neighbouring centres held out, further
progress into the gap was, in daylight at least, extremely
arduous. Against these machine gun nests the most gallant
efforts to advance with infantry weapons not supported by
artillery had proved unsuccessful. The German rearguards
had displayed resolution and had repeatedly sacrificed themselves. Fighting for time, the enemy had in many cases
forced from us more of that priceless asset than we were
disposed to yield, and he had maintained unbroken a screen
behind which he had withdrawn his guns and main force.

Under these conditions the attacking troops were called
upon for strenuous and incessant labour. Nor had the cost
been light. The Corps casualties amounted to over 600
officers and nearly 11,000 men. Of the 3 New Zealand infantry brigades, the 1st had lost 10 officers killed and 36
wounded, and 110 other ranks killed and over 500 wounded.
The 2nd Brigade had 7 officers killed and 28 wounded, 150
men killed and 650 wounded. In the 3rd Brigade, 14 officers
and 120 men had given their lives, and 34 officers and close
on 600 men had been wounded. The Division had lost some
2 dozen prisoners.

But despite German science and stubbornness there could be no doubt as to the satisfactory results of the battle. "The troops of the Third and Fourth Armies, comprising 23 British Divisions, by skilful leading, hard fighting, and relentless and unremitting pursuit, had driven 35 German Divisions from one side of the old Somme battlefield to the other, thereby turning the line of the River Somme. In so doing they had inflicted upon the enemy the heaviest losses in killed and wounded, and had taken from him over 34,000 prisoners and 270 guns."[1] The IV. Corps alone had captured nearly 8000 prisoners. Of these the New Zealanders' share amounted to 47 officers and just over 1600 men.

In the battle the Division had experienced its share of checks and disappointments, but these were outweighed by its repeated successes. In common with the other troops engaged it had found that the transition from trench warfare to a battle of movement involved certain novel and at the outset somewhat bewildering features. Above all, the speed necessary to secure surprise and exploit success had allowed no place for elaborate deliberations and had rendered it in many instances impossible for battalions or even brigades to give other than verbal orders. It was thus inevitable that the men should get little previous information. This involved obvious disadvantages. But all difficulties incident to the change were surmounted with remarkable and admirable rapidity. Competent observers noted the facility with which subordinate commanders grasped hurriedly-sketched operations, and with which units of all arms, after one or two days of open warfare, achieved a high degree of mobility. The mass of comprehensive detailed and precise reports forwarded by artillery and infantry officers and by Intelligence personnel on our own and the enemy's positions and movements constitutes a striking testimony to the adaptability of officers and men to novel circumstances.

1 Official Despatch.

CHAPTER XII

THE BATTLE OF HAVRINCOURT-EPEHY

The positions on which the enemy had been driven back at the close of the Battle of Bapaume (21st August-1st September), the second stage of the British offensive, he appears to have intended to hold firmly for the time. Under cover of strong resistance from his rearguards he proposed to make a gradual and deliberate withdrawal to the Hindenburg Line, saving equally guns men and material. But the development of the Battle of the Scarpe (26th August-3rd September), the third stage of the British offensive, precipitated his movements. By our success on the Scarpe the northern hinge of the Hindenburg Line itself was broken, and his organised positions west of it were turned for many miles southward. His plans had to be summarily revised and his armies to be withdrawn hastily on the famous fortress and its outlying bulwarks. In this chapter we are to trace 3 distinct phases of activity, in which the New Zealand Division was engaged during the part it played in the fourth stage of the British offensive. Firstly it was to attack the enemy in semi-prepared positions where, till the disaster on the Scarpe caused him to reconsider his policy, he had intended to make a tentative stand. Then, as he retreated on the Hindenburg Line outposts, it was to carry out a rapid pursuit under conditions closely approximating to open warfare. Lastly, in a distinct reversion to the trench warfare type of operation, it was to assault these outposts with a view to obtaining a position for attack on the main Hindenburg Line beyond.

For 2nd September the IV. Corps proposed to continue the policy of pressing the enemy withdrawal in co-operation with the Corps on the north and south. On the right the 42nd Division was instructed to capture Villers-au-Flos; on the left the 5th Division was to take the high ground east of Beugny with Delsaux Farm. The New Zealand Division in the centre would conform with the more important movements on its flanks by an advance driving the enemy off the bare, broad crest overlooking Haplincourt. Both flank Divisions were assisted by tanks. Exploitation was to be carried eastward if possible. Of the 5 field artillery brigades at the disposal of the Division, 2, the 2nd (Army) and 3rd Brigades, were earmarked to support the Division's operations. The 1st Artillery Brigade and an (Army) brigade supported the 42nd Division's attack. The other (Army) brigade co-operated with the 5th Division.

On the evening of 1st September, the 2nd Infantry Brigade took over the whole Divisional front, placing 2nd Otago[1] on the right and 1st Canterbury on the left. The battalions marched up round the outskirts of Bapaume, which was being heavily shelled and bombed by aeroplanes. Hostile artillery was similarly active in the forward area, and before relief was completed 2nd Otago had sustained several casualties. Batteries moved up behind Fremicourt.

In accordance with plans, the attack was launched at 5.15 a.m on 2nd September. Working in close conjunction with the 5th Division, 1st Canterbury advanced with 1 company over its entire front. The left, clearing up the rows of shellholes and disconnected trenches, reached the objective without much difficulty. The right was held up short of it by a nest of machine guns and by the guns of the 2 disabled enemy tanks which lay in a sunken road just beyond the brow of the hill.[2] 120 prisoners were captured with 16 machine guns. 2nd Otago, in co-operation with the 42nd Division also attacked with 1 company. There had been perhaps an error on the outgoing battalion's part in defining their line, or advanced parties of the German garrison had been pushed further forward during the hours of darkness. In any case, opposite Otago's right the enemy not merely held the crest where the 1st Brigade had experienced so much trouble during the previous afternoon but occupied in some strength positions that fell "within" our barrage line. It took some time and trouble to dispose of these posts, and meanwhile the barrage had swept well ahead and passed beyond the machine gun nests about the Haplincourt road. Their intense fire frustrated attempts by the weakened platoon on the right to reach the final objective. Meanwhile a fine instance of leadership and determination had been shown on the left. The platoon commander had been early wounded, and Sergt. R. D. Brown was left in command of the platoon, now isolated on both flanks. He led his men in a charge on a cross-roads in front, taking over 50 prisoners and several machine guns. He then found that the enemy

1 Major W. G. A. Bishop, M.C., temporarily commanding, vice Lt.-Col. Pennycook, killed 24th August.
2 p. 455.

were strongly entrenched behind him and between him and 1st Canterbury, but he re-organised the platoon and maintained his position, till later it was found possible to send reinforcements.   The 42nd Division early cleared Villers-au-Flos, but its capture did not silence the machine gun nests which lay about the Haplincourt road between the village and Otago's right.   An anti-tank gun was extremely active also from beyond Villers-au-Flos, and heavy fire from high-velocity guns in   addition   made   Otago's   position   most   uncomfortable. Infantry unaided could not hope to cross that open country, and it was decided to make a fresh effort later in the day with a further barrage.

At 12 noon a weak enemy counter-attack at the junction of 1st Canterbury with the 5th Division about Delsaux Farm was repulsed, and prisoners were captured.   This flank was strengthened by further machine guns.   An hour later 2nd Otago reopened the attack on their objective.   The 42nd Division, now in possession of their objective, had restored the 2 field artillery brigades lent to them. These were consequently available for intensifying the barrage which was described by the Corps artillery representative, who chanced to witness it, as the best barrage that he had ever seen.   The attacking line was similarly strengthened.   A fresh company was employed with 2 platoons of the original company and with a third from another company.   The group of huts on the Haplincourt road half a mile west of Haplincourt was strongly held, and a sunken road running at right angles to the main road was full of machine guns.   Pressing the attack vigorously, however, Otago cleared hutments and sunken road and then pushed on, still under machine gun fire, to another sunken road beyond.   Here they were but a little short of the line aimed at.

All through the afternoon the Canterbury company had been struggling with the hornets' nest about the tanks.   The position was in itself formidable and most difficult of approach. In the end they had recourse to artillery.   A platoon from one of the support companies came up to lend a hand, and a barrage was put down at 6 p.m.   Cpl. P. S. Putman working his section round the flank under heavy fire succeeded in killing or capturing the crews of the flank machine guns.   The remainder of the garrison then surrendered readily.   Together with the tanks Canterbury captured 30 prisoners with 4 machine guns, bringing their total bag to 150 prisoners and 20 machine guns.   They had also secured a field gun.   Taking advantage of this barrage and the enemy's preoccupation, Otago also made a further advance and secured the line of their objective. To them too the Germans now offered but feeble resistance, and swelled Otago's captures for the day to a grand total of 200. They claimed in addition 60 machine guns, the sunken road alone yielding 17, 3 trench mortars and much other material. By nightfall the 2nd Brigade was established in advance of the objective assigned. The 5th Division had taken Delsaux Farm, but were checked by heavy fire in front of Beugny.

It had been originally intended that the Corps should confine itself on 3rd September to consolidating the ground gained and the clearing of enemy "pockets." Later in the evening of the 2nd, however, it was decided that the 5th Division should take Beugny, which in view of our capture of the high ground south might prove now to be defended with less resolution. Two brigades of the New Zealand artillery were lent for the operation. Less important tasks were assigned to the other 2 Divisions. The 42nd Division would be satisfied with securing a position favourable for an attack on Barastre. The New Zealanders would establish themselves in the valley below the slopes on which their line now rested. They were not to go even as far as Haplincourt village and wood which had been reported full of machine guns and were to be bombarded.

During the night 2nd/3rd September the enemy made no attempt to recover the ground lost during the day, and his artillery and machine gun fire were not above normal. He was indeed in no position to strike back, for that day English troops and Canadians had broken the Drocourt-Quéant Line in the north, and as a repercussion of the blow, his whole front along the Fourth and Third Armies was being hurriedly withdrawn. Before dawn his fire died away, and soon after day broke vast coils of smoke from burning dumps could be seen rising behind his lines in Vélu Bertincourt and elsewhere. Patrols pushed forward with alacrity and found Haplincourt and its wood clear.

After a hasty breakfast the main advance was continued. A troop of Scots Greys attached to the 2nd Brigade was allotted to the 2 battalions in the line for the purpose of establishing liaison with flank units. The 2nd (Army) Artillery Brigade was detailed to support the pursuit. It was an ideal autumn day. The sky was flecked with gossamer clouds, and a few slight showers cooled the air. Haplincourt

was occupied by 7 a.m.   By 8.20 a.m. the 42nd Division had
reached Barastre and were through Haplincourt Wood, while
on the left, Beugny, yesterday so formidable, fell without
opposition to the 5th Division.   In the centre the New Zealanders moved forward rapidly.   Many fires started by the
enemy were still ablaze when passed.   By 9.30 a.m. 1st Canterbury reached the western edges of Vélu Wood and the
outskirts of Bertincourt with little resistance.[1]   Their left
was slightly troubled by machine gun fire from Vélu.   In
Bertincourt itself and on the high ground east of it there
were a few machine gun posts.   Ere long, however, Scots
Greys patrols reported that Bertincourt was clear of the
enemy, who were holding the high ground and the Bapaume-
Péronne railway east of it, and before noon the village was
in our possession.   The left too had cleared the intricacies
of Vélu Wood, and the whole line reached the railway.   We
were now among the old British rear lines which had gone
down before the avalanche in March.   Over these lines the
returning tide was now to flow strongly, till 3 days later
it beat against the barrier of the Trescault Ridge.   The enemy
had succeeded in destroying or withdrawing most of his
material, but on the Bertincourt station platform 1st Canterbury found a 5.9-in. howitzer.

A halt had been ordered east of Bertincourt for the
purpose of reorganisation, while patrols were to be pushed
forward to cover further advance.   It so chanced that at this
stage the first real opposition was encountered.   In front of
the railway the ground falls to the hollow, below the surface
of which is hidden the tunnel of the Canal du Nord.   Beyond
the hollow it rises again to the picturesque village of Ruyaulcourt, slightly under a mile east of the railway.   Here the
enemy's rearguards were still in strength.   His field artillery
fired over open sights at our patrols. Our Lewis guns engaged
and silenced them, but the Germans were able to man-handle
them out before our own artillery could destroy them.   There
was ample evidence of numerous machine guns in the gardens
and outhouses on the western edge of Ruyaulcourt.   The 5th
Division was well up on the left, but the right was not yet
in line.   We could therefore afford to wait quietly till dusk,
keeping clear of Bertincourt, now under heavy hostile shelling.

When the protective darkness fell, patrols were pushed
forward to penetrate Ruyaulcourt and gain the Pauper and

---

1 By the evening of 19th March 1917, during the German retreat, the
British infantry had reached the line Barastre-Vélu with cavalry in touch with the
enemy at Bertincourt.

Ponder lines of trenches east of it. The village was, however, held, though not in great strength, and the patrols for the most part were checked at the western entrances. Our main force rested in a trench system and along the railway east of Bertincourt. During the day, in addition to the 5.9-in. howitzer, 1st Canterbury captured 14 prisoners, 14 machine guns, and some trench mortars. The outpost line for the night was covered by the 2nd (Army) Artillery Brigade, and the main line of defence in rear by the 1st and 3rd Artillery Brigades and one of the 2 (Army) brigades attached. The other rejoined its Division. General Russell's Headquarters moved this day to Fremicourt, and Corps Headquarters were making final arrangements for their great bound forward on the following day from Marieux to Grévillers.

In view of the enemy's retirement the Third Army had issued orders for the advance to be continued on the following day (4th September), with the additional and thrilling instruction that the XVII. Corps on the north should move on Cambrai. When the enemy's main line of resistance was located, our advanced guards were to engage it closely but to refrain from attacks on a large scale until a properly organised operation was sanctioned by the Army. It was expected that the Germans would stand at bay on the Scheldt Canal to Banteux and the Hindenburg Line thence northwards. But till the enemy's line of resistance should be definitely located the bulk of the heavy artillery would be rested and reorganised. Similarly all heavy tanks and whippets were withdrawn into Army reserve for rest prior to major operations. The Corps right was directed to move on the trenches east of Metz-en-Couture, the New Zealanders in the centre on the trenches at the eastern edge of Havrincourt Wood, and the left on the trenches east of the Canal du Nord and north-east of Havrincourt village. If resistance should be offered to the New Zealanders in the Wood, it would be turned from the north and the south by the flank Divisions. Troops were to be kept in depth.

In the evening (3rd September) the 37th Division relieved the 5th in the left sector. With the New Zealand Division troops of the 3rd Hussars replaced the Scots Greys as a substitute for Divisional cavalry. The 2nd Brigade made arrangements to relieve 2nd Otago and 1st Canterbury, who had borne the burden of the hard fighting of the 2nd and the arduous patrol work of the 3rd.

Apart from considerable gas shelling the night was quiet, and the weather remained fine. During the hours of darkness the enemy fell back from Ruyaulcourt, and 1st Canterbury patrols pushed through it and in the morning established posts on its eastern outskirts. Sniping and machine gun fire, however, were active from Pauper Trench in front. In it our Lewis guns killed several Germans. With the dawn the British balloons rose startlingly close behind the front line and were ineffectually attacked by enemy aircraft. In the early morning 1st Otago[1] on the right and 2nd Canterbury[2] on the left passed through the leading troops on the railway and resumed the advance at 7 a.m. There was no barrage. Each attacking battalion was supported by a section of 18-pounders and by machine guns and light trench mortars. By 7.30 a.m. they had crossed the hollow and cleared Ruyaulcourt, in which a few machine guns remained till the last moment that permitted retreat, causing some annoyance to 1st Otago's flank in the open country south. At the other end of the line Canterbury's left pressed on to the high ground north of Ruyaulcourt, and after half an hour's bombardment of Pauper Trench the 2 front Canterbury companies attacked and cleared it, taking some 50 prisoners, with machine guns. They were now on bare gentle slopes overlooking a shallow valley. On the far side the ground rose on to an undulating tract of pasture ground. Beyond it some 1500 yards distant from our patrols was the dense bulk of the great Havrincourt Wood, in which Byng had hidden his tanks for Cambrai in 1917.

With hands up a large number of Germans came forward over the valley, in which they were securely hidden from their artillery and machine guns, but an untimely activity on the part of our own guns, misapprehending their intention, drove them back. From the western edge of the Wood enemy field guns fired salvoes on our advancing patrols, but were silenced by our admirably handled machine guns and forward sections of artillery. Particularly fine work was done by Lt. J. Mayer, of the 2nd Battery. One of his guns was destroyed, and he had serious casualties in men and horses, but in face of heavy fire he kept his section close up to the infantry.

More formidable even than the German field guns were the machine guns on the fringe of Havrincourt Wood

1 Major Hargest, vice Lt.-Col. Charters, on special duty.
2 Major Wilson, vice Lt.-Col. Stewart, on leave.

and in sunken roads across the fields. Such as were located by patrols and failed to yield to infantry pressure were engaged and were knocked out by the closely following 18-pounders. Others it was extremely difficult to detect. The right Canterbury company was commanded by 2nd Lt. G. Hartshorn, who repeatedly made daring reconnaissances for this purpose. In one of these he ran against a German machine gun post which was firing in another direction. He rushed it single-handed, capturing 11 prisoners and the machine gun. Hartshorn was later seriously wounded, but refused to leave his company till it was properly consolidated for the night. In the same way a Canterbury n.c.o., Cpl. M. O'Grady, in order to locate and bring Lewis gun fire on troublesome machine guns only some 200 yards away, got up from cover on 2 separate occasions during the afternoon and ran in the open to attract their fire. On both occasions the enemy disclosed his positions, and under cover of Lewis guns from a flank the infantry rushed and cleared them.

By the early afternoon the left Canterbury company, in line with the 37th Division troops, had reached within 600 yards of the Wood. The right was still somewhat in rear in touch with 1st Otago, who had successfully cleared resistance in a chalk-pit south of Ruyaulcourt, but were harassed by heavy enfilade machine gun fire from the huts on the road leading to Neuville-Bourgonval. That village itself was strongly held, and for the moment checked the 42nd Division. The Otago patrols, among whom a party led by Pte. A. G. Akroyd was conspicuous for resourcefulness and initiative, were withdrawn, and the area was searched by artillery. On a renewed advance, only 1 machine gun was in action, and under cover of Lewis gun fire the resistance was overpowered, and the gun and crew captured. Till Neuville-Bourgonval should be cleared by the 42nd Division, the right flank was flung back astride the road.

The capture of Neuville-Bourgonval, however, might prove no easy task. Soon after 1 p.m. numbers of the enemy were seen advancing in open order towards it from the east, but they were dealt with by our artillery, machine gun and Lewis gun fire, and dispersed. In the evening (7.15 p.m.) the 42nd Division attacked the village under a particularly heavy barrage and succeeded in capturing the northern half. 1st Otago co-operated on the left and advanced their line on the northern outskirts, capturing 45 prisoners. The southern

portion remained with the enemy. As a result of his resistance in and about Neuville-Bourgonval, there was a considerable re-entrant in the right of our line, where Otago, in
touch with the 42nd Division, lay astride the road leading to
Metz-en-Couture. Beyond our right the Germans had posts
in the southern part of Neuville-Bourgonval and a strong
garrison in the trench system east of the village.

During the day the enemy's artillery had been active with
guns and howitzers of all calibres up to 8-in. over the whole
area, and especially in the neighbourhood of Ruyaulcourt.
Together with a liberal profusion of gas this shelling continued throughout the night, but the troops were well spread
out and casualties generally light. In the open, splinters flew
wide, and 2nd Canterbury lost 13 out of their 15 stretcher-
bearers. Patrols secured touch with the enemy on the edge
of the Wood. The 5th was spent for the most part quietly
in improving our positions. In the morning, however,
1st Otago set about straightening the re-entrant on the Metz-
en-Couture Road. Prisoners and a machine gun were captured
in small enterprises in which a very fine platoon commander,
2nd Lt. W. H. Junge, showed exceptional powers as a fighting
leader. In the late afternoon (5.30 p.m.), in view of readjustments on the Corps front, to be referred to presently,
the 42nd Division attacked on a larger scale. Three companies of Otago co-operated. Their objective was a trench
system between Neuville-Bourgonval and a sunken road that
ran parallel with the western edge of Havrincourt Wood and
crossed the Metz Road. Otago were entirely successful. Fifty
prisoners were captured in the trench and road, but unfortunately, while Junge was rounding up some Germans who
had surrendered, he was killed by a machine gun firing from
the Wood. The 42nd Division fulfilled their task of
completing the capture of the village prior to handing over
the line.

On the left, 2nd Canterbury patrols had during the day
located enemy machine guns on the edge of the Wood. These
had been shelled by heavy artillery at 5 p.m. The barrage
for the Otago attack came down on part of the German
position facing Canterbury, and the latter's right, seizing the
opportunity, also swung forward. The movement was covered
by the Lewis guns of the left company. The 5 p.m.
bombardment had destroyed the German machine guns,
and our casualties were extremely light. 17 prisoners and 2
machine guns were captured. Many of the enemy were killed

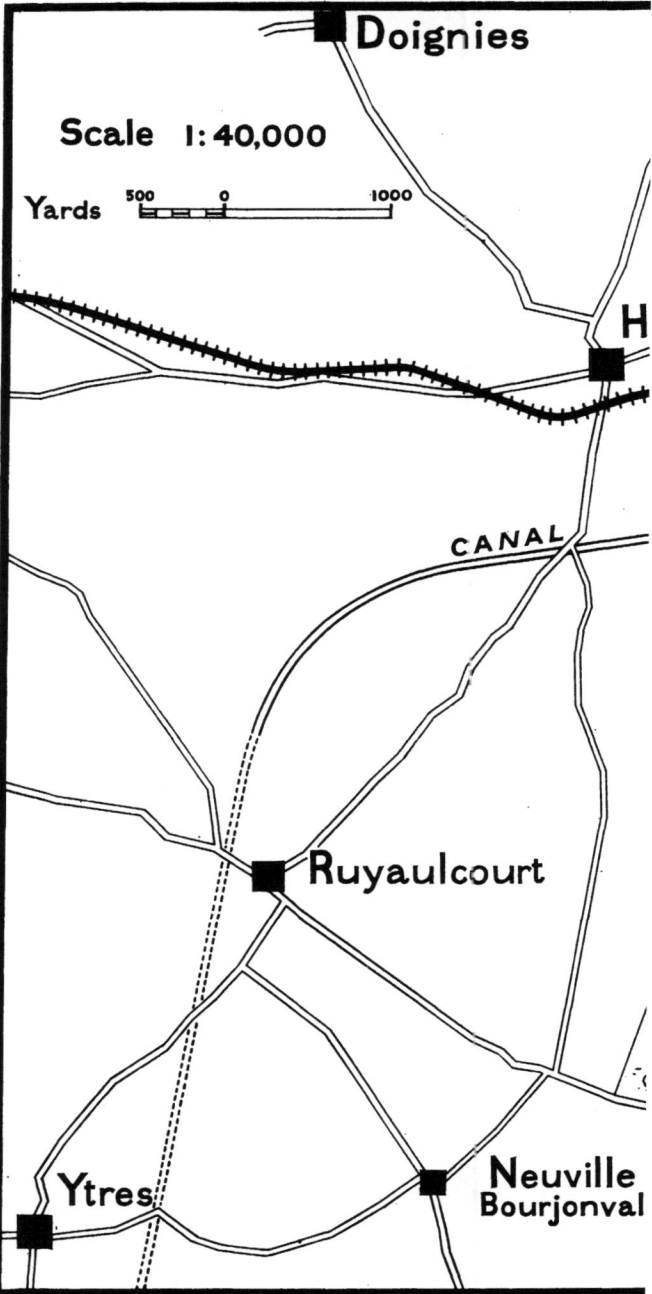

Doignies

Scale 1:40,000

Yards 500 0 1000

H

CANAL

Ruyaulcourt

Ytres

Neuville
Bourjonval

HAVRIN

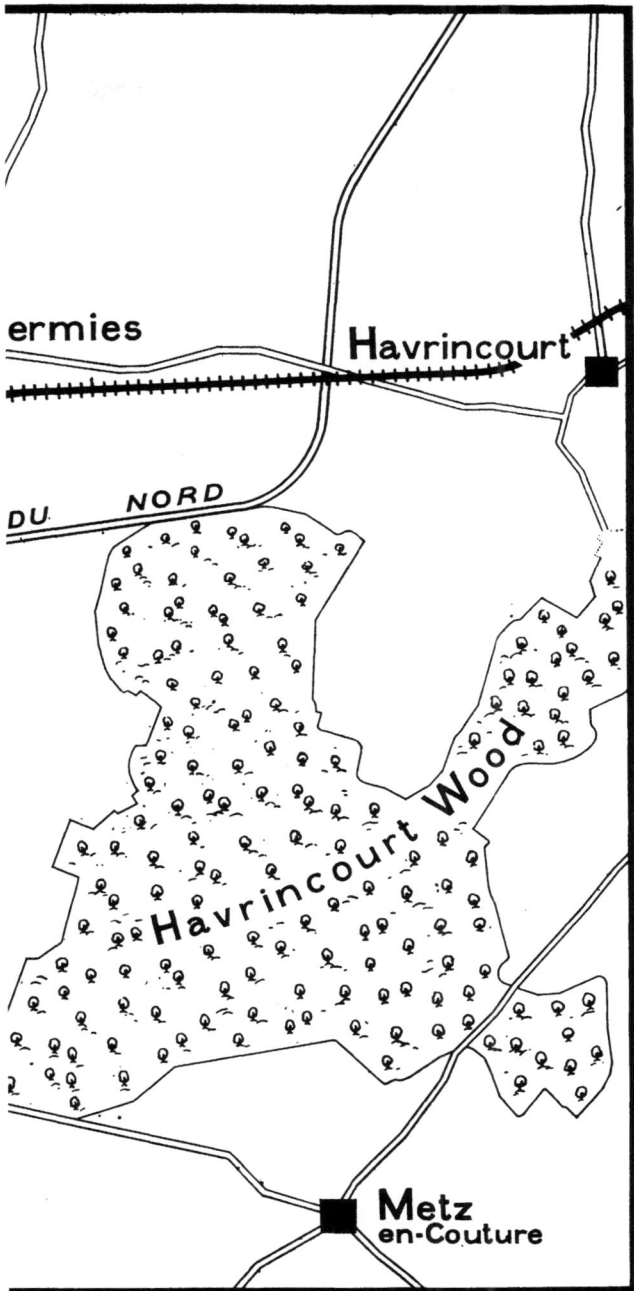

ermies

Havrincourt

DU NORD

Havrincourt Wood

Metz
en-Couture

by rifle fire. By 7 p.m. the line was established all along the sunken road 600 yards from the Wood.

The V. Corps on the right were now also over the Canal du Nord, and the VI. Corps on the left had reached its western bank about the great spoil-heap near Hermies. Here the deep trough of the canal might prove a serious obstacle, but it was not yet certain that the enemy would contest it. Corps Commanders were instructed to continue to adhere to the principle of pressing the enemy with advanced guards, with the object of driving in his rear guards and outposts and ascertaining his dispositions. Troops were to be rested as much as possible, resources conserved and communications improved with a view to a vigorous resumption of the offensive in the near future. As many Divisions and artillery brigades as possible were to be withdrawn into reserve for rest and training.

In accordance with this policy, the Corps front was on the night 5th/6th September reconstituted on a 2-Divisional basis. The 37th took over the northern sector of the New Zealand line, which extended southwards to include that of the 42nd Division. This increase of frontage necessitated the employment by the leading brigade of 3 battalions in the line. The remaining battalion would be in support. A battalion of the support brigade was allotted as reserves. 2nd Canterbury's line down to Matheson Road was handed over to the 37th Division, and it side-stepped southwards. Similarly 1st Otago extended their right to take over part of the 42nd Division's position east of Neuville-Bourgonval. The remaining 1000 yards were given to 1st Canterbury who came in on the right. 2nd Wellington was placed at General Young's disposal as a mobile reserve.

The 3 field artillery brigades covering the 42nd Division's front passed under General Napier Johnston's command. The second of the 2 British (Army) brigades hitherto attached to the Division was handed over to the 37th Division. A battery of 9.2-in. howitzers and a brigade of R.G.A., consisting of 3 batteries of 6-in. howitzers, was affiliated to the Division. The 2nd (Army) Brigade, 1 of the British field artillery brigades, and the 3rd Brigade covered the front, while the remaining 3 brigades remained in Divisional reserve but were maintained in action for S.O.S. On the following day, in conformity with Army instructions, 1 of the 42nd Divisional Artillery brigades was withdrawn, and the remain-

ing 2 brigades with the 1st N.Z.F.A. Brigade were superimposed over the whole front.

While these various readjustments were in progress, the
2nd Canterbury area and Ruyaulcourt were heavily gassed,
and the infantry reliefs were considerably hampered and
delayed. This artillery activity covered a further enemy
withdrawal south of Havrincourt Wood. The shelling eased
off towards morning, and patrols early reported signs of
evacuation.

While making a personal reconnaissance at 10 a.m. of a
Strong Point in the trenches east of Neuville-Bourgonval,
Major Hargest, his intelligence officer, and a sergeant ran
unexpectedly into and took prisoners a party of 5 Germans
with a machine gun. Shortly afterwards in the same vicinity
another small Otago party under 2nd Lt. A. E. Byrne
captured 21 Germans. These, however, were the final rearguards. Infantry patrols and a section of Otago Mounted
Rifles, now attached from the XXII. Corps Mounted Regiment
as Divisional cavalry, were pushed forward as a screen, and
the other troops followed. The advance continued throughout
the day, 6th September, with little opposition.

Under a blue sky and scorching sun 1st Otago moved with
remarkable rapidity. They were supported most effectively
by a section of the 9th Battery (2nd Lt. A. F. Downer)
which over open sights engaged enemy infantry and two
77-mm. guns in Metz. Here the battalion was for a time
checked, but by the late afternoon had succeeded in enveloping the village. Metz had been captured by the British in
the first week of April 1917, in the last stages of the German
withdrawal on the Hindenburg Line, and had been fortified
by them with 2 lines of inner and outer defences. Otago
carried the inner defences shortly after 6 p.m. Enemy
resistance, however, was appreciably stiffening, and a section
of Otago Mounted Rifles, attempting to reconnoitre Gouzeaucourt, came under heavy machine gun fire. Towards evening
the German guns bombarded Metz, where a large mine crater
was blown at the cross-roads, with marked vindictiveness.
The outer defences were part of the long line of old British
trenches which had been set as a distant objective for the
advance on 4th September. It extended southwards over the
Fins and Revelon Ridges and northwards along the eastern
edge of Havrincourt Wood. Despite the increasing fire, however, both right and centre battalions pushed on these trenches,
and by nightfall 1st Canterbury held the Quivering and

Quotient sectors east and south-east of Metz, 1st Otago the Quack and Quality positions to the east and north-east.

Meantime on the 2nd Canterbury front energetic reconnaissances by O'Grady and others established that the enemy still held Havrincourt Wood strongly as late as 3 p.m. It was no part of our purpose to force a passage at a costly price if the Wood could be enveloped. Shortly afterwards, however, signals were given by an aeroplane that the enemy was moving. At 5 p.m. our posts were on the western edge with fighting patrols among the trees. In combination with the troops on the left, 2 companies began to work through the forest. By 10 p.m. after an arduous and perplexing passage they had penetrated to within 50 yards of their objective in the important Quaff Trench which continued Quality northwards on the eastern edge of the Wood. Here the German rearguards proved too strong to be pushed without proper reconnaissance. Two Canterbury platoons had gone astray in the dense bush, and touch had been lost with the 37th Division. The line was consolidated for the night with a defensive flank formed by the support companies. Throughout the remainder of the night officers' patrols fruitlessly scoured the Wood in search of the lost platoons and the 37th Division troops on the left.

Losses throughout had been slight. 1st Otago captured 70 prisoners with 26 machine guns and a 5 9 in. howitzer. 1st Canterbury similarly secured numerous machine guns and two 77-mm. guns. Even 2nd Canterbury in the fastnesses of the Wood had contrived to capture a few prisoners. Nowhere till the close of the day had opposition been severe, and the line had been advanced over 2 miles. No more illuminating evidence of the aggressiveness vigour and dash of the New Zealand battalions could be cited than the reiterated admonitions addressed to them by the Divisional staff against undue impetuosity. The infantry were most efficiently backed by artillery and machine guns, and the very rate of progress saved casualties, for on repeated occasions the Germans put down barrages on ground over which the advance had already passed, thus providing object lessons to the gunner of the futility of map-shelling and the essential importance of observation of fire.

During the night, 6th/7th September, 1st Canterbury had been unable to secure touch with the enemy, but 1st Otago patrols penetrating the fringe of Gouzeaucourt Wood and working north of it were much hampered by fire. Just before dawn, 7th September, the active machine guns in Quaff ceased, and 2nd Canterbury carried it with slight resistance and pushed on to the eastern edge of the Wood. In the daylight they regained touch with the 37th Division. The lost platoons returned at 7 a.m. All 3 battalions were now confronted by the Trescault Ridge, and our advance had nearly reached its limits. Along this important height machine guns were in great force, and field guns in Trescault village on the north sniped over open sights down the valley at our patrols. Our 18-pounders "pasted" the trenches, and howitzers bombarded the enemy field guns. These latter were silenced, but machine guns and well-posted snipers made progress infinitely difficult. By noon, however, posts were established in front of Havrincourt Wood. The right and centre of our line pushed well into the valley and into the subsidiary southern corridor which held the greater part of Gouzeaucourt Wood, a long segment of thick bush straggling eastwards up the ridge. The enemy appeared to reinforce his already numerous machine guns, but we succeeded in establishing posts inside the edge and round the southern fringe of Gouzeaucourt Wood. The Rifle Brigade, however, were to relieve in the evening. In view of the difficulty of handing over these advanced posts about Gouzeaucourt Wood, it was decided to withdraw them on to the Quotient Quack Quality and Quaff trenches on the near side of the valley. The weather had turned colder, and much rain fell during the day.

While the infantry and artillery had been straining hard after the retreating enemy, the vast and complex machine of the administrative services had worked at intense pressure and with gratifying smoothness. Field ambulances followed close in rear. Engineers reconnoitred dugouts, searched for booby-traps, constructed defensive posts, and repaired roads. Not the least of their responsibilities was the supervision of the water supply. They cleared wells, tested the water, and put up notice-boards giving the results. They erected power-pumping plant and hand-pumps, and installed storage-troughs and water-cart filling-points. The whole rear area indeed seethed with the active movement that attends an advancing army. The effect on the German prisoners is happily illustrated by the remarks of an intelligent Guards n.c.o. captured a few days later in the neighbourhood:

"Passing back under escort I saw things that I could scarcely believe—such transport, such horses, such men and these masses of artillery! I compare them with our wretched iron-wheeled transport, skidding all over the place and blocking the roads in wet weather, our scanty and badly-fed horses, and those boys pretending to be Guards.

"We still have a certain amount of artillery, but you must have five guns to our one, and we are not well off for shells, whilst you seem to have an endless supply.

"No! Germany is defeated, and the sooner we recognise it the better, but you will admit we have put up a good fight. No nation could have done more."

The infantry relief was carried out in pitch darkness, and the South Island battalions withdrew to the position of support brigade. The Rifle Brigade took over the line with the 2nd, 3rd, and 4th[1] Battalions, in that order, from south to north. The 1st Artillery Brigade batteries were now on the western edge of Havrincourt Wood, the 2nd between the Wood and Metz, 1 of the 2 attached 42nd Divisional brigades south of Metz, with the other attached brigade and the 3rd Brigade superimposed further in rear.

The morning of the 8th broke very cold with a high wind from the south. Whatever hopes the Rifles had of emulating the rapid progress of the 2nd Brigade were doomed to disappointment. There was no abatement of the enemy's fire, and our posts on the forward slopes under Havrincourt Wood were aggressively sniped and machine-gunned from the high ridge over the valley. It became increasingly manifest that we were at length approaching the main line of resistance.

The enemy was now indeed only 3 miles from the Hindenburg Line itself. The Trescault Ridge,[2] in conjunction with similar positions southward about Epehy and with the obstacle of the Canal du Nord northwards beyond Havrincourt village, presented itself as a strong forward defence line which might be calculated on to withstand even prepared attacks, and act as a buffer to the main line of resistance behind. Eastwards the Trescault Ridge fell towards the Couillet Valley, through which ran the Péronne-Cambrai railway. Its general conformation was like an elongated right hand, with a long forefinger (Trescault Spur) pointing due north towards the village of that name, and the bent knuckles of the middle and fourth fingers projecting north-eastwards in the Beaucamp

1 Major Barrowclough, vice Lt.-Col. Beere, wounded 26th August.

2 It is convenient to apply this name to the whole of the high ground between Gouzeaucourt and Trescault, and reserve the name Trescault Spur for its proper use as designing the northern extremity of this ridge.

and Borderer Ridges towards Beaucamp village and Villers-Plouich respectively. West of Gouzeaucourt village, which lay in the upper Couillet Valley, the wrist joined a wide tableland.

The ridge, along whose crest ran the road from Gouzeaucourt to Trescault, was fortified by old British trenches. On its eastern brow was the strong and important African Trench running north and south along the ridge and overlooking Gouzeaucourt village. African Support on the western slopes above Gouzeaucourt Wood commanded the top of the ridge. Further north Lincoln Reserve and other trenches continued African Trench along the knuckles of Borderer and Beaucamp Ridges. There also on our side of the main spur, some 200 yards under the crest, ran a chord line connected in its turn with the African system southwards, and known as Snap Trench. Further down the slope lay Snap Reserve. A multitude of saps ran up from Snap Reserve to Snap Trench, and the German position on this western slope was further strengthened by many deep-sunken roads whose banks afforded admirable vantage points from which to rake our advance with grazing machine gun fire. Of these roads, 2 ran towards Gouzeaucourt, 1 eastwards from Metz and 1 south-eastwards from Havrincourt Wood. These were cut at right angles by an old British "corduroy" road traced along the hillside and parallel to our own positions and to African Support and Snap Reserve which lay just above it. At the junctions of this old road, with the Metz Road at Queen's Cross, and the Wood Road at Dead Man's Corner, the Germans had by digging into the steep banks improvised redoubts which they held in force.

The first effort on the high ground was planned for 9th September when the V. Corps on the right proposed to carry the part of the tableland west and south-west of Gouzeaucourt, including African Trench as far north as the Metz Road. The New Zealanders were instructed to protect the V. Corps' left flank by capturing and holding African for another 1000 yards northwards, thence refusing their left along a convenient communication sap down to Dead Man's Corner, and thereafter down the Wood Road back to the south-east edge of Havrincourt Wood. With this object in view the 8th was spent for the most part in necessary preparations. Patrols from the 2nd Rifles, however, penetrated Gouzeaucourt Wood, and a small party under Rflmn. J. C. Dibble surprised and dispersed with Lewis gun fire an enemy attack on an isolated British post to the south. Later these patrols were forced back by superior numbers of the enemy working round their right flank. In the evening they again penetrated part of the wood, and it was only after dark, when they were withdrawn in conformity with barrage plans, that the enemy reoccupied it in strength.

For the forthcoming attack the 4th Rifles on the left in front of Havrincourt Wood were not affected. The 2nd Rifles on the right would carry African System and the communication trench to Dead Man's Corner and clear that Strong Point. The 3rd Rifles[1] in the centre would form a 1200 yards' defensive flank from the cross-roads to Havrincourt Wood. Arrangements had been made for heavy artillery to bombard trenches and roads on the eastern slopes of the ridge, the Couillet Valley, and the outskirts of Gouzeaucourt. A creeping barrage would support the main New Zealand attack on the 2nd Rifles' front. A standing barrage would be placed on Snap Reserve in front of the left battalion. Protective curtains of machine gun fire were also provided.

The night was again intensely dark, and the assaulting companies had no little difficulty in reaching their assembly positions amid the wire and shellholes on the western edge of Gouzeaucourt Wood. Each section, however, was in its place some 20 minutes before zero. The attack was delivered at 4 a.m. During the previous day enemy aeroplanes had seen much movement of troops tanks and transport behind our lines, and our assault was expected. Determined to retain Trescault Ridge, the Germans did not commit its defence to the 44th and 225th Divisions that had the last few days opposed us and were exhausted by the pressure of hard rearguard actions and by lack of food. They had brought up fresh from refitting and rest the 113th and the Jäger Division, 2 of their strongest corps d'élite at this time. The latter especially was a magnificent body of men, fully equal to the Guards and reserved for the most vigorous work. On these troops the retiring rearguards of the 44th and 225th Divisions now fell back and passed into reserve. Large numbers of machine guns also were sent up to strengthen the all-important positions on the ridge, and the new garrison of tried and confident veterans were ordered to hold their ground at all costs. When our guns opened, the enemy's answering barrage fell immediately. It was directed, however, rather on Metz and Havrincourt Wood in rear than on the lower slopes of the ridge where our troops were assembled, and though inflicting casualties among the storming

1 Major Murphy (transferred from the 2nd Bn.), vice Lt.-Col. Bell, wounded 7th Sept.

riflemen it was not of undue intensity. But the fire of the enemy's massed machine guns leapt at once into a tremendous concentration which in daylight must have blotted out any assault. As it was, the darkness which the assembling troops had cursed so bitterly as they stumbled about the old entanglements now proved their salvation. It was lit only by the German flares and the bursts of howitzer shells on the hillside in front and valley behind. Much of the enemy's machine gun fire was consequently high and passed over their heads.

The 2nd Rifles employed 2 companies, using a support company to mop up Gouzeaucourt Wood and assist the leading companies in an emergency. The right company was commanded by an extremely gallant and capable officer, Lt. D. Kennedy, M.C., who prior to the attack had made a fine personal reconnaissance of the position. Faced by the impenetrable dark thickets of Gouzeaucourt Wood, his company boldly pressed in 2 columns up the Metz Road towards Gouzeaucourt and along another smaller track through the trees. The garrison at Queen's Cross was killed or captured in a brief struggle, and African Support was won after stubborn fighting. It was still dark, and the company, which had crossed several trenches on the way, believed and reported that they were in African Trench itself. Some 70 prisoners were captured, consisting mostly of Jägers, but including some men of the 6th (Dismounted) Cavalry Division. There was no sign of the troops on either flank. The V. Corps' assault had been unable to make progress, and the 2nd Rifles' left company, skirting the north edge of the wood and coming under intense machine gun fire from Dead Man's Corner, had been forced into the cover of shellholes round its north-eastern edge. When dawn came, Kennedy realised that he was not in his final objective, but with the company already isolated and with African Trench in front stoutly held, no attempt at further progress could for the moment be contemplated. It would be no mean achievement to hold the ground already won, for both flanks were in the air, and in his rear there was a strong German garrison in the southern part of Gouzeaucourt Wood, which the support company had not thoroughly cleared. The support company, indeed, had suffered somewhat heavily, and the company commander was the only officer left.

Part of this company, however, were to strengthen Kennedy's left. For, about 7 a.m., seeing the left company checked Sergt.-Major G. F. Webster and Sergt. T. R. Kennerley rushed forward with the right half of the company to occupy their place in African Support. They were covered by Kennedy's fire and carried the position. Each of the 2 leaders captured 2 machine guns and killed their crews. An attempt was at once made to help the left company by bombing up African Support towards Dead Man's Corner. Led by a fearless n.c.o., Cpl. G. Fruin, a little party reached this point. They captured 2 machine guns and 16 prisoners, and killed many of the retreating enemy. This deadly Strong Point cleared, 2 platoons of the left company also were able to reach African Support, and led by 2nd Lt. R. G. Bates, D.C.M., bombed past Dead Man's Corner northwards up the trench itself for 200 yards beyond. Their bombs were already running short, so here they established a block.

Before fresh supplies of bombs could reach them, the enemy fell on them from the northern end of the trench in overpowering strength and with inexhaustible quantities of bombs, and the mingled personnel of the left and support companies were driven back down African Support southwards. The hold on Dead Man's Corner was lost. Very hard fighting ensued about 1 p.m. Pressing his advantage, the enemy forced the posts established towards Dead Man's Corner to fall back nearer Gouzeaucourt Wood. All his efforts to recover the southern portion of African Support were in vain. On the contrary, repeated sorties led by Fruin[1] and by n.c.o.s of the right company made desperate attempts to clear the communication trenches leading up to African. Their pressure was not adequate, however, to dislodge the enemy from his strong position, though they forced him to invoke artillery protection.

While the left of the 2nd Rifles' line in African Support fought with great tenacity, the chief honour of the day undoubtedly belongs to the right company. Inspired by their commander's personality, Kennedy's men held their ground without losing an inch. They killed many of the enemy on their right and repulsed repeated counter-attacks from in front and from the flanks. Mention should be made of an act by C.S.M. P. A. Scully, who commanded a platoon in our support line. With 1 man he was returning from the front line after taking up a load of bombs, when he observed a machine gun firing from the flank. He at once rushed it, and bombing the crew killed them and captured the gun. In the evening the V. Corps troops came up as far

---

1 Fruin died of wounds after further conspicuously gallant work on the 12th.

as Queen's Cross, and to them the 40 Germans, who had all
day been contained by the right company in the southern
portion of Gouzeaucourt Wood, now surrendered. Whole
droves of our heavy shells passed overhead towards
Couillet Valley, but on the ridge the enemy's defence was
not shaken. His contact aeroplanes flew low over our positions. The valley and Queen's Cross were bombarded heavily
with gas and high-explosive. About 7 p.m. he made a final
effort to drive us back.

Under cover of a heavy bombardment he attacked our
whole front from African Support to Dead Man's Corner,
pressing down the saps with great vigour. Everywhere he
was completely repulsed, except before Dead Man's Corner,
where he temporarily compelled 1 post to withdraw. At
dusk the riflemen recovered it. During the day the 2nd
Rifles lost an officer and 14 men killed, 68 men wounded and
2 missing. Of the 150 prisoners captured by the brigade
nearly all were taken by the 2nd Battalion.

While this fiercely-contested battle raged on the 2nd
Rifles' front, the 3rd Battalion on the left was very much less
successful. The right company, held up by the 1917 British
entanglements and coming under heavy fire from Dead Man's
Corner, not yet contained, managed to approach the objective.
The left company suffered severely from machine guns on the
crest and in Snap Reserve and advanced positions which the
barrage chanced to miss. Only a handful reached their goal.
Reinforcements were at once hurried up, but these also lost
heavily. Almost immediately the enemy counter-attacked,
and the left company was forced back to the starting line.
Several wounded men lay still out in the open, 200 yards in
advance of our line. Desperate efforts to rescue these resulted
only in additions to the casualty roll. Sergt. J. Keatley had
gone back with despatches to battalion headquarters. He
was already wounded in the face, but returned to the line.
He now went out himself, under a hail of bullets, and
rescued first 1 and then another wounded man. On reaching a third he found him already dead.

This check in turn exposed the right company's posts.
They withdrew towards the eastern edge of Gouzeaucourt
Wood and took up a position about a hedgerow some 300
yards in front of their original line. Touch was maintained
with the 2nd Battalion, and a defensive flank on the north
was put round the wood. Here they were heavily bombarded and subjected to salvoes of small bombs of combined

gas and explosive which burnt the grass and earth black and caused considerable casualties. Four prisoners were taken. The 3rd Battalion lost an officer and 25 other ranks killed, and 4 officers and 66 other ranks wounded.

The stubbornness of the opposition and the number of counter-attacks attested the enemy's anxiety to maintain intact a deep outpost zone in front of his main line of resistance. Intercepted wireless messages in themselves indicated more and more clearly that the disorganisation of the German Command and troops, resulting from the last fortnight's operations, had been rectified, and that systematic opposition must be expected. In these comparatively local operations of the 9th the Division's role had been dissociated from the IV. Corps and co-ordinated with the action of the V. Corps on its right. Plans were already, however, completed for a resumption of the general advance of the Army with a view to carrying this outpost zone, including the Trescault Ridge, as a first step to the breach of the whole Hindenburg Line. These operations were to be followed some days later by a Fourth Army advance from Gouzeaucourt southwards beyond Epehy with a similar object.

The Third Army blow was to be delivered by the IV. and VI. Corps. The right flank was to be protected by the capture of the Trescault Ridge. For this purpose the 37th Division, on the left of the IV. Corps, and troops of the VI. Corps thence northwards would carry out preliminary operations with the object of securing favourable attack positions. The main attack would take place on 12th September. Then, at one and the same hour, the 62nd Division of the VI. Corps would assault Havrincourt village, and in a movement from the south-west, so as to turn the village of Trescault, the New Zealand and 37th Divisions would storm the Trescault Ridge. The right flank of the New Zealanders would be protected by an advance of a company of the 38th Division on the left wing of the V. Corps south of Gouzeaucourt Wood. The V. Corps also agreed to prolong the barrage on our right flank and to maintain a standing barrage for 2 hours after zero on African Trench, south of the portion to be attacked by them, and on Gouzeaucourt village and the approaches from it to the ridge. All brigades of heavy and field artillery now out of the line for rest or training were instructed to be in action on the night 10th/11th September, and certain batteries were ordered to move forward to advanced positions. Several of these were overlooked from high ground to the south, and hence a proportion of our guns would be compelled to remain silent till the moment of attack.

The 37th Division already on 9th September had by peaceful penetration reached the north-eastern edge of Havrincourt Wood, and by the evening of the 11th both it and the VI. Corps were in position. The New Zealanders were already as far forward as possible, and the intervening days were spent in effecting local improvements. The 3rd Battalion quietly effected considerable progress towards the objective of the 9th north of Gouzeaucourt Wood The 2nd Rifles consolidated their position in African Support, placing light mortars on their right flank and to deal with Dead Man's Corner on their left. One of their patrols, under Cpl. N .G. Stone, had won and occupied this Strong Point on 10th September. But on the evening of the 10th the enemy made a final costly effort to recover African Support. In captured British helmets his infantry rushed Dead Man's Corner and regained it. Then they bombed fiercely from it and from African Trench towards the Support line, but were repulsed with Lewis gun fire and chased back to Dead Man's Corner and their trenches with grenades. By nightfall on the 11th the V. Corps left had joined up with Kennedy in African Support. Renewed attempts to cross the crest and penetrate African Trench in front were foiled.

As compared with the operation of the 9th, the task now set the Rifle Brigade was at once larger and differently orientated. Instead of forming the left protective flank to an attack southwards, they formed part of the right protective flank to an attack on a more considerable scale northwards. Instead of using 2 battalions, all 3 were now to advance and carry the ridge in conjunction with the 37th Division on the left. The 2nd Battalion on the right holding African Support had a single and straightforward objective in the capture of African Trench. North of Gouzeaucourt Wood, in the centre of the line where the 1st Battalion[1] would pass through the 3rd, and on the left, where the 4th would cross the valley under Havrincourt Wood, our troops would be required to carry 2 objectives. The 1st Battalion after clearing Dead Man's Corner had its first objective in Snap Reserve, and its second in Snap Trench. On the extreme left, the first objective of the 4th Battalion was also Snap Reserve, but its

---

1 Major N. F. Shepherd, vice Lt.-Col. Austin, wounded 1st September for the fourth time. Lt.-Col. Austin did not rejoin his Bn. See footnote p. 513.

2ND LIEUT. H. J. LAURENT, V.C.

JÄGER PRISONERS PASSING HAVRINCOURT WOOD

CAPTURED GUNS TURNED ON THE GERMAN LINE

REPAIRING BROKEN SIGNAL WIRES

final objective lay beyond Snap Trench, here bending inconveniently far westwards, and was fixed in the crest road, some 300 yards east of it, which led from Gouzeaucourt to Trescault. The road junction known as Charing Cross, where this road intersected the track from Havrincourt Wood to Beaucamp, marked the boundary in the final objective between the New Zealanders and the 37th Division. Heavy and field artillery and machine guns would co-operate. 3 brigades of field artillery and 3 batteries of heavy artillery were placed under the C.R.A., in addition to the 3 New Zealand brigades. A section of machine guns was put at the disposal of each attacking battalion to assist them in holding the objectives during and after consolidation. A company of the 3rd Battalion garrisoning the centre of the present line was allotted to each of the 2nd and 1st Battalions as reserves.

The weather had turned cold and stormy, but the morning of 12th September was fair and cool. At zero, 5.25 a.m., the supporting artillery broke into a destructive fire on the German positions. The 3 batteries of 6-in. howitzers bombarded the enemy's field guns and selected targets in Couillet Valley. Along the New Zealand objectives the 6 field artillery brigades swept African Trench and Snap Reserve and provided a creeping barrage. The 4.5-in. howitzers opened on the first objective, and then on the 1st and 4th Battalion fronts, when the 18-pounder creeping barrage approached within 200 yards, lifted on the second objective, in order to ensure our men's safety, subsequently lifting again from the second objective in the same way on to selected targets beyond. Two machine gun companies provided an elaborate machine gun barrage. Four medium trench mortars bombarded Dead Man's Corner, a second cross-roads, and trenches 500 yards further north. Six light trench mortars co-operated in bombarding Dead Man's Corner itself and other Strong Points along the slopes.

In front of the 2nd Battalion the barrage rested on its opening line for 6 minutes, and then lifted on to African for 15. Under its cover the 2 attacking companies pushed their way through the wire in front of African Support and "got close down to the barrage in splendid style." On the barrage lifting from African they poured into the trench on its heels and worked deadly execution among the Germans. The right company alone killed from 60 to 80. The company of the 38th Division on their flank did not succeed in coming forward, and Kennedy's right again remained exposed.

After their experience on the 9th the right company had been determined to make no mistake this time about reaching their final objective. Part of one platoon, amounting to 12 men, under Sergt. Harry John Laurent, had been ordered to push beyond it as a fighting patrol. Laurent chanced to cross at a portion which was ungarrisoned and where the wire had been obliterated. Not recognising in the shallow and battered trench the notorious and formidable African, he passed far beyond it, losing some men from fire on the way. Marvelling that they saw no sign yet of African, his party went 700 yards beyond it and were fast approaching a sunken road near Gouzeaucourt, on which, with trench elements in front, the enemy rested his support line. Laurent saw now that he had come too far, but before withdrawing he resolved to attack the hostile supports. Shells and machine gun fire had reduced his party to 7, but each man was a fighter of proved courage and skill. Quickly and coolly making his dispositions, he led the charge. The fighting that followed illustrates well the effect of surprise and dash. The little party played havoc in the support line, killing some 20 of the enemy and taking the whole of the remainder prisoners. They were now being fired at from all sides, and their captives showed signs of making trouble. A grizzled senior officer, probably a company commander, was found at a telephone summoning assistance. He was shot dead by Rflmn. M. Healy, who had already killed 10 of the enemy by bullet and bayonet. The telephone wire was cut, and a few of the more fractious prisoners were killed. The remainder thereafter quietened down and were hurried to our lines. The bag amounted to 111 rank and file, and an officer with 2 messenger dogs. On the way back 1 of their captors was killed. This extraordinarily enterprising and successful achievement won Laurent the Victoria Cross.

Meanwhile the left company had carried the northern part of African Trench to the battalion boundary, killing large numbers of the enemy and taking 46 prisoners. Its outer flank also was exposed owing to the 1st Battalion right company swinging northwards, and down this gap almost immediately strong German bombing parties came from the continuation of African Trench itself in Lincoln Reserve, and from a communication sap. They suffered heavy casualties, but force of numbers enabled them to work round our rear. Under this pressure, the left company recoiled on the sunken Wood Road which ran obliquely midway between

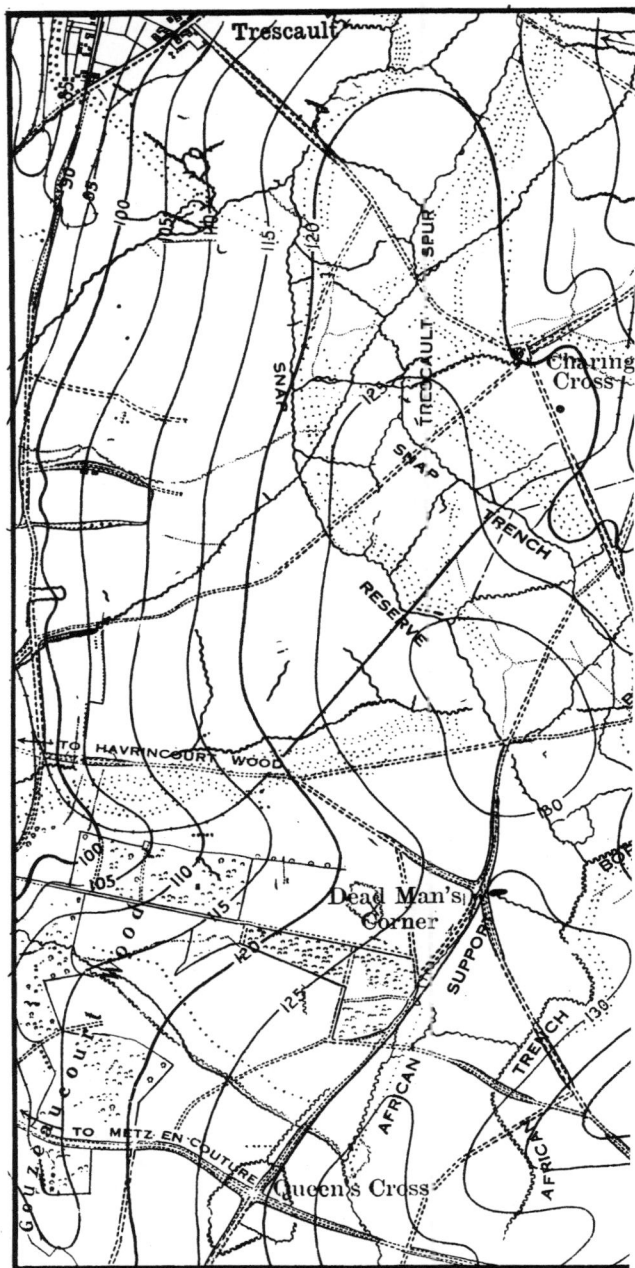

Trescault

Charing
Cross

TRESCAULT SPUR

LYNS

SNAP

TRENCH

RESERVE

TO HAVRINCOURT WOOD

Dead Man's
Corner

SUPPORT

AFRICAN TRENCH

AFRICA

Gouzeaucourt Wood

TO METZ EN COUTURE

Queen's Cross

35

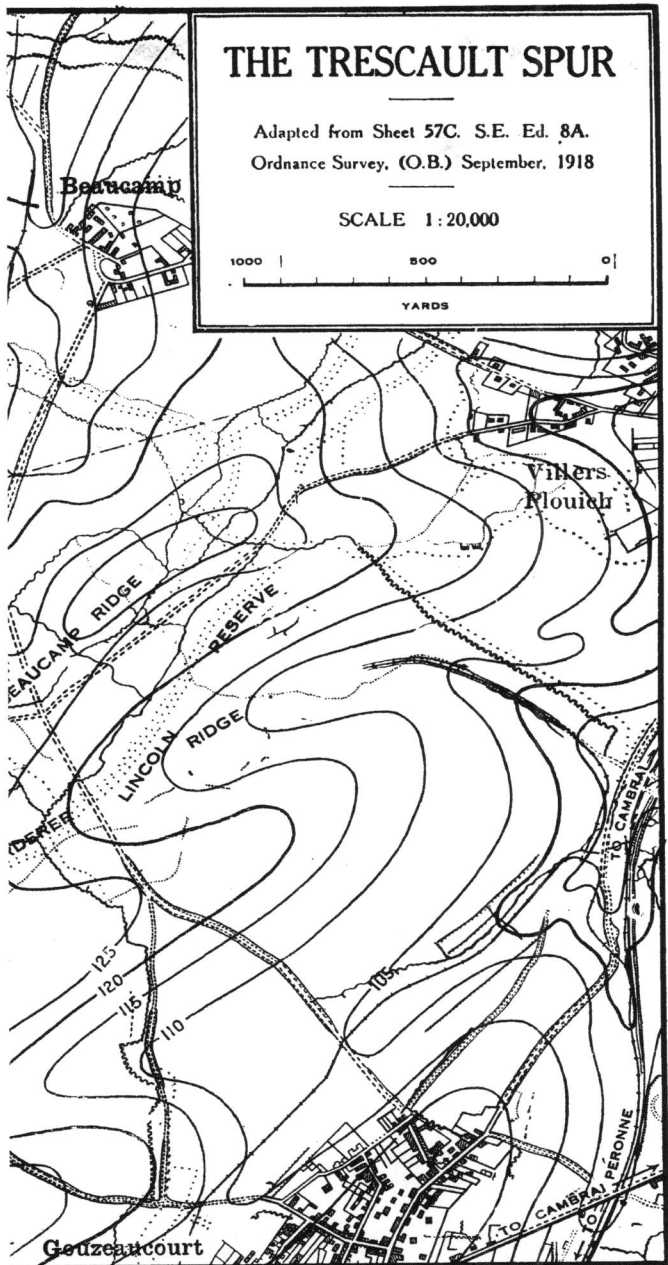

THE TRESCAULT SPUR

Adapted from Sheet 57C. S.E. Ed. 8A.

Ordnance Survey, (O.B.) September, 1918

SCALE 1:20,000

YARDS

African Trench and Support to Dead Man's Corner. The riflemen tried repeatedly to win back the lost trench but failed.

Since coming into the line the endurance of the 4th Battalion on the left in Havrincourt Wood and on the forward slopes east of it had been severely tested. The Wood itself had been continually drenched with gas, and our forward posts were commanded by the enemy on the Trescault Spur. They had therefore welcomed the prospect of capturing the hill and being relieved from German observation. Following now close behind the barrage, the troops of the 1st Battalion in the centre and of the 4th Battalion on the left advanced evenly and steadily uphill towards their first objective in Snap Reserve. At one point the 4th Rifles' advance was held up by the fire of 2 German machine guns. L/Cpl. W. F. Turner rushed forward with his Lewis gun, and though under direct and very heavy fire kept his gun in action and eventually silenced the enemy guns, thereby enabling his platoon to capture the position. Generally, not more than the usual difficulties were encountered, and both battalions reached their first objective along the whole front and up to time. Green flares notified our success to the watchers on the other side of the valley. The protective barrage remained for 10 minutes 200 yards east of the first objective, and the position along Snap Reserve was thoroughly cleared. On the lifting of the barrage and on our infantry movement towards the second objective, extraordinarily heavy machine gun fire from Snap Trench and the systems on Beaucamp Ridge at once lashed the parapets and made progress over the open utterly impossible. Pressing up the saps parties of the 1st Battalion succeeded in securing a footing in part of their final objective and in intermediate trenches. Sergt. E. S. Ellingham with remarkable resolution eventually, after 3 unsuccessful attempts from which only a handful of men survived, established a post in a commanding position. A small group of the 4th Rifles at one time appear to have reached Charing Cross. But, for the most part, the tide did not succeed in rolling further up the hill from Snap Reserve. Repeated efforts were made by Sergt. C. K. Jennens, Cpl. E. C. Fletcher, L.-Cpl. W. McIntyre and L.-Cpl. G. A. Papworth, M.M., to eject the enemy from the saps connecting Snap Reserve and Snap Trench, but the ensuing bombing encounters achieved no result.

35

While their strenuous efforts were making little headway, the right company of the 2nd Rifles in African were being very hard pressed. On this part of the sector in particular the Jägers displayed their traditional resolution and staunchness. After the left company's reverse, both Kennedy's flanks were now exposed. On the right the enemy pressure from Gouzeaucourt by various covered approaches became insistent. By 8 a.m. the hostile artillery fire, which from the outset had been fairly heavy, had slackened. Blasts of machine gun fire, however, swept the whole position incessantly, and the wide shallow trench littered with the German corpses was open to enfilade sniping and machine gun fire from both flanks.

During the morning the enemy counter-attacks were stopped dead, and the pressure was relieved by a successful thrust, carried out by a support platoon (Sergt. A. I. Batty), who captured 26 prisoners and 7 machine guns. In the early afternoon, however, after repeated efforts, the Jägers fighting with grim determination forced the exposed right of the 2nd Rifles back a little way north of the Metz Road. Our men, among whom Sergt. F. Ellery was prominent, "did extremely well," and after being twice pushed north bombed their way down again to the Metz Road. But then their bombs ran out, and they were gradually driven up African to a point some 200 yards south of the Wood Road held by the left company. To this narrow sector both the Wood Road from Dead Man's Corner on the left and another sunken road on the right extremity afforded approach from the support positions under a certain degree of cover. It was in addition served by a communication trench in the centre between the roads. Here bombs could be rapidly brought forward, and here all the enemy's efforts from both flanks and from the front were defied.

Throughout the day the response of our artillery had been prompt and effective, and now in the early afternoon they covered the approaches from Gouzeaucourt with a particularly excellent barrage which appreciably lessened the German aggressiveness. Despite continued enemy shelling, 2nd Lt. L. R. Pulham of the 6th Battery maintained his wire and sent in admirable reports of the positions of the hostile machine guns. While the riflemen themselves gave abundant credit to the fine standard of the work done by the artillery and machine guns, no praise could be too high for the magnificent stand which the 2nd Rifles, and in particular their right company, made throughout this fiercely contested day. Only skilful dispositions saved heavy casualties. They got off cheaply with 11 men killed and an officer and 44 men wounded. Kennedy's position was taken over in the evening by platoons of the 3rd Battalion company attached as reserves. For his splendid leadership throughout this fighting he received the D.S.O.

In maintaining communications through the gassed and shelled valley and Gouzeaucourt Wood, runners and signallers showed qualities of even more than their wonted energy and determination. One or two instances of the spirit which animated them may be quoted. After the hostile barrage had broken all forward line communications, Sergt. R. V. Manson, M.M., of the Divisional Signal Company went out early to get the lines through and worked unceasingly for $7\frac{1}{2}$ hours under the gas and shell bombardment. By that time he had restored the communications. On one occasion during the period he was gassed and fell unconscious. Half an hour later he was brought-to by the explosion of a shell alongside him and continued his work. Later in the day he organised a party to lay new lines to the left and centre battalions and again carried out his work despite the enemy fire. Rflmn. G. Burgess of the 2nd Rifles was employed as a linesman, mending and laying telephone wires between battalion headquarters and the headquarters of companies. Breaks in the wires were recurring almost unceasingly. Burgess was out day and night following the lines and restoring communications. Towards the end of the operations he was almost dead with exhaustion and lack of sleep, yet continued to perform his trying work steadily rapidly and uncomplainingly. Others, such as Rflmn. M. Berry, of the 3rd Rifles, were at times out for 5 hours on end.

At 7 p.m. a further attack was made on the left by the 4th Battalion to establish their line in the final objective. Stubborn resistance was again encountered, but by 7.30 p.m. they occupied Snap Trench from inside the area allotted to the centre battalion as far as the northern boundary. During the day Cpl. A. Gillam had been conspicuous for good work. When his platoon was held up by an enemy's Strong Point with 3 machine guns, Gillam and another man worked round to a flank of the position and then with great dash rushed the machine guns across the open. Throwing bombs into the sap, they jumped in and shot or bayoneted the entire garrison of 3 officers and 12 men, saving many casualties to their comrades and enabling the advance to be resumed. The Gouzeaucourt-Trescault road in front, the battalion's ultimate objective, was found to be impossible, but an advanced post was established 100 yards west of Charing Cross. Orders were received from Division that for the moment no further effort was to be made to reach the objectives. Units were to reorganise and consolidate. The right flank in particular was to be protected by mortars. In view of the possibility of further enemy pressure, immediate counter-attack troops were to be detailed and kept within striking distance of the crest.

While arrangements were being made to give effect to these instructions, the Germans launched another thrust at the centre of the line. At 10.30 p.m. the enemy poured up his saps from Borderer and Beaucamp Ridges and recovered the southern portion of Snap Trench on the centre battalion's front, forcing the garrison as far back as the "corduroy" road running north from Dead Man's Corner. There touch was effected by means of a communication sap with the 4th Battalion's right in the northern part of Snap Trench. Casualties were by this time considerable. The 4th Battalion had lost 2 officers and 18 men killed and 3 officers and 46 men wounded. In the 1st Battalion 2 officers and 22 other ranks had been killed, 4 officers and 73 men were wounded and 14 men were missing.

The enemy's losses were incomparably heavier, as was subsequently attested by the evidence of his captured cemeteries where cross after cross bore the name of a soldier of the Jäger Division with the date of 12th September. In the course of the stubborn day's fighting the Rifle Brigade captured close on 400 prisoners and about 1500 yards of trench objective. While not attaining their full purpose, they had won a footing in African Trench, cleared once for all Dead Man's Corner, and now held the northern part of Snap Trench to the left boundary. Here they were in touch with the 37th Division, who had reached their final objective north-east of Trescault village, and here they commanded good observation over Beaucamp Ridge. Northwards the VI. Corps had effected a breach in the Hindenburg Line itself and after a severe struggle carried the greater part of Havrincourt village. The results of the Havrincourt phase of the battle were sufficiently satisfactory, as bringing our assault positions within measurable distance of the enemy's main line of resistance.

The unremitting effort of his troops during the last 3 weeks was recognised by General Hart in a Special Order:
"I congratulate all ranks upon their splendid work during the recent operations.

"The Brigade took part in 8 engagements within a period of 22 days, capturing 1281 prisoners and very large quantities of war material.

"The gallantry skill determination and endurance displayed under strenuous conditions is worthy of the highest praise."

During the night (12th/13th September) the 1st Infantry Brigade relieved the 3rd. It was raining heavily, and conditions were wintry. There was considerable shelling, and bombing fights were in progress during the relief, which was not completed till 4.30 a.m. The 1st Brigade held the line with 1st Auckland on the right, 1st Wellington in the centre, and 2nd Wellington on the left.

The following day was wet and stormy, and the greasy mud in the sloping trenches on the hillside made movement slow and laborious. Despite discomfort and the fatigues of a trying relief, the 1st Brigade battalions had no intention of sitting still. Possibly they underestimated the difficulties, but in the case of 1st Auckland on the right and 1st Wellington in the centre it was desirable to improve the positions taken over from the Rifles. From the early hours of the morning they pushed posts forward and made preparations for a larger effort in the afternoon. At 3.30 p.m. after sharp bombardment of the numerous machine gun posts by artillery and light trench mortars, 1st Wellington, in the centre, in conjunction with the left company of 1st Auckland, initiated concentric bombing attacks to recover the southern part of Snap Trench. Wellington met with very strong resistance. A record is preserved of the consummate gallantry shown by L./Cpl. L. Greenbank. Leading his section, he rushed a machine gun post. Then, in spite of heavy casualties, he continued the attack with his 2 remaining men, bombed a superior enemy from their strong position, and gained his objective. Another post was established on Beaucamp Ridge, but after being held against repeated attacks it was eventually withdrawn. A portion of Snap Trench, however, was won, and 2nd Lt. R. L. Okey contrived to extend it to a stretch of 200 yards. While consolidating he was driven out. He immediately counter-attacked and reoccupied his gains. Eight prisoners were captured in the Wellington attack, but on the whole the progress effected was inconsiderable, and one platoon, counter-attacked from 3 different directions, fought its way out with heavy casualties, having 13 men missing. On the right 1st Auckland for the moment achieved

better results in African. They sent a bombing party to work
north from their existing foothold, and another party to work
south into it from the sap running from Dead Man's Corner.
These effected junction, and a further 400 yards of African
were now in our hands.

Later in the evening the Jägers girt up their loins for a
final and decisive effort. Shortly after 6 p.m. under cover of
a heavy barrage, a party of 50 attacked 2nd Wellington near
Charing Cross, but were driven off by our fire. In all 3
separate assaults were made on 2nd Wellington. The S.O.S.
was put up, and the enemy retired, suffering casualties in
our barrage. A little later it was the turn of 1st Auckland.
Their newly won section of African was heavily counter-
attacked by troops pressing down Lincoln Reserve and
communication saps from the north.   Our posts were
driven down African to their old footing between the sunken
roads. Even this last stronghold was to be lost. At 1.45 a.m.,
14th September, supported by liquid fire, the enemy again
attacked with the result that he regained the whole of African
Trench and forced our posts back to African Support. Thus
here the crest of the ridge once more became No Man's Land,
and extended observation was rendered impossible for either
side. At 4.30 a.m. a further determined counter-attack, also
with liquid fire, was delivered on the 1st Wellington line in
the centre at the point where Okey's platoon still guarded
their gains. It was beaten back. The Jägers were indeed
worthy foemen, and the balance of honours did not lie overwhelmingly in the New Zealanders' favour. Stubborn resistance in African was to be offered also to the 5th Division
who, attacking it on 18th September in the Epehy phase of
the battle and again on the 27th in the opening move of the
attack on the Hindenburg Line, succeeded in carrying it only
in the morning of the 28th.

All these German attacks had been accompanied by intense
hostile artillery activity, especially on our battery areas. An
unusually heavy gas bombardment in the early morning of
14th September on the 2nd (Army) Brigade area caused
exceptionally severe casualties. All officers and men of the
15th Battery at the guns were gassed. The area was
evacuated. In their new positions the 18-pounder batteries
were shelled by two 28cm. howitzers, and 1 gun was blown
about 30 yards from its pit.

In the evening of 14th September, 5th Division troops
relieved the 1st Infantry Brigade in the line, and the com-

mand passed to the new Division on the following day. Divisional Headquarters moved back to Favreuil and the infantry brigades to bivouacs round Biefvillers Bihucourt and Sapignies. The Divisional artillery for the moment remained in the line, but the D.A.C. came into reserve and was bivouacked between Favreuil and Sapignies. The 1st Artillery Brigade was withdrawn on the 19th, and the 3rd Brigade, less a howitzer battery, on the 20th. On the 16th the 2nd (Army) Brigade had come under orders of the V. Corps, and on the 21st it passed to the command of the XVII. Corps on the left of the Third Army.

On 18th September, on a 17 miles' front south of Gouzeaucourt, the Fourth and Third Armies undertook operations which were the second phase of the fourth stage of the offensive, in which the Havrincourt operations had been the first phase. They were successful over practically the whole front. In the Havrincourt-Epehy Battle (12th-18th September) the 2 Armies had captured nearly 12,000 prisoners and 100 guns. What was of no less importance was that the stage was now set for the attack on the Hindenburg Line and other artificial obstacles, the smashing of which was a necessary prelude to the final and overwhelming blows of October.

CHAPTER XIII

THE BATTLE OF CAMBRAI AND THE HINDENBURG LINE

The successes won in August and the first half of September by the British and French in the centre of the line and by the Americans at the St. Mihiel salient enabled Foch to prosecute with a minimum of delay the great strategic plan designed to drive the German Armies back on the line of the Meuse. North of the Ardennes the main lateral line of German communications from Lille to Metz was served from the east by railways having their heads at Valenciennes Maubeuge Hirson and Mézières. Reduced to simple terms the Allies' plan was that the French and Americans in closely co-ordinated operations should strike in the direction of Mézières, forcing the enemy back on the Ardennes, and that the British should simultaneously advance towards Maubeuge, threatening his main communications. If these conjoint and converging drives were perfectly timed and equally fortunate, the enemy would see position after position turned by a succession of rapid advances and would have serious difficulty in retreating without disorder and without the loss of a considerable portion of his effectives and material. At the same time, on the Flanders front the depleted German Armies would be driven towards Ghent by Belgian and other Allied forces.

In this grandly conceived scheme the most important role was entrusted to Haig's Southern Armies in the centre of the Allied Line. Success there, where the German Staff had their most highly organised defences, and where if anywhere they might reckon on holding their ground, would not only imperil the retreat of their forces to the south but react momentously on the German positions northwards. The difficulties of the task were proportionate to its significance. By the third week of September the left of the British line affected was indeed eastward of the Hindenburg System at Quéant, but was there barred from further advance on Cambrai by the deep trough of the Canal du Nord and by the marshes of the Sensée. Southward Rawlinson and Byng were confronted by the intact Hindenburg Line itself. On the Fourth Army front north of St. Quentin it was sited just east of the Scheldt Canal. On the Third Army front from

Bantouzelle northwards it lay west of the Canal. Part of the system had been successfully breached in the Cambrai Battle of 1917. What had been done already could be done again, but even granting the deterioration of German morale, the undertaking remained sufficiently formidable.

As the Germans for their comfort were at this trying time reminded, the Line was not composed merely of a single earthworks system. It was a deep fortressed zone laboriously entrenched and heavily wired, most skilfully sited to catch an attack with frontal and enfilade fire. In its prepared defences and behind the barrier of the Canal du Nord the Germans still believed that they could hold the Allied attack, and the strength of their positions was such as to cause their enemies careful and anxious deliberation. Even Foch, the very incarnation of the spirit of the offensive, was dubious as to the possibility of a break-through in a single operation. The British Cabinet left the decision to the men on the spot. Haig himself fully appreciated the strain put on his troops in the preceding battles, the difficulties of the undertaking and the unfortunate consequence of even a partial failure, but pressed for the enterprise as vital to the general scheme. After all his experiences of chequered fortune, Haig's decision spoke eloquently of his personal determination as well as of his strategic insight, and of his confidence in his weapons. Some little interval must elapse before the necessary preliminary measures were complete, but these were rapidly perfected.

Haig's plans were laid with consummate skill. Though no light obstacles confronted the Third and First Armies in the centre and left, the most formidable task lay before the Fourth Army on the right. There the intervening obstacles based on the Scheldt Canal necessitated prolonged artillery "preparation." Moreover, opposite the right of the Third Army, the Line overlooked the area of the Fourth Army into which it was necessary to move the latter's artillery. An advance by the Third and First Armies in the direction of Cambrai prior to the main attack by the Fourth Army presented therefore several advantages. The bombardment necessary to break the defences on General Rawlinson's front could be largely masked in a general preparation along the line of all 3 Armies, and the preliminary action of Generals Byng and Horne would serve as a diversion and attract the German reserves northward. Haig therefore proposed that the bombardment should commence on the night

26th/27th September, and that the 2 northern Armies, the Third and the First, should attack at dawn on the 27th, while on the Fourth Army front the bombardment should continue till the morning of the 29th when the main assault was to be delivered.

In this attack of the 27th the left wing of the Third Army, the VI. and XVII. Corps, would advance on the objectives of Flesquières Courtoing and Fontaine-Notre-Dame. If successful they would endeavour to gain the Scheldt in the neighbourhood of Marcoing and secure a bridgehead at Rumilly in the direction of Cambrai. The IV. Corps on the right would capture Beaucamp Ridge and Highland Ridge and clear the Hindenburg front system as far as Couillet Valley, while the V. Corps on the extreme right would make a limited advance in conformity. Should the advance of the VI. Corps in the centre on Marcoing be successful, the IV. Corps were to press forward and carry Welsh Ridge in order to protect the right flank of the VI. Corps.

The IV. Corps proposed to attack with the 5th Division on the right acting as a pivot to the general advance and with the 42nd Division on the left. The New Zealand Division was held ready to move at short notice to exploit success on either the 5th or the 42nd Division's front The 2nd Infantry Brigade was placed directly in Corps reserve, and on 26th September this Group comprising the 4 South Island battalions, a machine gun company, a light trench mortar battery, and a field ambulance, moved forward from the rest area behind Bapaume to the Bertincourt area nearer the battle. On the same day the 1st and 3rd Artillery Brigades returned to the line, the former to support the 42nd and the latter the 5th Division. The 2 New Zealand medium trench mortar batteries were also placed at the disposal of the 42nd Division.

The country separating the IV. Corps troops from the Scheldt Canal was a succession of ridges and valleys. Their right in the African Support and Snap Trench line rested on the high ground between Gouzeaucourt and Trescault. Northeast of Beaucamp was the isolated eminence of Highland Ridge on which in the initial stages of the attack on the 27th the Corps' right flank would be refused back to the south-west. Over this joint barrier advancing troops would drop into Couillet Valley through which the railway runs from Péronne to Cambrai. On the eastern side of the valley the ground rises on the right into Gonnelieu Ridge and on the left into

Welsh Ridge. Beyond Gonnelieu a wide plateau terminates in slopes overlooking the Scheldt, but beyond Welsh Ridge is the further shallow depression of Vacquerie Valley. Here the advance would have again to descend and then climb the Bonavis Ridge on the other side before it could command observation over the Canal.

The whole intervening country was covered with trenches and entanglements. First came the old British trenches as far east as Welsh Ridge, which the final developments of the 1917 Cambrai battle had, till the German 1918 offensive, left in our possession. Beyond were the intricate mazes of the Hindenburg system. The Canal runs roughly from south to north. The trend of the Line, in a north-westerly direction away from the Canal, was diagonal and not parallel to the IV. Corps' assault position. Various circumstances, however, made it necessary that our attack should be for the most part frontal. Of several roads crossing the area it is sufficient to notice 2. One of these is the sunken road which runs down Couillet Valley, parallel to the railway but slightly above it, along the western slopes of Welsh Ridge. This is Surrey Road. The second is the main highway from Gouzeaucourt to Cambrai. It leads first north-east as far as Bonavis village, passing just south of the township of La Vacquerie where Welsh Ridge joins Gonnelieu Ridge. Thus far it lies wholly on the high ground. At Bonavis it turns sharply north, drops down to the western reach of the Canal at Masnières and mounts the farther bank towards Cambrai, some 4 miles to the north. From the crest of the Trescault Ridge to the top of Welsh Ridge is, as the crow flies, 2¼ miles. A straight line measured from the top of Welsh Ridge to the Canal amounts to approximately the same distance.

On the general front of the Third and First Armies, the progress made on the 27th satisfied expectations. The Canal du Nord was crossed, 10,000 prisoners and 200 guns captured, and the line advanced beyond Flesquières and Bourlon and brought within assaulting distance of Cambrai. The IV. Corps on the right secured the flank of the main attack, but was unable to progress beyond their first objective. The VI. Corps did not succeed in capturing Marcoing. Thus the New Zealanders were not called upon.

During the night 27th/28th September, however, the 42nd Division succeeded in making further ground. They found resistance weakening. By the afternoon of the 28th the Corps reached Gouzeaucourt and Couillet Valley. Patrols of

the 42nd Division on the left had advanced towards Welsh
Ridge, meeting opposition, but it was confidently expected
that before nightfall they would master it, carry Welsh Ridge
and possibly reach Bonavis Ridge as well. On the same day
the troops northwards captured Marcoing and won a foothold
on the east bank of the Scheldt Canal, which after a short
westerly stretch here again turns northward. Time was now
ripe for the New Zealanders to be put into the battle.[1]

In preparation for this the 1st Brigade Group had moved
forward at 4.30 a.m. on the 28th to the Neuville-Bourgonval
area, the infantry being conveyed in a convoy of motor
lorries. The 3rd Brigade Group prepared to march up in the
afternoon.   Advanced Divisional headquarters was established in Vélu Copse. General Russell held a conference at
the 1st Brigade headquarters at noon and explained the
situation and the tasks of the Division to his brigadiers. The
5th Division on the right would advance between La Vacquerie and Gonnelieu towards Banteux. On the left the 62nd
Division of the VI. Corps would attack Masnières and
Rumilly. The New Zealand Division would pass that night
through the 42nd Division with the 2nd Brigade on the right
and the 1st on the left. In view of the 42nd Division's
progress, alternative plans were laid dependent on whether
the line to be taken over was still short of Bonavis or not.
Possession of Welsh Ridge seemed already assured.

In the former case, the Division would advance at 3.30
a.m. to carry La Vacquerie village, complete the capture of
Bonavis Ridge, and seize the crossings of the Scheldt Canal
between the villages of Vaucelles and Crèvecoeur. Should,
however, the Bonavis Ridge have been already captured by
the 42nd Division, our objectives were to be extended eastwards. Patrols would be rushed forward at once to ascertain
the situation on the Canal. Advanced guards would follow
at dawn, secure the crossings and establish posts on the high
ground beyond in order to deny observation of the river bed
to the enemy. The advance would then be pushed up to 3
miles east of the Canal. Five brigades of artillery were
available to support operations. A battery was placed at
the disposal of each infantry brigade for exploitation purposes. The remainder of the artillery was to be prepared to
move forward to positions to cover the Canal crossings,
should resistance be met with. Of the New Zealand artillery

1 During their period of training in reserve some battalions marched to the
1916 battlefield about Flers to revisit the scene of their former struggles and the
graves of old comrades.

only the 1st Brigade was present to support the attack, the
2nd (Army) Brigade being still detached with the XVII.
Corps[1] and the 3rd with the 5th Division. Two troops of the
3rd Hussars were allotted to each infantry brigade.

In accordance with these plans the 2nd Infantry Brigade,
now released from Corps reserve, moved up in rainy weather
during the forenoon to a concentration area behind Havrincourt Wood. In the late afternoon both assaulting brigades
marched forward along congested roads to the battle area.
Passing through Metz and rounding the southern edge of
Havrincourt Wood the 2nd Brigade climbed in gathering
darkness the familiar and bitterly-contested heights towards
Beaucamp. The rain had ceased. On the whole the night
was quiet, and it was on the battery areas further in rear that
the hostile aeroplanes sailing through a starry windless sky
dropped their bombs. Passing through Beaucamp, however,
2nd Otago was subjected to a brief bombardment by 5.9-in.
howitzers. The 1st Brigade was allotted a preliminary rendezvous area between the northern end of Highland Ridge and
Ribecourt. They turned up the valley east of Havrincourt
Wood towards Trescault, and as one of the battalions was
approaching Trescault, here too the enemy flung a shell-
storm on the village. In deviating round the outskirts to
dodge this, 2 companies bore somewhat too far north, and for
the moment lost touch with their unit. Such mishaps, inevitable in war, are not calculated to relieve commanding officers'
anxieties. Worse was yet to come, for on getting into touch
with the 42nd Division, it was found that the Lancashire
troops had met heavy opposition, and that so far from
occupying Bonavis they had been unable to clear Welsh
Ridge.

Plans were hurriedly modified. It was arranged that the
2 assaulting battalions of each brigade should form up
on Surrey Road and attack at 3.30 a.m. The 42nd Division
troops would be withdrawn half an hour before zero to below
Surrey Road, to enable our barrage to come down 200 yards
east of it. Thence the barrage would roll over the ridge
at the rate of 100 yards in 3 minutes as far as the forward
slopes of Bonavis Ridge overlooking the Canal, where it
would die away.

The plans settled, and the 2 lost companies of the
1st Brigade battalion recovered, the assaulting troops began
(12.30 a.m.) to move forward to their assembly position

1   p. 489.

between the high banks of Surrey Road. The night was now intensely dark. The shell-craters, old and new, and the wire entanglements were, even for seasoned troops, extraordinarily difficult to negotiate. All were in position, however, by 3 a.m. (Sunday morning). The support battalions moved into trenches on and behind Highland Ridge, which had fallen during the day. Each assaulting battalion had a section of machine guns and 2 light trench mortars. Despite the showers during the day, the ground was dry and was to facilitate rapid movement of troops guns and transport. At 3.30 a.m. there was a waning moon and a slight mist.

Almost as soon as our barrage opened, the enemy's heavy artillery bombarded the obvious assembly place in Couillet Valley, but his shells for the most part fell behind the attacking troops. 1st Canterbury, on the right of the 2nd Brigade front, attacked with 2 companies and carried Welsh Ridge without much difficulty. Cowed by the barrage and overwhelmed by the élan of the attack, the enemy offered little resistance. Nearer La Vacquerie machine gun fire became heavy, and the leading Canterbury companies cleared the ruins only after a lengthy and considerable struggle. On this line the 2 supporting companies were to have leap-frogged through them. Two platoons arrived. Time went on. There was no sign of the others. The original right attacking company, therefore, not satisfied with having done its own job, pushed on after the barrage and made substantial progress on the high ground due south of the village.

The remainder of the support companies had simply lost direction in the darkness. They were marching on compass bearings, but in that tangled and intricate country of trenches and wire-belts, running in every direction, they had swung southwards into the area of the 5th Division. Here the remaining 2 platoons of the one company encountered heavy fighting, and eventually, about 10.30 a.m., they were hemmed in by machine gun fire, surrounded and taken prisoners. Among the captured survivors were an officer and man, both wounded. These the Germans treated considerately and placed in a dugout, where they were recovered in our subsequent advance in the evening.

The other supporting company came in for equally stern fighting south of La Vacquerie but resolutely, yard by yard, driving the Germans before them, reached the Cambrai Road south-west of the village. Here, however, after beating off a counter-attack, they became exposed to reverse and enfilade machine gun fire, and were later withdrawn some distance to conform with the position of the 5th Division, who had been held up by deadly cross-fire from the ground south of La Vacquerie on the one hand and from Gonnelieu on the other. When the light dawned, some German posts on the eastern slopes of Welsh Ridge were found to have been overlooked, and one in particular, 1000 yards north-west from La Vacquerie, gave trouble, but was finally rushed by a patrol under cover of Lewis gun fire. In all, some 250 prisoners were captured. The fighting on this flank and the resistance offered to the 5th Division had left the position here somewhat unsatisfactory. To strengthen it, therefore, a company of 1st Otago was sent in the forenoon to the forward slopes of Highland and the rear slopes of Welsh Ridges, and in the afternoon 2 further companies were moved to Welsh Ridge.

On the left of the 2nd Brigade subsector no untoward incident marred 2nd Otago's success. Good Man Farm, at which cavalry and 42nd Division posts had been established during the previous evening and from which on account of our barrage they had been subsequently withdrawn, had not been reoccupied by the enemy. By 4.30 a.m. both assaulting companies had pressed over the crest of Welsh Ridge, stamping out inconsiderable resistance. Thereafter, as the light cleared, machine guns from about the village of La Vacquerie, not yet cleared by 1st Canterbury, from Vacquerie Valley, and from the Bonavis trenches beyond rendered progress in the open much more difficult. Strong bombing parties worked down the infinite maze of trenches in the Hindenburg Line to the sunken road in Vacquerie Valley, where touch was gained with the 1st Brigade on their left. Enfilade fire from the other flank, where for the moment nothing could be seen of 1st Canterbury, was becoming heavy and causing casualties. In spite of this, both companies pressed up the Bonavis slopes till within 400 yards from the crest. The 1st Brigade on the left were making unchecked progress, but the German machine guns on the right, south of La Vacquerie, were now in Otago's rear. The advance was therefore temporarily suspended till reinforcements could strengthen the right flank.

About 11 a.m. the support company thrown forward for this purpose had arrived, and the 2 assaulting companies, thus protected, fought their way on to the top of Bonavis Ridge. One company, shortly after taking 2 abandoned 77-mm. guns, was held up by heavy machine gun fire. Sergt.

R. B. Foote, though without previous training in gunnery, turned the captured field pieces on the hostile posts and drove the German garrison back over the ridge. By 1 p.m. 2nd Otago had cleared the summit and held the important Royal Trench on the Cambrai Road overlooking the Canal. Patrols pushed down the forward slopes to the outskirts of Lateau Wood, but were there met by intense machine gun fire, and for the moment no further progress was possible. 2nd Otago had taken nearly 600 prisoners, with 30 officers, together with 4 field guns, a howitzer, 2 trench mortars, and 30 machine guns.

The chief triumph of the day, however, was reserved for the 1st Brigade who, meeting opposition, swept it before them in seemingly effortless mastery. 2nd Wellington[1] was on the right and 1st Auckland on the left, supported by their sister battalions. As with the 2nd Brigade, their main difficulties in crossing Welsh Ridge were due to the darkness and not to the enemy. Shortly after 5 a.m. they were down in Vacquerie Valley, and their screen was breasting the slopes of Bonavis Ridge. Here one of the Wellington companies was momentarily arrested by machine gun fire from very close range, but 2nd Lt. D. G. H. B. Morison crawled along a sap and threw bombs into the post, thus enabling his platoon to advance above ground and capture the guns and crews. Before 8 a.m. 300 unwounded prisoners and 10 officers had passed the 1st Brigade headquarters, and many others were streaming in, carrying our wounded and their own. An enemy pocket in Vacquerie Valley, though surrounded, held out with determination till destroyed, not without risk to our own troops in the vicinity, by our heavy artillery.

Swarming up the Bonavis crest in the cool dawn the two 1st Brigade battalions completely overran the enemy. By 6 a.m. they were beyond the northern fringe of Lateau Wood, and over the Cambrai Road, and in those advanced trenches on the forward slopes which the British had won and held for 10 days in November 1917, till the German counter-stroke pressed them back on Welsh Ridge. 2nd Wellington, with 43 casualties, had taken over 250 prisoners, 20 field guns, and 29 machine guns. 1st Auckland, with similarly light casualties, secured an equal number of prisoners and machine guns, six 77-mm. guns, and 2 howitzers.

1 Major McKinnon, M.C., vice Lt.-Col. Cunningham, at Rest Camp.

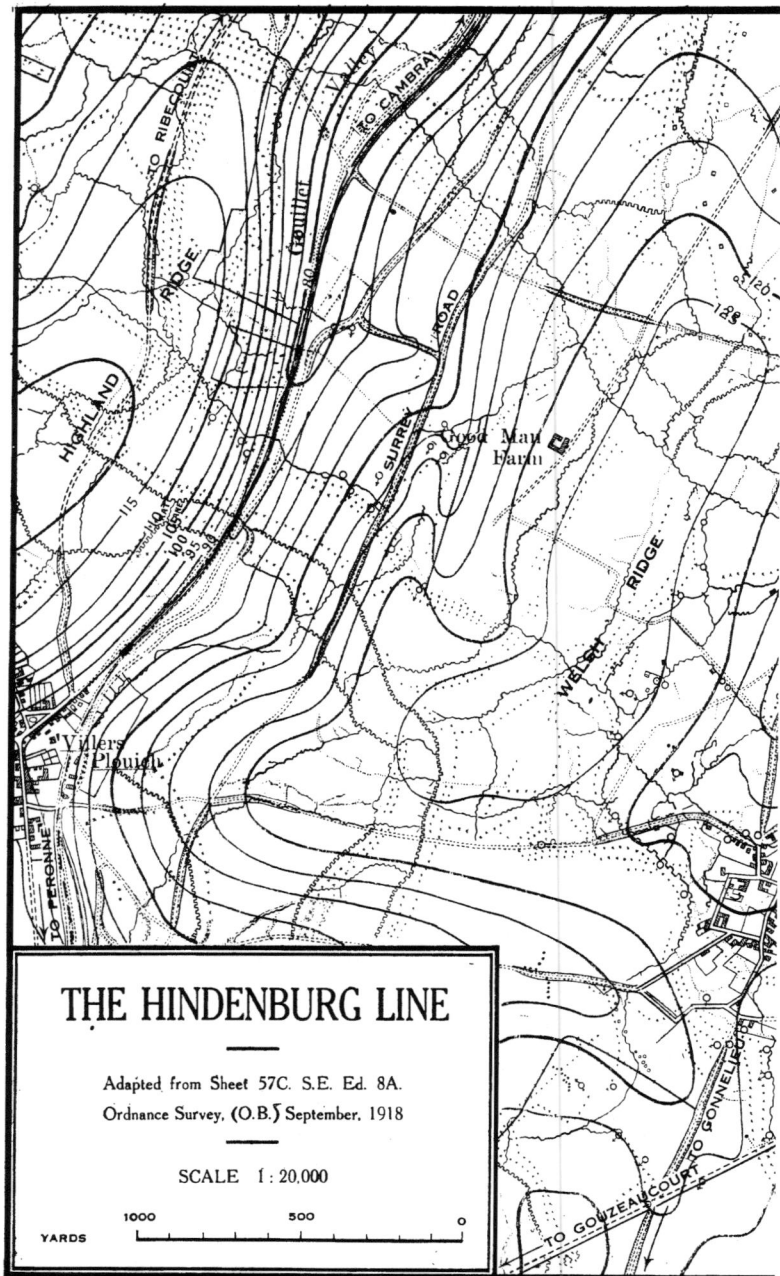

THE HINDENBURG LINE

—

Adapted from Sheet 57C. S.E. Ed. 8A.
Ordnance Survey, (O.B.) September, 1918

SCALE 1 : 20,000

YARDS

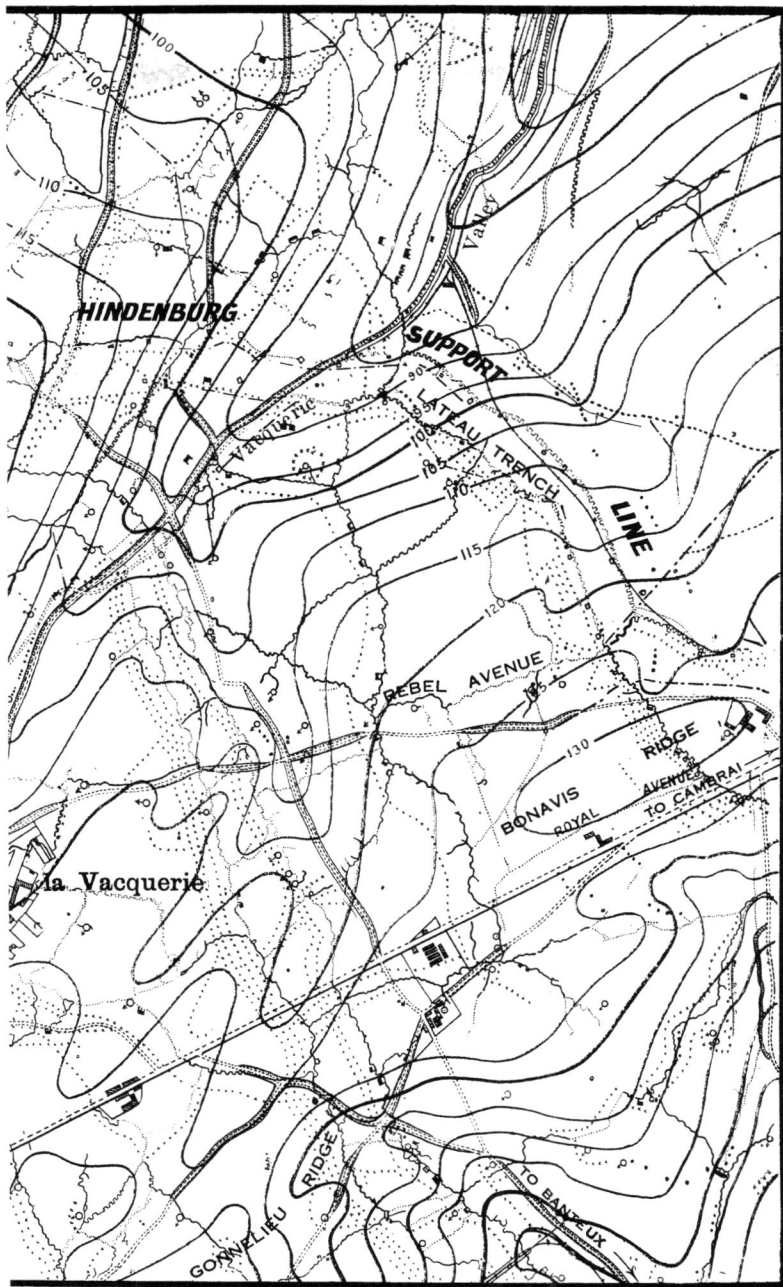

HINDENBURG

SUPPORT

PLATEAU TRENCH

LINE

Tadpole Pic

Valley

REBEL AVENUE

BONAVIS RIDGE

ROYAL AVENUE

TO CAMBRAI

la Vacquerie

GONNELIEU RIDGE

TO BANTEUX

100
105
85
110
115
90
100
105
110
115
120
130

On the extreme right of the 1st Brigade line, half a 2nd Auckland company, which had deviated too far south in the darkness, held the Bonavis ruins, where they secured the exposed flank till the 2nd Brigade came into line. The bulk of the 2 leading companies had become immerged in the front line. Following on with great rapidity, the remainder of 2nd Auckland on the left and 1st Wellington on the right had crossed Welsh Ridge at 6 a.m., where they mopped up some overlooked machine guns and took close on 50 prisoners. They now caught up the leading troops on the ridge and were eager to pass through, if these should be checked, and to make down for the Canal. 2nd Auckland on the left in particular pushed patrols through the 1st Auckland line of consolidation on the ridge down towards Crèvecoeur, where, as early as 8 a.m., they had secured 2 long-range guns,[1] captured a batch of prisoners, and were approaching the Canal.

But the whole 1st Brigade line was now somewhat disorganised both by the darkness and by the rapidity of the advance. On the left, touch was maintained with the VI. Corps troops, who had occupied Masnières but were held up by the trenches east of it and prevented from continuing their advance on Rumilly. On the right, however, there was a great gap about Bonavis village between the 2nd and 1st Brigades, and on the crest line itself men of 2nd Wellington, 1st Auckland and 2nd Auckland were much intermingled. Some reorganisation was therefore essential before pushing forward. The posts of 2nd Auckland were withdrawn by orders of Lt.-Col. Alderman (1st Auckland) to the line of the Cambrai Road.[2] The front was reorganised under the 2 original assaulting battalions, who took over for the moment the charge of making ground towards the Canal, thus leaving the supporting battalions ready for exploitation on its eastern side. Two 1st Wellington companies moved up to closer support on Bonavis Ridge. By noon, 29th September, the whole of the position was well consolidated, and the 2 support battalions were in readiness to press forward at a moment's notice.

During the forenoon the 7th Battery of the 1st Artillery Brigade moved into Couillet Valley and in the afternoon into

---

[1] Claimed also by 1st Auckland.
[2] Lt.-Col. S. S. Allen, whose opinion merits careful consideration, says (*2nd Auckland, 1918*, pp. 132, 133): "(This) extraordinary incident was the cause of robbing us of a very striking success. The Battalion's casualties were negligible. . . . There appears to have been little disorganisation. . . We might easily have secured the river crossings and Crèvecoeur." This is possible enough, though in the event of success they would almost certainly have had to face heavy counter-action.

Vacquerie Valley, where presently the rest of the brigade
also took up positions.   Advanced Divisional headquarters
was early established in Trescault.   The morning's work had
been extraordinarily successful.   Not less than 1400 prisoners,
with 2 naval guns, 30 field guns, and over 200 machine guns
had been captured by the Division.   Practically all objectives
had been secured at a light cost.   Particularly gratifying was
the fine dash and fighting spirit shown by lately posted
reinforcements.

On the line held by the 1st Brigade on the Bonavis Ridge
was a succession of trenches which were obviously not
German.   They greatly perplexed the North Island battalions
at the moment, and it was only later that men realised they
were on the furthest limit won by the 1917 Cambrai battle.
These trenches had been dug by the 12th Division.   Behind
our left flank in the Scheldt Valley was Masnières,
where a broken bridge had in 1917 prevented Byng's
massed cavalry sweep on Cambrai.   East of the Canal were
the last isolated trenches of the Hindenburg System, the
Beaurevoir-Masnières line, which a Canadian squadron had
then broken in a stirring charge.   At the time few if any of
the troops on the ridge knew this.   What they did most
thoroughly appreciate, was the sight of the smiling country
eastwards unscathed by war.   Behind them now was the
lacerated, too familiar, landscape of churned-up shellholes,
hideous walls of wire, miry battered ditches, the unsightliness
of stricken villages and blasted woods.   East of Bapaume
there had been a limited temporary approximation to normal
scenes, but even there the slopes were pocked with craters,
and the villages, though not levelled, had felt the heavy hand
of war.   Now, however, the attack had reached the threshold
of a new world, and fatigue was forgotten in tense exhilaration.   The grey lofty towers and spires of Cambrai were
clearly visible northwards, and great beacons of smoke told
of the destruction of dumps or the firing of the city.   Below
Auckland on this side of the Canal lay the 2 long streets of
Les Rues des Vignes, which had been held for an hour during
the 1917 Cambrai battle.   Half a mile further north on the
other side of the Canal, at the point where it turns westward
towards Masnières, was the village of Crèvecoeur.   A mile
up-stream from Les Rues des Vignes and opposite the 2nd
Brigade the village of Vaucelles nestled under protecting
tree-clad hills.   The Canal itself and the river which flowed
alongside were fringed with lines of poplars.   On the far

side, the ground rose steeply to the La Terrière plateau, broken by sunken roads and quarries. From it a broad spur running towards the Canal overhung Vaucelles on the south and looked on its northern slopes towards Les Rues des Vignes. The trees of Cheneaux Wood climbed up the lower hillside in a solid mass of greenery. Northwards the plateau fell towards Crèvecoeur and the village of Lesdain, further east. Stretching south from Crèvecoeur the wire of the Beaurevoir-Masnières line near the crest of the plateau was the one and only sign of prepared defences.

All this country over the Canal was full of German movement, and our patrols feeling down towards its banks saw guns limbering up for retreat eastward, and transport moving both east and west along the lower edge of Cheneaux Wood. Our machine guns, pushing aggressively forward, took up positions on the eastern slopes of Bonavis Ridge, engaging transport lorries, guns and motor tractors at ranges for the most part of between 1300 and 1400 yards, and scattering horses and personnel. In the afternoon, however, considerable forces of German infantry were dribbled up in small parties to contest the crossing. Movement became increasingly difficult. German guns began to shell the ridge. It was clear that the passage over the Canal would involve a separate operation. 1st Canterbury and 2nd Otago also were meeting fierce resistance about the Cambrai highway.

Meantime great events had been happening in the south. Just before 6 a.m. the Fourth Army had struck their blow on the Line, meeting for the most part with immediate and remarkable success. Satisfactory progress had also been made against stiffening opposition towards Cambrai. In the afternoon orders were issued by the Corps foreshadowing an advance on the 30th by all 3 Southern Armies. On the IV. Corps sector the 5th Division were during the night to complete the capture of the Hindenburg Line south-east of La Vacquerie. The New Zealanders were to strike early in the morning with the object of securing the eastern bank of the Canal between Vaucelles and Crèvecoeur and of establishing bridgeheads. In co-operation with the 5th Division on the right, the 2nd Brigade would throw its leading troops across the Canal, form a defensive right flank on the high spur above Cheneaux Wood, and pass through the Beaurevoir-Masnières line in the direction of a smaller copse, known as Pelu Wood, 2 miles beyond the Canal.

In view of the 5th Division's position and of the resistance still offered to the 2nd Brigade by strong enemy parties
on the western bank about Vaucelles, it was realised that the
New Zealanders' right wing would probably encounter difficulties.   More was to be hoped from the 1st Brigade movement against Crèvecoeur and Lesdain.   There it might prove
possible to exploit success towards the high ground north of
Esnes in conjunction with an advance of the VI. Corps and
cavalry on Wambaix.   A squadron of the 3rd Hussars was
attached to the 1st Brigade for the operation.

In his plans for the proposed advance General Melvill
ordered that 1st Wellington and 2nd Auckland, passing through
the original front line battalions, should make every effort to
secure the Canal crossings before dawn, and then attack with
the objectives of Esnes and the La Targette Road east of
Seranvillers.   2nd Auckland on the left was given a free
hand for exploitation and could move, if it proved possible,
in a northerly direction to threaten Cambrai.   A motor lorry
was provided to carry Lewis gun sections forward close
behind the cavalry.   2nd Wellington and 1st Auckland would
not move till Lesdain and Crèvecoeur were taken, but when
these villages were cleared, 2nd Wellington would watch the
right flank of the attack about Lesdain in case the 2nd
Brigade failed to cross at Vaucelles.   1st Auckland would
move also into a position of readiness behind Les Rues des
Vignes.   It was not at first proposed that there should be a
covering barrage, but at the request of the battalion commanders this was arranged for at very short notice.   The
hour of the attack was fixed for 5.45 a.m.

In the evening (29th September) rain began to fall
heavily about 5 p.m. and continued till midnight, making the
ground soft and muddy.   The night was again very dark.
Conditions seemed likely to favour an advance against
machine gun resistance, but there would be a difficulty in
maintaining direction.   As soon as dusk fell, the 2nd Brigade
battalions had begun to thrust towards the Canal.   2nd Otago
patrols endeavoured again to work towards Vaucelles, but
the enemy held the ground in force, and up to midnight no
material advance had been realised.

Shortly after midnight (29th/30th September), however,
the enemy began to evacuate the western bank.   As the
machine gun fire of his rearguards abated, 2nd Otago redoubled their pressure, and a strong patrol hurried the
German retreat towards the Canal.   The rain cleared about

4 a.m., and the morning was of delightful freshness. Before 5 a.m. an Otago patrol, under Lt. R. D. Douglass, after twice being driven back by direct machine gun and rifle fire, had covered the intervening 1000 yards and reached the bank opposite Vaucelles, where they found the centre span of the bridge destroyed. The reserve company was at once sent forward and reached the neighbourhood of the bridge by 6.30 a.m. The actual approaches were heavily swept by machine gun fire. A small party of Engineers, under Lt. T. K. 'Broadgate, endeavoured to reconnoitre the bridge, but were driven back, Broadgate being killed. Meantime, another Otago patrol, under Sergt. R. Fitzgerald, examined the whole Canal from Vaucelles to Banteux, in full view of the enemy. The footbridge at the lock north of Banteux was found mined. The wires and fuses were cut by Fitzgerald. Moving further south, they discovered 4 German sappers preparing to mine the traffic bridge from Banteux to Bantouzelle, and opening fire, killed 1 and forced the others to flight. Then crossing this bridge and boldly penetrating to the far side of Bantouzelle, the patrol safely returned to the battalion headquarters with most valuable information. Without delay 2nd Otago established posts on the western bank and were presently joined by 1st Canterbury. These also had moved at nightfall. Two companies had cleared the trenches east and north-east of La Vacquerie. Another, after fierce hand-to-hand bayonet work in the darkness, had reached the line of the Cambrai Road on 2nd Otago's right.

At dawn (30th September) the 5th Division had advanced under a barrage to reach their objectives of the previous day and make good our right flank. Under the protection of their barrage 1st Canterbury patrols also had moved forward over the Cambrai Road, overmastering half-hearted opposition, and shortly after 8 a.m. had gained the approaches to the Canal near a sugar factory on the northern outskirts of Banteux. Distant machine gun fire was encountered, but most of the enemy had already vacated the western bank. A few last rearguards were crossing the Canal by the foot-bridge at the lock nearer Banteux. Horses and transport were moving out of Bantouzelle, and infantry parties were retiring up the wooded slopes on the far side. At this particular point there was apparently nothing to stop further advance, but the troops on the right had met with consider- ably more resistance in the Hindenburg Line and had not been able to keep progress. Meantime the bridges were reconnoitred. The main factory bridge had been destroyed, but was just passable for infantry in single file. Across it and the footbridge, which was still intact, 2 platoons moved forthwith and occupied a line of willow trees 200 yards beyond the Canal. At 10.15 a.m., however, the enemy began to move back again. Considerable bodies re-entered Bant-ouzelle. A party approached the bridge with demolition material, but was scattered by our fire. There was no sign yet of the flank Division, so our bridgehead was temporarily withdrawn. An outpost line was established along the western bank to guard the crossings, and a defensive flank formed southwards. The whole position was consolidated pending further progress on the flanks.

In the late evening of the 29th the leading company of 2nd Canterbury had moved forward to Welsh Ridge, and soon after dawn on the 30th had passed through the rear companies of 2nd Otago in Rebel Trench and over the Cambrai Road into the long Lateau Trench that led towards Vaucelles. Should 2nd Otago succeed in forcing the passage, the Canterbury company was to cross over to the eastern bank and extend the bridgehead by the occupation of Vau-celles and the capture of the spur above it. Moving down the dilapidated Lateau Trench, the company was seriously incommoded by heavy machine gun fire from the eastern bank. It was immediately apparent that 2nd Otago had no chance of effecting a crossing. 2nd Canterbury accordingly at nightfall took over the front line in the hope that by the following morning the enemy might have withdrawn. Should resistance be maintained, a major operation would be neces-sary, in which, under cover of artillery fire, bridges could be flung over the deep unfordable Canal. At any time even unencumbered and active men, moving one at a time, would have difficulty in crossing the broken Vaucelles bridge. So long as a single hostile machine gun remained in action to guard it the passage was quite impossible. For the moment not less than 20 machine guns were located in the houses of Vaucelles and about the hedge-lined ditches which com-manded a clear view of the crossing.

While the 2nd Brigade advance was thus held up by obstacles which for the time were completely insuperable, the 1st Brigade attack also had encountered serious opposi-tion and failed to realise the sanguine expectations of the previous evening. In the darkness the brigade runners had gone astray, and it was not till 11.15 p.m. that orders reached

1st Wellington and 2nd Auckland. Very little time remained
to go into details with the company commanders. The brigade
order was misinterpreted by 1st Wellington, who supposed
that the attack was timed for 5 a.m. No barrage falling at
that time, the leading company, who were to cross the permanent bridge at Les Rues des Vignes and secure a bridgehead, believed naturally enough that the operations were
postponed and did not attack. Artillery fire fell, however,
further up-stream, and the right support Wellington company
made an independent advance in its direction to the edge of
the Canal. Deviating far away to the right, they cleared the
enemy's last foothold on the western bank in this area, taking
8 prisoners.

When it was found that 2nd Auckland had attacked independently, the main 1st Wellington advance was initiated
shortly after 6 a.m., and though harassed by fire from
artillery and machine guns on the eastern bank of the Canal,
parties occupied, about 8 a.m., Les Rues des Vignes, which
had already been mostly cleared by 2nd Auckland. But the
approaches over the slopes from the village to the Canal were
swept by extremely heavy fire and were all but impossible.
No hope of the actual crossing at this point could be entertained. Could it be achieved elsewhere? On their own
initiative 2nd Wellington sent a party up-stream to test the
bridge at Vaucelles, whence the 1st Brigade, after crossing,
could work north again on to their proper frontage. There
they were speedily satisfied that "nothing was doing." Meantime heavy machine gun fire and shell-fire enfiladed the 1st
Wellington troops in Les Rues des Vignes, causing casualties.
It was not till dusk that their patrols were able to work
down to the Canal and the shelter of its high bank.

In front of Crèvecoeur the Scheldt river makes a detour
eastwards of the Canal, thus leaving between it and the latter
a large marshy island which is connected with the eastern
bank of the river by a stone bridge. A subsidiary branch of
the river also cuts the island, so that to reach Crèvecoeur the
left of 2nd Auckland had to cross the Canal itself and the
2 branches of the river. Misfortune dogged 2nd Auckland
from the outset. The runners to the companies, like the
brigade runners, lost their way, and Lt.-Col. Allen was
obliged to modify his plans at the last moment. He employed
one company, the 15th (North Auckland), commanded by Capt.
J. Evans, to seize the Canal and river crossings and Crèvecoeur
itself. Two further companies were to continue the attack

beyond. Despite the short notice given the 15th Company
started punctually at 5.45 a.m., succeeded in crossing the
Canal by a permanent and a half-destroyed wooden bridge,
and by 6.30 a.m. had established themselves on the island.
One platoon on the left crossed the subsidiary branch by a
footbridge and made for the stone bridge. Their movement
was as yet not contested by the enemy. Wires could be seen
leading under the masonry, but risking the danger of mines
and booby-traps the leading patrol advanced straight on to
it. At that moment they were noticed. A blast of machine
gun fire came from the far bank, and several men were killed,
including the platoon commander and the senior n.c.o. An
enemy counter-attack was crushed by our Lewis guns, but the
number of German machine guns was considerable, and the
stream of lead made the bridge utterly impassable. The river
elsewhere was unfordable. The remainder of this platoon,
therefore, under Cpl. A. de B. P. Steward, took refuge in a
ditch in an angle between the 2 branches of the river.

Meanwhile the heavy fire of the aroused German posts
checked with loss the other 3 platoons on the western half
of the island, where the ground was destitute of cover. Steward
was anxious to let his company commander know the position
of the isolated and reduced platoon, but between them and
headquarters lay not only the deep river, where the footbridge was now raked with fire, but more than 100 yards of
open ground, already dotted with the dead of the other
platoons. Any such journey must be a most desperate undertaking. One of the private soldiers with Steward was a
certain James Crichton, who had been wounded in the foot
during the rush to the stone bridge. He now volunteered to
take the message. Removing his box respirator and helmet,
he lowered himself into the river and swam over, Steward
throwing his respirator and helmet after him. Now came the
open ground. Crichton picked up his respirator and helmet,
took a minute's breath, and dashed over the open to Capt.
Evans' headquarters. Machine gun bullets spattered up little
clouds of dust everywhere about him, and Steward and the
men watching him expected every minute to see him fall.
But Crichton arrived safely. Giving the written message,
he said not a word about his wound, but reported the mines
under the stone bridge. Capt. Evans asked him whether he
thought they could be removed after dark, having no intention of risking his men's lives in daylight under the hail
of machine gun fire. Crichton replied that it would be pos-

sible. Evans said nothing further, but sent a message to Steward bidding him hold his ground, and Crichton again made unharmed the perilous journey.

During his absence Steward, checking his platoon, had found some men missing, and Crichton now undertook to locate their whereabouts. He crawled nearer the bridge, machine guns opening every time that he exposed himself, but he found only dead. A hedge ran towards the bridge, with a shallow ditch on our side. By working along the ditch it might be possible to reach the bridge. Hugging the earth, Crichton came to the steep river bank, and in a flash dropped over it into the water. Here he was screened by the arch. He leisurely removed the 2 fuses and detonators of the mines and sank the mines in the water. The fuses and detonators he took back with him and showed to Steward. He crossed again through the undiminished machine gun fire to company headquarters, taking with him the proofs of his adventure. By this time he was not merely soaked to the skin, but his wound also had become acutely painful. Not even now, however, did he mention it. But it was no longer necessary to send him back to his platoon, and Capt. Evans, refusing to allow him to risk the journey again, detailed him as a stretcher-bearer to carry wounded back to the dressing station on the western bank of the Canal. Here his own wound was detected—a wound which the chaplain who had helped to dress his foot stated in his sworn evidence was one that most men would have "gone out with" immediately. He was evacuated. His outstanding gallantry and resourcefulness were rewarded by a V.C.

The rest of the isolated platoon held their ground all day, resisting attempts at envelopment, but were in the end surrounded. Of the survivors, some reached our lines and 11 were captured by the enemy. The other 3 platoons, though virtually cut off from the main line, held a commanding position with a good field of fire, and it was ultimately decided not to withdraw them. They were reinforced by 2 platoons of the reserve company. The remaining companies reached the western bank, but in the face of the machine guns an attempt to force a crossing either at Les Rues des Vignes or further north was out of the question. Major E. Sherson, reconnoitring the position on the island, was killed. In all, 2nd Auckland had lost in the 2 days' fighting 5 officers and 31 men killed, 6 officers and 112 wounded, and 11 men captured. They had taken 2 naval guns,[1] a 4.2-in.

1 p. 499.

howitzer with limber and 4 horses, four 77-mm. guns, 2
mortars, and 38 machine guns. In the latter part of the day
they were closely supported by the 3rd Battery, which had
moved over the Cambrai Road and had used the captured
howitzer and 77-mm. guns on their late owners.

The seriousness of the opposition at Crèvecoeur was not yet
realised at brigade headquarters, where it had been erron-
eously reported that the 62nd Division, on the right of the
VI. Corps, had made good progress towards Seranvillers.
Despite the check at Les Rues des Vignes it was still hoped
that by means of this bridgehead at Crèvecoeur it might be
possible to pour troops across and win the final objectives
about Esnes and the La Targette Road northwards. 1st
Auckland was accordingly warned to be ready to pass
through 2nd Auckland, and the squadron of 3rd Hussars,
now attached to the brigade, was instructed to cross the
Canal, gain touch with the VI. Corps at Seranvillers, and
facilitate the advance of the infantry. On arrival, however,
at 2nd Auckland headquarters, where the squadron commander was killed by a shell, the actual position was
explained, and the Hussars withdrew.

It speedily transpired that no hope could be entertained
of forcing a passage that day. Yet a foothold on the far
bank would be of inestimable value for a further advance.
Preparations were therefore made for a renewal of the attack
on the following day (1st October) by 2nd Wellington and
1st Auckland. Against a frontal assault the enemy position
was so strong as to be nearly, if not altogether, impregnable
without sustained artillery preparation. It was possible,
however, that it might be turned from the north, where the
VI. Corps had already gained a bridgehead beyond the Canal,
and where an attack would not be hindered by the water
barriers.

Plans were therefore adjusted on this basis. The 1st
Brigade would cross under cover of darkness to the north
bank on the western reach and assemble there in the VI.
Corps' sector to strike south-eastwards at Crèvecoeur. On
their left, the 3rd Division, relieving the 62nd on the right
flank of the VI. Corps, would attack Rumilly as a first objective and endeavour to exploit towards Seranvillers and
Wambaix. 2nd Wellington would take Crèvecoeur. 1st Auckland, on their left and in close touch with the 3rd Division,
would capture the high ground overlooking the Crèvecoeur
valley from the north and seize as their final objective the

A German Sap

PTE. J. CRICHTON. V.C.   [Photo Dobson

THE TUNNELLERS' BRIDGE, CANAL DU NORD

road running north from the Old Mill of Lesdain. If conditions favoured exploitation, patrols would be pushed out
towards the single and final Seranvillers trench line some 1000
yards beyond the objective and, if possible, still further eastwards.   The artillery arranged to support the New Zealand
attack by a barrage moving south-east on Crèvecoeur protecting 2nd Wellington, and by another co-ordinated with it and
moving due east in front of 1st Auckland.   A third, moving
north-east, supported the VI. Corps' operation.

Since it was desirable for General Melvill to have a
battalion in reserve, the brigade frontage was reduced.   A
2nd Canterbury company, in the evening (30th September),
took over the sector in front of Lateau Wood.   2nd Auckland,
extended southwards, took over the rest of the right battalion
area, thus holding the whole of the brigade front, and 1st
Wellington was accordingly brought into reserve.

Light showers of rain began to fall about 10 p.m. as the
2 assaulting battalions moved in pitch darkness to their
assembly position, crossing over by a wooden bridge to the
north bank of the Scheldt Canal.   Towards dawn (1st
October) the rain ceased, and the clouds cleared from a grey
sky with the promise of a fine day.   The battalions were in
position by 5.15 a.m.   2nd Wellington were on the right and
1st Auckland on the left.   At 6 a.m. our artillery opened
fire, the enemy guns at once answering along the line of the
Canal.   Closely following the barrage 2nd Wellington had
captured Crèvecoeur by 8 a.m., taking 150 prisoners.   Just
before reaching the final objective, 2nd Lt. H. Pettit pursued
a large party of the enemy along a sunken road, and over-
taking them captured 35 with an empty revolver.   Elsewhere
the enemy resisted stubbornly enough, and 2nd Wellington
had to fight hard, the enemy's shell-fire and enfilade machine
gun fire from the high ground southwards causing heavy
casualties.   Exploitation towards Lesdain was impossible, and
the situation did not permit of the employment of cavalry.

Between 1st Auckland and their objective on the Old Mill
Road lay 3 roads, first a track running diagonally across
the front to Rumilly, then a sunken road running due north
and marked by a crucifix, and lastly a further road also
leading due north.   The 2 latter roads would furnish
admirable facilities for checking direction, but in the sunken
Crucifix Road the Aucklanders were likely to meet opposition.
Two companies were ordered to seize the objective, detailing
platoons to safeguard the flanks.   Another company was

instructed to pass through them for exploitation towards
Seranvillers and Wambaix. Two machine guns were given
to each of the leading companies, and the exploitation
company was allotted 2 trench mortars.

A certain amount of opposition was encountered on the
Rumilly Road, but this was speedily overcome. The Crucifix
Road, as anticipated, was strongly garrisoned with at least
40 machine guns, and heavy fighting ensued before it was
cleared. Over 200 prisoners were captured here. The 2
companies, pressing on towards the third road, began to be
much troubled by machine gun fire from Seranvillers and
the left flank where the VI. Corps attack, delayed by strong
enemy resistance in the outskirts of Rumilly, had not made
progress. This third road was also held by the enemy in
force, and after seizing it the leading companies, now considerably reduced in strength, had reached the limit of their
powers. At this stage, therefore, the exploitation company
passed through them and attacked the final objective. Like
the third road it was occupied strongly, and from the 2 a
further large bag of prisoners was collected.[1] Many casualties also were inflicted on the enemy escaping towards Seranvillers. In crushing this stern opposition and securing their
final objective the Aucklanders had excelled their own record
in the battle, but their very success now left them in difficulties. On the right they were in touch with Wellington, but
their left, though to some extent protected by a flank
platoon, was very much exposed, and the anxiety of the
company commander was only too well founded.

For presently, about 8.30 a.m., a very strong counter-
attack developed from Seranvillers and the north. Intensely
heavy hostile shelling fell on the whole position back to the
Canal. Moving along the high ground on the left, the
Germans succeeded in working behind Auckland's left rear.
The open Old Mill Road was now hopelessly untenable, and it
was only by very bitter fighting that a proportion of our
troops fought their way back over the exposed third road to
the sunken Crucifix Road. Many were killed, and a few
captured. For a time the position was critical. The
Crucifix Road itself came under destructive enfilade
fire from the north. Unlike the 2 other roads, however,
it afforded some cover. It was held stubbornly, and
the depleted garrison was reinforced and shortly afterwards

[1] The prisoners captured by Auckland were taken to the 3rd Divisional cage
at Masnières. 163 prisoners only passed through the New Zealand cage.

relieved by the reserve company. The other Auckland companies were disposed in depth to meet further pressure. No infantry action, however, developed against the Crucifix Road. The shelling also began to slacken about 10.30 a.m., and had died away by 11 a.m. As the Auckland companies were now reduced to the strength of platoons, a 1st Wellington company (Capt. J. R. Cade) was sent forward before noon to reinforce them. This company in the evening took over the front line of the Crucifix Road.

The German counter-attack developed also on the Ruahine company (Lt. Temp.-Capt. W. R. Burge, M.C.) on 2nd Wellington's left flank. Ruahine lost half their effectives, but held on dourly, and their stand was largely instrumental in saving the whole line. Two platoons of the reserve 2nd Wellington company were sent forward to strengthen them. In the day's fighting 2nd Wellington sustained nearly 150 casualties. Those of 1st Auckland were considerably heavier. 2 officers, including Major G. de B. Devereux, had been killed, 8 wounded, and 2 were missing; 70 men were killed, 240 wounded and 10 taken prisoners. Normally, about this time, a company went into action with 3 or 4 officers and about 130 men. On relief, on 3rd October, the 1st Auckland company strengths were respectively 1 officer and 38 men, no officer and 29 men, 2 officers and 51 men, 2 officers and 39 men. The fortitude displayed by the regimental medical officer, Capt. P. A. Ardagh, M.C., in attending to wounded at an inadequately protected dressing station for 36 continuous hours, under the heaviest shell-fire, won him a recommendation for the V.C. and the grant of a D.S.O.

On the capture of Crèvecoeur and the clearing of the defences that had guarded the stone bridge, 2nd Auckland moved strong patrols across the river and extended the bridgehead south of the village. By noon (1st October) our lines ran solidly all round the eastern outskirts, with posts in the northern extremity of the Beaurevoir-Masnières line. Forward posts were established by 2nd Wellington well towards Lesdain and up the Seranvillers valley, and in the afternoon, the enemy artillery remaining quiescent, the position was strongly consolidated. A small party of Engineers under Lt. A. W. Thomas, M.C., had advanced with the 1st Brigade infantry and repeatedly done good work in removing demolition charges and delay-action mines from bridges and dugouts. Remaining from 30th September onwards on the Canal bank, they built under fire a footbridge across the river to the island and repaired a traffic bridge for the use of horses and transport. Other parties too of the Engineers were hard at work. They took in hand at once the placing of 2 pontoon bridges in position on the western bank of the Canal, in readiness to be thrown across when required. Conspicuously good work in this connection was done by Lts. W. S. Rae and M. K. Draffin and Cpl. A. T. Brokenshire, M.M. In the evening the artillery batteries moved forward to the depressions east of the Cambrai Road. The night was comparatively quiet.

On 2nd October Crèvecoeur and our battery areas were heavily bombarded throughout the day. The 7th Battery in particular received attention, but only 1 gun was destroyed. In the evening the battery moved forward just east of Les Rues des Vignes and became "silent." The 3rd Artillery Brigade, returning from the 5th Division, took up positions on the western bank of the Canal opposite Crèvecoeur.. On the same evening the 3rd Division of the VI. Corps captured Rumilly and advanced into line with the 1st Brigade, thus definitely securing the left flank. For the time being the Army policy was that our advance was not to be pressed. Artillery was to be brought up to deal with the enemy defences at the crossings over the Canal and to carry out vigorous counter-battery work. Constant vigilance was, however, to be maintained to detect any signs of withdrawal.

The 1st Brigade front was subjected to very heavy enemy artillery fire in the morning of the 3rd from 4 a.m. to 6 a.m. Unmistakable barrage lines were put down on the approaches to Crèvecoeur and to the Canal bridges, and Capt. Cade's company, though only just relieved and dog-tired, was sent forward again through the shell-fire to strengthen 1st Auckland. The hostile bombardment may have been meant to support a counter-attack, but no infantry movement developed. On the roads east of the Crucifix Road, where the Auckland dead lay from 1st October, the enemy were still in strong force, and rumours that reached the 1st Brigade headquarters of his withdrawal were unfounded. In the evening the Rifle Brigade moved up to relieve the 1st Brigade. Just prior to relief there was a particularly heavy enemy bombardment on our front line from Crèvecoeur northwards, and every indication foreshadowed an enemy attack. A slow fire was opened on S.O.S. lines by our artillery. The enemy shelling gradually died away, and his infantry did not leave

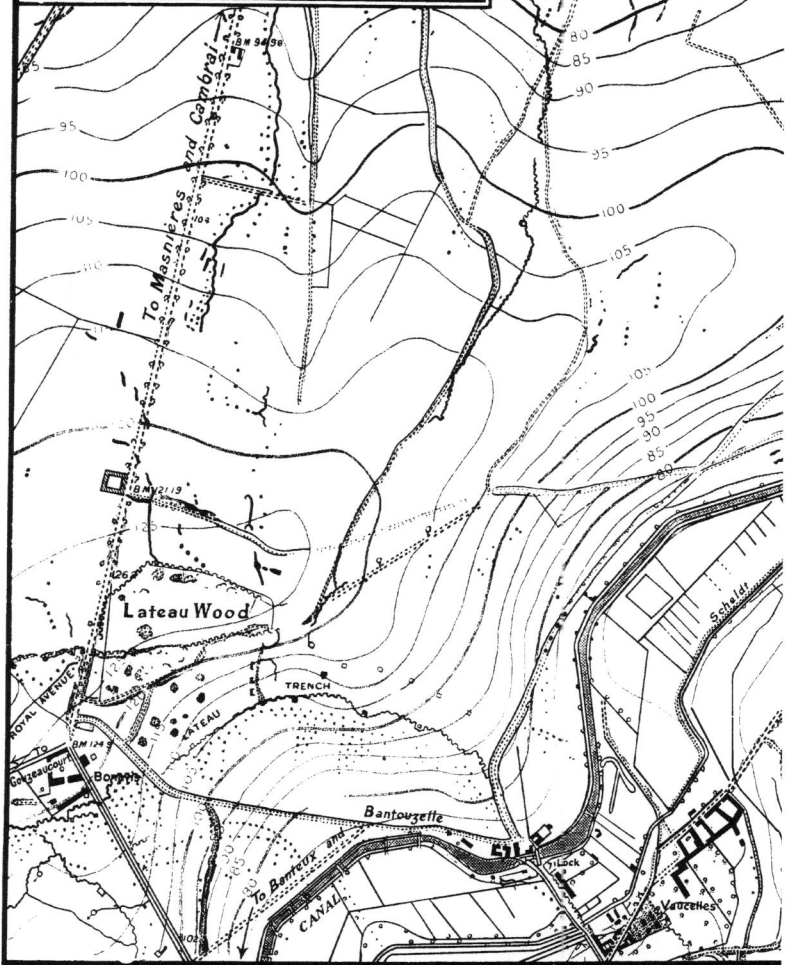

THE SCHELDT
CANAL

Adapted from Sheets 57ᴮ N.W. and S.W.
Ordnance Survey (O.B.), August, 1918
SCALE 1 : 20,000

YARDS   1000   500   0

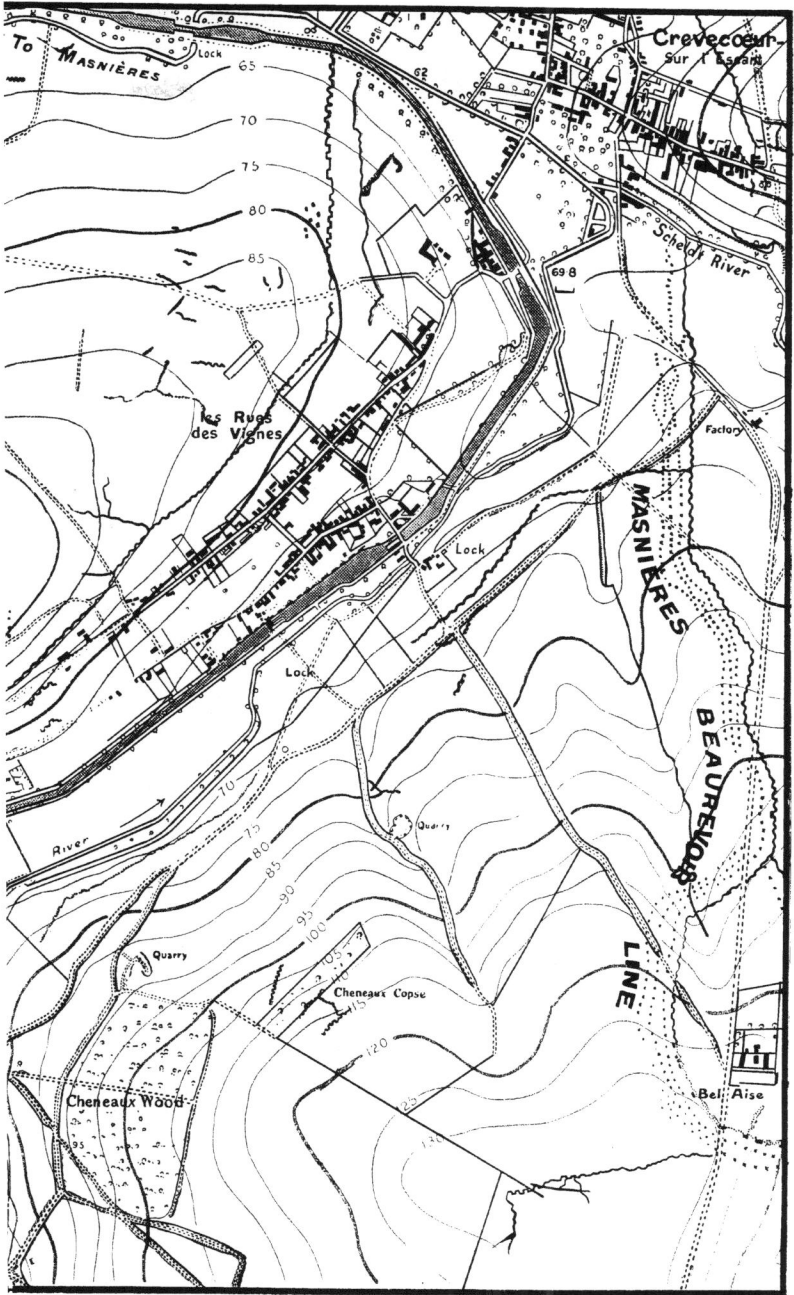

To MASNIÈRES

Lock

65

70

75

80

85

Crevecœur
Sur l'Escaut

Scheldt River

69 8

Factory

les Rues
des Vignes

Lock

Lock

MASNIÈRES

BEAUREVOIR

LINE

River

70

75

80

85

90

95

100

Quarry

Quarry

Cheneaux Copse

120

Cheneaux Wood

95

Bel Aise

their positions. The 4th[1] Battalion relieved 2nd Auckland and the 1st Battalion[2] 2nd Wellington. The 3rd Battalion took over the Crucifix Road positions from 1st Auckland.

Meantime opposite Vaucelles the 2nd Brigade had not succeeded in crossing the Canal. On 1st October it had side-slipped northwards. The 37th Division, relieving the 5th, took over the 1st Canterbury sector at Vaucelles, and 2nd Canterbury occupied the whole of the new brigade front south of Les Rues des Vignes. The change, however, offered even less facility for an advance, for 2nd Canterbury were now faced by the bridgeless Canal. Of the 3 spans of the bridge on the Tordoir Lock, at the southern end of Les Rues des Vignes, 2 had been blown up, and along the whole front the weedy muddy water was at least 5 feet deep. On the east bank also, though the enemy's movement was now restricted by the efficient fire of our artillery, he still held in strength his positions in Cheneaux Wood and about the quarries. From this high ground, the northern extremity of the La Terrière plateau, he could make no withdrawal without imperilling the last entrenched positions of the Hindenburg Line to the south.

Early in the misty morning of 4th October a silence of the enemy's guns appeared to betoken a retirement, but when the fog lifted there were indications that on the contrary he had even, possibly as a feint, strengthened his defences. His machine guns were as ever active against the forward Bonavis slopes south of Les Rues des Vignes, and large movements of troops in the rear areas suggested the possibility of counter-attack at Crèvecoeur.

While the whole of the Third and First Armies were by now similarly brought to a standstill, the Fourth Army had on 3rd October completed their task of breaching the Hindenburg Line by the capture of its last system opposite their front, 5 miles east of the Canal. The result of this last advance turned the enemy defences on the La Terrière plateau.

In the morning of 5th October the eagerly-awaited signs of withdrawal were forthcoming. 2nd Canterbury reported hostile shelling of Vaucelles and of the eastern bank in the neighbourhood. Without losing a moment, the right company commander (Capt. L. B. Hutton) went in person with a patrol southwards on to the 37th Division's front. Scrambling

---

1 Major Barrowclough, vice Lt.-Col. Beere, pp. 444, 473.
2 Lt.-Col. R. C. Allen of Auckland Regiment, now returned from New Zealand after wounds received at Messines, took over command on 30th September. See also p. 480.

over the Vaucelles bridge, before the troops on the spot moved, Hutton's party passed through the village, penetrated the near edge of Cheneaux Wood, and reached Fox Farm, south of it, without opposition. The patrol was followed by a 2nd Canterbury company, which crossed opposite the brigade front, 3 men at a time, on a German raft formed of a duck-walk supported by bundles of corks.

The platoon forming this company's advanced guard, under 2nd Lt. J. Mitchell, met with considerable resistance in the sunken roads on the slopes north of Cheneaux Wood. 5 machine guns and 15 prisoners were captured in successive encounters. On the fourth occasion, the German officer who commanded the machine gunners, after first holding up his hands, endeavoured to stab one of our party with a dagger. He raised his arm to strike, but L.-Cpl. M. H. Coppell, seeing his action, shot him dead instantly. Not a few other Germans were killed. A second company was diverted round to cross at Vaucelles. Meanwhile the Engineers had constructed a more substantial raft, on which the remaining companies, with a section of machine guns, ferried themselves across. 37th Division patrols were also now over the Canal and moving east.

Continuing their advance, the leading Canterbury company cleared the high ground about Cheneaux Wood, adding an officer and 22 men to their number of prisoners. On this spur they formed a defensive flank, and the support companies advanced on the Bel Aise Farm and the Beaurevoir-Masnières line with its 50-yard-wide belt of unbroken entanglements. This was the pivot of the enemy's withdrawal. Machine guns fired actively from it, but the patrols discovered saps giving approach towards the wire. Here they established the presence of a powerful garrison.

The necessity of guarding the right flank had swung the direction of the Canterbury movement some 600 yards southwards, but the 4th Rifles on the left swiftly filled the gap. For the Rifle Brigade, still being intermittently shelled with gas and high-explosive in the Crèvecoeur positions, were also able to make headway. One company of the 4th Battalion extended the bridgehead opposite Les Rues des Vignes and surprised a German post, capturing 18 prisoners and a machine gun. A second company moved over the Canal in support. Nearing the Beaurevoir-Masnières line, the leading company was counter-attacked on the left flank but drove off its assailants with the help of the support company. Two platoons actually entered the trench, but were later forced to fall back a distance of 150 yards, Rflmn. P. Henderson covering the withdrawal and crawling back later with his Lewis gun under direct and heavy fire. The left front line company, however, which had posts in the northern extremity of the Beaurevoir-Masnières line, succeeded in clearing it for 500 yards southwards. Owing to this hard fighting the 4th Rifles' casualties were fairly heavy, amounting to an officer and 5 men killed and an officer and 39 men wounded. The 1st Rifles' patrols in the centre met very strong fire from Lesdain, but reached its western outskirts, capturing 4 prisoners. On the left the 3rd Battalion gained some 500 yards in front of the Crucifix Road, but as the centre battalion could not make progress into Lesdain, the newly-established posts became exposed to the machine guns in the village and were withdrawn.

In view of the strength of the Beaurevoir-Masnières wire the enemy's position could not be rushed. But the advance already achieved facilitated immediately the Engineers' task of constructing bridges over the Scheldt Canal and river for guns and transport. Forward sections of artillery also could now be thrown over the Canal, and the fact that the New Zealanders and the 37th Division on their right had now room for deployment on the eastern bank would be of enormous assistance in the next movement.

The Battle of Cambrai and the Hindenburg Line closed on 5th October. Bitter resistance was being still encountered in the envelopment of Cambrai, but the strategic aims of the battle had been achieved, and the whole Hindenburg defence system was in our hands. From the various strong counter-attacks launched against us during the first 3 days of the battle along the Army front and from the fact that generally the bridges on the Scheldt Canal were only hurriedly destroyed, it seemed probable that the enemy had not only intended to hold up the British attack but had been confident of his power to do so. As late as 24th September Admiral Hintze had assured the Reichstag that the wall of bronze in the west would never be broken. It was now irretrievably shattered. With the passage of the Canal du Nord[1] and the

[1] The N.Z.E. Tunnelling Company had moved from Arras to Marieux in the IV. Corps area in August to work on the G.H.Q. line. They had followed up the advance, repairing roads water-mains reservoirs. On 28th September they began the erection of a bridge, capable of carrying the heaviest traffic, over the Canal du Nord near Havrincourt. It was completed on 2nd October. Sir Douglas Haig, General Byng, Mr. S. Gompers and others visited their work, and the Field-Marshal ordered Capt. J. D. Holmes, acting O.C. Company, to give the following message to his men:— "I wish to convey to one and all of the N.Z.E. Tunelling Company my appreciation of the excellent work done by the Company during the erection of the Havrincourt Bridge and also of the work done since the unit came to France." From several congratulatory messages, the following from the C.E. Third Army may be quoted:— "Congratulate you and your Company on completion of fine bridging feat." Photo opp. p. 509.

capture of the Hindenburg Line the first phase of the British offensive, the struggle in entrenched positions, was closed, and the menace to the enemy's railways and lines of communication became immediate. Except for the Beaurevoir-Masnières line and some other still less complete defences, no artificial obstacle barred the way to Maubeuge. Nor could the Germans find comfort in the north. The Flanders battle[1] commenced on 28th September. Ploegsteert Wood, Messines, and Polygon Wood were once more in our hands, and a large tract of country beyond the limits of the advance achieved in 1917. Threatened equally by this movement and by the progress on Cambrai, the Germans were already withdrawing south of the Lys, and by 4th October British troops were again in the old New Zealand area about Erquinghem Armentières and Houplines.

1   p. 490.

CHAPTER XIV.

THE SECOND BATTLE OF LE CATEAU

With the shattering of the Hindenburg Line and the corresponding movements southwards, it remained now only to develop and exploit these successes by co-ordinated movements on the part of the Americans French and British, with a view to realising Foch's strategical conception and thrusting the Germans back with deadly losses on the Meuse. Already in the first week of October at the southern end of the line the American and French advance had crossed the Aisne and threatened to turn Laon and the St. Gobain massif. If this right flank in the difficult country about the Meuse highlands could maintain sufficiently rapid progress, a trap was set for the German Army in which its retreat might be expected to degenerate into a rout. In any case, strong pressure applied without delay must shake the crumbling German Army to its foundations. The season, moreover, was now advanced. Some weeks still remained available before winter weather and shortened daylight would impede operations, but already at midnight, 5th/6th October, the approach of winter was heralded by the putting back of the clock an hour in the change from summer to normal time. For these reasons speed was more than ever essential. The combined attack was therefore fixed for 8th October. As it turned out, the Allies' full purpose was not to be immediately realised. The difficulties facing the southern horn of the pincers proved sufficient to retard its advance, and the German forces were saved for the moment from annihilating disaster. But the result was to make the enemy's position desperate. To the British attack carried out as part of these operations by the Fourth and Third Armies on a front of 17 miles, Haig has given the name of the Second Battle of Le Cateau.[1]

On the IV. Corps front the attack was entrusted to the 2 Divisions in the line, the 37th on the right and the New Zealanders on the left. The general direction was to the north-east in conformity with the movement for enveloping Cambrai. The New Zealand Division, therefore, by virtue of its position was given the main Corps objective, while the

---

1 As distinguished from the action near Le Cateau by the II. Corps, August 1914.

37th Division were to protect its right flank. The final line aimed at lay some 2½ miles to the east, on the western edge of the plateau bounded by the Scheldt and Selle. From right to left, it was traced first along a hedgerow south-west of Esnes. This hedgerow was some 200 yards east of a sunken road, itself lying parallel to and a corresponding distance beyond the single and last German trench which, running from southwards of Briseux Wood to Seranvillers, faced the Division across their whole front. Passing northwards, the line included the hamlet of Le Grand Pont, immediately to the west of Esnes, and the high ground beyond the Esnes Mill. Thence it ran along and beyond the Esnes-La Targette-Cambrai Road, the exploitation objective of the previous week, to the boundary with the VI. Corps. North of the boundary the 3rd Division on the right of the VI. Corps were to advance beyond Seranvillers. If opportunity offered, all Divisions would exploit eastwards, the New Zealanders by the capture of Esnes and the establishment of a line three-quarters of a mile east of the Cambrai Road, and the 3rd Division by an advance on Wambaix.

The New Zealand task was allotted to the 2nd Brigade on the right and the 3rd Brigade on the left, who were already in position in the 2 subsectors of the Division's line. An intermediate objective was selected for each brigade, but these, owing to the north-eastern direction of the whole advance, would not be in a straight line. A sunken road running south from Lesdain offered itself as a suitable inter-mediate goal for the 2nd Brigade. That of the Rifle Brigade lay further eastward in the Seranvillers trench line from their left boundary down to the precipitous right bank of the little stream which, rising beyond Esnes, flows round the north of that village and of Lesdain to the Scheldt about Crèvecoeur, and is called the Torrent of Esnes. On the first objective a varying pause was arranged in conformity with the general movement. Four tanks would co-operate with the Rifle Brigade in clearing Lesdain and were available, if necessary, to help the 2nd Brigade in clearing Esnes. The 3rd Division were also given 4 tanks to assist in mopping up Seranvillers.

Crèvecoeur was still persistently and violently shelled, so that its garrison was reduced to a minimum and its defence made dependent on machine gun fire from the flanks and a strong artillery barrage. It was discovered later that the enemy was already at work on extensive preparations for

studied demolition of the whole area in view of a retreat to
a position west of Caudry. In the Beaurevoir-Masnières line,
however, every indication pointed to a stand. Patrols continued to test the trenches and continued to encounter undiminished resistance. Aeroplanes also confirmed the presence of strong garrisons and the expenditure of considerable
labour on the trench. The openings of several new dugouts
showed up clearly.

In this last organised trench system and the positions
connected with it northwards there seemed to be sound
reasons for anticipating formidable resistance. Sufficient
artillery was therefore arranged to cope with it. Three
batteries of 6-in. howitzers were assigned to engage the
Beaurevoir-Masnières line and the series of roads eastwards.
These roads would receive also the special attention of the
light howitzers. The barrage would be provided by 6 brigades
of field artillery. The 2nd (Army) Brigade was still detached
with the XVII. Corps, but General Napier Johnston had at his
disposal 4 British brigades as well as the 1st and 3rd New
Zealand Brigades. In the meantime, medium and light
mortars were brought into forward positions to co-operate
with the artillery in cutting the extensive wire. The field
guns too moved to advanced positions. The 1st Brigade
guns were in new emplacements on 5th October, 2 sections of
the 7th Battery being held ready to support the assaulting
battalions of the Rifle Brigade. On the 6th a forward
section of the 13th Battery of the 3rd Brigade moved over
the Canal on General Young's front, and was followed on
the 7th by the remainder of the brigade. All other preparations were pushed on apace. In accordance with the
boundaries selected for the attack, the 37th Division on the
night 6th/7th October took over the southern extremity of
the 2nd Canterbury line opposite Bel Aise Farm. The
boundary between the 2 New Zealand infantry brigades
was similarly readjusted northwards. The Engineers were
engaged in the maintenance of existing bridges over the Canal
and the construction of new pontoon bridges south of Les
Rues des Vignes and in bringing up spare bridging material
to the western bank. Their work was constantly hampered
by shell-fire and called for no less patience than fortitude.

In the afternoon of 7th October General Young's Headquarters occupied a dugout in one of the quarries on the
hillside across the river. It was found prepared for
demolition, but the charges and fuses were removed without

accident. General Hart, too, moved in the evening to a battle headquarters in a quarry on the Rumilly track. In the late afternoon 1st Otago crossed the canal and river by the newly erected bridges and took over from 2nd Canterbury the right part of their line on the slopes north of Bel Aise Farm. The boundary of the 3rd Division was also shifted southwards to enable them satisfactorily to overlap Seranvillers. The 3rd Battalion of the Rifle Brigade garrisoning the left of the northern brigade subsector were not attacking. They withdrew 3 companies into reserve at 3 a.m., 8th October, and held the line with 1 company, thus facilitating the assembly of the assaulting troops of their own brigade and of the 3rd Division.

During the night 7th/8th October the enemy's artillery on the 2nd Brigade front was somewhat above normal. Whether by chance, or because some evidence pointed to our purpose, he shelled the assembly area intermittently. Crèvecoeur also received attention. The night was at first wet and dark. In the small hours, however, it brightened into unusual clearness, most helpful to the 2nd Rifles who moved up after midnight to the shallow sunken roads which formed their position of assembly. The few "cubby" holes available gave inadequate shelter, 1 company being practically in an open field and not a little troubled by the enemy machine gun fire. Fortunately, however, on this part of the front shelling had died down.

For the opening assault, in addition to the artillery, extensive use was made of machine guns and mortars. Two companies of machine guns were placed at the disposal of the Rifle Brigade for the purpose of the initial barrage, one company lifting forward steadily eastwards to extreme range—during the day it was to expend 80,000 rounds— the other sweeping the northern and southern outskirts of Lesdain. Two companies were earmarked to supply forward guns to the assaulting brigades. In the zero bombardment, mortars would prove valuable against the Old Mill of Lesdain and against a Factory which the Germans held in strength just west of Lesdain, opposite the junction of the 2 brigades. Mortars also as well as machine guns and forward sections of artillery were allotted to the assaulting battalions, to accompany them in their advance.

The attack was launched at 4.30 a.m., 8th October. The enemy's artillery response was immediate and fairly heavy, and the machine guns in Bel Aise Farm in particular swept the open

slopes falling towards the Lesdain valley.   From the outset
the attack moved forward with rapidity and certainty.   It
is sufficient to deal briefly with each unit in turn, beginning
at the right where 1st Otago lay on the northern slopes of
the plateau commanded from Bel Aise.   Over a large part of
their front they were faced by the unbroken wire of the
Beaurevoir-Masnières line, wholly impenetrable, had German
nerves been steady.   As it was, neither infantry nor
machine guns put up a stern resistance, and while Lewis guns
and bombs held the enemy down, the infantry hacked their
way through the entanglements and cleared the trench.
Only 1 post on their right near the farm provided a brief
check.   It contained 4 machine guns and a garrison of 40,
but after some trouble was surrounded and captured by 2
platoons under 2nd Lt. W. McKean, D.C.M., M.M.   The
barrage lifted 100 yards every 4 minutes, and by 5.40 a.m.
the leading company were on the first objective (the Red
Line) on the sunken road south of Lesdain.   From this
line on, it had been arranged that after the appointed pause
the barrage should move forward in the open country at a
faster rate of 100 yards every 3 minutes.   It was to include
a proportion of smoke, most serviceable in blinding and
bluffing disorganised resistance, and on the final trench was
to pause for 10 minutes.   On the Red Line a second 1st
Otago company passed through.   Skirting the north of Pelu
Wood, they covered the intervening ground and crossed the
surprisingly well-wired final trench with little opposition.
From there it was but a step to the sunken road and the
hedgerow which was their final objective.   They were on it
well up to time and with light casualties.   Behind them the
remaining companies consolidated in readiness to move
forward later in the morning, should conditions favour, to
the capture of Esnes.

2nd Canterbury had arranged for a medium trench mortar
bombardment of the wire in their sector on the 6th.   It
had been extremely successful.   Broad gaps and lanes were
distinctly visible from our trenches.   Through these openings
the 2nd Canterbury assaulting waves poured into the
Beaurevoir-Masnières line.   Here the enemy machine guns
were handled more stoutly than in the vicinity of Bel Aise,
and there were a few minutes of fierce resistance.   Two
machine guns particularly in the centre of the line, where the
wire chanced to be intact, proved a serious obstacle.   They
wiped out the sections of the first wave that charged them.

Sergt. R. C. Ecclesfield, however, with a couple of men
outmanoeuvred them.   Ecclesfield himself drew their fire
and engaged their attention in front, and the 2 men,
though fired on by rifles, worked round the flank and
liberally bombed the post. They then rushed it, captured
the 2 machine guns and took the crews prisoners.

At the outset of the attack 2nd Canterbury's left company already held the northern end of the Beaurevoir-
Masnières line won on the 5th, and their first obstacle was
the Factory.   The prearranged mortar bombardment at
zero proved effective, and in co-operation with the 4th Rifles
the company cleared the Factory without undue difficulty.
Several prisoners were taken.   After overcoming these
initial centres of resistance both Canterbury companies
moved on rapidly towards their first objective in the sunken
road on the outskirts of Lesdain.   The advance dipped down
into a deep valley and then mounted the other side where a
single field separated them from the road.   Little resistance
was shown.   A chance bullet shot Pte. J. Ward's rifle out
of his hand.   He could find no other to replace it, but
picking up a shovel continued on with his comrades, and
with this unorthodox weapon hammered in the heads of 3
Germans and killed them.   Only a few machine guns were
in action, and these were silenced by our machine and Lewis
guns and rifle grenades.   Crossing the field the Lewis
gunners dashed forward to the road.   Under the near bank
were deep and extensive dugouts, and the road itself was
packed with a mass of irresolute disorganised Germans.
Canterbury's Lewis gunners, Cpl. J. A. Auld, L./Cpl. H. Day,
and others enfiladed it from each flank, causing immediate
surrender, and the 2 companies secured between them over
200 prisoners.

Only a small proportion of the enemy preferred flight to
surrender.   These were now hurriedly running without arms
towards Esnes.   On them Pte. R. C. Butler and other Lewis
gunners, mounting the far bank and dashing forward,
inflicted severe casualties.   The Lewis gun fire assisted also
to cover the advance of the fresh company which here,
simultaneously with the 1st Otago company, "leapfrogged"
through.   Almost all semblance of opposition had disappeared.   The 2nd Canterbury company carried their second
objective easily, capturing 7 machine guns and 130 prisoners
and pushed on to a further short section of isolated trench
south of Esnes itself.   According to plan the fourth

Canterbury company followed up close behind, cleared Le Grand Pont village, still shelled by our heavies, and reached the high ground commanding Esnes from the north, where touch was established with the Rifle Brigade. It then crossed over the Cambrai Road and occupied a trench system on the north edge of Esnes. The right was for the moment refused on the north-western outskirts of the village till the time set for the 1st Otago exploitation troops to come forward. This company captured 5 machine guns, 3 mortars, and some 80 prisoners. Company Headquarters consumed with satisfaction an excellent breakfast prepared for the German officers. All through the morning invaluable service had been given on this flank by a boldly handled section of machine guns under Lt. A. R. Curtis. On repeated occasions they had engaged enemy machine gunners and infantry, whose bodies were passed in the subsequent course of the advance. Pushing his section well forward, this officer was now the first to locate a number of abandoned German field guns in a hollow north-east of Esnes. 3 of these the Canterbury company thereupon took over, 1 falling later to 1st Otago.

The Rifle Brigade attack was carried out with 3 battalions. The 4th[1] on the right was detailed first to capture Lesdain by an enveloping movement, and then to mop up the dugouts along the steep bank of the Torrent of Esnes up to a point some 1000 yards eastward, where the sharp north-easterly trend of the 2nd Brigade advance towards Le Grand Pont would then shut them out. In the centre of the line, the 1st Battalion would carry the Old Mill of Lesdain and push forward over the high ground north of the Torrent, in touch on the right, first with the 4th Battalion, and later, as the 2nd Brigade came up, with 2nd Canterbury. On the left the 2nd Rifles would with the 3rd Division on the north pass through the 3rd Battalion garrison .of our present front line, and then advance towards the Cambrai Road south of Seranvillers.

The 4th Battalion passed 1 company round the southern edge of Lesdain and another company through the northern outskirts. A light trench mortar was at the disposal of each company. The right company co-operated with 2nd Canterbury in the clearing of the Factory. Then crossing the network of light railways near it, the Rifles pressed on to prearranged positions along the southern edge of the village

1 Major Barrowclough, p. 513.

to the far side, whence they mopped up village and chateau, taking a large number of prisoners and 6 trench mortars. The left company similarly cleared the northern and north-eastern parts of the village and the cliffs of the Torrent of Esnes. They met with considerable resistance. They had a running fight all the way, and many enemy dead were left to mark the line of advance. In all, the battalion captured 19 officers, over 300 men, 6 mortars and over 30 machine guns. Of our own men 7 were killed, and an officer and 50 men wounded.

The 1st Battalion in the centre stormed the Mill, still smoking with the dust of the mortars' bombardment, and dealt in succession with a series of open and sunken roads crossing the line of advance. In the darkness the forward waves overlooked a pillbox from which the enemy, after they passed, directed a heavy fire on the supporting troops. Sergt. R. J. Sinclair without the slightest hesitation rushed the pillbox single-handed, killed the machine gun crew and captured the gun. On the left, both the leading company of the 2nd Rifles and a company detailed to follow it along the left flank appear to have pressed forward too impetuously into our barrage. They suffered somewhat heavy casualties. Both battalions, and in particular the 2nd Battalion on the left, were faced by German garrisons in the sunken roads. At one check on the left flank Cpl. S. J. Sapsford of the 2nd Rifles ran up a spur northwards with his Lewis gun, calling on 2 other crews to follow him with their guns. Standing up under heavy fire he located the enemy posts. He at once directed the fire of the other 2 guns and then himself fired his own gun with such good effect that the enfiladed Germans were routed, many being shot down as they ran away. Generally the powerful barrage and the dash of the riflemen were too much for the disheartened defence. On 2 successive roads before the Seranvillers trench, parties of 60 and 40, with numerous machine guns, surrendered practically without fighting to the left company of the 2nd Rifles.

Some 500 yards from the trench, however, the barrage, extremely dense and effective at the outset, had considerably diminished, and here in the clearing light numerous machine guns temporarily held up the advance and inflicted casualties. The wire, here as on the Otago sector of the trench, was strong, and the barrage was powerless to silence the machine guns which were particularly active against the 2nd

The Scheldt Canal and Vaucelles

GUNS CAPTURED NEAR ESNES

THE TRICOLOUR REAPPEARS IN BEAUVOIS

Battalion. Here, moreover, owing to the casualties incurred during the earlier part of the advance, the attacking line was thin. Part of the 2nd Rifles' support troops who were earmarked for the capture of the Cambrai Road moved forward into line with the leading company to aid them in the struggle for the first objective. Sergt. T. O'Neill, his platoon commander being seriously wounded, engaged the enemy with his 2 Lewis guns, and himself with a bombing section worked to the flank of the enemy trench, where he killed several of the garrison opposite him and took the remainder prisoners. At the same moment on the right, Sergt. H. L. Moyle with marked tactical skill swerved on to the 1st Battalion front, whose left flank was also checked, reached the Seranvillers trench and then pushed northwards. As he cleared the trench from the flank, the centre of the 2nd Rifles' line simultaneously worked forward directly on the position. Several machine guns and 40 prisoners were captured. Thus by 5.30 a.m. all 3 battalions of the Rifle Brigade were on their first objective in the Torrent of Esnes and the Seranvillers trench.

After the pause on the first objective the 1st and 2nd Rifles continued the advance on the brigade's reduced frontage towards the Cambrai Road and the final objective. Till 2nd Canterbury should come up, the right flank of the 1st Rifles was necessarily unprotected. It was guided by Cpl. C. A. Rowe. At one point it was threatened by a party of enemy in a quarry, but Rowe with 6 men rushed the position and captured over 20 prisoners. Like the South Island battalions, the Rifles now found the enemy's resistance broken. Practically the only trouble was caused by machine gun fire from Seranvillers, and this was ultimately silenced as the VI. Corps progressed. Several prisoners and machine guns were taken on a road which ran parallel to and about 200 yards west of the main road. Large numbers of the Germans gave themselves up without fighting. About this time the 1st Rifles' headquarters were heavily shelled, and all Lt.-Col. R. C. Allen's officers except 1 were casualtied. He himself was hit, but although suffering great pain superintended the evacuation of the wounded and remained at his post until the operation was completed.[1] Apart from this "crash" there was little evidence of the enemy's artillery. One battery of field guns in a sunken road just

---

1 Lt.-Col. Allen was again to show similar disregard to his own wounds in the operations prior to the attack on Le Quesnoy.

beyond the final objective shelled our advance from the Seranvillers trench and continued to fire at the Rifles' screen till, about 8 a.m., our scouts crossed the crest near the Cambrai Road. Thereupon 2nd Lt. A. L. McCormick, D.C.M., of the 1st Rifles, now the only officer left in his company, pushed out his Lewis gunners and engaged these field guns at point-blank range. For a moment the German fire forced our Lewis gunners and consolidating troops to fall back, but McCormick personally rallied them again, and his Lewis gunners shot down the enemy artillerymen. The gun positions were then occupied by a section under Cpl. L. G. McLean, till the line of outposts was established.[1] By 8.30 a.m. both Rifle Battalions were about 100 yards east of the Cambrai Road. The enemy appeared to be retreating hurriedly, and patrols were pushed forward by both battalions to keep in touch with him.

These patrols hardly moved forward, however, when heavy fire was encountered from machine guns in the direction of Longsart, and an embarrassing adventure befell the left company of the 2nd Battalion. One of their Lewis gunners, Rflmn. R. C. Ramsay, had run forward with his gun to silence an enemy field gun near Wambaix. At this moment 2 female British tanks, captured at some time and repaired and repainted by the Germans, suddenly appeared heading straight for the left company along the road that runs south-east from Wambaix. Their Lewis guns, converted to use German ammunition, sprayed the Rifles' posts vigorously and accurately. Several German field guns and machine guns supported the tanks' attack. Our own barrage had by this time practically died away. Nor had the company yet had time to consolidate. Taking cover, however, in the newly made shellholes, they fired at the vulnerable portions of the tanks. Ramsay out in front displayed conspicuous gallantry. Disregarding the approaching tanks, he continued to harass the field gun till he routed its crew. He then turned his fire on the tanks. They were now only some 150 yards away, and the situation was critical. Salvation came from an unlooked-for quarter. At this juncture 2 of our own male tanks, which had been engaged with the 3rd Division troops in clearing Seranvillers, nosed forward to the line of trees on the Cambrai Road. Here they quickly manoeuvred into position, and at a range of 300 yards laid out the females in quick succession. The

1 They appear to have been occupied later by the 2nd Rifles.

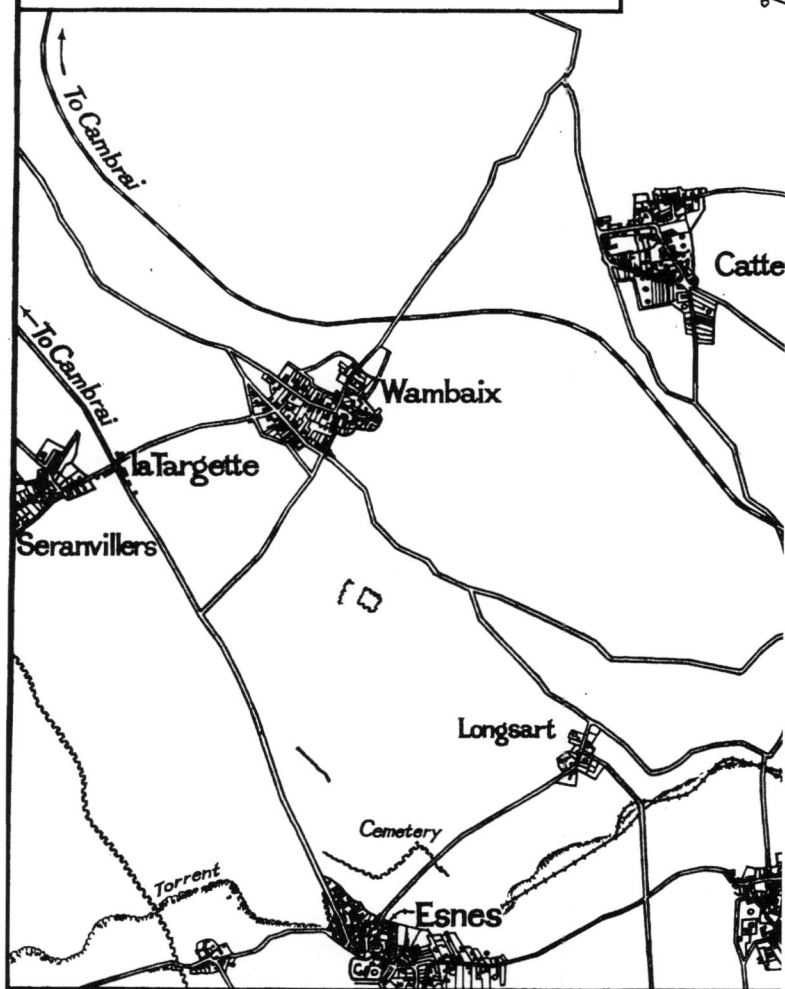

Scale - 1 : **40,000**

1000　　500　　0　　　　1000
YARDS

To Cambrai

To Cambrai

To Cambrai

Catte

Wambaix

laTargette

Seranvillers

Longsart

Cemetery

Torrent

Esnes

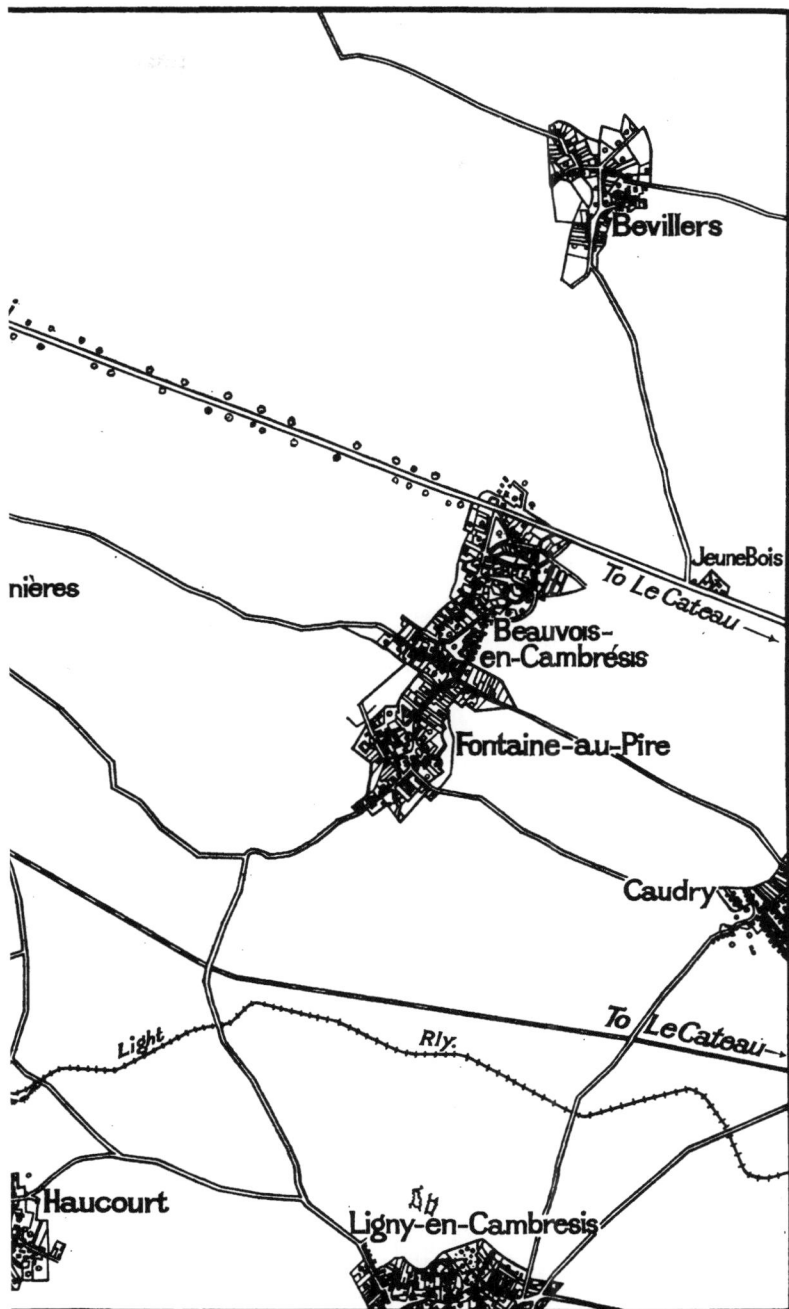

Bevillers

JeuneBois

nières

To Le Cateau →

Beauvois-
en-Cambrésis

Fontaine-au-Pire

Caudry

To Le Cateau →

Light   Rly.

Haucourt

Ligny-en-Cambresis

enemy crews poured out from the tanks and, in trying to escape, were wiped out by our Lewis guns.

Distant field and machine guns maintained a harassing fire, but were silenced by active sniping on the part of the Rifles' scouts and especially by forward sections of artillery now in position only half a mile behind the Cambrai Road. A daring and successful reconnaissance was made into Seranvillers by Cpl. J. C. Dibble, of the 2nd Rifles, with 3 men. He located enemy posts in various buildings and secured touch with the 3rd Division. The companies, somewhat mixed, were reorganised before noon. During the early afternoon they moved forward to their exploitation objective, 1000 yards further east, as far north as a mill near Wambaix, and took possession of abandoned German guns. On reaching this line it was found that opposite the 1st Rifles a party of the enemy, about 50 strong, were holding a well-wired isolated trench with 3 machine guns. As a frontal assault was impossible, Cpl. M. J. Mulvaney, D.C.M., a Lewis gunner, opened fire to cover a flank attack. He was immediately singled out by a German machine gun, but with his second burst of fire he killed the enemy Nos. 1 and 2 gunners. A moment later he disposed of the second machine gun in the same way. Thereupon the crew of the third gun took shelter. Mulvaney seized one of his men's rifles and with his No. 2 rushed the trench with fixed swords and forced the occupants to surrender.

No counter-attack developed against the Rifles themselves. About 5 p.m., however, a strong thrust was made from Wambaix against the VI. Corps front. A forward section of the 1st Artillery Brigade and the machine guns accompanying the Rifles did great execution in the enemy's ranks. But for the moment the Germans recovered part of Seran-villers. The Rifles' left flank, already much in advance, was accordingly withdrawn some 500 yards and refused thence back northwards along the Cambrai Road. At 7 p.m. under a barrage the VI. Corps again advanced on to the road.

In the enemy's shelling and machine gun fire and in our own barrage the 2 Rifle battalions attacking the final objective had lost fairly heavily. In the 1st Battalion an officer and 29 men had been killed and 8 officers and 227 men wounded. The 2nd Battalion casualties were 2 officers and 30 men killed or died of wounds, and 2 officers and 130 men wounded, and 4 wounded men also appear to have fallen into the enemy's hands south of Wambaix.   During the operation the Rifle Brigade had captured seven 77-mm. guns, a howitzer, several mortars and 89 machine guns, and by the close of the day their prisoners numbered over 800.

On the 2nd Brigade's front also the easy capture of the final objective had left the way obviously clear for exploitation.   At 9.30 a.m. the barrage reopened in front of 1st Otago, and the 2 fresh companies passing through our new outpost line by the hedgerow advanced on Esnes.   A certain amount of machine gun fire came from the south from Guillemin Farm and the Sargrenon Valley and from the high ground overlooking it which was not yet cleared. There was a handful of snipers in Esnes.   The village was, however, taken without trouble, and posts were established in a wide-flung line round it.   The 2nd Canterbury company north of Esnes, harassed during the interval by our own and the enemy's artillery and by the machine guns of German aeroplanes, swung up their right flank in conformity. Machine guns secured splendid targets in retreating enemy transport.   Special measures were taken to protect Otago's right flank, and in order to strengthen it further, the Canterbury company extended their right, now on the north-eastern outskirts of the village, down to the banks of the Torrent of Esnes.

Thus the 2nd Brigade's exploitation objectives were attained up to time, and the companies began to consolidate. When the enemy saw that the advance was stayed, he began to filter back.   The villages of Longsart and Haucourt further east were held in strength, and presently considerable machine gun fire and sniping developed from the high ground south of Longsart.   At 3.30 p.m. some 50 Germans advanced, possibly for a counter-attack, down the deep broken bed of the Torrent of Esnes, but were dispersed by our fire. Another smaller party approaching the advanced 2nd Canterbury company from the cemetery north-east of Esnes was beaten off by a patrol.   This little action gave a last fillip to the satisfaction inspired in this company by their long advance and the day's successes, and in closing a brief report the company commander (Capt. T. S. Gillies, M.C.) could not forbear adding: "Men in good heart, ready for anything."

In the evening the 37th Division attacked the high ground south-east of Esnes and relieved anxiety about the right flank.   During the day 1st Otago, losing 5 officers and 140 men, had captured over 100 prisoners, a field gun, and °

machine guns; 2nd Canterbury had 4 officers, including Major
D. A. Dron, M.C., and 32 men killed or died of wounds, and
4 officers and 110 men wounded. Having the good fortune
to find in their area the Lesdain Road dugouts, they had
secured a bag of nearly 500 prisoners, with 3 mortars and 24
machine guns, and the field guns discovered by Curtis.

The artillery had early moved well forward, and active
preparations were in progress for bringing up ammunition
to support the continuance of the attack on the following
day. On the cessation of the morning's barrage for the Rifle
Brigade, the 1st Artillery Brigade batteries moved to the
valley north-east of Crèvecoeur. One of the English brigades
attached to the Division simultaneously crossed the Canal,
and by 9 a.m. was in action north and south of Pelu Wood.
Shortly after midday both New Zealand brigades and 3 of
the 4 English brigades were in position east of the Canal and
on a corresponding line north of the Torrent of Esnes, the
remaining English brigade being temporarily retained by
Corps orders west of the Canal.

The night 8th/9th October was clear and the enemy's
bombing aeroplanes active. He shelled heavily his abandoned
dumps on the railway at Esnes and drenched our rear areas
with gas. Deep into the night patrols found his posts still
holding the sunken roads from Wambaix southwards. A
German machine gunner, carrying his gun, walked inad-
vertently into one of the 2nd Rifles' posts and was made
prisoner. The two 2nd Brigade support battalions and the
1 Rifle battalion, which would now adequately cover the
left brigade's shortening front, fully expected that their
advance would be contested.

The early hours of the morning were intensely cold with
the first frosts of autumn, and the troops waiting to continue
the attack had to stamp vigorously to quicken circulation.
At 5.20 a.m. the barrage started, lifting 100 yards every 3
minutes and preceded by a machine gun barrage 300 yards in
advance of and conforming with its lifts. The light mortars
bombarded the Torrent of Esnes. 2nd Otago on the right
and 1st Canterbury on the left passed through the 2nd
Brigade line and continued the advance, accompanied by
machine guns and attached sections from the 11th and 13th
Batteries. A squadron of 3rd Hussars was held in readiness
to follow the enemy and push out patrols if the situation
permitted. On the Rifle Brigade subsector the 3rd Battalion,
brought up from reserve and supported by a forward section

of artillery and a section of machine guns, similarly passed
through the 1st and 2nd Battalions. On their left the Guards
had relieved the 3rd Division. Of the anticipated enemy resistance not a sign was forthcoming. It became early apparent that the enemy had stolen away before dawn. Owing
to a shortage of reserves and the low strength of his
Divisions he was by this time experiencing the utmost difficulty in relieving or reinforcing his disorganised troops. At
the moment he was in no position to withstand an attack.
No rearguards remained to dispute progress, very slight
artillery fire was encountered, and the 38,000 shells of our
barrage were wasted. Speedily overrunning Longsart, by
9 a.m. the 2nd Brigade troops had reached the final objective
allotted, the Le Cateau-Cambrai railway. Under the bridge
on the Fontaine-au-Pire road 1st Canterbury found 4 artillerymen who claimed to have been on their way to rescue their
guns at Esnes, but were believed to have been a party left
for demolition. In close touch with the 2nd Brigade and the
Guards on either flank, the 3rd Rifles, suffering some casualties from our barrage,[1] reached their objective on the railway
south of Cattenières.

Our goal thus achieved, responsibility for the whole New
Zealand front was given to the 2nd Brigade, which taking
command of the 3rd Rifles became the advanced guard of the
Division. The 3rd N.Z.F.A. and an English artillery brigade,
both under Lt.-Col. McQuarrie, were made advanced guard
artillery, and during the day moved to Esnes and Longsart.
A line was roughly consolidated half a mile beyond the
railway, and patrols moved forward all along the front
towards Fontaine-au-Pire. On the high ground west of it
they began to encounter the first evidence of the German
rearguards. There were many machine guns in Fontaine-au-
Pire and Caudry, one of them firing from the steeple of the
Fontaine church. A patrol of the 3rd Hussars had already
galloped forward from the railway line, when our barrage
ceased. Disdaining to use low ground, they presented an
excellent target to the Fontaine machine guns, and an active
field gun followed their retirement, causing very severe losses.
It became necessary for the moment to suspend progress.
Towards dusk, however, a 1st Canterbury patrol succeeded in
penetrating the southern outskirts of Fontaine.

At nightfall (9th October) the 3rd Rifles were withdrawn,
and the 2nd Brigade battalions side-stepped to the north,

---

1   2 men killed, and 40 wounded.   The infantry complained of its erratic nature.

1st Canterbury gaining touch with the Guards on the left. Cold drizzling rain fell during the night, but blankets were now up for the supporting troops, who made themselves comfortable and slept peacefully on the quiet battlefield or under the almost forgotten luxury of a roof in undemolished villages. Vegetables from the gardens were "salvaged" to improve the evening meal, and old barrels were converted into bathing tubs. Under cover of darkness patrols pushed forward to envelop Fontaine-au-Pire, and found both it and Beauvois evacuated. The leading battalions therefore resumed their advance. There was some enemy shelling of Beauvois, but before daylight they had reached the Le Cateau-Cambrai Road. In Beauvois several civilians were found, who, when day dawned, gave their liberators a rapturous welcome.

At 3.30 a.m. (10th October) the advance was continued in "bounds" without a barrage. 2nd Otago crossed the Le Cateau Road between Caudry and Beauvois and, without opposition, reached the road running just west of Bethencourt northwards towards Quiévy. Here, however, the screen came under heavy machine gun and rifle fire from the direction of Quiévy and from rearguards in old "practice trenches" immediately in front. The forward artillery section rapidly came into action, and 4 Vickers guns also were hurried forward. Under this covering fire the trenches were cleared, and the troops swept down into the valley and up on the ridge north of Bethencourt. After a chilly morning the day had turned out beautifully fine.

In front of the same road where Otago had been momentarily arrested, 1st Canterbury met determined resistance at Herpigny Farm, which they carried at 10.20 a.m., several machine guns being captured and 1 man of the crews taken prisoner. On the road also 2 hostile posts were held strongly, but with the co-operation of Vickers and Lewis guns they were ultimately overpowered, and the road was in our hands at 2 p.m.

The 2 supporting battalions were by this time following up ready to move through when required, and before noon 1st Otago were passing through the right battalion on the railway north of Bethencourt. Skirting the village itself and Clermont Wood, they reached Clermont Valley. Here they took an abandoned field gun. Enemy artillery firing from the direction of Solesmes put a considerable barrage on this valley, but brushing all resistance out of their way, Otago advanced with exceptional rapidity and occupied Viesly. On

attempting to deploy from Viesly the right met heavy fire
from a cemetery on its southern outskirts. This was eventually mastered, and the line was established round the
eastern edge of Viesly from the cemetery to a large sandpit
on the north-east, whence it swung back to the north-west.

2nd Canterbury passed through the 1st Battalion after the
capture of Herpigny Farm and the road. The Guards were
experiencing stubborn resistance at Quiévy, and 2nd Canterbury were similarly exposed to heavy fire from Quiévy
itself and from about the neighbourhood of Fontaine-au-
Tertre Farm, now a mass of flames. Owing to their later
start and to this opposition they were unable to catch up
Otago, who therefore strengthened their long exposed left
with 8 machine guns, and specially directed their mobile
section of artillery to look after this flank. On Otago's
right the 37th Division had at an early hour enveloped
Caudry, and making fine progress were abreast with them on
the western slopes overlooking the Selle. In the afternoon
the 37th Division announced their intention of establishing
bridgeheads on the eastern bank of the river. To protect
their flank, 1st Otago moved forward in the evening to
within 400 yards of Briastre and consolidated a fresh line
there without opposition.

Throughout the day the advancing infantry had been
closely supported by the 13th Battery, which had made opportunities and used them for observed shooting. The rest of the
advanced guard artillery followed up early to the vicinity
of the Cambrai railway and later to Beauvois. At 2 p.m. the
1st Brigade batteries, too, had moved from their position of
assembly north-east of Crèvecoeur into action east of Beauvois. The 1st Infantry Brigade, marching up from the
reserve area, had reached Fontaine-au-Pire in the early afternoon, in preparation for passing through the South Island
battalions. About noon General Young had guaranteed to be
by the evening on the railway south of Quiévy. On that line
it was expected that the 1st Brigade would take up the
advance. But both front line battalions of the 2nd Brigade
were now considerably beyond this. 2nd Canterbury held
the Viesly-Quiévy spur, and 1st Otago were astride the
southern part of the Viesly—Fontaine-au-Tertre Farm spur
which had been decided on as General Melvill's first objective.
It had been originally proposed that the final objective of
the North Island battalions should be the line of the Selle
River. In view of the progress made on our own front and

by the 37th Division, this was now extended eastwards.
General Melvill was instructed to cross the river, secure
bridgeheads by daylight and be ready, if called upon, to
carry the high crests south-east of Solesmes. If conditions
warranted, cavalry might be pushed through to carry the
town from that direction. The Engineers were ordered to
repair at the earliest possible moment all bridges and communications and to arrange extra crossings over the Selle
for infantry and guns.

At 10 p.m. (10th October) the 1st Infantry Brigade were
beginning to pass through. The South Island battalions,
though tired and worn after their long marching and stiff
fighting moved back in exuberant spirits, singing and whist-
ling, to the houses in Beauvois, left in astonishing filth and
disorder by the retreating enemy. Casualties had been extremely light.

The 1st Brigade leading battalions were 1st Wellington on
the right and 2nd Auckland on the left. They had no formal
barrage, but the former was supported directly by a section
of howitzers, the latter by a section of 18-pounders. On the
infantry relief the 1st Brigade, N.Z.F.A., and an English
brigade became advanced guard artillery. The advance was
continued in the darkness with little opposition. Briastre
was cleared by Wellington patrols with some elements of the
37th Division, and Fontaine-au-Tertre Farm by Auckland in
conjunction with the Guards. Both battalions then moved on
to the line of the river. Except for stragglers, no Germans
remained on the western bank. In the morning it was found
that nearly 200 civilians were in Briastre. A handful of
Germans discovered hiding in cellars were taken prisoners.

The river Selle, one of the principal tributaries of the
Scheldt, flows northward along a deep valley and forms a
naturally strong position on which a retreating army can
stand at bay. About Solesmes its width varies from 25 to
35 feet. There is a good flow of water, and the stream is
mostly too deep to be fordable. On either side of the valley
the slopes rise up fairly steeply some 120 feet, completely
dominating the low ground by the river. Along the lower
slopes on the right or eastern bank run the main road and
railway from Le Cateau through Solesmes northwards to
Valenciennes. On 25th August 1914, during the retreat from
Mons, Solesmes had been the scene of a sharp rearguard
action by a brigade of the 3rd Division, who chanced now to
be in support to the Guards. On this line, which he had

then carried in the first flush of easy victories, the sorely-tried and disillusioned enemy now hoped to retard pursuit.

During the evening (10th October), despite opposition, Engineers of the 37th Division had thrown a narrow bridge over the river half a mile up-stream from the New Zealand boundary, and 4 of their infantry platoons were early in the night on the eastern bank. The 1st Wellington patrols reached the river about 1 a.m. The bridges opposite Briastre on our own front were down, and it was some little time before reconnaissance discovered the 37th Division's bridge. By 4 a.m., 11th October, however, 2 companies of 1st Wellington were over the river, the 2 leading platoons being commanded by 2nd Lt. S. S. Pennefather, D.C.M.[1] This force then proceeded to work back along the right bank to their own frontage. The left and leading company had reached the Factory in the low ground opposite Briastre, and both companies were beginning to cover their allotted fronts and deploy for their attack on the railway line, when the dawn disclosed them. At once heavy machine gun fire opened from the Solesmes road and railway. The left company was able to get under cover in and about the Factory and attached buildings, from which good observation and field of fire could be obtained both to the front and flanks. Pennefather held his men together and disposed them to meet counter-attack. The right company in the open suffered severely, and was forced to fall back on a sunken road near the river.

All along the eastern slopes the enemy was in strength. Contact aeroplanes reported also large bodies in rear. German artillery became active on our positions on the western bank. Further infantry movement was for the moment impracticable. On both company fronts several wounded lay out within 100 yards of the enemy's advanced positions. Very gallant rescue work in face of the German machine gun fire was to be successfully performed during the day by Cpl. H. B. Smith and Ptes. R. Campbell, M.M., and G. H. Buchanan. Pennefather himself went out no less than 11 times, and though fired on by machine guns from either flank at close range, succeeded in clearing the whole of his front of wounded. Under cover of the Factory Lt. A. W. Thomas, of the Engineers, and a small party of Wellington infantry constructed an improvised bridge of trees and rails, and across this after dusk the wounded were evacuated, and touch was maintained with the rear. Of the supporting

1   p. 245.

companies, one was disposed on the western edge of Briastre and the other through the village to secure touch with 2nd Auckland. There remained, however, a considerable gap astride the Selle river on the left of the Wellington outpost line on the eastern bank.

Like 2nd Canterbury on the previous afternoon, 2nd Auckland were still delayed by the obstinate resistance offered to their left and to the Guards west of Solesmes. They had accordingly to refuse the left flank, and for the moment relinquish any hope of crossing on their front to the east bank of the Selle.[1] Hostile artillery also harassed their left flank south of Solesmes and bombarded Viesly. Companies of both 2nd Auckland and the battalion in support suffered from this fire. The necessity for cover, or at least for concealment, was paramount. Part of 2nd Auckland's supports was therefore withdrawn behind the final ridge.

By 8.30 a.m. (11th October) the 1st Brigade batteries were in position behind Viesly, and the 15th Battery had a forward section just west of the village. They did much execution on the opposite hillside. Two further brigades of field artillery moved forward, and these, with the heavies, engaged the enemy's guns and the positions of his front line troops across the river and his support troops in the deep valleys eastwards. Our machine guns also, well sited on the forward slopes, inflicted several casualties. The German machine guns and snipers, however, were not silenced, and our infantry in the valley spent an unpleasant afternoon. From these commanding positions it was for many reasons most desirable to drive the enemy. At the same time it was impossible to undertake the operation off-hand in daylight.

Divisional headquarters was now at Beauvois and IV. Corps headquarters in Havrincourt Wood. At the latter place a conference was held during the afternoon. It was then arranged that the 2 Divisions in the line, co-operating with the V. Corps on the right, should at dawn on the 12th make another effort to reach the high ground on the eastern bank. With the Guards, however, still so far behind on the left, the New Zealanders' participation was ultimately modified, and it was decided that only the right battalion should move in order to protect the left flank of the 37th Division. 1st Wellington was ordered, therefore, to strike at the Belle Vue station on the railway, gain the spur just

---

1 In any case the crossing would have been very difficult, if not impracticable. The railway bridge over the Selle had been blown up, and the river, blocked by the debris, had risen considerably.

beyond it, and thence swing back their left north-west towards the river. Should little or no resistance be met with, patrols were to cross the spur and the valley beyond and occupy the next steep ridge to the north-east, thus directly threatening the investment of Solesmes.

The night was quiet. The survivors of the right Wellington company were relieved by 37th Division troops. The left company extended north to cover the allotted front. A company from support was brought over the river to deliver the attack, the left company being given certain tasks in co-operation. At 5 a.m., 12th October, our artillery and machine gun barrages came down on prearranged lines. It was likely that hostile enfilade fire from the road and railway beyond the northern limit of our operation might be troublesome, and special measures were taken to deal with these as far as Solesmes. For 5 minutes after zero, therefore, certain batteries were to bombard this part of the road, and then, lifting in conformity with the infantry advance, engage the railway, also north of the limits of the attack. Howitzers were to bombard the sunken roads in the valley beyond the spur for over 20 minutes.

Belle Vue was a name with sinister associations.[1] Now, again, as a year previously, Belle Vue machine guns bade our artillery fire defiance. From the station itself and from buildings on the Solesmes road, occupied in unexpected strength, they swept the low ground with a dense sheet of lead. The defences were held by troops of the German Jäger Division, that had contested so stubbornly with us the possession of the Trescault Ridge, and the garrison was at once powerful in numbers and of stout morale. By 8 a.m. the 1st Wellington right had reached buildings on the Briastre road 200 yards east of the river, where with some 37th Division troops a post was established. The left all but reached the road, which at this point bent nearer to the river. Eleven prisoners were captured, but the station at Belle Vue and the copse on the Solesmes road under the station remained in enemy hands. In answer to the attack Briastre was severely shelled all the forenoon, and Viesly intermittently bombarded with heavy guns. Attempts made by the enemy to work round the Wellington flank and attack from the rear were crushed.

At 8.30 a.m. it was seen that against the unexpected resistance even the strong barrage provided was inadequate.

[1] pp. 280 sqq.

A request was sent for concentrated artillery fire on the buildings. This was subsequently countermanded on a report that they had fallen, but at 11.45 a.m. all available guns were turned on the German positions. The fire, however, proved singularly ineffective, and the enemy machine guns were active as ever. We were in no position to safeguard the flank of the 37th Division, who had meantime captured the high ground south, nor had the V. Corps on their right made much progress. At 3 p.m., under a heavy barrage, the enemy launched a counter-attack with 3 battalions against the advanced and exposed troops of the 37th Division and recovered the heights, forcing the 37th Division back on the railway. 1st Wellington were thereupon withdrawn to their position of the morning.

For the moment the defences had triumphed, but their fall was only deferred. A further assault was arranged for 6 p.m. The difficulties were now fully recognised, and the attacking force was strengthened. Both Wellington companies would be used, and in addition 2 platoons of the reserve company were ordered to cross the river on the beginning of the attack and lend assistance if necessary. In the interval, concentrated and violent artillery fire was poured pitilessly on the station and on the enemy's positions about the road and railway. At 6 p.m. Wellington stormed again under barrages provided by the 1st Artillery Brigade and 2 machine gun companies, whose fire advanced at 200 yards' distance in front of the artillery barrage. The attached British batteries, as before, harassed the road and railway northwards. Our artillery fire was generally most effective, and in the 100 yards of railway line north of the level crossing at Belle Vue the foremost troops found on the permanent way itself 38 German dead. But in places the barrage fell somewhat short, or the attackers pushed into it too soon, most of our casualties being caused by our own guns. Despite the continued day's bombardment the Jägers fought with their traditional stubbornness, and lost heavily before they yielded the ground. The right company captured Belle Vue, establishing touch with the 37th Division. The left had more trouble. For some time a well-posted machine gun held up their attack. L.-Cpl. B. Quentin, who commanded a Lewis gun team on the left flank of the right company, held his ground firmly. The German machine gun was smothered with rifle grenades. Four survivors of its crew jumped out of their pit and rushed for their lines, but

Quentin shot all 4. The left company then cleared the copse
and the buildings on the main road. Near one of these
buildings another machine gun crew hung on with great
tenacity, but were eventually destroyed by a special party
from the 2 platoons of the reserve company. In all 10
prisoners were captured. Our new positions were consolidated by 9 p.m., and the Briastre river crossing thus secured.
In the day's attacks 1st Wellington had lost 28 other ranks
killed, 76 wounded, and 11 missing.

As the close of the Battle of Cambrai and the Hindenburg
Line had given us a footing on the east bank of the Scheldt,
so now the Second Battle of Le Cateau terminated in the
successful establishment on the IV. Corps front of a bridgehead on the Selle. The 2 front Divisions of the Corps could
now be relieved and the advance temporarily be discontinued
to enable road and railway communications in rear to be
re-established.[1] Corps Headquarters moved forward to Ligny.
In the evening, 12th October, which was again wet, the 42nd
Division took over the New Zealanders' line, and 1st Wellington, with the rest of the brigade, marched back to Fontaine-au-Pire. The New Zealand batteries also withdrew to
Beauvois. The D.A.C. came under the 42nd Division for
ammunition supply. On the river line the new garrisons on
the eastern bank consolidated their position, but the main
line of resistance was organised and entrenched on the
western bank. During a German counter-attack on the 13th,
repulsed at all other points, Belle Vue fell again for the
moment into enemy possession.

By that time the towns of Le Cateau and Cambrai had
been captured, and the Second Battle of Le Cateau (8th-12th
October) had closed. It was no fault of this brilliantly executed British thrust, for which as a classic example of the military art the French Staff expressed wholehearted admiration,
that the enemy was not forced to immediate surrender. Too
hard a task, however, had been set the Americans and French
southwards, and Ludendorff's day of final reckoning was postponed. None the less the sky was luridly dark for Germany.
While her Armies managed to hold Gouraud and the Americans, the British drive on the German centre and at the German
communications was striking into the enemy's vitals. They

[1] A single instance may illustrate difficulties. The Le Cateau road at Beauvois
runs along an artificial embankment across a small valley. In this embankment an
immense crater had been blown. On 12th October the whole of the available 2nd
Infantry Brigade transport together with G.S. wagons lent by the Corps was used to
cart material, and 200 men were employed from 7a.m. to 6 p.m. to fill it in. By that
time the road was available for single traffic.

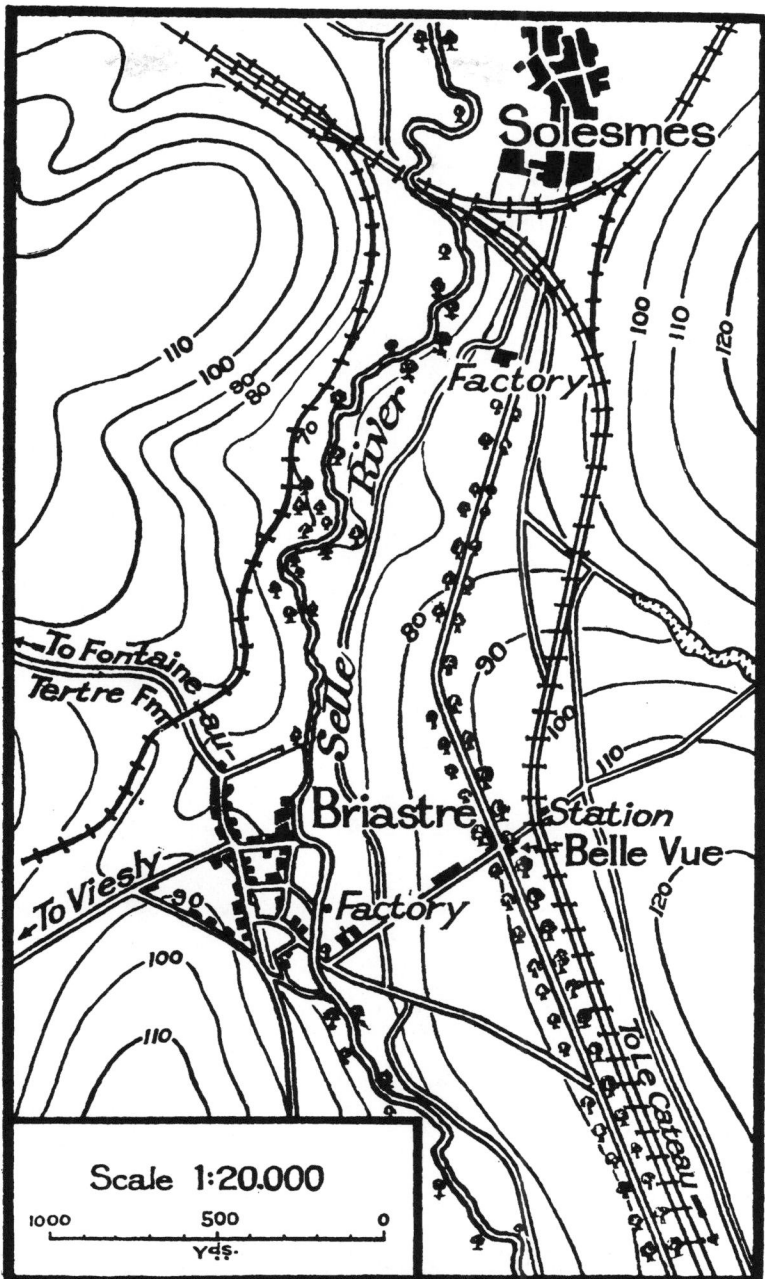

Solesmes

Factory

River

Selle

To Fontaine

Tertre Fm

Briastre · Station
Belle Vue

To Viesly

Factory

To Le Cateau

Scale 1:20.000

1000   500   0

YDS.

THE SELLE RIVER

THE CORPS COMMANDER AT A CHURCH PARADE

MACHINE GUNNERS IN A CAPTURED POSITION

were forced to evacuate the Laon salient, which by 13th October had fallen to the French. Apart from this, the immediate result of the British attack was the gain of the St. Quentin-Cambrai railway, the capture of 12,000 prisoners and 250 guns, and the establishment of a line along the Selle down to a point 7 miles below Solesmes. In the 5 days' fighting and pursuit the Division had advanced 11 miles, and at the cost of 536 casualties had inflicted very heavy losses on the enemy, in addition to capturing 13 field guns and over 1400 prisoners.

CHAPTER XV

THE BATTLE OF THE SELLE RIVER

Scarcely had the new trenches been dug about the Selle when, on 14th October, the Allied offensive broke out afresh with a large attack in Flanders. On the right flank, north of the Lys, 3 Corps of the Second Army participated. Ostend fell on the 17th. On the 20th the left flank reached the frontiers of Holland. The advance of the British on the right wing turned now the northern defences of Lille, as the southern defences had been turned in the Second Battle of Le Cateau. From his new salient between the Lys and the Sensée the German had no alternative but to withdraw. Lille was recovered on the 18th by General Birdwood's Fifth Army. On the evening of 22nd October the line of the Northern Armies lay along the Scheldt from Valenciennes to the east of Tourcoing.

Meantime, with the improvement of communications on the main battle front of Le Cateau, a fresh and deadly blow had been prepared and was being dealt by the 2 Southern Armies and the right wing of the First Army. The line aimed at was the Sambre-et-Oise Canal, the western edge of the Forêt de Mormal, and Valenciennes. Success meant the completion of another long stage on the march towards Maubeuge. The railway junction of Aulnoye, on the Sambre, where the Paris-Maubeuge railway crossed the lateral line from Hirson to Valenciennes, had already been repeatedly raided by our aeroplanes. If objectives were attained, it would now be brought under effective range of our artillery. As a preliminary phase of the advance, it was necessary to drive the enemy from his line on the Selle, and hence the whole operation, which lasted from 17th to 25th October, is defined as the Battle of the Selle River.

The preliminary attack was initiated south of Le Cateau on 17th October by the Fourth Army, in co-operation with a French Army on their right. Heavy fighting ensued, but by the 19th the attacking troops were on the Sambre-et-Oise Canal south of Catillon and thence held a line along the Richemont stream east and north of Le Cateau. The right flank thus secured, the main preliminary attack on the Selle

crossings was opened on the 20th, when the Third and the
right wing of the First Armies assaulted north of Le Cateau.
In this operation the IV. Corps used the 5th on the right
and 42nd Division on the left. Unless opposition should have
ceased, it was not proposed for this first day to advance on
the IV. Corps front beyond the high steep ridge south of
Marou and beyond the road from Marou to Romeries. The
attack would be continued on the 21st, but in the event of
serious opposition it would be undertaken by fresh troops.

The New Zealanders were accordingly ordered to be prepared to move through the 42nd Division on the night 20th/
21st October and continue operations on the following day.[1]
It was the Rifle Brigade's turn to be advanced guard. On
the 19th they moved forward from Esnes to Beauvois, whence
it was arranged that they should march on the 20th to the
Viesly—Fontaine-au-Tertre Farm Spur. There they would be
held in readiness to push forward at half an hour's notice.

While the New Zealand infantry were to play no part in
the opening moves, the artillery and certain other troops lent
active support to the 42nd Division. On the 16th[2] the 1st[3]
and 3rd Artillery Brigades began to cart ammunition forward
to selected positions, and after dusk on the 18th batteries
took a section into action east and south-east of Viesly, 1
gun of the 1st Battery being detached southwards for the
purpose of harassing the railway line south of Solesmes. The
balance of guns was brought in on the following day.[4] On
the 19th one of the machine gun companies moved into the
line to provide enfilade fire from the slopes north-west of
Briastre on the German positions across the river. Five New
Zealand medium trench mortars also supported the attack.
The 1st Field Company of the Engineers was put at the
disposal of the C.E., IV. Corps, for the purpose of constructing a tank bridge over the Selle at the earliest possible
moment after the advance on the 20th.

The heavy shelling on the river had barely abated when
the Engineers were hard at work on the bridge. By extraordinary exertions it was completed in 13 hours. This
rapidity of construction no less than the skilful and thorough
nature of the workmanship elicited warm congratulations
from General Harper and his Chief Engineer, who on the

---

1 On the 14th the Division had been visited by H.R.H., the Prince of Wales.
2 4th anniversary of departure of Main Body from New Zealand.
3 Major C. N. Newman, D.S.O., pending return of Lt.-Col. Symon, vice Lt.-Col.
Standish, proceeding on duty to New Zealand.
4 The 1st and 3rd Brigades formed part of a group commanded for the moment
by the old 2nd N.Z.F.A. Brigade Commander, Lt.-Col. Sykes.

21st personally witnessed the heaviest class of tank pass
safely over. On the following day the same company constructed a heavy traffic bridge in 15 hours. The 2nd Company was also now engaged in the maintenance of pontoon
and foot-bridges on the Selle. With regard to the support
rendered by the New Zealand artillery, particular mention
should be made of the extremely efficient shooting which a
forward section of the 3rd Battery (2nd Lt. R. C. Jamieson)
carried out on enemy parties engaged in digging trenches on
the Grand Champ west of Beaurain.

When the 42nd Division's infantry reached their objective,
the New Zealand batteries moved to the deep valley north-
east of the Belle Vue spur. Here during the night they came
under fairly heavy fire, and on the morning of the 22nd, in
dismal weather, the 1st Artillery Brigade especially were
intensely bombarded by guns of all calibres up to 8-in., firing
a large concentration of gas in addition to explosive. The
1st Battery sustained casualties in personnel and lost 11
horses. On this day the 2nd (Army) Brigade, after completion of its task with the XVII. Corps, rejoined the rest of
the New Zealand artillery in the line under the 42nd Division.
Lt.-Col. Falla now took command of the group comprising all
3 New Zealand and 2 English artillery brigades, Major Richmond assuming temporary command of the 2nd (Army)
Brigade.

In the preliminary attack on 20th October both front line
Divisions of the IV. Corps had succeeded in capturing their final
objective, but only after stubborn fighting. The general situation and the moving forward of our heavy artillery necessitated
a slight pause before the larger advance all along the line
towards the Mormal Forest and Valenciennes. It was arranged
that this grand attack should be delivered on the 23rd by
the Fourth Third and part of the First Armies on a frontage
of 15 miles. For this operation the IV. Corps, continuing to
strike north-east, proposed that a first limited stage of the
attack should be carried out by the 5th and 42nd Divisions
in the line, and that thereafter the 37th and New Zealand
Divisions should pass through them to a series of intermediate
objectives and on to the final objective. The advance of
20th October to the ridge south of Marcu and the south-
western outskirts of Romeries had brought the Corps line to
a distance of 2 miles east of the Selle. The task set the
leading Divisions for the 23rd was to carry Beaurain and
establish a line east of it with the left flank resting on

ONE OF THE SELLE BRIDGES

CHURCH IN SOLESMES

A GERMAN POST ABANDONED IN RETREAT

Romeries and facing the village of Vertigneul. On that line
there would be a certain pause, and then, following a preparatory barrage of 15 minutes, the 37th Division would pass
through the 5th on the right, and the New Zealanders through
the 42nd on the left. The proposed advance would cross a
succession of small rivers, all flowing roughly northwards,
and the rolling plateaus that separated their valleys. The
final Corps objective, forming part of the general line Mormal
Forest-Valenciennes, lay some 3 miles eastward on the watershed between the St. Georges and Ecaillon rivers. From that
high ground we would look down into the Ecaillon valley
and the large village of Beaudignies. The right Division was
covered by the artillery of the 5th and 37th Divisions, the
left by the 42nd 63rd and New Zealand Divisional Artilleries.

The New Zealand attack, originally allotted to the Rifle
Brigade, was eventually, owing to a temporary weakness of
effectives in the Rifle battalions, entrusted to the 2nd Brigade.
The operation was divided into 2 phases, the first objective
being the Neuville-Escarmain Road, on the watershed between
the Harpies and St. Georges rivers. General Young proposed
that 2 battalions should capture the first objective, and
the remaining 2 pass through them to the final line on the
watershed between the St. Georges and Ecaillon rivers. Each
battalion would be supported by a forward section of artillery
and a section of machine guns.

At 2 p.m. on 22nd October the 2nd Infantry Brigade Group
moved from Beauvois to an assembly area in the newly-
captured ground beyond the Selle river about the sunken
roads south-east of Solesmes. In addition to a machine gun
company, a light trench mortar battery, and a company of
Engineers, the Group comprised a squadron of the 3rd
Hussars and a troop of Otago Mounted Rifles. The concentrated force spent a miserable night under pouring rain.

On the 23rd the grand attack was opened by 2 Corps of
the Fourth Army at 1.20 a.m. and taken up at a later hour
by the Third Army. By 8 a.m. the 42nd Division were on
their objective. A protective barrage was maintained in front
for some little time, and on its cessation the command of the
5 artillery brigades covering the front passed to General
Napier Johnston. They were disposed in 2 groups. The 1st
and 3rd New Zealand Artillery Brigades composed the right
group under Lt.-Col. McQuarrie, and the two 42nd Divisional
brigades and the 2nd (Army) New Zealand Brigade made up
the left group under Lt.-Col. Falla. On the cessation of the

barrage, however, this last brigade moved forward immediately to positions of readiness, whence they could later advance towards Romeries in order to support the second phase of the New Zealand attack. The other 4 brigades, during the pause, fired a smoke screen and bombarded selected positions. About the same time General Russell's advanced headquarters were being opened at Prayelle.

The leading infantry, 1st Otago on the right and 2nd Canterbury[1] on the left, were now through the gas-drenched valley at Marou and close on their jumping-off line. The rain had cleared away and the morning was fine, but there was a heavy mist. It was still further thickened by the smoke barrage which was put down by our artillery from 7.15 a.m. till 8.35 a.m. on the valley south and north of Vertigneul to cover the approach of the 2nd Infantry Brigade Group. In this mist close touch was kept by means of advanced guards with the 42nd Division troops making the preparatory attack. In order to minimise casualties on the assaulting area, the battalions had been ordered so to time their march as to reach and be formed on their jumping-off line without superfluous delay prior to the moment of going forward at 8.40 a.m. In the case of both battalions the arrival was perfectly timed. The precaution proved justified, for just prior to our advance this line was heavily bombarded, more casualties being now sustained than during the actual attack. Within the short interval before the creeping barrage came down, small 1st Otago patrols, under L.-Cpls. W. Friend and N. Wright, cleared a pocket of enemy, about 80 strong, not far in front of the line of assembly.

Further to protect their deployment, 1st Otago made provision in case Beaurain and a quarry north of it were not cleared. The reserve company was held in readiness to meet awkward developments from this direction, and a strong patrol under Lt. F. M. Jenkins, D.C.M., acted as a flank guard. It was found unnecessary to call on the reserve company itself, but the flank guard was not to accomplish its duties without incident. In the mist it ran suddenly on an enemy machine gun post. The Division only rarely came across instances of German "treachery," but this was one of them. The 7 machine gunners held up their hands in token of surrender. Our men moved forward to take them prisoners. But seeing that they were dealing with only a patrol, the machine guns opened fire, and Jenkins was

---

1 Major Wilson, vice Lt.-Col. Stewart, in England on duty.

wounded. The post was rushed, and the Germans were one and all put to death.

At 8.25 a.m., while a certain proportion of the 4 artillery brigades continued the smoke screen for a short time further, sweeping so as to cover their batteries' front, the remainder, together with three 6-in. howitzer batteries, reopened the barrage for the New Zealand advance. Its opening line fell a short distance beyond the sunken road from Beaurain to Romeries. There the barrage halted for 15 minutes at a slow rate of fire, and then at 8.40 a.m. began to advance at a rapid rate of fire, lifting 100 yards every 3 minutes. The 4.5-in. howitzers fired 200 yards ahead of the 18-pounders, paying particular attention to sunken roads and ravines. These were dealt with also by the 3 batteries of 6-in. howitzers, whose fire advanced 800 yards in front of the 18-pounder barrage. In line with the 6-in. howitzers' fire a section of 60-pounders "walked up" the by-road which ran through Vertigneul to Pont-à-Pierres and thence along the main road to Beaudignies. The villages were shelled not with destructive high-explosive but with shrapnel, and were masked with smoke.

The 5th Division had been unlucky enough to be caught during assembly in an exceptionally severe bombardment. It was still uncertain whether they held their objective, and the 37th Division postponed their attack till 10 a.m. The New Zealand right would be consequently for the moment unprotected. In close touch, however, with the troops on the left, the 2nd Brigade, with the advance of the barrage at 8.40 a.m., moved forward under it through the 42nd Division.

The mist had by this time dispersed, and the day was gloriously fine. Isolated machine gun posts situated about hedges and in places of vantage offered resistance. The left 1st Otago company had advanced only a few hundred yards when a number of machine guns began to enfilade them. They were most skilfully outflanked by a platoon under Sergt. R. E. Fortune. Generally, however, there was not the stubborn fighting that had marked the action on the 20th. There was a momentary check on Otago's right owing to machine gun fire from Hirson Mill, just over the right boundary. L.-Cpl. H. Ingram led his section out till he gradually worked round the Mill, taking 10 prisoners and threatening to cut off the retreat of its garrison. The rest of the company pressed their advance under covering fire from the Lewis guns. The enemy thereupon vacated the Mill.

Otago's right flank then waded through the 12-feet broad Harpies river under fire and stormed the Cambrai-Le Quesnoy railway embankment beyond. Over the greater part of the Otago front the railway, crossing the river at the south-eastern corner of the Vertigneul woods, lay between us and the river and village. It formed an obvious and strong line of defence, but was carried without undue difficulty, several machine guns and 47 prisoners being taken. In Vertigneul itself resistance proved much less than anticipated. The numerous German dead attested the efficacy of the barrage. None the less, after the leading troops had passed, the ubiquitous sniper did not fail to emerge from his hiding place, and parties had to be sent back to clear the place thoroughly.

In the open country beyond the village machine gun fire from the crest in front became distinctly more troublesome, till the crews were knocked out by rifle fire. Over the right boundary also, towards Neuville, which the postponement of the 37th Division's attack left temporarily in enemy hands, a series of German posts were vigorously aggressive. The right company was forced to side-step to deal with them. This move, however, turned out a blessing in disguise, for on reaching the crest and moving over the plateau towards the Escarmain Road, Otago encountered severe machine gun fire. On the right boundary of their objective the Escarmain Road was crossed by 2 other sunken roads, and the junction of the different roads was marked by a crucifix and the Chapelle des Six Chemins. The roads themselves and the hedges in their vicinity were strongly held by machine guns. Instead of making a costly frontal assault, a platoon from the left company swept the position with fire. With the enemy thus engaged and diverted, the right company over the boundary was in a position to turn the flank, and the stronghold at the crossroads was captured with a minimum of casualties.

2nd Canterbury throughout met less resistance. They rapidly cleared the orchards, steep river banks and northern outskirts of Vertigneul, and passed forward between it and Romeries. The enemy in disorderly retreat before our barrage offered acceptable targets to Lewis guns and rifles. Only on the objective itself there was a short sharp struggle. 50 prisoners and 2 machine guns were captured here. 6 other machine guns with 3 trench mortars had been secured during the advance. Casualties were extremely light. Shortly after 10 a.m. both battalions had captured the brigade's first objective. Patrols were sent out in front, and the remainder of the troops dug in. The consolidation was hampered by active hostile artillery, and later in the afternoon by a large number of Blue Cross[1] gas shells.

On the cessation of the barrage covering this first New Zealand objective, one of the English artillery brigades moved speedily forward to the vicinity of the New Zealanders' jumping-off line south of Vertigneul to co-operate with the 2nd (Army) Brigade in supporting the attack on the final objective. Two New Zealand batteries also were rushed forward beyond Romeries and Vertigneul to give close and immediate help to the 2 fresh battalions. Till the advance was resumed, the other artillery brigades remained in their previous position and then moved forward in their turn east of Romeries and Vertigneul.

The whole of the newly-won ground, including the battery positions, was now being heavily shelled with gas and explosive. Vertigneul was particularly "unhealthy," and the supporting battalions as they came forward gave it as wide a berth as possible. Skirting it on the south, 2nd Otago deemed themselves fortunate in altogether avoiding casualties. 1st Canterbury similarly making a detour round the church lost a few men, but the advance was in no way disorganised.

Before noon both battalions, 2nd Otago on the right and 1st Canterbury[2] on the left, lay behind the Neuville-Escarmain Road in position to pass through at the appointed time of 12.12 p.m. The final objective lay nearly 2 miles away on the high ground this side of Beaudignies, and between them and their goal was the valley of the St. Georges river, where, if anywhere, the German might be expected to oppose them. Should, however, his resistance prove to be disorganised, the attack would exploit towards Beaudignies. The 2 brigades of field artillery supporting the attack, together with the additional forward batteries, all commanded by Lt.-Col. Falla, came under General Young's orders as advanced guard artillery. After establishing his headquarters with General Young, Lt.-Col. Falla took his battery commanders to reconnoitre positions for the next artillery advance. Riding forward briskly, they went right on to the Escarmain Road, where a few minutes after noon they found themselves among our foremost infantry fixing bayonets for the final attack.

1 A H.E. shell containing a gas very irritating to eyes and nose.
2 Major Stitt, vice Lt.-Col. Row, on leave.

On the right the 37th Division had reached the first objective at 11.30 a.m., and were now in line. The barrage protecting this second phase of the New Zealand advance was considerably thinner, but it was to prove more than adequate for the work in hand. Its rate was, however, only 100 yards in 4 minutes, and pressing forward and anxious to pass quickly the crest west of the St. Georges river, which the enemy artillery were shelling with some intensity, the 2 assaulting companies of each battalion chafed at its slowness. When at a later stage it died away, the advance pushed on with correspondingly greater rapidity. It was on this same crest that they first encountered appreciable weight of machine gun fire from the river valley itself and the German positions on the high ground east of it. Our infantry were admirably supported by the forward sections of artillery and by a machine gun company which boldly drove its limbers with the machine guns right up to the foremost infantry positions. Despite all this covering fire, however, the 2nd Otago patrols could only with great difficulty work down the forward slopes. The St. Georges valley and Le Mesnil Farm on the river bank were held by strong enemy rearguards, and although our machine guns and artillery harassed the German positions vigorously, the volume of the enemy's fire was not appreciably reduced. On the right company's front the slopes were bare of cover, and advance had to be suspended.

Under better cover, however, part of the left company, led by Sergt. J. J. Blackburn, worked steadily downhill. They crept along a hedgerow, climbed a garden wall and rushed the Farm, where they captured the bulk of a Battalion Headquarters, comprising 2 officers and 30 men. Moving then through the farm buildings, they crossed the St. Georges river to the other side. The remainder of the left company between the Farm and the little hamlet of Pont-à-Pierres, where the Beaudignies road crosses the river, were moving abreast with them. The right, on the exposed hillside, was still held up.

Climbing the eastern bank, these men found that the Germans had dug an improvised line of posts with a strong belt of wire in front all along the slopes overlooking the river and about the Salesches-Escarmain road, which ran parallel with it. Groups of these posts had been organised, each consisting of about 8 posts, and each post being held by 3 or 4 men. Protected by wire and manned by numerous machine guns, the whole formed an extremely formidable obstacle.

On the left of the line, however, a section of 5 men of the support platoon, under Sergt. F. C. Fergusson, stole up a hedge south of Pont-à-Pierres, crawled round the flank of the enemy position, and bringing a Lewis gun to bear at close quarters, charged and killed about 16 men in the garrison of the posts immediately adjacent. The remainder, with several machine guns, then gave themselves up.

As soon as the resistance slackened, the right 2nd Otago company, providing its own covering fire and rushing alternate sections down the slopes, plunged through the river and pressed up the eastern bank. By skilful Lewis gun tactics they advanced rapidly on the southern end of the line of posts towards Salesches. Heavy losses were inflicted on the enemy, and about 90 prisoners and several machine guns were captured. A vast number of expended cartridges lying in and about the pits indicated the severity of the opposition.

These defences carried, the main point of resistance did not now lie opposite the New Zealand front, but on the high ground beyond the right flank and about the outskirts of Salesches, which the troops of the 37th Division had not yet reached. Seeing this, and the possible effect of enfilade fire on the whole brigade advance, 2nd Lt. W. Murphy, on the Otago right flank, swung out a platoon, and attacking the superior enemy in enfilade, drove him off, capturing further prisoners and mopping up the northern part of Salesches. With little delay the main advance continued. By 2.25 p.m. the objective was taken, the right flank being refused for over three-quarters of a mile back to the northern outskirts of Salesches. The 37th Division, through no fault of their own but owing mainly to strong opposition encountered by the V. Corps on their right, had not yet come into line nor indeed were to do so till the following day. Till they should join us, the length of this right flank made for anxiety, which was not abated by evidence of German movement towards Salesches and an increase of hostile artillery and machine gun fire from that direction. To meet immediate emergencies a support company was brought forward. Meanwhile the 1st Canterbury line also was well advanced beyond the Division on the left. The 2 battalions, therefore, which had carried out the first attack in the morning and were now in support on the Neuville-Escarmain Road, were ordered each to move a company forward to keep close touch with the troops in front and to strengthen their flanks should the necessity arise.

The infantry were to be supported by harassing machine gun fire specially directed on the trenches in front of the villages and co-ordinated with the advance of the artillery barrage. The barrage would be provided by all 3 New Zealand artillery brigades as far as the Cambrai Road, when the 2nd (Army) Brigade would cease, in order to come into Divisional reserve and be ready to move forward at instant notice.

On the north the Rifle Brigade front amounted to 1000 yards and could be covered by 1 battalion. Warning orders were given the 1st Rifles[1] in the late evening. On definite information being received from the brigade at 1 a.m., the necessary instructions were issued to the company commanders already assembled at battalion headquarters. Expected guides from the leading troops failed to turn up, and the battalion moved off from their reserve position at 3 a.m., guided by their officers' compasses to their assembly area between the railway and the Cambrai Road. The company which had been in reserve to the 2nd Battalion[2] was made the left attacking company. Two of its platoons chanced to be engaged in "carrying" and found it impossible to assemble in time to advance with the rest of the battalion at 5 a.m.. It was only with the utmost effort and thanks to the energy displayed by Sergt. W. L. Free that they were able to follow the attack some 25 minutes after the barrage and reach the position for the final assault.

From the outset it was clear that the operation was to be no "walk-over." On the Cambrai Road just west of Fremicourt was an old British camp that had been used as rest billets for German troops in reserve. As protection against splinters from aeroplane bombs, the huts had been surrounded by the customary thick earthen walls. Over these several machine guns now fired at the 1st Rifles' screen. They were cowed, however, by the barrage and circumvented by an outflanking movement on the part of each company. On the other side of the road a large camouflaged Strong Point containing 3 machine guns was rushed without casualties by the left company. The Rifles were in touch with each flank, and the 5th Division troops on the left, accompanied by a tank, were making splendid progress. But Fremicourt itself presented an awkward problem. Our heavy howitzers had not yet lifted from its western edge, and their fire, while

1 Lt.-Col. Austin resumed duty this day.
2. p. 445.

MOBILE TRENCH MORTARS

RIFLEMEN WAITING THEIR TURN TO ADVANCE

THE LEVEL CROSSING, SEPT. 1919 (Looking towards Beaudignies)
[*Photo Capt. S. Cory Wright*

POST ON THE VALENCIENNES RAILWAY

tion. So now, ignorant of its fall, he moved back towards Beaudignies. At 9.15 p.m. a party ran against our post 200 yards east of the northern bridge. There was a sharp fusilade, and most unfortunately Sergt. Nicholas, V.C.,[1] was killed. On meeting resistance, however, the enemy sheered off down a side street of the village. Thereafter he contented himself with heavy machine gun fire from the high ground to the north-east. Later in the night the 1st Canterbury patrols pushed up the Le Quesnoy road and established a post 500 yards beyond Beaudignies. A German patrol attempting to approach this was repulsed with Lewis gun fire. Similarly 2nd Otago, shortly before midnight, pushed a support company through the front line and occupied 1500 yards of the Salesches-Beaudignies road, meeting little opposition and capturing 2 officers and 20 men.

Long ere this the 1st and 3rd Artillery Brigades and the attached British batteries had advanced to positions about Neuville and Vertigneul, where they were vigorously shelled, hostile fire being above normal all the afternoon. A battery of 60-pounders was temporarily posted to the Division, and while the remainder came into action west of Neuville, one section was ordered to go forward at the earliest moment to the St. Georges valley. Here the Engineer company forming part of General Young's Group was already beginning the construction of a light traffic bridge and making preliminary arrangements to throw a pontoon bridge across the river for field guns. By the following day they had constructed 4 trestle bridges and strutted the brick arches of such existing road bridges as had escaped demolition. On the main Beaudignies road at Pont-à-Pierres energetic preparations were in hand for the erection of a double-way heavy bridge of two 20-feet spans supported by a massive trestle pier. In the road itself by the bridge a mine had formed a yawning chasm 87 feet in diameter and 20 feet below the road level. A deviation therefore became necessary. This heavy bridge was completed on the 29th. The whole vicinity of Pont-à-Pierres was constantly and violently shelled and the bridges repeatedly damaged, if not destroyed. No unit, however, can boast of a higher standard of duty or hardier fortitude than the Engineers, who, making light of difficulties dangers and disappointments, persevered with, completed and maintained

---

1 p. 311. Nicholas' body was exhumed on the 29th and reinterred with military honours in Vertigneul churchyard, the service being conducted by the Bishop of Nelson.

their work. Special gallantry was shown by 2nd Lt. D. R. Mansfield and L.-Cpl. E. R. W. Pledger.

The day had been extremely successful. The 2nd Infantry Brigade had advanced 4½ miles, and pressing well beyond their final objectives had secured the Ecaillon crossings. Casualties had been very light. 1st Canterbury had captured just over 100 prisoners, and 2nd Otago just over 200. Many machine guns had been secured, and there had been, mostly in the St. Georges valley, a haul of abandoned guns. 2nd Otago had secured a field gun and 1st Canterbury an 8-in. howitzer, 2 "five-nines," 4 light howitzers, and a tank. In view of the disorganisation of the enemy it was determined to apply the last unit of energy left in the attack and maintain the pressure. After consulting the Divisional Staff, General Young sent orders over the telephone at 9.30 p.m. to 1st Otago and 2nd Canterbury to pass their support companies through the leading battalions and continue the advance. The objective to be gained by the dawn (24th October) was the sunken road which runs from Ghissignies past the eastern edge of Beaudignies. The companies would have to advance 1000 yards over unknown country to the line already established, and thence make good a further 1000 yards, the whole in the dark.

With the minimum of delay the troops were on the move. The character of the terrain was now markedly different from that of the wide open expanses over which the advance had hitherto been conducted. The country was very much closer. Beyond Beaudignies it was covered with successive thickly-set plantations orchards, and woods, and already the tall impenetrable hedges, that had grown up round old wire fences or were interwoven with German wire, constituted considerable obstacles. Careful, if rapid, reconnaissance and systematic touch were essential.

The 1st Otago companies, about 1 a.m., crossed the 2nd Otago outposts on the Salesches-Beaudignies road. The advance was led by parties supported by Lewis guns. The remainder of the 2 companies followed in artillery formation. It was a fairly clear moonlight night, but compasses had to be used for keeping direction. Extensive "practice trenches" west of Ghissignies had been vacated by the enemy. Meeting no opposition other than the natural difficulties of the country, 1st Otago passed through Saint Roch and the southern outskirts of Beaudignies and crossed the Ecaillon in the very early hours of the morning, taking up a position

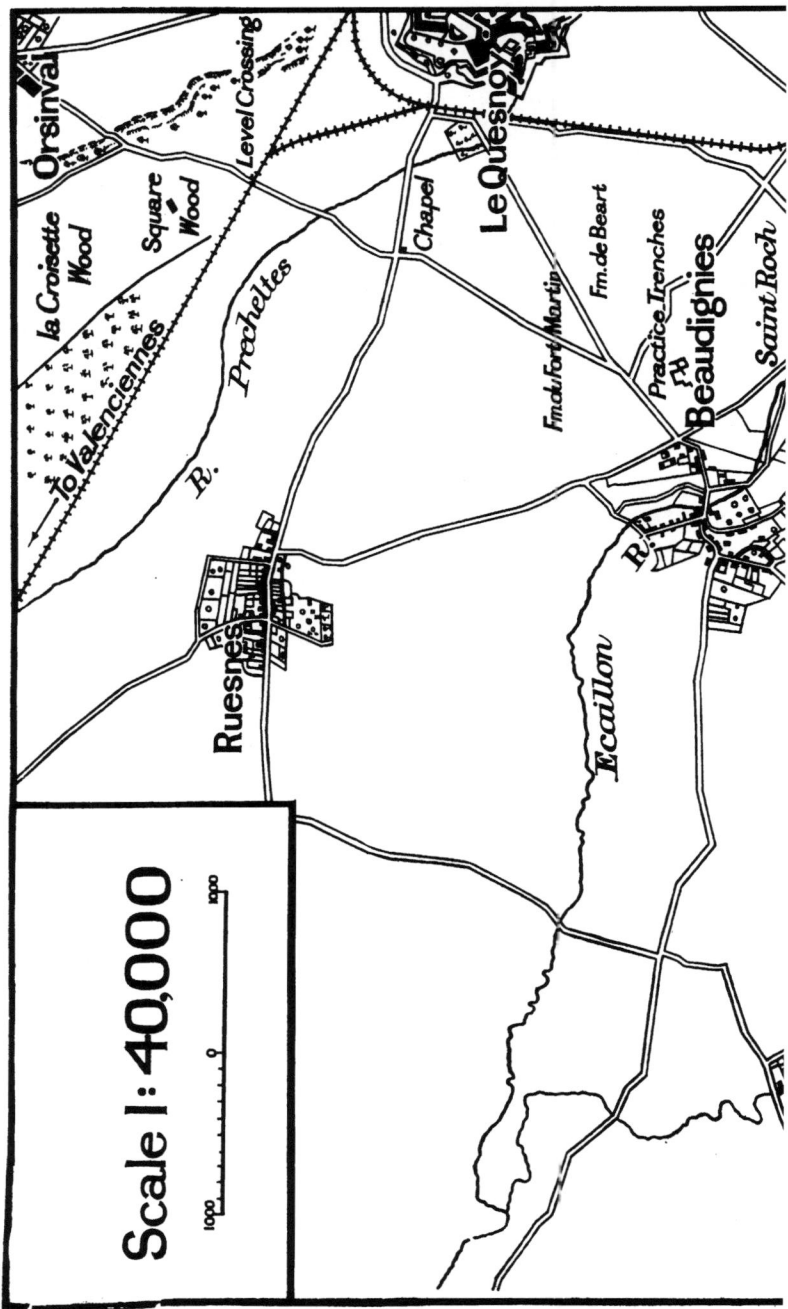

Scale 1: 40,000

Orsinval

la Croisette Wood

Square Wood

To Valenciennes

R. Prcheltes

Level Crossing

Chapel

Le Quesnoy

Fm.de Beart

Fm.at Fort Martin

Practice Trenches

Beaudignies

Saint Roch

Ruesnes

Ecaillon

R.

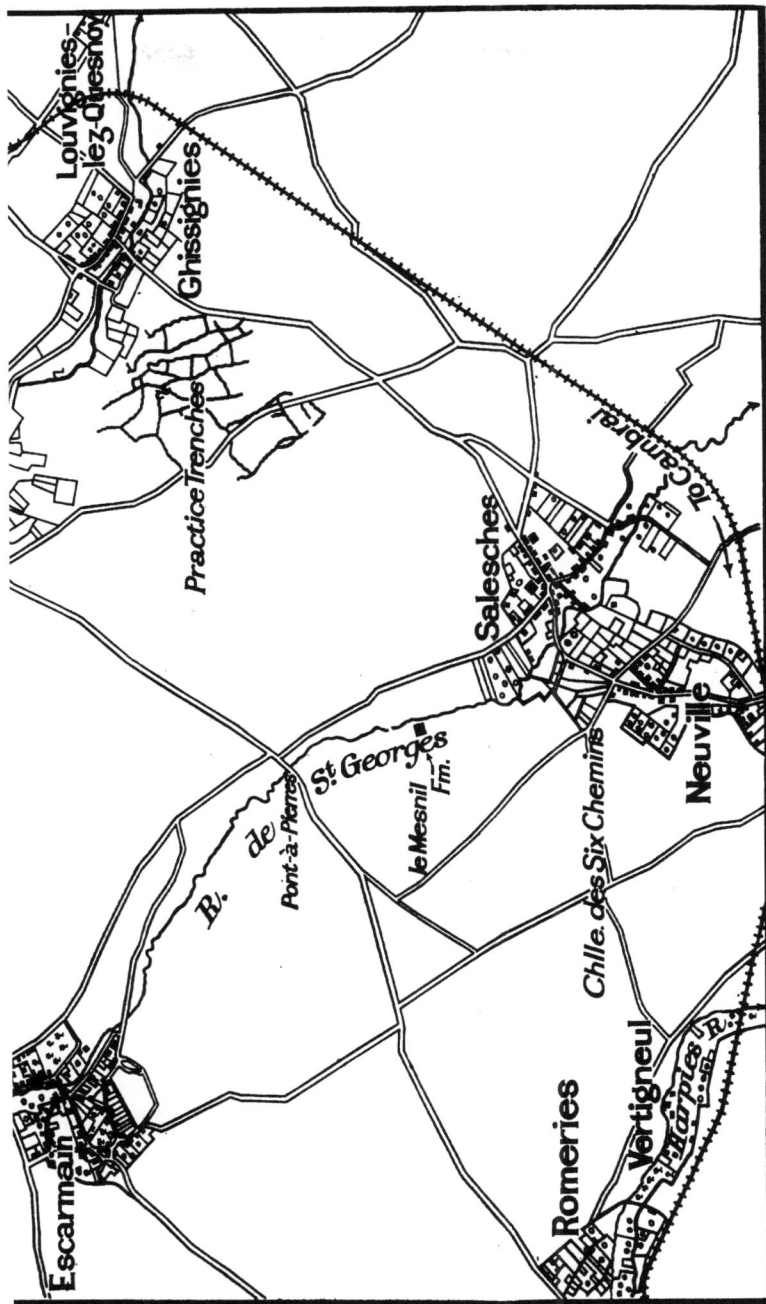

BEAUDIGNIES

forward of the Ghissignies road. With an earlier start
(10.30 p.m.) 2nd Canterbury reached the objective at 1 a.m.,
driving some 50 of the enemy before them. Touch was established between the 2 battalions.

The line, especially on the right, was now considerably
in advance of the flank units. In the Canterbury area an unexpected nest had been discovered still west of Beaudignies.
In front of Otago also the enemy was in considerable strength
on a sunken road eastwards and in isolated and inconsiderable "practice trenches" beyond an orchard just over the
Ghissignies road. It was known that both flank Divisions
were making an early attack. Patrols were pushed forward
in the meantime, and the companies waited for the dawn.

With the first glimmer of light (24th October) the flank
Divisions began to move forward into line. At 4.15 a.m. the
covering barrage of the 3rd Division on the VI. Corps right
overlapped our left and compelled 2nd Canterbury to withdraw temporarily some little distance to escape it. They
were soon back, however, in the sunken road, and by 9 a.m.
on the high ground north-east of Beaudignies. This movement, in combination with the Otago advance, compelled the
surrender of an enemy force of about 80 who had held an
orchard and now threw down their arms to Otago with the
utmost alacrity. On the left, 2nd Canterbury were much
assisted by the machine guns of the 3rd Division. These
swept the wooded valley of the Rogneau stream, which falls
north-west towards Ruesnes. Making the utmost use of outflanking movements against numerous enemy machine guns,
2nd Canterbury by nightfall had established outposts across
the valley, with their left flank over the Le Quesnoy-Ruesnes
road. During the day they captured an officer and 13 men,
with 9 machine guns. To the north and north-east the high
ground in their centre commanded a wide and diversified
view over rich peaceful country. But it was not in that
direction that the now exhausted men's eyes were turned.
Only a mile eastwards, between intervening coppices, could
be discerned the dense tree-tops which hid the ramparts of
the ancient and famous fortress of Le Quesnoy.

On the right flank 1st Otago, reassured by the appearance
of the 37th Division troops in the eastern outskirts of Ghissignies, advanced under cover of their Lewis guns on the
strongly held "practice trenches" beyond the road. Skilful
dispositions were made by Lt. H. R. Domigan, who commanded the assaulting company. Cpl. C. S. Moorhouse and

Pte. E. A. Richardson crawled forward with a Lewis gun
and covered the advance of the right platoon with enfilade
fire. In its turn the platoon brought enfilade fire to bear,
and the remainder of the company rushing forward carried
the position. In addition to 7 machine guns, 3 officers and
75 men were captured, and many others were killed.
On the next sunken road the right company was for some
little time checked. Repeating the successful outflanking
tactics of the previous day at the Chapelle des Six Chemins,
the left company manoeuvred forward, worked down to the
right and silenced the machine guns. Thereupon the companies without difficulty cleared the whole 1000 yards of road
from the right Divisional boundary to the Le Quesnoy
highway.

About 1000 yards from Beaudignies the Le Quesnoy road
passes uphill through a thin wood in which the Rogneau has
its source. The wood shelters 2 farms, 1 on each side
of the road. On the left the Ferme du Fort Martin abuts
on the road itself. South of the road the Ferme de Beart is
secluded within the wood. A patrol of 1st Otago, under
L.-Cpl. G. D. Tod, penetrated the wood, finding the De Beart
farm occupied by 2 civilians, the Fort Martin farm unoccupied, and the wood evacuated. On the eastern edge of
the wood, however, the enemy were located digging in.
Fairly heavy fire was directed from the Cambrai railway
embankment west of Le Quesnoy. Both flank Divisions were
now abreast, and in close touch with them the 2nd Brigade
line at nightfall ran from the Ruesnes road on the left to the
north-eastern extremity of the de Beart Wood on the Le
Quesnoy road and then through the trees. Outposts were
established on the eastern edge of the wood. At the nearest
point the line was only 1000 yards from the outer ramparts
of Le Quesnoy. During the 2 days' operations 1st Otago
lost 6 officers and 107 men, and captured close on 200
prisoners, with over 30 machine guns, a field gun, and 4 light
mortars. 2nd Canterbury had lost 2 officers and 130 men.
The enemy had given them little chance to get at close
quarters, but they had taken over 60 prisoners and 17 machine
guns, with 3 mortars.

On the infantry gaining the high ground beyond Beaudignies, the 2nd (Army) Brigade batteries, which had been
ordered to rendezvous at 6 a.m. on the main road through
Pont-à-Pierres, were rushed forward over the newly constructed bridge to the east bank of the St. Georges river. At

the storm-centre of Pont-à-Pierres the 6th Battery was caught in a sharp bombardment and lost 3 men and several horses killed. By 9 a.m. the bulk of the artillery was in the St. Georges valley. The line of the river continued to be heavily shelled. All teams were sent to the rear with the exception of those of the 9th Battery, which now moved still further forward to the northern outskirts of Beaudignies in order to be in close touch with the infantry.

In the evening (24th October), the South Island battalions and their affiliated units were relieved by the Rifle Brigade Group. The 3rd Battalion was placed on the right and the 4th on the left. The squadron of the 3rd Hussars and the troop of Otago Mounted Rifles passed under General Hart's orders. Following on the relief, the 3rd Artillery Brigade, with one of the 42nd Divisional brigades, both under Lt.-Col. McQuarrie, became advanced guard artillery, and on the same day the 1st Artillery Brigade went into reserve. Its casualties had been heavy, on the 24th the 1st Battery alone losing 1 man and 37 horses killed and 10 men wounded. There was a renewed violent bombardment on the Pont-à-Pierres crossings from 8 p.m. to 10 p.m., and the 2nd Rifles in the vicinity were much inconvenienced by gas. The rest of the night was marked by sporadic shelling, but was quieter. In the early morning (25th October) the fire became again intense along the line of the river.

By this time the Army objectives had been achieved generally all along the front. The line now ran from the western edge of the Mormal Forest past the western outskirts of Le Quesnoy and thence along the lower Rhonelle towards the Scheldt west of Valenciennes. On the New Zealanders' front the enemy was found to be established in strength along the Cambrai and Valenciennes railways. But northwards the 3rd Division had occupied Ruesnes and found indications in the forenoon of a further withdrawal. Immediately in front of Le Quesnoy the 3rd Rifles, apart from effecting local improvement in their position, could do little, but an advance might be effected round the town on the north. Orders were issued, therefore, for the 4th Battalion on the left to make good by the evening the line of the Valenciennes railway north-west of Le Quesnoy, after which the 2nd Battalion would pass through for exploitation.

Near the point where the Beaudignies road makes a sharp eastward turn before entering Le Quesnoy, the Cambrai railway, which faced the 3rd Rifles, splits into 2 branches.

One, carrying the traffic for Le Quesnoy, bends in a semi-circle round the town's north-western outskirts till the rails, turning south-eastward, reach the permanent way from Valenciennes. The second branch serves the northern traffic and continues north, meeting the trunk line about 1000 yards above the junction of the Le Quesnoy loop. Just above this northern junction the sunken road from Beaudignies to Orsinval, after crossing successively the Rogneau and the Precheltes, goes over the railway at a level crossing. Another 1000 yards further up the line towards Valenciennes the railway passes on its right La Croisette Wood. Of one or two small houses about the level crossing on the Orsinval Road we must notice a brick house on the far side of the line, occupied in peace time by an old couple who look after the gates at the crossing. The Orsinval Road, like most of the roads in the neighbourhood, is for the most part sunken, but just beyond the railway it is for some 20 yards on a level with the fields. Thereafter, again becoming deeply sunken, it leads down gently towards a well-defined mossy bank and hedge, with a belt of trees beyond. This hedge bank is almost continuous, but on the right of the road and at some distance from it is a gap of about 80 yards, below which the bank and hedge again continue south, merging eventually into plantations on the outskirts of Le Quesnoy. In the open field on the left of the road is a small square wood, some 300 yards east of the railway. On this level crossing and its vicinity the Division's efforts were to centre during the final movements of the battle itself and during the brief period of quiescence that followed.

In the afternoon and evening, 25th October, the 3rd Rifles advanced their line beyond the de Beart Wood and swung their right parallel with the Cambrai railway. In a small farm building at the eastern fringe of the wood they found 17 French civilians, men women and boys. The main building in the Ferme de Beart was, during the afternoon, fired and razed to the ground by German shells. By the evening the 4th Rifles succeeded in making the Precheltes stream north of the Orsinval Road, but machine guns on the embankment towards La Croisette Wood held them back from the railway. On the other side of the road, towards Le Quesnoy, the Germans were also in force in the whole triangle formed by the 2 railways, but the Rifles pushed well up the road itself towards the Level Crossing. The advance, though falling short of the objective, enabled the supporting artillery to move east of Beaudignies.

The 3rd Division, further distant from Le Quesnoy, had encountered less resistance. By 4.30 p.m., crossing the railway beyond Ruesnes, they occupied La Croisette village and were moving on the high ground east of the wood to outflank the enemy opposite their right at its southern edge. On the following day, 26th October, they proposed to advance on Orsinval and Villers Pol. The 4th Rifles were accordingly ordered to make a fresh bid after dusk, 25th October, for the Level Crossing, upon the seizure of which the 2nd Battalion would pass through them towards the Le Quesnoy-Orsinval road. The latter battalion was directed to push its left to the southern boundary of Orsinval, and at the same time to operate with patrols against the north and north-west of Le Quesnoy. A section of the Otago Mounted Rifles was placed at its disposal. It was hoped that, in view of the reported withdrawal on the left, the advance might be effected by methods of peaceful penetration.

Under cover of darkness, accordingly, the 4th Rifles renewed their movement against the Level Crossing. They rushed it, L.-Sergt. H. Moscroft heading the charge. Several enemy were killed without loss to the attack. A counter-thrust made about 2 a.m., after a heavy bombardment, was repulsed, German prisoners being left in our hands. The railway on each flank, however, was very strongly held, and the attack elsewhere being checked by intense machine gun and rifle fire, and at close quarters by bombs, the post at the Level Crossing had eventually to withdraw.

Meantime the 2nd Rifles had, shortly before midnight, come forward to follow through the 4th Battalion, exploit to the north of Le Quesnoy, and endeavour to penetrate the town from that direction. The enemy's guns were active. Gas was being sent over in salvoes, especially about Beaudignies, and the 2nd Rifles had to dodge storms of 8-in. shells on the road junctions. Their plans were that one company should move towards Orsinval along the sunken road, with a second following it to secure its left flank, and that a third should then exploit towards Le Quesnoy. At 3 a.m., 26th October, the leading companies moved to their assembly areas. Machine gun fire aimed at the 4th Battalion posts swept the approaches, and several men were hit. All companies, however, deployed in good time, and the telephone was run well forward along the Orsinval Road on our side of the Level

Crossing. On finding that the post at the Crossing had been lost, that we were not in touch on the left, and that there were no posts on the railway, the 2nd Rifles rapidly adjusted their plans to meet this unexpected situation. Two light trench mortars in the road were ordered to cover the advance by bombarding the railway and the high ground beyond it on the north of Le Quesnoy. The machine gun section attached to the battalion took up positions for a similar purpose. The first duty of the leading company was obviously to secure the Crossing and the railway junction just south of it, where the northern branch of the Cambrai line links with the main Valenciennes railway.

The 2nd Rifles' attack was launched at 5.15 a.m. The morning was very foggy, but as soon as ever the leading troops moved on the railway, heavy machine gun fire was opened at them from the Cambrai line embankment in their right rear. Our machine and Lewis guns, rifles and mortars replied from the Orsinval Road but were not able to dominate the enemy fire. The right platoon was practically annihilated and the centre held up. By 5.50 a.m., however, posts were established on the main railway line close to the junction. Resistance on the left was also heavy, but the line was cleared as far as La Croisette Wood. Outposts were thrown across the railway, and touch was secured with the VI. Corps. By 6.30 a.m. posts were held in the Square Wood and beyond it, and along the hedgerow from the sunken road as far as the gap in the hedge and bank.

Further progress, however, down the road proved impossible, and the passage of the gap, swept as it was by particularly heavy fire, appeared equally impracticable. None the less, another platoon (2nd. Lt. R. J. Richards) was sent forward at 7 a.m. Under all the covering fire which the platoon on their left could give, Richards' men made a very gallant effort to rush the gap to the belt of trees eastward. The enemy machine guns inflicted grievous losses. Some of the riflemen reached the edge of the belt of trees, where a slight hollow, carpeted with autumn leaves, gave shelter from the fire in front. The Germans, however, moved a machine gun down a dry ditch round their right flank, and against its enfilade fire our men had practically no protection. A scout from the platoon on the road endeavoured to reach them but could not. He reported that he could see only dead and wounded. He did not greatly exaggerate the actual situation. The Lewis gun was early knocked out of action, the Nos. 1 and 2 of the team hit, and Richards himself wounded in the jaw and neck. The party could neither advance nor withdraw. Two men volunteered to take back a message. One was killed; the other, although wounded, crawled back to the bank. Unless there was a marked turn of fortune, Richards and the few wounded survivors must fall into German hands.

Along the whole of the right flank the pressure from the direction of Le Quesnoy now grew overwhelming. Heavy and sustained fire from both railway lines forced the outnumbered and enfiladed post at the junction to fall back. The enemy began to move in behind the platoon on the Orsinval Road, and their position in turn became untenable. To prevent envelopment they withdrew under cover of its high banks towards the railway line just in time. The intense machine gun fire now directed over their heads across the sunken road did not matter, but the fire sweeping the open space at the Level Crossing, which they must pass, mattered very much. Every weapon available was turned on the enemy machine guns. They were silenced for a moment, and in that moment the platoon dashed safely across the line.

It was now 10 a.m. On our side of the railway line the sunken road was being severely bombarded by German light howitzers, field guns and mortars, and receiving in addition unwelcome and resented attention from some of our own 18-pounders. The enemy presently worked up the Orsinval Road on the other side of the line. His fire became increasingly violent, and it was evident that an attack was imminent on our own positions on this side of the railway. The 2nd Rifles strengthened their flanks by fresh posts of Lewis guns and prepared to meet it. About 10.30 a.m. a company or more of German infantry poured up the main railway from the direction of Le Quesnoy. About the junction the enemy swarmed over the embankment and reached some 50 yards further. There he was definitely held. At the Level Crossing he had won the brick house by 10.50 a.m. and was endeavouring, under cover of stick bombs, to cross to our side. An officer succeeded, but was instantly killed.

The watchful and active hostile machine guns on the Cambrai railway prevented a counter-attack over the open. The 3rd Artillery Brigade and the English batteries, however, which were now in action east of the Beaudignies-Ruesnes road, answered the S.O.S. signals by an effective barrage, and the enemy was in addition bombarded by the light mortars and by rifle grenades. Shortly after 11 a.m. his effort was broken, and his party at the junction withdrew, suffering several casualties as they recrossed the embankment. The junction was at once reconnoitred and found vacated, but a post here would be too exposed, and it was decided not to garrison it for the moment. The Level Crossing, however, was reoccupied and a strong post installed there so as to command the Valenciennes railway towards Le Quesnoy.

The enemy shelling had ceased as soon as his infantry came into action. It now reopened vindictively on the Crossing and our positions in the Orsinval Road, and continued intermittently during the afternoon. A further strong hostile attack was made after midday. It was for the most part shattered by the 2nd and 4th Battalions' fire. A handful of Germans reoccupied the brick house, but were driven out from it almost immediately. A third attack, shortly after 5 p.m., was repulsed with less difficulty. Two Lewis gunners of the 4th Rifles, A. G. Peat and F. Prince, had done particularly good service in moving their gun to a flank and enfilading the enemy's advancing troops. The check to our advance and the subsequent necessary withdrawal from the Orsinval Road across the railway left the posts in the Square Wood and beyond hopelessly isolated, and they must have been not a little uneasy about their position. There was no alternative for them but to retire. If the absence of cover made this impossible for them in daylight, it also prevented offensive movement against the wood by the enemy. At dusk they were successfully withdrawn through our posts in front of the railway between the Level Crossing and La Croisette Wood.

In the evening an overdue reorganisation was made. The 4th Battalion troops still in the sunken road at the Level Crossing were relieved, and the whole position was taken over by the 2nd Battalion. In the day's fighting 12 men of the 2nd Battalion had been killed, and an officer and 22 men wounded. Richards and half a dozen men, all wounded, were taken prisoners.

On 27th October the 2nd Battalion's left flank beyond the railway was improved and posts established to within 200 yards of the VI. Corps right, whose advance had been similarly arrested. The 3rd Battalion's posts now lay along the Precheltes and about 500 yards short of the Cambrai railway. No further enemy attack followed on the Level Crossing, but snipers in the excellent cover afforded by the railway embankments towards Le Quesnoy were markedly aggressive till overcome in the afternoon. The German machine guns and artillery remained abnormally active.

The enemy were known to be constructing a system of trenches on the line Mons-Maubeuge and were believed to contemplate also another as a temporary position west of Bavai. Till these were completed it was apparently his intention to stand on his present line. The increase of hostile fire and an extensive employment of mortars all along the front indicated that the tide of the battle had reached its limit. The attackers had no reason to feel dissatisfied. 20,000 prisoners and 475 guns had been captured. The objectives of the Armies had been attained and in places, as on the New Zealanders' front, exceeded. Haig marks 25th October as the final day of the Battle of the Selle.

The Rifle Brigade's effort was thus made when the action had already virtually reached its close. The Division, however, had been fully represented in the Corps' operations. The artillery and Engineers had borne an active share from the outset. The infantry's participation did not extend to the opening move of the 20th, and except for the Rifles' attack on the enemy's reorganised line was confined to the 2nd Brigade's advance on the 23rd and 24th. Its performance had, nevertheless, fully reached the level of the Division's best achievements up to this time. All objectives had been seized or passed with exemplary speed and precision. 524 prisoners and 8 guns, in addition to a vast array of machine guns and other trophies had been captured. 2nd Otago's skilful and resolute work at the St. Georges river, and 1st Canterbury's dashing and energetic seizure of the Ecaillon bridgeheads were exploits as gallant and successful as any in the long and honourable records of these battalions. Less dramatic but not less instinct with the soldierly spirit were the bold handling of the artillery, indefatigably eager and supremely competent to take advantage of fleeting targets and assist the line of bayonets; the staunch determination, true to death, of the Engineers at Pont-à-Pierres; and the impetuosity of the machine gunners, content only with a place in the foremost line. Nor did the administrative personnel escape dangers and fatigues or fail to overcome them. A single illustration must suffice. Rflmn. E. H. Nailer, a driver in the 3rd Rifles' transport, was engaged on 25th October in bringing up rations to the front line companies, when he came under heavy shell-fire at a cutting.

Here he passed a water cart which had been cut adrift by a fellow driver to save the horses. With consummate coolness and gallantry Nailer regotiated the cutting successfully and delivered the rations. Learning then that the fighting troops were short of water, he returned, hitched his team to the cart and went forward with it in turn. Shelling, though less heavy, had not ceased, and Nailer was wounded. None the less, he persevered with his errand, delivered the water, and brought his team back again to safety.

Pending the resumption of the advance the Division was organised in depth, and the front line was reconstituted on a 2-battalion basis. All necessary readjustments from a moving to a stationary warfare ensued. The consolidation of defences was taken in hand. Trenches were dug, not in continuous lines, but in section posts, arranged chequerwise. They were camouflaged to harmonise with their surroundings, and the excavations of shelters were covered to prevent tell-tale shadows in aeroplane photographs. Batteries of medium and light mortars were installed in or near the front line for offensive purposes. Forward sections of artillery, frequently changing their positions, were retained near the line for harassing fire, but the remainder of the 3 field artillery brigades, now covering the outpost line, withdrew into defensive positions. Of these 1 was superimposed for S.O.S. calls, the remaining 2 being placed in reserve positions to cover the second line.[1] The Engineer companies hitherto forming part of the infantry brigade groups reverted to the command of the C.R.E. Similarly the machine gun companies were restored to Lt.-Col. Blair's command, to whom with the change fell the responsibility of the machine gun defences. One company was detailed for the forward and one for the second line, the remainder passing into reserve. All possible precautions were taken to prevent casualties among men and animals. Thus the Engineers put in hand the construction of "elephant" shelters in the forward area and gas-proof protection east of the St. Georges river. Wagon lines also were withdrawn westwards.

The enemy's artillery meanwhile remained consistently active, particularly about Pont-à-Pierres. There was a very violent bombardment on the afternoon of the 27th, in which 8-in. shells and a heavy concentration of gas were included. A considerable number of artillery horses were killed. Troops

1 On 24th October the 7th Battery was selected to go to the Army Artillery School as a "model battery."

of 2nd Canterbury then in the vicinity of Pont-à-Pierres were forced to seek new bivouacs. The 2nd (Army) Brigade headquarters were also in the area affected. Lt.-Col. Falla was on the point of going to the N.Z.F.A. Depot in England in due rotation to relieve Lt.-Col. Symon, and Major Richmond had just taken command of the brigade. In the bombardment, together with other casualties, Major Richmond, gallant gentleman and exceptionally able gunner, was killed.

564

CHAPTER XVI

The Battle of the Sambre

The courses of the large rivers Sambre and Scheldt are so directed that between them is left a broad avenue where no great natural obstacle bars an invasion of France from the north-east. Here, on high ground between the smaller rivers of the Ecaillon and Rhonelle, stands the fortress-town of Le Quesnoy. Founded before the XI. century, it was a place of considerable importance in the ancient French Hainault. It was surrounded in the middle of the XII. century by extensive ramparts, which did not prevent its capture by several of the great captains in mediaeval and modern history. It had fallen, for example, to Louis XI. (1447), Henry II. of France (1552), the Spaniards (1568), Turenne (1654), Eugene (1712). In 1793 it had been captured by the Austrians, and with its recovery in the following year is connected one of the earliest recorded uses of telegraphy. Before it the English soldier had, in the year of Crecy (1336), been for the first time exposed to the fire of cannon.[1] The fortifications had been maintained and improved, notably by Vauban, who remodelled them in the light of developing military science, but already before the war were rightly considered obsolete. The town contained an arsenal, barracks, military and civil hospitals, and a municipal college. Its population of barely 5000 was mostly employed in the manufacture of iron ware, cotton thread, sugar, and leather. It is entered by 3 roads, 1 from the east, 1 from Orsinval and the north through the Valenciennes Gate, and 1 from the south-east passing between 2 lakes and entering by the Landrecies Gate.

The rolling countryside round the town, beautified at this season of the year with the brown and golden tints of the foliage, is generally well timbered, and some 3 miles to the south-east lie the western extremities of the great Forêt de Mormal, which eastward falls to the Sambre. Through the Forest, on 26th August 1914, the German cavalry and guns, followed by Jägers on motor lorries, had pressed hard on the British columns retreating from Mons. It is traversed by a

[1] Fortescue, "History of the British Army." Vol. I., p. 550.

first-class road from Le Quesnoy to Avesnes and by several second-class roads. In 1914 these roads had offered the only practicable passage for troops. Since then the Germans had felled large areas, but even in these thick undergrowth had risen, hardly less impenetrable than the virgin forest, and almost the whole of its 20,000 acres, with its bush marshes and streams, formed a most serious obstacle to military movement. Maubeuge, 15 miles due east from Le Quesnoy, is only 6 miles distant, as the crow flies, from the Avesnes-Bavai road which bounds the most easterly part of the Forest. Some 8 miles to the south-east of Le Quesnoy the Valenciennes railway and the Le Quesnoy-Avesnes road, after passing through the Forest and crossing the river Sambre, reach the Aulnoye junction, already under our artillery fire.

The enemy's position at the end of October cannot be defined more lucidly or briefly than in the words of the official despatch:—

"By this time the rapid succession of heavy blows dealt by the British forces had had a cumulative effect, both moral and material, upon the German Armies. The difficulty of replacing the enemy's enormous losses in guns, machine guns and ammunition had increased with every fresh attack, and his reserves of men were exhausted. . . . .

"The capitulation of Turkey and Bulgaria and the imminent collapse of Austria—consequent upon Allied successes which the desperate position of her own armies on the western front had rendered her powerless to prevent—had made Germany's military situation ultimately impossible. If her armies were allowed to withdraw undisturbed to shorter lines, the struggle might still be protracted over the winter. The British Armies, however, were now in a position to prevent this by a direct attack upon a vital centre, which should anticipate the enemy's withdrawal and force an immediate conclusion."

The general plan laid down for the British Armies was to continue their advance on the Aulnoye junction and other centres of communication about Maubeuge vital to the enemy, and, if possible, to cut the main avenue of escape for the German forces opposite the French and Americans. It was essential to strike with the least loss of time. A preliminary operation, begun on 1st November, brought up the left flank of the Third Army across the Rhonelle and gave the Canadians Valenciennes. South of Valenciennes the enemy made, on 3rd November, a limited withdrawal which did not extend

so far as Le Quesnoy and did not affect the New Zealanders.
"There were indications," writes the Commander-in-Chief,
"that a further withdrawal was contemplated both in the
Tournai salient, where the line of the Scheldt was turned by
our progress on the battle front, and also in the area to the
south of us, where the enemy's positions were equally
threatened by our advance. Our principal attack was ready."

It was to be delivered the following morning (4th November) along the front of the Fourth Third and First
Armies for a distance of about 30 miles from the Sambre,
north of Oisy, to Valenciennes, with the co-operation of the
French First Army southwards. The Sambre itself on the right
of the attack, the Mormal Forest, the thickset nature of the
country generally, and the successive river lines falling to
the Scheldt across the direction of the advance, threatened
to prove difficult obstacles. It was the Allies' intention,
however, now to secure that complete victory which had just
eluded their grasp in October and which would hurl the
Germans back on the Meuse. Nor were their hopes to be
disappointed or deferred. It should, moreover, be noted that
while the French and Americans were exercising great and
increasing pressure towards the Meuse, it was the decisive
operation now undertaken by the British Armies which definitely crushed the enemy's resistance, forced retreats in
front and on either flank, and compelled him to sue for an
armistice. Rich in dramatic values, the pursuit of the broken
forces of the invaders brought the Armies of the Empire back to
Mons and over the Belgian frontier. These final operations
are called the Battle of the Sambre (1st-11th November).

In the lull before the storm the Rifle Brigade continued
to hold the New Zealand line west and north-west of Le
Quesnoy. During the last days of October the enemy's
artillery was consistently active with explosive and gas.
General Russell accordingly ordered the evacuation of the
civilians from the Ferme de Beart and other houses east of
Beaudignies. From their positions across the railway the
enemy's machine guns were now less aggressive against our
posts but harassed our low-flying aeroplanes. In retaliation
a combined shoot was arranged for 29th October by artillery
and machine guns. Aeroplanes flew over the positions to
attract fire. The numerous German machine guns about the
Square Wood and the belt of trees by the Orsinval Road
refused to be drawn. In the railway triangle, however,
several, bolder or less sophisticated, opened fire, and locating

SUPPORT TROOPS, 4TH NOVEMBER 1918

"COOKERS"

THE INNER RAMPART (LE QUESNOY)

ANOTHER SECTION OF THE SAME

these the aeroplanes dropped light-signals and sent wireless messages to the batteries, which swept the hostile positions with destructive salvoes.

During the pause in our operations the Rifle Brigade carried out a series of raids, in which the 2nd Rifles in particular showed enterprise persistence and audacity. In the early morning (2 a.m.) of 29th October Sergt. S. Hartley and 10 men of this battalion, after 2 minutes' bombardment with light trench mortars, attacked an enemy machine gun post in the Cambrai line embankment. The German n.c.o. and 16 men who garrisoned the post at once fled. Hartley's party sped in pursuit. They overtook their enemy, killed 2 and captured a prisoner, whereupon they returned without loss to our lines. At 9 p.m. on the 29th Hartley again led a raid up the sunken road towards Orsinval. After a brief light trench mortar bombardment, with his 9 men he left our post at the Level Crossing and stole across the open ground to the deep banks of the road. Moving forward our men heard the enemy running down the road and gave chase. One or two Germans turned and wildly and blindly fired their revolvers into the darkness. There were several small shelters in the steep sides of the road, and the occupants of these also shot at the pursuers. Our men stopped for a minute to clear the road, killing 3 Germans in the dugouts and another on top of one of the banks. They then continued the pursuit. But the minute's delay and the fact that the enemy had flung off rifles and equipment allowed him to retain his lead, and when our men had penetrated 500 yards down the road they ran into a support post, whose fire prevented further progress and the capture of prisoners. They returned safely up the road.

During the same day a patrol had located 2 enemy posts about the near edge of Square Wood, some 300 yards away. These, it was found, could be observed from one of our own forward posts. It was decided to raid them in the early hours of the following morning. A covering party, with 2 Lewis guns, moved to a position whence in the event of emergencies they could support the operation. The enterprise itself was to be "silent." About 2 a.m. (30th October) the raiders moved into position. Nearing the posts they split into 2 parties, under Sergt. G. A. Jarvis and Cpl. M. Kerrigan, each with 2 men, the remaining 2 being kept in reserve. Both parties rushed the posts simultaneously. They met with a shower of bombs, but forced an entry. They slew nearly all the garrison, Kerrigan alone killing 5 and sparing 1, who

41

was wounded. The prisoner was sent back under escort of one of our men. As the other riflemen were looking for identifications and papers on the dead, they were interrupted by bombs thrown from posts nearer the wood. Without hesitation the raiders attacked these also, and after hard fighting killed some of their occupants and drove off the remainder. There were in the area altogether 8 or 10 small posts, but possibly all had not been occupied. About 30 Germans in all were encountered, of whom 15 were killed. But the raiders had not come off unscathed. Jarvis had received a stick bomb full in the chest and was very severely wounded, and another man also, hit in the thigh, was unable to move without assistance. Two more were wounded less severely, but were incapacitated and sent back to our lines.

The reserve men, hearing the fresh outburst of bombing, came forward to the posts which had been the original objective. There they found only the dead Germans. Failing to establish touch with their comrades in the darkness, they concluded that these had either driven the enemy away and returned already to our lines, or had been captured in a counter-attack. They also returned. Thus in the further posts nearer the wood Kerrigan was left alone with his 2 stricken comrades. Jarvis was quite incapable of moving, and was apparently dying. Kerrigan therefore assisted the other man in. With a stretcher-bearer he went back at once for Jarvis, but by that time the enemy had reoccupied the posts, and the rescue party was unable to approach them.

The 1st Rifles in the right of the line facing the Cambrai railway were less favoured by opportunities for these enterprises, but in the following night, 30th/31st October, they carried out a joint enterprise with the 8th Somersetshires on their right against the posts on the embankment. Protecting barrages were provided for the Rifles by the 3rd Artillery Brigade, machine guns and mortars. The New Zealand attack was carried out by 2 platoons, under Lt. H. Blackburne, on a front of 300 yards. Machine gunners accompanied them for the purpose of destroying captured enemy machine guns. The operation was a complete success. There was no hostile artillery fire. The garrison used neither rifles nor bombs, and only 1 machine gun fired. Some of the Germans ran up from the hedge at the foot of the railway embankment and disappeared down the other side amid saplings and thick undergrowth. 4 were killed, and the whole area was cleared in 25 minutes. The raiders returned without a casualty and with 3 prisoners and 2 machine guns. Another gun was rendered useless by the machine gunners attached to the party. The Somersetshires were equally successful.

Though the German movement amid the trees opposite our front was now very considerably restricted, our artillery were still favoured with targets, which the forward observation officers were quick to detect and engage. In the morning of the 31st, in particular, admirable shooting was directed by the forward observation officer of the supporting howitzer battery. With the 2nd Rifles' intelligence officer he went during the forenoon to our advanced post at the Level Crossing. This post commanded a good view of the enemy defences on the road to Orsinval. A telephone wire was run out to it. At least 1 German post was blown up, and the fleeing enemy was harassed with machine gun fire at 1200 yards.

On the same day the 2nd Rifles crowned their achievements by an enterprise marked by tactical skill and dashing leadership. Early in the afternoon, following on a medium trench mortar bombardment on the Cambrai line about its northern junction with the Valenciennes railway, 2nd Lt. W. E. McMinn, M.C., and 5 riflemen attacked a strong enemy post on the embankment. Bombarded by the mortars and sniped at just previously from the Level Crossing, the enemy's sentries on the railway had forsaken their posts. A separate party of Lewis gunners, under Rflmn. W. A. Wilson, was pushed well down the main line so as to enfilade the branch line. Covered by the Lewis gun, our raiders worked round past the junction to the embankment on the enemy side of the Cambrai line. McMinn himself stayed at the junction to co-ordinate the work of both parties. When the Lewis gun team saw that the raiders were in position, they fired several bursts along the cutting, bringing the astonished enemy out of his shelters and straightway forcing them into cover in the ditch. Our patrol on the embankment stood up and fired on the Germans. But they did not rush them. One or two of the Germans fired back, doing no more damage than breaking one of our men's bayonets.. But McMinn, afraid that his quarry would escape or even succeed in mopping up the patrol, dashed along the 100 yards of the line and attacked the Germans single-handed. His patrol on the embankment at once joined him. Several of the enemy were killed, and the remainder surrendered. Another German post

200 yards further south down the railway threatened trouble, and McMinn, covered by our Lewis gun, withdrew to the junction and thence round by the Level Crossing to the road. When his party was all in, the covering Lewis gunners followed. An officer and 37 men were taken prisoners. We had not a single casualty.

At 5.40 p.m. a further effort by the 2nd Battalion at the sunken Orsinval Road had to be relinquished owing to intense machine gun fire. The road had been bombarded during the previous day in short sharp bursts by our mortars and 18-pounders, and the enemy was now very alert. On this occasion he actually attempted to attack in his turn but, losing 3 men shot, desisted. Periodical bombardments on our positions were put down in considerable weight, and the German sentries and gunners were "jumpy" at the least noise. Our patrols remained active, but all attempts to effect surprise found his posts intently watchful, and McMinn's exploit was to prove the last of the Division's long record of successful raids. For the many preparations necessary in view of the forthcoming attack were beginning to claim undivided attention.

The role allotted to the Division was, in conjunction with the 37th Division on the right and the 62nd Division of the VI. Corps on the left, to attack and establish a line from the western edge of the Mormal Forest northwards through the more distant outskirts of Herbignies to the cross-roads at Tous Vents. This line was nearly 4 miles east of our present positions and $2\frac{1}{2}$ miles beyond the eastern ramparts of Le Quesnoy. Should opportunity offer, it was proposed to exploit success still further eastwards through the Mormal Forest.

Without intense bombardment, which would destroy historic monuments and material wealth and cause casualties among the civil population, a frontal assault on the fortress-town was impossible. It was arranged therefore to envelop it from the flanks. The attacking troops would move past on the south and north of it to a series of intermediate objectives, forming as they advanced flanks to face and eventually to encircle the town. During this movement the ramparts would be screened by smoke. The operations proposed fell into 5 phases.

(a) 5.30 a.m.—The Rifle Brigade, with 3 battalions in the line, would capture the railway and draw an arc round the western side of Le Quesnoy from south to north (the Blue Line).

(b) 7.29 a.m.—The reserve battalion of the Rifle Brigade would pass through the right battalion south of the town, and a battalion of the 1st Brigade, at 7.51 a.m., pass through the left battalion north of the town, both battalions establishing positions which would be in a level with and beyond the eastern ramparts, but not yet connected with each other. (The Blue Dotted Line.)

(c) 8.56 a.m.—Two fresh battalions of the 1st Brigade would pass through the Blue Dotted Line north of the town, gradually striking south-east as well as east, and meeting a further advance (beginning 8.47 a.m.) of the reserve battalion of the Rifle Brigade on the south of the town. The converging movements would meet on the Green Line, and the 1st Brigade take over the whole front. The Rifle Brigade would mop up Le Quesnoy.

(d) 10.20 a.m.—The same two 1st Brigade battalions would advance from the Green Line for the final objective. (The Red Line.)

(e) Should enemy resistance weaken, patrols would establish the Red Dotted Line some 3000 yards further eastwards.

From this point the 2nd Brigade would continue the advance. A troop of the 3rd Hussars was attached to the 1st Brigade, the rest of the squadron to the 2nd Brigade. A section of Otago Mounted Rifles was posted to each brigade. A proportion of Engineers and New Zealand Tunnellers were detailed to investigate mines in Le Quesnoy and in the area east of it. The remainder of the Engineers were held in readiness to prepare crossings over the Valenciennes-Aulnoye railway for the field artillery, and to carry out work on roads and bridges.

The attack was to be carried out under a somewhat complicated barrage of varying rates co-ordinated with the movement of the troops on either flank. General Napier Johnston had at his disposal the 3 New Zealand field artillery brigades, the 42nd Divisional and 2 further British R.F.A. brigades. Of these 7 brigades, all to be posted at first in the vicinity of Beaudignies, 5 would carry the attack forward to the Green Line, the remaining 2 being superimposed as far as the Blue and thereafter firing a smoke screen on the outskirts of Le Quesnoy. Definite stages were laid down for the artillery brigades to cease barrage work and follow up the advance. Three batteries of 6-in. howitzers were also available for the bombardment of special points. Prior to the attack, increase and decrease of artillery fire were equally forbidden, and in

all other ways the strictest measures were taken to preserve
secrecy. Ammunition was brought forward under darkness.
Road screens were erected to conceal such small movement
of troops as was inevitably necessary in daylight. Normal
wireless activity was maintained, and no additional stations
were allowed to come into action. Once the infantry advance
started, careful arrangements ensured touch being established
at a succession of selected points along our boundaries with
the Divisions on either flank.

In the first phase the Rifle Brigade proposed to attack
with 3 battalions in line, the 1st on the right and the 2nd
on the left crossing the railway and forming the first sectors
of the circle to be drawn round the town. The 4th, in the
centre, would also cross the railway and advance towards the
ramparts. The 3rd Battalion was in reserve. When, in the
second phase, the 3rd Battalion passed through and reached
the Blue Dotted Line, the 1st Battalion would immediately
take over the flank between the first and second objective
facing Le Quesnoy on the south. North of the town, it was
obviously convenient that from the 2nd Rifles' posts on the
Blue Line at the Valenciennes road onwards the whole
of the investment should be done by the 1st Brigade.

In addition to artillery support, it was provided that the
attack over the railway should be covered by the 2 medium
trench mortar batteries and by 2 batteries of light trench
mortars, whose barrages would conform with and advance
300 and 100 yards respectively in front of the field artillery
barrage. After completion of the barrage task, the 1st and
2nd Rifles would be allotted 2 light mortars and the 4th
Battalion 1. The attacks of the flank battalions would similarly be protected by barrages provided by 2 machine gun
companies conforming with the artillery barrage up to
extreme range and sweeping the outskirts of the town. In
addition, 8 other machine guns were for half an hour after
zero to enfilade the streets and ramparts. This task accomplished, these last would pass to their own company, which
was attached to the 2nd Infantry Brigade, while the company
co-operating with the 2nd Rifles on the north would be added
to the company supporting the 1st Brigade.

Certain adjustments had to be effected in the line.
During the evening of 3rd November the Rifles extended their
right 500 yards to secure elbow room south of Le Quesnoy.
In the more intricate ground to the north, the left was drawn
in to the Level Crossing, the 62nd Division taking over our

former positions thence northwards. On the same night the support and reserve field artillery brigades moved a section per battery into position about Beaudignies. The remaining sections followed on the eve of the attack. Advanced Divisional headquarters was at the same time established at Beaudignies, that of the Rifle Brigade at the Ferme du Fort Martin, and that of the 1st Brigade in a house on the Ruesnes road. The 1st Brigade troops, clearing Solesmes about 4 p.m., marched to orchards about Beaudignies, where they bivouacked for the night.

In the evening rain set in and lasted till about 3 a.m. Shortly before the attack our outlying posts were withdrawn to clear our barrage. Even now no indications pointed to an extension as far south as Le Quesnoy of the enemy's withdrawal opposite the VI. Corps front. Patrols reported his garrisons still in their posts. At intervals during the early hours after midnight he fired double red flares and periodically shelled with some intensity that area immediately behind the 2nd Rifles' assembly positions, from which his tormentors had been lately so active. A single shell, landing right in the sunken road, caused us 11 casualties. But he did not apparently anticipate an attack. At 5.20 a.m. 2 orange-coloured flares were fired as an all-clear signal.

Ten minutes later our guns and mortars opened together in a stupendous crash. The medium mortars alone fired a tornado of over 500 projectiles on the embankment. Drums of burning oil were projected on the ramparts. A display of the enemy's red and golden rain S.O.S. flares from the railway immediately followed. The German artillery's response was less severe on our front than on our battery areas. The 9th Battery had 2 and one of the English batteries 5 guns knocked out.[1]

The 1st Rifles[2] attacked with 3 companies. The objective of their right company was the Landrecies main road, some 1500 yards distant. Thence the proposed line swung back over the Le Quesnoy drill-ground in front of a large orchard to the railway embankment at the south-western edge of the town. Considerable machine gun fire was experienced from the right flank, and several machine guns on the railway line pinned the attackers for some minutes to the ground. One and all, however, succumbed to the Rifles' pressure. Against

[1] The 11th Battery's wagon lines were also heavily shelled in the early morning, 52 horses being casualtied.
[2] Capt. E. A. Harding, M.C., vice Lt.-Col. R. C. Allen, wounded on 3rd November.

one particularly aggressive post Sergt R. L. Ferguson led a small party which outflanked and silenced the gun. At another point on the railway embankment Cpl. M. J. Mulvaney, D.C.M., encountered a machine gun which was holding up the advance of the company on his right. Ordering his No. 1 to engage the gun, Mulvaney himself worked round to the left, and single-handed rushed the post, capturing the gun and its crew of 4. Here, also, Rflmn. E. W. Hallett dashed forward alone with his Lewis gun and put an enemy machine gun out of action. Then, springing to his feet and storming the post with his revolver, he killed 1 of the enemy and took the remainder prisoners.

In the orchard also some resistance was offered by a nest of machine guns. Lt. H. J. Thompson, who commanded the company concerned, disposed his platoons with such skill that all the machine guns, with a 77-mm. gun, fell into our hands, the artillerymen being shot down by Rflmn. J. R. Mason, who brought a Lewis gun round to the left flank. In the clearance of the orchard material assistance was given by the attached section of our own machine guns under 2nd Lt. A. W. Reynolds. Here an officer and 40 men were taken prisoners. The line then pressed forward towards their final objective. Near it Coy.-Sergt.-Major E. Olsen, when his company was held up by machine gun fire, acting on his own initiative, worked a section round behind the machine gun garrison. Then at a given signal the party rushed in and bombed 3 machine gun teams in succession, enabling their company to reach its objective. Elsewhere the 1st Battalion line was established with inconsiderable trouble.

After the forward companies had passed on to their objective, the reserve company moved forward to the railway, and to it was given the most piquant adventure that befell the battalion during the day. The 37th Division on our right had been temporarily checked in the vicinity of the chapel at the cross-roads on the Ghissignies-Le Quesnoy road, and between 7 a.m. and 7.30 a.m. a body of enemy, numbering 5 officers and 150 men, attempted to counter-attack about the cross-roads. Judging, however, by the sound of musketry and bombs on their right that they were liable to be outflanked, they determined to withdraw. By this time the day, beautifully clear at first after the night's rain, had become misty. The retreating Germans, not realising the extent of the New Zealanders' progress, thought to get back along the railway to Le Quesnoy. In the fog the reserve 1st Rifles' company, then resting on the railway line, received short warning of their approach. A platoon was immediately detached to deal with them. An admirably handled flank section under Cpl. C. Taylor turned a dangerous situation into a brilliant success, and within a few moments the whole body surrendered, with 2 machine guns. In all, the 1st Rifles' casualties amounted to 80, of whom 20 were killed.

In the centre of the line the 4th Battalion attack was also delivered by 3 companies, 1 from the hedge east of the Ferme de Beart, 1 from the high ground due west of the ramparts, and another down the Ruesnes road. All reached the objective of the railway line to the minute, and patrols at once pushed forward across an open stubble field towards the bank of trees which fringed the moat. What difficulties met them there and what progress they made will be narrated presently.

In the old troublesome ground of the railway triangle the 3 companies of the 2nd Rifles encountered stubborn opposition. In the darkness, a slight gap was created between the centre and left companies, and just opposite this gap unfortunately was an enemy machine gun, posted near the railway junction. It caused considerable casualties in the centre company before they stormed it. This company was engaged, too, in further fierce fighting in the railway triangle. When the right attacking platoon was put out of action, Sergt. J. Grubb, in the platoon on its left, covered its frontage with his own section and maintained touch with the right company. After clearing 2 machine gun posts he encountered a nest of 3. With the assistance of a light trench mortar he destroyed these and took the objectives of the casualtied platoon, with a large number of prisoners and several machine guns. On the rest of its front, owing to its casualties, the centre company had become disorganised, and some of its men passed on into our own barrage. Seeing the hard straits of this centre company, the reserve company (Lt. L. H. Denniston) had come forward of their own accord to strengthen the line, and their timely assistance facilitated the capture of the objective on the remainder of the central sector.

Part of the left company also came under heavy machine gun fire at close range, which inflicted casualties and held up the advance. Rflmn. C. Birch, a member of a light trench mortar team attached to the battalion, promptly volunteered to go forward and locate the machine gun. This he did with great coolness, and his comrades destroyed it with their

mortar bombs. Birch thereupon, completing his reconnaissance of the locality, captured a German officer and 27 men.
The remainder of the left company reached the Le Quesnoy-
Orsinval Road at 6.20 a.m. without any great resistance, and
took a fair number of prisoners. Here they were joined shortly
afterwards by the 62nd Division. The right company, like the
centre, had a hard struggle before they cleared their sector
of the railway triangle. They then threw out patrols to the
sunken road on the north-western edge of the town. It was
at this stage of the attack that a notable feat of arms was
performed by Sergt. W. P. McGillen. His men encountered
heavy fire from a German machine gun. In an exposed
position McGillen skilfully got his Lewis gun into action,
silenced the enemy gun and compelled the crew to retire to
a house in rear of the German position. Quickly following
up, McGillen personally rushed the house, killing 5 of the
enemy with a bomb and capturing 14 more.

Despite the resistance offered and some short shooting on
the part of our own guns, the 2nd Rifles accomplished every
part of their task. Thus all along the Division's front the
Blue Line was taken up to time,[1] large hauls of prisoners and
machine guns falling into our hands.

On the capture of the Blue Line the 4 British field artillery brigades advanced by batteries to the railway south-east
of Le Quesnoy and to the Ferme de Beart Wood, the Precheltes valley and the Level Crossing in order to carry on
the barrage supporting the 1st Infantry Brigade to the final
objective of the Red Line. While each battery moved forward, continuity of fire was maintained, the remaining batteries being distributed over their brigade's front and increasing the rate of their fire to compensate for the loss of
the battery on the move. Each battery as it arrived resumed
its task from its new position. The New Zealand artillery
brigades remained in their present positions, 2 firing the smoke
screen on Le Quesnoy and the third carrying the barrage on
to the Green Line to the limits of the guns' range.

The 3rd Rifles,[2] to whom it now fell to take up the action
south of the town, had been set in motion 5 minutes after zero,
and just as dawn was breaking their troops could be seen
advancing in perfect order over the low ridge west of the
railway. Here there was a little hostile shelling, and an
officer and 3 men were killed, but these were to be the only

[1] A nest in the Factory in the railway triangle was not completely cleared by the 2nd Rifles till 9.30 a.m.
[2] Major (Temp. Lt.-Col.) G. W. Cockcroft.

THE SLUICE GATE BRIDGE   [*Photo Capt. S. Cory Wright*

GENERAL RUSSELL ENTERS LE QUESNOY, 5TH NOVEMBER (Rainy Weather)

THE NEW ZEALAND FLAG PRESENTED TO LE QUESNOY

ARRIVAL OF PRESIDENT POINCARÉ

lives lost by the battalion during its last action. By 6.15 a.m. all companies were over the railway, and at 7.10 a.m. were assembled immediately in rear of the Blue Line. 1st Auckland in the same way, 15 minutes after our attack started, left the Beaudignies orchards. As they were crossing the Le Quesnoy-Ruesnes road, an enemy aeroplane flew low overhead, and heavy shelling immediately followed. Without serious losses, however, they reached their position of deployment in rear of the 2nd Rifles on the Le Quesnoy-Orsinval Road. To avoid losses through fire from the ramparts, this position had been defined well north of the town. The left Auckland boundary, in accordance with the pre-arranged plan, temporarily extended into the 62nd Division's area.

At 7.29 a.m., just as the reserve company of the 1st Rifles were dealing with the Germans on the railway, the second phase of our attack was initiated by the 3rd Battalion south of the town. The assaulting companies, with Advanced Battalion Headquarters, had already gone forward, and Major Cockcroft, with his intelligence officer, 2nd Lt. E. C. Drummond, were waiting for receipt of word from advanced headquarters to follow, when a curious and unlooked-for episode occurred. The morning mist was heavy, and it was difficult to see more than 40 yards. All at once Cockcroft and his party discerned a large number of men who, looming indistinctly through the mist, crossed from the south into our area in rear of our advancing front line companies. For a moment it was surmised that these were troops from the right Division who had lost their direction. Then the amazing truth asserted itself. They were Germans! Either as part of the counter-attack down the railway[1] or in an independent operation, the enemy force now threatened to intercept our supports from the assaulting companies. The Germans halted. They failed to notice the little group of riflemen. They were just preparing to place their machine guns ready for action when Drummond charged forward and fired his revolver into their midst. Completely bewildered, they surrendered, although fully armed, without more ado. They were found to number 4 officers and 70 men. No other noteworthy incident marked the 3rd Rifles' progress to the Blue Dotted Line, which before the scheduled hour was in their possession.

As soon as the advance to the Blue Dotted Line was on its way, the right company of the 1st Rifles proceeded to

1 p. 574.

occupy 600 yards of the Ghissignies road as far as the main
Landrecies road, at which point they would establish connection with the left of the 3rd Battalion on the second
objective. This movement was not effected without fighting.
On the Ghissignies road the enemy occupied the farms in
considerable strength and developed heavy machine gun fire
from them. 2nd Lt. J. L. Brown with several men worked
round behind the houses and rushed 3 machine guns in
succession, shooting down the gunners and taking many
prisoners.   Along this line the 1st Rifles' posts faced Le
Quesnoy and thus marked a further stage in the investment
from the south.

North of the town, in co-operation with the VI. Corps'
attack, the enveloping movement of 1st Auckland from the
Orsinval road was timed to commence 22 minutes later than
the 3rd Rifles' advance about the Landrecies road.   In
touch with the 62nd Division the two 1st Auckland assaulting
companies started forward at 7.51 a.m.   As in the assembly
position, so now in the advance, to avoid exposure to fire
from the direction of Le Quesnoy, a full 500 yards' distance
was maintained between our right flank and the railway.
The attacking troops were shrouded also by the mist as well
as by our smoke-screen on the ramparts.   Ramponeau, in
which were a certain number of civilians, was cleared about
8.30 a.m.   The battalion captured some 300 prisoners, and
50 machine guns.   Their casualties were under 50.   Throughout the attack Sergt. C. G. Buckworth had done fine work on
the left flank by personal reconnaissance and by bombing
attacks which resulted in the capture of several machine guns.
By 8.40 a.m. the second phase, the establishment of the Blue
Dotted Line, was complete.

The sun was now well up in the east, the mist had
dispersed, and the day was bright and warm.   At 8.47 a.m.
the 3rd Rifles continued their main advance south of the
town with the support companies.   One of these had
already passed through the left flank on the Landrecies road
and established strong points along the southern edge of
the 2 lakes in continuation of the line of investment begun
by the 1st Battalion.   This movement was now continued
along the road to Villereau, and at the same time the right
company advanced straight on the Green Line.   At the far
corner of the more easterly lake the 2 barrages sweeping round
Le Quesnoy north and south joined, and already through the
dust and smoke of the bursting shells glimpses could be caught

of the right flank of the 1st Brigade converging southwards. In the clearer light opposition was encountered from German posts and machine guns, which it was most difficult to locate. Rflmn. N. Coop, a No. 1 of a Lewis gun team, worked forward into the open to draw the fire of these guns and thus induce them to betray their exact positions. His fearless behaviour had the desired effect, and the No. 2 was enabled to bring his gun forward and put the enemy guns out of action.

Hostile fire was especially heavy on our right. Here Capt. F. E. Greenish's company had reached the line of the Chateau Montout, where they came into country devoid of cover and swept by machine guns from a commanding ridge directly in front of the Chateau. Greenish and his men without hesitation fearlessly went forward. The Germans withdrew from the position or surrendered, and the ridge was gained with surprising ease.

The Rifles' left met the 1st Brigade at the prearranged cross-roads beyond the far lake, and their right swung on with certainty and rapidity to the southernmost half mile sector of the Green Line. In the latter stages of the advance casualties had been negligible. In addition to the officer and 3 men killed at the outset the total losses for the day were only 45 men wounded. A field gun, a mortar, 17 machine guns, and over 300 prisoners were counted among their spoils.

1st and 2nd Wellington had left Beaudignies shortly after 6 a.m. and marched forward through a hostile barrage falling on the line of the Precheltes stream. With some difficulty in the fog and dense smoke barrage near Le Quesnoy, they reached their preparatory assembly position on the sunken Orsinval road north of the Level Crossing, where a week previously the Rifles had experienced such bitter fighting. Nine minutes after the 3rd Rifles' advance on the other side of the town the northern movement was resumed (8.56 a.m.) in close touch with the 62nd Division. 1st Wellington attacked on the right, and 2nd Wellington on the left. As they moved out in front from the 1st Auckland positions, Auckland commenced to trace the northern line of investment assigned to the 1st Brigade. The Auckland companies wheeled to the right to face Le Quesnoy, on the one hand linking up with the 2nd Rifles and on the other swinging up their outer flank towards the railway station on the north-east. The fortress was now almost surrounded. There remained only the narrowing gut due eastwards, rapidly being filled by the converging movements of the 3rd Rifles and 1st Wellington.

The two 1st Wellington assaulting companies were, as it happened, largely composed of men who had not been in action previously. Effectively assisted by machine guns, they moved at first parallel with and north of the Aulnoye railway. As they progressed, their right flank extended over the railway and met the Rifles' left on the cross-roads by the lake. Their country was for the most part open, but apart from a short fight on the Villereau road they had little trouble. At one point a brave action was performed by Sergt. R. Charteris, who rushed a machine gun post single-handed, putting the gun out of action and capturing the crew. The two 2nd Wellington[1] companies, though moving through the woods on the steep Rhonelle bank, also went forward without opposition as fast as the barrage would permit. In Villereau they found some 50 civilians and a small German nest of 2 officers and 22 men. By the appointed time of 9.25 a.m. both battalions were on the Green Line, where 1st Wellington immediately extended their right with a company under Capt. E. Whyte to the southern boundary occupied by the 3rd Rifles. Thus all along our line, now connected continuously throughout, the 1st Brigade troops were in position to carry out the fourth phase of the attack.

At 10.20 a.m. the advance was resumed from the Green Line by the 1st Brigade along the whole New Zealand front in touch with the troops on either flank. A section of the Otago Mounted Rifles was attached to 2nd Wellington and a section of a 3rd Hussars troop to 1st Wellington to maintain lateral communications, while the remainder of the 3rd Hussars troop maintained communication from front to rear, acting directly under General Melvill's orders. As the North Island Battalions passed through, one of the 3rd Rifles' companies was withdrawn out of the most forward positions to act as a battalion reserve, should the enemy attempt a sortie from Le Quesnoy. Though our line was now well over a mile beyond the town, there was no sign yet of its surrender. Completely invested but not bombarded, its garrison still resisted actively and was to resist for several hours longer. The British batteries were now in action about the Ferme de Beart Wood, and as soon as the 1st Infantry Brigade resumed their advance from the Green Line it was the turn of the New Zealand artillery brigades to come forward to positions from which to support exploitation

[1] Major McKinnon, vice Lt.-Col. Cunningham, seconded for duty to New Zealand.

beyond the final line. Lt.-Col. Symon[1] and his battery commanders, riding round north of Le Quesnoy, were held up by machine gun fire from the ramparts and forced to go round the southern side. The 2nd (Army) Brigade[2] reconnoitring party, similarly harassed, made a detour further north, and moving by Ramponeau and Villereau selected positions near St. Sepulchre east of Villereau. The leading battery was in action there about 1.30 p.m. The 1st and the 3rd Brigade batteries took up positions in the same vicinity. The 4 British artillery brigades remained for the moment north and west of Le Quesnoy to continue the barrage to the final objective. Lt.-Col. McQuarrie took over command of the advanced guard artillery consisting of the 3 New Zealand brigades. The resolution shown by the artillery in passing Le Quesnoy under machine gun fire in order to come forward and support their infantry was not the least notable performance of the day.

Up to this point the barrages had been of different rates co-ordinated with the advance of the flank Divisions on either side of the town and the converging movements of the 2 streams of New Zealanders. Thenceforward there was to be but 1 barrage moving at the uniform rate of 100 yards in 3 minutes. Forward sections from the 12th and 13th Batteries and a howitzer battery accompanied the 2 Wellington battalions. The barrage itself, as has been noted, was now provided by the 4 English artillery brigades. But the battalions were warned that it would die out on reaching the limit of the guns' range, and that the advance thereafter to the Red Line would be continued without a barrage and supported only by the fire of forward sections or batteries.

The 2 support companies of each Wellington battalion moved forward from the Green Line at 10.20 a.m. One of the 1st Wellington companies bearing too much to a flank left a gap. This was promptly filled by Lt. A. J. Nimmo, commanding one of the companies on the Green Line, who immediately rushed a platoon forward. The barrage, as the troops had been advised, was now thin. The enemy, however, though in considerable strength was disorganised and demoralised, and apart from the inevitable machine gun nests offered little resistance. Mopping up Potelle in their stride, the 1st Wellington screen saw in and near an orchard beside the Chateau striking evidence of the work of our artillery. Our

---

1 Reassumed command of 1st Artillery Brigade on 3rd Nov., vice Lt.-Col. Standish, returning on duty to New Zealand.
2 Major C. N. Newman, D.S.O., vice Lt.-Col. Falla, on duty to England.

batteries had very effectively "got onto" some German guns. The German gunners lay dead in a group. A few infantrymen also lay scattered about. The horses had been killed in the orchard. The men looked as if they had been running away when caught by our fire. Then passing through the woods on either side of the railway and along the Rhonelle banks, where they captured guns horses and limbers, 1st Wellington entered and cleared Herbignies without trouble. Many Germans had sought refuge in cellars and were mopped up by Sergt. H. O. D. Clark. Others yielded readily, a platoon under Sergt. S. J. H. Board capturing nearly 200 with 10 machine guns. Sergt. F. Baker, M.M., Sergt J. C. Short, L./Cpl. F. Lane, who hacked his way through a hedge to surprise an enemy machine gun, and Pte. W. G. Vial, who captured 2 machine gun posts in succession, were only the more distinguished of the many men who, during this irresistible onset, rushed and stormed the enemy's machine gun positions. At Herbignies, as in the other villages, the inhabitants pressed coffee milk and fruit on the hungry and thirsty infantry. Hospitality was not refused but was not allowed to delay the advance which, as ordered, reached the final objective (the Red Line) at 11.56 a.m.

Before 2nd Wellington the enemy had for the most part withdrawn. In the close country, however, a few Germans out of touch with their fellows were surprised. Four Wellington signallers under L./Cpl. J. H. Griffiths laying a telephone wire came on four 77-mm. guns still in action and firing over open sights. Griffiths promptly ordered his party to drop their wire and charge the guns. Most of the 10 artillerymen serving the guns fled at once. One or two vainly endeavoured to keep their assailants at bay by rifle fire. The guns with 2 prisoners were captured, whereupon Griffiths and his signallers continued their wire-laying.

It had been arranged that on the establishment of the final objective, should enemy resistance weaken, patrols were to be pushed forward to reach the exploitation Dotted Red Line, where the 2nd Brigade would "leap-frog" through to continue the advance. On the other hand, if resistance should be met in such strength as to check exploitation, a definite line was to be taken up and artillery brought forward preparatory to a formal attack during the afternoon. On the Red Line the Wellington companies were at once re-organised, and in close touch with the 37th Division 1st Wellington pushed forward patrols who about 2.15 p.m.

reached the road on the western edge of the Mormal Forest. There was no opposition except from a cavalry patrol which was fired on. 4 horses were killed and 2 prisoners taken. The 2nd Wellington patrols were on the left held up by machine gun fire from the flank, but on the right, in touch with 1st Wellington, they similarly were successful in reaching the western edge of the Forest. Scouts of both battalions, Ptes. L. G. V. Loveday and A. D. Anderson, on their respective battalion fronts penetrated deep into it. Loveday passing through a clearing came on 7 of the enemy. He shot 3 and took the remainder, including 2 officers, prisoners.

On the left flank 2nd Wellington patrols had early passed Le Carnoy, where a party under Coy.-Sergt.-Major J. H. Foster, coming under heavy fire from 2 machine guns in a house rushed and captured them. Scouts had actually reached the vicinity of Le Grand Sart, well beyond the exploitation line, but by the time permission had been received from Brigade Headquarters to occupy the village and the main advance was resumed, it was found that the Germans had come back in force to the neighbourhood of Le Carnoy and established strong machine gun posts. Against their obstinate fire little progress could be made in the daylight even with artillery support, and further advance was postponed till dusk. But officers and men were alike determined to set a seal on the day's work by reaching the exploitation Red Dotted Line on the Sarioton road during the night and clearing the high forest still unfelled east of Herbignies.

A light barrage was accordingly put down by the 2nd (Army) Brigade at 9.30 p.m. moving 100 yards every 4 minutes. 1st Wellington, further in advance, reached their goal by 11.30 p.m., meeting only 1 party of the enemy. 2nd Wellington continued the advance with 2 companies, one of the others forming a defensive flank on their unprotected north. By 1.30 a.m. they had reached the Sarioton road. Half an hour later the 37th Division were abreast on our right. It was much regretted that this most successful day was marred by the loss of Major McKinnon, commanding 2nd Wellington, and his adjutant, who were killed by an enemy shell when proceeding in the evening to advanced battalion headquarters. The other casualties in 2nd Wellington for the day amounted to just over 60. 1st Wellington had got off more lightly, an officer and 7 men having been killed, and 2 officers and 20 men wounded.

The Wellington Battalions' operations had yielded important captures.   2nd Wellington had taken 29 field guns, four 8-in. howitzers, 5 trench mortars, 33 machine guns, 400 prisoners.   1st Wellington claimed 45[1] field guns, 7 trench mortars, 60 machine guns, and several hundreds of prisoners, together with limbers water-carts and other material.

Meantime the persistent and obstinate efforts of the Rifle Brigade to clear Le Quesnoy had been for many hours frustrated by a tenacious defence and by the strength of the position.   The moat, unlike that under the Ypres walls, is not a single broad ditch but is divided into an inner and outer moat by a line of "demilunes" or disconnected fortifications which act as an outlying rampart.   The outer moat is about 50 feet wide and 36 feet deep.   The "demilunes" are some 20-30 feet high.   Their sides are faced with brick or sand-stone, supported by thick banks of earth.   In some places there is a single, in others a double line of these outlying bastions.   By some stretch of the imagination they may be compared to bold islets, but the banks and transverse walls, which connect them, and the trees and thick undergrowth which crown their summits and cover the earth banks make the whole of this outer rampart a bewildering labyrinth, in which, owing to circumscribed view and the different orientations of the various walls, it is extremely difficult to preserve an idea of direction.   Picturesque in appearance, they form also admirable defensive positions. They were now held in some strength as outposts by German snipers and machine gunners.[2]   Beyond them the inner moat lies at the foot of the rampart proper.   A small stream, a tributary of the Rhonelle, enters the fortress from the lakes south-east of the town by a sluice and flows along this inner moat, washing the foot of the final rampart.   This stream is about 7 feet wide, but on the western side of the town it runs mostly underground.   It leaves the fortress on the north by a second sluice.   It was considered not unlikely that the enemy would utilise this stream for flooding the inner moat, and a supply of cork mats had been obtained for crossing it.   He had, however, either neglected or been unable to strengthen the defence in this way, and the moat contained only the normal amount of water.   From the inner rampart a redoubt projected every 200 yards to give

1   These appear to include some claimed also by 2nd Wellington.
2   At one time they appear to have been loopholed every 40 or 50 feet, some loopholes being below the level of the ground to cover the moat, but most of them 5 feet above ground-level and capable of offering a good field of fire over the surrounding country.   These loopholes were now, however, bricked up.

flanking fire.   This final rampart was a solid continuous
brick wall about 60 feet high.   For crossing these defences
the Rifle Brigade had provided themselves with half-a-dozen
scaling ladders.

After reaching the protective line for the first objective
(The Blue Line), our barrage had searched the ramparts for
15 minutes and then ceased on the west and north-west faces.
Patrols went forward but met stubborn resistance, and to
enable the advance of the troops for the further objectives to
pass round the town's outskirts, it had proved necessary to
execute the arrangements made for putting down a heavy
smoke screen.   Under cover of this, Rifle patrols worked
forward to the outer moat.   Field and machine guns and
minenwerfer on strong commanding positions on the ramparts were extremely active, but once the investment had
been completed on the north and south the ultimate fall of
the town was only a matter of time.

It remained to be seen to which battalion of the Rifles
would accrue the distinction of first storming the walls.
The 1st Rifles on the south-west, like 1st Auckland on the
north-east, were too far distant to vie in the race for this
honour.   On the south-east, the 3rd Battalion had a chance
only if the bridge on the Landrecies road were unguarded.
Their reconnaissance patrols encountered hot machine gun
fire sweeping down the bridge and suffered casualties.   That
way was impregnably barred.   On the north the prospects of
the 2nd Rifles were brighter.   About 8 a.m. 4 men secured
a footing on the island ramparts, and captured a machine gun
which they tumbled down into the outer moat.   But machine
gun and rifle fire drove them back.   An organised attempt
was made later by one platoon covered by the fire of
another platoon, but the covering platoon was driven off by
fire, and such men as reached the foot of the bastions were
pinned there unable to get back or forward till the capture
of the town.   Other parties worked round the north-east
to the railway bridge, where a party of Engineers attached
to the battalion withdrew the charges under it.   Others again
gradually forced a way down the Valenciennes road and over
the railway crossing till they approached the cross-roads on
the northern outskirts.   One man is said actually to have got
into the town by climbing up some timber and to have shot
a sentry before being forced to withdraw.   Lt.-Col. Jardine
himself went from company to company, personally directing
operations and pushing his men forward from one position to

another.   Thus the 2nd Rifles began gradually to out-
manoeuvre the enemy.   For several hours, however, the
German machine guns in the outer rampart maintained sullen
and spiteful activity.   To deal with them, our mortars, who
had already from 9 a.m. rendered important service, were
worked up by stages to the cross-roads.   From this point
about 4 p.m. they put a fierce bombardment on the northern
ramparts.   The enemy machine guns were effectually silenced,
and it appeared that at last the 2nd Rifles' untiring efforts
were to be crowned by a triumphant entry into the town.
In view of their successes on its northern precincts a week
previously, no battalion would have grudged them the honour
of its capture.   They were, however, forestalled.

Fortune had not at first smiled on the 4th Battalion's
efforts west of the town.   As soon as the railway line was
taken, Lt.-Col. Barrowclough with his intelligence officer,
2nd Lt. L. C. L. Averill, M.C., and one or two members of
his staff left his overnight headquarters at Chapel Farm, 1200
yards west of Le Quesnoy down the Ruesnes road, and came
forward to the embankment.   He himself with Averill and 2
runners immediately set about locating the companies—no
easy task in the fog—and exploring the outer moat.   During
this reconnaissance they captured 2 Germans whom they bade
conduct them into the town.   The prisoners professed their
readiness to do this, but the route they followed, though
ultimately it was proved to be correct, seemed at the time
so long and devious that Barrowclough decided it would be
wiser to get a stronger party before trusting himself further.
By the time the additional men were secured, the enemy
machine guns had begun to play, and this bold attempt at a
coup-de-main had to be foregone.

All three 4th Battalion companies meantime had also
themselves been pushing patrols forward to explore the walls.
The left company, "C" (Lt. C. N. Rabone), when nearing the
outer moat had come under accurate machine gun and mortar
fire and were held up on the sunken road which runs round
the north-western side of the fortress.   Even apart from this
fire the way here was barred by a 40-feet broad expanse of
deep water which reflected in an unbroken mirror the rich
red of the brick rampart and the russets browns and yellows
of the trees.   Here the company could make no progress,
and here it remained practically isolated for the rest of the day.

"B" Company (Lt. V. F. Maxwell) in the centre and
"A" Company (Lt. H. S. Kenrick) on the right worked over

THE SOUTHERN FORESTER'S HOUSE, SEPTEMBER 1919
Photo Capt. S. Cory Wright

PRISONERS TAKEN NEAR LE QUESNOY

A NEW ZEALAND BATTERY

IN OPEN WARFARE

more passable ground and fared better. On the approach of
a strong patrol under 2nd Lt. F. M. Evans of the centre
company a German post on the low grass bank, which
borders a belt of trees before the outer moat, ran back
through the beeches, and Evans' men, followed shortly afterwards by the remainder of "B" Company, occupied this bank
and pushed through the spinney to the edge of the moat. The
right company halted for a time in the open field about 100
yards before the bank. Here Averill, searching for the
companies with a Headquarters runner, found them. A
platoon (2nd Lt. P. A. Lummis) was brought up to the outer
grass bank, and Lummis with Averill and his runner went
forward to reconnoitre the approaches towards the island
rampart. Dropping into the moat and momentarily perplexed by the intricacy of the trees banks and outlying
bastions facing them, they presently espied towards their
right an angle between one of the bastions and a traverse
wall, where the masonry had been broken and in part knocked
down. Making for this, Lummis suddenly through a rift in
the fog caught sight of a German post still on the outer
grass bank. The enemy had not seen them. Our little
party crept up quietly and rushed the post, capturing a
machine gun and 6 prisoners. Lummis' platoon then occupied
this position, and the rest of the right company presently
came up from the open field and lined the outer bank.
They were not yet in touch with the centre company. The
smoke was still very dense, and it was impossible to see
beyond 10 or 15 yards. Up to this time our advance had
been practically immune from German artillery fire. Now,
however, field howitzers began to shell fairly heavily the
outer moat. Fortunately some of the shells fell on the
bastions among the German defenders, who forthwith put
up a number of light signals, and the enemy's artillery ceased.

These movements had brought our lines to the edge of
the fortifications. Could we penetrate them? Snipers and
machine gunners were still in some numbers on the bastions,
but no enemy post appeared to linger now in the broken
ground of the outer moat itself. The approaches towards
the island ramparts afforded admirable cover and reasonable
freedom of manoeuvre. Under Barrowclough's personal
directions the centre company deluged one of the outer
bastions with rifle grenades, the light trench mortars not
being for the moment available, and Evans' platoon clambered
up its wall by a scaling ladder and occupied it. From here

Evans himself, with 4 men and a Lewis gun went forward to
reconnoitre further.   They reached the obvious gap which
Averill and Lummis had seen, climbed some 3 feet of broken
steps on to the buttress of another outer bastion and then
scrambled through the trees on its narrow top towards an
inner bastion.

It was close on 9 a.m., and the fog and smoke were
lifting.   The explorers were discovered and fired on by a
machine gun post on their right flank from the top of a
projecting salient of the final rampart.   They jumped into
a shallow hole.   After a moment, on the machine gun's ceasing
fire, Evans tried to scale the steep side of the inner bastion.
He was immediately shot through the brain and rolled back
dead into the hole.   One of his men in trying to get the
Lewis gun into action against the machine gun was similarly
shot through the head and killed instantly.   The other 3 men
were pinned to this very inadequate shelter in the heart of
the fortifications for 6 hours with their dead companions.
The latter were subsequently buried close to where they had
fallen.

With the dispersal of the fog the German machine guns
became at once more active, firing from all along the inner
rampart.   A nest harassing "A" company from a copse in
their right rear was cleared up by the 1st Battalion, but all
three 4th Battalion companies were unable to achieve further
progress, and any movement was now extremely difficult.
The Battalion had already done more than was asked of it,
and with the fate of the town sealed by our successful
advance round its flanks Barrowclough was too seasoned and
competent a soldier to throw lives away in a "heroic" frontal
assault.

While for the moment his men regained touch with each
other, reorganised and confined themselves to reconnaissance
and returning hostile fire, the influence of propaganda on the
stubborn enemy was being tried elsewhere.   Shortly after
11 a.m. 3 captured Germans were sent by the 3rd Battalion
through the Landrecies Gate into the town to explain the
hopelessness of the garrison's position and to invite surrender.
There was no reply to the message, and sniping and machine
gun fire continued well into the afternoon from the ramparts
on all sides of the town.   The 2nd Battalion also from the
north sent forward one of their prisoners through the
Valenciennes Gate without result, and the 3rd Battalion
again (3 p.m.) sent 2 more Germans, who this time returned

within half an hour saying that the men were willing to surrender but that the officers refused. About the same time the following message was dropped by one of our aeroplanes:—

AN DEN KOMMANDANTEN DER GARNISON VON
LE QUESNOY:—

Die Stellung Le Quesnoy ist jetzt völlig eingeschlossen. Unsere Truppen sind weit östlich von der Stadt. Daher werden sie ausgefordert sich mit Ihrer Garnison zu ergeben. Die Garnison wird als ehrliche Kriegsgefangene behandelt werden.

DER KOMMANDEUR DER ENGLISCHEN TRUPPEN.[1]

No white flag, however, appeared on the ramparts in answer. Machine gun fire continued active, harassing both the investing troops and movement on all roads within range. The Maoris of the Pioneer Battalion, early set to work on improving communications, had been subjected all the forenoon to bursts of this long-range fire. Artillery officers anxious to move up guns and ammunition without the necessity of a long detour were continually, if not impatiently, seeking information as to the prospects of the town's early fall. Shortly after noon, therefore, Barrowclough decided while avoiding unwarranted risks to make another attempt.

The reserve company, "D" (Lt. C. W. Birch), was brought up to the outer grass bank. A section of light trench mortars (Lt. I. P. Grant) had by this time joined the riflemen. Their fire and a miniature barrage of rifle grenades cleared in turn each outlying bastion of a not very resolute enemy. On these commanding positions and on the well-marked transverse wall, whose gap earlier in the day had promised an approach to the interior fortifications, Barrowclough placed all his available Lewis guns, thus developing an intense covering fire on the top of the final rampart. The inner island bastions in their turn similarly bombarded, the mortars directed their fire on 2 prominent salients of the main rampart on one of which was posted the machine gun that had pinned the survivors of Evans' party since the early morning. Their fire and the mortar bombs, though many of the latter failed to explode, succeeded in driving the German posts temporarily off the salients into the caverns

---

1 To the Commander of the Garrison of Le Quesnoy:—
    The position of Le Quesnoy is now completely surrounded. Our troops are far east of the town. You are therefore requested to surrender with your garrison. The garrison will be treated as honourable prisoners of war.
    The Commander of the British Troops.

under the wall on the town side. The German officers might stem the insidious influence of the 3rd Battalion's propaganda inside the town, but the 4th Battalion's fire had now cleared the ramparts and was powerful enough to prevent all but handfuls of the enemy from reoccupying them.

By 2.30 p.m. indeed the hostile machine guns gave practically no sign, and very little opposition was offered to our parties, mostly of the right company, in the broken outer moat and about the first line of the island bastions. The top of the main rampart appeared deserted. Barrowclough accordingly ordered Averill to take a Lewis gun section of the centre company and reconnoitre the inner line of island walls. Carrying the scaling ladder with them the party climbed without difficulty one of the outer bastions, pulled the ladder up after them, walked down an easy grassy slope on the far side unmolested, and along an 8-foot high bank to the second line of demilunettes. Scaling this also successfully they were now able to view the sheer face of the final rampart. The Lewis gun team was placed in a commanding position well screened by trees, whence they could provide directly covering fire. Averill himself picking up the ladder scrambled down the far side of the inner island bastion to a third somewhat ill-defined wall studded with trees. Here he met 2nd Lts. Lummis and E. P. Canavan who with a dozen men had reached the same spot from the obvious gap in the transverse wall. They were now on the western bank of the deep inner moat. The final rampart rose before them in an uncompromising cliff of red brick, completely unclimbable except at 1 spot. Here, midway between the 2 prominent and projecting salients, mentioned above, a narrow stone bridge, about a foot wide, spans the moat and is connected with the sluice-gate which controls the volume of the stream at the foot of the rampart. On the far side of the moat an inconsiderable ledge ran for some 10 yards along the side of the rampart to an arched opening which gives access to a stone stairway running up inside the rampart to the interior of the town. This opening had been blocked with timber by the faint-hearted enemy posts who had retreated from their isolated positions on the outer grass bank and the island ramparts. Only from the bridge could the 30-foot scaling ladder reach the top of the final wall.

After a careful scrutiny of this very unpromising problem Canavan followed by the others left the ill-defined wall and proceeded towards the sluice-gate bridge. Their approach was watched by a well-concealed German post which had returned to the top of the rampart. A shower of stick grenades fell about our party, causing no casualties but necessarily forcing them to drop the ladder and withdraw from their exposed position. They returned to the transverse wall to report in person to Lt.-Col. Barrowclough.

A council of war was at once held. To attempt to cross the knife-edge over the moat, rear the ladder against the wall in face of hostile resistance and mount 1 man at a time was at best a most hazardous enterprise. But it was obvious that here and here only was the wall assailable. Barrowclough therefore summoned Lt. Birch, the commander of the reserve company, and bade him detail a platoon to make a fresh attempt. The platoon would be divided into 3 parties, 1 to establish a footing at the top of the ladder, and the other 2 to seize the salients on either hand. Three or four men only would mount at a time owing to the flimsiness of the ladder. Birch detailed No. 14 platoon under 2nd Lt. H. W. Kerr, who selected 3 of his best men to climb the ladder with him. Averill was to accompany the party. The rest of the battalion waited by the transverse wall.

Everything that might help the scaling party in their desperate undertaking was done. A light trench mortar was brought well into the outlying ramparts, whence it poured in a brief sharp fusillade at the salients and the bombing post above the sluice-gate. The Lewis guns swept the whole of the parapet visible with heavy bursts of fire. Meanwhile Averill and Kerr were already working along the tree-covered bank to the edge of the inner moat. They picked up the ladder, and stepping on the knife-edge bridge in single file reached the sluice-gate. The whole place was ominously still but for the low gurgle of water in the moat below them. They hardly dared to hope that they would be left undisturbed by grenades. But no grenade fell from the empty silent rampart. Quietly they raised the ladder against the wall. It reached the top of the bricks with a foot to spare, resting against a 2-foot high grassy bank which crowned the rampart and prevented the projecting top of the ladder from being seen from the interior of the town. Two of the riflemen steadied the ladder on its insecure perch, and Averill started to mount it, telling the others that he would shout down to them from the top if all was quiet.

It was now about 4 p.m. Averill quickly reached the top of the brick-work, and stepped over the coping on to the grassy bank. Crouching behind it, he peered over. It was one of the most dramatic moments in the Division's history. There was an instant crashing through some brushwood on the far side, and Averill saw 2 Germans of the bombing post running off panic-stricken. He sent a revolver bullet after them. Kerr was now on the topmost rung. The 2 officers could see a pair of machine guns on the salient on their right pointing into the moat but abandoned. They stood up and walked over the top of the grass slope and down the other side towards the boulevard. They were greeted by a great jabbering of German. Kerr fired a shot at the man who appeared to be leader, but missed. The whole enemy party bolted at once into an underground cavern under the rampart.

By this time the remainder of the battalion were swarming up the ladder. They were led by Barrowclough himself, who took with him a signaller and signalling apparatus, in order to open communication with brigade headquarters from Le Quesnoy and establish the 4th Battalion's claim to the honour of the town's capture. The Germans recognising the *fait accompli* threw up the sponge, and some 15 minutes later the 2nd Rifles marched in through the Valenciennes Gate.

As the different bodies of our men passed up the various deserted streets to round up their prisoners, a door would open cautiously, a head of some civilian would peep out and immediately disappear again. In a few seconds the whole household would rush wildly into the streets, and in a few seconds more the whole street would be a tumultuous mass of indescribably excited townsfolk. The services of an English-speaking prisoner proved useful in extracting the numerous Germans who had sought refuge in the underground caverns below the wall and elsewhere. They were congregated in the Place d'Armes and sent back to the Divisional cage in batches of 50. Two or three houses had been fired by the enemy, and a large party of the prisoners was used to assist in extinguishing the flames. Others were employed in removing mines and booby-traps. The 2nd Battalion took in the northern outskirts of and in the town close on 200 prisoners, two 77-mm. guns, 3 mortars, and 27 machine guns. Their losses were 3 officers and 19 men killed, and 4 officers and 100 men wounded. The 4th Rifles lost 2 officers and a dozen men killed, and 40 men wounded. They captured 2 field guns, 8 mortars and 18 machine guns. In all some 700 prisoners were taken in Le Quesnoy itself.[1]

In the process of mopping up the town, the riflemen were at once assisted by civilians, eagerly indicating the lurking places of their late masters. They were also not a little embarrassed by the warmth of the welcome extended by the populace to their liberators. To the description given in the 4th Battalion diary nothing need be added:—"The civilian population gave the troops a wildly enthusiastic greeting, thrusting flowers cakes and flags upon the men. Old men and women, and not a few of the Mademoiselles pressed forward eager to shake hands with or embrace the Diggers." Within an hour of its fall the 4th Battalion cookers came steaming into the town.

At 11 a.m. the next morning an inevitable photograph was taken of the 4th Battalion formed up in the Square; "and then, preceded by the Mayor and Town Councillors and the band of the 2nd Battalion, the parade marched past the Brigadier and down a long lane of wildly applauding civilians across the ramparts and back to billets in Solesmes. There was not a vehicle in the transport but was flying the tricolour, and each platoon had its loads of flowers and flags and souvenirs from the delighted people."[2]

On the 10th President Poincaré paid an official visit, the New Zealanders forming a guard of honour on the Place d'Armes, and 4 days later General Hart and the Rifle Battalion commanders went back to Le Quesnoy from rest billets to receive a flag from the town and present in return a New Zealand flag.[3]

Shortly after the fall of Le Quesnoy the 2nd Brigade battalions marched up in the evening to Herbignies to obtain a short rest during the early part of the night before passing at dawn through the outposts of the 1st Brigade. Their advance was to be divided into bounds through the Mormal Forest, the first amounting to some 2 miles across a felled area mostly covered with dense fresh undergrowth. Here a road running north to Obies marked the western limits of

---

[1] The figure, 1000 in the Official Despatch, appears an over-estimate.

[2] In the same way when the 3rd Field Ambulance found the Hospital to have been left by the Germans in a filthy condition, "the Maire sent the Town Crier round for assistance, and a multitude of women children and boys appeared armed with rush brooms to clean the wards and rooms." The yards were later cleaned by prisoners.

[3] Local legends have already grown round the circumstances of the capture of Le Quesnoy. In Sept. 1919 an elderly quidnunc pointed out with assurance the tree which Averill's party had cut down against the rampart to effect the ascent.

2 tracts of virgin forest separated by a close jungle of
saplings.   On the road at each tract of forest was a
Forester's House.   This was the Black Line.   The second
bound, nearly a mile further east, was determined by a
road (the Yellow Line) which ran north to the village of
La Grande Rue across the whole front, and which delimited
the western edge of a final mass of virgin forest, stretching
unbroken, except for a well-marked clearing on the left
battalion sector, as far as the third objective (the Brown
Line) on the Bavai road, a mile and a half beyond the
second. Lastly, an exploitation objective was assigned on the
general line Pont sur Sambre—the western heights overlooking the Sambre—north of Hargnies (the Brown Dotted Line).
The reserve battalion of the 1st Brigade would safeguard the
northern flank, where the VI. Corps were not yet in line.
The 3 N.Z.F.A. brigades formed advanced guard artillery.
The 1st and 12th Batteries were ordered to give close
support to the right and left battalions respectively.   The
section of 60-pounders put at General Young's disposal was
instructed to come into action near Villereau on the morning
of the 5th.   The advance would be made in conjunction with
the 5th Division on the right, who were relieving the 37th
that night (4th/5th November), and with the 62nd Division
on the left.   On the following night the New Zealanders
were to be relieved by the 42nd Division.

From Herbignies the attacking battalions (2nd Otago on
the right and 1st Canterbury[1] on the left) moved forward at
3.30 a.m. to the Wellingtons' positions, along the road on the
north-western edge of the Forest.   The assembly was complete at 4.30 a.m.   The early morning was fine, but about
9 a.m. heavy rain began which continued all day, adding
greatly to the troops' difficulties in the dense forest, and
making roads and tracks impassable for motor cyclist despatch riders and transport, and all but impassable for
artillery.

Both battalions attacked with 2 companies.   Each
battalion's front was about 1500 yards.   The barrage fell at
5.30 a.m. extending 200 yards north of the Divisional sector
to protect the exposed left flank.   Remaining on its
original line for half an hour, it then jumped 500 yards
eastwards resting there for 10 minutes. A further lift brought
it another 500 yards forward where it played for 10 minutes
and then died away.

1   Major Stitt, vice Lt.-Col. Row, on liaison duties.

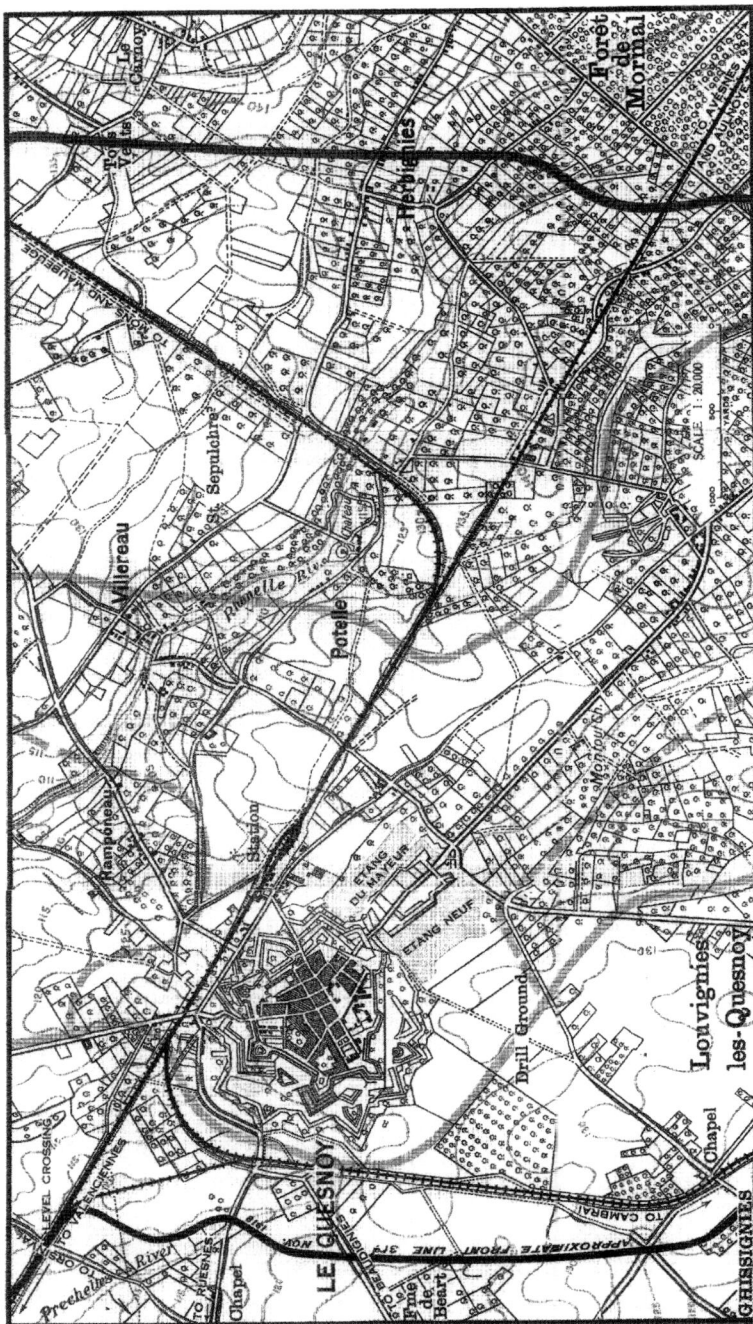

Forêt de Mormal

Herbignies

Le Carnoy

Tous les Vents

Le

St. Sepulchre

Villereau

Potelle

Rampouteau

Station

ETANG MAYEUR

ETANG NEUF

Montjoie

Louvignies les-Quesnoy

Drill Ground

Chapel

LE QUESNOY

GHISSIGNIES

Preche River

Chapel

Fond de Beart

APPROXIMATE FRONT LINE 3rd NOV.

SCALE 1: 20,000

Le Quesnoy

43

[Copyright

On the right 2nd Otago pushed forward rapidly to within half a mile of their first objective on the fringe of the southern tract of virgin forest. There, however, the Forester's House at an important cross-roads was held strongly, and the enemy had pushed machine guns some 200 yards down the road westwards. These machine guns were driven in, and Otago made ground steadily toward the main position where a crater near the House, the trees on each side of it, and rising ground beyond formed very strong positions. They were held by a considerable German rear guard. Here about 7 a.m. an aeroplane, hovering low over the tree-tops, saw little khaki figures making towards the House. The immediate approach to the enemy's defences offered little cover, and his resistance showed no sign of wavering. Speedier results in the long run were more likely to be obtained by a flank attack through the Forest supported by fire from in front. The extreme density of the brushwood and forest about the House made a joint operation impossible.

The first attempt to surround the enemy was made by the right company, but when within 50 yards of the position they were noticed and came under fire. The officer in command of the patrol and a man were killed. From this direction the road and a considerable stretch of bare sward had to be crossed at the closest of ranges in a final assault, and now that no surprise could be looked for, the effort of the right company was suspended. It was decided instead to capture the position from the left. A fresh barrage was arranged. Two platoons, making a wide flanking movement, pushed through the thickets and worked round the rear. When about 80 yards away the officer commanding the platoons was also killed by a sniper. But the enemy, now intensely nervous about his flanks and seeing his escape menaced, was satisfied with having checked our advance. Just before the House was rushed, its garrison fled through the trees too precipitately to take their machine guns with them. In the rest of the defences 2 machine guns and 30 prisoners were captured. It was now 11 a.m. The companies reorganised and went forward towards the second objective. Owing to the check at this southern Forester's House 1st Canterbury on the left had passed 2nd Otago on the Obies road. From this point on, however, Canterbury in their turn had heavy fighting in the wet forest, and Otago meeting practically no opposition, overtook and outdistanced them, and secured a

43

lead which they were to retain for the rest of the day. They reached the second objective without delay.

It had been proposed that on it the support battalions should pass through. As resistance, however, now appeared broken, 2nd Otago continued the advance, and 1st Otago followed behind them with a special charge of protecting their right. Troops of the latter battalion, deprived of the excitement of the pursuit that made amends for hardships, had nevertheless the satisfaction of coming across a small German nest and capturing it.

2nd Otago were by this time ahead not only of 1st Canterbury but also of the 5th Division, and additional precautions were taken to safeguard the right flank on the southern edge of the Forest. One of the support companies was brought up for this purpose, and the reserve company and attached machine gunners followed it. The advance from the La Grande Rue road (the Yellow Line) into the final mass of forest was resumed at 1.30 p.m. It was well that precautions had been taken on the right, for whereas the centre and left company moved on at first with little opposition, the flank guard company encountered from the outset heavy machine gun fire and determined resistance.

In this last battle, however, the dash and skill of Otago were not overshadowed by that unlucky star which had frustrated the heroism of the regiment's first essays in warfare on Gallipoli. The more open nature of this part of the Forest gave opportunity for manoeuvre, and each centre of resistance on its fringe was broken in turn. Like the other battalions engaged in these last 2 stirring days, 2nd Otago could record many incidents of epic prowess. Thus Sergt. L. R. Dickinson, M.M., had already during the action led a charge against an enemy position, capturing 25 prisoners and leaving many dead on the field. At this stage, noticing a large party out in the open, and not being sure as to their identity, he went out alone, to find that they were Germans. They opened fire and wounded him severely, but he returned to fetch a Lewis gun, and with it he dispersed the party. Pte. S. A. Noble, who was on the flank, saw through the trees a group of enemy 200 yards ahead. Running from tree to tree he came close enough to rush the party, capturing an officer and several men. At another point, where a well-posted machine gun checked advance, Cpl. E. Oxenbury took command of a Lewis gun section and by skilful manoeuvring brought fire to bear on the flank. He

then went back to his own infantry section and under cover of
the Lewis gun advanced to within rushing distance of the
German post, being all the time under heavy fire. Four of
his men were killed on the way, but Oxenbury and the
remainder rushed forward unhesitatingly, captured the gun,
and killed or wounded the crew. The centre and left
companies encountered little resistance till some 200 yards
from the Bavai road. Here a strong enemy position inside
the eastern edge of the Forest was cleared under cover of
Lewis gun and rifle fire. The defenders were mostly killed
or taken prisoners, 40 men surrendering under a white flag,
and the remainder were driven out of the Forest. The Bavai
road (the Brown Line) was reached at 3.45 p.m., and now
that the machine and Lewis gunners had at last clear fields
of fire, they inflicted heavy casualties on German parties
retiring across the fields towards the Sambre. Pickets
were established along the road. Neither of the flank
units was yet in line. The necessary defensive measures
were taken, and the approaches on the southern extremity
of the Forest were guarded by outposts half a mile clear of
it down the La Haute Rue road.

1st Canterbury on the left had at the outset met slight
opposition. The general direction of the enemy's retirement
was towards the north-east, and as the German rearguards
withdrew before 2nd Otago they crossed the front of Canterbury, whose Lewis guns secured not a few victims in parties
exposing themselves in the rides and tracks of the bush.
At 8.30 a.m. Canterbury was approaching the first objective
on the northern tract of forest. There round the northern
Forester's House the Germans were in force with several
machine guns. As with Otago, a direct approach could be
forced only with losses, but here there were greater facilities
for conjoint operations by both companies. About 9 a.m.
these had manoeuvred round on either flank and turned the
position. Five machine guns, a mortar and a considerable
number of prisoners were captured. The VI. Corps were
now over a mile in rear on the left, and Otago was for the
moment checked on the right, but the 1st Canterbury patrols
pushed resolutely into the depths of the unfelled forest.
Now fighting became much harder. The density of the trees
made connection between patrols a matter of the utmost
difficulty, and prevented the use of machine guns. 1st
Canterbury had to fight from tree to tree against a tenacious
defence, and it was now that their necessarily less rapid

progress enabled Otago to forge ahead   By 10 a.m.
battalion headquarters were established in the Forester's
House which about the same time came under minenwerfer
fire.   At noon it was subjected to an intense bombardment
by heavy and medium howitzers.   The support companies
then moving forward over some low ground west of the
House were caught in the outer fringe of the storm but
rushed up the slope and escaped severe casualties.   Gradually
clearing the Forest and driving the Germans before them,
the companies at length reached the La Grande Rue road.

In the latter part of this bound progress had been less
arduous, and the troops had set their hearts on pushing
further than the objective originally allotted them.   They
therefore entered the main mass of the Forest, penetrated
over half a mile and about 3 p.m. reached the edge of the
well-defined clearing.   Up to this time they had captured
150 prisoners, 16 machine guns, and a mortar.   In endeavouring to force the clearing, considerable opposition was met
from machine guns, and at length 2nd Canterbury[1] prevailed on the leading troops to stand fast and allow them to
pass through.

The 2nd Canterbury companies had been guarding the
left flank on the northern fringe of the Forest, and some time
transpired before they were assembled.   Without waiting
for the infantry the attached machine gun section under Lt.
Curtis appears to have pushed forward on their own
initiative, worked to the right and reached the Bavai road,
where they secured excellent shooting at enemy machine
guns and infantry.   In the meantime orders were received
that, in view of the forthcoming relief, no further advance
should be made after 4 p.m.   Exercising, however, the dis-
cretion given to the commander on the spot, the O.C. 2nd
Canterbury decided to make the Bavai road.   It was not
till close on dusk that his companies were able to move
forward.   By that time the Germans had withdrawn from
the clearing, which was crossed without trouble.   The
pouring rain, the blackness of the night, the dark dense wood
and thickets were in themselves very arduous obstacles.   By
9.30 p.m., however, the right had cleared the Forest and were
on the Bavai road with the enemy some 300 yards away
The left company also reached the road and established a
post on it, but a considerable pocket of the enemy still held
out with machine guns and mortars in the north-eastern

1   Major Wilson, vice Lt.-Col. Stewart, in England on duty.

corner of the Forest. Before dawn, 6th November, these had retreated into the open country eastwards, and the relieving Lancashire troops were able to form up on the Bavai road for the continuation of the advance. The brigade casualties had been remarkably slight. In all 2 officers and 18 men were killed, 5 officers and 130 men wounded.

Meanwhile 2nd Auckland,[1] who had spent the night in Villereau, successfully fulfilled their mission by picketing a series of heights on the left flank of the advance along a distance of 2 miles. For a short time they were troubled by German artillery, and there was an exchange of long-range machine gun fire, but no close contact was gained with the enemy who could be seen northwards on the VI. Corps front entering the houses and talking with the civilians. At midnight, 5th/6th November, these 3 battalions, 2nd Otago, 2nd Canterbury and 2nd Auckland, the last New Zealand infantry to be in the line, together with the support troops of the 2nd Brigade began to be relieved by the 42nd Division.

The role of the artillery was not yet completed. During the day several batteries had with immense exertions reached the western edge of the Forest. The 1st and 12th Batteries and the 2nd (Army) Brigade were detailed to support the 42nd Division's advance on the 6th and take part in the covering barrage. It was again a morning of heavy rain. The attacking troops, already exhausted by their long and trying march during the night, endured great hardships and encountered strong enemy opposition. The New Zealand batteries moving forward along the mined roads through the Forest were faced by difficulties of country that might have daunted even the most resolute. A bridge had been already blown up on the only serviceable road. A temporary structure of pick-handles and branches was improvised by 2nd Lt. C. S. Beilby of the Engineers and by the gunners, and meantime an inconceivably rough track through a forest clearing just served the advanced sections of the 2nd and 6th Batteries so that they might follow the infantry. By midday the remainder of the 6th Battery was over the bridge. One wagon capsised into the stream, and irretrievably damaged the makeshift crossing. But by the evening the New Zealand gunners and pioneers of the 42nd Division had succeeded in making a more substantial bridge. Two more wagons went over the side, but using partly this bridge and partly the track in the clearing the remainder of the

1 Major Sinel, vice Lt.-Col. S. S. Allen, on leave.

2nd (Army) Brigade had come into action about La Haute Rue by 7 p.m. Their performance was a supremely high instance of determination. In his report on the operations the commander of the 42nd Divisional brigade to which the New Zealand gunners were attached writes:—"The N.Z.F.A. also overcame very serious obstacles and evoked admiration for the way in which they did their work."

On the following day the 9th Battery, losing touch with the group under which they were working, pushed as far as the outskirts of Hautmont south-west of Maubeuge. The 1st and 3rd Artillery Brigades followed over the Bavai road, reaching the high ground north of the Sambre and carrying out a little harassing fire. The 2nd (Army) Brigade came into reserve. On the following day the 1st Artillery Brigade moved near Boussières, and on 9th November the 3rd Brigade went into billets at Hautmont. On that day the Corps line ran south of Maubeuge, and Maubeuge itself fell to the VI. Corps.

The advance of the VI. Corps towards the south-east was now beginning to squeeze out the IV. Corps. The former Corps were ordered therefore on the 9th to take over the command of the whole Army front, the IV. Corps becoming responsible for the defence of the Avesnes-Maubeuge-Mons road. On the 11th the New Zealand batteries moved back to Villereau towards the Divisional area.

The result of the brilliant and final victory of the 4th and succeeding days was to break once for all German resistance. Rawlinson and the French by their advance on the right had turned the pivot of resistance on the Sambre. Opposition had been shown to the First Army on the 5th and 6th, but by the 9th the enemy was in forced retreat along the front of the attack and to the extreme northern limit of the British sector, where the Fifth Army captured Tournai and the Second Army crossed the Scheldt and reached Renaix. On 10th November, with cavalry and cyclists preceding the infantry, the advance of the 5 British Armies had continued, reaching the environs of Grammont and Ath. In the early morning of the 11th the Canadians had captured Mons. "The enemy was capable neither of accepting nor refusing battle. The utter confusion of his troops, the state of his railways congested with abandoned trains, the capture of huge quantities of rolling stock and material, all showed that our attack had been decisive. It had been followed on the north by the evacuation of the Tournai salient and to the south, where the French forces had pushed forward with us, by a rapid and costly withdrawal to the line of the Meuse. The strategic plan of the Allies had been realised with a completeness rarely seen in war. When the armistice was signed by the enemy, his defensive powers had already been definitely destroyed. A continuation of hostilities could only have meant disaster to the German Armies and the armed invasion of Germany."[1]

Together with the Division and the Otago Mounted Rifles, the Cyclists[2] also had since August been engaged in the British offensive partly with the III. Corps (temporarily commanded by General Godley) but mainly with the XXII. Corps. On occasion they had experienced hard fighting. In this last battle also they took an active part, and one of their companies was actually in the outpost line near Givry when hostilities ceased.

If the Division felt some regret that this interesting experience was denied them, they had every reason to feel satisfaction with the result of their 2 days' operations. In their last action they had surpassed even their own high standard. They had seized all objectives assigned, and had driven a deep wedge with unrivalled rapidity into the German line. The passage of the Mormal Forest on the 5th under conditions of aggravated difficulty was in itself a notable performance; and, judged by material gains, the operations on the 4th were the most successful of all the Division's actions during the war. On that day they had advanced 6 miles, capturing Le Quesnoy Ramponeau Villereau Potelle and Herbignies with nearly 2,000 prisoners, 60 field guns, many complete with gunners drivers and horses, and hundreds of machine guns. The German Staff professed a belief in the deterioration of their enemies' morale. They were never more mistaken. The spirit animating the British Armies was of the highest. The élan displayed by every arm and every unit of the New Zealand Division received recognition in a unique order issued by General Russell on the 8th in Le Quesnoy:—"The Divisional Commander wishes to express to all ranks his appreciation of their work during the past fortnight's operations. At no time has the Division fought with more spirit and determination, nor have its efforts at any time been crowned with greater success. The Divisional Commander is convinced that the results achieved are due to the determination of every individual to do his utmost towards the common end."

1 Official Despatch.
2 Since 28th Sept. 1918 designated the New Zealand Cyclist Battalion.

CHAPTER XVII

CONCLUSION

On 11th November the Division for the most part was concentrated in the Corps rear area at Beauvois and Fontaine. The artillery was preparing to move back through Villereau to Le Quesnoy. The Engineers and Tunnellers, still in the forward areas about Le Quesnoy, were building bridges, repairing roads and erecting baths and laundries.

The telegraph message from the Corps announcing the Armistice was in these terms:—"Following from Third Army begins aaa Hostilities will ceases at 11.00 hours to-day November 11th aaa Troops will stand fast on line reached at that hour which will be reported by wire to Third Army aaa Defensive precautions will be maintained aaa There will be no intercourse of any description with the enemy until the receipt of instructions from Army Headquarters aaa Further instructions will follow aaa Advise all concerned aaa

IV. Corps

Time 0800 hours"

The news was received by the Division and by the Armies generally in a matter of fact way, totally devoid of any demonstration of emotion. A Divisional Service of Thanksgiving was held on 14th November.

It is interesting to note the composition of the Division at this date (11th November) and compare it with that of March 1916:

HEADQUARTERS

General Officer Commanding—Major-Gen. Sir A. H. Russell. K.C.B. K.C.M.G.

Aides-de-Camp—Capt. R. E. W. Riddiford, M.C.,[1] Lt. A. T. Williams

General Staff Officer, 1st Grade—Lt.-Col. H. M. Wilson, D.S.O., (British) Rifle Brigade[2]

General Staff Officer, 2nd Grade—Major H. M. W. Richardson, D.S.O., M.C., N.Z.S.C.[3]

General Staff Officer, 3rd Grade—Major O. Opie, R.N.Z.A.

A.A. and Q.M.G.—Lt.-Col. H. E. Avery, D.S.O., N.Z S.C.

D.A.A.G.—Major W. L. Robinson, N.Z.S.C.[4]

D.A.Q.M.G.—Capt. (Temp. Major) A. S. Muir

Intelligence Officer—Capt. S. Cory Wright, M.C.

[1] Died February 1919.
[2] Rejoined British Army, April 1919.
[3] Vice Major Eastwood, rejoined British Army, Oct. 1918.
[4] Succeeded in December by Capt. C. W. Salmon, D.C.M., who in turn was succeeded in February by Major J. B. Le Mottee.

Musketry Officer—(No appointment)
A.D.M.S.—Col. D. J. McGavin, D.S.O.[1]
D.A.D.M.S.—Capt. (Temp. Major) F. W. Kemp, M.C.[2]
A.D.V.S.—Major (Temp. Lt.-Col.) H. A. Reid
D.A.D.O.S.—Lt. (Temp. Major) C. I. Gossage
A.P.M.—Major C. A. Herman
Courts Martial Officer—(No appointment)

DIVISIONAL FIELD ARTILLERY

Commander—Bt.-Col. (Temp. Brig.-Gen.) G. N. Johnston, C.M.G., D.S.O., R.A.
Brigade Major—Major R. Miles, D.S.O., M.C., R.N.Z.A.
Staff Captain—Major W. G. Stevens, R.N.Z.A.
Staff Officer for Reconaissance—Lt. R. S. Park, R.N.Z.A.
Divisional Trench Mortar Officer—Major C. H. G. Joplin
Divisional Artillery Gas Officer—Capt. F. S. Wilding
1st N.Z.F.A. Brigade—Lt.-Col. F. Symon, C.M.G., D.S.O., R.N.Z.A.
2nd (Army) N.Z.F.A. Brigade—Lt.-Col. C. Sommerville[3]
3rd N.Z.F.A. Brigade—Lt.-Col. R. S. McQuarrie, M.C.
D.A.C.—Lt.-Col. H. C. Glendining, D.S.O., N.Z.S.C.

2 Medium Trench Mortar Batteries

DIVISIONAL ENGINEERS

Commander—Lt.-Col. H. L. Bingay, R. E.[4]

3 Field Companies
Signal Company

1st NEW ZEALAND INFANTRY BRIGADE

Commander—Lt.-Col. (Temp. Brig.-Gen.) C. W. Melvill, C.M.G., D.S.O., N.Z.S.C.
Brigade Major—Major W. I. K. Jennings, N.Z.S.C.
Staff Captain—Capt. F. S. Varnham, M.C.[5]
Musketry Officer—(No appointment)
Intelligence Officer—Lt. C. G. H. Robinson, M.C.
Bombing Officer—Lt. N. V. Le Petit
Gas Officer—2nd Lt. L. J. Mark
Transport Officer—Lt. L. M. Dixon, M.C.

1st Bn., Auckland Regiment—Lt.-Col. W. W. Alderman, C.M.G., A.I.F. Staff
2nd Bn., Auckland Regiment—Lt.-Col. S. S. Allen, D.S.O.
1st Bn., Wellington Regiment—Lt.-Col. F. K. Turnbull, D.S.O., M.C.
2nd Bn., Wellington Regiment—Major (Temp. Lt.-Col.) W. F. Narbey

2nd NEW ZEALAND INFANTRY BRIGADE

Commander—Lt.Col. (Temp. Brig.-Gen.) R. Young, C.M.G., D.S.O.
Brigade Major—Capt. (Temp. Major) A. S. Falconer, M.C.
Staff Captain—Major J. E. Barton, N.Z.S.C.[6]
Musketry Officer—(No appointment)
Intelligence Officer—Capt. S. G. McDonald, M.C.
Bombing Officer—(No appointment)
Gas Officer—2nd Lt. E. F. B. Waters
Transport Officer—Capt. J. G. C. Wales, M.C.

[1] Succeeded by Lt.-Col. Murray in January.
[2] There had been several changes in this appointment. Major A. V. Short, M.C., Major R. H. Walton, Major K. MacCormick, D.S.O., holding it in succession.
[3] See p. 141.
[4] Succeeded by Major (now Lt.-Col.) L. M. Shera, M.C., in November.
[5] Vice Capt. Holderness, to England on duty in October.
[6] Succeeded by Capt. S. G. McDonald, M.C., in December.

1st Bn., Canterbury Regiment—Lt.-Col. R. A. Row, D.S.O.
2nd Bn., Canterbury Regiment—Lt.-Col. H. Stewart, D.S.O., M.C.[1]
1st Bn., Otago Regiment—Lt.-Col. A. B. Charters, C.M.G., D.S.O.[2]
2nd Bn., Otago Regiment—Lt.-Col. J. Hargest, D.S.O., M.C.

NEW ZEALAND RIFLE BRIGADE

Commander—Lt.-Col. (Temp. Brig.-Gen.) H. Hart, C.M.G., D.S.O.
Brigade Major—Major D. E. Bremner, M.C., N.Z.S.C.[3]
Staff Captain—Lt. (Temp. Capt.) E. Zeisler, M.C.[4]
Musketry Officer—(No appointment)
Intelligence Officer—Capt. H. E. Crosse, M.C.
Bombing Officer—2nd Lt. C. A. Stringer
Gas Officer—Lt. A. M. Goulding
Transport Officer—Lt. V. Marshall

1st Bn., Rifle Brigade—Lt.-Col. R. C. Allen, D.S.O.
2nd Bn., Rifle Brigade—Lt.-Col. L. H. Jardine, D.S.O., M.C.
3rd Bn., Rifle Brigade—Major (Temp. Lt.-Col.) G. W. Cockcroft
4th Bn., Rifle Brigade—Lt.-Col. R. St. J. Beere

N.Z. Maori (Pioneer) Battalion—Lt.-Col. G. C. Saxby, D.S.O.[5]

3 Light Trench Mortar Batteries

N.Z. Machine Gun Battalion—Lt.-Col. D. B. Blair, D.S.O., M.C., N.Z.S.C.[6]

Divisional Train N.Z.—Lt.-Col. F. W. Parker[7]

1st N.Z. Field Ambulance—Lt.-Col. G. Craig
2nd N.Z. Field Ambulance—Lt.-Col. D. N. W. Murray, D.S.O.
3rd N.Z. Field Ambulance—Lt.-Col. J. Hardie Neil[8]

1 Mobile Veterinary Section
1 Employment Company

It was arranged that the opening stages of the advance into Germany should be carried out by the Second and Fourth Armies under the senior Commanders, Generals Plumer and Rawlinson, and that at a later stage the frontier should be crossed and the Cologne bridgehead occupied by the Second Army with the II. VI. IX. and Canadian Corps and the 1st Cavalry Division. The IV. Corps itself was transferred to the Fourth Army on 14th November, but in order to give the New Zealand Division the privilege of entering Germany the New Zealanders were marked for eventual transference to the II. Corps.

On 28th November, the day when the leading British cavalry reached the German frontier, the Division began its

1 Succeeded on 4th December by Major (now Lt.-Col.) Stitt. On Lt.-Col. Row's proceeding to England on 20th December, Lt.-Col. Stitt was posted to 1st Canterbury, Major Wilson assuming command of the 2nd Bn.
2 Succeeded in January by Major Bishop.
3 Succeeded in December by Capt. Zeisler.
4 Succeeded in December by Capt. H. E. Crosse.
5 Died in November and succeeded by Major (now Lt.-Col.) W. O. Ennis, D.S.O.
6 Succeeded in December by Major J. B. Parks, M.C.
7 Vice Lt.-Col. Atkinson, invalided in September.
8 Succeeded by Lt.-Col. H. J. McLean in November.

FIRST STAGE OF THE MARCH TO GERMANY (SOLESMES)

H.R.H. The Prince of Wales inspects 2nd Otago

The Y.M.C.A.

long march from Beauvois.   The 37th Division, which had
so often fought at their side, were at the moment in billets in
Caudry and adjacent villages.   They extended a most
cordial farewell.   Many of their battalions lined the roads,
and some of their bands marched 3 miles with the New
Zealand infantry.   The evidence of comradeship shown by
this fine Division was keenly appreciated.

The march continued in stages through the remainder of
France and across Belgium.   In Bavai on 1st December,
H.M. the King, accompanied by H.R.H. the Prince of
Wales and H.R.H. Prince Albert, visited the Divisional area
and attended a 2nd Infantry Brigade Church Service in the
Bavai Church.   Maubeuge was reached on 3rd December,
Charleroi on 7th December.   From that day the Division's
moves were ordered direct by the Fourth Army.   It
marched past General Rawlinson on 11th December on the
outskirts of Namur.   Huy was passed on 12th December, the
day on which the 1st Cavalry Division crossed the Rhine.
On the 14th the Division passed once more after 9 months'
interval under command of the Second Army.   After a
march of some 150 miles from Beauvois, Verviers near the
German frontier was reached on 19th December.   Everywhere received with the utmost enthusiasm and hospitality,
the Division was particularly touched by the warmth of the
reception given in Verviers.   Bunting was displayed pro-
fusely, and streamers bearing messages of welcome were
suspended across the streets.   Troops who chanced to halt
in the town for the customary 10 minutes at 10 minutes to
the clock hour went on their way, men rifles horses and
wagons decorated with flags and flowers.

This friendliness on the part of the inhabitants, the
beautiful scenery of the Sambre Meuse and Vesdre valleys,
the historic associations of Liège Namur and Charleroi made
the march interesting and enjoyable.   Much of it was done
in vile weather on bad roads.   Not unmindful of the strain
and sacrifices endured for so many months, the High
Command had laid it down that the comfort of the troops
during the march was to be the first consideration.   Supply
difficulties were, however, inevitably considerable and for the
time insuperable, and many men were forced to retain worn
out boots, which at the moment it was impossible to exchange.
Nevertheless march discipline was extraordinarily good.   All
the way 2nd Otago had not a single march casualty.

In the Verviers district the Maori (Pioneer) Battalion was detained for despatch to England. The artillery and part of the Train continued by march route to Cologne, but the infantry and the other troops proceeded from the German frontier by rail. On 20th December, passing through silent expressionless crowds, 1st Canterbury at the head of the 2nd Brigade Group was the first New Zealand infantry unit to cross the pontoon bridge over the Rhine. The Division was billeted in various suburbs. Divisional Headquarters were at Leverkusen, the 1st Infantry Brigade Group at Leichlingen, the 2nd at Mülheim, the 3rd at Bensberg. The artillery arriving on the 26th were quartered in Deutz and Mülheim.

In these areas the New Zealanders formed the reserve Division of the II. Corps. Certain precautionary measures were taken against an outbreak by the civil population or an armed rising. The Engineers established dumps in connexion with the organisation of the "B" Line Defences, Cologne Bridgehead, and large infantry parties cut pickets in the forests as stakes for our barbed wire entanglements. Numerous guards were maintained for various purposes. Sight-seeing was encouraged. Educational work replaced military training. Discipline was good, only 1 serious case affecting the good name of the Division.

No effort was spared to expedite demobilization. Already at the end of December the 1914-15 class and drafts of married men were sent to England. The first regular draft left on 14th January 1919, and from 28th January onwards drafts, varying from 700 to 1000 all ranks, were despatched weekly. The last draft was sent on 25th March.

During this process it was necessary to maintain the Division on a footing which would enable it to go into action at short notice. Certain changes in organisation were introduced with this end in view. Measures, however, were adopted to avoid transfers of personnel and to preserve for purposes of record the identity of units until final disbandment.

The artillery and D.A.C. were accordingly reduced first to a 4-gun and then to a 2-gun basis, two 4-gun batteries being formed in each brigade. The infantry were organised into 2 brigades. The 2 battalions of each Territorial Regiment amalgamated. The 1st and 2nd, and the 3rd and 4th Battalions of the Rifle Brigade were reconstituted as 2 battalions. The Rifle Brigade Headquarters and the units affiliated to the Brigade Group were disbanded. The new A and B Battalions (Lt.-Col. R. C. Allen and Lt.-Col. Jardine) of the Rifle Brigade were attached to the 1st and 2nd Infantry Brigades respectively. Medium and light mortar batteries were disbanded, the personnel being absorbed into artillery and infantry units. At a further stage all infantry units were reduced to a single brigade group by the amalgamation of the Canterbury and Otago Battalions, of the Auckland and Wellington Battalions, and of the A and B Rifle Battalions into a North Island, South Island and Rifle Brigade Battalion respectively, each then dealing direct with Divisional Headquarters. The Headquarters of the infantry brigades were then disbanded. A similar procedure was adopted with the Machine Gun Battalion. The Engineers, the Ambulances, and the Divisional Train were disbanded by units. Animals were disposed of, mainly for despatch to the United Kingdom. Ordnance equipment and all stores were handed in to the Army. As units gradually amalgamated or disbanded, the billeting areas were evacuated for the incoming troops of the 2nd Division. In the middle of February the 1st Infantry Brigade moved from the Leichlingen to the Bensberg area. By 9th March the Division was concentrated at Mülheim. Divisional Artillery Headquarters, artillery brigades, batteries and the D.A.C. were broken up on 18th March. A week later saw the disbandment of Divisional Headquarters, Headquarters of the Engineers and the remaining Engineer company, the Divisional Signal Company, the 12 infantry battalions, the Machine Gun Battalion, the last remaining Ambulance, the Headquarters of the Divisional Train, and the 1 intact Train company. The Division's 3 years' history comes to an end on 25th March 1919.

General Russell had already been compelled by illhealth to leave the Division on 1st February, when command was assumed by General Napier Johnston. General Russell bade his troops farewell in a singularly felicitous letter:—

"On leaving the Division after 3½ years[1] of command I wish to thank all ranks for their loyal support and to congratulate them on the success obtained. In the line and in action at all times they have earned the respect of their adversaries and the good word of those who fought at their side.

[1] *i.e.* including his command of the old N.Z. and A. Division in Gallipoli and Egypt.

"With one exception each objective has been gained, and that exception added yet fresh laurels for tenacity and resolution in face of insuperable difficulties.

"There is no distinction between one unit and another, between one branch and another. All alike, including the Staff, have done their share, working for the common end and together have earned a reputation of which their country is proud.

"This is all to the good. Now a word as to the future, where fresh problems are in front of us. Successes as real, if less dramatic, will surely be ours. The effect will be less evident, because each will have his own zero hour, but the success will be as great, if we continue to be animated by the same spirit of each for all.

"In conclusion, I wish you all a safe return to New Zealand and every prosperity and happiness in the future."

The demobilisation of the other New Zealand units in Belgium and France not incorporated in the Division proceeded concurrently. The Stationary Hospital[1] had moved from Amiens to Hazebrouck in May 1917, and thence to Wisques near St. Omer in September 1917, and was disbanded in December 1918. The Headquarters of the XXII. Corps were now at Mons, and in or about Mons were the squadron of the Otago Mounted Rifles, the Cyclist Battalion and the 2nd (Area) Employment Company formed of New Zealanders in 1917 and attached to the XXII. Corps. In the same neighbourhood was the N.Z. Tunnelling Company, who had been engaged with their usual conspicuous success in bridge-building at Solesmes Pont-au-Sambre Maubeuge and elsewhere. The Light Railways Operating Company, long stationed at Poperinghe, had followed the advance of the Second Army and were now employed on broad-gauge lines. The 5 Depot Units of Supply,[2] on arrival at Rouen in 1916, had passed under the command of the Inspector General of Communications. No. 1 had gone to the neighbourhood of Boulogne in April 1917. In 1918 No. 2 (Capt. D. Radclyffe) was at Ham, where becoming involved in the retreat of the Fifth Army it rendered valuable services. In 1916 No. 3 had gone to Marseilles, No. 4 to Hesdin, No. 5 to Boulogne. At Boulogne the Field Butchery was also quartered, employed in general work at the Base Supply Depot. The Field Bakery remained at Rouen. The

1 Lt.-Col. C. T. H. Newton had succeeded Lt.-Col. O'Neill, December 1917.
2 p. 16.

Sanitary Section was at Renaix with the XV. Corps. There was a New Zealand Veterinary Section in the Calais Veterinary Hospital, a New Zealand section attached to G.H.Q. 3rd Echelon, Rouen, and a small New Zealand Pay Staff in the Base Paymaster's Office at Boulogne. Finally there was the New Zealand Infantry and General Base Depot, whose functions had been largely usurped by the Entrenching Group,[1] and which in November was moved from Etaples to Rouen and redesignated The New Zealand Reception Camp. All these troops were now brought over to N.Z.E.F. establishments in England to await repatriation on a general policy of priority by length of service.[2]

The financial policy agreed on between the British Government and all Overseas Dominions with regard to the maintenance of troops during the war provided for a payment by the respective Dominion Governments for rations, clothing, personal equipment, horses, guns and equipment at contract rates. The maintenance and replacement of equipment and the expenditure of ammunition in France were covered by a pro capita rate which varied in accordance with the amount of ammunition expended at different periods. If thus in the financial burden of the war New Zealand bore her fair share, the scale on which reinforcements were sent forward from the training camps in New Zealand to the base in England and the regularity with which their arrival might be counted on were alike the envy and despair of the other Dominions. Throughout the whole of the war they had been despatched month by month in the average proportion of 10% establishment for infantry, 5% for artillery and 3%- to 4% for other arms. Exclusive of Imperial reservists and of New Zealanders serving in the forces of the Mother Country and other Dominions, the total number of troops and nurses provided by New Zealand, out of a population of slightly over a million, for foreign service from the outbreak of war to the Armistice amounted to over 110,000. The aggregate of troops and nurses actually despatched overseas exceeded 100,000. Of these two-thirds had enlisted voluntarily.

On arrival in England reinforcements were normally retained for a further period of 9 weeks' training prior to being sent to the field. From an early date this training

---

1 p. 328. On Lt.-Col. Mitchell's relinquishing command, it was commanded successively by Capt. (Temp. Major) E. C. Dovey, N.Z.S.C., Lt.-Col. J. A. Mackenzie, C.M.G., Major G. H. Gray, M.C.

2 The Maori (Pioneer) Bn. only were repatriated as a Unit.

at the base in England had been given by New Zealand
officers and n.c.o.s. All New Zealand troops were administered directly by the General Officer Commanding N.Z.E.F.
Establishments in the United Kingdom, the responsibility of
the War Office being limited to movements of troops by sea
and rail and to the inspection of training in order to ensure
similarity of system to that obtaining in the British Army.

By the end of 1918 the number of New Zealand camps
and establishments in England had been considerably
augmented. In September 1917 the Rifle Brigade personnel
had been separated from the 4th Infantry Brigade Reserve
Camp at Sling[1] and had been quartered at Brocton.[2] The
artillery since the spring of 1917 were trained at Ewshot.[3]
At the end of 1916, owing to the large number of casualties
at the Somme and the limited facilities then available for
evacuating sick or wounded to New Zealand, it was found
that existing hospitals and convalescent institutions were
becoming congested. As a measure of relief a Discharge
Depot (Major W. Kay), was formed at Torquay, where to
provide employment educational work was organised by the
N.Z. Y.M.C.A. and a farm of 800 acres leased by the N.Z.E.F.
An Officers' Convalescent Home and a Nurses' Home had
been established at Brighton. The Commanders of the
other more important camps and depots at this time were:—

N.Z. Command Depot, Codford—Lt.-Col. G. C. Griffiths
N.Z. Engineer Reserve Depot, Christchurch—Lt.-Col. G. Barclay, V.D.
N.Z. Signal Reserve Depot, Stevenage—Lt. (Temp. Capt.) T. L. R.
    King, M.C.
N.Z. Machine Gun Res. Depot, Grantham—Major L. C. Chaytor, M.C.
N.Z. Medical Reserve Depot, Ewshot—Major A. W. Izard
No. 1 N.Z. General Hospital, Brockenhurst—Col. P. C. Fenwick, C.M.G.
No. 2 N.Z. General Hospital, Walton—Col. E. J. O'Neill, D.S.O.[4]
No. 3 N.Z. General Hospital, Codford—Lt.-Col. G. Home, O.B.E.
N.Z. Convalescent Hospital, Hornchurch—Lt.-Col. C. H. Tewsley, C.M.G.

As demobilisation proceeded, the smaller establishments
were gradually absorbed in the larger. Owing to a congestion caused by strikes and consequent suspension of
shipping a further camp at Sutton Coldfield (Lt.-Col. J. A.
Mackenzie) was established during the spring of 1919 to
accommodate surplus personnel.

Administration in England, dealing with a multitude of
diverse questions such as personnel supplies ordnance con-

1 Now commanded by Brig.-Gen. Stewart, succeeded in turn by Brig.-Gen.
Young, and Lt.-Col. Stitt.
2 Now commanded by Lt.-Col. Shepherd.
3 Now commanded by Lt.-Col. Falla, succeeded by Major R. G. Milligan.
4 Succeeded in January 1919 by Lt.-Col. Home, command of No. 3 Gen. Hosp.
being assumed by Major (Temp. Lt.-Col.) H. M. Buchanan.

tracts accounts health—probably in no Force was more attention paid, for example, to dental work—wills records trophies, presented a never-ending series of intricate problems the solution of which was made more difficult by absence of precedents. They were one and all, however, handled by Brig.-Gen. Richardson[1] with confident and easy mastery, and with regard to the interests of the New Zealand taxpayer and the New Zealand private soldier. His administration was specially distinguished by economy foresight accessibility. Of his many services not the least valuable perhaps was a passionate zeal for the cause of education generally in the Force, and for the training of disabled soldiers in particular.

It seems not out of place here to allude briefly to the eminent and loyal services rendered to the New Zealand Force as a whole by General Godley. These did not generally meet due appreciation, partly because on him fell the onus of licking the splendid but undisciplined raw material into shape, partly owing to certain characteristics of temperament. Men who never saw him repeated garbled gossip from the strenuous days of training in 1914-15. Ignorance and rancour over grievances found in him a natural target for detraction. He was at once too far removed from a general contact which would have dispelled preconceived prejudice, and also of too strong a personality to court or care for popularity. When he liked, no one could be more gracious with an exquisite finish of manners, but as a rule, disdaining to lower the dignity of arms by an affectation of a quasicivilian camaraderie, which his nature did not allow him to feel, he appeared to the ordinary man somewhat devoid of human sympathy, aloof, austere, ambitious. Constitutionally not robust, of somewhat highly strung nerves, he was actuated by a natural inclination to severity of criticism and by a soldier's stern conception of duty. As its Commander he laid sure

[1] p. 17. His chief Staff Officers were:—
A.Q.M.G—Lt.-Col. (Temp. Col.) G. T. Hall, C.M.G.
A.A.G.—Major (Temp. Lt.-Col.) J. Studholme, D.S.O.
D.A.Q.M.G.—Major (Temp. Lt.-Col.) T. H. Dawson, C.M.G.
D.M.S.—Col. C. M. Begg, C.B., C.M.G. (succeeded Col. W. H. Parkes, C.M.G., C.B.E., in December 1918, died February 1919, succeeded by Lt.-Col. B. Myers, C.M.G.)
Matron-in-Chief—Miss M. Thurston, R.R.C.
D.D.S.—Lt.-Col. J. R. Rishworth, M.B.E. (succeeded by Lt.-Col. T. A. Hunter, C.B.E.)
Staff Paymaster—Lt.-Col. (Temp. Col.) J. W. Hutchen, C.M.G.
A.D.O.S.—Lt.-Col. H. E. Pilkington, R.N.Z.A., previously A.D.O.S., XIX. Corps.
Officer i/c Records—Lt.-Col. N. Fitzherbert, C.M.G.
Headquarters were transferred to Bloomsbury Square in November 1917. In March 1919 Brig.-Gen. Richardson was recalled to New Zealand on duty and succeeded by Brig.-Gen. Melvill and he in turn by Brig.-Gen. Napier Johnston.

foundations for the Division's later successes.   In common
with others he was not given in the tragic campaign at
Gallipoli opportunities of proving his abilities.   In France
as a Corps Commander he won an extraordinary high
reputation.   His faculty for grasping the most intricate
questions in a few moments was quite exceptional.   The
esteem with which he was held by the Army Commanders
and at the War Office, and his own perfect tact secured a
ready consideration from the Imperial Authorities for all
requests put forward in the interests of the N.Z.E.F.   He
rarely, and never if time permitted, took any important step
without consulting General Russell and General Richardson.
Amid his pressing duties he guided gratuitously the policy
of the N.Z.E.F. with a firm and wise hand and with an
unselfish devotion which were fully recognised by all qualified
to judge.   His services to New Zealand and to the Expeditionary Force stand above controversy.

The following extract from his Farewell Message to the
N.Z.E.F. may be quoted :—

"It has been a great privilege—a privilege I have most
fully appreciated—to have not only raised and brought
from New Zealand such a force, but to have had the
honour of holding the command of it throughout the whole
period of the war. . . . .

"In Gallipoli, Egypt, Sinai, Palestine, France, Belgium,
and the United Kingdom you have taken your full share
of the burden and stress of this war, and you have earned,
I believe without exception, the highest regard of all those
under whom and with whom you have served.

"You will leave behind you a reputation for discipline,
fighting qualities, steadiness, resource, initiative, hard
work, and gentlemanly conduct of which both you and
New Zealand have every reason to be proud. . . . .

"My four years as General Officer Commanding the
Forces in New Zealand and still more my nearly five years'
experience as General Officer Commanding the N.Z.E.F.
have specially impressed me with the natural capacity of
the New Zealander.   New Zealand, I am convinced, is able
and is destined to play a part in the world out of all
proportion to her size and population."

During the unsettling conditions attendant on the period
of repatriation from the English Depots every possible
measure was taken to facilitate the return to civil life.   A
Compulsory Educational Scheme was set in operation aiming

at the development of citizenship and at practical training
in civilian pursuits. As early as March 1917 the New
Zealand Y.M.C.A. had inaugurated educational training in
the hospitals in England, particularly in Hornchurch. This
was followed by the establishment of a school for disabled
soldiers in August 1917 and by a system of voluntary and
at a later stage compulsory education in the summer of 1918,
in both command and training depots and on transports.[1]
Following on a conference held in March 1918, on the eve of
the German offensive, similar educational work had been
carried on in the Division by the N.Z. Y.M.C.A.

With the Armistice a comprehensive compulsory scheme,
continued on returning transports, was enforced under
military control for all ranks. The administrative[2] and
educational staffs were drawn from the N.Z.E.F. A special
grant of £50,000 was made by the New Zealand Government
to cover expenses. In addition, as a free gift from the
Dominion to her soldiers, 50 scholarships of a value of
between £175 and £250 per annum were allotted to selected
candidates. Facilities for higher education and advanced
vocational training were given in a liberal spirit. Though
now losing the direct control which had been in their hands
up to the cessation of hostilities, the N.Z. Y.M.C.A. gave the
most loyal co-operation. No record of the Division would be
complete without a tribute to their unstinted and most
efficient ministration to the material mental and moral needs
of the troops, whether in front line trenches or at the base.

Throughout this period also sports and athletics were
actively fostered. Even during hostilities it had been
found possible in France on occasion to play Rugby Football
both in the Division itself and against British and French
teams. In England depots had early developed all branches
of athletics. Now with the Armistice a Sports Committee
was formed in England (Major J. A. Cameron being
appointed Sports Officer) for the purpose of systematic
organisation. The more important successes may be
briefly summarised. Sergt. M. Loveday, M.M., won the
King's Prize at Bisley. The Rugby Team secured the
Inter-Services and Dominions Rugby Championship, thereby
gaining the King's Cup and the right of meeting the French

---

1 Education Officer, Capt. J. R. Kirk.
2 Director of Education: Lt.-Col. (Temp. Col.) H. Stewart, succeeded by Major
(Temp. Lt.-Col.) E. H. Northcroft. Assistant Directors: for England, Lt.-Col.
Northcroft, succeeded by Lt. (Temp. Major) W. R. Tuck; for Germany, Capt. (Temp.
Lt.-Col.) H. E. Barrowclough; for Transports, Capt. G. E. Archey; for Disabled
Soldiers, Lt. (Temp. Capt.) N. Bell.

Army. They played the final of the Championship on 16th
April, met and defeated the French in London on 19th April,
travelled to Swansea and on 21st April avenged the All
Blacks' reverse in 1906. Of the 40 games played they won
35, drew 3 and lost 2. In rowing Sergt. D. C. Hadfield, the
N.Z. Champion Amateur Sculler, had a series of unchequered
triumphs. The 8-oar crew were unsuccessful in the King's
Cup race at Henley and in the International Race promoted
by the Americans, but won the Invitation 8-oared race at
Marlow and the Inter-Allied race in Paris in May. On
the track Sergts. G. P. Keddell, J. Lindsay, D. D. Mason,
J. H. Wilson, and H. E. Wilton well upheld the prestige of
New Zealand athletics, and following on their successes in
the Army Championship held at Aldershot in August were
selected to represent the British Army in the Inter-Services
Championship Meeting in September.

No unit as large as a Division can engage in 3 years of all
but continuous active fighting without experience of the
vicissitudes of war. In any reasonable operation skilful
preparation and gallantry can as a rule achieve success, but
occasions arise when a combination of factors over which no
control can be exercised frustrates the most skilful preparations and the most consummate gallantry. On other
occasions misfortunes must be ascribed to other reasons. In
the Division's history the only failure in a major operation
was at Bellevue,[1] and even in minor actions the number of
instances where full objectives were not attained is extraordinarily small. Almost exclusively its record is one of
success, and the rare failures may be boldly faced. As in
this narrative scrupulous care has been taken to avoid
magnifying successes, so failures have not been unduly
glossed over. It may be safely claimed that no Division in
the Armies of the Empire can lay bare every aspect of its
life to critical scrutiny with more assurance of winning
respect.

To the very remarkable and outstanding qualities of its
Commander the Division owed an inestimable debt. A born
leader of men, with natural gifts for the military art which
fell little short of genius and were developed by study and
experience, General Russell speedily enhanced in France the
high reputation already won on Gallipoli. By personal
acceptance of danger, untiring application to his duties, and

[1] pp. 280 sqq.

A Contrast: D.H.Q. September 1918

And January 1919 (Leverkusen)

NEW ZEALAND SENTRIES ON THE RHINE

DEMOBILISATION: TRANSPORT AT MÜLHEIM

intense devotion to his officers' and men's interests he set an example which could not have been bettered and which reacted with the most stimulating effect on all who even for a few moments came into contact with him. The personification of well-directed energy, he was invariably abroad at an early hour and not infrequently surprised his subordinate commanders still asleep. Ruthless determination on his part to attack and keep on attacking the enemy never resulted in hasty and improvised enterprises. All operations were undertaken with the utmost skill, thoroughness and attention to detail. He had a lightning insight into tactical situations, and phases of crisis or obscurity were powerless to shake his resolution or ruffle his composure. A severe and discriminating critic, not lavish of eulogy, and a most sagacious judge of men, he penetrated bluff and pretence and dealt short shrift to incompetence. As in action he showed all the finest qualities of the soldier, so in administration and in questions affecting civil life in New Zealand, his policy was statesmanlike in its breadth of view and sanity. Not the least marked of his intellectual qualities was his capacity for taking pains. On submitting questions to him, a subordinate could be assured that instead of superficial investigation they would be examined with a fullness and thoroughness which traversed every detail and envisaged every difficulty. Patient to hear the views of others, he had an unusual gift for getting down to bed-rock and for summing up and clarifying a discussion in a brief but illuminating sentence. Meeting all the insistent calls on his attention, he found relaxation in a study of ancient and modern thought, of history, economics and French literature. In character absolutely sincere, transparently honest, devoid of the slightest trace of self-seeking, he devoted his whole mind and thought to the common cause. Implacably hard and intent on efficiency he was at the same time frank straightforward and genial with a singular charm of candour and manliness. Not merely by position but by abilities and character he was far and away the dominating personality in the Division. Some measure of his prestige may be gathered from the indisputable fact that throughout the whole of the Division's history no whisper of criticism was ever raised against General Russell. There was indeed not an officer or man but felt unbounded confidence in and unlimited regard for their Commander. In his work he was supported by a highly competent Staff and by senior officers of proved merit.

The junior officers and the non-commissioned officers constituted one of the Division's strongest assets. Towards the end of the war officers were recruited almost exclusively from the ranks. Naturally mature for their years, trained in the stern school of practical experience, and privileged to take military courses in France and England, they possessed both personality and knowledge of their work on which company and battalion commanders could rely as on a rock.

From a young and virile people, predominantly agricultural, highly intelligent, of unusually fine physique, a race of horsemen farmers musterers athletes and Rugby footballers, it was only to be expected that its manhood, already subject to a compulsory system of military training, should yield sterling material for the purpose of war.

Such expectations were to prove not misplaced. No Army had a monopoly of gallantry and fortitude, which shone conspicuously against the dark background of battle both among our enemies and allies. Some few instances of New Zealand prowess have been given in these pages, many others are on record, many are known only to the dead, who fell as they performed them. But the unusually successful history of the Division presupposes the existence of other characteristics. Of these perhaps the most distinctive were aggressiveness resourcefulness and thoroughness. One and all were engrossed in a vigorous prosecution of the war. To this all other interests, such as leave or sport, were subservient. By its nature this history is mainly a record of the infantry, the drudge and queen of the battle, and of the other fighting arms, but the same ready initiative and the same earnest concentration on work were not less marked in the other branches of the service, in the brilliantly conducted administrative offices, the Medical and Veterinary Corps, Engineers, Train, Chaplains' Department, and all technical services. These qualities formed a central force of dynamic and unflagging energy permeating the whole body.

With a highly developed sense of esprit de corps, the troops generally impressed the outsider as stern dour and grim. On the march the cheerful and spontaneous gaiety of the English regiments was conspicuous by its absence. The undemonstrative reception of battalions returning after notable achievements suggested to an English observer the not inapt name of "The Silent Division." Characteristic too was a deep-rooted aversion to anything savouring of ostentation and "swank." From this and from the democratic traditions of national life arose a strenuously combatted inability, shared with other overseas troops, to achieve that polished finish in saluting, which is generally regarded as a hall-mark of military discipline. Yet throughout the war discipline both in the field and at the bases was extremely good, and was generally well maintained in England even under the irksome delays of repatriation. Countless unsought tributes were given to the good behaviour of New Zealanders in all places and under all circumstances, and while soliditary was preferred to superficial smartness, the Division practised in a very marked degree the virtues of precision orderliness and cleanliness whether in billets transport lines or trenches. In particular, the inspections held by General Russell in the last months of the war during periods of "reserve" would not have been out of place in the proudest barrack-square in England for minute perfection of equipment and for steadiness.

Innumerable references could be made to non-expert appreciation.[1] The tribute of a high authority cited by General Russell on his return to New Zealand indicated the measure of the regard in which the Division was held in France: "I think you may always claim that the Imperial soldier would sooner fight alongside the New Zealand Division or hand over to them or take over from them than from any other troops in the field."

On the same occasion as elsewhere General Russell himself bore witness to his troops: "They say a General leads his men. He does not really lead them, but he pushes them from behind, and when he has good boys like the New Zealanders he has no need to push them at all. He presses the button, and away they go, and sometimes they go too far."

In the German Intelligence captured at Hébuterne[2] occurs an appreciation which the events of the following months must have given the enemy no cause to modify:—"A particularly good assault Division. Its characteristics are a very strongly developed individual self-confidence or enterprise, characteristic of the colonial British, and a specially pronounced hatred of the Germans. The Division prides itself on taking few prisoners. A captured officer taken at the end of April did not hesitate to boast[3] of this while in the

1 Cf. a generous tribute paid by F. M. Cutlack, one of the Australian official correspondents, in *"The Australians"* p. 18, "The New Zealand Division, probably the all-round best and strongest Division in the British Army."
2 p. 402.
3 p. 383. Undue importance must not be attached to this remark.

prisoners' cage.   It is improbable that the New Zealand
Division, which is qualitatively and quantitatively much
stronger than the —th Division, should have taken over
only the same small sector occupied by the latter. . . . . .''
     With the scenes of the Division's earlier actions,
Armentières, Flers and the slopes in its vicinity, with Sailly
Ploegsteert Messines Basseville Gravenstafel Bellevue and
the Ypres ridges the name of New Zealand will be for all
time associated.   The epic fighting in 1918 is succintly
reviewed by General Harper, Commander of the IV. Corps,
in a farewell letter to General Russell, which may fittingly
close this record :—

     ''As the New Zealand Division is leaving the IV. Corps,
I desire to place on record my appreciation of the
valuable services they have rendered, and to thank all
ranks for the magnificent fighting qualities which they
have invariably displayed.
     ''The Division joined the IV. Corps at a critical time
on the 26th March, 1918, when it completely checked the
enemy's advance at Beaumont-Hamel and Colincamps,
and thus closed the gap between the IV. and V. Corps.
By a brilliant stroke it drove the enemy from the commanding ground at La Signy Farm and gained observation over the enemy's lines, which greatly assisted in
his defeat on the 5th April, 1918, when he made his last
and final effort to break our front.   Throughout the
summer the Division held portions of the Corps front
with but a short interval of rest.   During this period I
never had the least anxiety about the security of this
portion of the front; on the other hand, by carefully conceived and well executed raids the enemy was given
little respite, and identifications were procured whenever
required—in this connection I deplore the loss of that
brave man, Sergt. Travis, V.C.
     ''It was the ascendancy gained by this Division over the
enemy that compelled him to evacuate the ground about
Rossignol Wood.
     ''At the commencement of the great attack on 21st
August, 1918, only a minor part was allotted to the
Division, but subsequently on the night of 23rd August
the Division was ordered to attack, and swept the enemy
from Grévillers, Loupart Wood, and Biefvillers, and
gained the outskirts of Bapaume.   Stubborn fighting

was experienced around Bapaume, but eventually the enemy was overcome and pushed back to the East.

"From 24th August till 14th September the Division was constantly engaged, and drove the enemy back from Bapaume to the high ground west of Gouzeaucourt, where the heavy fighting occurred at African Trench.

"After a short period of rest the Division was put in again on 29th September to complete the capture of Welsh Ridge and to gain the crossings over the Canal de l'Escaut. A night advance over difficult country, intersected by the trenches and wire of the Hindenburg Line, was brilliantly carried out and entirely successful, and resulted in the capture of over 1000 prisoners and over 40 guns. On the 1st October the Division captured Crèvecoeur against strong opposition, and held it in spite of heavy shelling and several counter-attacks throughout the subsequent days, until the great attack on 8th October, when the Division broke through the northern portion of the strongly organised Masnières Line, and penetrated far into the enemy's line at Esnes and Haucourt.

"Going out to rest on the 12th October, the Division was again in the line on 23rd October and drove the enemy back from the outskirts of Romeries to Le Quesnoy. Finally on the 4th November the Division by an attack which did much to decide the finish of the war forced the surrender of the fortress of Le Quesnoy and drove the enemy back through the Forest of Mormal, the total captures of the IV. Corps on that day amounting to 3,500 prisoners and some 70 guns.

"During the period the New Zealand Division has been in the IV. Corps, they have captured from the enemy 287 officers and 8745 other ranks, 145 guns, 1419 machine guns and 3 tanks, besides much other material.

"The continuous successes enumerated above constitute a record of which the Division may well be proud. It is a record which I may safely say has been unsurpassed in the final series of attacks which led to the enemy's sueing for peace.

"In conclusion I wish to thank you and your Staff for the willing support which you have invariably given and the helpfulness shown in all circumstances.

"I send every man of the Division my heartfelt good wishes for the future."

Index

INDEX III

PERSONS AND PLACES

(Final or highest ranks are cited. In the verification of these and of initials much help has been given me by Lt.-Col. J. W. Hutchen and the staff of the War Accounts and Records Office, Wellington).

Ecaillon, R., 543, 550 sqq., 561, 564
Ecclesfield, 2nd Lt. R. C., 522
Eecke, 274
Egypt, ch. I pass., 607
El Ferdan, 3, 4
Ellery, Sergt. F., 484
Ellingham, 2nd Lt. E. S., 483
Ellmers, Cpl. R., 348
Emmerson, Rflmn. J., 152, 153
Engelbelmer, 340. 352, 356, 371
Ennis, Lt.-Col. W. O., 604
Epehy, 473, 479
Epernay, 380
Epsom, 17
Erquinghem, 26, 516
Erzerum, 11
Esnes, 502, 508, 518 sqq., 541, 619
Esson, Col. J. J., 16, 17
Estaires, 24, 58, 124, 139, 140, 376
Etaples, 16, 329, 609
Euston Junction (Colincamps), 348 sqq., 358
Evans, Lt.-Col. C. H. S., 59, 380
Evans, 2nd Lt. F. M., 587 sqq.
Evans, Major J., 505 sqq.
Ewshot, 610

Factory Corner, 69, 76, 82, 86, 87, 98 sqq.
Factory Farm, 185
Fairbrother, Sergt. R. E., 112
Fairweather, Pte. R., 432
Falconer, Major A. S., 60, 324, 330, 603
Falla, Lt.-Col. N. S., 15, 25, 141, 224, 253, 330, 374, 542, 543, 547, 563, 581, 610
Fanny's Farm, 197, 199
Favreuil, 435, 437 sqq., 449, 489
Fawcett, Capt. E. J., 286
Fenwick, Col. P. S., 19, 610
Ferguson, Sergt. R. L., 574
Fergusson, Sergt. F. C., 549
Ferme de Beart, 554, 556 sqq., 566, 575
Ferme de la Croix, 215, 220, 221
Ferme de la Hallerie, 27
Ferme des Deux Treilles, 36
Ferme du Chastel, 26
Ferme du Fort Martin, 554, 573
Fernandez, Cpl. J., 198
Ferret Trench, 90
Ferry Post, 12
Fins Ridge, 470
Fish Alley, 83
Fitzgerald, Sergt. R., 503
Fitzherbert, Lt.-Col. N., 611
Fitzpatrick, Pte. C. A., 190
Flattened Farm, 212, 213
Fleet Cottage, 273
Flers, 67 sqq., 76 sqq., 388, 442, 494, 618
Flers Trench System, 69, 78 sqq.
Flesquières, 492, 493
Fletcher, Cpl. E. C., 483
Fletcher, Lt.-Col. W. H., 164, 218
Flêtre, 225
Fleurbaix, 20, 27, 125, 146, 150, 155, 247, 374
Foch, Maréchal, 339, 372, 374, 379, 415, 416, 490, 491, 517
Fonquevillers, 340, 396, 419, 420
Fontaine-au-Pire, 530 sqq., 602
Fontaine-au-Tertre Farm, 532 sqq.
Fontaine-Notre-Dame, 492
Foot, Sergt. S. C., 238, 239, 241, 268
Foote, Sergt. R. B., 498
Ford, L.-Cpl. G. C., 453
Ford Trench, 391, 392, 408
Forester's House (northern), 594, 597, 598
Forester's House (southern), 594, 595
Fork Wood, 346, 389, 397, 409 sqq., 419

Forsyth, Sergt. S., 431, 432
Fort Trench, 78
Fortescue, Hon. J. W., 564
Fortune, Sergt. R. E., 545
Foster, Coy.-Sergt.-Major J. H., 583
Foureaux Wood, see High Wood
Fox Farm, 514
Francis, L.-Sergt., W. A., 146
Franks, Major-General, 124
Franvillers, 350
Fraser, Sergt. J. D., 221
Free, Sergt. W. J., 450
Frélinghien, 42, 47, 50, 136, 138, 175, 209 sqq., 229, 234, 245
Fremicourt, 449 sqq., 461, 465
French, Field-Marshal Viscount, 164
French Lane, 35, 83
Frickleton, 2nd Lt. S., 189, 190
Fricourt, 65, 67, 68, 89, 91
Fricourt Wood, 68, 71, 84
Friend, L.-Cpl. W., 544
Fromelles, 125, 130
Frost, Sergt.-Major W. E., 47
Fruin, Cpl. G., 477
Fulton, Brig.-Gen. H. T., 9, 15, 117, 192, 242, 324, 338, 359
Fusilier Trench, 392, 394
Fyfe, Lt. R. E., 412, 439
Gallipoli, ch. I pass., 27 sqq., 82, 259, 597, 607
Gapaard, 170, 210, 211, 217, 242, 243
Gard'ner, Lt.-Col. M.M., 15, 141
Garlick, Pte. F. T., 190
Gasquoine, Major G. K., 127
Geange, Pte. T., 264
Ghent, 490
Gheluvelt, 305, 308 sqq.
Ghissignies, 552 sqq.
Gibbs, Lt. W. G., 231
Gifford, Rflmn. P. H., 133, 134
Gilbert, Pte. G., 313
Gillam, Sergt. A., 485
Gillespie, Lt. C. T., 175
Gillespie, 2nd Lt. D. A., 128
Gillies, Capt. T. S., 528
Gilmore, Sergt. W. B., 93
Ginchy, 65, 88
Gird Trench System, 69, 86, 87, 91 sqq.
Glasgow Redoubt, 153
Glencorse Wood, 299, 320
Glendining, Lt.-Col. H. C., 224, 603
Godewaersvelde, 338
Godley, Lt.-Gen. Sir A. J., 2, 7, 10, 11, 14, 17, 35, 67, 129, 135, 139, 140, 178, 206, 209, 251, 322, 323, 377, 379, 601, 611, 612
Goldingham, 2nd Lt. K. A., 264
Goldstein, Major H. M., 241
Gommecourt, 340, 388, 389, 411, 413, 416
Gompers, Mr. S., 515
Gonnelieu, 493, 494, 497
Gonnelieu Ridge, 492, 493
Good Man Farm, 497
Goose Alley, 69, 80, 86, 91 sqq.
Gossage, Major C. I., 387, 603
Goudberg Copse, 289
Goudberg Spur, 278, 279, 289, 296
Gough, General, 61, 62, 226, 227, 333 sqq.
Goulding, Lt. A. M., 604
Gouraud, General, 538
Gouzeaucourt, 470, 473 sqq., 492 sqq., 619
Graham's Post, 46
Grammont, 600
Grant, L.-Cpl. A., 435
Grant, 2nd Lt. J. G., 456
Grant, Lt. I. P., 589

22086323R00462

Printed in Great Britain
by Amazon